PREFACE

When the first publication of *The Management of Nonprofit and Charitable Organizations in Canada* came out in 2006, it broke ground by being the first resource to address management of an increasingly complex sector. Since then the context within and around nonprofit and charitable organizations has continued to shift and change in response to such things as:

- Labour market information specific to the nonprofit and charitable sector showing skill requirements of employers as well as the nature of work and the ways in which it is carried out.

- Significant federal and provincial changes to social policies affecting funding and operational expectations associated with the sector.

- An explosion of social enterprises and social ventures that are changing how revenue generation by the nonprofit and charitable sector takes place.

- The accelerated move from paper-based media and fundraising to electronic social media and online giving platforms.

This third edition introduces new content on many of these themes. As well, information that is more fundamental has been updated with current research and practice ideas.

The third edition will be as valuable to managers and those studying the management of nonprofit and charitable organizations as previous editions. As the journey continues, this resource will offer multiple helpful perspectives.

Keith Seel, Ph.D.
Editor
Calgary, Alberta, 2014

CONTRIBUTORS

Carolyn Bodnar-Evans, M.Acc, CPA, C.A.

Carolyn Bodnar-Evans is Director, Finance and Administration with the Canadian Partnership Against Cancer (CPAC), a position she has held since 2009. CPAC is a federally funded health organization that works with Canada's cancer community to reduce the burden of cancer through co-ordinated system-level change. Carolyn has also worked with Dignitas International and served as the Chief Financial Officer of the Canadian Cancer Society and the National Cancer Institute of Canada from 1996-2005. Previous to that she held senior finance roles in the nonprofit sector in the areas of international development and the performing arts, serving with Save the Children Canada and Canada's National Ballet School. For over 25 years, she has actively contributed to the sector as a leader, board member, and academic lecturer with the University of Toronto and Ryerson University's nonprofit and voluntary sector management program. She also served on the Not-for-Profit Organizations Advisory Committee of the Canadian Institute of Chartered Accountants, and Ryerson University's Advisory committee for the Program in Interdisciplinary Studies in Nonprofit and Voluntary Sector Management Program.

Kathy Brock, Ph.D.

Kathy Brock is Professor, School of Policy Studies and Department of Political Studies, Queen's University. She came to Queen's mid-career in 1999 to head up the School of Policy Studies new initiative on the nonprofit sector and edited and co-edited a series of books and organized conferences on the nonprofit and voluntary sector. She served as the documentalist and advisor to the Federal Government-Voluntary Sector Initiative and helped found and served on the first and only national academic organization for the study of the nonprofit and voluntary sector (ANSER). She has also published widely on Canadian politics and government, federalism and constitutional matters, Aboriginal governance and issues and assisted suicide policy. Active in public affairs, she has served as an advisor to governments, Cabinet ministers, and an Aboriginal organization and on a number of national and local boards. She is currently Research Chair and both Executive and Board member of the Institute of Public Administration of Canada and on the Executive of the Canadian Association of Programs in Public Administration. A dedicated professor, she received the 2008 Pierre

De Celles IPAC Award for Teaching Excellence in Public Administration and the 2009 Frank Knox Award (Queen's University) for Teaching Excellence (Queen's).

Terrance S. Carter, B.A., LL.B., TEP, Trade-Mark Agent

Terrance S. Carter is Managing Partner of Carters Professional Corporation. Mr. Carter practises in the area of charity and not-for-profit law, and is counsel to Fasken Martineau on charitable matters. Mr. Carter is a co-author of *Corporate and Practice Manual for Charitable and Not-for-Profit Corporations*, a co-editor of *Charities Legislation & Commentary*, 2014 Edition, contributing author to *The Management of Nonprofit and Charitable Organizations in Canada*, and co-author of *Branding and Copyright for Charities and Non-Profit Organizations*, and Industry Canada's *Primer for Directors of Not-for-Profit Corporations*. Mr. Carter is recognized as a leading expert in Canada by *Lexpert* and *Best Lawyers in Canada* in the area of charity and not-for-profit law, and is a past member of the Technical Issues Working Group of Canada Revenue Agency's (CRA) Charities Directorate, Past Chair of the CBA National and OBA Charities and Not-for-Profit Law Sections. Mr. Carter is also a frequent author and speaker in the area of charity and not-for-profit law across Canada and internationally. He is the editor of www.charitylaw.ca, www.churchlaw.ca and www.antiterrorism.ca.

Karen J. Cooper, B. Soc. Sc., LL.L., LL.B., TEP

Karen J. Cooper is a lawyer with Drache Aptowitzer LLP and practises charity and not-for-profit law with an emphasis on tax issues from the Ottawa office, having formerly been a Senior Rulings Officer with the Income Tax Rulings Directorate of Canada Revenue Agency, as well as former counsel for the Department of Justice in tax litigation. Ms. Cooper also has considerable teaching experience, including presenting workshops for the Chartered Professional Accountants of Canada, as sessional lecturer at Carleton University School of Business teaching Business Law, and part-time professor at the University of Ottawa, Faculty of Common Law, and is a contributing author to *The Management of Charitable and Not-for-Profit Organizations in Canada* (LexisNexis Canada). Ms. Cooper has been recognized as a leading expert in charity and not-for-profit law by *Lexpert* and *The Best Lawyers in Canada*.

Michael H. Hall, Ph.D.

Michael H. Hall is Vice President, Program Research and Development at the YMCA of Greater Toronto where he provides strategic leadership to the YMCA's research agenda and the evaluation of its impact. Mr. Hall's career has focused on developing and mobilizing knowledge to strengthen the contributions that charities and community organizations make to the lives of Canadians. In addition to his many publications on philanthropy and nonprofit organizations, he played a key role in establishing and leading a series of foundational national research studies on giving and volunteering and Canada's charitable and nonprofit sector. His volunteer contributions include serving as the founding President of Parks and Recreation Ontario and membership on the boards of a number of nonprofit research associations and academic journals. Mr. Hall holds a Ph.D. in social psychology from York University.

Yvonne D. Harrison, Ph.D.

Yvonne D. Harrison is an Assistant Professor in the Department of Public Administration and Policy in Rockefeller College of Public Affairs and Policy, University at Albany, State University of New York (SUNY). Ms. Harrison has expertise in the governance and leadership of nonprofit and voluntary sector organizations, the adoption and use of information and communications technology by nonprofit and voluntary sector organizations, organization theory and the management of public-private partnerships. She and co-investigator, Vic Murray, have developed the Board Check-Up (www.boardcheckup.com) to help nonprofit and voluntary sector boards of directors assess and make decisions to improve governance effectiveness. This free online tool is a University of Albany sponsored research project (10-255) that has produced papers and reports on the issues that challenge boards and the impact of self-assessment from output (changes in governance practices) and process (board performance decision-making) effectiveness perspectives. Ms. Harrison brings expertise in Academic Service Learning from Seattle University, in Seattle, WA where she was Assistant Professor of Nonprofit Leadership and an Academic Service Learning Faculty Fellow focusing on designing education and research that meets student and community needs. She holds a B.S. in Nursing, a Master of Public Administration and Ph.D. in Public Administration from the University of Victoria, BC, Canada. Ms. Harrison is the author of a number of peer reviewed journal articles, book chapters, research reports, and other publications.

Andrea McManus, CFRE

Andrea McManus is known for her passionate belief in philanthropy and the value of the nonprofit sector in Canadian society. She is

President of The Development Group in Calgary and has worked with, trained and educated organizations and fundraisers throughout North America, the Caribbean, Mexico, Europe and Egypt. A highly strategic thinker, Ms. McManus works with organizations that span the nonprofit sector and is particularly dedicated to building long-term and sustainable capacity that are firmly anchored in a philanthropic culture that permeates all levels of the organization.

A leader in the nonprofit sector locally, nationally and internationally, Ms. McManus was the first person outside of the United States to hold the position of Chair of the International Board (2011-12) of the Association of Fundraising Professionals (AFP). She has sat on numerous local and national initiatives to strengthen the Canadian nonprofit sector and is currently a member of the Imagine Canada Ethical Code Advisory Committee, Canada Revenue Agency's Charities Technical Issues Working Group, Chair of the AFP Canada Government Relations Committee, is a trustee for the Alberta Cancer Foundation and member of the board of Student Energy. She was founding Board Chair of the Calgary Chamber of Voluntary Organizations.

Ms. McManus was recognized by the AFP Calgary Chapter as the 2007 Outstanding Fundraising Professional Award. She is an AFP Master Teacher and contributing author to four books on nonprofit management and fundraising, including *Excellence in Canadian Fundraising*, the first book published on fundraising in Canada for Canadian fundraisers. In 2012 Ms. McManus was the recipient of the Queen's Jubilee Silver Medal for her contributions to the Canadian nonprofit sector.

Dr. Agnes Meinhard

Dr. Agnes Meinhard is an Associate Professor of Organizational Behaviour and Theory in the Ted Rogers School of Management at Ryerson University. She is also the founding and current director of the Centre for Voluntary Sector Studies. She was instrumental in establishing Canada's first undergraduate interdisciplinary curriculum in nonprofit and voluntary sector management at Ryerson University. Dr. Meinhard's research encompasses a variety of topics including: the formation, growth and demise of voluntary organizations from a population ecology perspective; strategic responses of voluntary organizations to changing policy; volunteer behaviour and development; the role of voluntary organizations in integrating new immigrants and the unique characteristics of women's voluntary organizations. Her work has been published in the major nonprofit journals. Dr. Meinhard has been a three time recipient of Best Paper awards from the Administrative Sciences Association of Canada. She teaches courses in organizational behaviour, organizational theory and organizational leadership as well as nonprofit management.

Laurie Mook

Laurie Mook is Assistant Professor in the Nonprofit Leadership and Management program, School of Community Resources and Development at Arizona State University. She is also research associate at the ASU Lodestar Center for Nonprofit Innovation and Philanthropy. Prior to moving to Arizona, Ms. Mook was co-director of the Social Economy Centre of the University of Toronto. Ms. Mook is co-author of *What Counts: Social Accounting for Nonprofits and Cooperatives* now in its second edition (Sigel Press, 2007), *Understanding the Social Economy: A Canadian Perspective* (University of Toronto Press, 2009), and editor of *Accounting for Social Value* (University of Toronto Press, 2013). Her areas of interest are nonprofit management, social accounting, social economy and volunteerism.

Vic Murray, Ph.D.

Vic Murray is currently Adjunct Professor in the School of Public Administration at the University of Victoria and Professor Emeritus in the Schulich School of Business at York University. From 1983 to 1995, he was Director of the Voluntary Sector Management Program and professor of organizational behaviour and sociology at York University. He specializes in the study of leadership and management of voluntary sector organizations of all types with particular emphasis on the areas of board governance, strategic planning, inter-organizational collaboration and the assessment of organizational effectiveness. He is also an active consultant and volunteer in these areas.

As Director of the Nonprofit Leadership and Management Program at York University he developed several of the first certificate and master's level courses in that field. He is the author of numerous books, articles and papers in the fields of organizational behaviour and nonprofit management. He is currently co-director, with Professor Yvonne Harrison, of the Nonprofit Board Performance Self-Assessment Project (see www.boardcheckup.com).

Dr. Susan D. Phillips

Dr. Susan D. Phillips is Professor and since 2005 has been Director of the School of Public Policy and Administration, Carleton. She is also Research Associate of the Carleton Centre for Community Innovation (3ci). Her research focuses on philanthropy and the nonprofit sector, particularly the public policies and regulations that govern this sector and the role of foundations in place-based philanthropy. She is co-editor of the first international handbook on philanthropy, the *Routledge Companion to Philanthropy*, to be published in 2015.

Dr. Phillips is board member of the International Research Society for Public Management and member of the editorial boards of Public Management Review, Policy and Society, The Philanthropist, and the Canadian Journal of Nonprofit and Society Economy Research). She has been a member of Policy Advisory Committee of Imagine Canada, the board of Volunteer Canada, and a regular advisor to governments and national nonprofits. Dr. Phillips is leading the development of Carleton University's Master of Philanthropy and Nonprofit Leadership, the first graduate degree in philanthropy in Canada, which began in the summer of 2013.

Keith Seel, Ph.D., CVA, FRSA

Keith Seel is the Dean, Centre for Excellence in Foundational Learning at Bow Valley College. In this role he works extensively with the nonprofit sector and government to provide basic literacy education and upgrading for a diversity of students looking to either take additional education or to move to better jobs. Previously Mr. Seel was the Director, Institute for Nonprofit Studies at Mount Royal University where he was an active researcher into Canada's nonprofit sector. He focused on both governance and social policy issues within Canada's nonprofit sector. Mr. Seel is currently appointed to the Premier's Council for Alberta's Promise, an initiative designed to address the needs of children and children's service agencies in the province. He has served as the Chair, Human Resources Council for the Nonprofit Sector; board member of many nonprofit organizations for more than 30 years, and appointed to both the Alberta Council of Teaching Standards and the Persons with Developmental Disabilities Calgary Region Community Board. Mr. Seel is also the editor for *Volunteer Administration: A Profession* published by LexisNexis Canada.

Thea Vakil Ph.D.

Ms. Vakil is Associate Professor and Associate Director in the School of Public Administration, University of Victoria. She is also the Executive Director of the Centre of Public Sector Studies at the School of Public Administration. Ms. Vakil is a former senior executive with the British Columbia Government with extensive experience in a number of large portfolios including finance, organizational change, public policy, strategic planning and leadership development. She teaches widely in these and other areas at the School of Public Administration. Ms. Vakil served as the treasurer of a large non-profit organization in Victoria and has developed and delivered workshops in the public sector and the non-profit sector. She provides advice and support to community based organizations and has taught courses in strategic thinking and planning, policy analysis and management for community based organizations. She is a recipient of teaching awards from the Faculty of Human and Social Development and the Faculty of Business at the University of Victoria.

TABLE OF CONTENTS

Chapter 1

INTRODUCTION: WHAT IS SPECIAL ABOUT MANAGING NONPROFIT ORGANIZATIONS?

Vic Murray
University of Victoria

Keith Seel
Bow Valley College

"Running an organization like this can be really frustrating in these difficult times. Trying to provide the services our clients need, find funders who will support us and get enough good volunteers to help us out is not an easy job."

"We're here to serve our members but they never seem satisfied. They want more and more but don't want to pay for it."

"When volunteers and staff are working together on the same program it can get a bit tricky. Sometimes the staff wants to treat them as 'gofers' and sometimes the volunteers think the staff work for them."

"What is our mission? Sometimes it seems we change it for every funder to meet their expectations for partnerships and whatever issue has caught their attention."

"We used to be a small friendly organization where everybody helped everybody else and everyone had a say in deciding what we were going to do. But we've tripled in size in the last three years and things are getting a bit chaotic. I've also noticed more 'washroom grumbling'. I think we have to get better organized but I don't want to lose our old way of doing things."

The above are just a few of the kinds of remarks made by those who run Canada's nonprofit and voluntary organizations today. They reflect some of the special challenges that face leaders in this unique sector that comprises those organizations that are neither government-run nor private businesses. Comments like these have been made by those within the nonprofit sector for decades because the fundamental relationship between being a nonprofit organization, securing the resources to operate, and determining what service domain will be addressed is long standing. What has changed over time is the growth of Canada's nonprofit sector. In it are an estimated 165,000 organizations[1] that provide a vast array of services that affect the quality of life of almost all Canadians.[2]

With the growing awareness of the importance of this sector in society has come the realization that we know very little about how these organizations differ from those in business and government. Also, given that they provide paid jobs for over two million people, employ the services of some 19 million volunteers, and receive over $106 billion in revenues a year,[3] we need to pay more attention to what special problems they encounter as they seek to achieve their missions.

This book is an attempt to pull together what we know (and identify what we don't know) about managing nonprofit and voluntary organizations (henceforth referred to at times as "NPOs") in Canada. It is aimed specifically at those who are (or who aspire to be) in positions of leadership in these organizations: executive directors, members of boards of directors, program managers, volunteer leaders, and students in the many new university and college programs that have been created to prepare future leaders in this important sector.

We begin with a brief overview of just what the nonprofit and voluntary sector is (henceforth to be referred to simply as "the nonprofit sector"). How does it differ from the business and government sectors? How does it differ within itself? Next we will look at the special management challenges created by the unique characteristics of the sector for those in leadership positions within it. This will lead to the presentation of a simple framework for understanding these management challenges. It will be seen that this framework provides the basis for the organization of the remainder of the chapters in the book.

---

[1]   Imagine Canada (2014).

[2]   This number excludes an unknown, but probably very large, number of small, informal, "grass roots" groups that do not qualify as "organizations" but that help themselves and others in myriad ways.

[3]   Imagine Canada (2014).

HOW DO NONPROFIT SECTOR ORGANIZATIONS DIFFER FROM THOSE IN THE BUSINESS AND GOVERNMENT SECTORS?

There are many kinds of organizations in the nonprofit sector. They range from large and institutional bodies such as the International Red Cross to small and non-formal associations such as a self-help group of former alcoholics or a line dancing club. Some are entirely voluntary, such as a kid's hockey league while others are made up of all paid staff and no volunteers other than the board of directors, such as a children's mental health agency.

Even with this diversity, and on the understanding that one cannot generalize about all nonprofits, it *is* possible to describe how they resemble government-run services on the one hand and for-profit businesses on the other while being distinctly different from both in yet other ways. These unique differences create special kinds of leadership issues even though many other issues might be shared with the other two sectors. The main areas of difference lie in:

(a)   Organizational Mission and Values;

(b)   Organizational Goals and Strategic Priorities;

(c)   The Use of Volunteers; and

(d)   The Governance Practices of the Board of Directors.

Organizational Mission and Values

The ultimate purpose of government-run organizations is to serve the political process. They exist because legislators determine the services they are to provide and they survive only as long as political leaders want them to. Hence, they must always be conscious of the political agenda of elected officials. Business organizations, on the other hand, have the ultimate goal of making profits for their owners or shareholders. The growth or continued existence of a business depends on its rate of return on investment.

More than organizations in either of the other two sectors, those in the nonprofit sector are driven by a sense of mission — a strong commitment to "the cause" for which the organization was created, be it finding food for the hungry, "saving souls", showing great art, or finding a cure for cancer.

There is also a strong belief in certain values that must be upheld as the organization seeks to achieve its mission. One of the most important of these values for many is the "expressive" side of how the organization should work. In addition to achieving its goals in an efficient way, many NPOs want to provide an atmosphere in which staff and volunteers can develop a sense of community and mutual support. It is a major mistake for leaders of NPOs to act as though their only responsibility is to make their organizations "more businesslike". Ignoring the expressive dimension is to overlook a major factor influencing the organization's success.

In sum, then, the NPO's mission and values lie at the heart of its existence. They do not change at the whim of political leaders and do not depend on making surplus money. There are however, significant pressures — internally from the board and externally from service recipients, for example — to chase resources by changing the NPO's mission to fit a funder's criteria. This is known as "mission drift" and can mean that an organization that had a strong values base and focus will find itself some years later significantly removed from where it started. Staff and service recipients, not to mention funders and regulators may wonder if the NPO is still relevant or if it has lost its way. Resisting mission drift and keeping a strong focus on values is a challenge for leaders in NPOs.

This unique "mission and values driven" characteristic of most nonprofit organizations has both positive and negative implications for those who must lead them. For example, it is easier to attract and motivate staff and volunteers who believe in "the cause". Commitment can be harder to achieve in the other sectors where more people are likely to view their work as "just a job". But the same strong values can also make nonprofits more difficult to change because, without political masters or profit-seeking owners to drive them, they may find it easier to ignore signals from their environment that their missions may no longer be relevant to the needs of those they serve or that their programs are ineffective.

As well, like government organizations, the lack of a profit motive means that nonprofits can slip into operating inefficiently as long as there is a ready supply of money from their funders. For most businesses, competition and the market mechanism means that their income depends *directly* on their customers buying the products or services they offer. Declining sales sends the unavoidable signal that the business has problems. If the customer cannot be satisfied, the organizations in a competitive environment will eventually go bankrupt.

In both the public and much of the nonprofit sector, however, there is *no* direct connection between income and output. Except for nonprofits created solely to serve fee-paying members, the clients of most nonprofits are *not* the main providers of the organization's funds. Their money comes from funders who are not the organization's "customers". This has several implications for leadership:

- Nonprofit organization leaders must often be "Janus-faced" — having to look two directions at once. In order to get future funding they have to be able to keep funders satisfied that they are using their money the way they want it used; looking in the other direction they must provide clients the services they need and want. Sometimes these two groups, funders and clients, do not have the same agenda for the organization.

- Funders do not always demand efficient operations the way a competitive market place can "demand" efficiency from a business whose customers will desert it if they can find a better quality or lower priced product elsewhere. For many clients of nonprofits, there may not even be any "elsewhere" to turn to for the services they need. When this happens, special challenges arise in developing efficient operations.

- Because of the "power of the purse", much time can be taken up keeping funders happy resulting in a comparative neglect of the voice of the client or user of a nonprofit's services.

Organizational Goals and Strategic Priorities

How an organization achieves its mission depends on it having a set of more specific goals or objectives. In the public sector and many nonprofit organizations, these goals are often multiple, vague, difficult to measure and even, at times, mutually contradictory. Businesses, on the other hand, have the iron rule of "the bottom line" to hew to. For example, take the goal of a modern dance company which might be: "to bring the best and the latest developments in modern dance to the community". What does this mean exactly? Who should define "the best"?

Or how about a charity created to help those with certain health problems (*e.g.*, cancer, heart, kidney, diabetes) which has the goals of raising money to find a cure for the disease, educating the public about the disease, and helping victims of the disease deal with their affliction. Each of these goals is very general and it can be difficult to clearly measure progress toward them. It is also the case that, if more money is poured into one area, there may be less available for the others (so they can be mutually conflicting).

As another example, consider an international aid organization that may wish to be able to provide emergency help to developing countries where there is famine or disaster but also seek to provide longer-term aid that will allow people to help themselves in the future. Similarly, a community service agency may have the mission of improving the quality of life of the citizens of a given area but it has to decide what groups to serve (seniors? youth? immigrants? the poor?) and what services to provide. Too much for one group or one problem area may mean less for others.

Being very clear about what goals the organization should pursue and what priority each should have at any given time is one of the most challenging tasks for nonprofit leaders. They must constantly be asking themselves and their followers these questions:

- What services do we want to provide to whom at what cost?
- How will we raise the resources we need to provide these services?
- How will we measure our effectiveness and efficiency in carrying out these activities?

Considering Sustainability and Capacity

Two terms that have come to have great significance to the non-profit sector are *sustainability* and *capacity*. These two terms are significant for nonprofit leaders who must make choices about the ways that an NPO will create *outcomes* as a result of the activity it undertakes. Sustainability has to do with the level of activity and the resources required to carry that out. A common planning timeframe for NPOs is three to five years into the future. For some activities this timeframe makes sense while for others it does not. For example, if an environmental NPO wanted to develop a recycling centre for paint, sustainability concerns could be reasonably addressed in a five-year planning horizon. Funds could be raised, staff and volunteers put in place, systems for collection and distribution could be established. This could be sustainable for five years and then evaluated and a decision made about continuing on. However, if another environ-mental organization is looking at improving a watershed area, the timelines would be decades long. Accordingly, the decisions around what would be needed to be sustainable for that period of time would require considerable information and planning.

Relatedly the term "capacity" has to do with the resources that an NPO has that could be mobilized into activities. There is generally a view in the nonprofit sector that more capacity is better. More capacity translates into more financial, human, intellectual and other resources. Since resources are typically very limited for NPOs, decisions about the capacity that is required to carry out the mission often cross into a range of domains such as:

- Financial management;

- Human resource management;

- Fundraising;

- Partnerships and collaborative activity; and

- Ethics

Taken together, capacity and sustainability are two important parameters within which nonprofit organizations operate. Leaders in the nonprofit sector will find their roles increasingly focused on questions of capacity and of sustainability as resource constraints, social needs, environmental needs and economic needs bear down on nonprofit governance and operations.

Incidentally, it should not be inferred from the above that all nonprofits are inherently less efficient than businesses. If pressed by funders or concerned leaders, they have been shown to be as efficient as many businesses and more than some such as those which do not face a lot of competition.[4]

Use of Volunteers

Eighty per cent of Canadian nonprofit organizations depend on volunteers to help them operate with the remaining 20 per cent utilizing volunteers as members of their boards of directors. In this respect they are, of course, uniquely different from business and government organizations. Obviously, they do not have the expense of having to pay this part of their work force but it is erroneous to think that the use of volunteers is cost free. Successfully managing volunteers requires a

---

[4]   See B.A. Weisbrod, ed., *To Profit or Not to Profit: The Commercial Transformation of the Nonprofit Sector* (New York: Cambridge University Press, 1998).

considerable investment of both time and money if they are to be used effectively.

The biggest single difference between volunteer and paid staff is that the former do not *have* to be there in the way that an employee would be. This means that, whenever they become dissatisfied (or other activities become more appealing), they may leave. There are, however, positions held by volunteers where the level of responsibility and the consequences of not being present, a crisis line volunteer, for example, are high. The difference is that the kind of corrective action available to the NPO regarding an issue associated with the behaviour of a volunteer is significantly different in that financial penalties would not be applicable to volunteers.

It should be noted that the international professional association for the profession of volunteer administration — Council for Certification in Volunteer Administration — provides a body of knowledge[5] that clearly demonstrates that there are few real differences between the management of volunteers and the management of employees. Perhaps the most obvious single difference is that employees receive financial compensation where as volunteers do not. The relationship between a nonprofit organization and its volunteers is best when it is a contract relationship with clear roles, responsibilities, expectations and so forth. A poorly managed volunteer program brings risks to the NPO.

Consequently, considerable time and effort needs to be invested by a NPO in its volunteer program if:

- it is to generate the kind of outcomes expected, and

- brings minimal risk to the NPO.

Governance by a Nonprofit Board of Directors

All registered charitable organizations are required by law to have a board of directors as are NPOs registered as corporations under either provincial legislation or federal legislation depending on their mandate. Unlike their corporate counterparts, nonprofit board members are typically not financially compensated.[6] The nonprofit board, like its

---

5   See Council for Certification in Volunteer Administration. Online at: <http://www.cvacert. org/documents/CCVABOK2008-Final_000.pdf>.

6   Board members of *registered charities* are prohibited by law from being paid. In addition many other NPOs do not pay their board members. However, aside from registered charities, NPOs are not *legally prohibited* from paying their board members. For example, legislation

business counterpart, is legally responsible for the "governance" of the organization. This means it must ensure that the organization is achieving its mission and is being run in a fiscally and legally responsible way. Should the organization get into financial or legal difficulties, board members may be personally liable for any liabilities or damages that ensue if it can be shown that they failed to govern with "due diligence".

The problem often is, however, that board members are volunteers who often do not have extensive experience in organizational governance or as specialists in the mission of the organization. As a result, many boards experience difficulties in carrying out their duties. Too often there is confusion and conflict between some board members and the paid executives as to who is responsible for what. The latter may feel the board is meddling in matters they know too little about while the former may feel the managers should be more willing to bow to the board's ultimate authority. Managing the board by helping it to be clear about what its role is and ensuring that its members are able to carry out their responsibilities becomes, therefore, a critical task for the organization's leaders.

HOW DO NONPROFIT ORGANIZATIONS DIFFER FROM ONE ANOTHER AND WHAT DO THESE DIFFERENCES MEAN FOR THEIR LEADERS?

Let us now consider the ways that nonprofit organizations differ *from one another*. Each of these differences can create special problems or issues of leadership for those responsible for managing them.

Types of Nonprofit Organization

There are several different ways of categorizing the differences between organizations in the nonprofit and voluntary sector. Perhaps the most meaningful difference from the point of view of leadership issues is that between

- membership benefit organizations,

- public benefit organizations, and

- nonprofit social enterprises.

---

governing nonprofit *corporations* permits payment to directors. (See Chapter 5 for a full description of the various legal forms that nonprofits can take.)

Membership Benefit Nonprofits

Membership benefit nonprofits exist primarily to serve the needs of their members. They are usually created by and for members who make the conscious decision to join and often pay fees to do so. In many cases the members also do the work of the organization and manage it, all as volunteers (though larger and better off organizations, such as recreational or social clubs may hire both staff and managers).

In all membership benefit organizations the key leadership issue is member service — getting members and keeping them satisfied. Such organizations come the closest to resembling businesses of all nonprofits because their income in the form of membership fees depends directly on keeping the "customers" (*i.e.*, members) happy. If competition lures members away, the organization suffers (unlike the case of non-member based nonprofits where external funders may keep on providing money even when "clients" are unhappy).

Within the broad category of membership benefit organizations there are two sub-categories: those that are organized as "self-help" groups and those that are related to work and professional activities. Among the self-help groups are those that are organized for "expressive" purposes, to further personal interests such as spiritual needs or recreational interests. Examples are some churches,[7] sports clubs, outdoors groups, bridge clubs, *etc.* In these kinds of membership organizations, organized primarily for self-interest, the critical management task above all is keeping the members satisfied and watching out for competitive threats that might lure them elsewhere.

Another kind of self-help group is organized as an instrument for solving problems. Members join, not to have a good time, but to help themselves deal with difficulties that they have a hard time dealing with alone, such as loneliness, substance abuse (alcohol or drugs), abusive relationships (support groups for women), or neighbourhood security (such as Neighbourhood Watch groups). In many of these types of self-help organizations the members do not have much money. Thus they cannot afford to pay high membership fees. The special skill in running this type of organization lies in providing services on little or no income and getting work done through volunteers, many of whom have had little opportunity to learn the skills necessary to do the work required.

---

[7]   This would not include large, hierarchically organized religious organizations such as the Catholic or Anglican churches. These are closer to the service-providing organizations discussed below.

The work-related type of membership organization refers to trade and professional associations created to further the interests of members who are in the same business or occupation. Running a trade or professional association presents the leader with a number of special kinds of problems. Since members are interested primarily in what the organization can do for them professionally, they can be quite critical and very conscious of what they are getting for their fees (which can often be substantial). This easily leads to members protesting that they are not getting enough services for their dues. Trade and occupational associations are also prone to factionalism. Different groups of members have differing ideas about what the organization should be doing so keeping all the interest groups from attacking one another or trying to overthrow the current leaders can be a major problem.

Co-ops and Credit Unions also fall within the category of membership organizations. These have their own unique set of problems in that, not only must they continuously seek and satisfy members, but most of them also have to compete with for-profit businesses and financial institutions. As such, they also fall into the nonprofit social enterprise category discussed below.

Public Benefit Organizations

Public Benefit Organizations are the other major category of nonprofits. These are the typical "charities" created to provide services for persons other than those who run them or volunteer for them. This would include most social service organizations, cultural organizations such as museums, galleries or performing arts companies, health-related organizations such as the Cancer Society, civic benefit organizations such as the Red Cross, and many others. Their unique characteristic from a leadership point of view is that discussed earlier — the split between those who fund the organization (government grants and service delivery contracts, foundations, United Ways, public donors, *etc.*) and those who use its services. Leaders have to learn how to find, appeal to, and retain funders while not losing sight of the needs of clients. To dwell too much on one side of the equation to the exclusion of the other usually creates problems eventually.

Within the public benefit category, it is possible to distinguish between those organizations created primarily to provide services (*e.g.*, to immigrants, children at risk, the poor, seniors, *etc.*) and those created primarily to advocate a cause. Advocacy organizations exist to persuade governments or others to change their policies and/or "educate" the public to better understand and support their cause (e.g., environmental protection groups such as Greenpeace, anti-poverty organizations, etc.). Of course, many organizations of both member and public benefit types may have some element of advocacy in their agendas, however, this is not their primary reason for existence. In fact, they have to be careful about how much and what kind of advocacy they engage in because nonprofits that exist primarily to lobby governments are not allowed to become legally registered charities and give tax-deductible receipts for donations. And those that are registered, but become too active as advocates, will eventually lose their charitable status. See Chapter 5 for more on the legalities of advocacy activities.

Service-providing nonprofits are often organized around professional staffs that run the programs. Volunteers, if used, usually provide only assistance to the staff. One of the major dangers for leaders in these kinds of organizations is that the professional staff can lose touch with the clients. They end up providing these people with only what they, the professionals, think ought to be provided (in accordance with what they learn through their professional training) even when the clients may not want or need what they are getting.

The American scholar, John McKnight has taken this critique even further. He maintains that many social service, health and educational organizations have helped to create a "culture of dependency" in which the organization's clients are encouraged to believe they are weak, are "victims", and that, only by depending on the professional counsellors, social workers, care providers and the like, can they survive. If McKnight could have his way, most government and nonprofit social service providers would be dismantled and replaced by organizations headed by members of the community who would lead in helping community members by emphasizing their strengths and assets, rather than their weaknesses. Any help provided by "professionals" would be strictly on terms regulated by the persons with the problems rather than the other way around.[8]

Advocacy oriented public benefit organizations, because they are so strongly driven by people committed to "the issues", are more likely than others to suffer from factionalism. For example, in environmental organizations, it is common to find a split between "radicals", who want mainly to organize adversarial confrontations with those they see

---

[8]   See J. McKnight, *The Careless Society* (New York: Basic Books, 1995).

as "the enemy"; and "reformers" or "gradualists" who would prefer to work "within the system", negotiating improvements without trying to overturn the established order. Trying to find workable compromises among divergent factions is one of the most difficult challenges facing leaders in these types of organizations. A failure to do so frequently results in breakaway groups being formed or nasty internal squabbles being created that lead to large-scale resignations or dismissals.

Nonprofit Social Enterprises

According to the Institute for Nonprofit Studies, "a social enterprise (SE) is defined as a business venture, owned or operated by a non-profit organization that sells goods or provides services in the market for the purpose of creating a blended return on investment; financial, social, environmental, and cultural."[9]

Over the last decade the number of social enterprise nonprofit organizations, began to expand dramatically. Factors contributing to this growth include:

- An increase in the size of the nonprofit sector in Canada generally meaning more competition for a resource base that is largely unchanged. Opportunities for generating revenues independent of government and other funders have become more attractive.

- An emergence of more information about social enterprise such as the research profiles of social enterprises by province produced by the Institute for Nonprofit Studies.

- The formation of entities such as Enterprising Nonprofits (eNP), which is present in communities across Canada to promote, study, and connect nonprofit social enterprises.

A special challenge for leaders of social enterprise organizations is achieving a workable balance between the need to make the "business" aspect of the organization successful on the one hand and the goal of providing the best possible services for those the business is attempting to help.

---

[9]   P. Elson & P. Hall, *Strength, Size, Scope: A Survey of Social Enterprises in Alberta and British Columbia* (Port Alberni, BC: BALTA, 2010) at 10. For additional research on other provinces, see: <http://www.mtroyal.ca/ProgramsCourses/FacultiesSchoolsCentres/Institute forNonprofitStudies/SocialEnterprise/index.htm>.

Degree of Voluntarism

It has already been stated that a key distinctive feature of many nonprofits is their use of volunteers. Clearly when the ratio of volunteers to paid staff is high, such as in the Girl Guides or churches, the critical factor for success is managing them. This requires learning special skills and knowledge about:

- where to locate a reliable supply of good people;

- how to attract them to join;

- how to keep them once they have joined;

- how to make the best use of them (job design, training); and

- how to minimize volunteer-staff conflict in those cases where volunteers and paid staff must work together.

The Council for Certification in Volunteer Administration has done extensive work to establish the profession of volunteer administration. It offers a body of knowledge dealing with the successful management of volunteers.[10] In those organizations where the use of volunteers is low, there is greater dependence on a well-trained, highly motivated paid staff. Since many nonprofits often find it difficult to pay top wages, they depend on their employees being committed to the mission of the organization and therefore willing to do more than the bare minimum in their jobs. Thus, a key leadership success factor is being able to inspire staff to become committed to their work and the mission without many of the typical incentives of steady pay increases and opportunities for promotion (the expressive dimension of management identified earlier).

In those cases where there is a high proportion of professionally trained staff members (*e.g.*, teachers, nurses, social workers, doctors, psychologists, *etc.*) the "McKnight problem" discussed above, is an ever-present danger. It is all too easy for people who have received a credential to slip into the mind set that says they know it all and the client knows nothing. It is also, sadly, often the case that professionals in the course of their training unconsciously absorb a status ranking in which other professional groups are considered inferior to their own. Then, when these groups are required to work with one another, they clash. This is most common in the health field among doctors and the

---

[10] See K. Seel, ed., *Volunteer Administration – Professional Practice* (Markham, ON: LexisNexis Canada, 2013).

members of other health care professions but it can affect relationships between many occupational groups as well as those who come from other kinds of backgrounds, *e.g.*, people from nonprofit sector backgrounds working with those from business or government.

What all this means for the nonprofit leader is that team building and conflict management skills become highly important in staff management and in building collaborative relationships with external stakeholders.

Sources of Funds

Another way that nonprofit organizations differ is in terms of the sources from which they receive their money. We have already discussed the important distinction between those that are dependent mainly on fees paid by members and those funded by "outside" sources. Now we will consider the impact of having differing degrees of concentration in funding sources.

Many social service and health-related nonprofits are almost totally dependent for their existence on government grants or purchases of service. For example, they may run group homes for former patients with mental illness or provide children's services or family counselling on behalf of provincial social service departments. Organizations facing this type of funding environment have two kinds of special leadership problems. The first is the problem of over-dependence. As the old saying goes: "He who pays the piper calls the tune" so when programs are supported mainly by a single funder, that funder's agenda will have a significant influence on how they operate. If the funder's approach happens not to agree with that of the delivery organization, the leader is faced with a major dilemma — conform or terminate the contract. The former destroys the organization's independence; the latter may push it into bankruptcy. To navigate between these two extremes requires the leader to develop excellent skills in relating to these key outside funders so as to keep them "on board" in terms of what the organization is doing and trying to prevent major rifts from developing.

What about the other extreme where the sources of funds are many and varied with no one funder predominating? This is the case in those organizations that raise their money through appeals to the public (mail or phone campaigns, special events, *etc.*) plus seeking grants from United Ways (and similar "federated funders"), private foundations, corporations, the sale of services or products, and the like.

In this situation the secret to success lies in being highly skilled at fund development. As governments cut back their funding of nonprofits, many are being forced for the first time to become serious fundraisers yet have Chief Executive Officers who have never had to do this before. As a result, a whole new career path has arisen in the past 10 years for fund development specialists and consultants.

Degree of Resource Scarcity and Competition for Resources

One of the most common problems in many of today's public service nonprofits is having to cope with budget cuts due to reductions in government grants. When this occurs, most attempt to combat the situation by seeking alternative forms of income. This creates increased competition for the remaining resources. The number of mail, telephone, and Internet appeals for donations has increased many times in recent years along with every other known fund development method — appeals to foundations, sales, 'thons (run-a-thons, *etc.*), gaming (bingo, lotteries, *etc.*), corporate sponsorships, online auctions, and opening "profit making" side businesses.

The *Satellite Account of Nonprofit Institutions and Volunteering* (Statistics Canada)[11] shows that for 2009, the most recent survey year, sources of revenue for the core nonprofit sector are:

- sales of goods and services which account for 45.6 per cent of total income;

- government funding at 19.7 per cent;

- membership fees 15.9 per cent;

- donations from households 12.0 per cent; and

- investment income 4.9 per cent.

That nearly half of all revenues for the nonprofit sector come from sales shows that an entrepreneurial spirit is necessary to meet funding reductions from all levels of government.

Several leadership problems commonly arise when an organization is hit by hard times. Management often becomes obsessed with short-term money saving schemes to the exclusion of almost everything else, including concerns over client needs and quality service.

---

[11] See Statistics Canada, *Satellite Account of Nonprofit Institutions and Volunteering: 2007*, Catalogue No. 13-015-X (Ottawa: Statistics Canada, 2009). Online at: <http://www.statcan.gc.ca/pub/13-015-x/13-015-x2009000-eng.pdf>.

The phenomenon of the "bunker mentality" sets in during which top management stops communicating downward or listening to messages from below. This in turn creates major morale problems with staff and volunteers, especially when one of the actions taken is the laying off of staff.

It is a major challenge for nonprofit organization leaders to handle hard times with creativity and get through them with minimal pain. Conversely, the provision of adequate funds is no guarantee of a problem-free life. At the other extreme, when there is little or no scarcity and minimal competition from others for funds, equally serious problems can arise, namely those of slackness, inefficiency, and empire building. No one *intends* to be inefficient or "fat", but it is all too easy to think up reasons to expand employee numbers and other expenditures when there is little incentive to do otherwise. This in fact happened to some of the larger mainstream nonprofits just as it did to government and business organizations during prosperous periods in the past.

Age and Stage of Development

Organizations, like people, go through stages of growth, from birth, through adolescence to maturity, old age and even death. The movement through these stages for organizations is neither as inevitable nor as uniform in duration as it is for individuals. Nevertheless, each stage in an organization's life creates a probability that certain kinds of leadership problems will arise. In the case of nonprofits, a simple three-stage model will suffice to illustrate the point. When a nonprofit is new it is also usually quite small and must concern itself with basic survival. It usually does this by focusing strongly on "the cause" for which it was founded and a strong "missionary" flavour pervades its every action. While this commitment on the part of the founders provides much of the energy needed to get going, it can also mean that there is a tendency to ignore key stakeholders (volunteers, users of the service) unless they are supportive. Neglecting messages that are critical of what is going on can sometimes be fatal. This phenomenon is so common it has even acquired a name: "founder's syndrome" to refer to the unwillingness of some of those who start organizations to recognize the need for change and make room for new people with differing ideas.

Another tendency at the early stage of a nonprofit's life is for little attention to be paid to organization. The lack of formal job descriptions, structures, systems and policies, can cause terrible problems once the organization gets even slightly successful and grows past the stage when a small handful of volunteers or staff can cover everything informally. Miscommunication, confusion, and conflict abound because of gaps, overlaps, and poor memories.

Once the organization gets past its initial founding stage and begins to grow, it enters a transitional or "adolescent" stage. It is at this stage that the greatest risk of not surviving occurs. Several things have to happen before maturity can be reached. Often, initial funding dries up. In fact many foundations and government grants are given only as "seed money" to help in the early stages with the expectation that other sources will be secured after a few years.

The transition stage is also the point at which it is not uncommon for the founding head of the organization to retire, or sometimes even be forced to retire by the board, because of being unable to change with the times. It is a time when the founders may need to "let go" — to find their successors and delegate responsibilities to others. They will even *say* they are going to do this but, in the final analysis, cannot do it so keep second-guessing and contradicting the suggestions of the new leaders.

In the case of organizations started and run by volunteers, this is the stage at which many attempt to bring in a professional manager as paid head. These first paid staff often have a very frustrating time of it because some of the former volunteer managers cannot delegate their authority.

It is at this stage, too, when boards of directors can run into problems and become quite a headache for the paid CEO. In the early stage, the board often must be a "working board" whose members not only meet to discuss major policy issues but also manage important functions such as fundraising or some of the programs. But, as the organization grows and acquires more staff to do the actual work, the board could and should give up some of its involvement in everyday operations, keeping only those few things that staff cannot do and focusing more and more on purely "governance" issues. Often it has trouble doing this so it ends up dabbling in matters that belong to the CEO, second-guessing his or her decisions and generally being more of a nuisance than a help.

By the time an organization passes through the transition stage (and this can take quite a long time — or never — for some) it usually has grown quite large in terms of both budget and people. There are often multiple programs and quite a complicated formal organization structure with several levels of hierarchy, numerous departments or program groups, manuals of policies and procedures, *etc*. In other words, it has become a "mature bureaucracy" with all the dangers that entails — dangers such as tendencies toward empire building, loss of commitment to the cause, interdepartmental rivalries, *etc*. Some large, professionally staffed nonprofits also find it too easy to neglect what is happening to their environments until powerful external stakeholders create a crisis. For example, in the past many hospitals, social service agencies, universities and colleges, refused to believe that large scale government cutbacks would occur so did no planning in advance and were caught in a desperate crisis when budgets were finally slashed.

Summary

This section has outlined some of the major ways in which nonprofit organizations can differ from one another and some of the managerial and leadership issues that can come to the fore under these different conditions. Please understand that they will not always do so and that problems that are most common in one set of conditions can also occur, albeit less frequently, in other conditions.

OVERVIEW OF THE BOOK

The chapters that make up the remainder of this book focus on all of the unique aspects of the management of nonprofit organizations that were identified above. To get a better idea of how the chapters fit together, consider the following simple framework of the elements of nonprofit management — the things that leaders must pay attention to if the organization is going to survive and thrive (see Figure 1).

Figure 1: The Elements of Nonprofit Organization Management

External Elements   *Internal Elements*

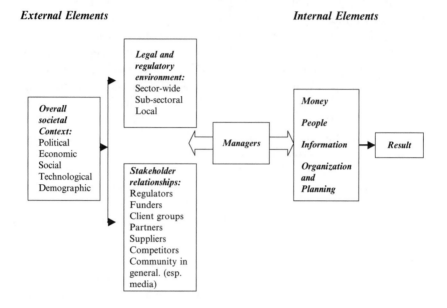

External Concerns

All nonprofit organizations exist in an external environment. It is made up of forces that will determine whether the organization survives or dies. The first responsibility of those who lead is to manage that external world. But few can do it alone. Leaders (and they may be one or several) need resources; therefore, their second responsibility is to manage the "inside" so as to secure, and get the most out of, those resources.

Figure 1 shows most of the elements of the external and internal worlds that must be managed. Looking first at the external world, there are, in the most general sense, a wide range of forces at work that strongly influence how we live as both individuals and organizations. Consider the following:

Politics

Political processes and ideologies matter greatly for many in the nonprofit world. For example, until the collapse of the Soviet empire, there was little in the way of a nonprofit and voluntary sector at all in most of the countries that made it up. This sector has been slowly emerging as these countries develop various forms of democratic political systems. Similarly, until the 1950s in Quebec, the provincial government formed a close partnership with the Roman Catholic Church, which, in effect, dominated the charitable sector for French Canadians.

In recent years, political ideology in Canada has shifted away from favouring the direct provision of many health and social services by government-run organizations. Instead many of these services have been devolved to nonprofit organizations but with government funding supporting them. Clearly, any nonprofit organization that receives money from, or is regulated by, governments must pay close attention to trends in political beliefs and attitudes.

Economics

The state of the economy in whatever regions nonprofits operate for fundraising or program delivery is another critical area to attend to. When times are tough economically (unemployment, rampant inflation, *etc.*), money is short, which makes it much more difficult to raise funds yet, paradoxically, creates a greater demand for services among whole sub-sectors of the nonprofit world. Conversely, "good times" (with high levels of employment, rising wages, *etc.*) can create the opposite problem of making it difficult to find and retain the best employees.

Social Values

These are another set of influences that are perhaps more subtle but no less real. They are the underlying beliefs, attitudes and values that are held in common by members of society in general and by various sub-groups within society. They make up what is generally known as the "culture" of society. Many of these are vital to the survival and growth of nonprofit organizations. For example:

- Beliefs about giving and volunteering — to whom and how much should one donate? Why volunteer and for what?

- Degrees of trust and respect that members of communities have for one another and for the social institutions they deal with such as governments, businesses, schools, hospitals. For example, according to Putnam, growing cynicism and feelings of distrust in the United States have led many to give up on all forms of participation in community life, from voting to volunteering.[12] Without this kind of involvement (or investment of "social capital" as Putnam calls it), the very basis of democracy is threatened. Since research comparable to Putnam's has not been done in Canada, it is unclear the extent to which his conclusions apply to this country, however, fragmentary evidence suggests that at least some areas of society such as large urban centres face the same declines.

Technology

The revolution in electronic information and communications systems (computers, the Internet, the World Wide Web, cell phones, social networking) has been a striking feature of modern society for the past 15 years and continues apace. Even the smallest NPOs can benefit from learning how to use this technology in communicating with volunteers, staff, funders, and other key stakeholders.

Demographics

A final broad contextual condition that NPO leaders must be aware of is population demographics. In recent years there has been a growing consciousness of the effect of changing population demographics on society. In the case of the voluntary sector, the two salient demographic segments are the aging baby boom generation, now mostly in its late 50s and early 60s, and rapidly approaching retirement, and the comparative dearth of young people available to fill their shoes when they go. Though retirees are not the greatest volunteers compared to other groups, their sheer numbers over the next decade will mean that many boomers will look to volunteering but with their usual attitude that nothing that has gone before could be of any value. Just as they had to "discover" relationships, birth, aging, menopause, *etc.* for themselves, so they will insist on discovering late life volunteering and put their own imprint on it. Probably they will be more demanding, want more say in what they do, be more impatient with poorly organized volunteer programs and, just maybe, prove to be more effective than those who have gone before.

---

[12]   See R. Putnam, *Bowling Alone: The Collapse and Renewal of American Community* (New York: Simon & Shuster, 2000).

The point about this review of broad environmental conditions in which NPOs exist is not to say that their leaders ought to try to change them (though as individuals they may well wish to join groups that do), but that it is often necessary to adapt to the pressures they bring to bear and that it is better to do this before they become major crises; hence the need to carry out regular "environmental scans" to spot critical threats and opportunities in the external world.

For most practical purposes, however, the external world impacts NPOs directly through the actions of its major stakeholders — those outside the organization who have an interest in it or whose support the NPO needs in order to survive. These stakeholders include: regulators; funders; client groups; partners; suppliers; competitors; and the community in general (especially the media and influential individuals who shape community opinion). It is a major part of the leader's job to learn what these stakeholders are doing, what their "agendas" are in areas that can impact the organization's functioning, what kind of influence they have and how they use it. This knowledge is necessary to enable the leader to effectively generate the support the organization needs.

Internal Concerns

To successfully manage the environment, NPO leaders need four critical internal resources: People; Money; Information; and Organization and Planning.

People

It is a cliché to say that without an adequate number of the right kind of volunteers and staff little can be accomplished. It is critical that the NPO manager understands how to attract, develop, and motivate staff and volunteers as well as help them to communicate effectively, work co-operatively together, and constantly be on the lookout for better ways to do things.

Money

Even though many small, all-volunteer organizations operate with very little money, most need *some* and, of course, those who employ staff and provide extensive services need a great deal. As mentioned, the unique feature of most NPOs is that their funds do not come from the users of their services, which creates the special challenge of fund development. The second key aspect of managing funds is the need to keep track of them through proper systems of money management — from budgeting to keeping records that can pass an external audit. The death knell of many NPOs is the charge that they mismanage or waste their funds.

Information

The key function of those who manage NPOs is making decisions: what programs to offer or terminate, whom to serve, *etc.* And the basis for effective decision-making is information. Leaders who do not obtain sufficient and accurate information about how their organizations are performing and what threats and opportunities they will face in the immediate future will not last long. This means that the design of proper information systems and a knowledge of the information and communications technology that they use are important.

Organization and Planning

Once an NPO grows beyond a very small handful of volunteers working together informally, it needs agreed-upon structures and processes regarding who will do what and who has the authority to make which decisions. It also needs to think about how to move forward in achieving its mission and put these thoughts in terms that all those involved can understand and subscribe to. This means developing plans and the policies and guidelines that will lead to their fruition.

OUTLINE OF THIS BOOK

Identifying the external and internal elements that leaders of nonprofit organizations must attend to in order to succeed is useful but says nothing about *how* they should handle them. It is the purpose of this book to provide an introduction to what it takes to manage each of these areas.

Chapter 2, "Nonprofit Organizations in Canada", looks at the broad environment by summarizing the latest information available on the size, scope, and importance of the sector as a whole. It also presents the challenges faced by many NPOs in seeking to achieve their missions in order that leaders can see how much they share with others who might seem to be in quite different lines of work.

Chapters 3 and 4, "Managing the Governance Function: Developing Effective Boards of Directors" and "Executive Level Management in Nonprofit Organizations" look at the central figures in the management of NPOs — the board of directors and the executive director. They focus on what each does and what makes the difference between those who create first-class organizations and the rest.

Chapter 5, "The Legal Context of Nonprofit Management", continues the examination of the larger context of the NPO world by focusing on its legal and regulatory environment — laws and regulations at federal, provincial, and even municipal levels — with which NPOs must comply in order to exist. It includes a review of the risks and potential liabilities that need to be considered when making crucial decisions.

Chapters 6 and 7, "Government and Community Relations" and "Resource Development Basics", look at how NPO leaders should relate to their critical external stakeholder groups: government regulators and contractors, potential partners, key community influentials, and the all-important people who provide, or have the potential to provide, needed financial resources to the organization.

The remaining chapters turn the focus inward to the four critical components of effective management within the organization.

Chapter 8, "Planning and Organizing for Results", addresses the constant challenge of deciding how best to achieve the organization's mission and designing a system of organization that will guide it toward the successful implementation of its plans.

Chapter 9, "Preparing for Impact: The Evolution of Evaluation in Canada's Nonprofit Sector", reviews one of the areas that many NPOs find the most difficult — tracking their performance and using this information both for internal decision-making purposes and for reporting to the external and internal bodies to whom its leaders are accountable.

Chapter 10, "Financial Management in Nonprofit Organizations", provides an introduction to what NPO leaders need to know about budgeting, controlling and accounting for the use of the ever-scarce funds they need to fulfill their missions.

Chapter 11, "Managing the Human Dimension in Nonprofit Organizations: Paid Staff and Volunteers", looks at the many factors involved in how to attract, retain, motivate, and make the best use of paid staff and volunteers.

Chapter 12, "Optimizing the Potential for Information and Com-munications Technology in Nonprofit Organizations", focuses on how managers can make the best use of the new technology that has been revolutionizing the way organizations work over the past 20 years with special emphasis on what is possible in the cash-short world of nonprofits.

Chapter 13 "Social Accounting" examines the concept of social accounting, which focuses on how a variety of stakeholders both contribute to it and are affected by it. This approach to accounting is associated primarily with nonprofit social enterprises though it has value for all types of NPOs. It represents an important and developing area requiring the attention of nonprofit leadership.

REFERENCES

P. Elson & P. Hall, *Strength, Size, Scope: A Survey of Social Enterprises in Alberta and British Columbia* (Port Alberni, BC: BALTA, 2010).

M.H. Hall *et al.*, *Cornerstone of Community: Highlights of the National Survey of Nonprofit and Voluntary Organizations* (Ottawa: Ministry of Industry for Statistics Canada, 2004).

Imagine Canada (2014), Research and Public Policy. Accessed online at: <http://www.imaginecanada.ca/node/32>.

J. McKnight, *The Careless Society* (New York: Basic Books, 1995).

R. Putnam, *Bowling Alone: The Collapse and Renewal of American Community* (New York: Simon & Shuster, 2000).

B.A. Weisbrod, ed., *To Profit or Not to Profit: The Commercial Transformation of the Nonprofit Sector* (Cambridge, MA: Harvard University Press, 1998).

Chapter 2

NONPROFIT ORGANIZATIONS IN CANADA

Michael H. Hall
YMCA of Greater Toronto

INTRODUCTION

Nonprofit organizations are key contributors to the social well-being of Canadians and are a significant component of the national economy. They are instruments of collective action that help people to come together and address the issues and interests that matter most to them. Canadians rely on nonprofit organizations to deliver a host of services in fields as varied as education, health, sports and recreation, social services, and arts and culture. As a result, Canada has one of the largest nonprofit sectors in the world.

This chapter provides an overview of national and international research (mostly conducted between 2003 and 2007) on the size and scope of Canada's nonprofit sector and the role it plays in Canadian society. It outlines the diverse areas in which nonprofit organizations work and shows how they vary in terms of the financial and human resources they rely upon to fulfill their mission. Lastly, it discusses the strengths that nonprofit organizations have and the challenges that they face as they work to fulfill their missions.

The overview draws on findings from four main Canadian research initiatives.[1] The main data source is the National Survey of

---

[1] In most of these studies organizations are referred to as "nonprofit and voluntary organizations". There are many terms used to describe the various organizations that are the subject of this chapter — voluntary, nonprofit, charities, third sector, civil society and community-based. The term "nonprofit" is used in this chapter. For a discussion of these terms and a rationale for using them, see A.R. Febbraro, M.H. Hall & M. Parmegiani (1999),

Nonprofit and Voluntary Organizations (NSNVO) conducted under the leadership of Imagine Canada by a consortium of nonprofit research organizations and Statistics Canada in 2003.[2] The NSNVO collected data from approximately 13,000 nonprofit organizations that were formally incorporated or registered with provincial, territorial, or federal governments. Estimates of volunteer hours come from the 2000 National Survey of Giving, Volunteering and Participating,[3] while estimates of the nonprofit and voluntary sector's contribution to the nation's gross domestic product are drawn from the *Satellite Account of Nonprofit Institutions and Volunteering*.[4] To provide comparative perspectives about the Canadian nonprofit sector the data from these studies were integrated with that collected on the nonprofit sectors of 37 countries around the world through the Johns Hopkins Comparative Nonprofit Sector Project conducted under the leadership of Lester Salamon, much of which has been reported elsewhere.[5]

The chapter begins by providing a definition for nonprofit organizations and outlining some of the common ways nonprofit organizations can be classified. Next, it reviews evidence about the economic impact that nonprofit organizations make and compares the size and scope of Canada's nonprofit sector with that of other countries. It then presents information about the key financial and volunteer resources that nonprofit organizations rely upon. The chapter concludes with a discussion of the strengths that organizations report they have and the challenges they face in their efforts to fulfill their missions.

The Voluntary Health Sector in Canada: Developing a Typology – Definition and Classification Issues (Ottawa: Canadian Centre for Philanthropy, Canadian Policy Research Networks, Coalition of National Voluntary Organizations, and Health Canada, 1999).

There has been little new research in this area since the publication of the first edition of this book. The statistics reported here are mostly unchanged with the main exception being revisions to estimates of contributions to the economy, which have been updated to 2007 based on the most recent report from the *Satellite Account of Nonprofit Institutions and Volunteering* from Statistics Canada.

[2] See M.H. Hall *et al.*, *Cornerstones of Community: Highlights of the National Survey of Nonprofit and Voluntary Organizations*, Catalogue No. 61-533-XPE (Ottawa: Statistics Canada, 2004).

[3] See M.H. Hall, L. McKeown & K. Roberts, *Caring Canadians, Involved Canadians: Highlights from the 2000 National Survey of Giving, Volunteering and Participating*, Catalogue No. 71-542-XPE (Ottawa: Statistics Canada, 2001).

[4] See Statistics Canada, *Satellite Account of Nonprofit Institutions and Volunteering: 2007*, Catalogue No. 13-015-X (Ottawa: Statistics Canada, 2009). Online at: <http://www.statcan.gc.ca/pub/13-015-x/13-015-x2009000-eng.pdf>.

[5] See M.H. Hall *et al.*, *The Canadian Nonprofit and Voluntary Sector in Comparative Perspective* (Toronto: Imagine Canada, 2005).

DEFINING AND CLASSIFYING NONPROFIT ORGANIZATIONS

Before providing a statistical portrait of the Canadian nonprofit sector, it may be helpful to explain how nonprofit organizations are being defined in the discussion that follows. As will be seen, the concept of a nonprofit organization is broad and includes a diverse set of actors.

Defining Nonprofit Organizations

Most of the research that is presented in this chapter employs the "structural-operational" definition of nonprofit organizations developed by Salamon and Anheier or some variant thereof.[6] This definition considers organizations to be nonprofits if they are:

- organized (*i.e.*, having some structure and regularity to their operations)[7]

- non-governmental (*i.e.*, institutionally separate from governments)

- nonprofit distributing (*i.e.*, do not return any profits generated to their owners or directors)[8]

- self-governing (*i.e.*, are independent and able to regulate their own activities)

- voluntary (*i.e.*, benefit to some degree from voluntary contributions of time or money)

It is important to recognize that relationships between nonprofit organizations and the state are dynamic and evolve over time. The extent to which government exerts or relinquishes control over specific

---

[6]   See L.M. Salamon & H.K. Anheier, eds., *Defining the Nonprofit Sector: A Cross-National Analysis* (Manchester, N.Y.: Manchester University Press, 1997).

[7]   The NSNVO excluded "grass-roots" organizations or citizens' groups that are not formally incorporated or registered with provincial, territorial, or federal governments. It also excluded some organizations that may be registered charities but are normally considered to be public sector agencies (*e.g.*, school boards, public libraries, and public schools). These types of organizations are also not included in the *Satellite Account of Nonprofit Institutions and Volunteering*.

[8]   A small number of co-operatives were included in the NSNVO. Jack Quarter notes that some co-operatives — including credit unions and groups that deal with farm marketing and food retailing — do allow members to hold shares in the organization. The mission of these organizations is typically not to maximize profits and, unlike the shares of a business, the shares of such co-operatives do not entitle holders to dividends of any year-end surplus. See J. Quarter, *Canada's Social Economy: Co-operatives, Non-profits and Other Community Enterprises* (Toronto: James Lorimer, 1993).

types of organizations can change their eligibility for inclusion in the nonprofit sector according to Salamon and Anheier's structural-operational definition. In applying this definition in the early 2000s, hospitals, universities, and colleges were included as part of the nonprofit sector.[9] Despite the fact that these organizations receive substantial amounts of public funding and are extensively regulated by government, they are generally governed by volunteer boards, registered as charities, and receive substantial contributions of volunteer time.

Although small in number, hospitals, universities and colleges are typically very large in terms of the size of their revenues and the number of people they employ. Although they are non-governmental in terms of being institutionally separate from government, they are nevertheless tightly controlled by government particularly in the case of hospitals and community colleges. It is helpful therefore to distinguish these organizations from other nonprofit organizations when presenting economic statistics because of their disproportionate impact. Economic statistics are presented in this chapter both for the entire nonprofit sector (with hospitals, universities and colleges included) and for what has been termed the "core nonprofit sector" (*i.e.*, all organizations except hospitals, universities and colleges).[10]

Finally, it is worth noting that the nonprofit sector framework is a specific framework for distinguishing and classifying social and economic organizations that dominates academic discourse in the United States and most of Canada. However, an alternative framework — the social economy — predominates in Quebec and in many parts of Europe.

One of the fundamental distinctions between these two frameworks is the role that the distribution of profits plays. In the Salmon and Anheier definition of the nonprofit sector, organizations are excluded if they distribute profits to owners regardless of whether or not they are driven by a social mission. As a result, organizations such as cooperatives, social enterprises and community economic development organizations are not considered to be part of the nonprofit sector. However, these organizations are usually considered

---

[9]   Hospitals, in particular, have became much more tightly controlled by government over the past decade and whether or not these institutions should be included in the nonprofit sector today is open for debate.

[10]   This follows the practice adopted by the *Satellite Account of Nonprofit Institutions and Volunteering*.

to be part of the social economy.[11] As a result, analyses of the social and economic contributions of the nonprofit sector will produce different (usually smaller) estimates than will similar analyses of the social economy.

Legal Distinctions

About half of all nonprofit organizations are formally registered as charitable organizations with the Canada Revenue Agency. In order to be eligible for registered charity status an organization's major purpose must fall into one of four areas: the relief of poverty, the advancement of education, the advancement of religion, or other purposes of a charitable nature beneficial to the community as a whole, including health. Charitable status provides two main advantages for organizations. It gives their donors access to tax incentives for the donations they make and enables organizations to access funding from charitable foundations which are restricted by law to registered charities and a small number of other "qualified donees".

Area of Activity

People commonly identify organizations according to their area of activity and are quite familiar with terms such as arts organizations, sports clubs, or social service organizations. Along these lines, this chapter employs a version of the International Classification of Nonprofit Organizations (ICNPO), a system developed by Salamon and Anheir and modified by Hall et al. for the Canadian context.[12] Table 1 outlines the 15 categories into which organizations have been classified based on their primary area of economic activity. While organizations may operate in more than one area (e.g., providing recreation opportunities and day care), they are classified into the single ICNPO category that describes where most of their time and resources are allocated.

---

[11] See J. Quarter, L. Mook & A. Armstrong, *Understanding the Social Economy: A Canadian Perspective* (Toronto: University of Toronto Press, 2009).

[12] See L.M. Salamon & H.J. Anheier, eds., *Defining the Nonprofit Sector: A Cross-National Analysis* (Manchester, N.Y.: Manchester University Press, 1997). See also M.H. Hall, *et al.*, *Cornerstones of Community: Highlights of the National Survey of Nonprofit and Voluntary Organizations*, Catalogue No. 61-533-XPE (Ottawa: Statistics Canada, 2004).

Type of Functions

Nonprofit organizations perform a variety of functions in Canadian life ranging from the provision of human and social services to offering vehicles for citizens to express their interests and address community needs through collective action and advocacy. Salamon has proposed two broad categories of functions:[13]

- **Service functions** involve the delivery of direct services such as education, health, housing, community and economic development promotion, animal welfare and social services.

- **Expressive functions** involve activities that enable the expression of cultural, spiritual, professional, and other interests and beliefs. Organizations serving expressive functions include sports and recreation groups, religious organizations, arts and cultural organizations, labour and professional associations, advocacy groups and those working on environmental issues.

Table 1: Nonprofit Organization Activity Types

Arts and culture	operate in general or specialized fields of arts and culture
Sports and recreation	operate in general or specialized fields of sports and recreation
Education and research	administer, provide, promote conduct, support and service education and research, excluding public school boards, universities, colleges, and postsecondary institutions
Universities and colleges	universities and colleges, postsecondary institutions
Health	engage in health-related activities, providing and administering both general and specialized health care services, as well as health support services, excluding hospitals
Hospitals	hospital facilities that provide inpatient or outpatient medical care, organizations and institutions providing social services to a community or target population
Social services	provide social services to a community or target population

---

[13] For a discussion of these functions, see L.M. Salamon, *America's Nonprofit Sector: A Primer*, 2d ed. (New York: The Foundation Center, 1999) at 15-17.

Environment	promote and provide services in environmental conservation, pollution control and prevention, environmental education and health, and animal protection
Development and housing	promote programs and provide services to help improve communities and promote the economic and social well-being of society
Law, advocacy and politics	work to protect and promote civil and other rights, advocate the social and political interests of general or special constituencies, offer legal services, and promote public safety
Grant-making, fundraising and voluntarism promotion	philanthropic organizations and those promoting charity and charitable activities, including grant-making foundations, voluntarism promotion and support, and fundraising organizations
International	promote cultural understanding between peoples of various countries and historical backgrounds, and/or provide relief during emergencies and/or promote development and welfare abroad
Religion	promote religious beliefs and administering religious services and rituals (such as churches, mosques, synagogues, temples, shrines, seminaries, monasteries, and similar religious institutions); and related organizations and auxiliaries of such organizations
Business and professional associations and unions	promote, regulate and safeguard business, professional and labour interests
Organizations not elsewhere classified	a small number of organizations that were unable to identify their primary activity within any of the specified activity categories

Source: Statistics Canada, National Survey of Nonprofit and Voluntary Organizations.

In the sections that follow, these various ways of classifying nonprofit organizations are employed to provide a portrait of their size and scope and the resources that they rely upon.

THE SIZE AND SCOPE OF CANADA'S NONPROFIT SECTOR

In 2003, there were an estimated 161,000 nonprofit organizations operating in the country. As Figure 1 shows, their activities are diverse and most organizations serve expressive functions. The two largest areas of activity involve expressive functions: Sports and Recreation (21 per cent of all organizations) and Religion (19 per cent). Social Service organizations are the next largest group comprising 12 per cent of all organizations.

Figure 1: Types of Nonprofit Organizations

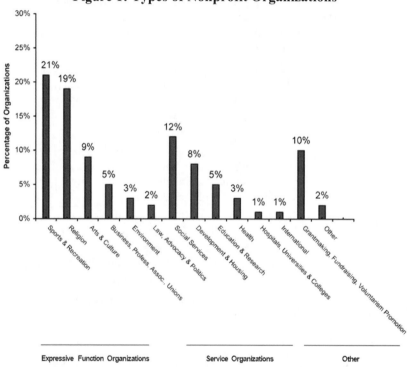

Source: Statistics Canada, National Survey of Nonprofit and Voluntary Organizations.

About half of all nonprofit organizations are registered charities. Their areas of activity reflect the requirement that they engage in specific types of activities to obtain charitable status. Registered charities make up over 70 per cent of all organizations operating in the areas of Religion, Social Services, Health, Hospitals, Universities & Colleges, Education & Research, International Development, and Grantmaking, Fundraising & Voluntarism Promotion. Over half of the Arts & Culture and Education & Research Organizations are also registered charities.

Geographic Area of Focus

The ability of nonprofit organizations to understand the needs of the communities in which they are based is often cited as one of their key strengths. Most non-profit organizations (64 per cent) operate at the local level serving a neighbourhood, town, or regional municipality. About one-fifth (19 per cent) serve a region, while about one in ten (9 per cent) serve a province or territory. A small minority operate in more than one province (2 per cent) or at a national (3 per cent) or international level (3 per cent).

Public versus Mutual Benefit

One of the questions that is raised about nonprofit organizations is the extent to which they exist to meet the needs of their members rather than to provide a larger public benefit. The NSNVO reveals a Canadian nonprofit sector that serves and is supported by the Canadian public. Most organizations (76 per cent) have individuals as members, collectively reporting a total membership of 139 million people (which indicates that many individuals hold multiple memberships in nonprofit organizations). Of those organizations with individuals as members, more than half (57 per cent) place no restrictions on membership and allow anyone to join. Only 27 per cent of all organizations report that their members receive special benefits or privileges from their membership, and 39 per cent indicate that their members benefit most from the services provided.

ECONOMIC CONTRIBUTIONS

Nonprofit organizations are significant players in the Canadian economy. In 2007, they accounted for 7 per cent of the nation's gross domestic product (GDP). These estimates do not take into account the value of volunteer activity, which could add an additional 1.4 per cent of contribution to GDP.[14]

---

[14] Statistics Canada's most recent report on the *Satellite Account of Nonprofit Institutions and Volunteering* did not calculate the value of volunteering because of data issues. The value reported is the contribution to GDP that was calculated in 2000.

Table 2: Economic Contribution of Nonprofit Organizations to the Canadian Economy

Total Nonprofit Sector

$100.7 billion added to national economy (excluding the value of volunteers)

7.0 % of Gross Domestic Product (excluding the value of volunteers)

2,073,032 full-time equivalent workforce

1,524,032 full-time equivalent paid employees

549,000 full-time equivalent volunteers

12.1% of the economically active population

Core Nonprofit Sector (excluding hospitals, colleges, and universities)

$35.6 billion added to national economy (excluding value of volunteers)

2.5% of the economy

1,541,345 full-time equivalent workforce

1,016,856 full-time equivalent paid employees

524,489 full-time equivalent volunteers

9% of the economically active population

Source: Johns Hopkins Comparative Nonprofit Sector Project, Statistics Canada Satellite Account of Nonprofit Institutions and Volunteering, 2000 National Survey of Giving, Volunteering and Participating, and National Survey of Nonprofit and Voluntary Organizations.

If one sets aside the one per cent of Canadian organizations that are hospitals, universities and colleges, the remaining organizations (the core nonprofit sector) contributed 2.5 per cent of the nation's GDP in 2007. The contribution of the core nonprofit sector is larger than many other well-recognized industrial sectors. It contributed more than two and a half times the amount of the agriculture sector and close to six times more than motor vehicle manufacturing even when the value of volunteering, which is considerable, is excluded (see Figure 2, below).[15]

---

[15]   Note that these data are for 2006 because 2007 data was not provided.

Figure 2: Comparative Contribution to GDP

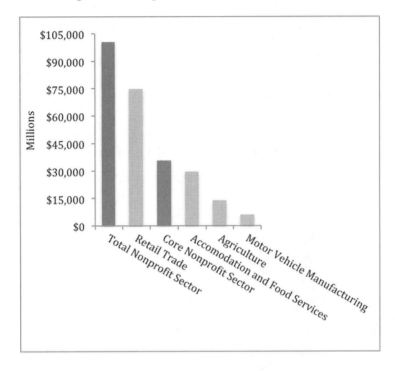

Note: Industry sector data is for 2006.

Source: *Satellite Account of Nonprofit Institutions and Volunteering: 2007*, Catalogue No. 13-015-X (Ottawa: Statistics Canada, 2009). Online at: <http://www.statcan.gc.ca/pub/13-015-x/13-015-x2009000-eng.pdf>.

A Growing Economic Contribution

From 1997 to 2007, the economic contributions of the core nonprofit sector nearly doubled in size growing by an average of 7.1 per cent per year. The rate of growth outpaced the 5.8 per cent average yearly growth in the economy as a whole.[16] In contrast, annual average growth in economic activity among hospitals, universities and colleges was 6 per cent less than that of the core nonprofit sector but close to the growth of the economy as a whole.

---

[16] See Statistics Canada, *Satellite Account of Non-profit Institutions and Volunteering: 2007*, Catalogue No. 13-015-X (Ottawa: Statistics Canada, 2009). Online at: <http://www.statcan. gc.ca/pub/13-015-x/13-015-x2009000-eng.pdf>.

A Substantial Workforce

The nonprofit sector is a major employer. With a workforce of 1.5 million full-time equivalent (FTE) paid staff and 549,000 FTE equivalent volunteers in 2003, it engages 12 per cent of the economically active population. To put this in perspective, the workforce is almost the size of the entire manufacturing industry in the country (see Figure 3).

Figure 3: The Relative Size of the Nonprofit Workforce (Paid Employees and Volunteers)

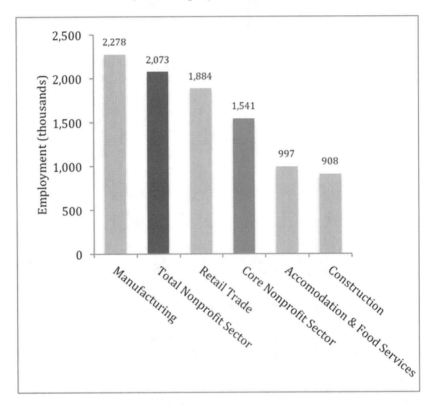

Source: Statistics Canada 2000 National Survey of Giving, Volunteering and Participating; and National Survey of Nonprofit and Voluntary Organizations. Statistics Canada CANSIM Table 282-0008.

The core nonprofit sector alone engages 1 million FTE paid staff and 524,489 FTE volunteers or 9 per cent of the economically active population. In 2003 its workforce was more than one and one-half times larger than the accommodation and food services industry and almost one and two-thirds larger than the construction industry.

INTERNATIONAL COMPARISONS

How does Canada's nonprofit sector compare to that of other countries? Is it bigger or smaller? Does it engage in the same types of activities? Answers to these questions are available from research conducted as part of the Johns Hopkins University, Comparative Nonprofit Sector Project (CNP).[17]

Of the 37 countries that participated in the CNP, Canada has the second largest nonprofit sector when expressed as a share of the economically active population.[18] Indeed, it is far larger than the nonprofit sectors in the United States, the United Kingdom, France or many other developed countries (see Figure 4, below).

---

[17] See M.H. Hall *et al.*, *The Canadian Nonprofit and Voluntary Sector in Comparative Perspective* (Toronto: Imagine Canada, 2005).

[18] The study included 17 advanced, industrial countries from North America, Western Europe and Asia; 15 developing countries across Latin America, Africa, the Middle East and Asia; and five countries in Central and Eastern Europe. International comparisons performed by the CNP exclude religious organizations.

Figure 4: Nonprofit Sector Workforce (Paid Employees and Volunteers) as a Share of the Economically Active Population, by Country

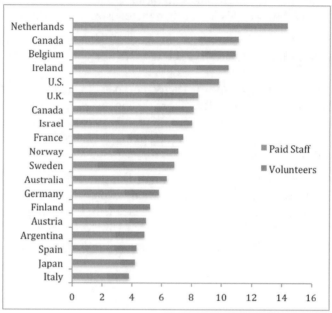

Source: Johns Hopkins Comparative Nonprofit Sector Project, Statistics Canada 2000. National Survey of Giving, Volunteering and Participating, National Survey of Nonprofit and Voluntary Organizations.

More Professionalized

The Canadian nonprofit sector is not only relatively large compared to many other countries, it is more professionalized and draws more on the efforts of paid employees. Three-quarters of the full-time equivalent workforce of Canadian nonprofit organizations is comprised of paid employees compared to 62 per cent in the 37 countries that participated in the CNP.

Canadian nonprofit organizations also engage more volunteers in their activities than do nonprofit organizations in many other countries. Three per cent of the economically active population in Canada contributes volunteer time to nonprofit organizations, an amount that is almost double the average for developed countries in the CNP (1.6 per cent) and larger than the overall CNP international average (2.7 per cent), but less than the amount of volunteer effort contributed in Sweden, Norway, the United Kingdom, France and the United States.

FINANCIAL AND HUMAN RESOURCES

Securing adequate financial and human resources is a key aspect of nonprofit management. With that in mind, it is useful to understand how nonprofit organizations are typically resourced and the particular types of resources that different types of organizations depend upon.

Financial Resources

Using 2003 data as our point of reference, most nonprofit organizations rely on two main sources of revenue — earned income and government funding (often in the form of payment for services delivered). Looking at the nonprofit sector as a whole, 49 per cent of all revenue comes from government compared to 35 per cent from earned income[19] and 13 per cent from private giving (*i.e.*, individual donations, foundation grants and corporate contributions).[20] With respect to government funding it is important to note that 83 per cent of all government funding comes directly from provincial or territorial governments.

For the core nonprofit sector, 43 per cent of revenues come from earned income, followed by 36 per cent from government and 17 per cent from gifts and donation. The most important sources of earned income are fees for goods or services (21 per cent of all revenues) and membership fees (16 per cent). Turning to government funding, almost one-quarter of all revenues for this group come from provincial governments and 9 percent from the federal government. The leading sources of revenue from gifts and donations are contributions from individuals (11 per cent of all revenues) and from corporations (3 per cent).

Nonprofit managers may find it informative to examine how the revenue profiles for their own organizations compare to those for their sub-sector overall. Government funding is dominant among social service and health organizations, hospitals, and universities and colleges (see Figure 5). On the other hand, earned income predominates

---

[19] The earned income category does not include payments from government for goods or services; such revenues are classified as government funding.

[20] See M.H. Hall *et al.*, *Cornerstones of Community: Highlights of the National Survey of Nonprofit and Voluntary Organizations*, Catalogue No. 61-533-XPE (Ottawa: Statistics Canada, 2004).

among sports and recreation, arts and culture, business, professional associations and unions, development and housing, and environmental organizations. Religious organizations are unique in their reliance on private giving as the primary source of their revenue.

Generally speaking, service delivery organizations rely more on government funding than do expressive function organizations, which rely more upon earned income and donations (see Figure 5). This undoubtedly reflects the role that these organizations play in delivering human and social services on behalf of government departments.

Figure 5: Sources of Revenue by Area of Activity

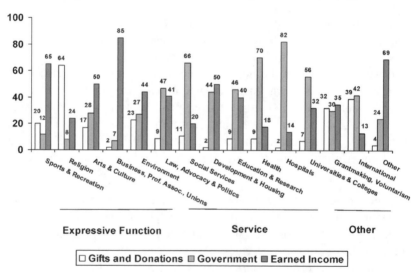

Source: Statistics Canada, National Survey of Nonprofit and Voluntary Organizations.

There are substantial variations among sub-sectors in terms of the amount of revenues that organizations receive. As Figure 6 shows, Hospitals, Universities, and Colleges have average annual revenues that far outstrip those of other organizations ($31.4 million and $24.7 million, respectively). Health organizations ($1.7 million average annual revenues), international development organizations ($1.2 million) and business, professional associations and unions ($1.3 million) have substantially larger revenues than other types of organizations. In contrast, sports and recreation, religious and arts and culture organizations have the smallest revenues. As will be seen, these organizations rely much more on volunteers to operate and much less on paid staff.

Figure 6: Average Annual Revenues by Type of Organization

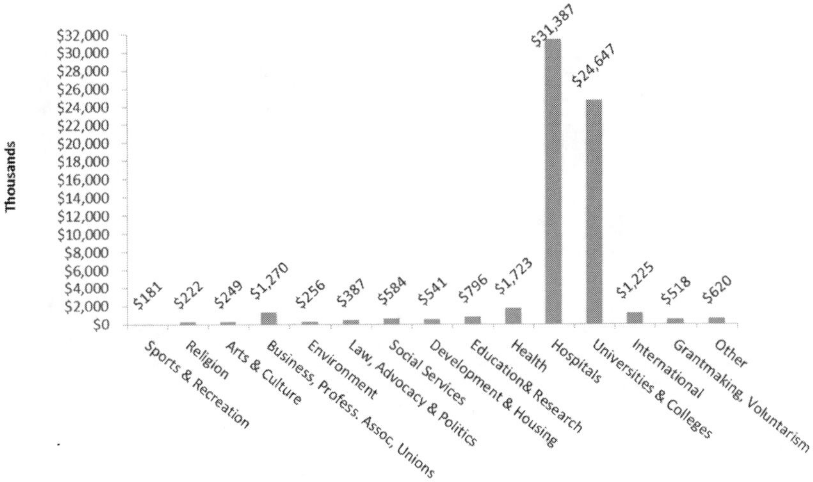

Source: Statistics Canada, National Survey of Nonprofit and Voluntary Organizations.

Concentration of Revenues

Large revenue organizations receive the bulk of resources in the nonprofit sector. As Figure 7 shows, the 1 per cent of organizations that have annual revenues of $10 million or more receive 58 per cent of all revenues in the nonprofit sector and the 7 per cent that have annual revenues over $1 million receive 84 per cent of all revenues. This concentration of economic activity is a pattern that is also found in the for-profit sector where small businesses predominate in terms of numbers, but a small number of large companies dominate economically. With 63 per cent of nonprofit organizations operating on revenues of under $100,000, it is clear that many nonprofit managers have to know how to operate their organizations without an abundance of resources.

Figure 7: Distribution of Revenues by Size of Organization

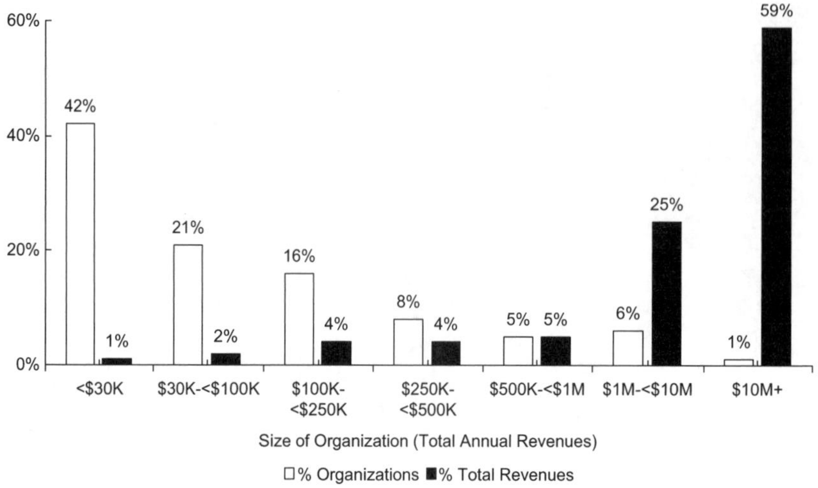

Size of Organization (Total Annual Revenues)

□% Organizations ■% Total Revenues

Source: Statistics Canada, National Survey of Nonprofit and Voluntary Organizations.

Human Resources

One of the unique aspects of Canadian nonprofit organizations is their ability to engage volunteers in their activities. In many nonprofit organizations, managers need to attend to two distinct types of human resources: volunteers and paid staff.

The majority of nonprofit organizations (54 per cent) rely solely on volunteers for their operations (see Figure 8) and only 12 per cent have paid staff complements of 10 or more. These volunteer-only organizations are most common among grantmaking, fundraising and voluntarism (82 per cent have no paid staff), sports and recreation (73.5 per cent), environmental, and arts and culture organizations (see Figure 9). Organizations with relatively large staff complements, on the other hand, are more likely to be operating in the areas of health, hospitals, universities and colleges and social services. Generally, service delivery organizations tend to have larger staff complements than expressive function organizations, with the exception of the development and housing sub-sector (56 per cent have no paid staff).

Figure 8: Distribution of Nonprofit Organizations by Staff Size

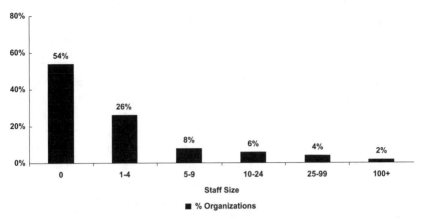

Source: Statistics Canada, National Survey of Nonprofit and Voluntary Organizations.

Figure 9: Size of Paid Staff by Area of Activity

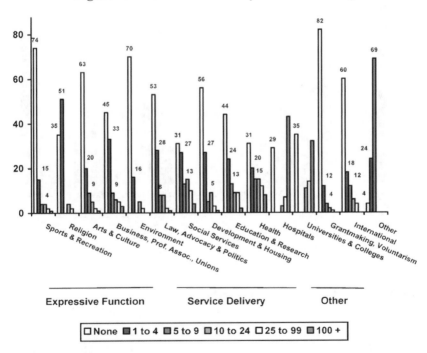

Source: Statistics Canada, National Survey of Nonprofit and Voluntary Organizations.

Volunteers perform a variety of functions. Most (93 per cent) are engaged in the delivery of programs and services or in fundraising and campaigning activities. Less than one in ten (7 per cent) participate in the governance of the organization by serving on boards of directors.

It is not surprising that the extent to which organizations have paid staff depends largely upon the size of their revenues (see Figure 10). Most organizations with annual revenues of $100,000 or less do not have any paid staff, while over one-half of the organizations with revenues between $100,000 and $250,000 have between one and four paid staff. In contrast, at least one-half of organizations with annual revenues of $1 million or more have staff complements of 25 or larger.

Figure 10: Paid Staff Employment by Size of Revenues

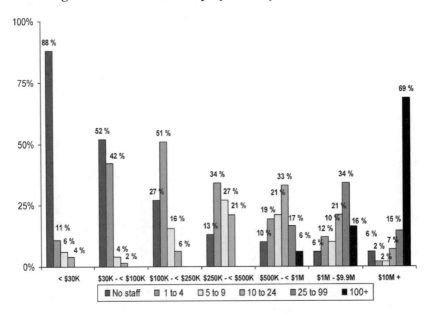

Source: Statistics Canada, National Survey of Nonprofit and Voluntary Organizations.

STRENGTHS AND CHALLENGES

While statistics on the size, scope and structure of the nonprofit sector in Canada are informative, they provide only part of the picture of organizational life within the nonprofit sector. A number of studies have provided a view from inside the organization about the strengths that nonprofit organizations have and the challenges they face. For example, Zarinpoush and Hall in their 2007 qualitative study observe that nonprofit leaders are:

> ... grappling with and adapting to a complex and changing environment, focussing on the need for a skilled and motivated workforce, looking for ways to expand their impact through collaboration, and working to improve their revenues through innovation and advocacy with their funders. They appear to be looking to the possibility of building new relationships with business and wary of their relationships with governments. And, finally, they are looking for ways to get the recognition from the public that they feel their organizations, staff and volunteers deserve.[21]

Before discussing in detail the research findings on the challenges faced by nonprofit organizations, we first focus on the organizational strengths that nonprofit leaders and staff identify.

Strengths

In a study involving a series of 36 focus groups conducted across Canada in 2002, Hall *et al.* found that nonprofit staff most frequently identified two main areas of strength in their organizations — their people and their relationships and networks with members, the community and other organizations.[22] Volunteers were most frequently mentioned as a strength with paid staff coming a close second. Participants often commented on the dedication and commitment of their volunteers and staff, as well as their teamwork, talent and professionalism, flexibility, efficiency, and their focus on the organization's vision. Zarinpoush and Hall also found that nonprofit leaders considered having professional and motivated paid staff as one of the great strengths of their organization, as well as board members when they had diversified skills and experience.

The second most frequently identified strength in the Hall *et al.* study was the relationships and networks that organizations have established with members, the community, and other organizations and their ability to draw on these relationships to support their work. Members were often recognized as a key underlying support for

---

[21] See F. Zarinpoush & M.H. Hall, *Leadership Perspectives: Interviews with Leaders of Canada's Charities and Nonprofit Organizations* (Toronto: Imagine Canada, 2007) at 18.

[22] See M.H. Hall *et al.*, *The Capacity to Serve: A Qualitative Study of the Challenges Facing Canada's Nonprofit and Voluntary Organizations* (Toronto: Canadian Centre for Philanthropy, 2003).

organizations and the value of having "broad and deep" community support was often noted. The ability to build networks with other organizations (both for-profit and nonprofit) was also reported to be one of their strengths insofar as they allowed organizations to access and share resources. Similarly, Zarinpoush and Hall report that nonprofit leaders identified their ability to collaborate as a key strength because it offered a way to both broaden the human and intellectual capital of the organization, to leverage resources, and to increase public confidence in the organization's work.

Nonprofit organizations also frequently identify their abilities in planning and organizational development as key strengths (Hall *et al.*; Zarinpoush and Hall). These strengths can help them to respond to a dynamic and changing nonprofit environment.

Challenges

The research that was conducted in the early 2000s shows that many nonprofit organizations were operating under strain even during a time of relatively strong economic growth. According to the 2003 NSNVO, those areas that appeared to pose the greatest problems involved recruiting and retaining volunteers, planning for the future, and obtaining funding.[23] Zarinpoush and Hall's 2007 study shows that many of these challenges remained four years later.

More recent research suggests that financial pressures are an enduring feature of organizational life for registered charities. Lasby & Barr (2013) report that in a series of surveys of charities conducted between 2011 and 2012, close to one-half of respondents predicted difficulty covering their expenses during the next two years with around 10 per cent predicting difficulty within the next quarter or sooner.[24]

The NSNVO explored a variety of possible challenges that organizations may experience as they attempted to fulfill their mission. The majority of organizations (56 per cent to 58 per cent) reported problems planning for the future, recruiting the types of volunteers the organization needed, and obtaining board members (see Figure 11, below). Close to one-half (48 per cent to 49 per cent) reported

---

[23]   See M.H. Hall *et al.*, *Cornerstones of Community: Highlights of the National Survey of Nonprofit and Voluntary Organizations*, Catalogue No. 61-533-XPE (Ottawa: Statistics Canada, 2004).

[24]   See D. Lasby & C. Barr, *Sector Monitor* 3:2 (Toronto: Imagine Canada, 2013). Online at: <http://www.imaginecanada.ca/files/www/en/sectormonitor/sectormonitor_v3_n2_2013.pdf>.

problems retaining volunteers, obtaining funding from other organizations such as government, foundations or corporations, and obtaining funding from individual donors. A substantial number reported that they were experiencing *serious* problems, particularly obtaining funding from individual donors (20 per cent report serious problems), planning for the future (15 per cent), and recruiting the type of volunteer the organization needs (15 per cent).

Close to 40 per cent of respondents reported problems with in-creasing demands for services or products, competition with other organizations for funding or revenues; difficulty earning revenues; difficulty adapting to change; lack of internal capacity; difficulty participating in the development of public policy; and difficulty providing training for volunteers (see Figure 12, below).

Figure 11: Top Six Problems that Keep Organizations from Fulfilling their Missions

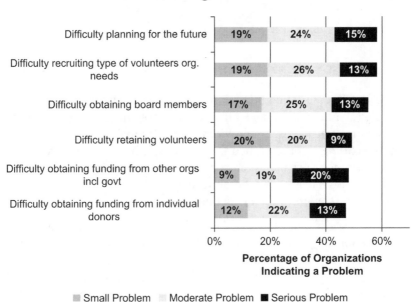

Source: Statistics Canada, National Survey of Nonprofit and Voluntary Organizations.

Figure 12: Other Problems that Keep Organizations from Fulfilling their Missions

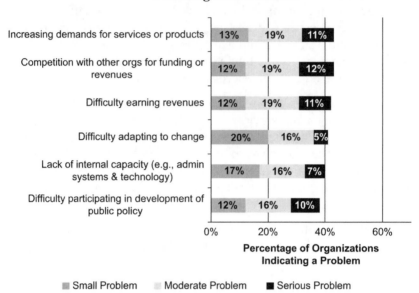

Source: Statistics Canada, National Survey of Nonprofit and Voluntary Organizations.

The NSNVO found that relatively few organizations experienced challenges in areas such as staff retention, obtaining the type of staff the organization needs, or providing staff training and development (less than 30 per cent identified these as problem areas). However, this also reflects the fact that over one-half of all nonprofit organizations have no paid staff. Larger organizations with paid staff were much more likely to report problems in this area.

Zarinpoush and Hall's 2007 study with a sample of leaders of larger nonprofit organizations found recruiting and retaining skilled staff to be their most frequently identified challenge. These leaders also frequently expressed concerns about organizational renewal and an aging workforce. Similarly, a 2008 survey of nonprofit sector employers found that nearly one-half of those reporting recruitment activity in the previous 12 months indicated that it was "difficult" or "very difficult" for their organization to find qualified people.[25]

---

[25] HR Council for the Voluntary & Non-profit Sector, *Toward a Labour Force Strategy for Canada's Voluntary & Non-Profit Sector: Findings from Canada-wide Surveys of Employer and Employees* (Report #2) (Ottawa: Author, 2008).

Problems with External Funding

The NSNVO found that the most serious problems were reported by organizations that relied on external funding from governments, corporations and foundations (see Figure 13). Almost two-thirds of organizations that received external funding reported that reductions in government funding were a problem and over one-third indicated that it was a serious problem. Six in ten reported problems arising from the unwillingness of funders to fund core operations with almost three in ten identifying it as a serious problem. Similar numbers reported difficulties because of an over-reliance on project funding. Close to half indicated problems arising from the need to modify programs in order to receive funding and just over four in ten reported problems with the reporting requirements of funders.

Figure 13: Problems Related to External Funding

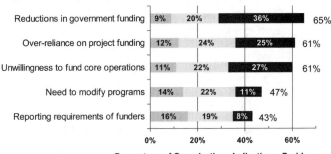

Percentage of Organizations Indicating a Problem

■ Small Problem   Moderate Problem   ■ Serious Problem

Source: Statistics Canada, National Survey of Nonprofit and Voluntary Organizations.

Note: Based on responses of 39 per cent of organizations that had been active for at least three years and that had received funding from governments, foundations, or corporations over that period. Government funding accounted for the bulk of their funding.

Zarinpoush and Hall's 2007 study reported similar findings with leaders of organizations that were financially dependent on government expressing concerns about their dependency and vulnerability to shifts in government priorities and funding. The biggest concern for leaders in these organizations was how to maintain their funding. Leaders noted problems with the lack of support for "core" activities and the inability of organizations to recover the full costs of delivering programs and services.

Organizations that rely on government funding appear to be still struggling to adapt to reverberations emanating from the radical cuts in government program spending that occurred during the 1990s. Between 1992 and 1999, total government program spending was reduced by approximately 20 per cent.[26] The funding regime for many nonprofits changed significantly and, as Hall et al.[27] and Scott[28] have noted, many are still attempting to cope with changes such as:

- reductions in funding;

- the introduction of competitive bid processes for government funding (particularly among health and social service organizations) that in some instances have included competition with private business;

- a move to fund projects rather than provide general support for an organization's activities;

- the restriction of funding to direct program costs, with little provision for infrastructure or the administrative overhead associated with program delivery;

- shorter duration of funding;

- frequently changing funding priorities;

- mandated collaborations with other organizations; and

- increasing requirements for financial accountability.

These changes combine to create a difficult operating environment for organizations that are delivering services on behalf of government. Unstable and short-term funding makes long-term strategic planning more of a guessing game than a rational process. It also undermines the ability of organizations to develop the human and intellectual capital they require. The administrative burden associated with acquiring funding, reporting on funding, and collaborating with others also appears to have increased. At the same time, fewer

---

[26] Measured as a percentage of GDP, government program spending fell from an all-time high of 43 per cent in 1993 to 34 per cent in 1999. See J. Stanford, "The Economic and Social Consequences of Fiscal Retrenchment in Canada in the 1990s" in K. Banting, A. Sharpe & F. St-Hilaire, eds., *The Review of Economic Performance and Social Progress – The Longest Decade: Canada in the 1990s* (Montreal: Institute for Research on Public Policy and Centre for the Study of Living Standards, 2001) 141-160.

[27] M.H. Hall et al., *The Capacity to Serve: A Qualitative Study of the Challenges Facing Canada's Nonprofit and Voluntary Organizations* (Toronto: Canadian Centre for Philanthropy, 2003).

[28] K. Scott, *Funding Matters: The Impact of Canada's New Funding Regime on Nonprofit and Voluntary Organizations* (Ottawa: Canadian Council on Social Development, 2003).

resources are available to support these activities or others that are equally important, such as the management and development of the organization's paid staff and volunteers.

Economic Challenges

Most of the research on Canadian nonprofit organizations has been conducted in periods of economic growth. As we have seen, nonprofit organizations reported considerable challenges fulfilling their missions even in a strong economy. But what happens to nonprofit organizations when the economy is in a recession as was the case in 2008 to 2009 or in a period of slow economic growth, which Canada has been experiencing since the recession? Unfortunately, we have little research to inform us.

Organizations that rely heavily on growth in charitable donations may not see the same growth that they have in the recent past. As Lasby (2011) reports there was strong growth in donations between 1995 and 2007 (with average annual growth of 6.7 per cent and 80 per cent growth overall).[29] However, during the 2009 recession donations declined by 6 per cent and in 2010 growth resumed at a more modest 4.6 per cent.

There has been little definitive research on the impacts of an economic downturn or the effect of a slow growth economy on nonprofit organizations. While a small number of studies were conducted during the recession these relied on convenience samples and were not broadly representative of the Canadian nonprofit sector.[30] These studies reported that a significant percentage of organizations had experienced increased demands for services or downturns in earned income, investments, and donations.

Lasby & Barr (2013) report findings from a series of biannual surveys from mid 2011 to late 2012 that focused on the impact of economic conditions on registered charities that have annual revenues

---

[29] D. Lasby, "Trends in individual donations: 1984-2010" *Research Bulletin* 15:1 (Toronto: Imagine Canada, 2011). Online at: <http://sectorsource.ca/resource/file/trends-individual-donations-1984-2010>.

[30] See, for example, Ontario Trillium Foundation, *Challenges and Opportunities for Ontario's Not-for-Profit Sector during Tough Economic Times* (Toronto: Author, 2009). Online at: <http://www.otf.ca/en/knowledgeSharingCentre/resources/challenging_times.pdf>; and Calgary Chamber of Voluntary Organizations, *Survey Findings: Impact of the Economic Downturn on Alberta's Nonprofits & Charities* (March 2009). Online at: <http://www.calgarycvo.org/wpcontent/uploads/2013/04/ReportonImpactoftheEconomicDownturnSurvey ResultsFINAL_01.pdf>.

of $30,000 or more and are not religious congregations. As they observe, charity leaders are "about as likely to report most external economic challenges as they have in the past".[31] About one-half of survey respondents reported increased demand for services and having difficulty fulfilling their missions in each of the surveys. The most noteworthy trend was a steady increase in those predicting difficulty covering expenses in the upcoming year (from 17 per cent in mid-2011 to 22 per cent in both mid- and late 2012).

CONCLUSION

Most Canadians are unaware of the economic and social contributions that Canada's nonprofit organizations make. Yet the activities of nonprofit organizations touch virtually every aspect of our lives. Nonprofit organizations enable Canadians to come together to provide opportunities for sports and recreation, advocate for social justice or the environment, encourage arts and cultural expression, provide food and housing to those in need, offer educational opportunities, provide health care and more.

Most organizations rely on modest resources and are driven by the energies and talents of volunteers. However, a small but significant number of organizations command substantial human and financial resources in pursuit of their missions.

The contribution of nonprofit organizations to the nation's economy far outstrips those of a number of more recognized for-profit industrial sectors. Without doubt, these contributions depend heavily on the talent and skills of the Canadians who manage the country's nonprofit organizations.

Nonprofit organizations can be broadly divided into two groups: volunteer-driven organizations and those that rely to some extent on paid staff for their operations. Volunteer-driven organizations tend to perform expressive functions and have relatively less in the way of financial resources. Paid-staff organizations, on the other hand, are predominantly (but not exclusively) service delivery organizations. Generally speaking, nonprofit managers are more likely to be found working within paid-staff organizations.

Just as in the business sector, the bulk of the revenues of the nonprofit sector go to a relatively small number of large organizations.

---

[31]   See D. Lasby & C. Barr, *Sector Monitor* 3:2 (Toronto: Imagine Canada, 2013) at 4. Online at: <http://www.imaginecanada.ca/files/www/en/sectormonitor/sectormonitor_v3_n2_2013.pdf>.

These larger organizations tend to receive substantial amounts of government funding, suggesting that there are substantial synergies between their interests and the interests of government. For nonprofit managers, the relationship with their government funders is likely to be a critical aspect of their work.

Counter to the common stereotype, nonprofit organizations do not rely extensively on donations or "charity" for their revenues. The largest source of revenue is earned income, which includes both the sale of goods and services and membership fees. This suggests that nonprofit managers require solid business skills to run their operations successfully.

Finally, the research indicates that nonprofit organizations face a variety of unique challenges that may tax the skills and talents of their managers. These revolve around the difficulty of planning in an uncertain resource environment, problems tapping the volunteer contributions that so many organizations depend upon, and, for those that rely on government funding, difficulties coping with a funding regime that offers little long-term stability and does not provide for the critical infrastructure that any organization requires to be effective.

However, nonprofit organizations have a number of assets that they can draw on to meet these challenges. The strengths they most frequently report are the skills, talent and dedication of the people they engage, their ability to develop and draw on networks and relationships to leverage their impact, and their readiness to collaborate to leverage the resources they have.

Canada's nonprofit organizations are a product of the efforts of the many Canadians, both volunteers and paid staff, who have come together to pursue common interests in communities across the country. What they have accomplished is impressive, building a collection of organizations that together comprises one of the largest nonprofit sectors in the world and appears to be a growing economic force (although economic data beyond 2007 is lacking). At the heart of it all are the volunteers, members, paid staff and nonprofit managers who give their talent, skills and energy to their organizations.

REFERENCES

Calgary Chamber of Voluntary Organizations, *Survey Findings: Impact of the Economic Downturn on Alberta's Nonprofits & Charities* (Calgary: Author, 2009). Online at: <http://www.calgarycvo.org/wp-content/uploads/2013/04/ReportonImpactoftheEconomicDownturnSurveyResultsFINAL_01.pdf>.

A.R. Febbraro, M.H. Hall & M. Parmegiani, *The Voluntary Health Sector in Canada: Developing a Typology – Definition and Classification Issues* (Ottawa: Canadian Centre for Philanthropy, Canadian Policy Research Networks, The Coalition of National Voluntary Organizations and Health Canada, 1999).

M.H. Hall *et al.*, *The Capacity to Serve: A Qualitative Study of the Challenges Facing Canada's Nonprofit and Voluntary Organizations* (Toronto: Canadian Centre for Philanthropy, 2003).

M.H. Hall *et al.*, *Cornerstones of Community: Highlights of the National Survey of Nonprofit and Voluntary Organizations*, Catalogue No. 61-533-XPE (Ottawa: Statistics Canada, 2004).

M.H. Hall *et al.*, *The Canadian Nonprofit and Voluntary Sector in Comparative Perspective* (Toronto: Imagine Canada, 2005).

M.H. Hall, L. McKeown & K. Roberts, *Caring Canadians, Involved Canadians: Highlights from the 2000 National Survey of Giving, Volunteering and Participating*, Catalogue No. 71-542-XPE (Ottawa: Statistics Canada, 2001).

HR Council for the Voluntary & Non-profit Sector, *Toward a Labour Force Strategy for Canada's Voluntary & Non-profit Sector: Findings from Canada-wide Surveys of Employer and Employees* (Report #2) (Ottawa: Author, 2008).

D. Lasby, "Trends in individual donations: 1984-2010" *Research Bulletin* 15:1 (Toronto: Imagine Canada, 2011). Online at: <http://sectorsource.ca/resource/file/trends-individual-donations-1984-2010>.

D. Lasby & C. Barr, *Sector Monitor* 3:2 (Toronto: Imagine Canada, 2013). Online at: <http://www.imaginecanada.ca/files/www/en/sectormonitor/sectormonitor_v3_n2_2013.pdf>.

Ontario Trillium Foundation, *Challenges and Opportunities for Ontario's Not-for-profit Sector During Tough Economic Times* (Toronto: Author, 2009). Online at: <http://www.otf.ca/en/knowledgeSharingCentre/resources/challenging_times.pdf>.

J. Quarter, *Canada's Social Economy: Co-operatives, Non-profits and Other Community Enterprises* (Toronto: James Lorimer, 1993).

J. Quarter, L. Mook & A. Armstrong, *Understanding the Social Economy: A Canadian Perspective.* (Toronto: University of Toronto Press, 2009).

L.M. Salamon, *America's Nonprofit Sector: A Primer*, 2d ed. (New York: The Foundation Center, 1999).

L.M. Salamon & H.K. Anheier, *Defining the Nonprofit Sector: A Cross-national Analysis* (Manchester, N.Y.: Manchester University Press, 1997).

K. Scott, *Funding Matters: The Impact of Canada's New Funding Regime on Nonprofit and Voluntary Organizations* (Ottawa: Canadian Council on Social Development, 2003).

J. Stanford, "The Economic and Social Consequences of Fiscal Retrenchment in Canada" in K. Banting, A. Sharpe & F. St-Hilaire, eds., *The Review of Economic Performance and Social Progress The Longest Decade: Canada in the 1990s* (Montreal: Institute for Research on Public Policy and Centre for the Study of Living Standards, 2001).

Statistics Canada, *CANSIM Table 282-0008 Labour force survey estimate (LFS) by North American Industry Classification System (NAICS), sex and age group, 2003 Employment Data.* Online at: <http://www5.statcan.gc.ca /cansim/a26>.

Statistics Canada, *Satellite Account of Non-profit Institutions and Volunteering: 2007*, Catalogue No. 13-015-X (Ottawa: Statistics Canada, 2009). Online at: <http://www.statcan.gc.ca/pub/13-015-x/13-015-x2009000-eng.pdf>.

F. Zarinpoush & M.H. Hall, *Leadership Perspectives: Interviews with Leaders of Canada's Charities and Nonprofit Organizations* (Toronto: Imagine Canada, 2007).

Chapter 3

MANAGING THE GOVERNANCE FUNCTION: DEVELOPING EFFECTIVE BOARDS OF DIRECTORS

Vic Murray
University of Victoria

As the 21st century moves well into its second decade, the challenges facing Canada's nonprofit and charitable organizations seem only to increase. For many, the causes they address are more important than ever and the demands for their services grow. At the same time, the resources available with which to meet those demands either shrink or remain stagnant. In this climate, it is more important than ever for nonprofit organizations (NPOs) to be wise, imaginative and nimble. Organizations that are unable to move quickly in making vital changes to their programs, resource development strategies and organizational systems are fated to suffer. The making of these kinds of decisions is what takes place in the world of governance and is the subject of this chapter — What is governance? Who should do it? What affects how well it is done?

WHAT IS GOVERNANCE?

Unfortunately, there is no single definition of the concept of "governance" that is universally accepted by all. For example, in the public sector, governance refers to the process of government policymaking and constitutes the "prescribed constitutional and statutory arrangements" among the various elements of government such as legislatures, the public service, the judiciary, *etc.* (Stone & Ostrower (2007, at 417)).

In the nonprofit sector, governance usually refers to how individual organizations make their "big picture" decisions. To quote one source: "Governance is the system and processes concerned with the overall direction, control and accountability of an organization" (Cornforth (2014, at 5)).

A key point to understand about governance in nonprofit organizations is that, although the board of directors is legally responsible for governance level decisions, in actual practice these decisions are often subject to the authority and influence of many other organizations and individuals both within and outside the organization. In fact, one of the dominant themes in the current research on governance is the exploration of the process in terms of *networks* of which boards of directors are only a part (Cornforth & Brown (2014)). However, because of the central role played by boards in this process, this chapter will focus on the practices of boards of directors that improve or detract from effective governance.

A FRAMEWORK FOR ANALYZING THE EFFECTIVENESS OF BOARDS OF DIRECTORS

Figure 1

A Framework for the Analysis of the Effectiveness of Nonprofit Organization Boards of Directors

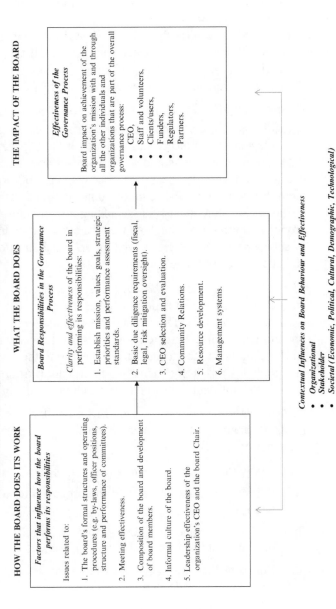

HOW THE BOARD DOES ITS WORK

Factors that influence how the board performs its responsibilities

Issues related to:

1. The board's formal structures and operating procedures (e.g. by-laws, officer positions, structure and performance of committees).

2. Meeting effectiveness.

3. Composition of the board and development of board members.

4. Informal culture of the board.

5. Leadership effectiveness of the organization's CEO and the board Chair.

WHAT THE BOARD DOES

Board Responsibilities in the Governance Process

Clarity and effectiveness of the board in performing its responsibilities:

1. Establish mission, values, goals, strategic priorities and performance assessment standards.

2. Basic due diligence requirements (fiscal, legal, risk mitigation oversight).

3. CEO selection and evaluation.

4. Community Relations.

5. Resource development.

6. Management systems.

THE IMPACT OF THE BOARD

Effectiveness of the Governance Process

Board impact on achievement of the organization's mission with and through all the other individuals and organizations that are part of the overall governance process:

- CEO,
- Staff and volunteers,
- Clients/users,
- Funders,
- Regulators,
- Partners.

Contextual Influences on Board Behaviour and Effectiveness

- *Organizational*
- *Stakeholder*
- *Societal (Economic, Political, Cultural, Demographic, Technological)*

As can be seen in the box on the right-hand side of Figure 1, the ultimate purpose of the board's work is to help the organization be more effective in achieving its mission. To do this, there are several critical areas of board responsibility (see middle box in Figure 1, above). These represent the "what" dimension of board effectiveness. Successful boards are those that have a shared understanding of what these areas are (both among themselves and with all those who relate to the board) and make the best-informed decisions about each of them. The basic seven areas of board responsibility are:

1. *Establishing the mission, vision and values of the organization and assessing the organization's performance in pursuing these.* This area refers to setting the overall purpose for the organization — why it should exist, who it should serve, what services it should provide and what values and ethical guidelines it should follow in providing them. It also includes the setting of objectives and the development of broad strategic plans for achieving the mission. To do this properly requires assessing how well the organization has performed in achieving the goals set as well as understanding the challenges and opportunities that lie ahead.

2. *Fiscal/legal oversight and risk assessment.* The board must ensure that the organization behaves in a fiscally and legally responsible manner. This includes such matters as overseeing operating and capital budgets, investments, property management and compliance with various laws applying to the organization. It also includes risk assessment — identification of areas in which there are significant risks to its assets, clients/users or reputation.

3. *CEO Selection and Evaluation*: Ensuring that the best person holds the position of chief executive officer and performs it at a satisfactory level of competence.

4. *Community Relations (also known as "Boundary Spanning")*:

    (a) Representing the interests of the organization to its external publics;

    (b) Building alliances and partnerships with others that benefit the community the organization serves; and

    (c) Ensuring that the interests of key external stakeholders are made known inside the organization.

5. *Resource Development*: Ensuring that the organization obtains adequate funds to enable it to achieve its objectives.

6. *Management Systems*: Ensuring that the organization is managed efficiently and effectively, *e.g.*, that it has the right administrative structures and policies, information systems, human resources policies, *etc.*

7. *Board Self-Management*: Activities aimed at ensuring the board itself is as effective as it can be, *e.g.*, recruiting, selecting and training its members, evaluating the effectiveness of its meetings and committees.

To know and share understanding of the board's areas of responsibility is important but the question remains: What has an impact on how well the board carries out these responsibilities? This leads to an examination of *how* boards should organize and operate in carrying out their duties.

The "how" dimension of board effectiveness has five elements (see left-hand box of Figure 1, above):

1. Issues related to the structure within which boards work such as the organization's constitution and by-laws, the number and nature of officer positions on the board and board committees.

2. The quality of board meetings.

3. Composition of the board (the "mix" of people making up the board's membership) and how well they are prepared for their positions.

4. The informal culture of the board. Behind the formal framework within which boards operate is an informal one that can be called the board's "culture". A culture is a set of behaviour patterns, attitudes, values and beliefs widely shared by a group, which influences their actions. Taken together, they represent the shared understanding of "how we do things around here". They are often taken for granted and are so deeply ingrained that group members are scarcely conscious of how they colour their views of the world.

5. Leadership of the board chair and the organization's CEO. The two positions that have the greatest influence on the way the board behaves are those of the board's Chair and that of the top paid manager of the organization — its CEO or Executive Director (ED).

At the bottom of Figure 1, it can be seen that boards do not work in a vacuum. The decisions they make in their areas of responsibility and the ways they structure themselves can be influenced by many factors external to them. Though they may often not be aware of it, a board's behavior may be affected by characteristics of the organization it governs — for example its history, size, the nature of its mission. The actions of external stakeholders such as funders, regulators and other organizations in the community or "industry" of which they are a part are also significant. Some of them have actual legal authority over some aspect of board responsibility while others have informal and powerful forms of influence. Finally, all nonprofit organizations exist within a larger society. Countries and communities can differ widely in the political and economic climate they create. Cultural values about the nature of charity, volunteering and the role of nonprofits create different environments for the NPOs within them (see Salamon & Anheier (1997)).

For the purposes of this chapter we will not enter into in-depth discussions of these contextual influences on governance. Those interested in the growing body of academic research on this topic should see Cornforth & Brown (2014). Because the focus of this book is primarily practical, the remainder of this chapter will deal with ways that boards can consciously choose to improve their effectiveness in the governance process. We begin with a general introduction to the role of boards in Canadian nonprofit organizations.

THE ROLE OF BOARDS OF DIRECTORS IN NONPROFIT ORGANIZATION GOVERNANCE

All registered charities in Canada as well as all organizations that are registered under federal and provincial legislation as nonprofit societies are required to have boards of directors.[1] The key questions are what the role of the nonprofit board should be and how it should operate so as to best fulfill that role.

Why are boards important? The simple answer to this question is that they are legally responsible for the actions of the organization. Their primary role is that of a fiduciary, which is to say that they are entrusted to look after the interests of the organization. In practical terms, this translates into making sure that the organization is achieving its mission, not wasting its money and not breaking any

---

[1]   This means that an unknown number of all-volunteer organizations that do *not* register under provincial or federal legislation do not require boards, though some may have them. Even so, if they want to survive, some of their members need to fulfill, however informally, the functions normally carried out by boards, which suggests that this chapter has relevance even for them.

laws. For more on the legal aspects of the board's role and the all-important question of the board's legal liability if it fails in carrying out its fiduciary responsibilities, see Chapter 5 of this book.

For years, many non-profit organization boards were content to define their fiduciary responsibilities in a minimalist way — keeping an eye on finances and listening to reports from paid and volunteer managers that assured them everything was fine. Occasional crises might arise, such as funding cuts, a poorly performing Executive Director or bad press, in which case the board would have to get involved with details and try to sort things out.

These kinds of "rubber-stamp" boards can still be found today though they are less and less common. The reason for this is that the world of most NPOs has become much more complex and challenging. Especially in the current environment of crisis and change, many programs supported by governments have seen their funding cut; competition has grown for all sources of funds and the needs of clients/users of the NPO's services are growing. All these trends leave Executive Directors feeling highly pressured. They could really use more help, so, logically, many start to expect more active assistance from their boards.

Added to this are new pressures from the outside world. There has been steadily growing public concern over the failure of the boards of *business* organizations to adequately check on the actions of their paid managers. The resulting corporate scandals have heightened the call for improved corporate governance. This trend, coupled with a few cases of blatant mismanagement in large nonprofits, has put pressure on NPO boards to pay more attention to the activities of their organizations.

The problem is that this increased emphasis on board involvement has had two kinds of effects. For some, the result has been a significant improvement in the success of the organization while for others board behaviour has created even more problems than existed before. When asked to describe "boards from hell" that they have known, Executive Directors rarely mention the passive, "rubber-stamp" boards of the past. More commonly they describe "micro-managing" boards that undermine the ED's authority and want to be involved in decisions on all kinds of day-to-day operating details. They also identify "erratic boards" that behave unpredictably — at some times dabbling in operational detail while at others wanting only to "rubber-stamp".

The remainder of this chapter looks at the critical dimensions of board effectiveness identified in Figure 1 and how they can be managed so as to produce a "high value added" board as opposed to a strictly "watchdog" board or one that actually creates "negative value", *i.e.*, is more trouble than it is worth. Before doing this, however, it is necessary to say a word about the current state of research into what is really known about what makes boards tick.

Since the 1980s, there has been a steady outpouring of books, articles, Websites and workshops aimed at telling those who provide leadership to boards how to do it better.[2] Over the same period, there has also appeared a much smaller body of literature reporting on empirical research into why boards actually behave as they do and the extent to which this behaviour affects the performance of the organization. With a few notable exceptions, the prescriptive literature blithely ignores the empirical literature and vice versa. Furthermore, though the research supports some of the suggestions of the "how to do it" literature, other studies do not and yet others raise questions about areas not even addressed by the "how to" experts (Murray (2004); Ostrower & Stone (2006); Cornforth & Brown (2014)). We will attempt to point out the connections between the two approaches to understanding boards as we proceed with this chapter.

We will now discuss the middle box of Figure 1, "What the board does". This identifies the major areas of board responsibility and the issues that can affect how well they carry them out.

WHAT THE BOARD DOES

Board Role Clarity

Without doubt, the single most common cause of boards contributing "negative value" to the organizations they govern is a lack of clarity over what responsibilities they should take on and what role they

---

[2]   There is not the space here to present a full overview of all the "how-to" literature on boards. For example, Amazon.com recently listed no fewer than 603 books under the heading "nonprofit boards of directors". Some good examples of recent Canadian books are Davidson, *et al.* (2013) and Gill (2005). Another standard Canadian reference is the series of booklets and bulletins published by the Alberta Culture and Community Spirit Program (2012 revised versions available online at <http://culture.alberta.ca/bdp/resources.aspx>). A useful publication from Britain is Tompkin (2013). Some worthwhile recent American publications include those by Board Source (2011), Thomas (2014), Trower (2012) and Wolf (2014). There are also numerous online sources. Probably the best single one is that of Carter McNamara of Authenticity Consulting: <http://managementhelp.org/freenonprofittraining/boards.htm>.

should play in dealing with them. Lack of clarity can occur when the board members themselves are unclear or differ from one another, or when the ED and managers have one set of expectations about board roles and responsibilities and the board Chair and members have another (Brown & Guo (2010); Herman & Renz (2000; 2008); Herman, Renz & Heimovics (1997)).

For example, when one mid-sized social service agency in a large Canadian city experienced a serious reduction in government funding for one of its programs, all agreed it was necessary to try to increase funds from other sources. A problem arose because the ED and management staff expected board members to get actively involved by approaching their contacts for corporate sponsorships and donations while board members thought their role was to simply approve fund-raising plans developed by staff while the actual activities would be carried out by others.

In another case, several members of the board of a small sport organization became annoyed with its one paid manager when he switched the supplier of team uniforms. The manager thought he had the authority to make such decisions but several members of the board thought he should have checked with them first.

One of the reasons for lack of role clarity in boards is that board members can actually play more than one role in the organization. The discussion of Figure 1 above has identified seven areas in which boards should have *some* kind of involvement. To be aware of these areas is important, but it does not indicate *how* they should be involved. It is common in writing about boards to talk only about the role of members as *decision-makers* acting as a group at formal board meetings. In addition, however, they may play two other critical roles in the organization: those of *advisor* and *implementer*. Thus, there are at least three roles that board members may play.

1. *Decision-Maker/Evaluator*: The most important thing to understand about the decision-making role of the board is the concept of delegation. Except in the smallest of NPOs, the board cannot make all the decisions needed to get things done. It must trust staff and volunteers to make many decisions that it will never hear about. When organizations employ an ED, the authority to make many decisions is delegated to that position and the ED may, in turn, delegate some of that authority to others. The only decision the board makes about all these delegated matters is whether they all add up to satisfactory performance for the organization as a

whole. This is the evaluation function of boards and it cannot be delegated. When the board *does* make decisions, it usually occurs only at the level of the whole board meeting in a formal session in which it votes on motions put forward to it. The evaluation aspect may take place in committees though the results of their assessments are used by the board as a whole.

The key issue with respect to the decision-making role of the board is what matters *it* should decide versus what it should delegate. How to resolve this issue is discussed below.

2. *Advisor*: In this role, board members provide information and expert advice to board decision-making meetings and to others such as the ED or other management staff. This role is usually played at the level of board committees who may develop recommendations for the whole board or ED. However, individual board members may also provide advice in two other ways:

    (a) In the form of knowledge gleaned through their training and experience; and

    (b) In the form of information gleaned from contacts in their networks. This latter contribution — the role of the board member in interacting with the outside world — has only recently been recognized as a vital part of the board's contribution (Renz (2006)).

3. *Implementer*: In a few instances, board members may actually carry out the activities required by the decisions they (or others) make. For example, they usually carry out the work of selecting future board members and selecting the ED. They may also approach prospective donors for funds or represent the organization in dealings with critical stakeholder groups. Implementation activities are usually carried out at the level of committees charged with specific tasks such as fundraising or board recruitment. Occasionally, individual board members may get involved in implementing decisions such as approaching prospective donors to ask for contributions or presenting briefs on behalf of the organization to government bodies.

BOARD DECISION-MAKING MODELS

Understanding the kind of matters boards might get involved in and the various roles the members can play is the first step to achieving clarity about what the board should do. However, the temptation is then to assume that there is a single pattern or model of board decision-making that is best for *all* NPOs. In spite of the assertions by some "how to do it" writers on boards that there is a "one best way" for all situations, the limited research on what makes for successful boards suggests that there is not (Nobbie & Brudney (2003); Murray (2004)). Let us look at several common models of board decision-making and discuss when each may be appropriate.

The Working Board. There are conditions when it is quite acceptable to have board members who simultaneously participate in setting strategic directions, managing the implementation of plans and actually "doing work". The term for a board like this is the "Working Board". A successful Working Board can exist when the nonprofit organization is new, small, all (or nearly all) made up of volunteers and offers services that are not numerous or complex. For example, many self-help groups, small advocacy organizations, housing co-operatives, collectives and sport organizations all operate very successfully with Working Boards.

In these conditions, board members are often the most committed and knowledgeable members of the organization and have worked up to the board as volunteers. It is not surprising, therefore, that some of them bring operational concerns to board meetings. In fact, at this stage, it may be impossible to differentiate between "the strategic" and "the operational" in any case. One botched special event fundraiser or one bad story about a mishandled client in the newspaper could end the organization's existence. Almost anything and everything has the potential to be "strategic". Getting established requires everybody with talent and energy to wear many hats.

All that is needed to create a successful Working Board is to make sure that everybody is clear about who can make which decisions and who is going to do what. There should also be basic agreement about what things are the most important (priorities). In general, *whole-board meetings* of working boards should still focus on governance issues — planning for the future, setting priorities and assessing performance. But time spent on apparent "details" is not necessarily wasted if the chair or others can spot the larger strategic issues that can be buried in them. In these kinds of small organizations the board can benefit by holding periodic special meetings of all active participants (such as other key volunteers and any staff) to discuss "how well are we doing in fulfilling our mission?" and "where do we go from here?"

The Working Board is *not* appropriate under conditions opposite to those that fit it best, that is, large organizations with a high proportion of paid staff and full-time managerial personnel who are operating many programs that take considerable skill and experience to implement. Most public institutions such as universities, hospitals and mid- to large-sized social service agencies fit these conditions. Such organizations cannot long tolerate the confusion created by board meetings, committees or individual board members trying to "micro manage" the organization's affairs when others are responsible, and better prepared, to do so.

The Governance-only Board. A Governance-only Board is one which restricts itself to providing broad, overall leadership to the organization by focusing primarily on issues that relate to the basic strategic question of "who is to receive what services at what cost?" (Carver (2006)). This means that decision-making/evaluating becomes the key role being played and that the first four of the responsibility areas (plus number seven) discussed above become the focus of the board's attention.

The dilemma facing the large, complex institutions that need Governance-only Boards, and one of the reasons they can so easily become rubber-stamp boards, is that most board members are busy civic leaders who, though great supporters of the organization, have very little time to become thoroughly knowledgeable about it or the sector in which it operates (such as healthcare, education or the arts). This makes informed debate about major strategic issues very difficult. For example, it takes a lot of expertise to know whether a university should open a new faculty or whether a hospital should convert 20 per cent of its beds from active to chronic care.

The secret of creating an effective Governance-only Board lies in developing a shared understanding of basic levels of policy, deciding which of them are "strategic" and devising information systems that supply valid data on past performance and future needs in ways that clearly relate to the basic strategic issues.

"Mixed Model Boards". Many boards in practice are neither purely working boards nor governance-only boards. They tend to be located between the two ends of the continuum. Sometimes they get involved in operational details while at other times they act more like governance-only boards. The movement between one state to the other can have several possible causes. Sometimes it may be due to the personalities of a few influential members who do not share a common understanding of how the board should operate. It can also occur

during periods of transition or crisis. As small, new organizations grow they often employ more paid staff and acquire professional managers. Paid staff handle most of the operating duties but board members who managed many things in the past still know a lot about how the organization works. They may even be needed to perform certain functions that are not yet being performed by paid staff, such as publicity, fundraising or government relations. These members of formerly successful Working Boards can, if the transition is not handled properly, run into increasing conflict with staff over who is to do what and who has authority to decide what.

At the other end of the spectrum, Governance-only Boards can revert to an erratic mixed model state during major crises such as the loss of large grants, financial mismanagement, serious labour unrest or the actions of militant client groups. Insofar as the paid managers have trouble handling these situations, the temptation on the part of board members to get involved in the direct management of operations is strong; indeed managers may ask for it and it may be necessary. Once the crisis is over, it is easy to allow things to keep going in a confused mix of Working and Governance-only modes.

The main solution to the problem of the confused board is to push it toward clarifying its role by fully embracing one or the other of the two basic models — "working" or "governance-only". However, if the conditions are too unstable or critical to allow this *or* the organization still must use some board members as volunteers to manage certain parts of the organization's operations, it is possible to sustain a Mixed Model that can work well. In this model certain board members or committees take responsibility for managing specific functions. If these are working committees, their chairs become *de facto* operating managers and, as such, should report to the ED. The remainder of the management functions continues to be played by paid managers who, of course, also report to the ED. At the level of the Whole Board, effort must still be made to focus primarily on strategic issues. In that sense, all boards must be governance boards at least part of the time. Insofar as possible, the operational committees and individual board members with specific operational responsibilities should work under the authority of the Executive Director.

The Mixed Model is a difficult one to implement successfully because there are so many occasions where confusion can arise, especially as the organization's environment continues to change. The secret of success lies in exceptionally full and open communication in which all parties feel free to raise questions over gaps or overlaps in authority and responsibility. There must also be high levels of tolerance for ambiguity. For example, even though meetings of the whole board are meant to be used for discussing major issues of policy and strategy, some board members will want to talk about matters pertaining to their responsibilities as *de facto* operational managers. They may thus seem to be cluttering the meetings with "managerial" details and undermining the authority of the Executive Director, if there is one. The key to success lies in training everybody — management and board alike — to recognize what is "strategic" and redirect the non-strategic matters to whoever is playing the role of the top manager.

In summary, there is no "one best way" of structuring the roles and responsibilities of a board of directors that fits all situations. The board cannot avoid its legal requirement of exercising "due diligence" in ensuring that the organization achieves its mission and does not get into financial or legal difficulties. However, the way it gets involved in the other responsibility areas discussed above, can be highly variable. The important thing to understand is that the board is part of the whole organizational system that includes paid mangers, staff and volunteers. All have roles to play in the process of deciding what to do and then implementing those decisions. Everyone must be clear about who will do the deciding, who will have input into those decisions, who will do the implementing and what information will be obtained to assess how well the decisions have worked out (see Harris (1993)).

We will now briefly look at each of the seven responsibility areas presented in Figure 1 at the beginning of this chapter and discuss how the board should approach each of them. We begin with the most of important of them all: the setting of the mission and strategic direction for the organization.

Board Responsibility Areas

Establish Mission, Vision, Values, Goals, Strategic Priorities and Assess Organizational Performance

A number of research studies have confirmed that the most effective boards are more likely to make regular efforts to focus on the "big picture" issues facing the organization — what its mission should be, what its vision for the future should be, what values it should adhere to, what its goals should be and how well the organization is performing (Bradshaw, Murray & Wolpin (1992); Cutt & Murray (2000); Herman & Renz (2000; 2008); Herman, Renz & Heimovics

(1997); Holland & Jackson (1998); Hough *et al.* (2014); (Paton (2003); Siciliano (1996; 1997)).

The questions can all be grouped under the heading of "strategic issues". What, exactly, is a strategic issue and what is not? Some time ago, the United Way of America suffered a grievous blow to its image and major loss of support when its executive director was found to be running up gigantic expense accounts by living lavishly while ostensibly on business. One could say this happened because the organization was lax in not having clear policies and controls regarding such expenses. Should the board have been responsible for deciding what such policies should be? Many would say, "No, this is a management matter" yet, in the end, the inadequacy of these financial controls had tremendous strategic consequences for the organization.

In general terms, this question of what is "strategic" has to do with levels of policy and each board must define what each level is for that organization and whether it should become involved in it. Then it must agree how far "down" the ladder of policy levels it will go in terms of what authority it will delegate to the CEO and what matters must be taken to board meetings for a vote. Finally, it must decide which level applies to any specific question. There are four basic policy levels:

(i) *Mission and Values.* The organization's mission statement reveals why the organization exists and what it is trying to achieve. It should be short, clear and inspirational. It is the ultimate criterion that the board should apply when deciding on major changes: "Are they consistent with our mission?" Any issue that suggests a change in mission must be brought to the board.

A statement of values makes clear the moral and ethical beliefs that underlie how the organization intends to approach its mission. Any issue that suggests a change in mission or values must be brought to the board.

(ii) *Strategic Priorities.* There are usually many ways to achieve the mission and an organization has only limited amounts of effort and money to expend. It cannot do everything that its clients, funders, members, volunteers or staff might want. There are usually only a small number of very broad strategic directions in which it might go at any given time. They involve answering the fundamental questions of "Who are we seeking to serve?"; "What services should we provide?"; "How should we provide these services?" and "What resources must we obtain in order to provide these services?" The answers to these questions must be identified and prioritized so everyone knows what is most important and what is less important.

For example, almost all nonprofit organizations must be concerned with getting enough money to operate. For many, raising funds is quite separate from deciding how to spend the money and these "how to spend" decisions may have only an indirect impact on how funders decide how much to provide (Cutt, Murray & Tassie (1996)). Hence, most organizations these days require a clear strategic objective specifying the amount of money they need and, in general terms, how they will go about obtaining it.

Setting priorities regarding what to spend the money on is a much more difficult task. For example:

- Charities set up to help the victims of various diseases and disabilities must always struggle to set priorities between the broad choices of: supporting research into cures and treatments, public education about the disease, and "patient services" (activities to make the lives of victims or their families easier).

- Performing arts and other cultural organizations must face the classic struggle between "artistic integrity" and "audience appeal", i.e., exploring new artistic frontiers that do not have mass appeal versus getting "bums on seats" by sticking with the most popular programs.

- International development organizations must choose between the basic options of long-term versus short-term forms of aid.

- Community service agencies with multiple programs have to decide which groups and social problems get what priority: for example, children-at-risk, new immigrants, single mothers, or poor and lonely seniors.

- Universities face continuous dilemmas in setting their admissions policies between "accessibility" and "student quality", i.e., making admission equally available to students from all backgrounds (including those from deprived conditions where prior education may have been of low quality) versus an emphasis on attracting only the "best and the brightest" (which often excludes many from deprived backgrounds).

For a fuller discussion of strategic planning, see Chapter 8 of this book.

(iii) *Program and Operating Policies.* Once the strategic objectives and priorities are identified, there are the decisions surrounding what particular programs, activities, or systems will best lead to the attainment of these objectives. Human resources policies must be decided (*e.g.*, compensation levels, benefit plans, selection criteria). Accounting systems must be put in place. Actual plays must be produced by the theatre company. Specific treatments must be chosen for the family violence program in the social agency.

(iv) *Rules and Procedures.* These are the myriad specific decisions that must be made to ensure that programs and operating policies are implemented consistently and at a high level of quality and efficiency.

Most boards find that, no matter how much they might agree that, at the whole board level, they will only discuss issues that represent policy levels (i) and (ii), they will sometimes start to discuss matters that seem "beneath" them. Skilled board leaders will be able to distinguish between an item that is truly a high-level policy matter and one that is not. They will then send the latter back to the CEO for decision if the board has adopted a governance-only model or, if it is a working board, identify it as an operational issue for an individual or committee to investigate.

Managers and committee members, on the other hand, must possess the equally special ability to spot a strategic level question in what appears to be a routine operational decision. For example, a question of whether to apply for funds from a government lottery commission may raise the much bigger question of the organization's values regarding obtaining money derived from gambling. A decision on whether to launch a pilot project for getting street kids off the street may contain the seeds of a radical reorientation of an entire agency. As Mintzberg points out in his book, *The Rise and Fall of Strategic Planning* (1994), the sources of information on strategic issues and ideas for strategic change are to be found in all parts of the organization. The great skill in leadership lies in recognizing this and knowing how to tap these sources.

A note on assessing organizational performance. A key determinant of how well boards set goals and establish priorities is the extent to which they seriously try to track the organization's performance in these areas. Inadequate information can occur because the main (sometimes only) source of information for many boards is the chief executive officer. CEOs may consciously or unconsciously filter what goes to the board so as to tilt the decision toward a predetermined outcome that they favour.

One of the biggest difficulties for boards is finding independent sources of information and ensuring that the information they do get from "the administration" is as complete and unbiased as it can be. Public auditors fulfill this function in the case of basic financial information. For other kinds of issues, alternative sources of information can include independently conducted client and donor satisfaction studies or information from umbrella associations of organizations in the same "business". It also behooves the board to carefully oversee the kind of information *systems* put in place for the organization, *e.g.*, ensuring that budgetary systems provide program and unit cost data; insisting on policy-oriented funding statistics and human resources information systems that monitor staff morale, absenteeism, etc. A full discussion of the challenges of evaluating organizational performance can be found in Chapter 9 of this book. For more on the special problems that confront boards in carrying out their due diligence in assessing performance, see Hough, *et al.* (2014).

Parenthetically, it should be noted that there can also arise the problem of *too much* information being presented to the board in a way that does not relate to strategic issues. The "snow job" (in which board members are buried in paper just before a meeting with no idea what parts of the pile are important) is a classic ploy of some chief executives trying to manipulate a board to "rubber-stamp" a particular recommendation. In other cases it occurs because the board itself is not clear about what it wants to see so the ED tries to cover all eventualities. Information overload may be reduced if the board chair insists that supporting information be provided in ample time to be digested before a meeting and that it explicitly connects to the issues under debate. Information not related to strategic issues would either be refused, included but not discussed unless someone has a problem with it (see "consent agendas" below), or presented in another forum outside of the board meeting.

Problems in the Fiscal/Legal Oversight Function of Boards and the Responsibility for Risk Assessment

Boards that are not capable of identifying and grappling with genuine strategic issues often fall back on an obsession with the organization's finances. If they cannot do anything else, they will make sure it does not go into debt. The problem here is that, if concerns about costs are abstracted from an overall perspective of the organization's strategic priorities, they can lead to poor policy decisions. For example, this can happen when the annual budget approval exercise for the board is disconnected from decisions about strategic priorities. As pointed out in Chapter 10 on financial management, all budgets contain implicit strategic plans within them in that they determine who gets what resources and the availability of money drives actions. This is the main reality for most operational managers and it heavily constrains their ability to accomplish whatever objectives may be laid out in a completely separate "strategic plan". Boards must insist that budgets and other financial information be presented in the context of the organization's strategic priorities.

However, guarding against financial mismanagement is only one example of risks of which boards should be aware. A comprehensive analysis of risks involves many other areas such as compliance with laws and the management of property, staff, volunteers, client relations, investments and others. For a full overview of all aspects of risk assessment see the Website of The Nonprofit Management Risk Center.[3]

The Responsibility for Selection and Evaluation of the Executive Director

Virtually all boards take this responsibility very seriously, at least the selection part. Yet, sometimes their choice turns out to be a poor one. Even more commonly, they fail to tackle seriously the job of reviewing the CEO's performance. This leads to frustrated chief executives who have no clear idea how they are doing in their boards' eyes. It also leads to major crises and lawsuits because the board fails to act on poor performance until too late, then fires the ED who promptly sues for wrongful dismissal on the grounds of never having been told he or she was performing poorly.

For more detailed information on how to carry out a good executive search and selection process see Chapter 11 on human resources in this volume. Suffice it to say here that, if it can possibly afford it, the board should obtain the services of experts in this area. But even this may lead to failure if the board is not clear about the organization's strategic priorities both at present and for the future. One of the major reasons that newly selected EDs do not work out is because they are chosen to lead the organization as it was, or is, but not the organization that will have to exist to succeed in the future.

As to the ED's performance evaluation, it simply must be taken seriously even though the temptation is to let it slip because leading board

---

[3]   <http://www.nonprofitrisk.org>.

members and the ED often develop a close relationship so such members may feel that formally assessing the ED's performance shows a lack of trust. Nevertheless, it is a temptation that must be resisted. Doing a proper job in this area means following the basics of good evaluation practice: jointly setting, with the ED, clear and reasonable objectives; providing the resources and necessary authority to achieve these objectives; agreeing beforehand on what would be reasonable indicators of success; then meeting periodically to review progress and decide what can be done to obtain improvement if it is deemed necessary. Usually this task is best done by a board committee. The choice of committee depends on the board's committee structure (see below). The whole board would come into play only in rare cases when serious performance problems persist over time and the possibility of dismissal exists, however the board should be given an annual report from the evaluating committee summarizing the results of the performance review.

The Board's Responsibilities for Community Relations

Research on board effectiveness has shown that paying attention to the boundary between the organization and its external environment is one of the most important things boards can do (see Freiworth (2014); Ostrower & Stone (2006); Renz (2006); Herman & Renz (2000); Stone *et al.* (2014)). This area of responsibility has two components: "Bringing the outside in" and "Taking the inside out". The topic is discussed in more detail in Chapter 6 of this book on government and community relations; however, a few comments are worth mentioning with respect to the specific role of the board in this area.

Problems arise in bringing the concerns of constituencies, stakeholders and the general community into important discussions on strategy when the board has no way to learn about them. This can happen because no members are close to these groups or because there is no training in how to approach them or any expectation that the board will do so. Solving the problem requires:

(a)   Re-examining the criteria for board membership so as to ensure that there is representation of people who know the concerns of key stakeholders;

(b)   Changing the board's own management system (see below) to ensure that there are formal occasions for board members (not only staff) to meet key external groups and prior training in how to relate to such groups.

The opposite problem to inadequately representing the interests of external stakeholders occurs when too many board members are explicitly appointed to represent such groups. The constitutions of some nonprofit organizations specify that certain board positions must be filled by appointees from designated stakeholder organizations. The difficulty occurs when such appointees pay attention only when issues arise that concern "their" interest group then contribute only that group's "line" on the issue. Such people are often not willing to modify their position based on dialogue or compromise for the good of the organization as a whole.

One method for tackling this problem (not guaranteed to succeed) is to include in the position description for board members a statement that all are expected to make decisions on the basis of what is best for the organization as a whole. This principle would be reinforced during orientation sessions for new members. An example of one such statement is as follows:

> *Board members are expected to make decisions based on the best interests of the institution as a whole and in keeping with its mission and objectives rather than on the basis of special interests. Members are also expected to support the majority decisions of the board and work with fellow board members in a spirit of cooperation.*

Such statements are of little use, however, unless the underlying board culture (discussed below) reinforces the value of putting the good of the organization first.

Turning to the "taking the inside out" side of the board's boundary spanning responsibility, the main problems are a lack of members willing or able to do it. This is usually a function best performed by individuals or a board committee (*e.g.*, community relations, government relations). If the board is made up primarily of "insiders" such as volunteers, clients, *etc.*, they may not have contacts with important outsiders. In other situations, members with excellent contacts (with the media, government officials, potential donors, *etc.*) may not be asked to do anything. "Community relations" must be a formally recognized, and planned for, board responsibility. If this responsibility is always an afterthought, it tends not be carried out successfully.

A special subset of the board's responsibility for community relations is that of building alliances and partnerships with other nonprofit organizations that have the potential to benefit (or harm) one's own organization. These become especially valuable in difficult economic times. Carefully crafted partnerships offer the potential for such things as the development of joint programs, the pursuit of common advocacy goals, the sharing of common resources and joint fundraising activities. A well-designed board can play a major role in introducing potential partners and persuading other boards to approve joint ventures.

The Board's Role in Resource Development

Again, for more detailed information on resource development see Chapter 7 in this book. Here we will concentrate on the difficult question of what role the board should play in this particular area of fundraising for the organization.

Surveys of board members and EDs assessing their satisfaction with the board reveal that most of them believe that boards should be "responsible" for fundraising but few think the board does a good job of it. This is largely because of confused expectations about what being "responsible" means. EDs often expect board members to both "give and get", *i.e.*, donate generously themselves and personally approach others for donations. In Canada, many board members expect the board to be involved in approving an overall fundraising strategy (and maybe in offering advice as individuals when it is being developed) but do *not* expect to have to "give or get" in the sense of actually donating money to the organization or asking their friends and associates for donations.

What are the various roles that boards can play in resource development?

Table 1: Board Roles and Responsibilities in Resource Development

Responsibilities	Roles		
	Board-as-a-whole	Committee	Individual board member
Approve strategy developed by others	Definitely	Never	Never
Participate in developing strategy	Possibly	Usually	Possibly
Help implement strategy	Possibly	Possibly	Possibly
Oversee implementation of strategy	Possibly	Usually	Never

It can be seen from the table above table that there that there are three possible roles for board involvement:

1. The board acting as a whole in the way it does during official board meetings.

2. A committee of the board or a special fundraising committee containing board members.

    NB: It is important to understand that fundraising committees do not have to be committees of the board and, if they are, they can contain some members who are not board members. Such committees should normally only help develop plans and policies to recommend to others for approval or assist in actually implementing fundraising activities.

3. Board members acting as individuals, for example, as they do when they make a donation to the organization or visit a potential donor.

Down the left-hand side of Table 1, it can also be seen that there are four possible levels of responsibility that can be taken up by the board:

1. Responsibility for reviewing and approving fundraising strategies, plans and policies developed by others such as fundraising professionals, a fundraising committee, *etc*. This is usually done at official meetings of the board as a whole.

2. Becoming involved in the *creation* of fundraising strategies, plans and policies, often within a fundraising committee.

3. Once plans are in place, there is the hard work of actually raising the money — holding special events, soliciting corporate sponsorships, applying for grants, running mail campaigns, asking potential big donors for support or just giving fundraisers contacts to approach. These tasks would usually be carried out through one of the board committees or by individual board members volunteering their time.

4. Finally, there is the job of tracking how well fundraising plans are working out — receiving and reviewing reports and suggesting changes if needed. This responsibility is often the job of a board fundraising committee but could, in some circumstances, be carried out by the board as a whole.

It is important to understand that there is no "one best way" when it comes to the board's involvement in fundraising. The content in each of the boxes in Table 1 represents common practice and should not be taken as the way it ought to be in all cases. Each organization must decide for itself which responsibilities should be carried out by whom and at what level — that of the board-as-a-whole, a committee or the individual board member. Where a board belongs on the fundraising involvement continuum depends greatly on a few factors:

- The ability of the organization to employ professional fundraisers. Such people are experts in developing plans and leading teams who will implement them. Small, new and low budget nonprofits can rarely afford this kind of support so the work has to be undertaken by volunteers and staff usually working in a committee structure. Board members can sit on committees and contribute as individuals.

- The level of commitment and experience/knowledge about fundraising among board members.

- The availability and expertise of other volunteers and external supporters and potential partners who could provide assistance in this area.

Once it is decided who should play what roles in doing what, the next job is making sure everyone is capable of performing those roles. In the case of fundraising, this can involve making the following changes:

- Developing criteria for board member recruitment and selection that identifies fundraising competency as a desirable skill for at least some members. If members will be expected to play a role other than general oversight, they should be ready and willing to do so.

- Provide training and development. Much of fundraising consists of learnable skills. Orientation and training for board members should address them.

- If the analysis of possible roles carried out in Table 1 reveals that a committee should be involved, be careful and thorough in defining its terms of reference so it does not tread on the toes of fundraising staff or take over the job of the board as a whole which is responsible for policy decisions made in this area of board responsibility.

In sum, expectations of the board's role in resource development must be decided upon and communicated without equivocation to all incoming board members. If applicable, individual members should be informed before they join that they may be asked, on a purely individual and voluntary basis, to approach people in their networks to discuss donations.

The Board's Role in the Development and Assessment of Management Systems

This refers to the processes and procedures used to manage the organization. They include the organization's systems of accounting and control, information systems that track program implementation and client demand and satisfaction, evaluation systems and human resources policies and practices. How deeply should boards become involved in decisions about these systems?

In small, mainly volunteer, organizations with working boards, the board and management functions are so intertwined in any case that the board is bound to be involved. This need not be a problem provided, as always, that there is a clear understanding of who is responsible for what.

The main problems in this area tend to arise in the Governance-only and Mixed Model Boards. Many of these boards contain genuine experts on various management subjects such as accounting, human resources, marketing, *etc.* Should the organization be prohibited from tapping this expertise? Not necessarily, but it should be at an individual level and in the form of advice on, or implementation of, a decision made by the designated manager.

At the whole board level, the question of management systems should come up only in the context of discussions regarding how the board is to *evaluate the performance of the organization.* As discussed, the board must assess how the organization is doing if it wants to set future directions. To do this requires information on many matters concerning the organization's environment and current performance. Thus it is appropriate for the board to decide what information systems are needed in order to reveal how well the organization is doing.

While Governance-only Boards generally should not get into debates as to whether this or that budgeting software package or program policy is best, they should insist that information of the kind they need for evaluation be provided and express their displeasure if current management systems fail to provide it. See Chapter 9 for a full discussion of evaluation.

HOW THE BOARD DOES ITS WORK

We now move on to a discussion of *how* the board should do its work. As can be seen in Figure 1, five sets of factors need to be considered.

Board Structure

The most important source of information on board structures is the organization's by-laws. This document is required if one wishes to formally incorporate as a nonprofit organization or become a registered charity. By-laws may be "bare bones" and include only what is required by the province of incorporation, Corporations Canada (for federally incorporated organizations) or the Canada Revenue Agency for those seeking tax exemptions for donors (see Chapter 5 for a full discussion of the legal aspects of incorporation). On the other hand some by-laws can be quite detailed. Going beyond basics has the disadvantage that making needed amendments can be bothersome. The details of what should be in an organization's by-laws will not be discussed here (see Alberta Culture and Community Spirit (2012)). However, the critical questions surrounding the board's structure are discussed below.

"Structures" are simply formal statements about who has the authority to do what in an organization. They become frozen in time as formal policies, procedures and organization charts, which then influence subsequent actions. For boards, structural issues include such questions as:

*   What is the best size for a board?

*   How many, and what kind of formal positions should exist (*e.g.*, chair, vice-chair, past president, president-elect, treasurer, secretary, vice-presidents, *etc.*)?

*   How many and what kind of formal board committees should exist and what authority should they have as compared to that of the whole board and the management team? Also, how large should they be and what should be the criteria for appointment to them?

Implicit in the above questions is the idea that there are right and wrong answers to them. Also implicit is the belief that if the "right" answers can be found, the board's problems will be solved and it will become effective: no more rubber-stamping or meddling, no more bad decisions or fundraising failures, *etc*. It turns out that none of these implicit assumptions is true.

Once again, research has found that there is no "one best way"; only structures and procedures that fit the circumstances of a given organization at a given time (see Bradshaw & Murray (1992); Herman & Renz (2000); Ostrower (2007); Ostrower & Stone (2010); Sonnenfeld (2002)).The following are brief comments on some of the pros and cons to consider when looking at various answers to these questions.

Board Size. The "how-to" books on boards are fairly consistent in warning against boards that exceed 15 or so people. This recommendation arises because the greater the number of people involved in the complex business of setting strategic direction (the board's #1 responsibility), the more difficult it will be to give them meaningful roles and arrive at a consensus on contentious issues.

Nevertheless, large boards (*e.g.*, 20 to 30) do exist. They often occur in part because it is believed that this is the way to gain the support of a lot of influential community leaders who will be useful in raising money and other purposes. They are also common in national NPOs who feel the need to have representation on the board from many geographical regions. Like the Canadian political scene, there is much suspicion of the agendas of other regions or central head offices, hence all must be represented. However, it should be realized that it is possible to get the support of prestigious people or input from all regions without resorting to the creation of unwieldy sized boards. One of the more common alternatives is to create Advisory Boards or Funding Campaign "cabinets".

Even large boards may be effective, however, as long as everyone recognizes and accepts that a smaller subset of board members (a "core group") will probably evolve (or may need to be created) to play a leadership role. The contributions from non-core-group members will come mostly at the individual and committee-identity levels. At these levels they can provide useful advice or contacts on request though, as noted, the same thing could be provided in other ways.

More generally problematic is the small board (fewer than six members) where there is a real risk that the board will not become aware of changing conditions that threaten the organization. They are also not very effective when the board needs to be a working board. Members tend to become overloaded with work and "burn out" can occur rapidly. However, many small boards, which are easier for a chief executive or board chair to control, are not necessarily a problem until a crisis hits. To cope in such situations requires the small board to ensure that it has independent sources of information and expert outside advice on how the organization is doing.

Formal Offices. The generally accepted recommendation is to keep formal offices to a minimum on the grounds that many of them have no real function other than ceremonial. At minimum, however, there must be a board leader (chair, president) and someone (usually a vice-chair) to step in if the leader cannot perform her or his duties. The vice-chair position is also useful as a way of grooming future chairs. A skilled treasurer is a very important office with the role of taking the lead in carrying out the fiscal oversight responsibility. The office of board secretary is often created for the purpose of keeping track of board decisions and other records. In governance-only boards, however, where there is usually professional staff employed, the taking of minutes may be delegated to administrative personnel, though the secretary can also fulfill a useful role as the person most familiar with the by-laws, board policies and precedent-setting earlier board decisions.

The main point is that the *functions* of chair, treasurer, *etc.*, must be performed; the actual titles used are not important. For example, in some small, simple, organizations all functions might reside in the offices of chair and vice-chair.

Other formal leadership positions in boards are usually those of the chairs of the board committees discussed below. The important requirement of all formal offices is that there be clear descriptions of the duties of the office and that provision be made for training those who fill these positions. Too often office holders take up their jobs without a clue as to what is required. With luck, they can learn by osmosis before a major issue arises, otherwise they can get themselves and their organization into serious trouble.

Board Committees. At one extreme in the "how-to" literature on boards are those, such as John Carver (2006), who state that the number of committees of the board should be kept to an absolute minimum. It is argued that committees do more harm than good because they either try to dabble in operations, thereby subverting the authority of managers, or make decisions on policy issues that are the responsibility of the whole board or the ED. The board and committees therefore end up duplicating each other's work and wasting everyone's time. These are real problems, but eliminating committees is not the only approach to solving them. In fact, in the Mixed Model and

Working Boards, as already pointed out, committees may be vital to the operation of the organization.

There are two basic types of committees:

(a) *Policy committees.* These are small problem-solving groups that can study important issues in depth and produce reports for the whole board with recommendations and supporting data. Note that they do *not* decide on policies; they only make recommendations to those with the authority to do so.

(b) *Working committees.* These are policy implementation groups that either assist paid staff in carrying out tasks that staff cannot do alone or are used instead of paid staff because none are available. Some argue that, strictly speaking, such operational committees should not be considered as committees of the board of directors, rather they should report only to managers. This is fine in theory but, in many organizations with Working or Mixed Model Boards, the best people to head such committees are already board members. Besides, in doing their work, operational committees often must make decisions that have large-scale implications. These level 1 or 2 policy issues must be recognized and brought to the whole board for discussion. A skilled board chair and trained committee chairs are the best judges of what is a major issue with strategic implications, and what is not.

Even in Governance-only Boards, some working committees may be needed at times to help with new operational activities in which the management has little experience, *e.g.*, a merger with another organization, a new kind of fund-raising activity, implementation of a pay equity program, property acquisition or investment decisions.

This said, there is much to support the commonly offered recommendation that *standing* committees (*i.e.*, permanent committees created by the organization's by-laws) be kept to a minimum in Governance-only Boards. Too many committees with titles such as Property Committee, Program Committee, Purchasing Committee, *etc.*, may have no clear function as either policy or working committees. Instead they waste the time of managers who have to think of things for them to do when they are not really needed, or they necessarily confuse the lines of authority of both managers and the whole board.

Many consultants urge that these useless standing committees be replaced by task forces to be created on an "as needed" basis with very clear terms of reference and deadlines for doing their jobs, after which they disappear. It is important to note that a big advantage of temporary task forces of the board is that their membership can more easily be augmented by well-qualified non-board members. At the extreme, only the chair need be a board member to bring any policy issues to the board.

Should boards using the Governance-only Board model have any standing committees, then? Since giving strategic direction is a key board responsibility, a good argument can be made for a Planning Committee to work with other strategically oriented groups in the organization (such as the management teams).It would work with these other groups to help define the issues, assemble relevant information and lay out options for the whole board to consider.

Often the role of taking the lead in strategic planning is played by the Executive Committee so it is worth saying a few words about the risks and benefits of such a committee. An Executive Committee is usually made up of those holding formal offices on the board (*e.g.*, President, Vice-President, Treasurer, *etc.*) and the chairs of standing committees. Its formal role is usually to look after board business between meetings and set the agenda for board meetings. The pitfall with Executive Committees is that they can become a powerful "inner cabinet" that arbitrarily makes decisions the board should make and skews the way issues are put before the board so as to favour a predetermined position. For this reason, some board experts advise against the existence of such a committee. On the other hand, someone must perform the function of setting the board agenda and ensuring that everything that goes before the formal board meetings is of sufficient importance and is well enough prepared and supported with good information. Leaving these matters solely up to the Board Chair and ED increases the possibility of just these two becoming the overly powerful "inner circle". Hence an Executive Committee with strictly limited powers as to what it can decide is probably a worthwhile entity especially for Governance Boards.

Because the board's responsibility for fiscal oversight is so critical, there is also usually a need for a Finance Committee provided it can be kept from making *de facto* strategic decisions when it reviews the accounts and budgets. Organizations with unique characteristics may well identify other areas where constant operational assistance from volunteer directors is required, thereby necessitating standing committees.

Finally, most boards need help to ensure that they manage themselves well. This self-help is sometimes provided in part by a standing committee of the board such as a Nominating Committee. It attempts to locate the best possible people to stand as potential board members. The trouble is that the conventional nominating committee does not go far enough. Who will arrange to have new board members oriented and trained? Who will take a lead in assessing the board's performance or deal with the cases of individual board members who fail to live up to the expectations for members? In some cases, these very important matters are the responsibility of the Executive Committee. In others, the terms of reference of the Nominating Committee are expanded and it is renamed as, for example, the "Board Development" or "Governance" Committee.

Terms of Appointment and Reappointment. It is the consensus of board management gurus that it does an organization good to get periodic infusions of "new blood" on the board to prevent it from becoming resistant to change. This suggests that boards should have a policy of appointing members for fixed terms of office (*e.g.*, of two or three years) and rules as to how many consecutive terms a member can serve. Of course the number of members turning over every year must not be too great so as to provide continuity of experience. This leads to procedures such as two- or three-year appointments with one-quarter or one-third of the board retiring each year. Reappointments can be made only for two further terms after which the person must retire for at least one term.

Such formal policies are potentially useful provided there is a ready pool of qualified candidates for board appointment. This may be the case either where membership on the board is eagerly sought by excellent people or where the organization has a "farm system". A farm system gets potential board members involved in the organization as volunteers and carefully develops and promotes them to the point where they become ready for board membership. It is especially useful for smaller, lower-profile organizations with working boards.

On the other hand, some organizations do not have limited term limits specified in their by-laws. They may be appointed for a fixed term but they can be reappointed endlessly until they choose to resign. Sometime the reason for this is that everyone gets comfortable with the "same old gang" and, if the organization is stable, no one feels a need to change anything. Others shy away from mandatory term limits because they fear (maybe with good reason) that it is too difficult to find a steady supply of committed and skilled new recruits every year. *If* this is true, it could be a valid reason for avoiding formal limits. In this case, however, vigorous and constant efforts must be made to educate board members in the latest challenges facing the organization so they will remain open to recognizing the need for change when it arises.

Effective Board Meetings

In many ways the most important work of the board occurs in the context of its formal meetings. Some of the critical issues that arise around meeting management are as follows.

Attendance. Poor attendance is usually an indication that a significant number of members are dissatisfied with the board and/or their role on it. Some consultants urge compulsory attendance rules as a way of getting the members out to meetings, *e.g.*, "Members must attend at least two-thirds of the meetings each year or resign unless a valid excuse is provided and accepted by the Executive Committee." This may get out the members but can mask the real problems behind low commitment.

Meeting Frequency and Times. There is definitely no fixed rule about the optimum frequency of official meetings of the whole board. Actual practice varies from monthly to annually. The governing criterion ought to be that the board should hold a formal meeting when it has enough business to warrant doing so. For working boards, this could be quite often. For many Governance-only Boards, even less often than monthly could sometimes be acceptable. Chairs and EDs can recognize if they are calling too many board meetings if they find themselves thinking, "Oh- oh, another board meeting coming up. How can we fill up the agenda this time?"

The goal of board meetings should be to focus on issues that have implications for the strategic direction of the organization. In the case of some Governance-only Boards in very stable environments, these might well crop up only three times a year: a meeting to approve the strategic plan; an interim progress report meeting; and an evaluation meeting to assess how well the organization has performed. These, however, are *official decision-making* meetings. But in today's fast changing and threat-laden world, this is usually not the situation.

Furthermore, many nonprofit organizations today find that it is useful to differentiate between decision-making meetings and another kind of board meeting held for the purpose of becoming informed about a single important strategic issue. These meetings are usually less formal discussions and feature input from invited staff or experts from outside. Specific motions are not debated; instead, information is provided, alternatives identified and opinions sought. This is all fed to relevant board or management working groups, which then develop specific policy recommendations in the context of the organization's strategic plan. Formal discussion and voting on such recommendations occurs at one of the decision-making board meetings.

The question of the *time of board meetings* is important when board membership is diverse and everyone's schedules do not fit the same period of the day, or day of the week (mothers caring for children unable to attend midday meetings, shift workers unable to attend evening meetings, or others unable to meet on weekdays). The organization must be conscious of the need to vary meeting times in such circumstances so all board members have an equally fair opportunity to attend. There is also the option of permitting, and arranging for, board members to attend virtually through the use of conference calls, Skype, *etc.* (See Chapter 12 for a discussion of the full potential of information and communications technology).

Meeting length can be another indicator of board mismanagement. Board meetings that regularly last longer than two hours can be an indication of problems. One thing that has been made clear by psychological research is that the ability of a large group of people to constructively contribute to a problem-solving discussion declines dramatically the longer a meeting wears on. This leads to the common ploy used by some manipulative executive directors seeking rubber-stamp approval of their recommendations on contentious issues. They ensure that these items are placed at the *end* of a long agenda. By that time, no one has the energy to think, let alone object.

More commonly, however, the problem of overly long meetings exists because either too much time is being spent on issues that do not need to be considered by the whole board, or there are too many items that involve long-winded reports "for information only". Alternatively, the regular occurrence of long debates that extend meeting times may indicate badly worded motions or poorly prepared reports that do not contain enough supporting data. When these kinds of long discussions occur often, attention should be paid to how to improve the work of the committees or managers who prepare the agenda items in question.

When board meetings go on too long because of too many items being presented "for information only", a solution increasingly adopted by many, is the introduction of a "consent agenda". The procedure is to include all items of information in the agenda sent beforehand to board members. When these items come up at the meeting, there is no oral presentation of the information. Instead, it is taken as understood that the information has been read and will only be discussed if anyone has a question or comment on it. This can save large amounts of time though the disadvantage of it is that it might hurt the feelings of those who prepared the reports and would like to have their "moment in the sun" before the whole board. Other ways of recognizing the work done by board members should be developed.

The flip side of meetings that go on too long is meetings that are too short. Meetings that the board rushes through in, say, half an hour could be an indication of a rubber-stamp board. If this happens regularly it might suggest that the board has been conditioned not to question whatever is put before it or simply that there is not enough business to warrant a meeting and there could be fewer of them.

Meeting Agenda Formats and Meeting Rules. One of the most common complaints of board members is that meetings are "not properly organized". Specific problems include the following:

- The agenda does not reach board members until very shortly before, or even at, the meeting so they have no time to prepare.

- The agenda contains too much information that is irrelevant to the issues to be discussed *or* there is not enough relevant information.

- The order of the agenda items places unimportant and routine items at the top while important ones are at the end, when energy tends to decline.

- Meetings fail to follow accepted "rules of order" so are too disorganized; *or*, conversely, are too rule bound, thereby preventing full and frank debate.

Except in rare emergency situations, there is really no excuse for not getting meeting agendas into the hands of board members at least five working days beforehand. Agendas should be organized so that items requiring decision are put at the top. All supporting material should be directly relevant to the impending discussion.

Even the most informal working boards should adopt one of the standard authorities on "rules of order", such as Roberts Rules[4] to be used as a guide in conducting official board meetings. This, however, does not mean that all meetings must be run in strict accordance with these rules. The rules are primarily of benefit when the items to be

---

[4]   See online at: <http://www.robertsrules.org/rulesintro.htm>.

discussed are likely to be highly controversial with a lot of disagreement among board members. As in any emotion-laden debate, rules are needed to make it fair. These would include: how often a person can speak, rules regarding how amendments to motions should be made, when and how a motion can be tabled, what constitutes being, "out of order", *etc*. In most non-crisis situations, however, a much more relaxed approach can be taken to meeting rules provided the board chair maintains an orderly, businesslike approach by keeping discussions on topic. Agendas that specify approximate times to be devoted to each item also help control disorganized meetings.

Board Composition and Development

Board Composition

Critical to having a successful board is getting the right people on it in the first place. The difficult part is deciding who will be "right" for the organization. Too often the tendency is to appoint members who resemble existing members or who are suitable for conditions as they were but who may not be suitable for a changing future. There is a good deal of advice available to those who are seeking to put together a successful board but there are only two universal criteria which are supported both by research and the "how-to" authors:

1.   Board members must be *committed* to the organization's mission, *i.e.*, they must believe strongly in what the organization is trying to do and seriously want to help. A board dominated by people who sit on it as a favour to a friend or because they believe it will look good on their resumé will not usually be effective.

2.   Prospective members must have the *time and energy* to devote to the board's business.

   Establishing board recruitment needs. The first step in finding the best potential members for a board is to be clear about the kind of people one is seeking in the first place. One way to do this is by compiling a board membership needs document. Table 2 provides one example of a simple recruitment needs grid.

Table 2: Sample Board Member Recruitment Needs Grid

Possible Criteria	Board Members						Gap
	A	B	C	D	E	F	(H, M, L)
Stakeholder Connections (Strong, Med, Weak)							
Clients/users/audience							
Funders							
Actual/potential partners							
Governments or other regulators							
Community leaders							
Other?							
Useful Skills							
Fundraising							
Public Relations/Community Relations							
Finance/accounting							
Planning							
Legal							
Marketing							
Human Resources							
IT/Project Management							
Other?							
Demographic Representation							
Gender balance							
Age balance							
Ethno-racial balance							
Socio-economic balance							

(H= High; M= Medium; L= Low)

Down the left-hand column of Table 2 are listed some of the kinds of background characteristics of individuals that might be important to have on the board and, more importantly, in a changing future environment. The actual ones chosen should be decided on by each organization as they might vary depending on local conditions.

Across the top of Table 2 are listed the names of the *current* board members. The committee doing the nominating then informally assesses the extent to which each member possesses each of the characteristics in column 1, "scoring" the extent to which it is present as being "high", "medium" or "low". A careful examination and discussion of the results of this process should give the committee an indication of the "gaps" in desirable background characteristics needed by the board at that time. This becomes the basis for the subsequent recruitment drive.

There are also many other important questions to answer when it comes to finding the ideal mix of people for a board. The main ones are discussed below.

Should boards be composed primarily of "important" people? Having many "big name" people on the board can help in giving a nonprofit organization credibility and a high profile in the community. And some, if not all, "names" have valuable talents. The dilemma is that many of these people are so busy they do not really have time to do much more than make token appearances.

Many organizations elect to keep the percentage of "prestige" members relatively small and tolerate their minimal involvement as the price that must be paid for their ability to provide contacts and credibility. The majority of the board carries the workload. Of course if the "busy names" become the majority of the board, this can often lead to a Rubber-Stamp board.

The other approach is to put the prestigious names on an "Advisory Board" comprising those who can give useful help with specific matters (such as fundraising) and heighten the organization's profile, but who are not expected to govern. A variation of this idea is the creation of a category of "honorary" board members who may be listed as board members but do not have voting privileges.

The Diversity Dilemma. It is generally agreed that boards should represent the diversity of the people that they serve but research has established that many boards do not achieve this representation (Bradshaw and Sukornyk, 2009). Instead, the majority of their members have similar backgrounds (usually middle class, middle-aged, well-educated, with business or professional experience and of European ethnic origin). To what extent this affects the board's, or organization's, performance depends on how diverse the populations are that the organization seeks to serve. The hypothesis is that a non-representative board will increase the chances that the agency will serve the needs of non-mainstream communities poorly. Put in positive terms, the advantage of expanding a board's diversity along ethno-racial, social class, gender and other dimensions is that this will improve the board's "boundary spanning" function and lead to better strategic leadership.

On the other hand, the fear associated with a very diverse board is that these new kinds of members will not always understand how the board operates and will not be able to see what is best for the organization as a whole. Again, there is no research evidence that this, in fact, happens. Differences in background may sometimes make it more difficult to develop a comfortable, open, problem-solving climate but it is not impossible. Given careful selection of the individual nominees and an adequate board development program, a diverse board can be much more effective than a homogeneous one.

A related question is how much the board should be made up of "stakeholders" who have specific interests in the organization, as opposed to more general "community representatives". Stakeholders consist of organized interest groups, *e.g.*, on a university board of governors, there would be representation from the student government, the faculty association, government ministries, the alumni association, support staff association and associations representing the community. Again, the positive side of organized stakeholder representation is it promotes "bringing the outside in" and "taking the inside out". Once more, the downside risk is the possibility that the representatives will feel they must act solely in what they see as the interests of the organized group they represent. Hard data on the extent to which this actually happens are very scarce. The probability is that problems arise only infrequently, but stakeholder organizations can cause major upheavals during crisis periods such as downsizing, opening or closing programs, or shifting attention from one client group to another. Again, great care in selecting the individual representatives and thorough board training in putting the interests of the organization first can help minimize the frequency of destructive approaches to conflict during periods of change.

How well should candidates know the organization? Another dilemma is the extent to which the board should consist of members who already have an in-depth knowledge of what the organization does and how it operates. For boards using the Working Board model, this is quite important, at least for selection of the majority of their members. For Governing Boards, it may be impossible, other than by choosing internal stakeholder representatives. A majority of Governing Board members will not be "experts" in the organization they govern. This raises the question: how can they provide strategic leadership? As noted, the solution to this problem lies in thorough orientation and provision of at least partially independent information systems for the board.

How much should "business skills" be emphasized? A related question is the extent to which board members should possess specific skills or knowledge based on their employment or training in areas such as law, accounting, marketing, human resources, public and government relations. One school of thought says this kind of talent is very useful for providing the executive director with invaluable free advice on all sorts of management issues. The other says it is overrated and runs the serious risk of creating a board which is going to be primarily interested in management issues and unable to focus on governance issues. Again, there are no data to support either of these assertions so probably there is not a universally correct mix. Organizations with Working Board and Mixed Models are, by definition, deficient in certain management skills so board members who can help fill such gaps are important. Even in large professionally managed institutions there can be certain areas of specialized knowledge that the organization cannot afford to pay for but which a board member might possess. The key in all cases is to train these useful specialists to understand that their expertise will be sought from them in the roles of advisors or implementers only, not as decision-makers.

What individual personal qualities to look for? Developing broad criteria for board selection such as those discussed above is important but, in the end, the most important criteria are those that are the most difficult to specify and measure in potential candidates for membership. These are the *personality characteristics* that one wants to see in board members. Everyone who has ever spent much time watching different boards come and go in an organization will agree that, some years, the majority of board members seems particularly quick to understand issues, creative, constructive in their handling of differences, and businesslike, while in other years, the opposite qualities prevail. Since most boards do not like to check carefully into the personal qualities of the people they nominate, it is almost a matter of chance how well the mix works out in any particular year.

What is needed, clearly, is: (a) an attempt to articulate the kinds of personality characteristics and personal values that are being sought; and (b) a serious attempt to state how they will be discerned in any given nominee. Under heading (a), the following are some of the qualities that are important for most board members: creative imagination, ability to see "the big picture", openness to change, ability to communicate and ability to work well with others and handle conflict constructively.

Regarding (b), there is not space here to provide a full review of the most valid methods for assessing these characteristics in people; most textbooks on human resource management will do that. Suffice it to say here that the essence of the process lies in how the candidates' past behaviour is checked through references. This process needs to be systematically thought out in advance and implemented with care. The all-too-common method of nominating someone whom one other board member believes "is a wonderful person" just is not good enough. These days, most people called to provide references are loath to communicate negative things, especially in writing. However, some might be more open in oral conversations and when asked questions that relate to specific actions, *e.g.*, "What role did 'x' play in your strategic planning process?" or "How was 'x' involved in your fund raising activities?"

A carefully designed board recruitment process looks something like this:

- It is carried out by a Board Governance (or Nominations) committee.

- The committee looks at the strengths of the existing board and tries to identify gaps in skills, abilities and back ground that need to be filled.

- A widely broadcast call for nominations is made highlighting the qualifications sought.

- Those making nominations are asked informally to provide information on why their candidate(s) is suitable.

- Assuming such information is available, others who know the potential nominee are asked (again, informally) how they perceive him/her.

- A short list of suitable nominees is created and ranked by preference. Each person on the list would then be approached in order by the board chair.

The Special Problems of Low Profile and Non-Popular Organizations. Unfortunately, for a large number of worthy but low-profile organizations that support causes that are not widely popular, the problem of board composition is not one of how to choose among a range of possible candidates. It is to find enough people of any kind who meet the basic criteria of commitment to the organization's mission and willingness to devote enough time and effort to the cause. This is a problem of recruitment, rather than selection. Solving it requires developing a focused, formal recruitment program for board members.

The usual method employed by successful nonprofits of this type is the "grow-your-own" approach. This is accomplished by concentrating on getting a lot of working volunteers to help with programs and projects. The best of these are then identified and systematically wooed and trained to accept increasing amounts of responsibility, including the leadership of others. Before long, those with skills and attitudes required on the board can be asked to join it (which, in these situations, is almost always a Working Board). In desperation, one can trust recruitment to the efforts of a few board members to pressure their friends to join, but do not expect a very effective board as a result.

A Final Word on Board Composition. Though there are no hard and fast rules about how a board should be made up, there is probably one generalization that fits all voluntary organizations that are facing rapidly changing, often threatening, environments: strive for balanced diversity. The exact *kind* of mix will vary from situation to situation, but a mix it should be. Older, younger; men, women; rich, poor; "old hands", "young blood"; business and non-business backgrounds; multi-ethnic and multi-racial — the criteria can vary. But only with a balanced mix can the organization improve its chances for getting the fresh ideas and specialized information it needs to cope with its changing world. Remember, however, that to make it all work, the board needs training in how to work together as a team and in how to discern the greater good of the organization as the basis for making all decisions.

Orientation and Development of Board Members

Even though boards may manage to find the ideal mix of skilled and committed people to become members, it may still end up losing them or having them perform ineffectively. This is because members do not know what is expected of them or lack the skill and knowledge needed to make good decisions. The most direct way to deal with this problem is through a well-planned system of board orientation, development and evaluation (Brown (2007); Brudney & Murray (1998); Green &

Griesinger (1996); Herman & Renz (1997; 2000); Herman, Renz & Heimovics (1997); Holland & Jackson (1998);Nobbie & Brudney (2003)). The components of such a system are:

- A board manual that provides full background information on the organization and its current programs and plans, descriptions of the position of board members, and outlines of the responsibilities of board officers and committees.

- A formal orientation program at which new board members meet top management officials, tour facilities and hear presentations on the organization's programs and background information on strategic issues. Also helpful here are informal "mentoring" programs that pair new members with current members. A good mentoring program will "train the trainer" by providing the mentor with a checklist of topics to discuss and the necessary information to cover.

- Periodic formal occasions at which the board assesses its own performance using feedback questionnaires covering much the same topics as the content of this paper. Feedback from the management team who interact with the board should also be obtained. Also useful in helping boards get a realistic picture of how they are doing is obtaining periodic feedback from key external stakeholders on how *they* view the board's work.Differences in perceptions of board effectiveness between the board, staff and external stakeholders are often an indicator of a potentially harmful situation that should be addressed.

One example of a board self-assessment tool is provided as an appendix to this chapter. An online version can be found on the Internet.[5]

There is also a need to assess the performance of individual board members. Again, this can be done by having individuals complete their own self-assessment questionnaire. It is remarkable how honest many are willing to be. However, attendance records and feedback from the Chair and Committee Heads can also be useful. The main problem is that assessing individual performance often feels like a very awkward thing to do because members are volunteers and often have a certain amount of prestige in the community. It is not impossible, however, if board members are shown when they join that there is a formal system of board self-evaluation and understand how the information obtained

---

[5]   See <https://www.boardcheckup.com>.

through it is to be used. Also, the board's by-laws must clearly specify what is expected of members in the way of attendance, behaviour in meetings and in the larger community. They should then specify the procedures to be followed in removing a member from the board if these responsibilities are not properly fulfilled.

The Informal Culture of the Board

So far, the critical factors that shape the effective board have been primarily "formal": they can be the subject of written statements in board by-laws and policy manuals. The roles and responsibilities of the whole board and its committees should be clearly set down; structures and procedures are best embodied in by-laws and board policy statements. The criteria for the composition of the board can be similarly published. However, even if all the "official" and "formal" policies, structures and procedures are ideal, the board may still fail to become a high value-added board. This is because, behind the formal framework, is an informal one which can be called the board's "culture".

A culture is a set of behaviour patterns, attitudes, values and beliefs widely shared by a group, which influences their behaviour. Taken together, they represent their shared understanding of "how we do things around here". They are often taken for granted and are so deeply ingrained that group members are scarcely conscious of how they colour their individual ways of viewing the world. Not all boards have strong, widely shared cultures, especially when they are new or when there are wholesale changes in their makeup. But most do eventually evolve, in an unconscious way, ways of thinking and feeling about how the board should function. Let us look at just a few of the more important elements of board cultures.

Informal Groups in Boards. One of the more common aspects of board cultures is the way they sometimes develop sub-groups within them — people who stick together more with each other than they do with other board members (Reid (2014)). Many of the "how-to" writers on boards deplore the existence of these "cliques" within boards on the grounds that they dominate board proceedings and shut out non-members. They urge that every effort be made to give all board members equal voice in decision-making. This is unquestionably a desirable ideal. Reality, however, is something different. Sub-groups emerge unbidden and usually without conscious intention within the board. Furthermore, they need not be all bad. One study (Murray, Bradshaw & Wolpin (1992)) found that over 60 per cent of a sample of 427 Canadian nonprofit boards of all types were seen as having "core groups" within them. Of those reporting core groups, 71 per cent said they were "a positive force for change". Many such groups exist because of differences among board members in the degree of commitment and experience they bring to the job. Groups with extra time and special expertise are often highly valuable advisors to both the board chair and chief executive.

This said, it must be realized that some core groups can be a strong force inhibiting needed change. In other situations boards may fracture into two or more *competing* cliques that often engage in destructive political conflict that can tear the organization apart. Leaders of boards must manage informal groups just as actively as they do other aspects of board work. Sometimes the issues surrounding sub-groups can be surfaced for leaders to deal with through board performance self-assessment exercises using tools like the one provided at the end of this chapter or online.[6] Team building exercises for the board can also lessen the influence of divisive cliques.

Elements of the How-To-Run-A-Meeting Culture. A stranger observing the meetings of the boards of several organizations with similar memberships, structures and operating policies may often note how they can differ. In one, for example, meetings of the whole board may be stiff and formal. Discussions consist of "speeches" each of which makes little reference to previous speeches. Expressions of disagreement are few and are quickly smoothed over. There is a tendency for the meeting to be dominated by a few "senior statesmen/women". In another board, governing the very same type of organization, the meetings are much more relaxed and informal, members appear to know and respect each other, one person's comments pick up on others adding to, or modifying, their ideas. Disagreements may arise but are "talked out" until there is consensus or the parties "agree to disagree" and a vote settles the matter without lasting rancour. Though some may participate more than others, everyone usually contributes something to the discussion and the ideas ofanewcomer have as much chance of influencing the debate as those of the old hands.

What we have here are cultural differences in shared beliefs about the way meetings ought to be conducted. The important elements of the meeting culture are: the formality of discussion, the inclusiveness of participation and the management of differences. They are strongly influenced by the leadership style of the board chair

---

[6]   See <https://www.boardcheckup.com>.

(see below) and can have a huge impact on the quality of the decisions reached by the board.

Openness to Change. Some boards come to view themselves as the "keepers of the flame". They have a strong sense of what has made the organization distinctive and successful in the past. Every proposal for change is scrutinized for evidence of a departure from tradition. At the other end of the spectrum are boards that have little or no sense of the organization's history or its basic mission or values so are willing to opportunistically take on every new program that looks as though it might bring money or popularity (a phenomenon known as "mission drift"). In between are those that intuitively understand the core values and mission but also appreciate that threats and opportunities in the environment require change, sometimes major change.

Acceptance of Diversity and Equity. Organizations may make official pronouncements about their commitment to increasing diversity and promoting equity in their treatment of clients, staff and volunteers. These may even be reflected in the board's membership as new members who represent different backgrounds are appointed; however, behind the formal are the informal attitudes toward these others that can be reflected in a hundred ways through tone of voice, choice of words, body language and what is left unsaid. That message may be one of non-acceptance and, if it is, the newcomers quickly pick it up. Confronted by such a culture, most tend to leave or try to "fit in", conforming to the others' expectations of how they ought to act.

Commitment to Action. One of the most important elements of some board cultures is the extent to which they have an orientation to action as opposed to "just talk". In one situation, new board members rapidly learn that the main role of board members is simply to express their opinions in board meetings. When it comes to taking an active role by digging up new information, consulting outside stakeholders, raising funds, sitting on task forces, *etc.*, everyone gazes fixedly at the ceiling until someone suggests that the executive director or other staff do the work. In others, the sense of partnership with management is pervasive. Members sense when and where they can help and step forward.

Deep-Seated Convictions About Board Roles and Responsibilities. It is quite common for boards to hold retreats at which they make firm resolutions to change the pattern of roles and responsibilities they use from, say, a Rubber-Stamp Board to a Governing Board, or from a Meddling Board to a clearer Mixed Model

Board. Reports are written and motions passed to this effect. Yet two or three years later they have drifted back to their old ways of rubber-stamping or meddling. Why is this? In all likelihood it is because the deeply held, shared beliefs about how boards ought to operate were never touched in the "change" exercise. The research of Holland, Leslie and Holzhalb (1993), Holland and Jackson (1998), Chait, Ryan and Taylor (2005) is especially useful in reminding us of how important it is for board members to share a sense of themselves as a "team" whose members trust and respect one another.

Building a team culture in boards is not something that happens automatically. Many members never get to know anything about one another beyond a vague familiarity with their colleague's official titles. Specially designed team building exercises can help change a culture of disassociation among board members. Note, however, that *overly* cohesive boards have risks as well in that they may reject ideas or people who differ too greatly from the norm, a phenomenon known as "group think" (Brown (2007)).

The Leadership of the Board Chair and CEO

Students of organizational culture are far from unanimous about how board cultures (or any others) are created and what makes them change. Without doubt, the characteristics of individual board members are important, which is why selection is so critical. So too are the formal policies, structures and procedures of the kind discussed throughout this chapter. But they are not sufficient to result in positive changes without leadership. There are two critical leadership roles that strongly influence board cultures: those of the board chair, or president (terminology varies, but this is the volunteer head of the board) and the organization's chief executive (the paid top manager where this position exists). (In organizations made up entirely of volunteer organizations, the chair usually fills both the top board and top management roles.) The way these roles are played can have a great deal of influence on the board's culture: when the two are played in complementary ways, the influence is multiplied; when they are in conflict, they can paralyze both the board and the organization.

An excellent book that summarizes the literature on leadership in nonprofits and reports research on the differences between effective and ineffective leaders in this sector is *Executive Leadership in Nonprofit Organizations by* Herman and Heimovics (1992). In condensed form, the way these two top positions influence board cultures can be described as follows:

The Chair

Recent research has shown that the chairperson of the board can have a considerable impact on its effectiveness. Between 2006 and 2009 Harrison and Murray (2007; 2013; 2014) studied the role and impact of 170 chairs of NPOs in the United States, Canada and Great Britain. It was clear that, not only are chairs largely responsible for the quality of the board meetings they lead but they can also be highly influential in a number of other, less formal, ways. In particular, their relationship with the CEO can be either highly supportive or, in the minority of cases, a major impairment to that person's effectiveness. Similarly, chairs may play a significant role in representing the organization in the outside community.

This research also revealed that it is the *informal* leadership behaviours of chairs that are the most important. Chairs who have the greatest positive impact are more likely to:

- Be trustworthy and calm

- Be a good listener and an effective communicator

- Clarify and help define issues

- Act as a coach or mentor when EDs wish it

- Develop a sense of team spirit in the board while making sure the talents of all board members are used and valued.

Turning to the main responsibility of chairs, that of actually chairing the meetings of the board, they will be effective or ineffective depending on how well they handle the following basic elements of meeting leadership:

- *Degree of Control.* Strict application of rules of order versus a looser approach. The more controlling the chair, the more likely the board climate will be formal and the greater will be the tendency to adopt a Rubber-Stamp model of operating. Conversely, overly loose control can lead to a Confused Board in which all members feel free to do and say whatever they want, for as long as they want to.

- *Degree of Organization.* Meetings start and stop on time, discussions end with clear action plans (who is going to do what and when), agendas are organized with items appearing in order of importance. The more organized the chair, the more boards will value commitment to action as opposed to "just talk".

- *Tolerance for Digressions.* This refers to how the chair handles discussions that wander off the topic. Too much tolerance breeds a "just talk" culture; too little can kill spontaneity and creativity.

- *Ability to Control Dominators and Disturbers.* If the chair cannot manage the tendency of a few members to dominate discussions by too much talk or personal attacks on the contributions of others, a culture will develop in which the majority of members (if they stay on) will feel there is no point in their saying anything.

- *Ability to Draw Out Non-Speakers.* Some board members are too inhibited to contribute so must be skillfully brought out of their shells. Unless this happens, a board can evolve into two cliques — the talkers and the non-talkers. Valuable input will be lost from non-talkers and some may eventually "blow up" in damaging ways.

- *Ability to Inspire and Motivate Commitment.* By far the most important function for the board chair to play is that of helping the board to articulate its vision and decide on the strategic paths to achieving the organization's goals. Some will try to do this through a form of personal charisma that inspires an unquestioning devotion on the part of followers. Without thinking too much for themselves, they buy the leader's dream and do whatever the leader suggests needs to be done to make it come true. The danger of this form of charisma is that it creates a Rubber-Stamp Board dominated by the chair. If and when the vision fails, it is very difficult for the board to see a new way. Usually the fallen leader leaves and most of the rest of the board follows or, if they do not, the board becomes paralyzed.

  There is another kind of charisma, however: that of the leader who has the talent to spark creativity in others; who can synthesize and articulate the contributions of others. The result is a vision and strategic plan in which the whole board, indeed the whole organization, feels ownership. If it experiences difficulties in implementation no one runs away or blames others, rather they pull together to make the necessary changes.

The Executive Director

The results of many research studies suggest that the way EDs lead is the single most important factor differentiating successful from less successful nonprofits (for more detail on this topic, see Chapter 4 in this book). Without doubt, EDs can strongly influence the ability of boards to play their roles effectively (Herman & Heimovics (1991); Murray, Bradshaw & Wolpin (1994); Cornforth (1999); Pettigrew & McNulty (1995)).

The reason EDs are so important to their boards is because of their power to control information. Because of the amount of time and energy they put into the organization, they simply know more about what is going on both inside and outside among critical stakeholders. This gives them a tremendous advantage in determining how problems are defined and tackled. For example, "Our problem is not enough money" versus, "Our problem is that our programs don't meet the needs of our clients" — both could be offered as "explanations" for bad publicity from dissatisfied clients. They also control what information is provided to analyze issues and what solutions will be seen as "feasible".

Experienced, long-tenure EDs who want to control and manipulate their boards so they become Rubber-Stamps, usually have little trouble doing so because they can influence who is invited to join, who is nominated to key positions as board chair and committee chairs and, as mentioned, they can control the board's agenda and its information resources.

On the other hand, EDs who want to ensure that board meetings are truly strategic will do so by involving members in information gathering and the creation of recommended actions well before complete reports and formally worded motions are put to a board meeting for approval. They will also be very aware of contributions that board members can make in their capacity as committee members and individuals with useful skills and knowledge. Those organizations that need a Working or Mixed Model Board will help train the volunteer/manager board members in how to distinguish between big-picture strategic issues and operational matters so that only the former are brought before the meetings of the whole board.

CONCLUSION

The task of improving the performance of nonprofit boards of directors is still more of an art than a science. There is still a shortage of solid, oft-replicated, research "proving" that boards will cause their organizations to perform better if they adopt certain structures or procedures or play certain kinds of roles rather than others. There is rather more support for the claim that boards with unclear roles that do not perform their basic due diligence duties and have an inability to focus on the "big picture" might well cause severe problems for the organizations they govern. Fixing these problems might move board performance from "awful" to "adequate". Getting to "outstanding" however requires each board to adapt to the contingencies of the context in which it finds itself — the state of the organization's external environment and the mix of resources, skills and abilities within the organization itself.

The key requirements of *all* those who have responsibility for the success of a nonprofit organization are to:

1.   Be aware of all the "players" who have an influence on the major decisions that affect the organization and those it serves.

2.   Decide what are the most important issues facing the organization.

3.   Identify who has the skills and knowledge needed to address these issues (and acquire such people if they are not already part of the organization).

4.   Ensure that they have the clear authority and resources needed to act.

5.   Have in place the best possible information systems for tracking progress.

In some organizations, the board that results from this approach will look a lot like that recommended as a universally valid best model (such as that put forward by Carver (2006)), while in others it will look like an old-fashioned work group that simultaneously engages in operational work and major policy setting. In between can be an almost infinite combination of mixed characteristics that defies easy labelling but that nevertheless works very effectively for the particular situation the organization is in.

REFERENCES

Alberta Culture and Community Spirit Program, *Board Development (Series of 5 booklets)* (Edmonton: The Muttart Foundation, 2012).

Board Source (USA): *Building Effective Non-Profit Boards*, online at: <www.boardsource.org/default.asp?ID=1>.

P. Bradshaw, V. Murray & J. Wolpin, "Do nonprofit boards make a difference? An exploration of the relationships among board structure, process and effectiveness" (1992) 21:13 Nonprofit and Voluntary Sector Quarterly 227-249.

P. Bradshaw & L. Sukornyk, "Results of a survey of diversity on Canadian nonprofit boards" (Paper presented at the annual conference of the Association for Nonprofit and Social Economy Research, Ottawa (2009)).

W.A. Brown, "Board development practices and competent board members" (2007) 17:3 Nonprofit Management and Leadership 301-318.

W.A. Brown & C. Guo, "Exploring the key roles for nonprofit boards" (2010) 39:3 Nonprofit and Voluntary Sector Quarterly 536-546.

J.L. Brudney & V. Murray, "Do Intentional Efforts to Improve Boards Really Work? The Views of Nonprofit CEOs" (1998) 8:4 Nonprofit Management and Leadership 333-348.

R.R. Chait, W.P. Ryan & B.E. Taylor, *Governance as Leadership* (Toronto: John Wiley and Son, 2005).

C. Cornforth, "Power Relations Between Boards and Senior Managers in the Governance of Public and Non-profit Organisations" (Paper presented to British Academy of Management (1999)).

C. Cornforth, "Nonprofit governance research: The need for innovative perspectives and approaches" in C. Cornforth & W. Brown, *Nonprofit Governance: Innovative Perspectives and Approaches* (London: Routledge, 2014) 1-14.

C. Cornforth & W. Brown, *Nonprofit Governance: Innovative Perspectives and Approaches* (London: Routledge, 2014).

J. Cutt & V. Murray, *Accountability and Effectiveness Evaluation in Nonprofit Organizations* (London: Routledge, 2000).

J. Cutt, V. Murray & W. Tassie, "Nonprofits Accommodate the Information Demands of Public and Private Funders" (1996) 7:1 Nonprofit Management and Leadership 45-68.

C. Davidson *et al.*, *Board Governance Resource Guide for Community Organizations* (Toronto: Community Literacy of Ontario, 2013).

J. Freiwirth, "Community Engagement Governance: Engaging stakeholders for community impact" in C. Cornforth & W. Brown, *Nonprofit Governance: Innovative Perspectives and Approaches* (London: Routledge, 2014) 183-209.

M.D. Gill, *Governing for Results* (Victoria: Trafford, 2005).

J.C. Green & D.W. Griesinger, "Board performance and organizational effectiveness in nonprofit social service organizations" (1996) 6:4 Nonprofit Management and Leadership 381-402.

M. Harris, "Exploring the Role of Boards Using Total Activities Analysis" (1993) 3:3 Nonprofit Management and Leadership 269-281.

Y.D. Harrison & V. Murray, "The best and worst of board chairs" (2007) 24:2 The Nonprofit Quarterly 24-29.

Y.D. Harrison & V. Murray, "Perspectives on the leadership of chairs of nonprofit organization boards of directors: A grounded theory, mixed method study" (2012) 22:4 Nonprofit Management and Leadership 411-438.

Y.D. Harrison, V. Murray & C. Cornforth, "Perceptions of Board Chair Leadership Effectiveness in Nonprofit and Voluntary Sector Organizations" (2013) 24:3 Voluntas 688-712.

R.D. Herman & R.D. Heimovics, *Executive Leadership in Nonprofit Organizations: New Strategies for Shaping Executive-Board Dynamics* (San Francisco: Jossey-Bass, 1991).

R.D. Herman & D.O. Renz, "Multiple constituencies and the social construction of nonprofit organization effectiveness" (1997) 26:2 Nonprofit and Voluntary Sector Quarterly 185-206.

R.D. Herman & D.O. Renz, "Nonprofit organizational effectiveness: Contrasts between especially effective and less effective organizations" (1998) 9:1 Nonprofit Management and Leadership 23-38.

R.D. Herman & D.O. Renz, "Board practices of especially effective and less effective local nonprofit organizations" (2000) 30:2 American Review of Public Administration 142-160.

R.D. Herman & D.O. Renz, "Advancing nonprofit organizational effectiveness research and theory: Nine theses" (2008) 18:4 Nonprofit Management and Leadership 399-415.

R.D. Herman, D.O. Renz & R.D. Heimovics, "Board practices and board effectiveness in local nonprofit organizations" (1997) 7:4 Nonprofit Management and Leadership 373-385.

T.P. Holland & D.K. Jackson, "Strengthening board performance: findings and lessons from demonstration projects" (1998) 9:2 Nonprofit Management and Leadership 121-134.

T.P. Holland, D. Leslie & C. Holzhalb, "Culture and Change in Nonprofit Boards" (1993) 4:2 Nonprofit Management and Leadership 141-156.

A. Hough *et al.* (2014), "Board monitoring and judgment as processes of sensemaking" in C. Cornforth & W. Brown, *Nonprofit Governance: Innovative Perspectives and Approaches* (London: Routledge, 2014) 142-160.

H. Mintzberg, *The Rise and Fall of Strategic Planning* (Toronto: Maxwell Macmillan Canada, 1994).

V. Murray, "Prescriptive and Research-Based Approaches to Nonprofit Boards: Linking Parallel Universes" (Paper presented to the annual conference of the Association for Research on Nonprofit Organizations and Voluntary Action, Los Angeles (2004)).

V. Murray, P. Bradshaw & J. Wolpin, "Power in and Around Boards: A Neglected Dimension of Governance" (1992) 3:2 Nonprofit Management and Leadership 165-182.

P.D. Nobbie & J.L. Brudney, "Testing the Implementation, Board Performance and Organizational Effectiveness of the Policy Governance Model in Nonprofit Boards of Directors" (2003) 32:4 Nonprofit and Voluntary Sector Quarterly 571-595.

F. Ostrower, *Nonprofit Governance in the United States* (Washington, D.C.: The Urban Institute, 2007).

F. Ostrower & M. Stone, "Governance: Research trends, gaps and future prospects" in W.W. Powell & R. Steinberg, eds., *The Nonprofit Sector: A Research Handbook*, 2d ed. (New Haven: Yale University Press, 2006).

R. Paton, *Managing and Measuring Social Enterprises* (London: Sage, 2003).

A. Pettigrew & T. McNulty, "Power and Influence in and Around the Boardroom" (1995) 48:8 Human Relations 845-873.

W. Reid, "Beneath the surface and around the table: Exploring group dynamics in boards" in C. Cornforth & W. Brown, *Nonprofit Governance: Innovative Perspectives and Approaches* (London: Routledge, 2014) 249-271.

D. Renz, "Reframing governance" (2006) 13:4 The Nonprofit Quarterly 12-16.

L.M. Salamon & H.K. Anheier, *Defining the Nonprofit Sector: A Cross-National Analysis* (New York: St. Martin's Press, 1997).

J.L. Siciliano, "The relationship of board member diversity to organizational performance" (1996) 15:4 Journal of Business Ethics 1313-1320.

J.L. Siciliano, "The Relationship Between Formal Planning and Performance in Nonprofit Organizations" (1997) 7:4 Nonprofit Management and Leadership 387-404.

M. Stone & F. Ostrower (2007), "Acting in the Public Interest: Another look at nonprofit governance" (2007) 36:3 Nonprofit and Voluntary Sector Quarterly 416-438.

M. Stone, B.C. Crosby & J.M. Bryson, "Adaptive governance in collaborations: Design propositions from research and practice" in C. Cornforth & W. Brown, *Nonprofit Governance: Innovative Perspectives and Approaches* (London: Routledge, 2014) 249-271.

J.A. Sonnenfeld, "What Makes Great Boards Great" (2002) 80:9 Harvard Business Review 106-113.

T. Tompkin, ed., *You and Your Nonprofit Board* (London: Charity Channel Press, 2013).

C. Trower, *The Practitioner's Guide to Governance as Leadership* (San Francisco: Jossey-Bass, 2012).

T. Wolf, *Effective Leadership in Nonprofit Organizations* (New York: Alworth Press, 2014).

APPENDIX

DIAGNOSTIC CHECKLIST FOR ASSESSING THE PERFORMANCE OF NONPROFIT ORGANIZATION BOARDS OF DIRECTORS[7]

Below are a number of statements that briefly describe issues related to the effectiveness of boards of directors of nonprofit organizations. Check the box that comes closest to describing the situation in your board as you see it.

If a question does not apply to your board (for example, if the question deals with board committees and you do not have any), simply leave it blank.

If your organization does not have a paid top manager (e.g., Chief Executive Officer, Executive Director), but does have a volunteer who fills that role, answer the questions related to the CEO with that person in mind.

Feel free to add comments at the end of each group of items checked if you would like to expand on your thoughts.

©2009
Prof. Vic Murray
School of Public Administration
University of Victoria
vmurray@uvic.ca

---

[7]   An online version of this Checklist can be found at: <https://www.boardcheckup.com>.

This questionnaire may be used free and without obtaining permission, however, it is requested that its authorship be acknowledged.

A. Issues Related to the Board's Overall Role and Responsibilities

Basic board responsibilities

	Agree Strongly	Agree Somewhat	Disagree Somewhat	Disagree Strongly	Not Sure
1. All board members are clear about what the role of the board ought to be.	☐	☐	☐	☐	☐
2. The Board and the Chief Executive Officer (CEO or Executive Director) sometimes seem to have different ideas about the responsibilities and authority each should have.	☐	☐	☐	☐	☐
3. The board tends to act too much as a "rubber-stamp" for decisions made by the organization's top management.	☐	☐	☐	☐	☐
4. The board never gets involved in making decisions about operational details that ought to be made by management.	☐	☐	☐	☐	☐
5. Board members are unclear about their legal liabilities and what protection they have against them.	☐	☐	☐	☐	☐
6. The board regularly ensures that an analysis is done of any serious risks that the organization might face and that a plan is in place to minimize these.	☐	☐	☐	☐	☐
7. The board does a very good job of ensuring that the organization's finances are being managed soundly.	☐	☐	☐	☐	☐

Board responsibilities for planning

	Agree Strongly	Agree Somewhat	Disagree Somewhat	Disagree Strongly	Not Sure
8. The board has not spent enough time establishing a clear mission and vision for the organization.	☐	☐	☐	☐	☐

	Agree Strongly	Agree Somewhat	Disagree Somewhat	Disagree Strongly	Not Sure
9. The board never seems to have time to explore external challenges and opportunities that the organization might face and decide whether these will require changes in its future direction.	☐	☐	☐	☐	☐
10. The board does not do a very good job of learning about the concerns of the communities that the organization serves and other stakeholders that impact the performance of the organization.	☐	☐	☐	☐	☐
11. The board regularly holds "creative thinking" sessions aimed at trying to find new ways the organization could develop.	☐	☐	☐	☐	☐
12. The board does little to learn about innovations tried by others that might help the organization.	☐	☐	☐	☐	☐
13. The board is provided with a clear picture of the organization's internal strengths and limitations in dealing with its external environment.	☐	☐	☐	☐	☐
14. The board has developed a clear, well-researched, strategic plan that sets out realistic goals and establishes priorities for the organization.	☐	☐	☐	☐	☐
15. Plans exist on paper but they don't get implemented at the operational level. Other concerns drive what actually gets done.	☐	☐	☐	☐	☐

The board's role in performance assessment

	Agree Strongly	Agree Somewhat	Disagree Somewhat	Disagree Strongly	Not Sure
16. The board makes regular attempts to assess how well the organization is doing in achieving its mission effectively and efficiently.	☐	☐	☐	☐	☐
17. The board does not get enough of the right kind of information to give it a clear picture of how well the organization is doing.	☐	☐	☐	☐	☐
18. The board regularly and systematically carries out assessments of the CEO's performance (e.g. Executive Director, President, etc.).	☐	☐	☐	☐	☐

The board's role in fundraising

	Agree Strongly	Agree Somewhat	Disagree Somewhat	Disagree Strongly	Not Sure
19. The board is confused about its role in fundraising for the organization.	☐	☐	☐	☐	☐
20. There is no overall strategy for fundraising that the board has approved.	☐	☐	☐	☐	☐
21. The board has problems engaging in actual fundraising activities.	☐	☐	☐	☐	☐

Please add any comments you might have on the clarity of the board's responsibilities and how well it carries them out.

B. Issues Related to the Board's Formal Structures and Operating Processes

The formal structure of the board

	Agree Strongly	Agree Somewhat	Disagree Somewhat	Disagree Strongly	Not Sure
22. The board seems too large and cumbersome to enable it to act as an effective decision-making body that can deal with complex issues.	☐	☐	☐	☐	☐
23. There are clear and well-used position descriptions for the positions of the board officers (e.g., Chair, Vice-Chair, Treasurer, Secretary, etc.).	☐	☐	☐	☐	☐
24. Administrative support for the board (secretarial assistance, record keeping, assistance in arranging meetings, etc.) is inadequate.	☐	☐	☐	☐	☐
25. Some board committees are not all that useful anymore.	☐	☐	☐	☐	☐
26. All board committees are quite clear as to their responsibilities and authority. There is no confusion over what the committees should decide compared to what should be decided by the board as a whole or by staff.	☐	☐	☐	☐	☐
27. Some chairs of committees are not very effective leaders in getting things done.	☐	☐	☐	☐	☐

	Agree Strongly	Agree Somewhat	Disagree Somewhat	Disagree Strongly	Not Sure
28. Some committees have members who don't pull their weight or don't have enough experience to be of much help.	☐	☐	☐	☐	☐

Board meetings

	Agree Strongly	Agree Somewhat	Disagree Somewhat	Disagree Strongly	Not Sure
29. The agenda for board meetings is provided to board members in plenty of time before the meeting.	☐	☐	☐	☐	☐
30. When the agenda does come, there is too much information to digest *or* not enough to adequately familiarize board members about the issues.	☐	☐	☐	☐	☐
31. The agenda for meetings is too full of "routine" motions or items "for information only" so there isn't time to discuss more important matters.	☐	☐	☐	☐	☐
32. The agenda items of greatest importance often come up too late in the meeting when board members are too tired to concentrate on them.	☐	☐	☐	☐	☐
33. We have no problems when it comes to attendance at board meetings; most members attend most meetings.	☐	☐	☐	☐	☐
34. Board meetings often go on too long.	☐	☐	☐	☐	☐
35. Once the board has finished discussing something, it is always quite clear who is going to do what and when.	☐	☐	☐	☐	☐
36. Discussions at board meetings rarely get off track.	☐	☐	☐	☐	☐
37. There is too much unconstructive arguing among some members during meetings.	☐	☐	☐	☐	☐
38. Meetings are run too informally, for example with more than one person talking at once, no time limits on discussions, a tendency for discussions to go off on unrelated tangents, etc.	☐	☐	☐	☐	☐
39. Meetings stick too much to formal "rules of order" so that thorough, probing discussions are discouraged.	☐	☐	☐	☐	☐

	Agree Strongly	Agree Somewhat	Disagree Somewhat	Disagree Strongly	Not Sure
40. A few members seem to dominate discussions and this discourages quieter board members from contributing.	☐	☐	☐	☐	☐

Please add any comments you may have regarding the structure of the board and its committees and the quality of its meetings.

C. Issues Related to the Composition of the Board and Development of Board Members

	Agree Strongly	Agree Somewhat	Disagree Somewhat	Disagree Strongly	Not Sure
41. Looking at the board as a whole, there is not enough "new blood" coming on to it to provide fresh energy and ideas.	☐	☐	☐	☐	☐
42. Recruiting high quality new board members is not a problem for us.	☐	☐	☐	☐	☐
43. We pay considerable attention to making sure we get the mix of skills and backgrounds we need in the new board members we recruit.	☐	☐	☐	☐	☐
44. The diversity of publics with an interest in this organization is not well represented in the make-up of the board.	☐	☐	☐	☐	☐
45. We don't do a very good job of orienting and training new board members	☐	☐	☐	☐	☐

Please add any comments you may have on the composition of your board and effectiveness of board orientation and development efforts for new members.

D. Issues Related to the Informal Culture of the Board

	Agree Strongly	Agree Somewhat	Disagree Somewhat	Disagree Strongly	Not Sure
46. Too many board members seem unwilling to devote much time or effort to the work of the board.	☐	☐	☐	☐	☐
47. The board handles crises well. It gets involved in helping to overcome them rather than depending on others to solve the problem.	☐	☐	☐	☐	☐
48. The board regularly attempts to assess its own performance and change itself if it thinks it can improve.	☐	☐	☐	☐	☐

	Agree Strongly	Agree Somewhat	Disagree Somewhat	Disagree Strongly	Not Sure
49. Board members tend not to be involved in representing the organization to the outside community nor do they try to bring the concerns of that community into the organization.	☐	☐	☐	☐	☐
50. As far as I know, many board members have contacts among people who might help the organization but they are not encouraged, or given the opportunity, to make use of them.	☐	☐	☐	☐	☐
51. Effort is regularly made to help board members get to know one another and develop "team spirit" in the group.	☐	☐	☐	☐	☐

Please add any comments you may have about the informal "culture" of the board and how it affects the board's performance.

E. Board Leadership Issues

	Agree Strongly	Agree Somewhat	Disagree Somewhat	Disagree Strongly	Not Sure
52. There is a kind of "inner group" that seems to run things on the board and those who are not part of it sometimes feel left out.	☐	☐	☐	☐	☐
53. The board chair tends to be overly controlling,	☐	☐	☐	☐	☐
54. The board chair is a bit too passive and disorganized in her/his leadership style.	☐	☐	☐	☐	☐
55. As far as I know, the board chair is quite willing to speak to board members who don't carry out their responsibilities properly.	☐	☐	☐	☐	☐
56. The board chair seems to "play favourites" among board members.	☐	☐	☐	☐	☐
57. As far as I know, the organization's Chief Executive Officer (CEO, Executive Director) is quite willing to consult individual board members for informal advice or assistance.	☐	☐	☐	☐	☐
58. As far as I know, the relationship between the CEO and the board chair is quite formal; they don't talk much "off the record".	☐	☐	☐	☐	☐
59. The CEO sometimes seems to be manipulating the board.	☐	☐	☐	☐	☐
60. The board chair is highly effective at running meetings.	☐	☐	☐	☐	☐

Please add any comments you may have about the leadership provided by the board chair and/or the chief executive officer of the organization.

OTHER CONCERNS AND SUGGESTIONS

Please note below any other concerns you have about anything that you think prevents the board from doing the best job it can and provide specific suggestions on how the board could become more effective.

Chapter 4

EXECUTIVE LEVEL MANAGEMENT IN NONPROFIT ORGANIZATIONS

Keith Seel
Bow Valley College

INTRODUCTION

Executive management in a nonprofit organization refers to the individual who has overall responsibility for the operations of the organization. While in very small, unstaffed nonprofit organizations, volunteers take on the responsibilities of the executive manager, it is typically the first paid position offered within these organizations as they grow. In this chapter, executive management refers to the most senior salaried staff position within the organization. As Boland (2013) describes the position:

> Accountable to a fully autonomous Board of Directors for executing the organization's mission, strategy and business plan. Working within broad strategic guidelines and Board policy leads the organization to attain short and longer-term strategic financial and operational goals and develop its organizational culture. Plans, directs and monitors all aspects of the organization's operational policies and the achievement of revenue/fund development objectives and initiatives, manages staff committees and develops business plans in collaboration with the Board. May liaise or advocate with various levels of government, community partners and other stakeholders to further the goals of the organization. Typical titles include: President, Chief Executive Officer or Executive Director.

Put differently, Heimovics *et al.* (1993, at 420) see executives of nonprofit organizations as being in the position of controlling the successes and failures of the organization that they have responsibility for. Further, these executives are "at the centre of the organization's information flow" (at 420). Because they are at the centre, nonprofit organizations often organize around the executive to "help reduce information uncertainty caused by the shifting nature of resource dependency" (at 420). Any way you look at the role of the senior executives in nonprofit organizations, they are the focus for decision-making, information flow, accountability, responsibility and relationships with the external world beyond the nonprofit organization.

This chapter is organized to give the reader a general overview of the executive director position within a nonprofit organization. The issues to be discussed are:

- the terminology associated with the executive position and in particular how one might understand the title "Executive Director" (ED);

- the role of the ED and how the position is situated relative to staff, the board, and the community;

- the relationship between the ED role and leadership responsibilities. The use of Canadian data from EDs provides a range of interesting perspectives on the competencies of an effective leader in the ED role;

- the determinants of ED effectiveness;

- what shapes the effectiveness of the board-ED relationship;

- the relationship between the ED and staff;

- the financial oversight responsibilities of the ED; and

- a brief exploration of challenges facing people in the role of ED and what might be done to meet them.

TERMINOLOGY

In the discussion that follows, the term "Executive Director" refers to the senior executive position in a nonprofit organization — paid or volunteer. For smaller organizations where a volunteer or a board member may fill a similar position, the chapter will be of value in defining the broad responsibilities associated with the role. Made up of two words, the title "Executive Director" covers many functional areas and indeed this range of activities is well demonstrated in Canada's nonprofit sector where a person having this title can for example, run a very small organization addressing issues of street teens through to a large national organization addressing a health issue. Table 1 below looks at the two words making up "Executive Director" and provides a suggestion of the diversity of activity implied in the title.

Table 1: Definitions of the Term "Executive" and "Director"

According to the Oxford English Dictionary:

As a noun, *executive* has the following relevant meanings:
1.   A person or group having administrative or managerial authority in an organization.
2.   The chief officer of a government, state, or political division.

As an adjective, *executive* has two related meanings:
1.   Of, relating to, capable of, or suited for carrying out or executing: *an advisory body lacking executive powers.*
2.   Having, characterized by, or relating to administrative or managerial authority: *the executive director of a nonprofit organization; executive experience and skills.*

As a noun, *director* means:
1.   One who or that which directs, rules, or guides; a guide, a conductor; "one that has authority over others; a superintendent; one that has the general management of a design or work".
2.   A member of a board appointed to direct or manage the affairs of a commercial corporation or company.

These definitions provide us with the origins of what is understood to be two common characteristics of EDs:

*   They hold the administrative or managerial authority in the organization.

*   They are appointed by a board to direct or manage the affairs of the organization.

What is not included in these definitions is any description of the context within which EDs use their authority to realize the mission of the organization — the fundamental raison d'être of nonprofit organizations.

THE ROLE OF THE EXECUTIVE DIRECTOR

Being an ED of a nonprofit organization is arguably one of the more demanding and complicated jobs that an individual could undertake. While there are tremendous rewards that come with the job — effecting change in the community, improving the lives of people, conserving the environment, or creating theatre, for example — there are also enormous challenges that need to be addressed.

Three broad categories of stakeholders and the interplay between them are the sources of the complexity faced by EDs. The first group is the staff and volunteers working within the organization; the second is the board of directors of the nonprofit organization; and the third is the community within which the organization operates, seeks funding, and other kinds of support. For each one of these groups the primary point of contact is the ED.

Figure 1 below shows the relationship of these stakeholder groups to the ED. The ED is in the centre of the picture, between each stakeholder group. The teardrop shaped areas represent the staff reporting up to the ED and the board who make policy decisions to be implemented by the ED. Surrounding the ED and the organization, is the ring of organizations (funders, other nonprofits, government, businesses, *etc.*) that have an interest in what the organization is doing and connect through the ED to initiate some kind of action. The cones surrounding the staff and board elements represent the web of not yet connected but potential board members and employees who need to be nurtured to fill the future needs of the organization. Again, it is typically the ED who must keep contacts and networks alive and interested in the work of the organization. Executive Directors are "sandwiched between internal and external demands, specifically: the needs of the clients they serve; the board members with whom the future of the organization and its mission resides; and, the government/funding agencies that affect their ability to carry out the work for their organization" (Seel & Angelini, 2004, at 8).

Figure 1: Representation of the Main Stakeholder Groups in Relation to the Executive Director

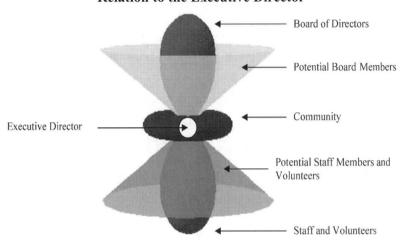

The role of the ED will now be explored using a number of different perspectives. These perspectives are intended to introduce and explore the range of concerns faced by an ED, such as addressing board-staff relations or weighing the benefits of forming a partnership with another organization.

LEADERSHIP AND THE EXECUTIVE DIRECTOR

The questions of what is a leader or what is leadership have many answers. To get a sense of the range of definitions consider Terry (1993) who sees leadership as something that reaches "across boundaries" to discover "what is really going on, then living the answer" (at 9). Compare that with Bailey (1989) who finds that leadership is inherently unethical as it strives to control followers: "Leadership is a form of cultivating ignorance, of stopping doubts, and stifling questions" (at 2). Or consider Kouzes & Posner (2002), who argue that leaders inspire a shared vision, model the behaviour they expect in others, take risks, enable others to act and to demon-strate caring and appreciation (at 13-20).

Schmid (2006) studied leadership styles and leadership change in human and community service organizations. He presents four quadrants created by looking at

- Is the leadership role task oriented or people oriented? and

- Is the leadership role internally oriented or externally oriented?

Figure 2: Schmid's Four Quadrant Model of Leadership and Patterns of Management

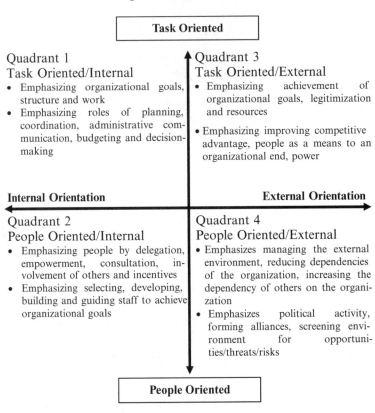

Adapted from Schmid, 2006

The quadrants also point to an evolution in the leadership context from a start-up organization (Quadrant 1) through to a mature organization (Quadrant 4) — though Schmid recognizes that such an evolution is not linear and often organizations move back to earlier stages for a variety of reasons.

The significance of what Schmid proposes is that leadership as not a constant and that over time an organization may need to seek out very different types of leaders. For executives this suggests that:

1. They reflect on the kind of leadership domain they prefer, *e.g.*, task oriented and internally focused or people oriented and externally focused.

2. They clarify the leadership role with the board of directors at the time of hire and regularly through the performance management process.

3. They are prepared to step away from an organization when it is clear that the time has come for a leadership style that is different than the one that the executive is able to provide.

Leadership is often compared or contrasted with management. Drucker (1999) succinctly defines management when he states, "It has to be *operational*" (emphasis in original, at 34). He continues:

> Management exists for the sake of the institution's results. It has to start with the intended results and has to organize the resources of the institution to attain these results. It is the organ to make the institution ... capable of producing results outside of itself [at 39].

What the two terms — leadership and management — tell us is that while management is a focused operational activity internal to an organization, leadership is a more diffuse activity focused on creating some kind of change in the world.

Executive Directors are viewed as leaders in their organizations — refining the vision, motivating people to perform effectively in realizing the vision, and being the public face of the organization. Moreover, the ED is expected to be a competent leader in the eyes of the stakeholders of the organization they lead. In Canada, the subject of the competencies required to be an effective leader were recently studied by the National Learning Initiative.[1] It generated these competencies through a first-ever "practitioner-driven voluntary sector leadership competency identification process" (at 10). Within this action research project, the sample was peer nominated and generated 396 nonprofit sector leaders. From this list, 64 EDs participated in one of several intensive two-day workshops held across the country. Within this group of executive directors, there

---

[1] The National Learning Initiative (NLI) grew out of the Voluntary Sector Initiative to address a national skills and learning framework for the Canadian nonprofit sector. The first focus area for the NLI was leadership development. The NLI undertook Canada's first practioner-driven leadership competency identification process. A national nomination process involved 136 nominators who identified 396 nonprofit sector leaders from which 100 individuals were invited to participate in one of seven regional two-day focus groups. Sixty-four leaders eventually participated.

was representation from a number of domains including: geographic, sub-sector, organization size, and service scope of organization (local through to international). Specific individuals were included to represent people with disabilities, aboriginal peoples, visible minorities, immigrants and francophones living outside of Quebec (at 10).

What this research showed is that leadership competencies of executive directors spanned four broad competency domains each with specific areas of competence. It should be noted that while the focus of the project was on leadership, several of the competencies are clearly managerial suggesting that EDs are often both a leader and a manager.[2] Table 2 summarizes the findings.

Table 2: Leadership Competencies of Executive Directors

Competency Domain	Areas of Competence
Vision and Alignment	• Vision — the leader is able to guide the development of and commitment to an inspired, achievable view of the future. • Ethical/value-oriented decisions — the leader guides the organization, individuals, or community through a structured decision-making process to resolve ethical and values-based issues. • Public action — the leader guides effective and innovative action based on sound public policy. • Public policy — the leader is involved in the development of public policy. • External relations — the leader builds external relations by collaborating with individuals, organizations and communities. • Global issues — the leader is aware of and takes action on global issues at a personal, organizational and community level. • Culture of learning — the leader sustains a culture of learning in their organization such that risks are taken and innovative ideas are nurtured and valued.
Strategies and Resource Management	• Fundraising — the leader optimizes diverse, effective and ethical fundraising approaches that enhance the vision of the

---

2 It should be noted that, while the following information comes from leaders believed to be effective and successful by the people nominating them, there is no claim in the project that individuals demonstrating these competencies have been proven to be effective.

Competency Domain	Areas of Competence
	organization while being responsive to, and respectful of donors' wishes. • Financial stewardship — the leader is a steward of financial resources, ensuring effective use of funds towards fulfilling the mission and accepts inclusive decision-making and accountability as cornerstones of practice. • Marketing and public relations — the leader guides a variety of marketing and public relations processes to enhance the organization's ability to communicate its vision and inspire others. • Information and communication technology — the leader optimizes information and communication technology opportunities and solutions. • Research — the leader optimizes research and its application to the organization. • Planning and evaluation — the leader guides responsive and inclusive planning and evaluation processes to achieve the mission.
Relationships	• Interpersonal relationships — the leader optimizes, sustains and grows interpersonal relationships and effectively negotiates relationship dynamics. • Communication — the leader is an excellent communicator in multiple media with people from diverse personal, social and cultural backgrounds. • Political acumen/savvy — the leader demonstrates political acumen by maintaining effective relationships among individuals, within the sector and beyond into the broader community. • Public persona — the leader represents as a public figure the interests, ideas and views of the organization and its constituents to the public while being mindful of diversities and complexities. • Human resources — the leader optimizes human resources and provides a collaborative and supportive environment in which to work. • Team development — the leader employs appropriate approaches to team development enhancing the potential for

Competency Domain	Areas of Competence
	creativity and productivity in the organization. • Healthy workplace environment — the leader builds and sustains a healthy workplace environment. • Collaboration — the leader encourages and supports collaboration, optimizes relationships between individuals, organizations and communities by developing shared strategies among a diversity of stakeholders.
Complexity	• Creative and innovative culture — the leader sustains a culture that celebrates creative decisions and innovative strategies, where individuals are inspired to find creative solutions to complex problems leading to long-term sustainability. • Adaptation to change — the leader guides adaptation to change by the organization and the people associated with it as well as with other organizations involved in broader change initiatives. • Interdependent perspective — the leader demonstrates interdependent perspective, recognizing the interdependence, self-organizing capacity and emergent elements of a complex system. • Multiple accountabilities — the leader ensures that multiple accountabilities are met and decisions are made with the understanding of the dynamic tensions among multiple stakeholders. • Awareness of context — the leader demonstrates an awareness of the environment and an ability to assess systems and structures. • Cooperation and competition — the leader excels at balancing the tension between cooperation/collaboration and competition/confrontation necessary to achieve the mission and sustain relationships.

Source: Adapted from NLI (2003).

This list represents the total number of competencies identified by the 64 EDs in the research project. No one ED could be expected to have all of the competencies. For each ED and for each organization the competency mix required to generate success would vary. For example, the competencies required by an ED of a small peer support group with no staff and minimal budget would likely be different from the competencies needed in the ED of a multimillion-dollar social service agency with hundreds of staff and several locations.

Case 1

Janet is the ED of a social service agency focusing on aboriginal issues, especially drug and alcohol addiction. The annual budget is $2.1 million and the agency employs 53 full-time and 17 part-time staff. A significant part of Janet's role is ensuring that the elders of different First Nations peoples are respected, meaning that attention has to be paid to traditional lands, the traditions of each of the First Nations represented as employees and as clients, as well as herself. Without proper respect being paid to the multiple stakeholders, the support of elders for Janet's agency could be withheld, meaning that important parts of the services being provided could not be offered. Balancing those concerns with the requirements of provincial and federal government funders is a skill that Janet has had to learn. She has had to become a skilled negotiator, able to move from specific service provision concerns to global issues of substance abuse among aboriginal people, in the midst of contract negotiations. She has also become a skilled collaborator, working with affiliated aboriginal service groups to jointly sponsor projects or submit funding proposals, while at the same time ensuring that her agency remains competitive in terms of service delivery costs, funding drives, and the acquisition of skilled staff. During a recent interview Janet commented that, "No one could have explained to me how complicated this job is or what I have to be able to address in a day. I have to inspire people, fund the money to buy coffee, and oversee our finances while working within native tradition."

Case 2

Henry is the part-time ED of an environmental agency addressing watershed issues along the East Slopes of the Rocky Mountains. The annual budget is $47,000 and Henry is the only employee. Roughly 35 volunteers stretching from the border with the Northwest Territories to the U.S. boarder assist with educational and advocacy initiatives. Most of Henry's time is spent working with volunteers in the field. He prepares information packages and workshop guides, and identifies political, business and other community contacts for the volunteers. Communication has been identified as an agency issue because it is hard to keep up regular contact with a widely distributed group and because the issues vary between regions in the agency's operational area. The focus on email communications is necessary but the agency cannot afford high-speed access so Henry runs most of the agency operations from his home. A space that the agency shared with other small nonprofit groups will be closing, meaning that he will have to turn his home office into the mailing address for the agency. Henry has had one face-to-face board meeting, with monthly phone meetings scheduled as people are available. Since all of his board members are also doing volunteer work in the local community, he knows that his working board is stretched in terms of the time that they can give to the agency. Henry finds that the part-time nature of his work is a barrier to achieving the mission of the agency. He noted that, "The most stressful part of my job is knowing that we could do more if we just had the resources. There is only so much I can do on 20 hours per week."

Besides identifying competencies, the NLI project looked at how the competencies were manifested within the life of the ED. The leadership exhibited by EDs took place at four different levels: personal (as understood through beliefs and values), organizational, community, and global. Figure 3 represents the overlap of the leadership competencies and the different levels at which the competencies could be demonstrated. Further examination of these competencies is worthwhile because, in the summary that follows, we get a sense of not only how the ED has to connect with the stakeholders shown in Figure 1, but, we also begin to understand some of the behaviours associated with being an effective ED.

Figure 3: Leadership Competencies And The Levels At Which They Could Be Demonstrated

Source: From NLI (2003, at 14).

PERSONAL BELIEFS AND VALUES

Values and beliefs are at the root of any action taken by an ED. The NLI project demonstrated that EDs as leaders acted from a personal values base that had the following dimensions:

- social responsibility
- sustainability and self-sufficiency
- building capacity
- individual ethical and principled behaviour
- inclusion and diversity
- courage (NLI, 2003, at 14)

Personal beliefs and values lay behind the actions of EDs as they attempted to shape the culture of their organizations so that it would see itself as having a broadly conceived social responsibility to the community. Other values fostered the organizations' sustainability and led to practical activities such as reducing the organizations' reliance on single funders and more sophisticated analysis of the dynamic systems associated with exchange mechanisms within the nonprofit sector.[3]

Executive directors also needed to have personal values that made them aware of issues of power or discrimination when working with vulnerable or at-risk people in the community. Finally, at the level of values, the ED needed to have a strong sense of ethics and the courage to act properly even when such actions could disadvantage the ED or their organization.

The leadership competencies suggested by EDs in the study are unique in the Canadian literature. Kramer (1987, at 244) observes: "Large or small, most voluntary agencies are unusually dependent on the quality of their executive leadership, and therefore, more subject to idiosyncratic rather than structural factors." In effect, the ability, skill, or competency of the ED is of more significance in the nonprofit sector than elsewhere. Considering what an ED ought to be competent in is important both for aspiring EDs and the governors of nonprofit organizations who must hire and evaluate them. A unique combination of ED competencies will exist for each nonprofit organization. The assumption is that an ED with the right set of competencies should be effective. Are we correct in making that assumption?

EXECUTIVE DIRECTOR EFFECTIVENESS

Figure 1 portrays three major areas where ED effectiveness could be examined:

1. effectiveness with the board of directors;

2. effectiveness with staff and volunteers; and

3. effectiveness with the community.

Before looking at these areas in greater detail, it should be stated that the question of ED effectiveness is part of the greater issue of nonprofit organizational effectiveness. Herman & Renz (1998, 1999) advance the position that nonprofit effectiveness is not only multidimensional;

---

[3] The nonprofit sector, sometimes called the voluntary sector, third sector or independent sector has notably different ways of securing the resources it needs compared to either the private sector or the public (government sector). A fundamental difference is that many in the non-profit sector receive donations and, if registered with the Canada Revenue Agency, can issue a tax receipt to donors. Restrictions differentiating the nonprofit sector include the fact that a registered charity must be "non-distributing" meaning that, if there is money left over at the end of the year, it goes to charitable activities **not** to shareholders as might be the case in the private sector.

it is also idiosyncratic to the organization being examined. In other words, not only is the notion of effectiveness made up of many dimensions, each organization will have its own bases of effectiveness. Interorganizational comparisons of effectiveness may not be possible except in a relative sense.

How one looks at a nonprofit organization determines what one would observe when assessing effectiveness. The goal model of nonprofit organizations (Seashore, 1983) assumes that a nonprofit organization has a stated purpose and that effectiveness can be measured based on the attainment of goals. A problem with this is that, with several stakeholders, many nonprofit organizations might have several goals, some of which could be mutually contradictory (Green *et al.*, 2001). The decision-process model (Seashore, 1983) examines the relationship between ends that the nonprofit organization would like to achieve and the means by which the organization reaches those ends. This model focuses on internal processes linking means and ends. Insofar as operational processes are more effective, it is assumed that the nonprofit organization will achieve its desired ends (Green *et al.*, 2001).

In both of these models, the ED is a central figure. For many, an effective ED would also mean an effective nonprofit organization — at least within the scope covered by the models above. More specific research demonstrates particular aspects of ED effectiveness that refine our understanding.

THE BOARD AND ED EFFECTIVENESS

The relationship between EDs and their boards is a foundational one for any nonprofit organization. The ED is usually the only employee hired, evaluated, and if necessary terminated, by the board. While in practice the ED is commonly a major contributor to policy it is the board that represents the "policy" or "governance" activities of the organization and the ED is the bridge between governance and operations (the juncture of the two tear-drops in Figure 1). Even though connected through the ED, the board and staff domains have been shown to be "independent and distinct factors" to which the ED must attend. (Herman & Heimovics, 2005, at 157). Given this, how might we assess ED effectiveness with the board?

Herman and Heimovics (2005, 1990a, 1990b) after sustained work in the area of executive leadership in the nonprofit sector, conclude that effective EDs "develop their boards' abilities to carry out their duties and responsibilities" (2005, at 157). In comparing effective executives with those who were not effective (1990) it was found that effective executives actively provided more support and leadership to their board. This characteristic was labelled as "board-centred" and meant that the executive director took on the responsibility for supporting and facilitating board work along six dimensions (Herman & Heimovics, 2005, at 158):

1. facilitating interaction with board relationships;

2. showing consideration and respect toward board members;

3. envisioning change and innovation for the organization with the board;

4. providing useful and helpful information to the board;

5. initiating and maintaining structure for the board; and

6. promoting board accomplishments and productivity.[4]

Strategic planning is one area where the connection between the ED and the board is especially important. Herman and Heimovics (2005) found that a dominating ED is much less likely to be a facilitator with the board and less likely to show consideration and respect for the autonomy of the board.

While formal planning efforts of the organization should be a shared responsibility, an imbalance of responsibility, ownership, or power can have dramatic results. For example, it would not be surprising to learn that EDs are most satisfied when the planning efforts actually produce change. However, in their review of 154 United Way affiliates, Webster & Wylie (1988) found that only half of the formal plans they produced led to any change whatsoever. Challenges such as unclear roles and responsibilities, or poor communication, between the board and the ED appeared to contribute to this lack of success.

The complexities of the Board-ED relationship were brought into greater resolution by Murray, Bradshaw & Wolpin (1992), who inquired into the relationship between power distribution and performance.

---

[4]   It is interesting to note that from the point of view of the ED, what makes a "good board" ranges widely. Chait, *et al.* (2005, at 11) found that for some EDs a good board is a compliant board, that is, the board takes direction from the ED. On the other hand, Fletcher (1992) found other EDs felt that a good board was a board that takes its governance responsibilities seriously, chooses members carefully, participates in strategic planning, has high attendance at board meetings and has an experienced executive focused on good board behaviour.

They surveyed EDs of 417 health and social welfare nonprofit organizations. Most identified their organization as having either an ED-dominated board or a power-sharing board (defined as organizations in which the ED and the Board shared in the making of major decisions). Power-sharing boards were strongly associated with the perception that the board was effective. However, a board that was dominated by the ED was shown to result in the ED having the perception that the organization was effective. While this research has some issues with a sampling bias, it does bring to light a most interesting tension experienced by EDs — does an ED work to ensure that the organization is seen to be effective (which could mean dominating the board agenda or at least ensuring that the board is compliant) or does the ED share power with the board which may enhance board effectiveness but not necessarily organizational effectiveness. Of course, the ideal solution should be that, what the ED does improves both the organization and board effectiveness.

Effectiveness as something that both the board and the ED contribute to in a nonprofit organization is challenging to understand. To a large measure it is the interplay between the ED and the board that determines the effectiveness of the organization. Green *et al.* (2001), note that the primary measures of effectiveness as "focus on the activities specified in the organization's mission, goals, and objectives are often difficult to assess fully" (at 460). Green *et al.* (2001), repeated an earlier study (Green & Griesinger, 1996) to explore how boards and EDs view each other and how they perform individually and together — that is to say, how effective they are as a team. The research used two models for understanding how nonprofit organizations function:

1. Goal Attainment Model. This view holds that nonprofit organizations have a purpose, stated in the mission for example, and that effectiveness can be determined by measuring how well the goals set to achieve the mission have been attained. A challenge with this model is that a complex organization may have multiple goals, some of which could be in conflict with one another. Also as Gruber (1986) observed, there may be problems with this model because it may be difficult to distinguish between values and goals in a nonprofit organization.

2. Decision-process Model. This model examines the relationship between the means — the processes, resources, *etc.*, — needed to undertake an activity, and the ends, the outcome(s) arising as a

result of the activity. Building on Drucker (1974, 1990) this approach uses processes as proxy measures of success because, it presumes, if the processes are performed well the organization is more likely to achieve the ends it wants.

Green *et al.* (2001), were able to show that:

- Boards felt that they did more than the ED gave them credit for … the reverse was also true.

- EDs believed they should have more responsibility and authority than boards acknowledged.

- EDs agreed with boards that boards needed to attend more to board performance issues and that EDs should do more to evaluate board performance.

- EDs felt that they should have more input into recruiting new board members than the board did.

- EDs wanted the board more involved in evaluating the ED.

- Boards felt they and the ED should do more to represent the organization to the community. EDs felt that they were performing this function at an appropriate level.

Throughout their research, Green *et al.* (2001), found a constant theme within ED comments: EDs wanted "more responsibility than the board members believed appropriate", and EDs believed that, "they should have more responsibility or authority than board members acknowledged" (at 465). The research concluded that:

> Although the research has uncovered several areas of tension between board members and [EDs] in the organizations studied, they appear to be related to the overlap and lack of clarity about respective roles as well as differences in the evaluation of actual role performance. There was not a clear pattern of either the presence or absence of tension necessarily translating into effectiveness with the organization [at 473].

THE ED-STAFF RELATIONSHIP

The National Survey of Nonprofit and Voluntary Organizations (Statistics Canada, 2004) found that only 1 per cent of the 161,000 nonprofit and voluntary organizations in Canada have budgets over $10 million. More that two-thirds have budgets under $100,000. Depending on the size of the nonprofit organization, the extent to which the ED is involved in any of the elements of the overall planning framework (see Figure 4) will vary. In a very large nonprofit, the ED will have staff or even departments responsible for such things as financial planning or human resources. In a very small nonprofit, those tasks may be the responsibility of the ED him- or herself.

The ED fills the top management role in the organization and is typically the highest paid employee. As such, the ED delegates responsibilities, oversees the human resources and volunteer resources of the organization, and coordinates the overall performance of activities by employees and staff towards achieving the mission.

In an effort to give EDs ready access to human resources management information and processes, the Human Resources Council for the Nonprofit Sector (HR Council) was formed with support from the Government of Canada. The HR Council initiative identified major human resources issues within the nonprofit sector then built an information base to improve human resource capacity of nonprofit organizations — the HR Toolkit.[5] Much of what has been collected on their Website is focused on the responsibility that the ED has for such things as hiring, termination and performance management. The list below is what HRVS identifies as the primary human resources management activities that one can associate with the ED role:

- How many staff will be required to achieve the strategic goals of the organization?

- What jobs will need to be filled?

- What skill sets will people need?

- How does the current economy affect our work and our ability to attract new employees?

- How do current technological or cultural shifts impact the way we work and the skilled labour we require?

- What changes are occurring in the Canadian labour market?

- How is our community changing or expected to change in the near future?

- Why diversity at work matters (HR council, 2014).

---

[5]   <http://www.hrcouncil.ca>.

Boards of directors commonly state through policy that these areas are the responsibility of the ED. These responsibilities are situated within the overall strategic plan of the organization and tied to other focal areas of planning such as financial or operational plans. One way of viewing these responsibilities, is shown in Figure 4, below.

Figure 4: Situating Human Resources Management Within a Planning Framework

Arising out of the human resources management plan are a number of activities that can occupy a significant portion of the ED's time. The figure below categorizes these activities and suggests that to be effective in managing staff and volunteers, the ED must have considerable skill and aptitude in working with people.

Figure 5: Human Resources Practice and Activity Areas Requiring Ed Involvement

Human resources practice	Human resources activity
Staffing *Meeting staff requirements*	Job Analysis Job Design Job Descriptions Recruitment Selection Orientation
Training and Development *Developing effective staff*	Training Employee Development
Compensation and Benefits *Establishing fair compensation*	Job Evaluation Compensation Plan Benefits Retirement Plans
People Management *Building effective employer/employee relationships*	Work Plans Supervision Performance Management Recognition Conflict Resolution Discipline Termination Day-to-Day HR Administration
Workplace Management *Creating a good place to work*	Work-life Balance Health and Safety Diversity

Source: HRVS, 2005.

Executive Director perceptions of their role in the human resources function are at best mixed. In-depth work with a small group of EDs (Seel & Angelini, 2004) suggests that:

- EDs feel that they have little control over circumstances affecting personnel due to funding limitations or lack of time, for example.

- Isolation is a concern for EDs. Being the only person in that position, the ED becomes counsellor or confidant to all but lacks that kind of support him- or herself. Being able to manage the concerns and issues of each staff person and board member requires tremendous personal strength.

• Many EDs do not fully understand how to delegate so as to accomplish the mission through other staff or volunteer positions within the organization. This can mean that the ED feels responsible for "doing it all themselves" and suffers the stresses of trying to live up to that expectation.

THE ED AND FINANCIAL OVERSIGHT

After oversight of the staff of the organization, financial oversight is the next most important area of ED responsibility. Many might in fact argue that in terms of the time required and the significance of financial resources for the sustainability of the organization, financial oversight is the most important area of ED responsibility. As discussed in more detail in Chapter 10, typical areas of concern are cash and accrual accounting, financial statements (balance sheet, income statements, statement of cash flows), financial statement analysis, financial modelling and endowment management.

In principle, the ED has responsibility for overall financial management and accounting for the nonprofit. The financial responsibilities that need to be undertaken by the ED are:

• ensuring that managers have support for decision-making in financial areas appropriate to their level role, and responsibility;

• ensuring the availability of timely, relevant and reliable information — financial and non-financial — to staff and board;

• contributing to the identification and management of risks to the organization, its employees, volunteers and clients;

• helping the organization make efficient, effective and economical use of resources;

• enabling managers to account for their use of resources;

• establishing a supportive control environment;

• ensuring the organization complies with authorities and laws and regulations; and

• safeguarding the assets of the organization through appropriate controls, processes, and procedures.

It cannot be expected that every ED will have a strong financial background. What can be expected is that the ED knows how to oversee and guide the processes necessary to ensure that an appropriate degree of financial oversight is in place. Working with the board and other staff or volunteers, the ED should be able to state what their skill level is with financial accounting, be supported in identifying and receiving any necessary training and/or recruiting the needed skills into the organization. Executive Directors with no financial experience can still be effective if they recognize what they do not know, find theneeded skill sets and bring them to the table and then deploy those skills in the ways needed to ensure that the various tasks are accomplished.

Financial management is differentiated from the accounting function. For EDs, it is likely that the financial management practices and activities will be of greater importance on a day-to-day basis. While the accounting and audit sides of the organization's finances are very important, the ED by law or by choice will have to involve bookkeepers and independent auditors. Figure 6 outlines common financial management practices and associated activities that are likely to be encountered by an ED.

Figure 6: Financial Management Practices and Activities Involving the Executive Director

Financial Management Practice	Financial Management Activity
Management of Resources *The guidelines for* *managing finances*	Policy and procedures Process management Quality management Strategic planning Efficiency and effectiveness measures Staffing, roles and responsibilities
Risk Management and Control *Establishing risk factors and* *controlling for them*	Risk assessment Audit Insurance Organization structure and support Control mechanisms Investments
Information *Ensuring transparency and* *accountability to stakeholders*	Budgeting Reporting Support for decision-making Compliance Information systems
Accounting *Building effective* *employer/employee relationships*	Accounting system Chart of accounts Reporting

As with financial accounting, not every ED will have financial management experience. While financial accounting requires very specific skills (e.g., a chartered accountant is required to conduct the financial audit of the organization), financial management is somewhat broader in scope. The emphasis within financial management is on the oversight of processes and systems within an organization rather than the actual line-by-line work of balancing the books. As shown in Figure 6, the areas of practice and associated activities do require particular managerial skills. If EDs do not possess them they must recognize the need to obtain assistance from staff, volunteers, or board members.

THE ED AND THE COMMUNITY

The community surrounds the nonprofit organization, as shown in Figure 1, and the ED is the principle point of contact with it. How the ED handles this role is determined by a number of factors. Some EDs act like travelling salespeople, taking what their organization has to offer and bringing it to the wider community. These EDs seek out opportunities to talk about the work of their organization and may bring important information back into it for consideration or action. Other EDs take a much more internal role, rarely making forays beyond their organization, working on the inside, focusing on services and the systems needed to operate them. While these two examples are generalizations, they do reflect the fact that there is no one way EDs behave in their role as the point of community contact.

The work that an ED undertakes to complete the link between the organization and the community has political characteristics. In their research into the determinants of effectiveness in the ED role, Heimovics, Herman & Jurkiewicz (1993, 1995) found that effective EDs are more likely to employ a "political" view of their work as part of a more complex multiframe perspective (Bolman & Deal, 1991) than a group of executives not identified as effective. What this means is that effective EDs recognize the need to address "conflict or tension over the allocation of scarce resources or the resolution of differences" (Heimovics et al., (1993, at 421)). Such EDs respond to these issues by coalition building, mobilizing various constituencies, creating mutual commitments to future oriented goals as well as negotiating and bargaining for the resources needed to accomplish their organization's mission (at 426).

In working with staff, board, and the community, then, EDs are most effective when they are actively bargaining, negotiating, networking, building alliances, addressing conflicts between stakeholders, and addressing resource allocation disputes. An ED that does not understand this political frame is "risking their organization's viability *and* its leadership effectiveness" (emphasis in original, at 425).

CHALLENGES

Very real challenges face EDs. Some of those have been alluded to already in this chapter. Recent research with EDs (Seel & Angelini (2004, 2005)) identifies challenges as seen from the perspective of the EDs themselves. Using a peer learning circle model (Suda (2001); O'Donnell & King (1999); Wade & Hammick (1999)), Seel and Angelini worked with a diverse group of nine EDs from large and small nonprofit organizations (budgets ranged from $285,000 to $1.4 million) operating in the areas of seniors, persons with disabilities, aboriginal issues, multicultural issues, youth, and community development. Over an 18-month period, the study probed deeply into the dimensions of job satisfaction and job quality. Emerging from this research were a number of challenges commonly faced by EDs:

- *Isolation.* Executive Directors experience isolation in two ways. First, an ED is the only person with that title and associated responsibilities in the organization and does not feel part of the staff or board team. Executive Directors have a partial existence in both worlds but reside in neither. Second, they feel isolated from other EDs in other organizations because the opportunity to network or even just communicate with others in the same role is practically nonexistent.

- *Powerlessness to effect change.* Executive Directors reported feeling powerless to effect meaningful organizational change because the power to do so was seen as resting primarily with the board. Whether or not this is true is immaterial since it caused EDs to behave as if they had no power to change their organization and their role in ways that would improve job satisfaction and job quality.

- *Lack of a Clear Role.* Executive Directors commonly expressed lack of clarity about the roles and responsibilities of the board and the ED. Very little relationship was reported between the EDs' written job descriptions and what they actually carried out. In large measure this is due to the board either not being familiar with the responsibilities the ED has or being unclear about what they want the ED to focus on (*e.g.*, fund development, building a stronger organization, advocacy, or outreach).[6]

- *Tunnel vision.* The demands of the job for an ED are great and very little time remains for reflection on how they are performing their jobs or on how the organization as a whole is functioning. There are many paths to achieve a goal or the mission, however, EDs can be carried along by the current of daily affairs and not have the opportunity to consider other approaches.

- *Everybody's counsellor/confidant.* Being an ED means that all interpersonal issues eventually find their way to your desk. This is especially true for smaller organizations. The ED will be sought out for support, as a counsellor when an employee needs guidance, as a confidant when personal issues emerge and so on. Board members seek out the ED for the same reasons and sometimes as a sounding board for understanding the inner workings of the board. While an ED has need for someone to act as their counsellor or confidant, it emerges as a problem should such a person be in the same organization. While it may be appropriate for a staff member to discuss a conflict with another staff member, it would not be appropriate for an ED to go to staff and divulge problems he or she was having with an employee. The lack of an outlet for personal stresses and concerns is itself a source of stress.

- *Compensation.* While pay was not a dominant determinant of whether an ED stayed or left, it had the potential for being the "final straw". Other components of job quality (staff relationships, hours and scheduling, organizational structure, for example) ranked as more important aspects for EDs considering whether to stay with an organization or leave. An unsatisfying job in a low quality workplace could not pay sufficiently to retain an ED. That said, low compensation is a very real barrier to individuals faced with yearly inflation, mortgages and cost-of-living expenses. Reasonable pay is important to a high-quality and satisfying job.

- *Unreasonable expectations.* Internal and external stakeholders from employees and the board to funders and the government, make claims on the ED's time. When resources do not allow for

---

[6] For more information on job descriptions specific to these board expectations, see the HRVS Website at: <http://www.hrcouncil.ca>.

sharing these responsibilities with other staff, the ED bears the load and all of the responsibility. If there are inadequate systems or resources through which some of the work associated with these expectations could be delegated, the quality of the ED job drops. What we call "burn out" happens when well-intentioned people working hard to meet all the demands made of them have nothing left to give to the organization or themselves.

Solutions to each of the challenges identified above will be unique to each nonprofit organization. What is apparent is that open communication between the ED and all the staff, board, and community members is critical to resolving misunderstandings, clarifying perceptions, and achieving the best leadership possible from the ED.

CONCLUSION

This chapter has examined the executive-level management as represented by the ED in nonprofit organizations. The role is a challenging one with broad accountabilities to multiple stakeholders combined with specific responsibilities unique to each organizational setting. There are nuances to the ED role not found in executive management in either the private or public sectors, such as the unique relationship that needs to be cultivated with volunteers both at the program level and most significantly at the governance level. While no one body of knowledge is specifically tied to becoming an ED, we can see from the literature covered in the chapter that there are skills and competencies, even predispositions, that suggest what is required for an ED to be effective.

Executive Directors are unique in that they are hired by, and accountable to, the board of directors. It is the board that sets the parameters of the role and establishes responsibilities for the ED. If the boards are not up to the task of creating a reasonable position with their organizations, they should not be surprised if those hired as EDs do not perform as expected, express dissatisfaction with the job or eventually leave the organization. A board that takes the time to understand what it wants of its ED will seek to create a culture or climate within the organization that supports the work that the ED must undertake to move the organization towards achieving its mission. Such a board will be more likely positioned to enjoy a good working relationship with the ED and be able to retain that individual for a longer period of time. Success for an ED in a nonprofit organization is closely tied to board effectiveness.

REFERENCES

F. Bailey, *Humbuggery and Manipulation: The Art of Leadership* (Ithaca, NY: Cornell University Press, 1989).

P. Boland, *Boland Survey of Not for Profit Salaries and Human Resource Practices – Position Descriptions* (Calgary, AB: Peter T. Boland & Associates Inc., 2013). Online at: <https://secures5.brinkster.com/boland survey/positionlookup.asp#101>.

L. Bolman & T. Deal, *Reframing Organizations* (San Francisco: Jossey-Bass, 1991).

R. Chait, W. Ryan & B. Taylor, *Governance as Leadership* (Hoboken, NJ: John Wiley & Sons, 2005).

P. Drucker, *Management: Tasks, Responsibilities, Practices* (New York: HarperCollins, 1974).

P. Drucker, *Managing the Nonprofit Organization: Principles and Practices* (New York: HarperCollins, 1990).

P. Drucker, *Management Challenges for the 21st Century* (New York: HarperCollins, 1999).

K. Fletcher "Effective Boards: How Executive Directors Define and Develop Them" (1992) 2:3 Nonprofit Management and Leadership 283-293.

D. Forbes "Measuring the Unmeasurable: Empirical Studies of Nonprofit Effectiveness from 1977 to 1997" (1998) 27:2 Nonprofit and Voluntary Sector Quarterly 183-202.

J.C. Green *et al.*, "Local Unit Performance in a National Nonprofit Organization" (2001) 11:4 Nonprofit Management & Leadership 459-476.

J.C. Green & D.W. Griesinger, "Board Performance and Organizational Effectiveness in Nonprofit Social Service Organizations" (1996) 6:4 Nonprofit Management and Leadership 381-402.

M. Gruber, "A Three-factor Model of Administrative Effectiveness" (1986) 10:3 Administration in Social Work 1-24.

M.H. Hall *et al.*, *Cornerstones of Community: Highlights of the National Survey of Nonprofit and Voluntary Organizations*, Catalogue No. 61-533-XPE (Ottawa: Statistics Canada, 2004).

R.D. Heimovics, R.D. Herman & C. Jurkiewicz, "The Political Dimension of Effective Nonprofit Executive Leadership" (1995) 5:3 Nonprofit Management & Leadership 233-248.

R.D. Heimovics, R.D. Herman & C. Jurkiewicz, "Executive Leadership and Resource Dependence in Nonprofit Organizations: A Frame Analysis" (1993) 53:5 Public Administration Review 419-427.

R.D. Herman & R.D. Heimovics, "Executive Leadership" in *The Jossey-Bass Handbook of Nonprofit Leadership and Management*, 2d ed. (San Francisco: John Wiley & Sons, 2005) 153-170.

R.D. Herman & R.D. Heimovics, "The Effective Nonprofit Executive: Leader of the Board" (1990) 1:2 Nonprofit Management and Leadership 167-180.

R.D. Herman & R.D. Heimovics, "An Investigation of Leadership Skill Differences in Chief Executives of Nonprofit Organizations" (1990) 20:2 American Review of Public Administration 107-125.

Herman, R.D. & D.O. Renz (1999), "Theses on Nonprofit Organizational Effectiveness" (1999) 28:2 Nonprofit and Voluntary Sector Quarterly 127-126.

R.D. Herman & D.O. Renz, "Nonprofit Organizational Effectiveness: Contrasts Between Especially Effective and Less Effective Organizations" (1998) 9:1 Nonprofit Management and Leadership 23-38.

Human Resources Council for the Nonprofit Sector (2014), online at: <http://hrcouncil.ca/hr-toolkit/planning-strategic.cfm>.

J. Kouzes & B. Posner, *The Leadership Challenge* (San Francisco: Jossey-Bass, 2002).

R. Kramer, "Voluntary Agencies and the Personal Social Services" in W.W. Powell, ed., *The Nonprofit Sector: A Research Handbook* (New Haven, CT: Yale University Press, 1987) 240-257.

V. Murray, P. Bradshaw & J. Wolpin, "Power in and around Nonprofit Boards: A Neglected Dimension of Governance" (1992) 3:2 Nonprofit Management and Leadership 165-182.

National Learning Initiative (September, 2003). *Voluntary Sector Leadership Competencies: Examples, Current Challenges, Complexities and Learning Outcomes.* A collaborative project of the Association of Canadian Community Colleges and the Coalition of National Voluntary Organizations.

A. O'Donnell & A. King, *Cognitive Perspectives on Peer Learning* (Mahwah, NJ: Erlbaum, 1999).

H. Schmid, "Leadership Styles and Leadership Change in Human and Community Service Organizations" (2006) 17:2 Nonprofit Management and Leadership 179-194.

S. Seashore, "A Framework for an Integrated Model of Organizational Effectiveness" in K.S. Cameron & D.A. Whetten, eds., *Organizational Effectiveness: A Comparison of Multiple Models* (New York: Academic Press, 1983).

K. Seel & A. Angelini, "Strengthening the Capacity of Executive Directors: A Review of the Effectiveness of the Peer Learning Circle Process One Year Later" (Paper presented at the ARNOVA Conference, Washington, November 19, 2005).

K. Seel & A. Angelini, "Strengthening the Capacity of Executive Directors" (Paper presented at the annual conference of the Association for Research on Nonprofit Organizations and Voluntary Action, Los Angeles, November 21, 2004).

L. Suda, "Learning Circles: Democratic Pools of Knowledge" (2001) 12:3 ARIS Resources Bulletin 1-4.

R. Terry, *Authentic Leadership — Courage in Action* (San Francisco: Jossey-Bass, 1993).

S. Wade & M. Hammick, "Action Learning Circles" (1999) 4:2 Teaching in Higher Education 163-178.

S. Webster & M. Wylie, "Strategic Planning in Competitive Environments" (1988) 12:3 Administration in Social Work 25-43.

Chapter 5

THE LEGAL CONTEXT OF NONPROFIT MANAGEMENT

Terrance S. Carter, B.A., LL.B., TEP, and Karen J. Cooper, LL.B., LL.L., TEP

INTRODUCTION — DEFINITIONS AND LEGAL ENVIRONMENT

Nonprofit organizations come in many shapes and sizes and are referred to in this chapter by different names depending upon the context of the discussion, particularly with respect to the legal environment surrounding the discussion. It is important to recognize that while all charities are nonprofit organizations, not all nonprofit organizations are charities. As such, care should be taken when referring to such organizations, as both have different legal definitions, privileges and responsibilities. Additionally, despite the significant growth in number and size of charitable and nonprofit organizations in Canada,[1] changes to the legal framework from both the federal and provincial governments are not fully modernized as one would expect, and the charitable sector still relies heavily on concepts from the 17th and 19th centuries (Bourgeois (2012, at 2)). This is particularly so for members of the public, who often use the terms of nonprofit organizations and charities interchangeably.

---

[1] For example, Statistics Canada released the results of its survey of charitable and nonprofit organizations in 2004, which indicated that there were approximately 161,000 such organizations in Canada in 2003. These organizations had revenues totalling $112 billion ($10 billion of which came from individual donations), and they drew upon 2.1 billion volunteer hours and 139 million memberships. See M.H. Hall, *et al.*, (2004), at 7, 9 and 10. See also latest survey, M.H. Hall, *et al.*, (2009) released by Imagine Canada on June 8, 2009.

Defining Charitable and Non-profit Organizations

Both charitable and non-profit[2] organizations operate on a nonprofit basis in that both must devote all of their resources to their activities and neither may distribute any of their income to their members, officers, directors, or trustees. Both are exempt from tax on their income, with some exceptions for non-profit organizations, and both will often have similar governance structures. Charitable and non-profit organizations are, however, two distinct types of legal entities with different legal obligations and rights. An organization which has charitable purposes is much more limited in the types of activities it can engage in, but, in return, receives substantial advantages in carrying out its purposes by being able to issue charitable receipts for income tax purposes in response to donations that are received.

At law, charity has a specific meaning that often eludes the popular conception. For an organization to be considered charitable at law, its activities must be undertaken to achieve a charitable purpose. At present, only four categories of charity are recognized in Canadian law. In the seminal decision *Special Commissioners of Income Tax v. Pemsel*,[3] Lord MacNaughten identified four "heads" or categories of charity:

- relief of poverty;

- advancement of education;

- advancement of religion; and

- other purposes beneficial to the community not falling under any of the preceding heads.

This definition is generally mirrored in Ontario's *Charities Accounting Act*,[4] and although the *Income Tax Act* does not make specific reference to these categories, both the Charities Directorate of Canada Revenue Agency (CRA)[5] and the courts rely on the same categories in regulating the sector. The Supreme Court of Canada, in *Vancouver*

---

[2]   The defined term in paragraph 149(1)(*l*) of the *Income Tax Act*, R.S.C. 1985, c. 1 (5th Supp.) (ITA) is "non-profit," not "nonprofit" or "not-for-profit." Where "non-profit" is used in this section rather than "nonprofit" it is used to identify the entity that is separate and distinct from a charity for tax purposes.

[3]   [1891] A.C. 531 (H.L.) (*Pemsel*).

[4]   R.S.O. 1990, c. C.10 (CAA).

[5]   See the Canada Revenue Agency Guidance CG-019 on "How to Draft Purposes for Charitable Registration" available online at: <http://www.cra-arc.gc.ca/chrts-gvng/chrts/plcy/cgd/drftprpss-eng.html>.

Society of Immigrant and Visible Minority Women v. Canada (Minister of National Revenue — M.N.R.),[6] clarified the Canadian approach to recognizing charities, noting that while the ITA focuses on the character of the activity undertaken by the organization, linking them to the categories established in *Pemsel,* the focus should be on the purpose in furtherance of which an activity is carried out in order to determine whether charitable status should be granted. An organization with objectives and activities that fall into one of these four categories will qualify as a registered charity for the purposes of the ITA. As we discuss in further detail below, a registered charity may take one of three legal forms depending upon the types of activities undertaken and the relationship between the organization and its main source of funds: a charitable organization, a public foundation, or a private foundation.

Under the ITA, a "non-profit" organization is defined as a

> ... club, society or association that ... was not a charity ... and that was organized and operated exclusively for social welfare, civic improvement, pleasure or recreation or for any other purpose except profit, no part of the income of which was payable to, or was otherwise available for the personal benefit of, any proprietor, member or shareholder ... .[7]

The ITA clearly establishes that, for its purposes, non-profit organizations and charities are two mutually exclusive categories of organizations. As such, any organization whose objectives and activities fall exclusively within the four categories of charity discussed above is not a non-profit organization and should seek registration as a charity under the ITA in order to avoid being taxed on its income. Although a non-profit organization, like a charity, has tax-exempt status and does not pay tax on income or capital gains (except income from property of an organization whose main purpose is to provide dining, recreation, or sporting facilities),[8] the non-profit organization is not able to issue charitable receipts to donors for income tax purposes.

For example, in a 2007 decision of the Supreme Court of Canada, the Court considered whether an Ontario amateur youth soccer association qualified as a registered charity within the meaning of the ITA. The letters patent provided, in part, that the organization had the following objects:

---

[6]   [1999] S.C.J. No. 5, [1999] 1 S.C.R. 10 (*Vancouver Society*).
[7]   ITA, s. 149(1)(*l*).
[8]   ITA, s. 149(5)(*e*)(ii).

(a)   to fund and develop activities and programs to promote, organize, and carry on the sport of amateur youth soccer;

(b)   to fund, promote, and develop local amateur youth soccer programs and coaching appropriate to different age groups and different levels of ability to increase participation in the sport of soccer.

In *A.Y.S.A. Amateur Youth Soccer Association v. Canada (Revenue Agency)*,[9] the Court found that the promotion of amateur sports, in and of itself, was not a charitable purpose and that sports organizations may only become registered as a charity if sport is ancillary to another recognized charitable purpose, such as education or relief of the disabled. As a result, most sports organizations do not qualify as registered charities and will be considered non-profit organizations.[10] Other examples of non-profit organizations include recreation or hobby groups, social clubs or fraternal lodges, certain music or arts festival organizations, professional or political organizations, and many others.

LEGAL ENVIRONMENT

Added to the confusion of language, which is often misunderstood and misused, is a legal environment, which is also complex, confused and underdeveloped. According to Donald Bourgeois (2002, at 5):

> The confusion in the law and the failure to amend the statutory provisions to address and to take into account changes in society has made it more difficult for directors, officers and members to understand their legal obligations and roles. Individuals who participate in charitable and not-for-profit organizations are, for the most part, sincere in their attempts to make improvements to society, communities and institutions. They are not as often prepared for the potential legal, financial and practical consequences of their involvement. They may be "at sea" and unsure of what steps to take to address problems or issues.

Contributing to this confusion is a patchwork of federal and provincial legislation that has not been fully modernized. Instead, problems have been addressed through policies and practices that have developed over time. At the federal level, significant changes have been made

---

[9]   [2007] S.C.J. No 42, 2007 SCC 42 (S.C.C.).

[10]   Note that the ITA (s. 149(1)(g)) provides a specific tax exemption for registered Canadian amateur athletic associations (RCAAAs). The definition of a "RCAAA" found in s. 248(1) of the ITA requires that the association promote amateur athletics on a national level and that the association qualify as a nonprofit corporation in accordance with paragraph 149(1)(*l*) of the ITA.

and proposed with respect to the regulation of charities and its supporting corporate law. Following years of policy development, public
consultation, and legislative drafting, a new *Canada Not-for-Profit
Corporations Act* was enacted by Parliament in 2009,[11] which will
ultimately replace Parts II and III (which govern federal non-share
capital corporations) of the *Canada Corporations Act* (CCA),[12] which
was first enacted in 1917 and substantively unchanged since that time.
In Ontario, similar changes have been made but are yet to come into
force (see further discussion below). Every federal Budget since 2004
has seen amendments to the ITA related to the compliance obligations
of charities and/or requirements for charitable gifts. The new and
proposed changes aim to provide a more flexible process for incorporating and governing non-share capital corporations and increased
compliance for charities, but have also introduced a substantial level of
complexity that makes it very difficult for those involved with the
nonprofit sector to fully understand their legal obligations.

Applicable Federal and Provincial Legislation

There is a plethora of legislation that is applicable to both charitable
and non-profit organizations, whether it is at the federal or provincial
level, and the directors and members of these organizations must be
aware of how the legislation will impact on their operations.[13] Although space does not permit a full discussion of the applicable
legislation, the following provides a brief summary of some of the
more important pieces of it.

Income Tax Act

The ITA is relevant to charitable and non-profit organizations because it
provides valuable tax benefits to this sector. In addition to determining
whether an organization is a charitable or non-profit organization, the
ITA places certain obligations upon directors of organizations, some of
which continue for a period after the individual ceases to be a director.
Directors are not only liable for ensuring employee source deductions
are remitted to the government, they must also ensure the charity complies with numerous reporting requirements. Directors may also face

---

[11]   *Canada Not-for-profit Corporations Act*, S.C. 2009, c. 23. The new *Canada Not-for-Profit
Corporations Act* received Royal Assent on June 23, 2009, and came into force on October 17,
2011.

[12]   R.S.C. 1970, c. C-32.

[13]   For a useful resource in this respect, see Carter, Hoffstein & Parachin (2013).

fines and imprisonment where they are involved in making false or deceptive statements in any return required under the ITA or willfully evading compliance with the ITA. To avoid liability, a director needs to show that positive steps were taken, including a degree of care, diligence and skill, to ensure that the corporation complied with the ITA's requirements. The ITA has corresponding regulations[14] that must also be complied with.

Canada Not-for-Profit Corporations Act

Prior to the coming into force of the *Canada Not-for-Profit Corporations Act* (CNCA)[15] on October 17, 2011, all federal non-share capital corporations had been incorporated under the *Canada Corporations Act*, which used an out-dated letters patent system of incorporation for charities and not-for-profit corporations.[16] The CNCA has replaced the letters patent system with a system based on Articles of Incorporation similar to the structure of the for-profit Canadian Business Corporations Act model and is viewed as being more modern than the pre-existing legislation.[17] The CNCA outlines how non–share capital corporations are to be governed and the rights and obligations of directors and members. It also has regulations that must be complied with.[18] Corporations that are currently incorporated under the CCA must be continued under the new CNCA by October 17, 2014 or they will face dissolution.

Personal Information Protection and Electronics Documents Act

The *Personal Information Protection and Electronics Documents Act* (PIPEDA)[19] applies to any organization that collects, uses or discloses personal information in the course of commercial activities. Charities that engage in commercial activities should consider the implications of PIPEDA. PIPEDA's definition of "commercial activity" includes the "selling, bartering or leasing of donor, membership or other fundraising lists",[20] and therefore, the transfer of a donor list by a charity will trigger

---

[14] C.R.C. 1978, c. 945.

[15] S.C. 2009, c. 23.

[16] Carter, Hoffstein & Parachin (2013) at 12-13.

[17] For a detailed discussion about the *Canada Not-for-profit Act*, see Bourgeois (2012) at 28-46; and Carter, Hoffstein & Parachin (2013) at 13-16.

[18] *Canada Not-for-profit Corporations Regulations*, SOR/2011-223.

[19] S.C. 2000, c. 5.

[20] *Personal Information Protection and Electronics Documents Act*, S.C. 2000, c. 5, s. 2(1).

the application of PIPEDA. When PIPEDA does apply to an organization, it requires that certain measures be implemented by the organization to ensure that personal information is protected and secured.[21]

Charities Registration (Security Information) Act

The *Charities Registration (Security Information) Act*[22] was created by the *Anti-terrorism Act*.[23] The *Charities Registration (Security Information) Act* is intended to provide a means to ensure that charities do not directly or indirectly fund terrorist activities. In particular, it provides a two-step process whereby a registered charity or an applicant for registered charity status may, respectively, be de-registered or denied charitable registration for supporting terrorist activities.

Competition Act

The *Competition Act*[24] is a federal statute, the purpose of which is to encourage competition and to prohibit unfair business practices. The term "business" is defined in subsection 2(1) to include "the raising of funds for charitable or other non-profit purposes". Therefore, the *Competition Act* currently provides for a variety of rules that regulate the fundraising activities of charities, including rules that regulate telemarketing, promotional contests, lotteries and the making of representations to the public. In addition, any charity carrying on a business activity will be required to comply with the *Competition Act* regarding the manner in which the business activity is carried out.

Lobbying Statutes[25]

The federal *Lobbying Act*[26] and its regulations establish the general rule that certain persons who communicate with federal "public office holders" regarding proposed changes to the law or other matters of public policy shall file an annual return with the federal government. The persons required to file such returns include incorporated charities that employ individuals to make such communications and individuals

---

21   See Carter, Hoffstein & Parachin (2013) at 42.

22   S.C. 2001, c. 41, s. 113.

23   S.C. 2001, c. 41.

24   R.S.C. 1985, c. C-34.

25   See Carter, Hoffstein & Parachin (2013) for this discussion and additional information.

26   R.S.C. 1985, c. 44 (4th Supp.).

who, for payment, make such communications on behalf of charities. In addition to complying with this statute, charities engaged in lobbying activities need to be mindful of the restrictions imposed upon them further to the so-called "doctrine of political purposes". Ontario's *Lobbyists Registration Act, 1998*[27] contains similar provisions to the federal *Lobbying Act* that apply in relation to lobbying directed at the Ontario government.

Provincial Legislation

Like their federal counterpart, each of the provinces has enacted legislation setting out the requirements for incorporating and maintaining a corporation. Issues concerning directors' rights and obligations are covered in detail.[28] Ontario's new *Not-for-Profit Corporations Act* (ONCA) will likely come into force in 2015 and will replace the current Ontario *Corporations Act* (OCA).[29] Unlike the CNCA, a nonprofit created under the OCA will not be dissolved if it fails to continue, but its letters patent and bylaws will be deemed to be amended to comply with the ONCA, after a period of three years after the ONCA is proclaimed, which may result in uncertainty as to what provisions apply.

In Ontario, the *Trustee Act*[30] establishes that directors of a charitable corporation have the power and duty to invest the assets of the corporation as a prudent investor would. This includes the power to invest in mutual funds and the power to delegate investment decision-making to qualified investment managers, provided the corresponding statutory requirements are strictly complied with. Other provinces have similar legislation.[31]

---

[27]   S.O. 1998, c. 27, Schedule.

[28]   See, *e.g.*, Alberta's *Societies Act*, R.S.A. 2000, c. S-14; British Columbia's *Society Act*, R.S.B.C. 1996, c. 433; Saskatchewan's *Non-profit Corporations Act, 1995*, S.S. 1995, c. N-4.2; Manitoba's *Corporations Act*, C.C.S.M. c. C225; Ontario's *Not-for-Profit Corporations Act, 2010*, S.O. 2010, c. 15 [not yet in force]; Québec's *Companies Act*, R.S.Q., c. C-38; New Brunswick's *Companies Act*, R.S.N.B. 1973, c. C-13; Nova Scotia's *Societies Act*, R.S.N.S. 1989, c. 435; Prince Edward Island's *Companies Act*, R.S.P.E.I. 1988, c. C-14; Newfoundland and Labrador's *Corporations Act*, R.S.N.L. 1990, c. C-36; Yukon's *Societies Act*, R.S.Y. 2002, c. 206; Northwest Territories' *Societies Act*, R.S.N.W.T. 1988, c. S-11; and Nunavut's *Societies Act (Nunavut)*, R.S.N.W.T. 1988, c. S-11.

[29]   R.S.O. 1990, c. C.38. For a discussion about the new *Not-for-Profit Corporations Act, 2010*, see Carter, Hoffstein & Parachin (2013) and Bourgeois (2012).

[30]   R.S.O. 1990, c. T.23.

[31]   See, *e.g.*, Alberta, R.S.A. 2000, c. T-8; British Columbia, R.S.B.C. 1996, c. 464; Saskatchewan, S.S. 2009, c. T-23.01 ; Manitoba, C.C.S.M. c. T160; New Brunswick, R.S.N.B. 1973, c. T-15; Nova Scotia, R.S.N.S. 1989, c. 479; Prince Edward Island, R.S.P.E.I. 1988, c. T-8;

Provincial Legislation Aimed at Regulating Charities

There are a few provinces with statutes aimed at regulating the charitable sector. In Ontario, in addition to the *Trustee Act,* the *Charities Accounting Act*[32] sets out certain requirements for operating a charity and limit the activities in which a charity may participate. Failure to conform to the requirements of this legislation may result in the province cancelling the corporation's letters patent and liability for the directors. Alberta regulates the fundraising activities of charities through the *Charitable Fund-raising Act,*[33] while Saskatchewan's *Charitable Fund-raising Businesses Act,*[34] focuses its attention on fundraising businesses, not charities. Manitoba regulates fundraising activities through the *Charities Endorsement Act,*[35] requiring ministerial authorization to solicit funds. Prince Edward Island's *Charities Act*[36] makes distinctions between solicitations by charities and appeals by religious institutions (churches, synagogues, mosques, *etc.*) for financial support.

As legislation is not uniform across the country, charitable and non-profit organizations should enquire as to the governing legislation in their own jurisdiction. These will be in addition to any laws of general application that also apply to the activities of nonprofit organizations.

LEGAL STRUCTURES FOR NONPROFIT ORGANIZATIONS

Overview of Types of Legal Structure

Just like a for-profit business, a nonprofit organization must determine the appropriate legal structure to meet its needs. Not all nonprofit organizations are created equal, and as such Canadian law provides four different legal structures for nonprofit organizations: a trust; an unincorporated association; a corporation without share capital; or a co-operative without share capital. Not only will the legal structure chosen dictate the rights and responsibilities of the organization and its directors, it may also impact on donations and grants from other

---

Newfoundland and Labrador, R.S.N.L. 1990, c. T-10; Yukon, R.S.Y. 2002, c. 223; Northwest Territories, R.S.N.W.T. 1988, c. T-8; and Nunavut, R.S.N.W.T. 1988, c. T-8.

[32]   R.S.O. 1990, c. C.10.

[33]   R.S.A. 2000, c. C-9.

[34]   S.S. 2002, c. C-6.2.

[35]   C.C.S.M. c. C60.

[36]   R.S.P.E.I. 1988, c. C-4.

bodies. When starting a nonprofit organization, the organizers must consider a number of factors in order to choose the necessary structure to carry out its goals. The factors to consider include (see Burke-Robertson & Drache (2002, at 1-3)):

- the purposes of the proposed organization;

- whether the purposes will be of short or long duration;

- the proposed size of membership (if any);

- whether the organization will be of national or local concern;

- whether the organization will be called upon to enter into contracts or hold real property;

- whether it will incur debts or liabilities for which the contracting members or directors may be personally liable;

- the tax treatment of the organization; and

- whether registration as a charity is desired because of ability to issue receipts or because funders require it.

Once these factors are determined, the various legal structures should be examined in order to assess their advantages and disadvantages in relation to the needs of the organization.

As Burke-Robertson notes, "the appropriate form of legal structure may also be dictated by the existing legislation and regulations governing the activities of the particular type of not-for-profit organization" (at 1-3). For example, if one is organizing an agricultural society in Manitoba, they must refer to the requirements under the *Agricultural Societies Act.*[37]

Trusts

The trust is one form of legal vehicle for charitable organizations, which, because of its greater flexibility and fewer administrative burdens, may be seen as an attractive alternative for organizations that are made up of only a few people. The option of a trust is not available to nonprofit organizations by virtue of the definition in paragraph 149(1)(*l*) of the ITA. While many academics consider the nature of a trust to be hard to define, it is generally regarded as the relationship between the settlor (the donor) and the trustee, where the trustee holds

---

[37]   C.C.S.M. c. A30.

the trust property for the benefit of some persons or for some objectives in such a way that the real benefit of the property accrues to the beneficiaries of the trust rather than the trustee (see Waters (2005, at 3-4); Radu (2009, at 128-130)). While the trustee's actions are governed by the *Trustee Act*,[38] in order for the trust property to vest in the trustee, the trust must meet the common law requirements. To properly be recognized as a trust, the trust document or instrument must include what the courts refer to as the three certainties: certainty of intention, certainty of subject-matter, and certainty of objects.[39] This requires the trust document to set out the purposes or objectives of the trust, the property to be held in trust, and to identify the beneficiaries of the trust or a means by which to determine who will be the beneficiaries (Bourgeois (2012, at 2); Waters (2005, at 132 ff.)).

In situations where there will be a limited number of individuals wishing to aid in the administration of a non-profit or charitable endeavour, a trust is a useful vehicle, as involvement in the trust is limited to the trustees. For example, the Kadey Family Charitable Trust is administered by two members of the Kadey family.[40] Although the trust is a convenient vehicle, both statutory and common law requirements place substantial fiduciary obligations upon the trustee, including the following three fundamental duties (Waters (2005, at 852)):

> First, no trustee may delegate his office to others; secondly, no trustee may profit personally from his dealings with the trust property, with the beneficiaries, or as a trustee; thirdly, a trustee must act honestly and with that level of skill and prudence which would be expected of the reasonable man of business administering his own affairs.

Although there are statutory provisions governing trust documents and duties of trustees, and the common law related to the administration of trusts has developed over hundreds of years, the primary terms of a trust are to be found within the trust document itself. Apart from the

---

[38] *Trustee Act*, R.S.O. 1990, c. T.23; *Trustee Act*, R.S.A. 2000, c. T-8; *Trustee Act*, R.S.B.C. 1996, c. 464; *Trustee Act*, S.S. 2009, c.T-23.01; *Trustee Act*, C.C.S.M. c. T160; *Trustees Act*, R.N.B. 1973, c. T-15; *Trustee Act*, R.S.N.S. 1989, c. 479; *Trustee Act*, R.S.P.E.I. 1988, c. T-8; *Trustee Act*, R.S.N.L. 1990, c. T-10; *Trustee Act*, R.S.Y. 2002, c. 223; *Trustee Act*, R.S.N.W.T. 1988, c. T-8; *Trustee Act* (Nunavut), R.S.N.W.T. 1988, c. T-8.

[39] *Faucher v. Tucker Estate*, [1993] M.J. No. 589, [1994] 2 W.W.R. 1 (Man. C.A.).

[40] See 2011 Registered Charity Information Return for the Kadey Family Charitable Trust, available online at: <http://www.cra-arc.gc.ca/charitylists/>.

general duties imposed by law, the trustee must follow the terms of the trust or risk allegations of breach of fiduciary duty.[41]

Unincorporated Association

An unincorporated association is defined as "a group of two or more persons united together by mutual consent in order to determine, deliberate and act jointly for a common purpose" (CED 2008 at §1).[42] In many respects, it is like a business partnership, however, it is not formed for the purposes of profit.[43] In an unincorporated association, the members may be governed by a contractual arrangement, which is commonly referred to as a "Memorandum of Association", a Constitution, or by-laws.[44] Both documents set out the purpose or "objects" of the organization and how it is to be managed or operated, providing great latitude for the creation of an organization since the only limitation is that the objects must be lawful.

As is demonstrated by the above example, a Memorandum of Association must include a clause stating that no gain, dividends, or income will be paid to members of the organization, and that all profits or any income must be used to promote the organization's objects. The nonprofit organization's objects cannot include the carrying on of a profit-making business.

Unlike some of the other legal structures that are available for nonprofit organizations, an unincorporated association does not have the legal capacity to sue or be sued.[45] The contractual nature of the organization creates a legal relationship among the members, but does not create a legal person (Bourgeois (2012, at 21)).[46]

Corporation without Share Capital

A corporation without share capital (or a non-share capital corporation) is akin to the traditional corporate structure, except that the members (who are similar to shareholders) do not benefit financially

---

[41] See Bourgeois (2012) at 123-125.

[42] See also *Orchard v. Tunney*, [1957] S.C.J. No. 26, [1957] S.C.R. 436 (S.C.C.).

[43] A partnership is not a structure available to either a nonprofit or charitable endeavour because, at law, a partnership requires a profit-making intention. See Bourgeois (2012) at 24.

[44] By-laws are sometimes a more detailed document separate from the constitution or memorandum of association: Bourgeois (2012) at 24.

[45] See, *e.g.*, *S. (J.R.) v. Glendinning*, [2000] O.J. No. 2695, 191 D.L.R. (4th) 750 (Ont. S.C.J.).

[46] See also Bourgeois (2008).

from the organization. A corporation without share capital can be incorporated federally, under the CNCA, or provincially, under the applicable provincial corporate legislation such as the new ONCA. The decision to incorporate federally or provincially (or both) will be determined by the organization's purposes, the legislative authority under which they fall, and the scope of the organization's activities, *i.e.*, whether it is a local organization or one crossing multiple jurisdictions. Under the CNCA and the ONCA, incorporation is "as of right", unlike the old letters patent system under the CCA where it was a privilege.

Although terminology and procedure will vary from jurisdiction to jurisdiction, in order to become a corporation without share capital, multiple persons[47] must file articles of or an application for incorporation with the appropriate authority (*i.e.*, either a Minister or Lieutenant Governor) under the applicable legislation.[48] In order to obtain a certificate of incorporation or letters patent, the organization must set out the purposes of the corporation, which will describe the scope of its proposed activities. If the purposes are deficient, the only way to change them is through articles of amendment or an application for supplementary letters patent. As such, careful consideration must be given to the drafting of the purposes of the corporation in order to ensure all activities will be covered and that it will qualify either as a registered charity or a non-profit. As will be discussed in greater detail below, the process of incorporation results in the creation of a separate legal person and provides the members with protection from liability.

Co-operative without Share Capital

A co-operative without share capital (such as a nonprofit housing co-operative) is a special type of corporation, which in Ontario is created under the *Co-operative Corporations Act*[49] or federally under the *Canada Cooperatives Act*[50] if it meets the requirements of subsection 3(2) of the Act. Although co-operatives both with and without share capital are

---

[47] The exact number of persons required to incorporate depends on the jurisdiction. For example, to incorporate federally, three or more persons are required, whereas in British Columbia, five or more persons are required to incorporate a Society. Under the CNCA only one person is required to incorporate a non-soliciting corporation.

[48] The one exception to this is the utilization of an "unlimited liability company" in Nova Scotia, under the *Companies Act*, R.S.N.S. 1989, c. 81.

[49] R.S.O. 1990, c. C.35.

[50] S.C. 1998, c. 1.

intended to be operated "as nearly as possible at cost",[51] a co-operative without share capital cannot distribute any surplus or dividends to its members, unlike a co-operative with share capital. Co-operatives without share capital must be organized, operated and administered according to basic principles set out in the legislation: each member or delegate has only one vote, and no member or delegate may vote by proxy.[52] Provisions enabling a small fixed percentage of any surplus to be distributed to members do not apply to a co-operative without share capital. The legislation also places restrictions on the conversion or dissolution of such corporations; upon dissolution the remaining assets can only be distributed to similar organizations or charitable organizations.

Advantages and Disadvantages of Different Legal Structures

One of the primary advantages of organizing as a non-profit organization, regardless of its structure, is being exempt from income tax imposed under the ITA.[53] A charitable organization is also exempt from income tax.[54]

Apart from the income tax benefits that accrue by obtaining non-profit status, the advantages and disadvantages of the different legal structures should be examined in order to determine if the structure is appropriate for the needs of the organization. Some of the important considerations include set-up costs, legal capacity, liability and perpetual existence.

Set-up Costs

As would be expected, the more formal the organization's legal structure, the more expensive it will be to establish. Accordingly, a trust or unincorporated association is relatively inexpensive to set up as compared to the cost of the incorporation process for a corporation without share capital or a co-operative without share capital. However, there are significant benefits in choosing the corporation options as outlined below.

---

[51]   *Co-operative Corporations Act*, R.S.O. 1990, c. C.35, s. 1(1) "co-operative basis" (d).
[52]   *Ibid.*
[53]   ITA, s. 149(1)(*l*).
[54]   ITA, s. 149(1); ITA s. 149(1)(*f*).

Legal Capacity

Legal capacity refers to the organization's ability to be recognized at law, *i.e.*, whether it is a separate legal entity with the capacity to commence or defend a lawsuit, enter into contracts, or own land in its own name. Without delving into legal theory, only a "person" can have rights and responsibilities. Incorporated entities are recognized by law as "persons" capable of obtaining these rights and responsibilities. Although in some respects a trust is considered a separate entity (*i.e.*, for income tax purposes) for many other purposes the trust is not considered a legal entity.[55] Rather it is considered a relationship between the trust property, the trustee who holds legal title to the property, and the beneficiaries of the trust who hold equitable title to the property. Since the trust property vests in the trustee, there is no trust without the trustee. As such, the trust can only sue, be sued or enter a contract through the trustee who performs these actions on behalf of the trust. An unincorporated association is also not a legal entity, and therefore is incapable of holding title to property or exercising any other legal rights. Property is held in trust and legal acts are carried out by individual members of the group whose actions would be governed by the by-laws of the association.

The main advantage of having a separate legal entity incorporated for the purpose of carrying on charitable or nonprofit activities is that it is the entity which will enter into contracts or carry out the activities and, therefore, the entity which may ultimately be sued for any damages caused by the entity, thus providing some protection for individual trustees and members against future liability. In other words, failure to obtain legal capacity for the organization means the individual members will be personally liable for any damages resulting from the organization's activities, as the organization will not have the capacity to be sued.

Liability (Organization, Directors, Officers, Members)

Liability can come in many forms, whether it is for failure to follow statutory rules, breach of contract, negligence, or intentional harm. Whether individual members, directors, or the organization will be held responsible will depend on the legal structure. As a separate legal entity, an incorporated corporation without share capital will be held answerable and responsible for any act, default, obligation, or liability

---

[55]   Bucknall (2002). See also *United Service Funds v. Richardson Greenshields of Canada Ltd.*, [1987] B.C.J. No. 1391, 40 D.L.R. (4th) 94 (B.C.S.C.).

of the corporation, and the individual members are absolved of responsibility. This does not mean that directors or officers can escape liability, as personal liability may arise in the execution of their duties where their conduct falls below the prescribed standard of care. For example, under sections 145 and 146 of the CNCA, directors can be personally liable if they authorize payments contrary to the Act or if there are unpaid employee wages. When performing their duties in the course of their employment, section 148 states that directors must act honestly, in good faith, and exercise the care and skill of a reasonably prudent person. According to the CNCA, officers also must use the care and skills of a reasonably prudent person. On the other hand, the members of the corporation are not liable for the liabilities of the corporation pursuant to subsection 36(1) of the CNCA.

Although the duties of a trustee are similar in nature to those of the director and officer, a trustee's exposure to liability is greater as he or she is the only legal person in the trust and is generally held to a higher standard of care. In addition, a trustee will only be reimbursed for those expenses that are properly incurred. Expenses that are improperly incurred become the sole responsibility of the trustee (Waters (2005, at 1151)).[56] Members are at greatest risk in an unincorporated association, which has no legal status apart from that of its members. As such, an association cannot incur liabilities or be convicted of an offence; instead, the members of an unincorporated association may be held personally liable for the acts or omissions of the organization.

Perpetual Existence

As a separate legal entity, a corporation without share capital can, theoretically, have perpetual existence, so that changes in the membership will not affect its continuity. Similarly, there are provisions in the *Trustee Act* to appoint successor trustees when a trustee dies, retires, refuses to act, or is incapable of acting.[57] An unincorporated association on the other hand cannot have perpetual existence, as it is indistinguishable from its members. When the members no longer exist, neither does the association.

---

[56]   See *Trustee Act*, R.S.O. 1990, c.T.23, s. 23.1.
[57]   *Trustee Act*, R.S.O. 1990, c. T.23, s. 3.

As a result of the advantages noted above, specifically relating to the protection from liability and perpetual existence, incorporation is generally preferred.

Nonprofit Corporate Structures for National Organizations[58]

The business sector has utilized multiple corporations for years to contain liabilities and to protect assets. Nonprofit corporations, though, have been generally slow to establish and implement multiple nonprofit corporations to the same end. The traditional use of a corporation by nonprofits has been focused almost exclusively on obtaining limited liability protection for its members, and very little thought has been given to the benefits associated with carrying on operations within a separate corporation in order to contain liabilities and to protect assets while addressing the common nonprofit purpose that may be found on a national or multi-jurisdictional basis. Such an organization can be based on one of two models: the national association model or the centralized chapter model.

National Association Model

The national association model involves multiple legal entities that are organized at various levels, such as incorporated provincial associations or incorporated local organizations. The national association model will have a governing body, normally established as a federal corporation, to act as the umbrella body over its member organizations, whether those members are corporations or unincorporated associations. An example of this model could be several local churches that are part of a large national denomination.[59] A member organization will normally have either a name or nonprofit purpose that is similar to that of the governing national association.

The primary benefit of utilizing the national association model is that of reduced liability exposure for the organization by containing the liability attributable to each member organization within a separate corporate entity. As such, the claims made against one member organization do not necessarily affect the assets of other member organizations or that of the governing body.

---

[58] See Carter (1998; 2001); Godel (2007); Bourgeois (2012) at 97-104.
[59] Bourgeois (2012) at 97.

The most obvious problem with the national association model is that a governing body can easily lose control over its separately incorporated member organizations if appropriate steps are not implemented to ensure that the member organizations are subject to appropriate contractual and/or licensing control mechanisms. In this regard, the national organization can lose goodwill and other intangible assets such as trademarks through the actions of the local member.

Centralized Chapter Model

The centralized chapter model involves one legal entity acting as a single nonprofit organization across Canada, normally involving multiple divisions at either the provincial, regional, or local level, as is the case with the Canadian Cancer Society. Those divisions are often referred to as chapters or branches. However, none of the chapters or branches are themselves separate legal entities. Instead, the chapters or branches are a part of a single legal entity.

The most significant benefit of the centralized chapter model is that by requiring only one corporation, it is much easier to maintain a higher degree of control over chapters or branches without the necessity of contract or licence agreements that are otherwise required with the national association model. In addition, by utilizing only one corporation to carry on operations on a national basis, there is generally more symmetry and coherence to day-to-day operations and control of personnel. This model also avoids the risk of losing assets, goodwill, donor base, or trademarks to a "renegade" member organization, since everything is legally owned by the single national corporation. A chapter or branch would have no legal right to take any assets on its own if it were to leave the national organization.

The most fundamental problem inherent in the centralized chapter model is that by having only one corporation, the liabilities that occur in the operations of one chapter will expose all of the assets of the national organization to claims arising out of activities of that one chapter, even though other chapters may have had nothing to do with the incident in question. Similarly, even if the incident involves a national program involving all chapters, there is no ability to protect specific assets of the national organization, since all assets are owned by the national organization.

Association Agreements

An association agreement is often referred to as a "chapter agreement", an "affiliation agreement", or a "membership agreement". The content of the agreement, not the terminology used to describe it, is what is important. The agreement sets out the contractual relationship between the governing association and its member organizations. Some of the more important considerations include:

- a recognition that despite the similar purposes, the two organizations are recognized at law as being separate and distinct corporate entities with separate boards of directors and that they are to remain independently responsible for the management and governance of their respective operations;

- an indication that the contractual relationship contained in the agreement does not constitute either a partnership or a joint venture arrangement between the parties;

- the term of the agreement;

- the basic requirements of the association relationship;

- the rights that flow from the association relationship;

- the actions by the member organization that would terminate the association relationship and the consequences that flow from termination;

- a mechanism for indemnification;

- the maintenance of documents, books, and records;

- provisions requiring compliance with various statutory obligations (*i.e.*, tax laws, anti-terrorism legislation, *etc.*); and

- a mechanism for conflict resolution.

REGISTERED CHARITIES UNDER THE *INCOME TAX ACT*

Types of Registered Charities

As discussed above, there is an important distinction between non-profit organizations and registered charities in Canada. The definition in the ITA of a non-profit organization is a negative one in the sense that a non-profit organization is one that is *not* a charity within the meaning of section 149.1(1) of the ITA.[60] If an organization has charitable purposes, it must be a charity and should seek registration under the ITA to avoid being taxable. Next, a charitable organization has to determine what type of registered charity will best suit its objectives:

- a charitable organization;

- a public foundation; or

- a private foundation.

Amendments to the ITA seem to be blurring the distinction between the types of registered charities, particularly between a charitable organization and a public foundation (see, *e.g.*, Man & Carter (2005a; 2005b)).[61] Nevertheless, the choice of charitable structure is important because it will determine which rules in the ITA will apply. The following general discussion of the differences between the types of registered charities will be followed by a more detailed summary of the specific rules affecting registered charities.

Charitable Organization

Under the ITA, a charitable organization is one that devotes all of its resources to charitable activities carried on by the organization itself[62] —

---

[60]   ITA, s. 149(1)(*l*).

[61]   On June 26, 2013, Bill C-48 received Royal Assent. Bill C-48 proposed various amendments to the ITA that have impacted the operations of registered charities in Canada since their first introduction in 2002.

[62]   The definition of "charitable organization" in s. 149.1(1) provides as follows:
"charitable organization", at any particular time, means an organization, whether or not incorporated,

  (*a*)   all the resources of which are devoted to charitable activities carried on by the organization itself,

  (*b*)   no part of the income of which is payable to, or is otherwise available for, the personal benefit of any proprietor, member, shareholder, trustee or settlor thereof,

  (*c*)   more than 50% of the directors, trustees, officers or like officials of which deal at arm's length with each other and with

   (i)   each of the other directors, trustees, officers and like officials of the organization,

   (ii)   each person described by subparagraph (*d*)(i) or (ii), and

   (iii)   each member of a group of persons (other than Her Majesty in right of Canada or of a province, a municipality, another registered charity that is not a private foundation, and any club, society or association described in paragraph 149(1)(*l*)) who do not deal with each other at arm's length, if the group would, if it were a person, be a person described by subparagraph (*d*)(i), and it is generally considered to be a "doing" organization. A charitable organization may be established as a corporation, an unincorporated association, or a trust. It cannot be controlled by a group of related directors/trustees,[63] and, like a non-profit organization and the other types of registered charities, no part of its income may be payable to or otherwise available for the personal benefit of a proprietor, member, shareholder, trustee, or settlor.

Charitable Foundation

The ITA provides that a charitable foundation is an entity that is created and operated exclusively for charitable purposes,[64] which may be either a public foundation or a private foundation. While they may carry on a limited number of charitable activities, charitable foundations generally provide funds to other charitable organizations or "qualified donees" so that those organizations may carry out their charitable activities. In this regard, charitable foundations are commonly considered "granting" or "funding" organizations. A charitable foundation may be established as either a corporation or a trust, but not as an unincorporated association.

There are two types of charitable foundations: a public foundation[65] and a private foundation. Like a charitable organization, a public

---

(*d*)   that is not, at the particular time, and would not at the particular time be, if the organization were a corporation, controlled directly or indirectly in any manner whatever

   (i)   by a person (other than Her Majesty in right of Canada or of a province, a municipality, another registered charity that is not a private foundation, and any club, society or association described in paragraph 149(1)(*l*)),

      (A)   who immediately after the particular time, has contributed to the organization amounts that are, in total, greater than 50% of the capital of the organization immediately after the particular time, and

      (B)   who immediately after the person's last contribution at or before the particular time, had contributed to the organization amounts that were, in total, greater than 50% of the capital of the organization immediately after the making of that last contribution, or

   (ii)   by a person, or by a group of persons that do not deal at arm's length with each other, if the person or any member of the group does not deal at arm's length with a person described in subparagraph (i).

[63]   The details of this requirement are discussed below.

[64]   The definition of "charitable foundation" in s. 149.1(1) is as follows: "'charitable foundation' means a corporation or trust that is constituted and operated exclusively for charitable purposes, no part of the income of which is payable to, or is otherwise available for, the personal benefit of any proprietor, member, shareholder, trustee or settlor thereof, and that is not a charitable organization".

[65]   The definition of "public foundation" under the ITA s. 149.1(1) is as follows: "public foundation", at a particular time, means a charitable foundation

foundation cannot be controlled by a group of related directors/trustees. A private foundation is defined in the ITA as simply a foundation that is not a public foundation. Generally, a private foundation is an entity established for philanthropic and/or tax planning purposes by a wealthy family or corporation that may be controlled by them.

Specific Rules Affecting Registered Charities

Relationship between Directors/Trustees and Control

Apart from the distinctions based on the difference between "doing" and "funding" entities, the most important requirement distinguishing a charitable organization and public foundation from a private foundation is the relationship between the directors/trustees and control of the entities. The ITA currently provides that more than 50 per cent of the directors, trustees, officers or like officials of charitable organizations and public foundations must deal with each other and with each of the other directors, trustees, officers or like officials at arm's length.[66] As a

---

(*a*) more than 50% of the directors, trustees, officers or like officials of which deal at arm's length with each other and with

    (i)   each of the other directors, trustees, officers and like officials of the foundation,

    (ii)   each person described by subparagraph (*b*)(i) or (ii), and

    (iii)   each member of a group of persons (other than Her Majesty in right of Canada or of a province, a municipality, another registered charity that is not a private foundation, and any club, society or association described in paragraph 149(1)(*l*)) who do not deal with each other at arm's length, if the group would, if it were a person, be a person described by subparagraph (*b*)(i), and

(*b*) that is not, at the particular time, and would not at the particular time be, if the foundation were a corporation, controlled directly or indirectly in any manner whatever

    (i)   by a person (other than Her Majesty in right of Canada or of a province, a municipality, another registered charity that is not a private foundation, and any club, society or association described in paragraph 149(1)(*l*)),

        (A)   who immediately after the particular time, has contributed to the foundation amounts that are, in total, greater than 50% of the capital of the foundation immediately after the particular time, and

        (B)   who immediately after the person's last contribution at or before the particular time, had contributed to the foundation amounts that were, in total, greater than 50% of the capital of the foundation immediately after the making of that last contribution, or

    (ii)   by a person, or by a group of persons that do not deal at arm's length with each other, if the person or any member of the group does not deal at arm's length with a person described in subparagraph (i).

[66]   ITA s. 251(1) provides that related persons do not deal at arm's length with each other and s. 251(2) provides that persons may be related by blood, marriage or common-law partnership or adoption. There are also detailed rules in ss. 251 (am. S.C. 1994, c. 7, Sch. II, s. 195; S.C. 1998, c. 19, s. 242; S.C. 2000, c. 12, ss. 140, 142; S.C. 2001, c. 17, s. 192; S.C. 2013. c. 34, s. 361), and 256 (am. S.C. 1994, c. 7, Sch. II, s. 198; S.C. 1994, c. 21, s. 114; S.C. 1995, c. 3, s. 55; S.C. 1995, c. 21, s. 44; S.C. 1998, c. 19, s. 246; S.C. 2001, c. 17, ss. 194, 231; S.C. 2005, c. 19, s. 55; S.C. 2009, c. 2, s. 78; S.C. 2013, c. 34, ss. 37, 364), dealing with factual

result of recent amendments to the definitions, charitable organizations and public foundations cannot also be controlled directly or indirectly by a person who has contributed amounts to the organization that total more than 50 per cent of the organization's capital, unless the contributor was either the federal government, a provincial government, a municipality, another registered charity that was not a private foundation, or a non-profit organization.

These amendments were intended to ensure that in certain circumstances large donations were not prohibited or inadvertently caused the organization to be deemed to be a private foundation by virtue of such gifts. However, due to the inclusion of the phrase "controlled directly or indirectly in any manner whatever" in the new definitions, the convoluted rules in the ITA in relation to "control" will now apply.[67] The practical application of these rules in the charitable context is unclear, since the rules are premised upon application to commercial arrangements in a business context rather than for registered charities. (See Couzin (2005); Loukidelis (2004)).

As such, directors and officers of registered charities will need to carefully review these rules when establishing charitable organizations and public foundations involving a major donor or when receiving a donation from a major donor who contributes more than 50 per cent of the capital of a charity in order to ensure that the charity in question will not inadvertently be caught by these rules and be designated a private foundation. As well, the current relationships between entities in multiple corporate structures should also be reviewed in order to assess whether this new control test may have an undesirable effect.

Disbursement Quota Rules

All registered charities are required to annually expend a portion of their assets in accordance with a disbursement quota (DQ), which is a prescribed amount that registered charities must disburse each year in

---

non-arm's length and factual control which are relevant for determining whether corporations deal at arm's length with individuals or other corporations, but are beyond the scope of this text.

[67]   Section 256(5.1) provides as follows:

For the purposes of this Act, where the expression "controlled, directly or indirectly in any manner whatever," is used, a corporation shall be considered to be so controlled by another corporation, person or group of persons (in this subsection referred to as the "controller") at any time where, at that time, the controller has any direct or indirect influence that, if exercised, would result in control in fact of the corporation ...

order to maintain their charitable registration.[68] The purpose of the DQ is to ensure that most of a charity's funds are used to further its charitable purposes and activities; to discourage charities from accumulating excessive funds; and to keep other expenses at a reasonable level".

Registered charities are required to expend at least 3.5 per cent of their assets that are not used directly in their charitable activities or administration (commonly referred to as "investment assets"). The value of the assets in this regard is based on the average value of the charity's assets that are not used directly in its charitable activities or administration in the 24 months immediately preceding the taxation year.[69]

Related Business

Charitable organizations[70] and public foundations can carry on related businesses.[71] If charitable organizations and public foundations carry on *un*related businesses, their charitable status may be revoked.[72] Private foundations, however, may not carry on any business activity, otherwise their charitable status may be revoked.[73]

Political Activities

All registered charities are required by law to have exclusively charitable purposes (*e.g.*, relief of poverty, advancement of education, advancement of religion and other purposes beneficial to the community).

---

[68] Prior to the 2010 *Income Tax Act* changes, there was an 80 per cent disbursement quota that required charities to spend 80% of receipted donations. The 80 per cent rule was found to be too complex and in 2010 the 80 per cent rule was eliminated as well as concepts of enduring property, ten year gift, capital gains pool, and specified gift. See Theresa L.M. Man, "Disbursement Quota Reform: The Ins And Outs Of What You Need To Know" (Paper presented at the 2011 National Charity Law Symposium, May 6, 2011). Online at: Carters Professional Corporation <http://www.carters.ca/pub/article/charity/2011/tlm0506.pdf>.

[69] The 3.5 per cent DQ does not apply if the amount of property owned by a charitable organization is $100,000 or less ($25,000 if a public or private foundation). The detailed method for the calculation of the 3.5 per cent DQ is set out in ss. 3701 and 3702 of the *Income Tax Regulations*, C.R.C. 1978, c. 945 (am. SOR/87-632, s. 1; SOR/94-686, ss. 22(F), 51(F), 73(F), 79(F); S.C 2007, c. 35, s. 76; S.C. 2010, c. 25, ss. 84, 85).

[70] Paragraph 149.1(6)(*a*) of the ITA.

[71] See Canada Revenue Agency Policy Statement CPS-019 entitled "What is a Related Business?" dated March 31, 2003, for a discussion of what CRA considers to be a related business, available online at: <http://www.cra-arc.gc.ca/chrts-gvng/chrts/plcy/cps/cps-019-eng.html>. See also *Alberta Institute on Mental Retardation v. Canada*, [1987] F.C.J. No. 286, [1987] 3 F.C. 286 (F.C.A.) and *Earth Fund v. Canada (Minister of National Revenue)*, [2002] F.C.J. No. 1769 (F.C.A.).

[72] Paragraphs 149.1(2)(*a*) and 149.1(3)(*a*) of the ITA.

[73] Paragraph 149.1(4)(*a*) of the ITA.

In order to determine whether a charity is constituted exclusively for charitable purposes, the CRA will look at the stated purpose of an organization and the organization's current activities. A political purpose that is not in a charity's governing document but that the charity still pursues can become an unacceptable "unstated political purpose".[74]

According to CRA, activities undertaken by a registered charity can be categorized as charitable activities, political activities, or prohibited activities. A charitable activity is an activity undertaken to achieve a charitable purpose. If a particular activity is considered by CRA to be charitable, then it is permitted without limits. For example, communication with a public official or the public by a charity regarding an issue related to the charity's purposes can be a charitable activity under certain circumstances. The communication would need to satisfy the following requirements: (1) it would need to relate to and be subordinate to the charity's charitable purpose; (2) be well reasoned; and (3) not contain information that is false, inaccurate or misleading.

With regard to political activities, there is currently no definition in the ITA of "political activity". However, CPS-022 provides that an activity is presumed to be a political activity if a charity:

- explicitly communicates a call to political action (*i.e.*, encourages the public to contact elected representatives or a public official and urges them to retain, oppose, or change the law, policy, or a decision of government);

- explicitly communicates to the public that the law, policy or decision of any level of government in Canada or a foreign country should be retained, opposed or changed; or

- explicitly indicates in its material that the intention of the activity is to incite, organize or put pressure on governments to retain, oppose or change the law, policy or decision of any level of government in Canada or another country.

A charity may engage in political activities provided that:

- The activities are non-partisan (as discussed below).

- The issue in question is connected to the charity's purposes.

---

[74] Canada Revenue Agency, Policy Statement, CPS-022, "Political Activities", online: Canada Revenue Agency <http://www.cra-arc.gc.ca/chrts-gvng/chrts/plcy/cps/cps-022-eng.html>.

- The activities are subordinate to the charity's purposes.

- The charity's views are based on a well-reasoned position.

- The activities fall within expenditure limits under the ITA.

With regard to the expenditure limit, where a charity takes part in political activities, in general it must devote substantially all (*i.e.*, 90 per cent or more) of its resources to charitable activities.

Prohibited activities are those activities that are either illegal or involve partisan political activities, which are not permitted at all. According to subsections 149.1(6.1) and 149.1(6.2) of the ITA, and the CRA Advisory on Partisan Political Activities, "partisan political activity" involves the "direct or indirect support of, or opposition to, any political party or candidate for public office".[75]

Charitable Activities

As noted above, charitable organizations primarily carry on their own charitable activities. They may give funds to other qualified donees but may not disburse more than 50 per cent of their income annually to qualified donees,[76] unless the qualified donees are also associated charities.[77] Public foundations, however, are required by CRA to give more than 50 per cent of their income annually to other qualified donees. This requirement is not explicitly set out in the Act, but implied by virtue of the requirement in section 149.1(6)(*b*) of the ITA that charitable organizations may not disburse more than 50 per cent of their income annually to qualified donees and the definition of "charitable foundation" in section 149.1(1) of the ITA, which provides that a charitable foundation is "not a charitable organization" (Man & Carter (2005b)).

---

[75] Canada Revenue Agency, Advisory on Partisan Political Activities, online: Canada Revenue Agency <http://www.cra-arc.gc.ca/chrts-gvng/chrts/cmmnctn/pltcl-ctvts/prtsnctvts-eng.html>.

[76] Paragraph 149.1(6)(*b*) of the ITA. Section 149.1(1) of the ITA provides that "qualified donees" are organizations that can issue official donation receipts for gifts that individuals and corporations make to them under ss. 110.1(1)(*a*) and (*b*) and 118.1(1). These consist of registered charities in Canada, registered Canadian amateur athletic associations; housing corporations resident in Canada constituted exclusively to provide low-cost housing for the aged; Canadian municipalities; the United Nations and its agencies; universities that are outside Canada that are prescribed to be universities the student body of which ordinarily includes students from Canada; a municipal or public body performing a function of government in Canada that has applied for registration; a foreign organization that has applied to the Minister for registration under subsection (26).

[77] Paragraph 149.1(6)(*c*) of the ITA.

Private foundations may carry on their own charitable activities, and may give funds to other qualified donees. It is not clear from the Act whether there is any requirement on private foundations to give more than 50 per cent of their income annually to other qualified donees. As explained above, CRA takes the administrative position that the language in the definition for "charitable foundation" implies that public foundations must disburse at least 50 per cent of their income to qualified donees. CRA also takes the administrative position that since the definition of "private foundation" in section 149.1(1) of the ITA provides that a private foundation is a charitable foundation that is *not* a public foundation, private foundations are not required to give at least 50 per cent of their income annually to other qualified donees.

Borrowing

Public and private foundations are prohibited from incurring debts other than debts for current operating expenses, the purchase and sale of investments or the administration of the charitable activities.[78] These restrictions do not apply to charitable organizations.

Control of Other Corporations

Public and private foundations are prohibited from acquiring control of any corporation.[79] Failure to comply with this restriction may lead to revocation of a foundation's registration. Generally, control occurs when the foundation owns 50 per cent or more of a corporation's issued share capital, having full voting rights under all circumstances. However, a foundation that has not purchased more than 5 per cent of these shares but is given a block of shares that brings up its total holding to more than 50 per cent will not be considered to have acquired control of the corporation.[80]

The restrictions that apply to foundations do not apply to charitable organizations. This means that, for purposes of the Act, charitable organizations are permitted to acquire control of a corporation. As such, CRA suggests that a charitable organization may operate a business through a taxable share capital corporation with the charitable

---

[78] Paragraphs 149.1(3)(*d*) and 149.1(4)(*d*) of the ITA.
[79] Paragraphs 149.1(3)(*c*) and 149.1(4)(*c*) of the ITA.
[80] *Ibid.* See Jane Burke-Robertson, Terrance S. Carter & Theresa LM. Man, *Corporate and Practice Manual for Charitable and Not-For-Profit Organizations* (Toronto: Thomson Carswell, 2013) at 2-25, 2-26.

organization retaining control over the taxable corporation "through share holdings or a power to nominate the board of directors".[81]

The following table summarizes some of the specific rules affecting registered charities, including recently enacted amendments and proposed amendments.

Table 1: Rules Affecting Registered Charities

Characteristics	Types of Registered Charities		
	Charitable Organizations	**Public Foundations**	**Private Foundations**
(1) Relationship between directors/ trustees and control	More than 50% of the directors of charitable organizations and public foundations must deal with each other and with each of the other directors or trustees at arm's length. A person or a group of persons not dealing with each other at arm's length may contribute more than 50% of the charity's capital as long as such a person or group does not control the charity in any way or represent more than 50% of the directors, trustees, officers and similar officials of the charity (amendment retroactive to January 1, 2000).		No requirements — may be closely held.
(2) Disbursement quota rules	All must expend an amount equal to 3.5% of its assets that are not used directly in its charitable activities and administration. If the value of the assets is below $100,000 for charitable organizations ($25,000 for private and public foundations), then the 3.5% quota does not apply.		
(3) Related business	Can only carry on related businesses		Cannot carry on any business
(4) Political Activities	Can only devote 10% or less of their resources to permitted political activities, which does not include illegal or partisan activities.		

---

[81]   See CRA Policy Statement CPS-019 entitled "What is a Related Business?" dated March 31, 2003 at paras. 47 and 48, available online at: <http://www.cra-arc.gc.ca/chrts-gvng/chrts/plcy/cps/cps-019-eng.html>.

Characteristics	Types of Registered Charities		
	Charitable Organizations	**Public Foundations**	**Private Foundations**
(5) Charitable activities	Primarily carry on their own charitable activities, may give funds to other qualified donees, may not disburse more than 50% of their income annually to qualified donees, unless they are associated charities.	Public foundations must give more than 50% of their income annually to other qualified donees.	Private foundations primarily fund other charities.
(6) Legal structure	Must either be corporations, unincorporated associations or charitable trusts.	Must be either corporations or trusts.	
(7) Borrowing	No restriction.	Cannot incur debts other than debts for current operating expenses, the purchase and sale of investments, or the administration of the charitable activities.	
(8) Control of other corporations	No restriction.	Cannot acquire control of any corporation. Generally, control occurs when the foundation owns 50% or more of a corporation's issued share capital, having full voting rights under all circumstances. There is an exception where a foundation has not bought more than 5% of these shares and is given a bloc of shares that brings up its total holding to more than 50%, it will not be considered to have acquired control of the corporation.	

Regulatory Regime

Interim Sanctions

Prior to the 2004 Federal Budget, the only sanction available to CRA in regulating registered charities was the revocation of a charity's registration (Canada, Department of Finance (2004, at 338)). Revocation occurred sometimes inadvertently as a result of a failure by the charity to file an information return or because the charity was being discontinued, and was only invoked rarely by CRA in situations of serious non-compliance and only after a lengthy audit process. To provide an alternative to the revocation of charitable status for less severe non-compliance, the ITA now provides for intermediate sanctions (which includes financial penalties or suspensions).[82] In the situation of a failure to file an information return on time, the registered charity will be subject to a monetary penalty of $500. A registered charity may also face a suspension of its ability to issue tax receipts and to receive funds from other charities for one year if it fails to comply with certain verification and enforcement provisions of the Act (e.g., fails to keep proper books and records) or fails to file an accurate information return. Private foundations that carry on a business or public foundations and charitable organizations that carry on unrelated business will be subject to a monetary penalty equal to 5 per cent of their gross revenue from such business activities and a repeat offence of the first infraction will carry a monetary penalty equal to all of the charity's gross revenue from the offending activities as well as a suspension of its ability to issue tax receipts.

Similarly graduated monetary penalties will be applied to registered charities if:[83]

- a charitable foundation acquires control of a corporation;

- a registered charity confers on a person an undue benefit (essentially, transfers resources of the charity for the personal benefit of a member, director or trustee of the charity which could include excessive salaries, or interest free loans);

---

[82] "Guidelines for applying sanctions" by Canada Revenue Agency is available online at: CRA <http://www.cra-arc.gc.ca/chrts-gvng/chrts/plcy/nwsnctns-eng.html>; and "Penalties and suspensions" of Canada Revenue Agency, available online at: CRA <http://www.cra-arc.gc.ca/chrts-gvng/chrts/plcy/csp/pnlts-eng.html#pnltrc>.

[83] For the percentage of the penalty, see "Penalties and suspensions" of Canada Revenue Agency, available online at: CRA <http://www.cra-arc.gc.ca/chrts-gvng/chrts/plcy/csp/pnlts-eng.html#pnltrc>.

- a registered charity issues improper receipts;

- a person provides false information for the purposes of a tax receipt, which could include incorrect valuation information of either the property gifted or the advantage received by the donor when making the donation; or if

- a registered charity makes a transfer to another registered charity for the purpose of delaying expenditures on charitable activities.

In addition, if a charitable foundation acquires control of a corporation a second time within the span of five years, if false information has been provided and the amount of the penalty imposed is in excess of $250,000, or if a charity has received a gift and issued a receipt on behalf of a registered charity under suspension, the registered charity will also face suspension of its ability to issue tax receipts and to receive funds from other charities for one year.[84]

Appeals Process

The appeals regime is intended to make the appeal process more accessible and affordable for registered charities and unsuccessful applicants for charitable status. Previously, the only avenue for challenging CRA's decisions on charitable matters was through the Federal Court of Appeal. Currently, CRA's existing internal objection review process extends to notices of a decision by CRA regarding the refusal, revocation or annulment of a charity's registration, the designation of a charity as a private or public foundation or a charitable organization, income tax assessments and reassessments of tax and penalties, and notices of suspension of tax-receipting privileges. Filing a notice of objection to the Minister of National Revenue with the CRA Appeals Branch is a required step before an appeal may be brought to the courts.[85]

If a charity disagrees with CRA's decision resulting from an objection, appeals in respect of decisions concerning refusals to grant registered charitable status and revocation of registered charitable status will continue to be made to the Federal Court of Appeal. However, with respect to the imposition of the monetary penalties

---

[84] Intermediate sanctions, such as penalties and taxes, are found in ss. 188.1 and 188.2 of the ITA.

[85] "Objections and appeals: Registered charities, registered Canadian amateur athletic associations (RCAAAs), and other listed qualified donees" of Canada Revenue Agency available online at: CRA <http://www.cra-arc.gc.ca/gncy/cmplntsdspts/chrts-eng.html>.

and/or the revocation tax or suspension of its tax receipting privileges, a charity may appeal the decision to the Tax Court of Canada under either the informal procedure (expected to apply if the amount of penalties or tax is less than $12,000 per assessment) or general procedure.

Fundraising Policy

Fundraising is not a charitable purpose in itself; however, charities can fundraise when doing so is within CRA's legal parameters, which are outlined in CRA's fundraising policy.[86] A charity's fundraising activity is unacceptable when it is:

- one of the charity's purposes
- an unrelated business
- deceives the public
- provides more than just an incidental private benefit
- illegal and against public policy

CRA's policy on fundraising by registered charities lists certain indicators of unacceptable fundraising, which are considered by the CRA when it evaluates a charity's fundraising activities. The policy also lists factors that may influence the CRA's evaluation, such as the small size of the charity.

RISK MANAGEMENT AND LIABILITY

The operations of nonprofits have become complex and the possibility of litigation against them occurring as a result of their operations is greater than ever before. The exposure of nonprofits to liability goes further than the loss of assets and/or the insolvency or winding up of a nonprofit. Directors may also personally face legal actions against themselves by donors, members, third parties, and governmental authorities for breach of their fiduciary duties or even breach of trust in failing to adequately protect or apply the assets of a nonprofit. Given these increases, there is a greater need to protect assets from lawsuits and creditors on a pro-active basis.

---

[86] See CG-013, "Fundraising by Registered Charities", available online at: <http://www.cra-arc.gc.ca/chrts-gvng/chrts/plcy/cgd/fndrsng-eng.html>.

Black's Law Dictionary defines "risk" as the "chance of injury, damage or loss", and it defines "risk management" as the "procedures or systems used to minimize accidental losses".[87] Although the levels of risk are subjective and difficult to quantify for such a diverse sector as the nonprofit sector in Canada, it is important for directors and members to understand the impact of risk on the operation of their organizations. As most directors and managers already understand, risk cannot be completely eliminated, but it can be managed through conscientious and careful planning and organization. Liability and risk management must be reviewed from many different standpoints, including from the level of the organization or corporation and from the level of directors and officers.

Level of the Organization/Corporation

Choice of Non-profit or Charitable Structure

As was discussed above in the section "Legal Structure for Nonprofit Organizations", the choice of the appropriate non-profit or charitable structure is a primary consideration for managing risk and liability. Depending on the choice of legal structure, risk and liability will rest with different parties. For instance, an unincorporated association has no legal capacity to sue, be sued, or to contract, and only derives its existence from its members. As such, the unincorporated association can bear no liability for the acts or omissions of its members; instead it is the individual members who will ultimately be liable (Bourgeois (2012 at 23, 228)). Like the unincorporated association, a trust has no legal personality. Thus, all actions are carried out by the trustee, who must bear the liability for any acts or omissions. However, the trustee acting in accordance with its obligations and authority as trustee is entitled to be reimbursed for reasonable expenses, so the trust and/or the beneficiaries may ultimately bear the financial liability for any claim (Waters (2005)). A corporation without share capital, on the other hand, *is* a separate legal entity from that of its members, and therefore has the legal capacity to sue, to be sued, and to contract with other parties. With legal capacity, the incorporated corporation without share capital bears the liability for breach of contract, negligence, or other suable actions of its directors, officers, members, staff, volunteers and agents.

---

[87] *Black's Law Dictionary* (1999), *s.v.* "risk" and "risk management".

Vicarious Liability (Directors, Officers, Staff, Volunteers)

Vicarious liability imposes liability upon an employer or principal for the conduct of an employee or agent, on the grounds that the employer or principal should be held accountable for losses to third parties that arise from the actions of the employee or agent. Unlike the principle of personal liability, vicarious liability does not require that the employer or principal actually cause the loss sustained by the third party. Liability is imposed on the employer or principal with the rationale that the loss is the result of a reasonably foreseeable risk and attributable to the employer's or principal's activities, and that it is reasonable that the employer or principal should be liable for the risk.

From a public policy point of view, vicarious liability is designed to ensure that parties undertaking risky enterprises take all reasonable measures to reduce the risk. It is a form of risk allocation, in keeping with the logic behind tort law in Canada; namely, losses will be suffered in our modern world, and we should be aware of the losses we cause, and should try to reduce the risks of such losses, or compensate for them when appropriate.

In the seminal case of *Bazley v. Curry*,[88] the Supreme Court of Canada provided a two-part approach for determining whether and when vicarious liability should be imposed on an employer.[89] First, a court should determine whether there are precedents that unambiguously determine whether vicarious liability should be imposed under the circumstances in the case. Second, "[i]f prior cases do not clearly suggest a solution, the next step is to determine whether vicarious liability should be imposed in light of the broader policy rationales behind strict liability."

In general, vicarious liability will be imposed by the courts where the plaintiff can establish the following: (1) the relationship between the tortfeasor (*i.e.*, the employee) and the person against whom liability is sought (*i.e.*, the employer) is sufficiently close; and (2) the wrongful act was sufficiently connected to the conduct authorized by the employer. To determine whether a sufficient connection exists under part 2 of the test referred to above, the Supreme Court of Canada has set out some factors to consider:

---

[88] [1999] S.C.J. No. 35, [1999] 2 S.C.R. 534 (S.C.C.) (hereinafter "*Bazley*").

[89] *Ibid.*, at para. 15. See also *Jacobi v. Griffiths*, [1999] S.C.J. No. 36, [1999] 2 S.C.R. 570 at para. 31 (S.C.C.).

- the extent to which the wrongful conduct may have furthered the employer's enterprise;

- the extent to which the wrongful act was related to friction, confrontation or intimacy inherent in the employer's enterprise;

- the opportunity that the enterprise of the employer or principal affords to the employee or agent to abuse his or her power;

- the extent of power conferred on the employee in relation to the victim; and

- the vulnerability of potential victims to wrongful exercise of the employee's power.[90]

Recent case law has affirmed that charities and non-profit organizations can be held vicariously liable for the conduct of their employees and agents, and they do not enjoy any special "immunity" on account of their nonprofit status.[91] As a result, charities and non-profits have a significant obligation to carefully supervise and monitor the conduct of their employees, especially where those employees are in a position of power and authority over others. The importance of such supervision and implementation of risk management mechanisms — such as a policy against child abuse — cannot be understated.[92]

However, in addition to these due diligence steps, it is important for charities to assess and, if necessary, modify their organizational structure so that, in the event that a tort claim is successfully brought against the charity, liabilities may be contained and charitable property protected.[93]

Anti-terrorism Legislation Compliance

A discussion of anti-terrorism legislation compliance may seem odd in a work about nonprofit organizations, yet they, with charities and non-governmental organizations (NGOs), have been identified as a "crucial

---

[90] *Ibid.*, at para. 41.

[91] See, *ibid.*, where the Supreme Court of Canada rejected the argument that nonprofit organizations should be shielded from tort liability in the public interest. See also *John Doe v. Bennett*, [2004] S.C.J. No. 17, [2004] 1 S.C.R. 436 at para. 24 (S.C.C.), where the Supreme Court of Canada confirmed that nonprofit status in itself would not be sufficient grounds to obviate a finding of vicarious liability. For more information see Mervyn F. White, "Supreme Court of Canada Brings Clarity to Vicarious Liability of Churches in Canada" (2005), *Church Law Bulletin* No. 11, online at: <http://www.carters.ca/pub/bulletin/church/2005/chchlb11.htm>.

[92] Carter (2008).

[93] *Ibid.*

weak point" (Financial Action Task Force (2002a)) in money laundering and terrorist financing initiatives in the international community, and are thus subjected to increasing scrutiny by government.[94] The fear remains that "non-profit organizations that engage in raising or disbursing funds for charitable, religious, cultural, educational, social or fraternal purposes, or for the carrying out of other types of 'good works' [will be] ... misused or exploited by the financiers of terrorism".[95] In addition to sham organizations, the international community has witnessed instances where terrorist organizations were supported without the knowledge of the donor or directors of the organization.[96]

Although nonprofit and charitable organizations were not the primary target of the far-reaching counterterrorism legislation that was introduced in Canada following the terror attacks on New York and Washington, D.C., on September 11, 2001, the organizations and directors of those organizations have much to fear should they become the unwitting assistants of terror organizations. Nonprofit organizations should be aware of some of the key pieces of legislation that were affected by Canada's *Anti-terrorism Act*,[97] including the *Criminal Code*[98] and the *Proceeds of Crime (Money Laundering) and Terrorist Financing Act*.[99] Of particular note in the *Criminal Code* amendments is the introduction of offences for "facilitating" a terrorist activity or organization.[100] Despite government claims to the contrary, these poorly drafted sections may ensnare otherwise innocent organizations that unknowingly assist terrorist organizations.

The *Proceeds of Crime (Money Laundering) and Terrorist Financing Act* also places a heavy burden on organizations that deal in

---

[94] An important resource in this respect is <http://www.antiterrorismlaw.ca>. In particular, see, *e.g.*, Carter (2005) and Chapter 18: Anti-terrorism and Money Laundering Issues for Charities in Jane Burke Robertson, Terrance S Carter & Theresa LM Man, *Corporate and Practice Manual for Charitable and Not-For-Profit Organizations* (Toronto: Carswell, 2013).

[95] Financial Action Task Force *Combating the abuse of non-profit organizations: Best practices* (2013) para. 3, available online at: FATF-GAFI <http://www.fatf-gafi.org/media/fatf/documents/reports/Combating_the_abuse_of_NPOs_Rec8.pdf>.

[96] See, *e.g.*, Financial Action Task Force, *Report on Money Laundering Typologies 2002-2003* (2003), online at: FATF-GAFI <http://www.fatf-gafi.org/media/fatf/documents/reports/2002_2003_ML_Typologies_ENG.pdf>. See Financial Action Task Force *Terrorist Financing,* (2008), online at: FATF-GAFI <http://www.fatf-gafi.org/media/fatf/documents/reports/FATF%20Terrorist%20Financing% 20Typologies%20Report.pdf> for case studies.

[97] S.C. 2001, c. 41 (proclaimed in force December 24, 2001).

[98] R.S.C. 1985, c. C-46.

[99] S.C. 2000, c. 17.

[100] See, *e.g.*, *Criminal Code*, R.S.C. 1985, c. C-46, at ss. 83.18, 83.19, 83.21 and 83.22 (all enacted 2001, c. 41, s. 4).

large financial transactions to retain detailed records and report information to the Financial Transactions & Reports Analysis Centre of Canada (FINTRAC). Failure to do so carries significant penalties and the possibility of seizure of funds.

These provisions highlight the need for due diligence on the part of the nonprofit organization. Not only should there be strict controls on the financial operations of the organization, but the operational side of the organization needs to be carefully managed. Policies demonstrating intent to comply with anti-terrorism legislation should be in place and nonprofit organizations should be able to document their administrative, managerial and policy control over their operations. This necessarily includes auditing or investigating other organizations with which the nonprofit organization works, overseeing activities conducted, and accounting for funds expended.

Before 2009, there was very little practical guidance for charities or nonprofit organizations with respect to compliance with anti-terrorism legislation and due diligence procedures. In April 2009, Canada Revenue Agency released "Checklist for Charities on Avoiding Terrorist Abuse" (the "Checklist")[101] in order to provide guidance to Canadian registered charities in identifying vulnerabilities to terrorist abuse and developing good management practices. Though the Checklist falls short of providing comprehensive guidelines for compliance with Canada's complex body of anti-terrorism legislation, the Checklist is an important first step in assisting charities to develop due diligence procedures.

The full extent to which the government will enforce anti-terrorism provisions against unwitting organizations remains to be seen. However, a growing aspect of the federal government's anti-terrorism initiative is the designation of organizations to a list established under the terrorism provisions of section 83.05 of the *Criminal Code*. The entities on this list include widely recognized foreign organizations, such as Hezbollah and Al-Qaeda, and the World Tamil Movement, which was a Canadian nonprofit organization. The list currently includes 50 entities that are deemed to have facilitated or been associated with terrorist activities.[102]

---

[101] Available online at: <http://www.cra-arc.gc.ca/chrts-gvng/chrts/chcklsts/vtb-eng.html>.

[102] Carter, S.S. (2008). The currently listed entities Webpage is available online at: Public Safety Canada <http://www.publicsafety.gc.ca/cnt/ntnl-scrt/cntr-trrrsm/lstd-ntts/crrnt-lstd-ntts-eng. aspx>.

As a further illustration of the government's enforcement of these anti-terrorism provisions, on March 14, 2008, the first person in Canada to be charged under Canada's anti-terrorism financing laws was arrested in New Westminster, British Columbia. The accused, a Toronto area resident, was charged with committing an offence under section 83.03(b) of the *Criminal Code* — the section that makes it an offence to provide, or make available property or services for terrorist purposes. It is alleged that the accused solicited donations in British Columbia for the World Tamil Movement (WTM), a humanitarian organization, which the police claim is the leading Liberation Tigers of Tamil Eelam ("LTTE") front organization in Canada.[103]

Level of Directors and Officers

Roles and Duties of Directors and Officers

The most basic role or duty of a director of a nonprofit organization is to manage the affairs of the corporation.[104] In essence, the directors are the guiding minds of the corporation, while the officers and staff manage the day-to-day operations. Managing the affairs of the corporation encompasses a broad spectrum of duties, including: ensuring the organization adheres to and carries out the goals of the corporation; setting long-term objectives in accordance with these goals; ensuring financing stability; assessing the corporation's performance; establishing policies; and being the public face of the corporation (Burke-Robertson & Drache (2002, at 5-1 and 5-2)). Any or all of these duties may be limited by the organization's by-laws; however, the directors must always be able to demonstrate that they "manage or supervise the management of the activities and affairs"[105] of the corporation in accordance with the governing legislation.

In managing the affairs of the corporation, a director has a number of fiduciary duties, including: a duty to act honestly; a duty of loyalty; a duty of diligence or to act in good faith; a duty to exercise power; a duty of obedience; a duty to avoid conflict of interest; a duty of prudence; and a duty to continue. Many of these duties are self-

---

[103] Carter, T.S. & S.S. Carter (2008).

[104] See, *e.g.*, *Canada Not-for-profit Corporations Act*, S.C. 2009, c. 23, s. 124. A useful reference tool in this respect is available online at: Industry Canada <http://www.ic.gc.ca/eic/site/cd-dgc.nsf/eng/h_cs04953.html>.

[105] *Canada Not-for-profit Corporations Act*, S.C .2009, c. 23, s. 124 (CNCA). Also refer to s. 21 of the Ontario *Not-for-Profit Corporations Act, 2010*, S.O. 2010, c. 15 (ONCA) [not yet proclaimed in force].

explanatory, but some comments are warranted. The duty to exercise power is essentially a requirement that the director fulfills his or her role, pursues the organization's objectives and does not fail to supervise delegated tasks. Similarly, the duty to continue requires a resigning director to ensure there is an adequate replacement. Resignation will not avoid liability and may constitute breach of fiduciary duty where the director put his or her own interests ahead of those of the corporation.

Standard of Care and Duty of Care

The standard of care is a legal concept referring to the degree of care expected of an individual in relation to a duty to other individuals. An individual will only incur liability where his or her conduct falls below that which is expected by the community. Texts and case law generally do not discuss the standard of care expected of a business corporation, let alone a nonprofit corporation. As such, any discussion of standard of care will generally relate to that which is expected of directors and officers. This is likely because the corporation is a fictionalized person while a trust or unincorporated association has trustees and members standing in front of them. Conceptually, it is difficult to apply a standard of care to a fictional person, but the courts will hold a corporation both directly and vicariously liable for the acts or omissions of its directors, officers, staff and volunteers. In assessing liability against a corporation, the court will apply the "reasonable person" standard; that is, whether the corporation acted in the same manner as a reasonably careful person in the circumstances (Osborne (2003)). For example, a court (and therefore an effective risk manager) would ask: "Did the nonprofit corporation exercise reasonable care in training its staff?"

The duty of care of directors and officers is now codified in the new CNCA and ONCA. Under the CNCA, directors and officers are required to act honestly and in good faith with a view to the best interests of the corporation, and to exercise the care, diligence and skill of a reasonably prudent person in comparable circumstances.[106] These duties are judged on an objective standard of care. In other words, in determining whether a director or officer has breached his or her duty to the corporation, the court will test the person's actions against that of a reasonably prudent person. This standard is lower than the

---

[106] CNCA, s. 148(1).

common law subjective standard of care, assessing a person's actions against what may reasonably be expected from a person of his or her knowledge and experience.

As well, directors and officers are required to comply with the CNCA and its regulations, the articles, the by-laws and any unanimous member agreement.[107] Directors (but not officers) are subject to additional duties under the CNCA. For example, directors must be informed about the corporation's activities and to ensure the lawfulness of the articles and the purpose of the corporation.[108]

In meeting their duties, directors and officers would not be liable if they have exercised the care, diligence and skill that a reasonably prudent person would have exercised in comparable circumstances, including reliance in good faith on reports prepared by professionals. Directors (but not officers) may also rely on the corporation's financial statements prepared by the corporation's public accountant.[109]

The ONCA provides that every director and officer has a duty to act honestly and in good faith with a view to the best interests of the corporation. They must also exercise the care, diligence and skill that a reasonably prudent person would exercise in comparable circumstances, which, like the CNCA, reflects an objective as opposed to a subjective standard of care.[110] The ONCA also provides directors with a reasonable due diligence defence. This defence applies where a director has exercised the care, diligence and skill that a reasonably prudent person would have exercised in comparable circumstances.[111] However, in spite of requests by the nonprofit sector, the ONCA does not contain a partial liability shield similar to that which is found under the Saskatchewan *Non-profit Corporations Act, 1995,*[112] that would otherwise limit the liability of directors or officers for non-pecuniary and pecuniary losses stemming from acts or omissions of the corporation or of any of its directors, officers, employees or agents.

Liability of Directors

Enhanced corporate governance is a popular slogan for both business corporations and nonprofit corporations. Good governance, which includes such principles as participation in decision-making;

---

[107] *Ibid.*, s. 148(2).

[108] *Ibid.*, s. 148(3).

[109] *Ibid.*, s.149 and s. 150.

[110] ONCA, s. 43(1).

[111] *Ibid.*, s. 44.

[112] See s. 112.1(1) of Saskatchewan's *Non-profit Corporations Act, 1995,* S.S. 1995, c. N-4.2.

accountability and transparency; responsive, effective, and efficient performance; and sound rule of law, is the responsibility of the directors. In the absence of a limitation on liability for directors (which is available only in Saskatchewan, as previously discussed),[113] acting in good faith will not be sufficient to avoid liability. As such, directors who do not perform to the expected standard of care may be liable for the damages that result from their actions.

Additionally, both provincial and federal statutes impose liability on directors in specific circumstances. For example, directors of nonprofit corporations are jointly and severally liable to employees for unpaid wages to a maximum of six months wages while they are directors and for the two years after their director position ends.[114] On a related issue, they are liable for the corporation's failure to remit an employee's source deductions to the tax authorities, along with interest and penalties.[115] Directors will also be held liable for the corporation's failure to meet reporting, record-keeping, or filing requirements under various pieces of legislation.[116] As such, directors are subject to both pecuniary and criminal liabilities.[117]

Rights and Powers

It goes without saying that directors would be unable to effectively carry out their duties without concomitant rights and powers. Given the heavy burden directors carry with respect to liability for their actions and the actions of the corporation, directors have a right to

---

[113] In Saskatchewan's *Non-profit Corporations Act, 1995*, directors and officers of non-profit corporations are not personally liable for acts or omissions connected with their responsibilities, but note that this immunity only applies to acts done in good faith and not to fraud or the taking of profit. (Government of Saskatchewan, Ministry of Justice, The Non-profit Corporations Act, 1995 <http://www.justice.gov.sk.ca/Non-profit-Corporations-Act-1995>).

[114] Industry Canada, Corporations Canada, New Legislation, Canada Not-for-profit Corporations Act guide available online at: <http://www.ic.gc.ca/eic/site/cd-dgc.nsf/eng/cs05004. html#fnb46-ref>. See also, *Canada Not-for-profit Corporations Act*, S.C. 2009, c. 23, s.146; Ontario *Not-for-Profit Corporations Act, 2010*, S.O. 2010 c. 15, s. 40 [not yet in force].

[115] ITA, s. 227.1(1).

[116] See, *e.g.*, CNCA, s. 262 or ITA, s. 238.

[117] Although there are no statistics on the number of directors that have had pecuniary and criminal liabilities imposed upon them, there are some interesting examples. In *Ontario (Public Guardian and Trustee) v. National Society for Abused Women and Children*, [2002] O.J. No. 607 (Ont. S.C.J.), the three directors of the charitable organization were ordered to repay the nearly $1 million they funneled into non-arm's length fundraising corporations and were prohibited from acting as directors of any other charitable organization until the funds had been repaid. Noting that only $1,365 of the nearly $1 million raised made its way to charitable work, the court stated (at para. 1) "A distinct odour emanates from the facts of this case."

unimpaired access to all resources of the corporation in order to effectively perform their duties. This necessarily requires access to books and records, notice of meetings, an equal right to vote at the meetings, and a right to inspect and approve or disapprove the minutes of previous meetings of the board.

Like the director's rights, the powers complement their duties. In this respect, directors have the power to manage the affairs of the corporation, the power to borrow money in accordance with statutory procedures, the power to make investments on behalf of the corporation and the power to dispose of property.[118]

Statutory Protection

Unlike their business counterparts, there has been little in the past in the way of statutory protection for directors of nonprofit organizations. However, section 149 of the CNCA and section 44 of the ONCA now provide a limited due diligence defence for directors when they exercise the care, diligence and skill of a reasonably prudent person, which includes relying in good faith on financial statements and reports from officers or persons whose professions lend credibility to the statements made by them, such as lawyers and accountants.

There is a common law rule prohibiting directors of nonprofit organizations from profiting or benefiting directly or indirectly from their position. Should any benefit accrue, the director would be in breach of his or her fiduciary duty and would be held accountable to the organization for the benefits received. This translates into a practice of avoiding conflicts of interest or even the appearance of a conflict of interest. The CNCA aims to prevent conflicts between the corporation and directors, so a director must disclose to the corporation any conflict of interest,[119] although for charitable corporations such disclosure is not sufficient to permit a benefit to be paid to a director without court approval.

---

[118] See CNCA ss. 28 and 33.
[119] CNCA, s. 141.

Other Means of Reducing Risks

Indemnification, Insurance and Risk Transfer[120]

Indemnification and insurance are key considerations for both the nonprofit organization and any individual considering being a director.[121] Indemnification is the process by which the corporation agrees to cover the cost of, or compensate the director for, any loss or damage sustained as a result of the acts or omissions of the director in his or her capacity as a director of the organization.[122] Of course, this would not cover illegal acts or omissions, or directors who are in breach of their fiduciary duty. In order for a nonprofit corporation to provide indemnity for its directors, such a power must be included in the organization's by-laws. This provides a measure of protection for the director, thereby enabling the organization to attract capable individuals to the position. It may also be prudent for individuals who consider becoming a corporate director (whether it be for a for-profit corporation or a nonprofit corporation) to obtain personal indemnity agreements from the corporation. This agreement will increase a director's likelihood of avoiding personal responsibility for the legal costs associated with possible claims arising from his or her responsibilities as a director.[123] However, such an indemnity is worthless if the organization does not have sufficient assets to cover significant claims, which is likely the case if there is a sexual abuse claim.

Insurance, on the other hand, could prove to be an important safety net if the nonprofit corporation is involved in risky operations that could result in significant claims made against the organization and its directors. There are a variety of types of insurance an organization should consider obtaining, depending on the size and type of its activities. In addition to general liability insurance, directors and officers liability insurance (D&O) is one type that is appropriate for all nonprofit organizations, as it provides protection in relation to the board's acts or omissions, and any activities conducted under the auspices of the board of directors.

---

[120] For a useful resource in this respect, see Carter & Demczur (2008).

[121] See CNCA s. 151 about indemnification of directors or officers. A corporation can purchase insurance, compensate directors for losses suffered while completing their directorship duties, or advance funds to directors for the costs spent defending themselves in a lawsuit. See Industry Canada's explanation of important CNCA sections available online at: <http://www.ic.gc.ca/eic/site/cd-dgc.nsf/eng/cs05004.html#fnb48>.

[122] *Black's Law Dictionary* (1999), *s.v.* "indemnification" and "indemnify".

[123] See Oh (2009).

Regardless of the type of insurance obtained, directors should review the policies in order to determine any limitations. These limitations may be in the form of the type of activity covered, the number of claims permitted in a time period, or the timeframe in which an action will be covered (*i.e.*, whether the policy will provide coverage in 2014 for an incident that occurred in 1995, or if a policy purchased in 2014 will cover any claims made in 2018 as a result of incidents occurring in 2014).

Another method of reducing risk that should be considered is risk transfer. In some cases, charities and non-profit organizations may want to develop and administer effective liability shields in the form of informed consents, disclaimers, releases, waivers and indemnities for program participants as necessary. In this regard, liability risk can be transferred from the organization and its directors to program participants.

Due Diligence in Operations (Maintaining the Corporation)

Exercising due diligence is the most effective way for directors to protect themselves from liability. The directors must also carry out their due diligence to protect the interests of the organization and its charitable purposes (Bourgeois (2006 at 219)). Due diligence includes utilizing the rights and powers of the director and seeking professional advice when necessary. However, it will not provide a defence for all statutory violations, *i.e.*, failure to comply with the anti-terrorism legislation. As Bourgeois notes (2001, at 17):

> Due diligence is both a question of fact and of law. What is due diligence will depend on the circumstances, the type of organization and the activities undertaken. In general, directors or officers will meet their obligations if they act *reasonably, prudently and sagaciously* and within the law, including the objects of the organization and the scope of their position or office.

(Emphasis added.)

As such, directors will be exercising due diligence in circumstances in which they fulfill their primary duty of managing the affairs of the corporation. As noted above, this necessarily includes ensuring that meetings are held as required, that the director attends the meetings and is prepared to discuss matters, that corporate records are duly maintained, and that reports are submitted as required. There is the accompanying need for ongoing training and education in order to ensure directors maintain and enhance their skills and knowledge in the area of the organization's operation, as well as the applicable legislation and case law. In certain circumstances, it will be necessary for the directors to obtain advice from qualified professionals, which can assist in insulating directors from liability. Such circumstances include situations requiring legal, accounting, or financial expertise.

Legal Risk Management Committees

Another means of reducing risk is through establishing legal risk management committees to conduct the reviews of the organization's policies, activities and associations, and identify risk areas. These committees should conduct a comprehensive audit of the corporation's assets, structure, legal relationships (contractual and non-contractual), and particularly activity-related risks, and the committee should advise the board on implementing due diligence and risk management procedures.

Crisis Management Committees

Like any other organization, charities and non-profits face the possibility of dealing with sudden emergencies or disasters that threaten their ability to survive. For example, an organization may run out of funds causing it to be unable to meet payroll requirements. Or perhaps a nonprofit has been publicly accused of wrongdoing directly or indirectly leaving the organization with significant damage to its credibility and reputation. In these circumstances, the organization will be better equipped to survive the catastrophe if it has an existing crisis management plan.

While a risk management committee tends to concentrate its efforts on avoiding risk in everyday and urgent matters, crisis management committees focus more on events and circumstances that have the potential to completely disrupt an organization's operations. A crisis management committee should consist of a group diverse enough to consider a full range of crises that an organization might face. Some potential disasters that the committee should consider in developing strategies include: death or injury of a key individual; loss of access to the use of facilities and equipment; loss of crucial information; and intense media scrutiny leading to irreparable damage to a charity's reputation.[124]

---

[124] A useful resource in this respect is: <http://www.imaginecanada.ca>.

Independent Legal Advice

Directors should obtain independent legal advice in situations where they may be facing a high degree of exposure to personal liability. As noted above, simply resigning is not necessarily a measure that will insulate a director from potential liability. As such, before considering resigning from the board, a director should obtain independent legal advice.

Size of the Board

Careful consideration should be given to the appropriate number of directors required to effectively operate the nonprofit corporation. A smaller board will give directors more effective control over the management of the corporation's affairs, and will help reduce the number of individuals who will be exposed to liability.

Transfer of Assets

No proactive or due diligence steps can completely shield a director from all potential liability. In circumstances where the organization participates in high-risk activities, *i.e.*, work with children, it may be advisable for the director to transfer his or her personal assets to his or her spouse in advance of joining the board in order to aid in shielding the assets in the event of a finding of liability. However, such an action is not advisable after the director has joined the board as it may be viewed as a fraudulent conveyance in order to avoid creditors.

Checklists

The use of a checklist in order to ensure the nonprofit corporation has complied with all legal requirements is an effective tool in any corporation's risk management strategy. Whether it is prepared by the directors or available through professional advisors, a checklist can guide the board through its duties to ensure all bases are covered. A sample Legal Risk Management Checklist for Charities is available at <http://www.charitylaw.ca>.

REFERENCES

Black's Law Dictionary (1999), 7th ed. (St. Paul, MN: West Publishing, 1999).

D.J. Bourgeois, *The Law of Charitable and Not-for-Profit Organizations*, 4th ed. (Markham, ON: LexisNexis Canada, 2012).

D.J. Bourgeois, *Halsbury's Laws of Canada*, 1st ed. "Charities, Associations and Not-for-Profit Organizations" (Markham, ON: LexisNexis Canada, 2008).

D.J. Bourgeois, *Charities and Not-for-Profit Fundraising Handbook* (Markham, ON: LexisNexis Canada, 2006).

D.J. Bourgeois, *Charities and Not-for-Profit Administration and Governance Handbook* (Toronto: Butterworths, 2001).

D.J. Bourgeois, *The Law of Charitable and Not-for-Profit Organizations*, 3d ed. (Toronto: Butterworths, 2002).

B. Bucknall, "Conventional and Unconventional Parties: How Documents Are Engrossed and Executed" in P.M. Perell & S.H. Troister, eds., *LSUC Special Lectures, 2002: Real Property Law* (Toronto: Irwin Law, 2002).

R.J. Burke-Robertson & A.B. Drache (2002), *Non-Share Capital Corporations* (Toronto: Carswell, 2002).

R.J. Burke-Robertson, T.S. Carter & T.L.M. Man, *Corporate and Practice Manual for Charitable and Not-For-Profit Corporations* (Toronto: Thomson Carswell, 2013).

Canada, Department of Finance, *The Budget Plan, 2004* (Ottawa: Department of Finance Canada, 2004).

Canadian Encyclopedic Digest, "Associations and Not-for-Profit Corporations", vol. 1, title 1 at §1 (Toronto: Thomson Carswell, 2008), available on Westlaw Canada.

T.S. Carter, M.E. Hoffstein & A.M. Parachin, eds., *Charities Legislation & Commentary, 2014 Edition* (Markham, ON: LexisNexis Canada, 2013).

T.S. Carter, "First Charge Laid Under Canada's Anti-Terrorism Financing Regime" *Charity Law Update*, March 2008 at 7, online at: <http://www.charitylaw.ca>.

T.S. Carter & S.S. Carter, "First Canadian Non-Profit Added to Terrorism List", *Anti-terrorism and Charity Law Alert* No. 15, June 25, 2008, online at: <http://www.antiterrorismlaw.ca>.

T.S. Carter & J.M. Demczur, "Legal Risk Management Checklist for Charities" and "Legal Risk Management Checklist for Not-for-Profit Organizations" October 2008, online at: <http://www.charitylaw.ca>.

T.S. Carter, "Strategies for Protecting Charitable Assets Through Multiple Corporate Structures" (Toronto: The Canadian Institute, 2008).

T.S. Carter, "The Impact of Anti-terrorism Legislation on Charities: The Shadow of the Law" September 27, 2005, online at: <http://www. antiterrorismlaw.ca>.

T.S. Carter, "Risk Protection" in P. Broder *et al.*, eds., *Primer for Directors of Not-for-Profit Corporations (Rights, Duties and Practices)* (Ottawa: Industry Canada, 2002).

T.S. Carter, "Pro-active Protection of Charitable Assets: A Selective Discussion of Liability Risks and Pro-active Responses" (Paper presented to the Law Society of Upper Canada, November 20, 2001).

T.S. Carter, "Fit to Be Tithed 2: National and International Charitable Structures: Achieving Protection and Control" (Toronto: Law Society of Upper Canada, 1998).

R. Couzin, "Some Reflections on Corporation Controls" (2005) 53 Can. Tax J. 305-332.

Financial Action Task Force, *Combating the Abuse of Non-Profit Organizations: Best Practices* (Paris: FATF Secretariat, 2013), online at: FATF-GAFI   <http://www.fatf-gafi.org/media/fatf/documents/reports/ Combating_the_abuse_of_NPOs_Rec8.pdf>.

Financial Action Task Force, *Terrorist Financing* (Paris: FATF Secretariat, 2008), online at: FATF-GAFI <http://www.fatf-gafi.org/ media/fatf/documents/reports/FATF%20Terrorist%20Financing%20Typo logies%20Report.pdf>.

Financial Action Task Force, *Combating the Abuse of Non-profit Organisations: International Best Practices* (Paris: FATF Secretariat, 2002(a)), online at: FATF-GAFI <http://www.fatf-gafi.org/media/ fatf/documents/recommendations/11%20FATF%20SRIX%20BPP%20S RVIII%20October%202003%20-%20COVER%202012.pdf>.

Financial Action Task Force, *Report on Money Laundering Typologies 2002-2003* (Paris: FATF Secretariat, 2003), online at: FATF-GAFI <http://www.fatf-gafi.org/media/fatf/documents/reports/2002_2003_ML_Typologies_ENG.pdf>.

L. Godel, "The How, Why and When of Using Multiple Corporate Structures" (2007) 21:1 The Philanthropist 18-35.

M.H. Hall *et al.*, *Cornerstones of Community: Highlights of the National Survey of Nonprofit and Voluntary Organizations* (Ottawa: Ministry of Industry for Statistics Canada, 2004).

M.H. Hall *et al.*, *Caring Canadians, Involved Canadians: Highlights from the 2007 Canada Survey of Giving, Volunteering and Participating* (Ottawa: Minister of Industry, 2009).

J. Loukidelis, "Comments on Certain Proposed Tax Rules Applicable to Charities: Gifts to Foreign Entities, Large Gifts and 'Split Receipts'" (2004) 18:4 The Philanthropist 261-302.

T.L.M. Man & T.S. Carter, "A Comparison of the Three Categories of Registered Charities" *Charity Law Bulletin No. 73*, July 21, 2005, online at: <http://www.charitylaw.ca>.

T.L.M. Man & T.S. Carter, "How do Charitable Organizations and Foundations Differ Under Income Tax?" *Lawyers Weekly* 25:16 (2 September 2005).

E.S.J. Oh, "Comment on Delaware Decision and Possible Need to Consider Director Indemnity Agreements" *Charity Law Bulletin No. 157*, February 25, 2009, online at: <http://www.charitylaw.ca>.

P.H. Osborne, *The Law of Torts*, 2d ed. (Toronto: Irwin Law, 2003).

C. Radu, "Public/Private Foundations – Issues and Planning Opportunities" (2009) 57 Can. Tax J. 119-142.

D.W.M. Waters, *Waters' Law of Trusts in Canada* (Toronto: Thomson Carswell, 2005).

Chapter 6

GOVERNMENT AND COMMUNITY RELATIONS

Kathy L. Brock
Queen's University

INTRODUCTION: MANAGING UP AND OUTWARDS

Change is a constant in the world of nonprofit organizations, particularly in their relations with other organizations and the public. Citizen demands shift according to population trends and preferences, causing nonprofit organizations to frequently reassess their programs, services and methods of operation. Economic trends may cause organizations to review their operations. These forces may cause nonprofit organizations to build new alliances, merge, reconsider existing relationships, or even cease operation.

In many cases, societal and economic changes may force changes in relations with governments but governments may also impose new demands or pressures through new contracting, funding, or accountability arrangements, by re-evaluating current services or program delivery, or by requiring nonprofit organizations to fulfill new roles in either the policy process or society. Managers of nonprofit organizations are expected to balance these shifting requirements. The most successful managers will respond positively to the new environments, ensuring their organizations are flexible in operations yet remain true to their missions and founding ideals.

This chapter examines the changing world of nonprofit organizations and the challenges affecting managers as they position their organizations to survive and thrive in this inconstant social, economic and political environment. Managers are increasingly expected to build more effective alliances within the nonprofit sector but also with the public and corporate sectors if they are to serve Canadians in an efficient and satisfying manner. To function effectively in this increasingly integrated world, an understanding is required of four dimensions of the changes as Figure 1 indicates.

Figure 1: Four Dimensions of Change Facing Canadian Nonprofit Organizations

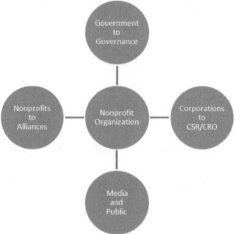

First, both the federal and provincial levels of government are moving away from traditional "command and control" models of government to what is known as a "governance model". This requires more reliance upon external organizations to advise on policies and deliver services and programs to the public. This shift requires the movement from traditional hierarchical relationships in which the government actors define the nature of the relationship to negotiated arrangements between the two sectors. However, in spite of this trend, tensions abound as governments often still attempt to retain control and enforce accountability requirements that are not negotiated but imposed and at variance with the nature of the service or program. Defining the relationship between the two sectors in largely instrumental terms, that is, according to what the two sectors can do for each other, further complicates the role of nonprofit organizations in the policy process by leaving the questions of advocacy and critical analysis of public policies in abeyance. Managers must cope with this ambivalence in the relationship and strive to negotiate flexible arrangements that meet citizen requirements.

Second, pressures are building on nonprofit managers to look to the corporate and business sector as allies in serving Canadians. Traditionally the two sectors have been viewed as more competitive and even antagonistic towards each other, pursuing objectives that are at variance. The "market failure" theory of nonprofit organizations characterized them as providing programs and services where the private sector had failed to offer a commercial variant of those goods or where public needs were created as a byproduct of the operation of the private sector.[1] In both cases, the nonprofit organizations were often critical of the operation of the private sector and profit motive. However, as public resources to nonprofit organizations have become increasingly constrained and as the corporate sector is engaging in more socially responsible endeavours and shifting towards more strategic investment in the nonprofit sector,[2] managers of nonprofit organizations must strive to develop relations with private sector actors that benefit both partners and enhance their operations but remain loyal to their principles. This is not an easy task, and one made more difficult by the contraction in the corporate sector in recent times.

Third, nonprofit organizations are building relations, both wanted and unwanted, with other nonprofit organizations. Increasingly, both public and private funders of nonprofit organizations are exerting pressure on their managers to look to creative means of co-operating with other organizations in order to reduce overlap or duplication in services or to rationalize management structures. The ultimate objective is to use funding dollars more efficiently and effectively. At the same time, many managers of nonprofit organizations are identifying benefits in partnering at the subsectoral level and reaching out to other organizations, independent of their funding situations.

A critical factor affecting the ability of organizations to forge strong alliances is the cost both in terms of dedicated monetary and personnel resources and the time required to nurture the relationships. However, relationships between individual organizations, networks at the community level, and sectoral alliances and multi-sectoral coalitions at the provincial and federal levels are all becoming increasingly necessary to the vibrancy and sustainability of the nonprofit sector.

Fourth, as nonprofit organizations exercise more influence in policy design, development and delivery, they have come under more scrutiny. The governance and accountability scandals affecting a small minority of nonprofit organizations in Canada and the United States in

---

[1]   The "market failure" theory of the nonprofit sector has been largely developed by economists and posits that nonprofits arise where the private sector fails to meet needs due to insufficient market incentives. For a discussion of earlier explanations of nonprofit, private and public sector relations see Young (1999); *cf.* Weisbrod (1988).

[2]   For comments on this trend see Austin and Seitanidi (2012a, 2012b).

the 1980s and 1990s created a new attentiveness in the media that has only been heightened with the increasing role of nonprofits in delivering services to needy portions of the population both home and abroad. As the level of public donations to nonprofit organizations increases, this scrutiny is intensified. Not only is the office of the Auditor General examining the relationships established between nonprofit organizations and government departments more closely and providing a source of material to the media, the media are tracking nonprofit organization performance on a more sustained and regular basis. Managers must adapt to the sometimes capricious but more often insightful and thoughtful world of investigative journalism. This requires developing good media relations skills — quick judgment, clear soundbites and sensible responses to probing questions, among other things.

The requirements imposed on managers of nonprofit organizations by the shifts in these relationships cannot be underestimated. Already coping with heavy workloads, managers must develop new skills and adapt to unstable environments. The first step, in not just coping but thriving amidst these challenges, is to understand the nature and significance of these shifts. This chapter begins that process but focuses primarily on relations with governments owing to their importance. While much of the focus is at the federal level of government, similar relationships and challenges exist at the provincial level of government.

GOVERNMENT TO GOVERNANCE: TRENDS IN GOVERNMENT–NONPROFIT RELATIONS

Nonprofit organizations are being increasingly drawn into the orbit of government. At the most sustained and complex level, these bisectoral arrangements involve multiple nonprofit organizations in delivering advice and engaging in policy development in areas ranging from international affairs and trade to childcare, to sports policies, to railway safety, to emergency response preparedness, right up to redefining the overall relationship between the two sectors.

In many cases, nonprofit organizations execute government policies through the provision of services to citizens. These relations tend to draw specific organizations into direct relations with specific government departments through contractual arrangements. In other cases, organizations may consider themselves independent of the governments and quite rightly may not be engaged in policy advice or service delivery. However, they are still increasingly affected by governments through the myriad of legislative arrangements and regulations governing their daily operations.

Relations between the two sectors have been further embedded as public funding of nonprofit endeavours has grown and nonprofit organizations have become more dependent on public sources of revenue. Finally, the identification of the nonprofit sector as an entity and important force in the Canadian economy has meant that the operation, capacity, reach and impact of the sector is being more carefully monitored than ever before with manifold policy implications that this data will yield. In times of economic downturn, the level of monitoring only increases even as public funding wanes.

As a result, senior officials and managers in the nonprofit world must pay increasing attention to trends and shifts in government and the economy, and in legislation affecting them or the sector as a whole. While the main responsibility for monitoring the relationship may be efficiently relegated to larger, well-resourced nonprofits or to umbrella organizations, managers of nonprofits are advised to keep abreast of new developments as they affect their particular organizations and to ensure that their interests are not overlooked or adversely affected. To perform this monitoring role effectively, nonprofit managers should have an understanding of:

- the pressures on government towards change and engagement of the nonprofit sector;

- the types of relationships being forged; and

- the challenges facing the two sectors as they strive to co-operate, including the recent attempt to redefine the parameters of governmental-nonprofit sector collaboration and co-operation. Each topic is addressed below.

Accountability, the Westminster Model of Government and Nonprofit Services

In a globalized and more competitive environment, governments are increasingly expected to build community, position their countries economically, and ensure national security in all its forms, all while their capacity is being diminished through reorganization, streamlining, and reducing expenditures (Reich (2001, at 207-10); cf. Krugman (2013)). The devolution of powers to external agencies and other governments has become a normal process of operation. The result is the increased need of government departments for collaboration with external agencies in the private and nonprofit sector and special operating agencies (Webb (2005)). The role of government becomes one of surveillance and monitoring to a greater extent and less of direct action and involvement as a service provider with the citizenry.

The paradox is that government not only remains answerable for these policies, services, and the quality of life enjoyed by citizens, but also must confront new expectations that are being formed. The emergence of an audit society, a citizenry that is more aggressive and less deferential, involves:

> ... demands for greater transparency in the conduct of public business by political and administrative officials, increased public access to government information, more explicit standards of public service entitlements and rights, enhanced citizen consultation and engagement in policy development and in the design and delivery of public services, and, among other things, public reporting on the performance of government ... .

(Aucoin & Heintzman (2000, at 245); Dean (2007)).

The result is a system that is measured less in terms of process and inputs and more in terms of outputs and outcomes. Efficiency and performance evaluation become the hallmarks of government action. Accountability is the rule.

What is accountability in government? The constant is that accountability literally means "to hold to account", or "capable of explanation". In a political system like the Canadian one characterized by the Westminster parliamentary model of government, accountability translates into: the ability of citizens to hold governments responsible for their expenditures, policies and programs through elections; the ability of politicians to oversee and ensure the responsiveness of the administrative branch of government to the public; and the power of the courts and tribunals to ensure that elected and non-elected public officials act in conformity with the powers of their offices. While the first two forms of accountability have traditionally operated in a hierarchical authority structure, the latter has imposed a horizontal check on the actions of government.

The notion of accountability within government has changed with the move towards governance as the accepted mode of operation (Sutherland (1991); Peters & Savoie (1999); *cf.* Thomas (1998)). Aucoin and Heintzman identify three central tenets of accountability within the parliamentary system as: "to control for the abuse and misuse of public authority"; "to provide assurance in respect to the effective use of public resources and adherence to public service values"; and, "to encourage and promote learning in pursuit of *continuous improvement* in governance and public management" (Aucoin & Heintzman (2000, at 244-45, emphasis in original)). They suggest that there is an inherent tension between these purposes of accountability but that improved performance and measurement (read efficiency) are not necessarily antithetical to improved accountability.

Hierarchical models of control and the objective of assurance can be balanced with efficiency and more horizontal modes of governance. Decentralization does not always equate with improved efficiency, just as hierarchy, uniformity and central control may be efficient and responsive to public need. Similarly, managing for outcomes and outputs may become just as ossified as a system of accountability measured on inputs and process. Good governance requires a certain fluidity and the right balance of the three purposes.

This change in government operations has had an impact on the relationship between the nonprofit sector and government as well as on the internal operations of the sector and organizations. To justify funding nonprofit organizations to provide services and programs previously administered by the public sector, governments must provide public assurances that the organizations will be held accountable for the efficiency and quality of those services and programs. Thus, while governments might be attracted by the flexibility enjoyed by nonprofit organizations in delivering goods and services, they will require certain operational methods to remain standard, such as financial management and accounting practices, key policy objectives including equity, forms of program evaluation and measurement, and adherence to human rights and environmental objectives.

Government requirements for accountability have been largely accepted by nonprofit organizations but do cause consternation for five principal reasons (see Table 1). First, greater accountability to the public sector is not uniformly embraced across the nonprofit sector. While many nonprofit organizations have generally been improving their accountability mechanisms, others have eschewed transparency and public accountability in favour of retaining their status as private organizations and adhering to internal codes of good practice consistent with their missions.

Table 1: Comparing Past and Present Accountability Requirements

Accountability within the Nonprofit Sector	
New Requirements	Traditional Requirements
Public, Transparent	Private, Internal Scrutiny
Formal Structures, Hierarchical	Informal Structures, Flexible
Shared Arrangements, Cooptation	Independence, Advocacy
Market Ethos	Community Ethos
Professionalism, Responsibility	Responsiveness, Collective Decision-making

Second, stricter public sector reporting requirements can increase bureaucracy within agencies at the cost of flexibility, informality, internal control over operations and responsiveness to members or beneficiaries. For example, an organization may perceive a need in the community that was not identified when the funding grant application was submitted and approved, and thus be constrained in its ability to respond to that need by the terms of the grant.

Third, dependence on government funding and entering into shared arrangements with government departments may compromise an organization's independence and its ability to serve as an advocate for the sector or to criticize government policy in that area. Organizations may become stakeholders in policies instead of agents of change and improvement. Certainly organizations speak of a hesitancy to engage in political activity given the restrictions on charities at the federal level of government. But even at the provincial level, if organizations perceive that they may be adversely affected by a negative perception in government created by their adoption of a public stance on an issue, they will be less likely to go public on the issue. Public debate suffers.

Fourth, in the quest for efficiency, governments have imposed upon nonprofit organizations principles of "new public management" including the market ethos,[3] transforming citizens into consumers and

---

[3]   "New public management" refers to a new paradigm in government operations. It embraces: providing high quality services valued by citizens; increasing the autonomy and decision-making authority of public managers; measuring and rewarding organizational and individual performance; investing in the necessary human and technological resources to enhance performance; and valuing competitiveness and openness with regards to the delivery of public services by the nonprofit, private and public sectors. For a good, practical discussion of these values, see, Blakeney & Borins (1998), esp. at 156-158.

beneficiaries of services into clients. And yet, this designation may obscure the more meaningful and personal relationship between the nonprofit organizations and their members or community served. For example, a home care organization may find itself constrained in the ability to allow its workers time just to chat with clients and limited to providing the specified meal or cleaning service even though the personal chats have a positive effect on the mental and emotional state of their clients.

Fifth, to meet the externally driven notions of accountability and efficiency, nonprofits may be obliged to move away from traditional strengths such as diversity and a democratic (or grassroots) ethos. Hierarchical decision-making with clearly defined points of responsibility becomes the norm instead of collective decision-making with diffuse responsibility. Professionalism instead of responsiveness becomes the standard. However, a well-governed organization will understand how to balance professional norms with community responsiveness by knowing when to ease the rules.

These concerns are valid and require vigilance among organizations as they adapt to the changing environment. However, there are key benefits for organizations in improved and closer relations between the nonprofit and public sectors. For example, public funding provides a measure of financial security for organizations to achieve their goals, particularly after an organization establishes a good reputation with a department. Federal and provincial government improvements to contracting-out procedures and clarification of performance measures enhance the desirability of such contractual arrangements. Further, meeting public sector requirements for accountability and establishing a record with public partners, improves organizations' chances of securing funding from or collaborating with other nonprofit or private sector organizations. Finally, these relationships may result in closer harmonization of public and nonprofit objectives and definitions of public service, to the benefit of both, and most of all, to the Canadian public.[4] How to maximize the benefits of relationships and minimize the tensions is the focus of the rest of this section.

---

[4] For an excellent guide on introducing and improving accountability measures in nonprofit organizations, see online at: Voluntary Sector Initiative <http://www.vsi-isbc.org/eng/funding/financial_guide/index.cfm>.

Understanding the Nature of the Relationship with Government

Traditionally, relationships between nonprofit organizations and governments have been characterized as conflictual or competitive. In this view, organizations were cast as critics of the state or as being threatened by state intervention. However, in a seminal study of the relationship between the state and the nonprofit sector, Benjamin Gidron, Ralph Kramer and Lester Salamon refuted this depiction in favour of a much more complex characterization of it (Gidron, Kramer & Salamon (1992)). They argue that the relationship between the state and the nonprofit sector will be influenced by the functions each side performs, the method of financing, the historical context, as well the political culture and social context of the relationship. In Canada, this would mean that, while some generalizations about the relationship might be made for the nonprofit sector at the federal level, these assumptions would not hold for the relationship between the state and sector in each province. Indeed, variations would even occur at the local or municipal level.

The relationship is even more complex. Since both governments and organizations have multiple roles, it is "quite possible for third sector organizations to have one set of relationships with government with respect to their service functions and another with respect to their representational or advocacy functions" (Gidron, Kramer & Salamon (1992, at 11)). While organizations might be critics of government policies and attack the very departments that fund them, governments may be equally torn between supporting organizations that deliver their programs and enforcing regulations. In the case of the Federal Government — Voluntary Sector Initiative ((VSI) 1999-2005), which brought together senior representatives from both sectors to redefine their relationship for the future, officials found themselves negotiating as equals at the VSI table but then dealing with each other in contractual arrangements at the level of department-to-organization with all the tensions implicit in those relations. This experience has been replicated in provinces like Newfoundland and Labrador, Alberta, Saskatchewan and Manitoba where initiatives similar to the VSI have been undertaken.[5]

---

[5]   The VSI was a joint endeavour between the Canadian government and national voluntary organizations to redefine the entirety of their relationship and set down good practices. It culminated in a bisectoral accord establishing the principles of a future relationship, two code of good practices to help implement those principles, and a multitude of changes ranging from introducing new technologies more widely in the sector to regulatory reforms, to the addition of the nonprofit sector to the satellite accounts of Statistics Canada, to the first survey of the nonprofit and voluntary sector in Canada, among other things. For indepth discussions of the VSI by two observers and advisors, see Brock (2001, 2004, 2005) and Phillips (2001, 2003).

To make sense of the complexity in these relations, Gidron, Kramer and Salamon offer four basic models of the types of relationships that can exist between the state and sector but then distinguish between two types of functions involved in service delivery, namely, the financing and authorization of services, and the delivery of services. Table 2 captures these models and their variations.

Table 2: Models of Government-Nonprofit Sector Relations

Function	Model			
	Government Dominant	Dual	Collaborative	Third Sector Dominant
Finance	Government	Government/ Third Sector	Government	Third Sector
Delivery	Government	Government/ Third Sector	Third Sector	Third Sector

In the Government Dominant model, typical of modern welfare state arrangements, the government is the main provider of both funding resources and services to the public, with the nonprofit sector playing a largely supplementary role determined by the state. In the case of the Third Sector Dominant model of relationships, typically found where there is opposition to a large role for the state in social welfare provisions, organizations play the key role in financing and delivering services.

In the Dual Model, the state and sector operate relatively autonomously of each other, both providing services and financing their operations. The sector might be either supplementary or complementary to the state but will be principal in its areas of operation.

In the Collaborative Model, both act but tend to work together and most often with the state as funder and sector organizations as service providers. The degree of autonomy and shared functions will be dependent on negotiations. The political appeal of organizations combined with the difficulty of governments in monitoring sector organizations means that the collaborative arrangements are more common than is usually assumed (Gidron, Kramer & Salamon (1992, at 16-19)).

In their study of state-sector relations in Canada, Susan Phillips and Katherine Graham accept that collaborative arrangements have become more common (Phillips & Graham (2000)). They suggest that it is useful to distinguish among the types of collaborative arrangements by placing them on a continuum as Figure 2 does.

Figure 2: Types of Collaborative Arrangements

Insular ➡➡ "Collabitation" ➡➡ Partnership ➡➡ Merger

At one end of the continuum, organizations operate autonomously with little or no collaboration with government, other organizations or the private sector. In the second phase, "collabitation",[6] organizations co-operate in some areas of the relationship but are competing for resources. The third phase foresees more co-operative relations with greater sharing of resources, risk, information and decision-making authority between the state and organizations. While equality is an ideal in a partnership, it cannot be assumed and the degree of equal authority in the relationship will depend on the negotiated terms. In the extreme form, collaboration can lead to mergers. State-imposed accountability requirements have meant that organizations are locked into the collabitation model of relations predominantly.

In positioning itself with the state, a nonprofit organization should first understand the fundamental nature of the relationship and how much power it has in the relationship. To do this, the nonprofit executive will ask the following type of questions: What is the best possible funding arrangement? Is the sector influential enough to negotiate more autonomy? How much does the state require its services? Are there other organizations that are likely to be competing for the same contract or resources? If so, are they better positioned? Is collaboration among competing organizations possible or desirable? Questions like these will determine the parameters of the relationship and inform any funding negotiations between the organization and government.

The second step in understanding the nature of the relationship is to examine the service or function involved. Is it one the state has traditionally provided? If so, more state control might be expected. Is it new? Does the organization have expertise needed by government? If so, the organization can assume more dominance in the relationship and negotiate for more autonomy. Is it an area better shared by both state and sector organizations? If so, the lines of decision-making and

---

[6]   The authors constructed this term to capture the idea of both collaboration and competition.

the scope of authority of both actors must be clearly delineated to ensure lines of responsibility are clear and conflict is minimized.

The third step in an organization's calculations concerns its advocacy or representational role. Where the state is dominant and the organization is more dependent on state funding and authorization, or where the organization has become a stakeholder in policies through shared authority, the organization will need to be more circumspect in its public criticism of government. As autonomy increases, organizations have more latitude to criticize government policies and programs, bearing in mind that positive relationships are more likely to develop in future when the criticisms are judiciously and discreetly offered and, on the state side, capable of acceptance.

The nature of the relationship between the state and organizations, and in particular the ability of organizations to perform an advocacy role, is heavily influenced in Canada by the federal regulatory regime in operation. A. Paul Pross and Kernaghan Webb document the regulatory reach of the federal government on the nonprofit sector in a groundbreaking study (Pross & Webb (2003)). They argue that viewing federal authority over the nonprofit sector as largely determined by its constitutional jurisdiction over taxation is misleading and too narrow. Instead, they identify a more comprehensive but often conflicting regulatory regime that encompasses seven areas of authority over charities and nonprofit organizations:

- Accountability
- Regulation of access to policy formulation
- Corporate status
- Direct funding
- Tax expenditure funding
- Regulation of lobbying
- Regulation of participation in elections

Each can impact on organizations and affect their operations in important ways. Given that provincial legislation for nonprofits may incorporate or mirror federal legislation, it is important to understand this regime.

The first two forms of regulatory measures range from the requirement for filing a tax form each year, to the obligatory audits and evaluations associated with government grants and programs, to adherence to criteria to maintain access to policy formation, to more informal requirements to ensure trust and co-operation between nonprofit and public officials. Corporate status for nonprofit organizations is desirable, especially to limit directors' liability, facilitate legal transactions, secure government contributions funding or raise the level of public donations by establishing a reputable form, and to ensure organizational stability and structure. However, acquiring such status may be expensive, confusing and time-consuming for many organizations while yielding few direct benefits (Pross & Webb (2003, at 77-79)). This process and the terms have been clarified under the *Canada Not-for-Profits Corporations Act*,[7] as requested by nonprofit sector leaders during the VSI but some ambiguity remains.

Similarly, obtaining recognized status under the *Income Tax Act*[8] may result in direct benefits for organizations, including the ability to issue tax receipts for donations in addition to being exempt from paying taxes (this latter provision applies to registered nonprofit corporations whether or not they are charities under the *Income Tax Act*). However, as with corporate status, obtaining charities status may be time-consuming, expensive, confusing, and imposes restrictive standards on the expenditure of funds, including the obligation to spend money as promised when raised, the duty to spend a majority (usually 80 per cent) of funds on charitable activities, the restriction on political advocacy (10 per cent of resources), and the need to meet a public benefits test.

Some of the burdens of charitable status were eased by federal activity flowing out of the VSI, including streamlining of the tax form, making the process for application and appeals of charitable status more transparent, and creating a nonprofit advisory board to the Canada Revenue Agency.[9] However, the advisory board has since been disbanded and still more work is required to enable nonprofits to obtain the full benefits of this tax expenditure (Levasseur (2012, at 181)). It should be noted too, that size of a charity or nonprofit organization will affect the application of these regulations.

The other three federal regulatory measures can circumscribe the behaviour of charities in important ways. While the impact of contribution agreements is discussed below under challenges facing nonprofits, it is important to mention the impact of regulations on electoral participation and lobbying.

---

[7] S.C. 2009, c. 23.

[8] R.S.C. 1985, c. 1 (5th Supp.).

[9] For a discussion of changes to federal regulations affecting corporate and tax status, see online at: Voluntary Sector Initiative <http://www.vsi-isbc.org/eng/regulations/index.cfm>.

The federal *Lobbying Act*[10] requires the formal registration of lobbyists who are attempting to influence government policy and who are either employees of an organization with part of their duties dedicated to that purpose or consultant lobbyists acting on behalf of an organization. However, as Pross and Webb point out, the requirements for registration are ambiguous and do not affect activities like "appearances before inquiries, parliamentary committees, and so on" (Pross & Webb (2003, at 98)). New regulations and guidelines clarify registration while adding to the complexity of this web of rules by including measures to strengthen transparency, enforce compliance and monitor public office holders more closely. Given the limited amount of "pure lobbying" done in the sector, the legislation has limited effect on organizations. However, managers of nonprofit organizations would be well advised to consult the registrar about the need to register if they do wish to influence government policy on contentious or important political issues.

In a similar vein, electoral regulations affecting the ability of nonprofit organizations to advertise during elections or engage in partisan activities do not apply to the vast majority of nonprofits (Pross and Webb (2003, at 101-04)). While advocacy organizations might see a benefit in direct partisan engagement in an election, most organizations would value their nonpartisan status. The regulations on partisan activities do not impede the ability of organizations to track issues during campaigns and conduct public awareness campaigns of party positions and issues. However, the caution is for nonprofits to remain objective, not critical or partisan lest they run afoul of election guidelines (Lawlor and Crandall (2011 at 509)).

While federal regulations are significant and may be considered to constitute a "regime" governing nonprofits as Pross and Webb conclude, most nonprofit organizations will have more daily interaction with provincial/territorial and municipal levels of government. For example, the *National Survey of Nonprofit and Voluntary Organizations* found that: "Most organizations rely more on provincial government funding than they do on funding from federal or municipal sources" (M.H. Hall *et al.* (2004, at 25)). Further, most organizations provide their services locally (about 64 per cent), regionally (about 19 per cent) or province-wide (about 9 per cent), thus necessitating more contact with the provincial and local levels of government (M.H. Hall *et al.* (2004, at 15)).

---

[10] R.S.C. 1985, c. 44 (4th Supp.).

The variations among these jurisdictions are too numerous to allow a summary here, however, nonprofit managers should inform themselves of the regulatory policies and practices within their own jurisdictions and govern themselves accordingly. Most governments at the provincial and territorial level have branches or units within government departments that deal with the nonprofit sector and can direct organizations to other areas of government that will affect their operation in most areas of nonprofit activities.[11] The table below provides a list of departments with primary responsibility for the nonprofit sector.

Some provinces, like Newfoundland and Labrador and New Brunswick have formally assigned responsibility for the voluntary sector to specific Ministers. Manitoba has taken the unusual step of dedicating a portal to the nonprofit sector. The Alberta and B.C. governments engaged in initiatives similar to the federal VSI but the B.C. initiative is in a hiatus at time of writing. Most provinces house responsibility for the sector within other ministries. For example, Ontario houses support for the nonprofit organizations in Community and Social Services and support for volunteerism in the Ministry of Citizenship and Immigration but the relationship with the nonprofit sector is complex and distributed among many departments (Brock (2010)). The trend in governments seems to be away from dedicated ministries and incorporating units responsible for nonprofit organizations into other departments. The difference between the current phase of government relations and the phase before the federal VSI is that governments are more conscious of the sector as a sector in its own right and of its potential as a partner.

Table 3: Provincial and Territorial Authorities

Provincial or Territorial Government	Lead Department or a Good Starting Point for Nonprofit Organizations
Newfoundland &Labrador	Minister Responsible for the Office of Public Engagement including the Volunteer and Non-profit Sector
Nova Scotia	Labour and Advanced Education, Volunteerism/Nonprofit Sector Division
Prince Edward Island	Department of Innovation and Advanced Learning Multiple departments have ties

---

[11] See the work of Peter Elson who is trying to chart the provincial and territorial regimes (Elson (2013)).

Provincial or Territorial Government	Lead Department or a Good Starting Point for Nonprofit Organizations
New Brunswick	Minister Responsible for Citizens' Engagement (Premier) Minister Responsible for Healthy and Inclusive Communities
Québec	Comité ministeriel de la solidarité
Ontario	Ministry of Citizenship and Immigration, Support for Nonprofit Organizations Ministry of Community and Social Services
Manitoba	Non-Profit Organization (NPO) Portal Ministry of Culture, Heritage, Tourism and Sport
Saskatchewan	Ministry of Social Services, Community-based Organizations
Alberta	Ministry of Culture, Community and Voluntary Services Alberta Nonprofit/Voluntary Sector Initiative
British Columbia	Ministry of Social Development and Social Innovation Government Non-Profit Initiative (dormant)
Nunavut	Ministry of Culture and Heritage
Northwest Territories	Ministry of Municipal and Community Affairs, Volunteerism and Youth
Yukon	Ministry of Community Services, Nonprofit Organizations/Societies

For practical advice on managing the government-nonprofit relationship at any level of government, nonprofit leaders should consult *Collaboration on Policy: A Manual developed by the Community-Government Collaboration on Policy*.[12] Developed by the Community Services Council, Newfoundland and Labrador and the Caledon Institute of Social Policy, the manual provides illustrative examples of successful initiatives in community development undertaken by the two sectors.

---

[12]   Online at: <http://www.caledoninst.org/Publications/PDF/772ENG.pdf>.

Challenges in Developing and Maintaining Relationships with Governments

The challenges in developing and maintaining relationships with governments will depend largely on the nature of the relationship. Is it primarily a policy, service delivery, funding or advocacy relationship? In many cases, organizations may have multiple relations with government departments and may have to manage competing sets of requirements. This section reviews some of the challenges in each type of relationship briefly.

There are three main challenges in developing and maintaining a policy relationship with government:

(1)   An organization must gain access to the relevant government actors in a policy field. While access to politicians may help place an issue on the policy agenda, to maximize influence over the longer term, organizations should build relations with senior officials in the departments. Obtaining access involves establishing an organization's legitimacy and policy research and development capacity in the area of interest. In an environment where there are a number of organizations operating, influence will be diluted by conflicting advice to officials. In these cases, organizations are most effective if they co-ordinate policy advice.

(2)   The second challenge involves maintaining policy access. This is critical to long-term policy influence since legislative or regulatory changes can be ongoing or take place over a number of years and through a number of changes of government. Maintaining good policy relations with senior officials involves adequate resources to track changes and monitor government activity and to conduct research, to deliver reliable advice, and to understand what is negotiable and what is not in any policy discussions. While most of the relationship will occur in private or semi-private meetings, organizations should be prepared to make submissions to parliamentary committees or inquiries, and, when necessary, to use the media responsibly to build support on an issue.[13]

(3)   Finally, organizations must assess the quality and extent of their influence on a policy issue when determining whether to engage.

---

[13]   The use of media or public lobbying tactics requires discretion since embarrassing officials is likely to produce resistance or resentment in government officials towards the organization. If an organization releases any information officials consider private, then trust will decline, and in turn erode the relationship.

Are they merely being brought into policy discussions by officials to legitimize a chosen policy route or is their advice genuinely sought? The answer will determine whether and how they allocate resources to a policy relationship.

The types of relationships constructed and maintained between the public and nonprofit sector to deliver services are as varied and intricate as the nature of services available to Canadians. The nature of the relationship will depend on the funding relationship, the type of service, the relative strengths of the bureaucracy and nonprofits, the importance of the issue to the political agenda, and the working relationships established between the public and nonprofit actors. However, three areas are especially important.

First, who is in control? Is the organization an agent of the public sector or is it an actor with decision-making authority? Which role is more acceptable and desirable for solid or improved service delivery?

Second, when agreeing to engage in service delivery, an organization must provide a realistic assessment of its strengths and capacity. Can it manage the service without overtaxing its resources or detracting from service provision in another area of operation? Are the public sector resources adequate to sponsor the service, including the internal costs to the organization? The terms must be carefully negotiated.

Third, organizations must learn to say no when arrangements are not adequately resourced or the mission and objectives of the nonprofit will be compromised unduly. Before refusing contracts, however, organizations should consider whether changes could be negotiated to make an arrangement more acceptable. In this case, a strong policy relationship with the relevant department and officials will be important.

The funding relationships between the federal government and nonprofit community have undergone significant changes in recent years. As the Canadian Council on Social Development has documented, funding matters. It is not just the amount of funding that makes a difference, but the type of funding regime (Scott (2003 and 2003 Summary)). In this seminal work, Scott tracks the shift from core funding to project funding, noting the impact that this change has on the ability of organizations to maintain operations and their missions as their administrative functions are starved of resources. Instability of funding, shorter funding terms, increased reporting requirements, and the need to collaborate with other organizations to secure funding add to the operation costs of organizations which are not compensated in the contracts gained. Although the sector is resilient and has adapted remarkably well to the pressures, all things considered, Scott names some worrisome trends including: volatility of resources which affect an organization's stability and capacity to provide consistent quality in services; mission drift as organizations vie for funding; a loss of infrastructure that sustains the organizations; reporting overload caused by the concurrent loss of staff and multiple reporting requirements and forms by multiple funders; precarious financial structures and dependence on maintaining multiple funding sources to survive; an advocacy chill as organizations attempt to maintain good relations with multiple funders with divergent directives; and human resource fatigue in an increasingly competitive and onerous environment. Akingbola adds that the impact on staffing patterns is also troubling (Akingbola (2004)). The pressure of the new funding regime identified by Scott constrains the creative and longer-term work that has characterized the sector.

A key point of tension in the funding relationship between the federal government and the nonprofit sector has been the move towards contribution agreements and away from sustaining grants. Contribution agreements are favoured within the public sector as a means of ensuring stricter performance measures and reporting requirements consistent with the Auditor General's guidelines. These contracts involve specified terms and outputs and strict reporting requirements (usually quarterly progress reports, financial reports and an independent assessment). Eligibility requirements for organizations are also strict. Protracted negotiations and public sector approval of the agreements, heavy reporting requirements (often disproportionate to the amounts involved), lapses or delays in funding as reporting documents are filed and approved, monitoring of contracts and inconsistent standards for approval, as well as changing requirements in the agreements, have produced frustration for both public and nonprofit sector officials whose common objective is to ensure funds are available for the provision of reliable, stable and worthy services and causes. However, the auditor's chill in the public sector has meant that these accountability measures are likely to remain despite efforts made in the VSI to streamline negotiations and provide more flexibility in funding arrangements. The cause for optimism is that increasingly, government departments are moving to multi-year agreements, allowing organizations for longer-term planning.

How can nonprofit managers cope in this increasingly volatile, competitive and unpredictable funding environment? Marilyn Struthers advises organizations not just to cope with change and strive for stability but also to accept change as the constant and recognize it as an opportunity to thrive. She identifies four main characteristics of organizations that enable them to obtain financial vibrancy, defined as "the capacity of an organization to transition from one sustainable moment to the next" (Struthers (2004, at 2-3)). First, organizations must build an organizational culture and architecture that allows for fluidity in roles that can be adapted to build links with other organizations without losing identity or mission focus. These linkages may include umbrella organizations, networks of information sharing, global ties with similar organizations, strategic alliances, in-kind exchanges, joint ventures and collaborative planning in addition to developing a long-term, networking relationship with funders. Second, they must engage in strategic planning with multiple stakeholders, including reflection upon and learning from past experiences, and focusing their missions. Third, they should pursue funding sources that "further their mission while generating revenues such as fee-for-service projects, developing research capacity or marketing training" rather than developing adjunctive activities that raise funds (Struthers (2004, at 8)). Finally, they should "have a strong and creative understanding of organizational financial management and accountability", that results in a deliberate resourcing strategy consonant with missions and values (Struthers (2004, at 9)). Developing these traits will prepare organizations to enter into a more creative and productive alliance with funders.

From the United States has come an even more controversial recommendation. Dan Pallotta argues that it is wrong to ask charities to be more efficient in a changing social and economic environment without allowing them access to the tools of the free market. He suggests that charities, and by association nonprofits, have to be integrated into the economy and allowed to use the tools they need to address social needs. Such tools include compensation for executives, risk-taking, long-term vision, advertising and capital investment (Pallotta (2008, at 8-9, 35-36)). Similarly, the standard for assessing the work of charities and nonprofits cannot be the simple market test of efficiency but must be multifaceted and include effectiveness of service (Pallotta (2008, at 168-76)). Enabling charities to function more like profit organizations would require regulatory reform but also a re-engineering in thinking about the nature and purpose of the charitable, nonprofit sector. This thinking is consistent with the blurring of lines between the public, private and nonprofit sectors and the move towards social entrepreneurship.

Nonprofit organizations must be innovative and active in the new funding regime, even if they are not willing to go as far as Pallotta suggests. This includes monitoring government department Internet sites for new funding opportunities, foundations and granting agencies for changes in programs and requirements, and sharing possible funding opportunities with other organizations. Given constrained resources in organizations, collaboration among organizations in sourcing and applying for funding maximizes opportunities for securing new streams of funding. It can also include risk-taking and innovation in structure. For example, when public sector funding to the arts community was becoming more constrained and less dependable in Alberta in the 1990s, the Glenbow Museum undertook the innovative step of moving to nongovernmental organization status, which allowed it to compete for international funding and broadened its activities to include international co-operative endeavours. This strategy was successful and resulted in new and exciting art exhibits but was not sustained.

If a relationship between the nonprofit sector organizations and government is one based on advocacy, it does not necessarily mean that it is adversarial. In many cases, government officials will rely on organizations to speak on behalf of a segment of the public and to help improve policy by doing so. In some cases, governments will fund organizations to represent a part of the population that is underrepresented or marginalized in the policy process. At other times, organizations with relationships that are primarily service-driven, will need to perform an advocacy role to secure needed changes in that service. In other cases, organizations may find their advocacy activities unpopular with policymakers and will fight to be heard. In these types of relationships, organizations must ask whether the most effective means of securing needed changes is through quiet diplomacy or public vehicles such as the media or demonstrations. In many cases, the answer will depend on whether the organization is in the relationship for the longer or shorter term.

In all of the relations built between nonprofits and governments or between nonprofit and government funders, one ingredient is critical to success; nonprofit organizations must be true to their mission and purpose but flexible in the means of obtaining their objectives.

PARTNERING WITH THE CORPORATE SECTOR: FROM ANTAGONISTS TO ALLIES

The relationship between the nonprofit and for-profit sectors has never been a simple one. On the one hand, nonprofit organizations have often found themselves in operation to serve the very people that private enterprise has "failed". Thus, some nonprofit leaders have emerged as trenchant critics of the corporate sector for its failure to engage in sustained and positive community action and for the social costs of doing business. On the other hand, traditionally, many nonprofit organizations and businesses have worked together, sometimes warily, to provide services and benefits to Canadians. Examples of these partnerships include corporate donations to non-profits enabling them to conduct their work, joint partnerships in activities such as the CIBC Run for the Cure, and corporate promotion of charitable activities.[14] But much of their relationship has been predicated on independent coexistence.

These relationships are currently in transition. As governments have shifted from hierarchical modes of operation towards governance and horizontal relations, nonprofits and businesses have had to re-evaluate and re-orient their policy and public roles. Nonprofits and businesses have moved towards viewing each other as allies more than antagonists with the urging of governments.

The Shift Towards Partnerships

Corporations and nonprofit organizations are increasingly moving to more co-operative and sustained arrangements. The pressures towards greater nonprofit and corporate co-operation derive from different sources. As forces of globalization have increased economic pressures domestically, corporations and nonprofits have realized the need to work together to ensure national competitiveness and to mitigate the fallout from corporate failures. New technologies have encouraged citizens to expect more not just of their governments but also of corporations and nonprofits in addressing social problems. Citizens increasingly expect seamless services requiring the three sectors to work together. Social activists, environmentalists and the Aboriginal community have all engaged in sustained action against corporations to impress upon the public and the corporations the costs of doing business and the need for co-operation with communi-ty organizations.

---

[14] In the first case, the relationship is monetary. In the second case, officials from both sectors will be involved in planning, running and participating in the event. In the third case, a corporation will take an active role and have a vested interest in the promotion of a cause, much like The Body Shop does with respect to women's health.

Each sector is re-evaluating its relationships as well. Governments have been reducing funding for nonprofits, requiring them to look to the corporate sector for more sustained sources of revenue while encouraging corporations to accept more responsibility for social ills. Corporations have found that mere association with good causes through cheque-book charity or through occasional alliances is no longer sufficient to ensure a positive public image (Dunham & Pierce (1989); Forcese (1997); Global Business Responsibility Resource Centre; Selley (1998); Verschoor & Entine). Socially conscious employees and shareholders increasingly expect corporations to engage in building community relations.

For their part, nonprofit organizations have realized that the relationship is not just one of dependence on businesses for funding, but a mutual one in which they can provide businesses with community knowledge and more legitimacy as creators of social value (Daw (2006)). Cross-sectoral co-operation is also necessary to begin to address increasingly complex, polycentric public policy issues that affect all segments of society.

Two examples illustrate the increasingly intertwined relationships and roles of the three sectors. When a tsunami hit Southeast Asian countries at the end of 2004 and when Hurricane Katrina struck New Orleans in 2005, military and state aid agencies teamed with nonprofit organizations that had valuable local knowledge and networks, and with businesses that had necessary technologies and skills, to provide relief in a more effective and immediate manner than any sector alone could provide (Chikoto *et al.* (2013)). In 2013, when flooding reached disastrous proportions in Alberta, nonprofits worked with public and private organizations to restore services and return people to their homes. Despite differences and tensions, the three sectors are learning to act together to serve citizens better.

The Types of Relationships

Co-operation among the sectors can take various forms. Given that public nonprofit relations have been addressed extensively above, this section will concentrate on the main types of relationships emerging between the private and nonprofit sectors. Three main categories of relationships have emerged: independents, competitors, partners or allies and dependants. Each has its strengths and its points of caution for the sector.

Table 4: Nonprofit-Private Sector Relationships

Nonprofit-Private Sector Relationships		
	Autonomy High	Autonomy Low
High Market Power	Independent	Partners
Low Market Power	Competitors	Dependent

First, nonprofit organizations and private businesses may exist as independent organizations with little contact and limited consciousness of each other. Both types of organizations will be autonomous and enjoy a defined space in the marketplace of public goods. This type of relationship is more traditional and less common in an increasingly integrated world.

Second, nonprofit and for-profit organizations may still operate as competitors in key areas of public service as well as in new areas as the public sector devolves responsibilities. In this case, organizations from both sectors retain their autonomy but have reduced market power because they are competing for space. For example, in recent years the provision of home care services to the elderly and sick has been the locus of increasing competition between the nonprofit and for-profit sectors. In one case study in which the Victorian Order of Nurses faced competition from for-profit organizations for public contracts, the nonprofit experienced lowered efficiency and higher costs in providing services to a smaller, more dispersed community. The agency was forced to seek commercial opportunities and charge fees for services, thus fundamentally altering the culture of the organization in the eyes of its employees (Tindale & MacLachlan (2001, at 199, 200-201, 204-208)). In another study of nonprofits and for-profits providing home care services in the same community, Luc Thériault and Sandra Salhani noted the emergence of a two-tier structure of services: poorer service recipients could not afford the costlier and often more extensive services offered by private care firms. They emphasized that nonprofits could maintain their organizational culture and level of services if they did not overstep their capacity to provide services and developed extensive networks with other providers. This study concluded that co-operation between all three sectors is developing as the need for home care services increases (Thériault & Salhani (2001, at 232-233, 243-245)). Even competitive relations may produce opportunities for co-operative and productive relations (Marshall *et al.* (2012, at 371)).

Third, partnerships and alliances between the two sectors can assume a wide range of forms. While they might relinquish autonomy in of co-operative action, they will command a greater share and more power in the marketplace than if they acted alone. Martha Parker, then Executive Director for Volunteer Calgary, observed in her study of partnerships between nonprofits and for-profits that corporate involvement may ascend from arm's length to full engagement, as Figure 3 illustrates (Parker (2000, at 37)).

Figure 3: Partnerships Between Nonprofits and For-profits

Cheque Book ➡➡	Strategic ➡➡	Community ➡➡	Corporate ➡➡	Corporate
Philanthropy	Philanthropy	Investment	Social Responsibility	Citizenship

Cheque-book philanthropy is the "old" style of corporate interaction with worthy causes in the sector. Strategic philanthropy is becoming more prevalent. Corporate dollars are targeted with investment strategies to build corporate image, and employees may volunteer for good causes as a formal or informal part of their corporate duties. Cause-related marketing, where a corporation attaches its logo to a nonprofit cause to publicly associate sympathy for the issue with its products as a means of market retention or expansion, is an example of strategic philanthropy (Daw (2006)). Community investment is the next stage, where corporations identify causes that are related to their business objectives, are proactive in the investment strategies by seeking out partners, are more closely involved in the activities undertaken within the partnership, and expect greater accountability and performance results. In the areas of corporate social responsibility and corporate citizenship, corporations integrate social values into business functions, adopt social audits, implement sound social, environmental and ethical practices, and demonstrate leadership working in tandem with the other sectors.

Nonprofit partnering develops along a parallel continuum according to Parker, as Figure 4 demonstrates (Parker (2000, at 38)).

Figure 4: Nonprofit Partnering

Service ➡➡	Strategic ➡➡	Partnerships ➡➡	Nonprofit ➡➡	Nonprofit
Provider/	Positioning	&	Social	Citizenship
Entitlement		Collaborations	Responsibility	

At the lower end of the spectrum, nonprofits operate in isolation and are dependent on key funders while focusing on their missions and performing good works. At the level of strategic positioning, nonprofits begin to diversify their funding needs and compete for corporate dollars. They may engage in some sectoral collaborations but will maintain a focus on their missions and markets. At the level of partnerships and collaborations, nonprofits demonstrate knowledge of community issues valuable to corporate partners, are proactive, engage in enterprising thinking including brand equity, build business capacity, supportive organizational culture and cross-sectoral partnerships, and adopt more accountability measures. They adapt business practices to serve their causes. In the cases of social responsibility and citizenship, nonprofits develop and share best practices, adopt value-added strategies, contextualize their narrower organizational interests within broader social issues, commit to building community capacity and promoting civil society, and demonstrate leadership while working with the other sectors.

Organizations interested in partnering arrangements with corporations or private sector organizations now have access to a plethora of reliable Internet sites offering good sensible advice on these arrangements. Some consulting firms have been created to provide advice on a fee-for-service basis and through blogs.[15]

In the fourth type of relationship, nonprofits are in a dependent relationship with private corporations and fall on the left side of the Parker continuum. In this case, nonprofits rely on the corporate partner for funding and lose autonomous decision-making power as a result. They also have lower market power since their ability to act is circumscribed by the funding relationship. As Parker indicates, nonprofits may emerge from positions of dependency and isolation to equality with the other sectors in serving citizens.

Finding the Right Partner

Partnerships can be beneficial to nonprofits when right, and disastrous if poorly chosen. Some cautionary notes must be sounded in reviewing relations between nonprofits and for-profits. Nonprofits need to develop and maintain a clear understanding of both their mission and their capacities before engaging with for-profits. In some cases, a

---

[15] See for example, "How to Choose and Approach a Corporate Partner for Your Nonprofit" at: <http://mashable.com/2011/05/27/non-profit-corporate-partners/>.

dependent funding relationship may serve the needs of the nonprofit and its clients. To engage in a more extensive relationship might jeopardize the existing quality of services. However, suspicion of the corporate sector or its motives should not hamper an organization from developing better or closer ties with for-profit funders or partners when the ability of the organization to execute its mission will be improved.

As nonprofits engage more closely with corporations, though, they will need to research the relationship for their interests in more depth and engage in discussions with other stakeholders about the terms of the partnerships. Part of the analysis involves an assessment of the benefits that the nonprofit brings to the relationship: too often these aspects are undervalued and underexploited. And, as in any relationship, know your partner and the skeletons in the closets. The better prepared the nonprofit is to engage with corporations, the better the alliance will fit its objectives. This means learning to say "no" when the fit is wrong.

Alliances may turn sour because of personalities, mission drift, conflicting objectives and interests, or changes in circumstances. In these cases, nonprofits must be prepared to cut ties. Corporations can be seductive but if enticing incentives to partner distort the culture, mission, or operation of the nonprofit in unacceptable ways, nonprofits must remain virtuous and cultivate other more satisfying, even if less exciting, relationships.

A crucial ingredient for building relationships between for-profits and nonprofits is mutual self-interest. Based on their extensive involvement with these alliances in the United States, Shirley Sagawa and Eli Segal concluded that:

> In working more closely together, organizations need not, and should not, abandon their central missions. Over-commercialization of nonprofit organizations could undermine their legitimacy, discourage donors and volunteers, and cause them to neglect those who are hardest, and costliest, to serve. Businesses that put social change ahead of profits risk losing shareholders and customers, and ultimately, threaten their own survival. The key is for business and social sector organizations alike to strike the right balance as they move in these new directions.

(Sagawa & Segal (2000, at 238))

Sagawa and Segal remind nonprofit and for-profit organizations of several elements that have to be watched in order to sustain their joint ventures all captured by the acronym "COMMON": **c**ommunicate with each other and internally; seek out new opportunities and grow in the relationship; ensure both sides mutually contribute to and benefit from the relationship in ways appropriate to their organizations; engage at multiple levels and identify champions of the relationship and cause in both organizations; keep the relationship open-ended with the termination point when it is not longer working or with the possibility of renewal if a termination date has been set for a specific exchange; and, create new value for both partners (Sagawa & Segal (2000, at 213-33)).

Corporate and nonprofit partnerships face a serious challenge in Canada. The recent economic downturn combined with the forces of globalization have resulted in two challenging trends. First, corporate restructuring and consolidation have meant that smaller and rural communities have lost many of their immediate ties with the business community. Head offices often make decisions on partnering and levels of donations, with the discretion of regional managers increasingly diminished.[16] The personal faces of nonprofit and for-profit organizations are lost in this new world. Thus, to a greater extent than ever before, nonprofits need to engage in proactive partnering strategies involving *other* nonprofit organizations when they approach for-profit partners with potential common interests.

Second, there has been a loss of corporate headquarters in this country (Brock, Brook & Elliott (2003, at 18-20)). Again, this increases the competitiveness of the donor and partnering pool. However, in these relationships, local nonprofits can offer valuable local knowledge not available as readily to corporate headquarters located outside the country or within large urban centres to ensure more effective use of corporate resources. Nonprofits should not discount partners from "away".

A more positive development involves the creation of Corporate Responsibility Officers in large corporations. Under this rubric, corporations have merged investor, government and community relations with social responsibility objectives. This development is in keeping with the trend towards more social partnerships and social innovation in the private sector as a means of enhancing legitimacy

---

[16] This fact emerged twice during the interviews Jan Elliott, David Brook and I did with voluntary sector leaders on globalization (Brock, Brook & Elliott (2003, at 18-20)). In addition, work with voluntary sector boards in Kingston has revealed that the discretion of regional managers in banks and corporations is limited to under $5,000, thus limiting local control over dollars spent.

and reputations in the marketplace. However, it offers entrepreneurial nonprofit organizations opportunities for building sustainable and meaningful relationships with private companies that extend beyond the more limited goals of corporate social responsibility towards social change and innovation.[17]

BUILDING WITH OTHER NONPROFITS: THE CHALLENGES OF FORMING ALLIANCES

Nonprofits can form alliances with each other. These relationships may take the form of umbrella organizations, coalitions to lobby funders or policymakers, strategic alliances, joint endeavours, and even mergers. The previous sections of this chapter have indicated that the incentives for nonprofits to ally with other nonprofits are growing. The tougher investment and business climate at the end of the first decade of this century provides an incentive to organizations to merge, ally with others, or face closure.

Katherine Scott explains what is old and new in these pressures for nonprofits (Scott (2003, at 51)):

> Increasingly, public and private funders are encouraging nonprofit and voluntary groups to form partnerships or coalitions to advance their work. Nonprofit and voluntary groups have always worked with a variety of partners — including community representatives, other nonprofit and voluntary organizations, local business and funders — to develop and implement programs. As well, nonprofit and voluntary organizations have a long history of joint advocacy, working with various communities of interest to promote change, such as alleviating child poverty or expanding public support for the arts. What is new is the call by funders to submit joint funding proposals in an increasingly wide range of areas.

Nonprofit organizations are using past techniques to adapt to the new funding environment but the "forced" alliances are not always the best arrangements for citizens being served. For example, if two agencies have similar missions but serve different populations, the alliance might result in compromises in service delivery that disadvantage some of the recipients. This is particularly the case with respect to ethnic and racial minority services versus services provided to the general population. Similarly, two organizations might provide

---

[17]   See, for example, Corporate Responsibility Officers association (CROA), online at: <http://www.croassociation.org/>.

services that appear similar but are different in operation. Public choice is reduced and quality of service delivery might suffer as operations are rationalized. Finally, two organizations in a region might provide the same service but the geographic and cultural needs of the recipients might be different. This is particularly apt in the case of rural and urban organizations.

The ingredients for successful alliances have been outlined in the sections on government and corporate relations. However, some characteristics of relationships among nonprofits should be mentioned before examining some of the questions surrounding these alliances.

First, nonprofits co-operate. As the National Survey of Nonprofit and Voluntary Organizations documented (M.H. Hall *et al.* (2004, at 25)):

> A substantial amount of funds is transferred among nonprofit and voluntary organizations. The primary function of some registered charities is to provide funding to other organizations. In addition, organizations may operate as part of a larger network of organizations and may, for example, transfer funds to the national arm of their organization. Finally, organizations may also transfer funds to pay for services provided by other organizations. Twenty-seven per cent of all nonprofit and voluntary organizations transfer or disburse funds to other organizations. These transfers make up almost $4.7 billion ... or 4% of total revenues.

Second, while about one-quarter of organizations identify collaborating with other organizations as a problem, this does not rank as a serious concern very often (only 2 per cent) for organizations and remains relatively low on the list of problems and challenges facing organizations (M.H. Hall *et al.* (2004, at 43-44)).

How well are these relationships working? In a survey of civil society leaders, Don Embuldeniya reflected on the quality of these relationships. Since the 1980s, organizations have increasingly been forming umbrella and networking organizations to support and promote volunteerism, fund development and leadership. However, civil society leaders have questioned the capacity of these organizations to represent members effectively. Only 57 per cent of leaders suggested that umbrella organizations have the capacity (financial and human resources, knowledge, information technology) to represent the interests of their members. On the positive side, approximately 65 per cent believe that these organizations integrate members into decision-making (Embuldeniya (2001, at 11-12)).[18]

---

[18] This was a targeted survey of 104 key leaders.

Similarly, while leaders realized the benefits of alliances among organizations, they were skeptical of the ability of organizations to form those alliances. About three-quarters of leaders said that organizations "seldom or only sometimes collaborate across different subsectors to further social and community well-being", over 50 per cent believe organizations seldom or only sometimes join alliances with other organizations and almost 50 per cent believe organizations join with citizens (Embuldeniya (2001, at 12-13)). And as the National Survey discovered, these alliances are most problematic for organizations whose primary activity areas include international aid (40 per cent), law, advocacy and politics (35 per cent), universities and colleges (39 per cent), health (32 per cent), and social services (30 per cent). The least problematic for collaboration were the areas of development and housing (14 per cent) and religion (14 per cent) (M.H. Hall *et al.* (2004, at 46)). Over a decade later, these problems remain.

Forced arrangements raise more concerns than voluntary partnerships. Nonprofit leaders recognize and acknowledge the benefits of sharing information and best practices especially as resources are more constrained and the strategic value of alliances in achieving policy or practical changes or delivering services. Where time and resources are available to prepare and build these alliances, they tend to be more successful. While territorial or personality clashes may impede the formation of alliances among nonprofits, generally the culture is one of co-operation.

However, in the case of funder-imposed partnerships, more problems arise. While such alliances may be useful for leveraging funders' dollars, in many cases what appear to be logical alliances among organizations may be costly in execution or inefficient in operation.[19] Rarely do funders cover the real costs of building partnerships or merging organizations. In some cases, organizations need to resist forced arrangements but to explain their reasons to funders. While organizational differences are unlikely to be compelling, inefficiencies and cost arguments may be persuasive. Where resistance to proposed alliances is strong, funders should be prepared to re-evaluate their reasons for promoting the alliance. Is it in the best interests of the community or are the reasons ones of administrative convenience for the funder? In any case, Struthers' recommendation for a sustained

---

[19]   For a discussion of nonprofit concerns with forced partnerships, see Scott (2003, at 51-52).

dialogue between funders and organizations is important in assessing the value of consolidation in the sector.

In many cases, the most effective alliances among nonprofits are coalitions, networks and umbrella organizations. In these cases, nonprofits retain autonomy but share the benefits of collective action. Coalitions among a number of organizations at the national or provincial level provide the critical mass to influence policy trends and decision-making processes. Advocacy networks offer opportunities for soft power strategies to influence policy without jeopardizing individual relations of nonprofits with state actors (Acosta (2012, at 156)).

PUBLIC AND MEDIA RELATIONS: WITH INFLUENCE COMES SCRUTINY

Nonprofit organizations are subject to a higher level of public scrutiny than ever before in the history of the sector. Media are regularly tracking the performance of organizations, particularly in the aftermath of large-scale fundraising. International and domestic agencies track donations to organizations and the expenditure of those funds. For example, after the tsunami disaster in Southeast Asia, the United Nations created a monitoring agency to track donations made to provide relief efforts. Media outlets reported extensively on donations, expenditures, and the state of relief efforts at both the six-month and one-year anniversaries of the tsunami. And the public is watching; direct access to information about organizations is increasingly accessible through convenient technologies. Organizations need to build their media and public profiles.

One tendency that organizations need to struggle against is the perception that the media are a threat. The qualitative portion of the National Survey of Nonprofit and Voluntary Organizations reported that organizations worry about fair media coverage (M.H. Hall *et al.* (2003, at 18)):

> Media coverage of nonprofit and voluntary organizations often focuses on problems rather than the contributions of these organizations. Many participants suggested that a broad-based public relations campaign could counteract bad press, raise awareness of the value of the sector, and educate the public about the actual cost of, and need for, basic administration. A number of participants, often from smaller communities, reported difficulties in fundraising because of negative media depictions of fiscal inefficiencies and mismanagement.

Negative media reports contributed to public misperceptions about the needs and work of the sector, thus discouraging donations and volunteers.

Despite these fears, the sector is beginning to understand the potential of the media as an ally in delivering the good news of the sector to the public. This is occurring at two levels. At the national level, a sector-wide public awareness campaign was conducted under the aegis of the VSI to extol the variety and extent of ways in which the sector contributes to the quality of life in Canada. Similarly, national surveys have been released to maximize media attention to the contributions of the sector to Canadian social and economic life.

At the organizational level, nonprofits are also learning to use the media to their benefit. While larger organizations have traditionally had strong public relations campaigns, smaller and medium-sized organizations are increasingly realizing the need to reach the public beyond featured events like fundraisers. A sustained event such as Volunteer Week is one method, but other tactics include keeping interested media reporters informed of organizational activities, goals and contributions, and exemplary volunteers. Boards often include a public relations expert to ensure a positive media presence and to track media coverage. While some leaders might be hesitant about encouraging media coverage since they cannot control the stories, Sandra Beckwith reminds them that these uncontrolled stories can actually have more credibility than advertising or mail-outs because they are independent (Beckwith (2006, at 3)).

There are three immediate benefits to sustained media relations. First, media reports tend to be better informed and more accurate with regular familiarity. Organizations can provide often-harried reporters with good leads or ideas for feature or human interest stories, thus saving them time. Second, trust is built between the media and the nonprofits. Third, if a relationship has been established between an organization and the media, then reporters are more likely to call that organization when negative or "hot" stories surface about that organization or the sector. This provides organizations with a critical opportunity to offer needed commentary or refutations of any inaccuracies. In these cases, nonprofit leaders must be careful not to appear defensive or too aggressive, or to avoid the media, but must respond with honest answers that reinforce the positive image of the organization and sector. The "right spin" is one that treats the topic in a fair and practical manner. When handled well, the relationship can be a positive and mutually beneficial one.

Finally, nonprofit organizations need to develop a strong public presence through social media outlets, Web portals blogs, and dedicated Websites. However, to be effective, Websites must be kept current and accurate. The social media presence should be regular, not intermittent. Further, organizations must strike a balance between providing public information available to all interested parties and select information available only to members. If a Website or public information is too readily available, the incentive for membership in an organization may be less compelling. Well-used, social media and new technologies can be effective means of publicizing organizational goals and leaders' messages to the public and, when interactive, can keep leaders informed of changes in public opinions or member preferences. Creative nonprofit leaders can also use social media to secure funding for projects through crowdsourcing techniques or to secure public action on important causes. Social networking is a must for nonprofits hoping to survive today.

Social media provides more opportunities for engaging youth. This is a "turned on" generation and more likely to access information through the social media including Facebook, Twitter and YouTube among others than newspapers (see Chapter 12 in this book). Organizations must deliver their message in the way they expect. Organizations would do well to cultivate "e-volunteers" — those volunteers that might not be willing to be present physically but will make substantial contributions over the Internet. It is just a matter of tracking the times (Briones *et al.* (2011, at 37-43).

CONCLUSION

Building government and community relations requires nonprofit organizations to use their resources strategically and wisely in an increasingly complex world where the roles and responsibilities of the three sectors are eroding and blurring. While larger organizations will have more capacity to respond to challenges and adapt to changes, smaller and medium-sized organizations can target their efforts and create alliances to support their work. Dialogue, clarity of mission, knowledge of the broader community, and flexibility in action will be traits that allow organizations to take advantage of the opportunities embedded in the changing relations between nonprofits and the external world.

One last word of caution is warranted. On a sombre note, Robert Reich, looking at the changing world of community relations in the United States, warned that (Reich (2001, at 208-209)):

> Nonprofit leaders, likewise, are immersed in continuous efforts to lure talent and money. "To direct an institution nowadays you have to be an opportunist," says Marcia Tucker, former director of the New Museum of contemporary art in New York. "You have to use every social situation to think about fundraising and social contacts." While university deans busily court faculty stars (increasingly, as has been observed, in … bidding wars), most college presidents are consumed by the task of raising funds. "One has to be a beggar, a flatterer, a sycophant, a court jester," notes Leon Botstein, president of Bard College. The great visionary university presidents who once changed America's thinking on weighty matters … have been replaced, for the most part, by a generation of leaders whose vision is focused on raising large donations.

His words ring true as much today as they did in 2001. Positioning an organization, whether a university or a health agency or a small social service provider, for dollars and donations may take precedence over developing a vision. When organizations focus on developing relations to build donations and image instead of using their vision to drive their relations, the community suffers.

REFERENCES

R. Acosta, "Advocacy Networks through a Multidisciplinary Lens: Implications for Research Agendas" (2012) 23:1 Voluntas: International Journal of Voluntary and Nonprofit Organizations 156-181.

K. Akingbola, "Staffing Retention and Government Funding. A Case Study" (2004) 14:4 Nonprofit Management and Leadership 453-465.

P. Aucoin & R. Heintzman, "The Dialectics of Accountability for Performance in Public Management Reform" in B.G. Peters & D.J. Savoie, eds., *Governance in the Twenty-First Century: Revitalizing the Public Service* (Montreal and Kingston: McGill-Queen's University Press, co-published by Canadian Centre for Management Development, 2000) 244-280.

J.E. Austin & M.M. Seitanidi, "Collaborative Value Creation: A Review of Partnering Between Nonprofits and Businesses: Part I Value-Creation Spectrum and Collaboration Stages" (2012) 41:5 Nonprofit and Voluntary Sector Quarterly 726-758.

J.E. Austin & M.M. Seitanidi, "Collaborative Value Creation: A Review of Partnering Between Nonprofits and Businesses: Part II Partnership Processes and Outcomes" (2012) 41:6 Nonprofit and Voluntary Sector Quarterly 929-968.

S. Beckwith, *Publicity for Nonprofits: Generating Media Exposure that Leads to Awareness, Growth and Contributions* (Chicago: Kaplan Publishing, 2006).

A. Blakeney & S. Borins, *Political Management in Canada*, 2d ed. (Toronto: University of Toronto Press, 1998).

R.L. Briones *et al.*, "Keeping Up with the Digital Age: How the American Red Cross Uses Social Media to Build Relationships" (2011) 37:1 Public Relations Review 37-43.

K.L. Brock, "Capturing the Complexity of the Ontario Government Relationship with the Social Economy Sector" in L. Mook, J. Quarter & S. Ryan, eds., *Researching the Social Economy* (Toronto: University of Toronto Press, 2010) 131-153.

K.L. Brock, "Judging the VSI: Reflections on the Relationship between the Federal Government and the Voluntary Sector" (2005) 19:3 The Philanthropist 168-191.

K.L. Brock, "State, Society and the Third Sector: Changing to Meet New Challenges" (2001) 35:4 Journal of Canadian Studies 203-220.

K.L. Brock, "The Devil is in the Details: The Chrétien Legacy for the Third Sector" (2004) 9:1 Review of Canadian Studies 263-282.

K.L. Brock, D. Brook & J. Elliott, "Globalization and the Voluntary Sector in Canada" (Ottawa: Public Policy Forum, 2003).

G.L. Chikoto, A-A. Sadiq & E. Fordyce, "Disaster Mitigation and Preparedness: Comparison of Nonprofit, Public and Private Organizations" (2013) 42:2 Nonprofit and Voluntary Sector Quarterly 391-410.

Community Services Council NL and Caledon Institute for Research on Social Policy, *Collaboration on Policy: A Manual developed by the Community-Government Collaboration on Policy*, online at: <http://www.caledoninst.org/Publications/PDF/772ENG.pdf>.

J. Daw, *Cause Marketing for Nonprofits: Partner for Purpose, Passion and Profits* (Hoboken, NJ: John Wiley and Sons, 2006).

T. Dean, "Modernizing Public Sector Organizations" in *Five Trends that are Transforming Government* (Ottawa: Public Policy Forum, 2007).

R.B. Dunham & J.L. Pierce, "Social Responsibility and Managerial Ethics" in R.B. Dunham & J.L. Pierce, eds., *Management* (Glenview, IL: Scott, Foresman and Co., 1989) 96-113.

P.R. Elson, "Third Wave, Third Sector: Comparative Provincial Governance of Third Sector Relations" (Paper presented to the 101st Annual Conference of the Canadian Political Science Association, Victoria, British Columbia, June 2013).

D. Embuldeniya, *Exploring the Health, Strength and Impact of Canada's Civil Society* (Toronto: Canadian Centre for Philanthropy, 2001).

C. Forcese, *Putting Conscience into Commerce* (Montreal: International Centre for Human Rights and Democratic Development, 1997).

B. Gidron, R.M. Kramer & L. Salamon, "Government and the Third Sector in Comparative Perspective: Allies or Adversaries?" in B. Gidron, R.M. Kramer & L. Salamon, eds., *Government and the Third Sector: Emerging Relationships in Welfare States* (San Francisco: Jossey-Bass, 1992).

Global Business Responsibility Resource Centre, *Corporate Citizenship*, online at: <http://www.corporate-citizenship.net>.

M.H. Hall *et al.*, *Cornerstones of Community: Highlights of the National Survey of Nonprofit and Voluntary Organizations* (Ottawa: Ministry of Industry for Statistics Canada, 2004).

M.H. Hall *et al.*, *The Capacity to Serve: A Qualitative Study of the Challenges Facing Canada's Nonprofit and Voluntary Organizations* (Toronto: Canadian Centre for Philanthropy, 2003).

Joint Coordinating Committee (2002), "Progress to Plan Report", Ottawa, September 5, 2002.

P. Krugman, *End This Depression Now* (New York: W.W. Norton, 2013).

A. Lawlor & E. Crandall, "Understanding Third-Party Advertising: An Analysis of the 2004, 2006 and 2008 Canadian Elections" (2011) 54:4 Canadian Public Administration 509-529.

K. Levasseur, "In the Name of Charity: Institutional Support for and Resistance to Redefining the Meaning of Charity in Canada" (2012) 55:2 Canadian Public Administration 181-202.

A. Marshall *et al.*, "An Examination of 'Irregular' Competition between Corporations and Nongovernmental Organizations" (2012) 23:2 Voluntas: International Journal of Voluntary and Nonprofit Organizations 371-391.

D. Pallotta, *Uncharitable: How Restraints on Nonprofits Undermine their Potential* (Medford, MA: Tufts University Press, 2008).

M. Parker, *Partnerships: Profits and Not-for-Profits Together* (Edmonton: Muttart Foundation, 2000).

B.G. Peters & D.J. Savoie, eds., *Governance in a Changing Environment* (Montreal and Kingston: McGill-Queen's University Press, 1995).

S.D. Phillips, "From Charity to Clarity: Reinventing Federal Government-Voluntary Sector Relationships" in L.A. Pal, ed., *How Ottawa Spends 2001-2002* (Toronto: Oxford University Press, 2003) 145-176.

S.D. Phillips, "In Accordance: Canada's Voluntary Sector Accord from Idea to Implementation" in K.L. Brock, ed., *Delicate Dances: Public Policy and the Nonprofit Sector* (Montreal and Kingston: McGill-Queen's University Press, 2003) 17-61.

S.D. Phillips & K. Graham, "Hand-in-Hand: When Accountability Meets Collaboration in the Voluntary Sector" in K.G. Banting, ed., *The Nonprofit Sector in Canada: Roles and Relationships* (Montreal and Kingston: McGill-Queen's University Press, 2000) 149-190.

A.P. Pross & K.R. Webb, "Embedded Regulation: Advocacy and the Federal Regulation of Public Interest Groups" in K.L. Brock, ed., *Delicate Dances: Public Policy and the Nonprofit Sector* (Montreal and Kingston: McGill-Queen's University Press for the School of Policy Studies at Queen's, 2003) 63-122.

R.B. Reich, *The Future of Success* (New York: Alfred A. Knopf, 2001).

S. Sagawa & E. Segal, *Common Interest, Common Good: Creating Value Through Business and Social Sector Partnerships* (Boston: Harvard Business School Press, 2000).

K. Scott, *Funding Matters: The Impact of Canada's New Funding Regime on Nonprofit and Voluntary Organizations* (Ottawa: Canadian Council on Social Development, 2003).

K. Scott, *Funding Matters: The Impact of Canada's New Funding Regime on Nonprofit and Voluntary Organizations – Summary Report* (Ottawa: Canadian Council on Social Development, 2003).

D. Selley, "Social Accounting and Auditing: Has the Time Come at Last?" *Management Ethics* (December 1998), online at: <http://www.ethicscentre.ca/EN/resources/december%201998%20methics.pdf>.

M. Struthers, "Supporting Financial Vibrancy in the Quest for Sustainability in the Not-for-Profit Sector" (Paper prepared for the Community of Inquiry Symposium, Toronto, July 2004).

S. Sutherland, "The Al-Mashat Affair: Administrative Responsibility in Parliamentary Institutions" (1991) 34:4 Canadian Public Administration 573-603.

L. Thériault & S. Salhani, "At the Loose End of the Continuum: Two Nonprofit Organizations Delivering Preventive Homecare Services in Saskatchewan" in K.L. Brock & K.G. Banting, eds., *The Nonprofit Sector and Government in a New Century* (Montreal and Kingston: McGill-Queen's University Press, 2001) 215-254.

P.G. Thomas, "The Changing Nature of Accountability" in B.G. Peters & D.J. Savoie, eds., *Taking Stock: Assessing Public Sector Reforms* (Montreal and Kingston: McGill-Queen's University Press, 1998) 348-393.

J.A. Tindale & E. MacLachlan, "VON 'Doing Commercial': The Experience of Executive Directors with Related Business Development" in K.L. Brock & K.G. Banting, eds., *The Nonprofit Sector and Government in a New Century* (Montreal and Kingston: McGill-Queen's University Press, 2001) 189-214.

C.C. Verschoor & J.H. Entine, "Social Auditing: Oxymoron or Wave of the Future?" in *Values: A Publication of US Trust*, online at: <http://www.jonentine.com/articles/social_auditing.htm>.

K. Webb, "Sustainable Governance in the Twenty-First Century: Moving Beyond Instrument Choice" in P. Eliadis *et al.*, eds., *Designing Government: From Instruments to Governance* (Montreal and Kingston: McGill-Queen's University Press, 2005) 242-280.

B. Weisbrod, *The Nonprofit Economy* (Cambridge, MA: Harvard University Press, 1988).

D.R. Young, "Complementary, Supplementary, or Adversarial? A Theoretical and Historical Examination of Nonprofit-Government Relations in the United States" in E.T. Boris & C.E. Steuerle, eds., *Nonprofits and Government: Collaboration and Conflict* (Washington: Urban Institute Press, 1999) 31-67.

Chapter 7

RESOURCE DEVELOPMENT BASICS

Andrea McManus, CFRE
The Development Group, Calgary

WHAT IS "RESOURCE DEVELOPMENT"?

The changes in the nonprofit sector over the past two decades, and particularly the decrease in government funding and the significant growth in the number of nonprofit organizations, has forced organizations to look at diversifying their funding bases. A dramatic outcome of this shift has been the way organizations both think about and approach the development of new funding resources and, in particular, their philanthropic-based revenue.

This chapter provides an overview of non-government funding with primary focus on an organization's fundraising and philanthropically based activities.

Clarifying Terminology

Broadly termed as "resource development", the pursuit of new funding sources can include everything from fees for service to numerous forms of fundraising to more entrepreneurial ventures. The terminology can differ from organization to organization and, while there are more overlaps and similarities than differences, it is worth clarifying these various terms.

The most commonly used terms found in Canadian nonprofits are "resource development", "fund development", "institutional advancement" and "fundraising".

Resource development is the broad umbrella under which a variety of non-government funding sources are collected and pursued. According

to the Association of Fundraising Professionals (AFP) Online Dictionary, resource development refers to *"the practice of identifying,
cultivating, and securing financial and human support for an organization"*: AFP 1996-2013.[1]

Organizations that call their function resource development will
typically utilize a broad approach that includes both philanthropically
based revenue and more entrepreneurial methods such as fees-for-
service, gift shops, cause marketing (alignment of a corporate brand or
product with a cause for marketing purposes), or social enterprise (a
business within the nonprofit that promotes mission awareness and/or
raises financial revenues).

Fund development refers to a system that raises philanthropic and
sponsorship support for an organization. It is a process, certainly part
art and part science, but one that moves in an orderly and logical
sequence. It starts with preparation and planning, moves to execution,
is controlled at various points throughout, is tracked, evaluated, and
measured, and then moves back to renewal of the plan. This "cycle" is
not haphazard, nor is it reactive (although crisis fundraising, by its
nature, is reactive to such things as natural disasters). Rather, it is a
thoughtful, relevant connection of activities in a program that raises
financial and human support for a nonprofit organization. Fund
development is by far the most commonly used name for this function
in Canadian nonprofit organizations and, by and large, resource
development and fund development are used interchangeably and
usually referred to as "development".

Institutional advancement is a term most commonly used to refer
to fundraising in post-secondary education organizations such as
universities and colleges. Advancement is a strategic, integrated
method of managing relationships to increase understanding and
support among an educational institution's key constituents, including
alumni and friends, government policy makers, the media, members of
the community and philanthropic entities of all types.[2]

The primary core disciplines of educational advancement are
alumni relations (in educational organizations), communications,
marketing and fundraising. Communications and marketing usually

---

[1]   AFP Fundraising Dictionary online at: <http://www.afpnet.org/files/ContentDocuments/
AFP_Dictionary_A-Z_final_6-9-03.pdf>.

[2]   Council for Advancement and Support of Education (CASE), online at:
<http://www.case.org>.

also include public relations, external relations and government relations.

In this model, the department is generally referred to as the "advancement office" or "the external relations" department. The use of the term "advancement" is enjoying increased use outside of the post-secondary world as more and more nonprofits understand that, if they wish to maximize their potential, an integrated model delivers better results. However, this integrated philosophy is also key in both of the previous two models.

Fundraising is one outcome of all three models that describes the actual activities directly involved with raising resources for the work of the organization and can be done by professional staff or by volunteers. There are different fundraising methodologies (direct mail, telemarketing, online giving, sponsorships, major gifts) in a fund development program and each of them has its own targeted constituents, strategies, measurements and cycles.

UNDERSTANDING THE DIFFERENCES BETWEEN NONPROFITS AND REGISTERED CHARITIES

There are approximately 165,000 nonprofit and voluntary organizations operating in Canada in 2012. Of these, about 85,000 are registered charities and the remainder have nonprofit status.[3] The distinctions between the two types of organizations are important for resource development.

A nonprofit organization can be created through a variety of statutes at either the provincial or federal level. Registered charitable status can only be given at the federal level through application to the Canada Revenue Agency (CRA). Once a nonprofit is given registered charitable status and a registered charitable number, it is then able to provide tax receipts for philanthropic gifts that donors can use for personal tax credits. Unregistered nonprofits cannot issue a tax creditable receipt.

There are a few important things to know about the issuance of charitable receipts:

- Charitable tax receipts can only be issued for a contribution that meets the conditions of a "gift" as defined under tax legislation.[4]

---

[3]   Imagine Canada Website: <http://www.imaginecanada.ca>, Research and Public Policy.

[4]   "Registered Charities and the *Income Tax Act*", Canada Revenue Agency, RC4108, at 5.

- The gift must be transferred by a donor to the registered charity.

- The gift must be given voluntarily by the donor.

- No consideration can be provided in return for the gift.

- Charitable tax receipts can be issued for in-kind contributions of product or materials (the donation of an item for an auction, a building, or a piece of art) but cannot be issued for the gift of services (contribution of 10 hours of consulting time, labour to install new flooring). Charities will typically handle this kind of situation through a simple cheque exchange; the services are provided and billed for, the charity pays the bill, and the provider donates the same amount back in exchange for a tax receipt.

- Corporate gifts that sponsor an event, name a building, or for which public recognition is a condition of the gift do not qualify for a charitable tax receipt. According to CRA this constitutes a marketing benefit and does not meet the gift definition. If a corporation takes a general business (non tax-creditable) receipt, the gift is then exempted from the gift receipting limitations.

There are other considerations that charities must take into account, such as the format and content of tax receipts as well as other kinds of contributions that do not meet the gift standard, and charities should be aware of all of these requirements. These can all be obtained from the CRA Website.[5]

While there are certainly advantages that nonprofits with registered charity status enjoy when it comes to philanthropic fundraising, this in no way precludes other nonprofits from successfully diversifying their revenue base. In fact, not having the limitations that come with charitable status allows nonprofit organizations to be more entrepreneurial and market-driven in expanding their resources.

TYPICAL SOURCES OF INCOME

The National Survey of Nonprofit and Voluntary Organizations provides us with a good picture of how organizations are funded (M.H. Hall *et al.* (2004 at 23-25)). Forty-nine per cent of all revenues reported by all nonprofit organizations (including hospitals, universities and other large institutions) come from governments. Of that, 40 per cent is from

---

[5] <http://www.cra-arc.gc.ca/chrts-gvng/menu-eng.html>.

provincial sources, 7 per cent is from federal sources and 2 per cent is from municipal sources. Earned income from non-governmental sources accounts for 35 per cent of revenues and includes such items as charitable gaming (1 per cent), membership fees or dues (11 per cent), fees for goods and services (20 per cent), and earnings from endowments or investments, including interest income (4 per cent).

The remaining 13 per cent (9 per cent excluding religious worship organizations) of all revenues comes from gifts and donations and breaks down as shown in Table 1.

Table 1: Sources of Gifts and Donations for all Canadian Charities

Source	Percent-age
Individual donations	8%
Fundraising organizations and family community foundations	1%
Disbursements from other nonprofit organizations	3%
Corporate sponsorships, donations or grants	3%

These numbers apply to all nonprofit organizations and within this group there are some common generalizations (M.H. Hall *et al.* (2004, at 23-25)):

- Smaller organizations rely more upon gifts and donations for revenues than do larger organizations.

- Larger organizations, particularly hospitals and universities, rely more on government funding but get a far greater share of the total value of gifts and donations than do the smaller organizations.

- Registered charities rely more on government revenues (54 per cent of their total revenues) than do other organizations (39 per cent) but also depend more on gifts and donations — 18 per cent compared with 4 per cent for non-charities.

- Other organizations rely more on earned income from non-government sources (53 per cent of revenues versus 25 per cent for charities).

There are a number of different sources for earned income other than fundraising.

More recent numbers are available through *The Satellite Account of Nonprofit Institutions and Volunteering* published by Statistics Canada in 2009 shows the sources of revenue for the core nonprofit sector (excluding the larger health care and post secondary institutions):

- sales of goods and services account for 45.6% of total income

- government funding at 19.7%

- membership fees 15.9%

- donations from households 12.0

- investment income 4.9%.

FIGURE 1

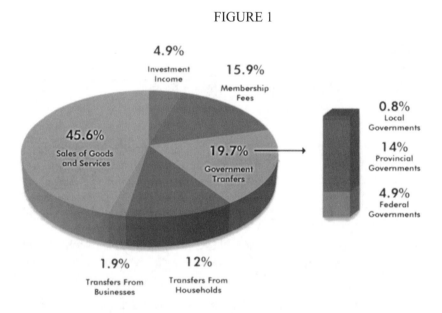

There is a multitude of ways that nonprofits can earn income. Some have been around for decades and others are just emerging. Table 2 lists some of these and their key characteristics:

Table 2

Type of Earned Income	Key Characteristics
Fees for service	Sliding scale (social service organizations) or flat rate (typical of sports groups/ associations)
Gaming	Raffles, bingos, casinos and lotteries of all sizes. Tend to be labour intensive and rely heavily on volunteers. Exception is large-scale lotteries, which are higher risk and require not only a large natural market but also a significant upfront investment.
Auxiliaries/Guilds/ Friends of	Typically found in health-related, cultural or recreation/environmental organizations and can range from an unstructured "friends of" group to a legally constituted, separate charitable organization. They may raise money for specific aspects of a charity's mission, *i.e.*, acquisition of art or a piece of medical equipment.
Membership Fees and Dues	Many nonprofits are member-based and these members can play an active role in the organization's affairs. Some organizations, such as the YMCA or volunteer centres, charge annual member fees that provide access to reduced fees for some of their services and other member-only benefits. Others, such as social service agencies or sports groups, offer membership more as a way to generally support the organization's mission. Either way, membership fees can be not only a source of revenue but, because they usually come from the people closest to your organization, a source of future philanthropic support.
Social Enterprise	Entrepreneurial ventures such as thrift shops, parking revenue and consulting services have been used by nonprofit organizations for many years as a way of diversifying revenues while balancing the demand for service and funding needs of nonprofit organizations.
	"Social enterprise" has emerged as a way for nonprofits to adopt more entrepreneurial and innovative revenue-generating strategies. However, there is much debate on what exactly social enterprise is and who should be

involved. The most common interpretation is an initiative that is set up to fulfill the mission and generate revenue. From a corporate perspective it is "doing good by doing well". There are, of course, both advantages and disadvantages to social enterprise. Table 3 outlines the most commonly considered ones that nonprofits may encounter (Williams (2005, at 23)):

Table 3: Social Enterprise Advantages and Disadvantages

Advantages	Disadvantages
• May bring in more revenue to the overall agency • The agency may become more self-sufficient • Financial diversification • Increases the agency's visibility • Expansion of contacts within the community including donors • Develops skills and knowledge within the organization • Opportunity to be innovative in developing services/programs • Puts the agency on the same playing field as the other sectors giving more credibility and power to influence policy change • Will not have to always dance to the funders' tune	• Lose focus or change mission and philosophy of the agency • Level of human resource expenditure • Level of financial start-up expenditures • Too much — not only an expert in running an organization, but now also need to be expert as an entrepreneur • Internal philosophical conflicts • Risk of financial loss if the venture is not successful • Risk of increased financial expenditure if the venture requires unanticipated subsidization • Board liability • It is a big structural change • It is a big cultural change (changes relationships with all stakeholders) • Just another phase, wait it out until the next flavour of the decade

If a nonprofit chooses to enter into the world of social enterprise, wherever your particular activity falls on the spectrum, it should make that choice after in-depth consideration of what will work for that particular organization, in terms of risk, support to target population, mission, mandate, and values. In 2003 CRA changed the *Income Tax Act*[6] to allow charitable organizations and public foundations to carry on related businesses that accomplish or promote their charitable objectives. A related business is a commercial activity (*i.e.*, revenue generating) that is either related to a charity's purposes or substantially run by volunteers. Registered charities need to take CRA requirements into account when considering social enterprise as a revenue generating opportunity.

There are numerous other sources of income that fall under the umbrella of fundraising. These include grants from foundations, corporate gifts, special events, direct mail, door-to-door campaigns, and telemarketing, to name a few. They are discussed in more detail later in this chapter.

RECENT TRENDS IN FUND DEVELOPMENT

Understanding the environment in which you are operating is key to strategic planning for any organization. For nonprofit organizations, understanding their giving and fundraising environments, both from a trend and a competitive perspective, is critical to assessing what your fundraising potential is and how best to achieve it. Key trends include:

Giving is rebounding in Canada. Charitable giving in Canada decreased substantially after the 2008/09 recession. In 2008 giving was down 5.6% and in 2009 down a further 5.4%. The trend is now upward and 2010 showed a 6.5% increase over the previous year with a total of $10.6 billion, which is comparable to what was given in 2007. Approximately 24 per cent of Canadian tax filers claim charitable donations, an increase of close to 100 per cent since 1997 and a 12 per cent increase since 2004.[7] Additional research conducted by the Association of Fundraising Professionals (AFP), an international association that represents fundraisers around the world, presented in its annual 2012 State of Fundraising review, reveals that fundraising revenue in Canada continues to increase year-by-year. Nearly six in 10 charities surveyed (58 per cent) raised more in 2012 than they did in 2011 from contributions, marking the first time since 2006 that significantly more than half showed such positive results.

---

[6]   R.S.C. 1985, c. 1 (5th Supp.).

[7]   See online at: <http://www.statcan.gc.ca/daily-quotidien/081104/dq081104b-eng.htm>.

However, there is also a stagnant trend in the number of tax filers (donors) who are claiming charitable gifts on their return. The percentage of Canadians claiming charitable tax credits has decreased from the low of 30 per cent in the late nineties to 24 per cent in 2007 (noting that Canadian couples can maximize their tax credits by claiming all charitable contributions on one return). At the same time, the number of Canadians over the age of 15 who give either money, gifts in kind or volunteer remains steady, and impressive, at approximately 84 per cent. Giving, both in number of tax filers and percentage of income, varies by province or territory. This information is available through Imagine Canada.[8]

Anecdotally, total giving in Canada is estimated to be more in the $15 billion range and reflects all financial gifts, tax receipted or not and including sponsorship dollars. According to The Fraser Institute, the extent of generosity in the United States is over three percentage points higher: 26.7 per cent of U.S. tax filers donate to charity compared to 23.3 per cent of Canadians. The gap between these two countries widens when considering the depth of the generosity of each. In 2010, Americans gave 1.38 per cent of their aggregate income to charity. This rate of giving is more than double that of Canadians, who gave 0.66 per cent of aggregate income to charity in 2010 (Fraser Institute, The 2012 Generosity Index). (The differences between the countries might be because Canada has a long tradition of government (tax) supported social services, health care, and education and thus many Canadians believe they support these services through their taxes, which are generally higher than in the United States.)

Individuals provide by far the largest portion of charitable gifts. Every year, approximately 74 per cent of total donations come from individuals, 14 per cent comes from corporations and 12 per cent comes from foundations. According to KCI Philanthropy, one of the leading fundraising consultancies in Canada, individual giving at the large gift level continues to grow exponentially. In the first three months of 2012 there were at least 43 gifts of more than $1 million made to Canadian charities by individuals, corporations and foundations, totalling $275 million. And more than $1 billion is given annually through direct response (mail, online, text). This is often surprising news to the leadership of many organizations, who assume that corporations and foundations are the best prospects for major

---

[8]   See online at: <http://www.givingandvolunteering.ca>.

sources of funding. It should be noted that it is difficult to assess the true value of corporate contributions because it can be sourced from so many pots within the corporate structure (community investment budget, marketing and executive). Nevertheless, it is generally accepted that, even if we were able to identify the total amount, it would not vary the picture by much more than 1 to 2 per cent.

The fundraising profession is growing. There has been a huge growth in the fundraising profession itself. In 1995, 214 Canadian fundraisers were members of the AFP. By mid-2013, this had grown to over 4,000, an increase of over 1,800 per cent. Fundraisers are better educated, have greater training and have more ongoing professional development opportunities. Organizations are responding to the increased competition for funds and the retreat of government funding by hiring professional fundraisers. As a result, more people are coming into the profession from all walks of life, many as a second career. There are also far more educational opportunities for fundraisers available in both Canada and the United States. An individual interested in fundraising as a career can take a certificate course at a local community college, a degree at a university or a Master's degree in Philanthropy and Nonprofit Leadership Program at Carleton University in Ottawa. Within the profession there is also a certification process. The Certified Fund Raising Executive (CFRE) benchmarks the achievements and expertise of fundraisers with a minimum of five full years in the profession. The Advanced Certified Fund Raising Executive (ACFRE) is an advanced credential for professional fundraisers with a minimum of 10 years' experience.[9]

Nonprofit fundraising activities show increased strength and professionalism and philanthropy is increasingly becoming a core source of funding for registered charities. Nonprofit organizations have become more strategic and professional in the way in which they plan and implement their development activities, the way they staff and resource their programs, and also in the way in which they work with donors. Cultivation of donors and solicitation methods have become more personalized, more strategic, and more professionally conducted.

---

[9]   Additional information about credentialing and educational opportunities can be accessed at: <http://www.afpnet.org> (the oversight body for the ACFRE credential); <http://www.cfre.org> (the oversight body for the CFRE credential and for information about U.S.-based educational opportunities); and <http://carleton.ca/mpnl> about the Carleton MPNL Program.

Organizations better understand the value of research and the importance of stewardship.[10]

More organizations are also hiring professional fundraisers to lead and manage their development activities. A 2002 study conducted by the Association of Fundraising Professionals (AFP) and Canadian Policy Research Networks (CPRN) (CPRN/AFP Study) found that almost one-quarter (24 per cent) of its respondents (fundraising professionals) were working for organizations that had been involved in fundraising for less than 10 years (McMullen (2003, at 13)). This was most common in organizations in the social services sub-sector. While there are no statistics on the number of Canadian nonprofits that employ professional fundraisers, extrapolation of the membership numbers of various professional associations (AFP, AHP, CASE) cross-referenced with the number of nonprofits that actually have staff (a very small percentage) would lead us to believe that there may be about 15,000 professional fundraisers in Canada working for about 12 to 15 per cent of the 85,000 registered charitable organizations.

One significant negative trend however, is the transient nature of the fundraising profession. The findings of the CPRN/AFP study were more recently substantiated in *Underdeveloped: A National Study of Challenges Facing Nonprofits* released in 2013 by CompassPoint and the Evelyn and Walter Haas, Jr. Fund (Underdeveloped Report). While the data is U.S.-based, it is highly likely that the numbers, disturbing as they are, would be similar in Canada. Nonprofits are struggling with the high turnover and long vacancies in development positions and a shocking 50 per cent + development directors plan to leave their current job within a two-year period. There are a variety of reasons for this but the primary factor is considered to be the lack of fundraising leadership at the top levels of the organization.

There is a greater focus on leadership. A demonstration of internal leadership has always been an important factor in an organization's ability to raise philanthropic revenue. With the increasing sophistication of donors and professionalism of fundraisers, this has become even more paramount. Donors expect an organization's key leadership (staff and board) to be visible, engaged, and a part of their relationship.

At the same time, it has become more challenging to recruit volunteer leadership. People have busy lives and, when they do volunteer

---

[10] Stewardship focuses on the whole relationship and recognizes that a donor has invested in your organization. Donor recognition is a part of stewardship as is accountability and trust.

for an organization, they want that experience to be meaningful. They expect to be strategically used and professionally supported.

Six Key Fundraising Principles

1.	People give to people.
2.	Much comes from few.
3.	Wealth is not always obvious.
4.	It's not about the money, it's about building the relationship.
5.	Fundraising is not a stand-alone activity.
6.	Philanthropy is something to be proud of, and fundraising enables philanthropy.

Fundraising can be a new and unfamiliar area for those nonprofit leaders who do not come into their positions with much experience in raising money either through fundraising or by more entrepreneurial means. Establishing a fundraising focus within a nonprofit, or enhancing a program that is already in existence, can be a challenging, and sometimes intimidating, undertaking. Assessing your strengths and weaknesses, your competitive position in the community, and what is going to work for a particular nonprofit organization are all factors for consideration. The following six key fundraising principles apply across the board to all fundraising and are important to recognize as your program develops:

People give to people. People give for all kinds of reasons but individuals in particular give for specific reasons. While there is no quantitative research available on this subject, anecdotal and experiential evidence tells us the following:

- The number one reason people give to a particular organization is because they or someone close to them has been touched by the cause that organization represents. For example, they or a family member, had cancer, they have a child with a disability, they attended a particular university or their mother/father/husband/wife/child/friend received exemplary care at a particular hospital.

- People give to other people, not to organizations. Too many organizations make the mistake of telling potential donors about how great their organization is. What donors want to hear about are the people your organization helps, how effective your organization is at providing services to them and the benefits to the community as a result of what your organization does. People want to give to the people for whom your organization is there to provide help and services. How your organization recognizes the gift and stewards the donor relationships (use of the gift, effectiveness, accountability) will help that donor to make the gift to your particular organization — usually after the donor has decided to make a gift to your general cause.

- People give because they are asked. All too often nonprofits make the mistake of not asking people to give to their organization. Whether this is board members, volunteers, prospects, clients, or current donors, if you do not ask you will not likely receive. People are generous and like to help others, but they need to be directly asked.

- Who asks is important. People like to see volunteer and staff leadership committed to the cause and "walking the talk". Having the right person cultivate and ask potential donors demonstrates credibility and worthiness of the cause.

- People do not make donations primarily because of the tax credit they receive. The tax credit is a bonus. They give to help, or build, or care for, or invest. However, the tax benefits are often a factor in determining the size of a gift, particularly when an individual is making a planned gift such as a bequest or a gift from assets, such as securities, real estate, or life insurance.

Much comes from few. The Pareto Principle, or 80/20 rule, created by Italian economist Vilfred Pareto in 1906 and later expanded upon by American Dr. Joseph Juran, is an accepted mathematical formula that describes how 20 per cent of something is always responsible for 80 per cent of the results. The 80/20 rule can be applied to just about anything: 20 per cent of the people in a business make 80 per cent of the decisions; 20 per cent of the people hold 80 per cent of the wealth; and 20 per cent of the work consumes 80 per cent of your time. The 80/20 rule is equally applicable to fundraising and is a key principle of fund development upon which goals and strategies are based. A successful fund development program will receive 80 per cent of its donations from 20 per cent of its donors. This is true pretty much across the broad spectrum of any fund development program and particularly so in major gift and campaign fundraising. An analysis of the 2003 CRA data on charitable contributions reveals that 25 per cent of all donors gave 82 per cent of the value of all donations. And this breakdown is consistent from year to year. In large capital campaigns, the trend is to an even wider ratio with 90 per cent or more of the gifts coming from 10 per cent or fewer of the donors.

Wealth is not always obvious. Too many organizations spend too much time trying to secure donations from the "usual suspects", *i.e.*, the high-profile community individuals who are known to have both influence and affluence. A look at CRA data for 2003 provides a different reality — 94 per cent of individuals with incomes over $75,000 claimed a charitable donation in that year and, on average, gave .32 per cent of their income to charities. In contrast, 76 per cent of individuals with incomes of less than $25,000 made a similar claim and, on average, gave 1.38 per cent of their income to charities. Clearly, there is generosity at all levels.

There is also wealth in less than obvious places. The high-profile community leaders (the "usual suspects") may very well be doing good works for many other organizations in the community but you can be sure that there are an even greater number who are trying to get them on their board, as a donor, or to head up their campaign. Charities need to take a broader view. There are many generous individuals with less, or less obvious, wealth but who still have the means and the interest to support your organization, and businesses that may not be the corporate leaders but still have a strong sense of community. The challenge for a nonprofit is to identify its potential donors and then find an approach to them.

It's not about the money, it's about building the relationship. With the growth of the fundraising profession, its increasingly professional approach to the discipline, and the greater knowledge and expectations of donors, organizations have realized that they need to pay more attention to donors and to building relationships with them in order to sustain their support. Donors are an organization's friends and play a large and vitally important role in organizations in which they invest. They contribute to an organization because they believe in the cause. At the same time, they do not always understand or accept the professional approach to fundraising and, in fact, can be suspicious of it. Getting to know and understand your donors, particularly at the higher giving levels, is key. Relationship, or donor-centred, fundraising is now a hallmark of successful programs that requires a nonprofit to look beyond the money transaction and respect donors as stakeholders in your mission.

Fundraising is not a stand-alone activity. One of the biggest mistakes a nonprofit can make is to treat fundraising as if it operates in a silo, separate and distinct from everything else that happens in your organization. Henry Rosso, in his groundbreaking and authoritative book, *Achieving Excellence in Fundraising*, says (Rosso (2003, at 27)):

> Fundraising cannot function apart from the organization; apart from its mission, goals, objectives and programs; apart from a willingness to be held accountable for all of its actions ... Fundraising by itself and apart from the institution has no substance in the eyes and heart of the potential contributor.

In order to achieve success, fundraising must work in synergy and collaboration with strategic planning, governance, and program planning and execution. And, it will involve and engage other staff, volunteers, and the board in all of these activities. The fundraiser is the professional manager, but the whole organization has a role to play in ensuring the cause is worth investing in and providing the opportunity for donors to make that investment.

Philanthropy is something to be proud of, and fundraising enables philanthropy. Philanthropy is often defined as "the gift of time, talent and resources", in the dictionary as "love of humankind" and also as "voluntary action for the public good through voluntary action, voluntary association, and voluntary giving" (Payton (1988)). People who give to organizations do so because they believe in something. They are proud of their act of philanthropy and consider it a privilege to be able to help and to make change. Ethical fundraising is the process that enables philanthropy, the presentation of the opportunity to make a gift. It is the responsibility of the nonprofit organization, board and staff, to approach its fundraising activities by seeking to match a prospective donor's interests with the needs of the organization and to do so in a way that does not demean the act of asking but presents the opportunity to support the cause with pride.

OVERVIEW OF A DEVELOPMENT PROGRAM

Nonprofit organizations come in all sizes and shapes. So too do development programs. Clearly, what is necessary in terms of staff, resources, volunteers, planning, evaluation, and communication to reach the large financial goals of a major university is not going to be what is required, let alone even feasible, for a small, grassroots nonprofit that has much smaller goals and no staff. Nevertheless, good and ethical fundraising is a component of all development programs, no matter the size of the organization or its financial goals.

In order to be successful and sustainable over the long term, to have renewal and growth, to develop mutually beneficial relationships with donors and to be accountable to those donors, a development program must integrate a diversified funding base with a number of fundraising vehicles rather than relying on just one method such as special events or direct mail or major gifts.

Donors can be grouped into broad categories, *i.e.*, individuals, corporate/business, foundations, groups/associations, for the purposes of broad strategies and evaluation. An integrated development program recognizes that there are different motivations for giving and preferred vehicles for giving. Some people prefer to handle their philanthropic giving by buying tickets or donating auction items to special events, some prefer giving at the door, some via direct mail, some like to give monthly and others once a year. An increasing number of people are making their donations online. The onus is on the nonprofit to offer a diverse number of vehicles that appeal to a broad base of donors.

CATEGORIES WITHIN AN INTEGRATED DEVELOPMENT PROGRAM

Organizational needs are typically classified into four specific categories: ongoing annual needs, special purpose needs, capital needs and endowment needs. The corresponding fundraising programs are typically the annual fund, major gifts program, capital campaigns, and planned giving. The "donor pyramid" is a conventional model that illustrates how an organization uses these fundraising programs to move a donor up the ladder in terms of both involvement and level of giving. It is also a key underpinning for all development planning. With the emergence of major giving it has become more common for donors to come into the pyramid at any level. Nevertheless, the concept of the pyramid still has value to demonstrate the inter-relationships between the various pieces of a development program.

Figure 2: Pyramid of Giving

Annual Giving

Ongoing annual financial needs arise out of the annual budgeting process and relate to that portion of a nonprofit's annual programs, services, and operating costs that are not covered by core grants or other forms of earned revenues. Some programs and services may need to be fully funded through fundraising revenues, others partially funded and others may not require any philanthropic support. In many organizations, core operating costs are not fully funded and fundraising is also required just to pay staff, buy copier paper, and keep the lights on.

An annual gift is one that is reasonably expected to be given year after year. Most annual gifts are small but the important thing for the annual giving program is that there are gift renewal mechanisms in place. Like anything else, it costs more to get the gift in the first place than it does to renew that gift. An annual development program that does not include a planned and proactive renewal program is neither cost-effective nor strategic.

A *successful* annual fund can provide several benefits such as:

- a reliable base of funding on an annual basis;

- a foundation for all other fundraising;

- support for annual operating and program needs that are not funded by other means;

- a source for "undesignated" gifts that can be used by the organization where most needed;

- an excellent way to attract greater numbers of new donors into the organization with potential to move up the giving pyramid toward the major gift status; and

- an increase in the profile of your organization in the community on a mass-market basis.

Most annual giving occurs in non-face-to-face activities such as personalized mail, special events, door-to-door campaigns, face-to-face or street fundraising, telephone solicitation, e-philanthropy, or other mass promotional opportunities such as organizational newsletters. Although personal fundraising is by far the most effective, it can also be the most expensive, particularly in human resources (staff and volunteers). Since annual gifts tend to be much smaller, the mass-market appeals can make sense from a cost versus benefit perspective.

Typical annual giving vehicles include:

Direct Response. Direct mail is one of the most commonly used fundraising vehicles by large and small organizations alike. According to Tech Web Direct,[11] direct response is "an information-driven marketing process, managed by database technology that enables marketers to develop, test, implement, measure and appropriately modify customized marketing programs and strategies" and typically includes mail, phone, radio/TV/Print, Web/email, and mobile/texting.

FLA Direct, a former Canadian direct marketing firm, measured the Canadian direct mail market between 2003 and 2007 and found that:

---

[11] Website at: <http://www.techwebdirect.ca>.

- one in three Canadian adults made contributions to charity through the mail in 2007;

- direct mail donations accounted for approximately $1.32 billion, or 25 per cent of all charitable revenue; and

- while the participation rate in direct mail was declining (35 per cent in 2003 to 33 per cent in 2007) total giving still represents a significant piece of the Canadian giving pie.

Tech Web Direct estimates that there is still over $1billion given annually by Canadians through some form of direct response and this vehicle represents the majority of first time gifts for most nonprofits.

Regular, targeted solicitation strategies can be an effective way to bring in new donors, upgrade or renew current donors and past donors who have not given to your organization for a few years, and create awareness for your cause.

The two key aspects of any individual direct response piece are having a compellingly written letter and making sure it is sent to the right people. Nonprofits can create their direct response pieces in-house or with the aid of a direct response specialist. Lists can be bought from list vendors or drawn up internally. This can be as simple as identifying the key stakeholders for your nonprofit (volunteers, suppliers, names supplied by volunteers) or purchasing lists from list vendors according to very specific criteria relevant to your particular cause. There are also mailing vendors who are able to take care of the actual distribution of a direct mail piece.

Direct response can be undertaken by any size organization, from large hospitals who do grateful patient mailings and universities who do alumni direct response marketing, to much smaller organizations who may only reach out at Christmas or for special appeals. Many organizations, particularly those that are organ or disease related, choose a particular month around which to create awareness (April is the Canadian Cancer Society's Cancer Awareness Month, January is Alzheimer Awareness Month sponsored by the Alzheimer Society of Canada) and will then conduct a number of events in that month that might include a special acquisition appeal (to acquire new donors), events, phone, online and door-to-door solicitation.

Direct mail itself can be expensive, particularly in the early stages, and organizations need to thoughtfully consider the risks and rewards. Direct mail is about building a long-term relationship with donors so they become annual contributors. To achieve success, nonprofits have to make a long-term commitment. The first year of any direct mail program may only break even or it could lose money. The second year is likely to be marginally better but it may take five years or more until the program reaches its maturity both in scope and revenues. Regardless, the key is to integrate direct response donors into all of the other fundraising tools in your toolbox.

The age-old question about direct mail is: *how often is too often?* Charitable organizations may be concerned that by mailing a solicitation to their donors more than one or twice a year they might be seen as intrusive and this could result in turning donors off. However, what many organizations find is that frequency of approach during the year actually increases the annual renewal rate of existing donors. This stands to reason since a donor is being given more than one opportunity during the year to make a gift — at a time when it is more convenient or to an appeal that resonates more with them. Furthermore, there tends to be a direct correlation between the frequency of giving during a calendar year and donor loyalty over time. Those donors who make multiple gifts during the year are self-identifying themselves as ones who feel more connected to the cause and are possible candidates for personal giving options. And if you did not ask more than once, you would not know this.

However, when conducting a direct response program where there will be multiple "asks" during the year, it is essential that the donor data system be structured in such a way as to honour donor requests such as not sending mail, mailing only once per year, or even, where possible, mailing at a preferred time of year. Those donors who may be offended by too many mailings should be given an option to join a monthly giving program. This could be the right solution for them and a big win for the organization.

Special Events. Special events can figure prominently in many development programs and not at all in others. What they should not be is the primary or sole method of raising funds. Events can be expensive and labour-intensive, requiring both significant volunteer and staff time, and have no guarantee of success. They are one of the least cost-effective ways of raising money but can also be one of the most effective at raising profile and, if directly mission-related, awareness of the cause. Events tend to be more about raising friends than raising money.

Events come in all sizes and shapes and include everything from runs/walks to gala dinners and balls. Online events (Movember, Weekend to End Breast Cancer) have become hugely successful programs for organizations and almost every event now will have an online component — everything from ticket purchase to an advance online auction. Many organizations may use an annual signature event to define themselves with the public and to raise dollars. Key considerations for event fundraising include:

- Know why you are having an event. Is it to raise money or raise friends and awareness? Or a combination and, if so, in what mix?

- Have a clear understanding of who your event is targeted to. An event targeted towards twenty-somethings is going to be much different from an event targeted to an older, more sedate crowd.

- Clearly outline the roles and responsibilities between staff and volunteers.

- Have an event plan and a timeline for key activities to keep everyone on the same page and on track.

- Have an event budget so both staff and volunteers know what resources are available and what the net financial goal is.

- Make sure the event is appropriate for your organization. Creativity and innovation can make or break an event but it must be aligned with your organization's values and not offend your key stakeholders in any way.

The two main sources of revenue for events are ticket sales and sponsorships. In order to maximize results it is often a good strategy to target one or the other as the source of revenue that will cover all the event costs, leaving the other as net profit.

Telemarketing/Phone Solicitation. Telephone solicitation remains a vital component of many development programs and is particularly effective for renewal and upgrading of current donors, for membership associations, for donor clubs and for recapturing lapsed donors. A combined mail/on-line/phone campaign can yield even better results. Using phone solicitation for acquiring new donors through cold calls can be both expensive and inefficient. Privacy has become more of a concern to people and many dislike being called at home; the increased use of voice mail and call display makes impersonal phone solicitation challenging. Nevertheless, thousands of nonprofits of all sizes raise millions of dollars each year by telephone solicitation.

Historically, a telephone solicitation program was conducted by volunteers but the majority of nonprofits now hire telephone canvassers or use a professional telemarketing company. A common exception to this is phone-a-thons, used by causes that have wide public appeals, such as those often conducted by community partners for children's hospitals. Universities have long used student canvassers to solicit support from alumni. They are paid for their services but the function is overseen internally.

There are advantages and disadvantages to both models but, in most cases, inhouse programs should only be considered if a nonprofit is willing to invest the time and resources to ensure success.

Table 4: Telephone Solicitation

	Advantages	Disadvantages
Conducted inhouse	• Can recruit, train, and supervise callers yourself • Offers more day-to-day control over activities • Can write your own script • Less costly • Highly interactive and personal	• Can be difficult to recruit trainers • Need to have staff to train and supervise callers • Recruitment is ongoing • Need equipment and space for call centre
Conducted by outside vendor	• Vendor hires, trains, and supervises callers • Vendor will take care of all administrative functions, tracking, and reporting data • High cost efficiency (technology, technique, and experienced staff)	• Less control on day-to-day basis • Can be more costly, particularly in the early stages • Less commitment to your cause

Selection of a vendor needs to be done carefully and involves checking references, quality control processes, pricing, reliability and success rates. It is helpful to talk to other clients. Pricing is a key factor. In the past many vendors billed on a percentage of dollars raised and this often resulted in the vendor taking an unreasonably high portion of the funds raised. (See, the section of ethics and percentage-based fundraising for additional information.) Flat-fee contracts are now the norm and provide safety nets for nonprofits and assurance to donors that a greater percentage of their donation will go to the cause (depending, of course, on how much is raised). Commercial telemarketers will charge the same rate regardless of how much is pledged and ultimately collected so a phone campaign could cost 20¢ for every dollar raised or 45¢ for every dollar raised, depending on the purpose of the campaign and the targeted list.

Door-to-door Campaigns. There are far fewer door-to-door campaigns in the 2000s than there were in the 1980s. The major challenge with a door-to-door campaign is finding the volunteers to do the canvassing, and many nonprofits are not comfortable with hired canvassers. Very few charitable organizations continue to canvass with volunteers but many, such as the Salvation Army, have discontinued their door-to-door campaign because of this issue. Safety of canvassers has also become of increasing concern.

Nevertheless, door-to-door campaigns remain solid fundraisers, particularly for many smaller, community-based organizations, such as local sports groups, that have the capacity to draw from an invested group of volunteers within a localized geographic area. In larger urban areas door-to-door campaigns are now almost solely conducted by larger organizations but in smaller communities they are still feasible for many organizations.

E-philanthropy and Social Media. Online capacity and social media have had a significant impact on fundraising in a number of ways. One of these is the emergence of e-philanthropy, or the use of the Internet to build donor relationships with supporters of a nonprofit organization. Websites are key information tools for the nonprofit to communicate its cause and its needs and for donors who want information about an organization or a particular cause. Now widely used for ticket sales and disaster relief,[12] online giving is favoured by donors of all ages and is a fundamental staple of almost all development programs. Social media such as Facebook, Twitter and Pinterest have

---

[12]   In 2005, the American Red Cross reported that it received nearly 50 per cent ($762.5 million) of the total donations ($1 billion +) in the first two weeks after Hurricane Katrina online.

become integral components of many charities, to both raise money and build relationships.

There are a number of online giving portals that charities can register with as a cost-effective alternative when it does not make sense to establish an online giving mechanism through its own Website. One such portal is CanadaHelps.org. Established in 2000, CanadaHelps has facilitated over $300 million in donations to Canadian charities annually.[13]

Face-to-face/Street Fundraising. Still relatively new in Canada, F2F or on-street fundraising has long been a staple in Europe and Asia and is making an appearance in many Canadian cities. Solicitors tend to be young people, are very well-trained and focused on signing up donors for monthly giving. It is most commonly used by global non-government organizations (NGOs) but universities and larger institutional charities are experimenting with this strategy.

Major and Special Giving

There has been an explosion of major gift fundraising in Canada and of the number and value of major gifts given. Rather than relying on many small gifts from a large number of donors, major gift fundraising focuses on strategically identifying and cultivating donors with the potential to contribute significantly greater amounts to an organization. Over the past decade the number of major campaigns with $100 million plus goals has increased exponentially. In response, so has the giving by Canadians. While billion dollar campaigns are more frequent the vast majority of charities would never have the need or capacity to set a goal of that size.

There are a variety of financial needs that a nonprofit has that are most suitable to a major gift program. Current programs and services, special projects, seed money for new projects, research, endowments and capital needs are examples. Many organizations are now permanently in "campaign" mode and run concurrent campaigns that are really ongoing major gift programs. Characteristics of major gifts include:

• They are typically one-time gifts as opposed to gifts that an organization can reasonably expect to receive annually.

---

[13] Website at: <http://www.canadahelps.org>.

- They are almost always designated, *i.e.*, one that the donor is making for a specific purpose, and the gift the nonprofit is morally obligated to use according to the donor's intent.

- They can be made from cash or assets (gifts of appreciated securities, real estate, art).

- They are almost always the result of a face-to-face cultivation and solicitation.

- They are generally the top 10 to 20 per cent of gifts received.

Major gift programs have become a critical component of non-profit development programs of all sizes for two main reasons. First, they are the most effective way of building what could be long-term relationships with donors to an organization and, second, because major gift fundraising is an individual, face-to-face exercise, it is the most cost-effective way of raising money.

What constitutes a major gift varies from organization to organization. In smaller organizations they could start at $1,000 and in larger institutions at $50,000. Historically, major gifts tended to come from donors who had made several smaller annual gifts to a nonprofit over time. Today, however, major gifts can come from current donors or first time donors. Current donors are still the best prospects for greater giving and individuals, corporations, and foundations are all potential prospects for major gifts.

There are a number of vehicles through which major gifts are solicited and received:

Major Gift Program	A major gift program is a seamless, ongoing series of activities that is specifically focused on identifying potential major gift prospects, cultivating their interests, and matching them to a nonprofit's needs before soliciting them for the gift.
Major Gift Campaign	A major gift campaign utilizes the same series of activities as a major gift program but it is packaged as a time-sensitive campaign. This may be for a special project such as research, a new program or programs, or expansion of current activities.

Capital Campaign	A capital campaign is a one-time, intensive effort to raise a specific dollar goal for a specific bricks and mortar project. It could be a new building, renovation of an existing building, a new wing of a hospital or a combination of capital and program needs. A capital campaign is a focused project in and of itself that is strategically planned and executed, generally relies heavily on volunteers, and has a beginning and end.
	An organization considering a capital campaign is generally wise to first conduct a feasibility or planning study into the community's interest and willingness to participate. Feasibility studies are a worthwhile investment that test the goal, the potential leadership, the case, and the timing, and should be conducted by an outside consultant to ensure objectivity.
Endowment Giving	An endowment fund is a self-sustaining funding source based on the interest from invested money. It can be extremely helpful in providing long-term financial stability in the present and future. Gifts to an endowment are not subject to a charity's regular disbursement quota and are invested in stocks, bonds, and other vehicles. With the exception of a small percentage of assets as required by the *Income Tax Act*, the principal remains intact in perpetuity and the interest is spent on charitable purposes.

An important method of creating an endowment fund is by utilizing the resources of Community Foundations. These organizations exist in many areas of Canada. They solicit donations from many individuals and then provide grants to causes specified by the donors or by the foundation itself. Most community foundations are willing to talk to specific nonprofit organizations about housing and administering endowment programs for them.[14]

Typical endowments are endowed chairs at universities, which can be set up with a lead donor and then many other smaller donors (*e.g.*, an endowed research chair in pediatric oncology). Another

---

[14] See Community Foundations of Canada Website at: <http://www.cfc-fcc.ca> for additional information.

example is an operating endowment, which a nonprofit would hold for long-term sustainability purposes and for which it would solicit donations from a variety of sources. (Often undesignated bequests will go directly into an operating endowment.)

An endowment can also be created for a fixed term — until a specified period of time elapses or until a specified event occurs. In the meantime, it functions as a true endowment as discussed above. Some nonprofits choose to set up a quasi-endowment, or a reserve fund that, while they treat it is an endowment, it is not subject to endowment tax regulations.[15]

Endowments are largely derived from gifts from individuals. Corporations and foundations will usually exclude this type of giving from their guidelines because of their long-term nature and, particularly with corporations, the difficulty in providing recognition.

Endowments can be held and managed internally but many organizations prefer to have them managed externally by a community foundation, private foundation or private investment firm where the expertise and capacity to do so already exists.

Planned Giving. Frank Minton and Lorna Somers define planned giving as "… the process of designing charitable gifts so that the donor realizes philanthropic objectives while maximizing tax and other financial benefits" (Minton & Somers (1997)). Planned gifts are either current or deferred major gifts. Current planned gifts are given from current assets such as securities or real estate and timed to minimize any capital gains tax and obtain full benefit of the tax credit. Deferred gifts are gifts that are committed to in the present but the value of the gift is not received by the charity until some time in the future. Deferred gifts can be through bequests, charitable remainder trusts, life insurance policies, or gifts of residual interests.

There has been much discussion about the transfer of wealth between generations over the next several decades, with some estimates as high as one trillion dollars. This, combined with a change in Canadian tax law that removed the capital gains tax on donations of securities to registered Canadian charities, has fuelled a steep rise in the incorporation of planned giving into development programs. A 2006 study conducted by Imagine Canada on behalf of

---

[15] For information on 10-year gifts and endowments see the CRA Website at: <http://www.cra-arc.gc.ca>.

seven umbrella organizations and associations[16] found that donations of securities increased noticeably between 2004 and 2006; that the percentage of charities receiving donations of securities increased from 43 per cent to 49 per cent; the number of donations of securities more than doubled; and the total value of donations of securities donations also doubled. Gifts of securities have only continued to become a significant source of revenue for many charities and, while there was a noticeable drop during the economic crisis of 2008/09, they have by and large not only retained but continued to grow their popularity.

The surge of planned giving activity initially resulted in a sub-specialty of the professional fundraiser, the gift planner, within the development office. However, the current trend is to fully integrate gift planning into major gift programs in recognition that a donor can and often wants to give in a variety of ways. Regardless of size of organization, all nonprofits can incorporate some element of planned giving into their fund development program without a specialist on staff. Bequests and gifts of securities are easily handled by most organizations. The more sophisticated vehicles call for outside legal or financial expertise and are usually proactively promoted by organizations with specialized gift planners on board.

There are several resources available for nonprofits interested in implementing a planned giving program. The Canadian Association of Gift Planners (CAGP)[17] has numerous resources available and operates Leave a Legacy Councils in many communities. These councils provide a professional resource for nonprofit gift planners as well as public activities such as Wills Workshops to educate donors on making bequests. Many of these Wills Workshops are hosted in conjunction with local community foundations, which are also good resources for planned giving information.

IDENTIFYING DONORS

Successful fundraising is predicated on the building of relationships with donors who have the most potential to support your organization. While there is a whole universe of potential donors for nonprofit organizations, identifying the donors who are going to be interested in

---

[16] M. Lasby & M.H. Hall, *Charitable Gifts of Securities: Implications for Canadian Organizations* (Imagine Canada, 2007), available online at: <http://www.nonprofitscan.ca> and <http://www.afpnet.org>.

[17] Online at: <http://www.cagp-acpdp.org>.

your particular cause, have both the ability to give to you and the connections to your organization is something that must be done in a focused, thoughtful, and strategic manner. Broad categories of donors include individuals, corporations/business, foundations and other groups/associations. Within each of these categories there are sub-categories that apply to individual nonprofits, as shown in Table 5.

Table 5: Identifying Donors

Individuals	<ul><li>alumni (universities, colleges, private schools)</li><li>clients and potential clients (social service agencies)</li><li>members (religious organizations, environmental groups, membership-based organizations, professional associations, sports and recreation)</li><li>patients (health care)</li><li>current and former staff</li><li>current and former volunteers</li><li>parents/family of clients, members, students, patients</li></ul>
Corporate/Business	<ul><li>corporations that operate in the area</li><li>small- and medium-sized businesses that operate in the community</li><li>businesses with which someone connected to the organization may have a relationship, i.e., business owned by a board member or volunteer</li><li>businesses that provide supplies, equipment, or services to the organization</li></ul>
Foundations	<ul><li>the local community foundation</li><li>private family foundations</li><li>foundations set up by other nonprofits that may grant outside of their connected institution</li></ul>
Groups/Associations	<ul><li>United Ways and other federated funding organizations</li><li>service clubs</li><li>employee groups</li><li>professional associations</li><li>community groups</li></ul>

This list is not exhaustive by any means. Individual nonprofits will each have their own stakeholder groups. The key is to identify them from the inside out. Start with those closest to your organization, the prospective donors who have the greatest potential for your own organization.

Figure 3: Constituencies and Energy of an Organization

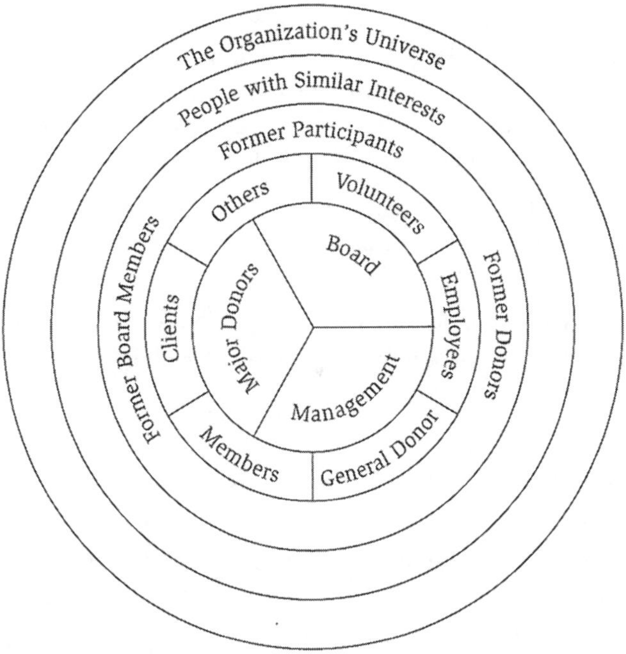

Source: © 2002, The Fund Raising School at the Center on Philanthropy at Indiana University. Reprinted by permission.

The concentric circles developed by The Fund Raising School[18] illustrate the constituencies and energy of an organization. The closer a person is to the organization (the middle of the circle) the greater the energy, the stronger the bond, and the greater potential for obtaining donations. As one moves outwards, the energy and the bonds weaken and the potential for recruiting donors is lessened.

---

[18] The Fund Raising School, 2002, at 2-17.

Individual Donors

Individual donors are the mainstay of almost all development programs. From small annual donors to major gift donors, individuals consider their gifts to be investments in the cause of the organization. The *2010 Canadian Survey of Giving, Volunteering and Participating* reveals that 89 per cent of donors gave because they felt compassion for those in need and that 85 per cent gave because they personally believed in the cause. On the other hand, only 23 per cent (or one in five donors) gave because of the tax credit they would receive.[19] For the most part, experience confirms these statistics and tells us that the vast majority of people give to organizations they believe in or by whose cause they have been personally touched.

In 1994 Alan Prince and Karen File studied more than 800 individuals and developed seven basic profiles for major givers (Prince & File (2001)):

1. *The Communitarians* — people who give to charities because of a strong sense of community and a desire to help build or enhance that community.

2. *The Devout* — people who generally give to their church or for other religious or spiritual reasons.

3. *The Investors* — people who give because it is good business to do so. These are often corporate leaders and people to whom the charity's cost-effectiveness will be an important factor.

4. *The Socialites* — people who give through their leadership and attendance of special events.

5. *The Altruists* — people who give because of a strong moral sense that it is the right thing to do.

6. *The Repayers* — people who give because they have benefited from a cause, a program or an organization's services.

7. *The Dynasts* — people who give through family foundations or from a strong family tradition.

These profiles are helpful in understanding why people give and how they should be approached, but for each nonprofit identifying the potential group of donors in the community who might be interested in

---

[19]   CSGVP, 2010, available online at: <http://www.givingandvolunteering.ca>.

the specific organization and then identifying their individual motivations is the key to success. Simply meeting and talking to them, possibly utilizing such techniques as focus group interviews, is the best way to learn about these motivations.

Donors are also more knowledgeable and sophisticated about their giving. The accessibility to information through the Internet, the increase in natural disasters and media coverage on the sector have all resulted in a higher sector profile and more information for donors to use in deciding where to contribute and in planning their giving.

Corporate Donors

Corporate giving has changed dramatically in the past two decades from simple donations to a more marketing-driven model. Donations programs are now a part of strategically focused community investment programs and come under the banner of corporate social responsibility initiatives. Many companies have strict guidelines about what they will give to and where their interests are, or are not, and these are tied to its "triple bottom line" (economic, social, and environmental returns on investment). Many companies also realize that community involvement is important to their employees and so has value in the recruitment and retention of their workforce. It also has a positive impact on their public image and can be used to support the company's marketing efforts. As a result, corporate philanthropy has by and large merged with the marketing and community relations functions and is tied much more closely to the company's bottom line.

For the nonprofit organization, this necessitates a much more strategic approach to securing corporate support. Research is a must — the lack of homework on the part of an organization will be clear to the company's community investment staff. Like individuals, corporate donors now have clearly defined outcomes they expect the nonprofit to achieve and will scrutinize the use of their funds to a greater degree. Figure 4 illustrates the continuum of corporate philanthropy and the framework within which corporate giving tends to occur today.

Figure 4: Continuum of Corporate Philanthropy

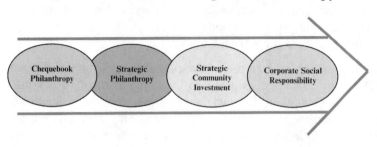

• Financial donations	• Focus area	• Linked to business	• Integrated
• Traditional causes/approaches	• Employee volunteerism	• Proactive	• Value add strategies
	• Image	• Stakeholder involvement	• Social vision

Source: The Strategic Giving Group, The United Way of Calgary and Area: <http://www.calgaryunitedway.org>. © 2006 United Way of Calgary and Area. Reprinted by permission.

To identify potential corporate donors, a nonprofit needs to have a clear understanding of what the opportunities for each partner are.

Table 6: Identifying Opportunities for Companies and Nonprofits

What Companies Might Be Looking For:	What Nonprofits Might Need:
• Engage employees, build a true partnership • Build brand awareness • Enhance image or reputation • Increase profits • Increase employee morale and attract and retain employees • Attract investors • Create public trust and goodwill now and in the future • Gain competitive advantage	• Secure needed revenue • Diversify revenue base • Enhance reputation • Increase public awareness of the organization and the cause • Attract volunteers and donors • Gather in-kind resources or services • Build capacity

Corporations are more likely to give to specific program or capital projects and much less likely to give undesignated operating support money. There are a number of ways in which they may make contributions.

Sponsorships. A rapidly growing form of corporate giving, companies sponsor everything from special events to special projects. Sponsorship is a pure marketing endeavour for which a company will require public recognition. Nonprofits should look for companies that align with their cause, where their cause may support a company's brand and where there are natural synergies between the nonprofit and the company.

In-kind Donations. In-kind giving is one of the largest forms of support by companies. Everything from furniture to media buys to personnel secondments can provide a source of non-financial but needed resources that assist a nonprofit in fulfilling its mission.

Matching Gifts. Many companies have programs that will match the contributions that employees make to nonprofits up to a certain amount.

Cause Marketing. The phrase "cause-related marketing" was first used by American Express in 1983 to describe its campaign to raise money for the restoration of the Statue of Liberty. Every time someone used an American Express card, the company made a one-cent donation to the Statue of Liberty. The result was a sizeable donation to the project as well as a significant growth in both cardholders and card usage.

Since that time, cause marketing has come into its own and become a viable part of many nonprofit fund development programs. Today, it annually raises over $4 billion (Daw (2006)) in marketing support (cash and awareness) for North American nonprofit organizations through creative, innovative, and mutually beneficial partnerships.

In her 2006 book, *Cause Marketing for Nonprofits: Partner for Purpose, Passion and Profits*, Jocelyne Daw, Vice-President Enterprises at The Glenbow Museum in Calgary, defines cause marketing as "… a corporate-nonprofit partnership that aligns the power of a company's brand, marketing and people with a nonprofit cause's brand and assets to create shareholder and social value and to publicly communicate values" (Daw (2006, at xvii)).

Cause-related marketing initiatives come in many forms. Traditionally, cause marketing referred to a for-profit company associating itself with a nonprofit organization by promoting a product and raising money for the nonprofit at the same time. Most common are agreements to donate a percentage of the purchase price of a specific object to a specific organization or project. An example is McDonald's McHappy Day®, which invites local celebrities and community leaders to serve on a specific day and $1 of certain products sold on that day is donated to charity. McHappy Day® has raised more than $25.9 million for children's charities in Canada since its inception in 1977. Other initiatives include affinity credit cards, long distance telephone services and special offers of services by professionals (dentists, lawyers).

Cause marketing has continued to evolve and to build on the brand and assets of both the nonprofit and the business to achieve greater awareness, enhance mission fulfillment and raise revenues by working together. The CIBC Run for the Cure is one such cause marketing initiative. Started in 1992 by a small group of volunteers who wanted to raise awareness for breast cancer, it now involves over one million participants and raises in excess of $30 million each year to support breast cancer research and educational initiatives.[20] CIBC aligned itself with the run from the start and has brought its considerable assets, marketing power and reach, staff support (the CIBC team is 10,500 strong), and funding, to promote the run, the breast cancer cause, and CIBC as a community-minded and caring company.

Cause marketing can bring many benefits to a nonprofit but also comes with challenges and risks. *Cause Marketing for Nonprofits* points out that there are benefits beyond just dollars, including validation of a nonprofit's activities, help in achieving its mission, the creation of brand awareness, the dissemination of information, the opportunity to change behaviour and attitudes, the bringing of valuable corporate expertise and finally, the leveraging of additional resources.

For corporations, as Daw says, "the more active cause-marketing relationships give the company a competitive advantage by creating tangible value and increasing their profitability by helping them attract employees; selling products; managing their reputations; increasing their bottom line; appealing to employees, customers, and stakeholders; and securing the license they need to operate in many markets" (Daw (2006, at xvii)).

While cause-related marketing can be an excellent source of long-term returns with minimal long-term effort, the nonprofit must

---

[20] Canadian Breast Cancer Foundation, Website at: <http://www.cbcf.org>.

still think carefully about whether or not such a partnership will work for it. Questions to consider include:

* What is it you have to offer a potential cause marketing partner?
* Who are good potential partners for your organization?
* Is there a good alignment of values between the organizations so that the nonprofit's vision, mission and values are not undermined?
* What is required in terms of internal infrastructure to support the relationship?
* How much time will it take?
* Are there staff in place to support and manage the program?

Foundations

Foundations exist to contribute financial resources to charitable organizations. They are almost always governed by strict guidelines that define their areas of interest, the types of programs they will and will not fund, their geographic scope of giving, and their application process. Grant applications are typically detailed in nature and differ from foundation to foundation. Foundation fundraising can be a time-consuming undertaking and, in order to maximize results, thorough research into potential foundation funders is critical. There are a number of databases available as a good resource for researching foundations and their giving records. Imagine Canada's *Directory to Foundations*[21] and Metasoft's *The Big Database*[22] are two that provide a good first overview of potential funders. Additional research is strongly recommended so that only those foundations with demonstrated potential for interest in the organization's cause are targeted. A broad, mass appeal to foundations is not recommended nor is it a good use of resources.

Groups and Associations

Every community has its share of Kinsmen Clubs, Rotary Clubs, Lions Clubs and a good variety of community groups that can provide both financial and volunteer resources to a nonprofit. As these groups are largely volunteer run and managed, access to them is best achieved by volunteers from the nonprofit. While many of these groups provide

---

[21] Online: <http://www.imaginecanada.ca>.
[22] Online: <http://www.bigdatabase.ca>.

small grants, some have the potential and preference for larger grants. For example, more affluent Rotary Clubs will often make a smaller number of larger grants to fewer organizations and Kinsmen Clubs will often tend to align themselves with a particular cause.

There are also federated funding agencies in most communities across Canada such as the United Way/Centraide that run annual campaigns to raise funds from a broad community base and then invest it back into that community. United Ways typically limit their funding to social service agencies, and the more progressive ones will also identify key community issues and fund solutions-based initiatives that draw on a diverse number of community partners.

FUNDRAISING FOR CORE OPERATING NEEDS

Fundraising for core costs can be extremely challenging because they are not as exciting to donors as special projects and programs. They are, however, essential and legitimate components of the projects and programs that donors do like to fund. While fundraising for undesignated dollars helps to cover the lights, heat or rent, the better way to approach core costs is to ensure that they are fairly allocated across the spectrum of programs and services a nonprofit offers. Rather than operating with a line item budget, nonprofits are better positioned if they operate with project-oriented budgets. Project accounting is widely used by business and government and is completely ethical and legal for use by a nonprofit. The goal is not to trick donors but to present the true costs of a program. For further discussion of this form of budgeting and accounting, see Chapter 10.

IDENTIFYING WHAT WORKS FOR YOUR NONPROFIT

Identifying the development approach that offers the best return on investment and is suitable for a particular organization is the key to success. While diversity is always important, each fundraising vehicle needs to be designed in a way that capitalizes on the organization's strengths and its financial and human (staff and volunteer) resources. While not exhaustive, Table 7, below outlines the financial and human resources generally required for each type of fundraising and how they might apply to different sized nonprofits.

Table 7: Identifying What Works

Type of Fundraising	Financial Resources	Human Resources	Suitable for
Annual Giving			
Direct Response	Significant upfront investment of dollars over multiple years with no guarantee of return in early years.	Small, irregular mailings can be done by volunteers. Larger programs require staff to either run inhouse or manage an outsourced campaign; no volunteer involvement necessary.	All sizes of nonprofits but difficult for all-volunteer organizations to conduct a program with regular mailings.
Telemarketing	Significant investment in equipment, space and administrative infrastructure. Hired callers add to costs.	Recruiting volunteers to make calls can be challenging. Staff to run inhouse program or monitor outsourced one. Outsourcing requires no volunteers.	Volunteer phone solicitors effective way to thank and renew donors. All nonprofits can run an outsourced telephone solicitation if budget allows.
Door-to-door Campaign	Investment in materials and administrative infrastructure. Hired canvassers add to costs.	Recruitment of volunteers can be challenging. Safety is an issue. Require staff to plan program, recruit and monitor, and do follow-up.	Small organizations typically depend on volunteers. Larger nonprofits can handle volunteer or hired canvassers.

Type of Fundraising	Financial Resources	Human Resources	Suitable for
E-philanthropy/Social Media	Investment in continuous Website upgrades and capability and administrative infrastructure.	Staff to monitor must be dedicated and knowledgeable; minimal volunteer involvement.	All organizations, either through their own Website or a giving portal.
Face-to-face/Street	Almost always outsourced.	Minimal internal other than gift processing. Most gifts are monthly so ongoing communications and data processing are key.	Organizations with a broad and deep profile and appeal.
Major gifts			
Major Gift Programs and Campaigns	Materials, research, cultivation activities.	Volunteers play a key role in identifying, opening doors and cultivating prospects. Can be volunteer only or staff/volunteer mixed.	Suitable for all organizations tailored to size.
Capital Campaigns	Can require significant costs in materials, training, campaign counsel, recognition.	Staff and volunteers together. Difficult to do all-volunteer campaign (will take longer and may flounder without staff direction).	Suitable for all organizations tailored to size.
Endowment Giving	Financial costs are generally associated with other vehicles.	Same as for major gifts.	Same as for major gifts.

Type of Fundraising	Financial Resources	Human Resources	Suitable for
Planned Giving	Start-up costs in materials, information, available technical expertise. The more complex the offerings the more costly the program.	Same as for major gifts.	Same as for major gifts. Being more proactive in encouraging bequests a good starting point for smaller nonprofits.
Sponsorships	Recognition, event planning. Costs are part of event budget.	Can be volunteers or staff or mix. Sponsor support should usually be staff.	All sizes. Sponsor/nonprofit alignment and clear goals are key.
Cause Marketing	Research, cultivation, negotiation, travel, administrative oversight.	Requires staff to implement and monitor on a larger scale.	Appropriate to size. Small organizations on a local level; larger nonprofits have regional and national potential.
Social Enterprise	Research, start-up costs, administrative oversight.	Generally requires staff to implement and monitor.	Medium to larger organizations.
Foundations	Research, grant preparation.	Generally staff though volunteers ok on small scale.	All organizations.
Groups/Associations	Minimal financial costs.	Staff and volunteers.	All organizations.

RESOURCING THE DEVELOPMENT FUNCTION

Organizational Structure

There are two possible frameworks within which the development function can take place on behalf of a nonprofit. The function can operate as a separate department within the organizational hierarchy or it can function within a separately instituted organization or foundation. A nonprofit can opt to establish a parallel foundation for a variety of reasons. These are the pros and cons to be considered:

Table 8: Parallel Foundation Pros and Cons

Pros	Cons
• Can help make fundraising happen faster • Provides the opportunity to recruit a separate set of influential leadership just focused on fundraising, particularly when the governing board does not have profile or does not consider fundraising part of its job • Recruitment can be easier because leaders do not need to be consumed by other governance issues • Formalizes the separation between operating, endowment, and/or capital funds • Places the funds out of sight of government encroachment • Eliminates bureaucratic restrictions • Protects assets in the event of a legal suit	• The establishment of a separate legal entity requires by-laws, separate board meetings, minutes, annual meetings, financial statements, tax returns, and other government-related documents • Requires recruitment, orientation and support of a completely different set of volunteer leaders • It can be challenging to ensure that the mission, goals, and objectives of the two organizations do not diverge over time • There is a more stringent disbursement quota applied to parallel foundations than there is to a registered charity • A foundation does not always increase fundraising results. Commitment and planning are still a prerequisite

Some nonprofits choose to set up a small "f" foundation that is not legally constituted, but nevertheless operates as a foundation with a separate leadership group and single focus. Others utilize Community Foundations as the home for certain kinds of funds.

Staffing

The growth in fundraising and of the fundraising profession has resulted in staffing challenges for nonprofit organizations. The 2003 CPRN/AFP Study (McMullen (2003, at ix)) found that slightly more than 40 per cent of the fundraisers surveyed had 10 or more years of experience while 29 per cent had less than five years. This correlated to organizational size with 43 per cent working for small organizations that generated less than $250,000 annually and having less than five years' experience. Even though 60 per cent worked for organizations that had increased their fundraising staff in the previous two years, the majority (60 per cent) worked in establishments with fewer than 25 paid staff (McMullen (2003, at 13)). Of these, we can reasonably assume that a strong majority are working in one-person development shops, likely with no or part-time administrative support. In the current climate, the number of job opportunities far outstrips the number of experienced and qualified fundraisers and this, along with a number of other factors, has led to a high level of transience in the profession and escalating salaries, often higher than program heads. The Underdeveloped Report (at 252) provides valuable insight into the challenges with fund development and leadership and underscores the necessity of development as a core function that is supported from the top.

Professional staff are essential if an organization wants to build a long-term, sustainable development program. Almost equally as important is the need for support staff. Development is a labour-intensive undertaking where quality and timeliness of data and attention to detail are crucial. Receipting, recording, reporting and supporting donors are time-consuming activities that are most cost-effectively done by including qualified administrative support in the staffing plan in order to ensure that the professional fundraiser is spending time on the initiatives designed to bring in revenue rather than the details that support it.

Non-staff Resources

In addition to staff resources, a development budget should include a realistic level of expense to support the function. In addition to the standard operational expenses, fundraising materials, prospect and donor research resources and databases, cultivation activities, volunteer support and training, postage, meetings, marketing and community relations, and professional development and training all need to be included in the expense budget.

Technology is an essential management tool for development. There are many fundraising software programs available at various price ranges. While small organizations may be able to use programs such as Excel or Microsoft Access to manage their information, most will eventually grow out of their capacities, requiring a specialized database program. The purchase of a fundraising software program should be done after a thorough assessment of an organization's development program and its data management needs and, most importantly, should be considered as a necessary investment that will produce a future return. Individual software packages will have their own Websites but information about assessing an organization's needs and identifying the right package can be obtained through the AFP Resource Centre[23] or in the archives of Charity Village®.[24]

Fundraising Costs

Donors and the public expect that most of the money they contribute will be spent on a charitable purpose. While this is a reasonable assumption, it is complicated by the fact that there is such limited awareness as to the true cost of either the programs they are supporting or the reasonable costs of fundraising itself. The bottom line is that, like any other for-profit or government enterprise, it costs money to make money and nonprofits need to be transparent and realistic about how they present these costs. Fundraising cost effectiveness is a very complex issue and there are many factors involved for individual organizations: the age and size of the organization; the size of its donor base; its mix of fundraising programs and the maturity of individual programs; the maturity and effectiveness of its staff; the time it takes to see returns; and anomalies of giving such as the receipt of a large bequest. This, and the fact that there are a variety of different kinds of funding models used by organizations, often results in comparing apples and oranges and making it very difficult to establish a set of guidelines that are reasonably applicable to all organizations. Organizations also have different cost issues and may treat revenue streams differently. Large endowment investment returns may be included or may be held in a separate foundation. Office space can

---

[23] Online at: <http://www.afpnet.org>. There is a nominal fee for non-members.

[24] Online at: <http://www.charityvillage.ca>.

be provided or not. Nevertheless, the sector does need to develop better benchmarks and standards to communicate to donors that it is fundraising in an efficient and effective manner. There are a number of things nonprofits should do to provide a more realistic picture:

- Establish targets that are appropriate and achievable (based on track record and resources), not just numbers that make up a gap in the budget.

- Implement project accounting to capture the true cost of programs.

- Report on individual programs rather than on fundraising as a single entity.

- Evaluate, measure and report fundraising costs on a three-year rolling average as opposed to an annual basis.

- Report on other things besides the "cost of dollar raised" such as fundraising achievements, historical trends, and the acquisition and retention of donors.

Fundraising costs can range from as low as $.12 to $1.50 per donation for individual methodologies and anywhere from 5 per cent to 35 per cent of overall fundraising revenue. James Greenfield, one of the leading authorities on fundraising cost-effectiveness, provides the following guidelines for fundraising programs that have been active for a minimum of three years. (Note: these are based on U.S. studies and experience but are also applicable to Canadian practice.) These guidelines are the result of a number of national studies and from Greenfield's own considerable years of experience (Greenfield (1996, at 281), and additional sources).

Table 9: Reasonable Cost Guidelines for Solicitation Activities

Solicitation Activity	Reasonable Cost Guidelines
Direct mail (acquisition)	$1.25 to $1.50 per $1.00 raised
Direct mail (renewal)	$0.20 to $0.25 per $1.00 raised
Membership associations	$0.20 to $0.30 per $1.00 raised
Activities, benefits, and special events	$0.50 per $1.00 raised (gross revenue and direct costs only)
Donor clubs and support	$0.20 to $0.30 per $1.00 raised

Solicitation Activity	Reasonable Cost Guidelines
Volunteer-led personal solicitation	$0.10 to $20 per $1.00 raised
Corporations	$0.20 per $1.00 raised
Foundations	$0.20 per $1.00 raised
Special projects	$0.10 to $0.20 per $1.00 raised
Capital campaigns	$0.10 to $.20 per $1.00 raised
Planned giving	$0.20 to $0.30 per $1.00 raised

AFP has produced an informative and helpful paper on fundraising costs that is very useful in understanding the complexities of, and identifying a reasonable approach for, an organization and its board. ("Measuring and Reporting Fundraising Costs: A Canadian Perspective", online at: AFP <http://www.afpnet.org>).

Canada Revenue Agency has developed a policy "Fundraising by Registered Charities" that provides consistency in reporting methods and an educational and informational tool for donors. The guidance recognizes that costs can vary program by program and charity by charity and sets a "benchmark" of 35 cents on the dollar as "reasonable".[25] Nevertheless, the scrutiny by the public is at an all time high and there are numerous 'watchdog' organizations that provide additional information to donors. Boards and leadership must be ever vigilant to ensure that reasonable financial guidelines are in place that allow fundraising to occur in a strategic and professional manner while providing the accountability and expectations required by donors. It has never been more of a balancing act.

PLANNING AND EVALUATING DEVELOPMENT ACTIVITIES

Philanthropic Culture

As outlined earlier in this chapter, a development program should be integrated within your organization and not function in isolation. Development is an organizational process that involves just about all aspects of the nonprofit. Growing your mission, leadership at all levels, and strategic planning are all impacted by your success at fundraising. A respect for the philanthropic process, an awareness of the fundraising requirements and activities, and an appreciation

---

[25] Online at: CRA <http://www.cra-arc.gc.ca/chrts-gvng/chrts/plcy/cgd/fndrsng-eng.html>.

throughout the organization of its (not the fundraiser's) need for support enable development to flourish.

Planning and Implementation

Successful fundraising is not about a quick hit. It is about thoughtful planning and meticulous execution and, in fact, the planning is where most of the activity happens. Development needs to be part of the larger organizational system as the workings of one function affect what happens in other functions. In *Strategic Fund Development*, author Simone Joyaux lists a number of initiatives for a chief executive to ensure a philanthropic culture and a development program that is integrated throughout the organization (Joyaux (2001, at 7)):

- Help board and staff to see the links between fund development and other institutional functions, to identify and resolve systemic issues at various points.

- Make sure the fundraising staff understand the program and relate well with the program staff.

- Involve your fundraiser in board selection, recruitment and development.

- Insist that fundraising staff work with all other staff, including program and marketing, to identify the agency's constituents, find out their interests and needs, and brainstorm how the agency can respond.

- Show your staff — janitor, receptionist, direct service personnel, trustees, chief executive, bookkeeper — the role they play in fund development.

- Listen to your fundraiser's thoughts about program quality and community perception.

- Expect your fundraiser to be actively involved in the community, serving on boards and exploring community issues, trends, and solutions.

The CPRN/AFP study and the more recent Underdeveloped Report revealed that fundraisers were more likely than other Canadian workers to be considering a job change. More than 50 percent reported that they had looked for a job in the previous year and these numbers held across the sub-sectors. Further, 46 per cent of these cited frustrations with the work environment, 36 per cent cited a lack of recognition, and almost 30 per cent said that it was because they faced unrealistic expectations or their workplace was unsupportive (McMullen

(2003, at 68-70)). Clearly, the quality of the work environment plays an important role.

Strategic and Annual Planning

A healthy nonprofit that knows the direction it is heading is one that embraces strategic planning. Development should be a part of the organizational strategic planning process from the outset. It only makes sense that if the direction involves programs, services, or buildings that require philanthropic revenue, development should be included. Development staff provide a touchstone to the community, can most effectively represent the views of your donors and feed external views and information back into the process.

In addition to strategic planning, development requires a clearly written plan complete with goals, strategies, tactics, target markets, cultivation, communication and solicitation strategies, the case for support, benchmarks of success, evaluation mechanisms, timelines, resources and responsibilities. The annual development plan is based on past results, current and future trends (internal and external) and future goals. A growth in goals will likely entail a growth in staffing and/or other resources. The planning cycle will generally start mid-year in concert with the budget planning process and be completed prior to the commencement of the next year, providing the framework for the development program. Like the strategic planning process, a sound development plan is developed with the input and participation of the whole organization.

Evaluation and Measurement

The annual development plan should be measured and evaluated on a regular, ongoing basis separate and apart from the financial reporting of the organization. Key performance measurements include gross revenues, net revenues, number of new donors, percentage rate of renewed donors, percentage rate of lapsed donors, cost of fundraising, average gift sizes and expense versus income. These measurements should be conducted across the program as well as by individual program. There is much more to development than the dollars raised and future performance is dependent on solid information about the past.

ROLES AND RESPONSIBILITIES

Fundraising can be completely done by volunteers (as in many smaller nonprofits), by a combination of staff and volunteers, or solely by staff (generally in bigger organizations with larger development offices). The majority of Canadian nonprofits have no professional staff and rely heavily on volunteers to raise money through their community networks. In most other organizations, fundraising can be led either by volunteers with support from staff, or, less common but increasing with the professionalization of fundraising, staff led with support from volunteers. Characteristics of these two models are shown in Table 10.

Table 10: Roles and Responsibilities of Volunteers and Staff

Volunteer Led/Staff Supported	Staff Led/Volunteer Supported

• Volunteers fulfill governance and leadership roles that determine vision, direction, and broad strategies for fundraising activities such as:
  • Approve annual financial and non-financial goals
  • Lead and own strategic planning process
  • Define and redefine mission, vision
  • Annual joint retreat.
• Volunteers play a lead role in external championing of organization, opening doors, cultivation initiatives and solicitation of larger gifts.
• Staff provide professional expertise and management of fundraising process.
• Volunteers and staff share ownership for success of program.
	• Volunteers operate in service volunteer capacity only (no governance or leadership).
	• Staff set goals (with appropriate internal collaborations), define program initiatives, set budgets, manage and direct the process.
	• Staff are responsible for program growth, vision, development, and policies.
	• Staff provide professional expertise and management of fundraising process.
	• Volunteers involved selectively and appropriately with key asks. Includes developing cultivation and solicitation strategies collaboratively with staff. Solicitation generally conducted jointly.
	• Staff own and manage program success. Volunteers contribute to success.

The development professional, the Chief Executive Officer or Executive Director and volunteer leadership all play key roles in successful fundraising.

Table 11: Key Roles in Fundraising

Development Professional	• Sets strategic direction • Responsible for planning and execution • Leads, enables and supports volunteers • Maintains infrastructure • Conducts evaluation and reporting • Identifies strategic issues for board discussion and action • Proposes and tests goals and directions
Chief Executive Officer	• Sets strategic direction • Ensures resources are in place • Champions program • Participates in cultivations and solicitations • Chief representative of the organization
Board as a Whole	• Ensures the nonprofit is worthy of investment by donors • Endorses goals and direction • Adopts plan as part of budget process • Participates in strategic discussions regarding strength and weaknesses, progress, trends and implications
Individual Board Members	• Carry out specific activities such as identification of potential donors, cultivation and solicitation of donors • Are accountable for fulfilling commitments made • Make personal gifts

There is always much debate about the role of boards in fundraising. The CPRN/AFP Study and the more recent Underdeveloped Report reveal that almost half of all respondents (47 per cent) said that their board members did not play an active role in fundraising while only 37 per cent agreed that their board members were active. As well, 30 per cent did not think that board members had realistic expectations of fundraising activities, with goals being set too high (McMullen (2003, at 44)). Clearly, for many managers and fundraisers in organizations the lack of board engagement is an issue.

The expectations are fairly widespread that board members have a responsibility to lead by example (give personally), provide contacts, open doors and cultivate others, and generally to act as an ambassador for the organization. The way this is done varies with different sizes and types of organizations and the model of governance used. Each organization needs to set expectations and responsibilities that work for it. The key is to have these discussions in advance of major fundraising and particularly during board recruitment, not after an individual has joined the board.

The role of volunteers and board members may also change over time. A nonprofit that has never had the need to raise money may now find itself facing that requirement. Or a nonprofit that has done all of its fundraising at the staff level and is facing a large expansion or building campaign will likely need to reconsider its model. These are discussions that are held at the board level. The result could be that the board changes its fundraising responsibilities or finds other leadership volunteers to do the job. Some board members may leave the board as a result.

Giving by board members can be another controversial topic. While we do not know what percentage of nonprofit board members actually give to their organization, common wisdom holds that you start with those closest to you and then go out to the community. But is this reality? We at least know from experience that there is a moral authority attached to a nonprofit that can say that 100 per cent of its board contributes to the organization on an annual basis. And, a request for support by a board member or campaign volunteer who has given himself or herself clearly carries more weight than from one who has not contributed. There are several other compelling reasons supporting board engagement (both time and money):

- Board members are usually better positioned in the community to open doors and make contacts than just relying on the development professional or the Executive Director.

- Board members can extend the reach of the development activities into broader networks.

- Commitment by board members demonstrates a belief in the cause, *i.e.*, walking the talk.

- It is usually very de-motivating for other fundraising volunteers if they are volunteering their own time and money and board members are not.

Development Committees

Some nonprofit boards choose to have a standing development committee that is responsible for leading fundraising activities. This can work well as it provides focus and clear lines of responsibility for reaching the goals. However, it can also be detrimental to overall success if it means that fundraising is delegated to a small group that ends up working in isolation from the rest of the board. Development committees are also known to have become mired in minutiae rather than focusing on the identification, cultivation and solicitation of donors. Strong leadership and clear responsibilities, supported by firm staff direction (if applicable) are necessary to ensure a development committee lives up to its potential benefits.

ACCOUNTABILITY, STEWARDSHIP AND ETHICS

Accountability and Stewardship

The 2008 study *Talking About Charities: Canadians' Opinions on Charities and Issues Affecting Charities*, found that 84 per cent of Canadians think charities are honest about how they spend their donations and 77 per cent of them trust charities "some" or "a lot" and this number has remained about the same since its initial survey in 2000.[26] Notwithstanding that these are impressive numbers, the issue of accountability continues to rise in public awareness, particularly as it relates to governance and fundraising activities. The increased competitiveness for funds combined with the more knowledgeable donor has raised expectations and guaranteed that accountability is no longer optional. Donors are asking more questions before and after making their gifts and have higher expectations of the organizations

---

[26] *Talking About Charities: Canadians' Opinions on Charities and Issues Affecting Charities* (The Muttart Foundation, 2008), available online at: <http://www.muttart.org/surveys>.

that they choose to support. They increasingly consider their contributions to be an investment in the mission of the organization and, as such, view themselves as stakeholders in that organization.

Nonprofits are the stewards of the philanthropic dollars contributed by its donors and, as a result, have a responsibility to maintain that relationship and that trust through ethical fundraising and accountability to its donors.

Stewardship presupposes that as soon as a donor makes a gift that donor immediately becomes another prospect and the organization must earn the donor's trust and prove itself worthy of future investment. Good stewardship includes:

- the policies that govern investment practice;

- the use of sound financial and management practices;

- the honouring of donor intent;

- the acknowledgement and recognition processes for gifts; and

- transparent and accountable financial reporting.

Ethical Fundraising

Ethical fundraising is a fundamental underpinning of trust, donor relationships, and long-term success. Regardless of the size of the community, the donor sphere is small. A perceived or actual unethical act by the nonprofit can have long-term and severe consequences for fundraising. Fundraising is about relationships; ethical fundraising is about building and maintaining trust.

There are a number of codes that an organization can adopt and operationalize into policy as Step 1. Step 2 is to ensure that all staff and volunteers are aware of these policies and of the organization's commitment to ethical fundraising. Some of the codes and principles governing ethical fundraising are as follows:

- *The Code of Ethical Conduct and Standards of Practice* of the Association of Fundraising Professionals applies to individual professional fundraisers and commits them to serving the ideals of philanthropy. Among other things, it places the responsibility for ensuring that all solicitation materials are accurate and truthful, that contributions are used according to a donor's intent, that confidential and privileged information will be protected and that gift conditions will not be altered without donor permission, squarely on the fundraiser.[27]

- *The Ethical Fundraising and Financial Accountability Code* of Imagine Canada outlines the commitment of charities and their boards to fundraising practices that respect donors' rights to truthful information and to privacy. It also commits board to managing responsibly the funds entrusted to them by donors and to report their financial affairs accurately and completely.[28]

- *The Accountable Not for Profit Organization* is a statement of principles that outlines the operations and procedures a charity takes to show it is accountable to donors, the people it serves, and the general public.[29]

- *The Donor Bill of Rights* sets out commitments to donors' rights.[30]

In addition, there are codes governing prospect research, planned giving, and e-philanthropy, all of which can be obtained from different Websites or through links from the above-noted sites.

Percentage-based Fundraising

A key tenet of all codes is the prohibition of percentage- (or commission-) based fundraising. First promulgated by the AFP Code, this ban is based on the belief that for professional fundraisers charitable purpose, not self-gain, is paramount and that if percentage-based compensation is used:

- charitable mission can become secondary to self-gain;

- donor trust can be unalterably damaged; and

- there is incentive for self-dealing to prevail over donors' best interest.

AFP also believes that percentage-based compensation produces reward without merit and can encourage abuses, imperil the integrity

---

27 This code can be found online at: <http://www.afpnet.org>.
28 This code can be found online at: <http://www.imaginecanada.ca>.
29 This code can be found online at: <http:// www.afpnet.org>.
30 This can be found online at: <http://www.afpnet.org>.

of the voluntary sector, and undermine the philanthropic values on which the sector is based.[31]

In 2005, the Uniform Law Commission of Canada developed a proposed Uniform Charitable Fundraising Act that, if adopted by individual provinces, will regulate fundraising activities. The proposed Act includes a ban on percentage-based fundraising.

Canada Revenue Agency Fundraising Guidelines

In 2009, the Canada Revenue Agency released guidelines for reporting fundraising expenses on a charity's T3010. These guidelines, while not legal requirements, are intended to be used by the public in determining whether a registered charity's fundraising is acceptable.[32]

Privacy Legislation

In 2000 the Canadian Government enacted PIPEDA, the *Personal Information Protection and Electronic Documents Act*,[33] to guide the use of personal information. Several provinces have enacted their own legislation, which complies with the federal legislation. In provinces that do not have provincial legislation the federal Act applies. The Privacy Commissioner subsequently ruled that fundraising is not a commercial activity within the definition of the Act and is therefore exempt from most of its provisions. However, there are still implications for the collection and use of data that nonprofits must comply with.

Canadian nonprofits that are subject to provincial privacy legislation that has been deemed to be substantially similar are exempt from PIPEDA with respect to the collection, use, or disclosure of personal information within the respective province. However, PIPEDA still applies to federal work and collection, use, or disclosure of personal information outside the province of operation.

---

[31] AFP "Position Paper: Percentage-Based Compensation", available online at: <http://www.afpnet.org/Ethics/EthicsArticleDetail.cfm?ItemNumber=734>.

[32] See CPS-028, Guidance on Fundraising by Registered Charities, effective June 11, 2009. Online at: <http://www.cra-arc.gc.ca/tx/chrts/plcy/cps/cps-028-eng.html>.

[33] S.C. 2000, c. 5.

FUTURE TRENDS

The face of development has changed significantly in the past 10 years and indicators lead us to believe that the pace of change will not only continue but will likely increase. Three trends that will have impact on a nonprofit's ability to earn revenues and fundraise effectively in the future include:

The Economy. In late 2008 the world economy suffered a downturn that shook the underpinnings of economic stability for almost every country to a degree never before experienced. The impact on the Canadian nonprofit sector has been significant resulting in increased demand for services coupled with reduced revenues from all traditional sources. In previous downturns, however, giving has remained relatively stable and nonprofit organizations have generally been able to weather the economic impacts. An economic crisis is not the time to downsize fundraising staff or reduce fundraising programs. Donors still give during a recession. They may take longer to make decisions — they will definitely make more strategic decisions — and they may make smaller gifts. It is an opportunity to focus on building stronger relationships with your current donor base, take the time to strategically plan current and future activities, and build your internal capacity and case for support.

Human Resource Challenges. Professionalization of fundraising is occurring at a rapid pace. The number of organizations involved in fundraising and requiring professional fundraisers will continue to outstrip the availability of experienced individuals even as the profession itself continues to grow. This places pressure on the organization to offer competitive compensation packages (including salaries, benefits, and professional development opportunities) and a quality of work environment (realistic expectation, organizational support, and leadership) to recruit and retain fundraisers.

A Growing Awareness of Philanthropy. The sophistication and expectations of donors will continue to grow. Access to more information fuels the expectation that information will be forthcoming, transparent, and readily available. The Canadian nonprofit sector is proactively working to increase awareness of its role in our society. As the sector profile rises, Canadians will continue to become more knowledgeable, ask more questions and develop deeper bonds with the organizations in which they invest. They will have a greater sense of the role of philanthropy and the philanthropic process. The onus will be on the development program to respond to these expectations and retain donor loyalty.

The Changing Donor. Donors have moved from loyalty to an organization, to loyalty to a cause, to viewing themselves as "stakeholders" and "investors" in making change. With the advent of the Internet, the access to incredible amounts of information, and the general savviness of the giving public, donors are more active and strategic in their giving. With the younger generation, the term "donor activist" has surfaced as a way to describe the commitment donors are willing to make to invest in change, and the expectations they have to be actively involved, beyond their financial gift, in making that change happen.

E-philanthropy/Social Media. This is already a rapidly growing vehicle, and nonprofits will have to embrace e-philanthropy to remain competitive. Still in its relative infancy in Canadian organizations, e-philanthropy, and particularly social marketing initiatives, offer wider reach and the opportunity to retain donors as they become more mobile in a global world.

REFERENCES

AFP, *State of Fundraising 2007 Report* (Alexandria, VA: Association of Fundraising Professionals, 2008), online at: <http://www.afpnet.org>.

J. Daw, *Cause Marketing for Nonprofits: Partner for Purpose, Passion, and Profits* (Hoboken, NJ: John Wiley & Sons, 2006).

Fraser Institute, *Charitable Giving in Canada and the US: The 2008 Generosity Index* (Vancouver: The Fraser Institute, 2008).

J.M. Greenfield, *Fund-Raising Cost Effectiveness: A Self-Assessment Workbook* (New York: John Wiley & Sons, 1996).

M.H. Hall *et al.*, *Cornerstones of Community: Highlights of the National Survey of Nonprofit and Voluntary Organizations* (Ottawa: Ministry of Industry for Statistics Canada, 2004).

M.H. Hall *et al.*, *Highlights from the 2000 National Survey of Giving, Volunteering and Participating* (Ottawa: Imagine Canada, 2000).

S.P. Joyaux, *Strategic Fund Development: Building Profitable Relationships that Last*, 2d ed. (Gaithersburg, MD: Aspen Publishers, 2001).

KCI, *Philanthropic Trends*, Ketchum Canada Inc. (Spring 2005), online at: <http://www.kciphilanthropy.com/english/explore/trends.html>.

K. McMullen, *A Portrait of Canadian Fundraising Professionals* (Canadian Policy Research Networks Inc./Association of Fundraising Professionals, 2003), online at: <http://www.cprn.org/doc.cfm?doc=347& l=en>.

F. Minton & L. Somers, *Planned Giving for Canadians*, 2d ed. (Waterdown, ON: Somersmith, 1997).

R.L. Payton, *Voluntary Action for the Public Good* (New York: American Council on Education/Macmillan Publishing, 1988).

A.P. Prince & K.M. File, *The Seven Faces of Philanthropy: A New Approach to Cultivating Major Donors* (San Francisco: Jossey-Bass, 2001).

H.A. Rosso & Associates, *Achieving Excellence in Fund Raising*, 2d ed. (San Francisco: Jossey-Bass, 2003).

S. Williams, *Social Enterprise: The Three P's: Philosophy, Process and Practicalities* (Edmonton: The Muttart Foundation, Fellowship Series, 2005).

FURTHER RESOURCES

Web-based Resources

Canada Revenue Agency (CRA): <http://www.cra-arc.gc.ca>.

Association of Fundraising Professionals (AFP): <http://www. afpnet.org>.

Association for Healthcare Philanthropy Canada (AHP): <http://www. ahp.org>.

Council for Advancement and Support of Education (CASE): <http:// www.case.org>.

Canadian Association of Gift Planners: <http://www.cagp-acpdp.org>.

Community Foundations of Canada: <http://www.cfc-fcc.ca>.

Charity Village: <http://www.charityvillage.ca>.

Imagine Canada: <http://www.imaginecanada.ca> and <http://www.givingandvolunteering.ca>.

Print Resources

Social Enterprise

S. Williams, *Social Enterprise: The Three P's: Philosophy, Process, and Practicalities* (Edmonton: The Muttart Foundation, Fellowship Series, 2005).

Cause Marketing

J. Daw, *Cause Marketing for Nonprofits: Partner for Purpose, Passion and Profits* (Hoboken, NJ: John Wiley & Sons, 2006).

R. Steckel, *Filthy Rich: How to Turn your Nonprofit Fantasies into Cold, Hard Cash*, 2d ed. (Berkeley, CA: Ten Speed Press, 2001).

Fundraising

K. Burnett, *Relationship Fundraising: A Donor-Based Approach to the Business of Raising Money*, 2d ed. (San Francisco: Jossey-Bass, 2002).

J.M. Greenfield, *Fundraising Cost Effectiveness: A Self-Assessment Workbook* (New York: John Wiley & Sons, 1996).

S.P. Joyaux, *Strategic Fund Development: Building Profitable Relationships That Last*, 2d ed. (Gaithersburg, MD: Aspen Publishing Inc., 2001).

G. Perry, *Fired-Up Fundraising: Turn Board PASSION into ACTION* (New York: John Wiley & Sons, 1996).

H.A. Rosso and Associates, *Achieving Excellence in Fundraising*, 2d ed. (San Francisco: Jossey-Bass, 2003).

Planned Giving

F. Minton & L. Somers, *Planned Giving for Canadians*, 3d ed. (Waterdown, ON: Somersmith, 2008).

Chapter 8

PLANNING AND ORGANIZING FOR RESULTS

Thea Vakil
University of Victoria

INTRODUCTION

This chapter discusses how nonprofit organizations should decide on which strategic direction they should take and how they can best be organized for optimal performance. The chapter is concerned with those organizational characteristics that are separate from the people populating the organization yet are indispensable for meeting the organization's objectives. Organizational characteristics refer to aspects of the nonprofit organization that describe its form, structure and strategy as well as the subcomponents of strategy: planning, programs and projects. Each of these topics will be addressed in this chapter to assist nonprofit leaders in deepening their understanding of organization strategy and structure and enhancing their ability to consciously use organizational attributes to achieve the organization's vision.[1]

The chapter begins with a general discussion about the importance of strategy, strategic thinking, and the need to create a strategic vision for the nonprofit organization. It then moves to the strategic planning process, its major components, and the steps involved in putting a strategic plan in place, including project management. Planning strategically may have significant consequences for the organization's operations, structure and processes, so the second part of the chapter provides an overview of the more common structures and processes in

---

[1] The term "nonprofit leader" denotes executives responsible for the operations of the nonprofit. This chapter uses the titles Chief Executive Officer (CEO) and Executive Director (ED) interchangeably.

nonprofits in order to inform a possible redesign of the organization flowing from the strategic direction of the organization.

STRATEGIC MANAGEMENT

Nonprofit organizations are created to achieve a specific purpose. The purpose may be modest and small scale, *e.g.*, establishing a neighbourhood safety program, or large and ambitious such as the Red Cross or UNICEF. Nonprofits articulate their purpose in mission statements and it is this mission that guides their programs and activities. But mission alone may not be enough. Nonprofits also need to make sure that mission connects to strategy so one does not lose sight of the other. For example, the mission of SOS Kinderdorf, a nonprofit established in Austria in 1949, was "to provide orphaned, abandoned and destitute children with a new and permanent home, and to lay a sound foundation for a useful and productive life". Kinderdorf created children's villages all over the world to provide shelter and care. However, because in developing countries no schooling was available and shelter alone would not have been enough to lead to a useful and productive life for children there, the organization established kindergartens and schools. By 1990, about 40 per cent of its budget was being spent on schools and medical centres. While these activities were consistent with the mission, the organization now only dedicates 60 per cent of its budget for its original purpose of providing homes (Rangan (2004)).

Sometimes missions need to shift, such as when the original purpose of the organization has been achieved. The mission of the "March of Dimes" in the early 1950s, for example, was to fund rehabilitation centres and job training for individuals suffering from poliomyelitis. After the Salk vaccine (discovered in 1954) was adopted as a prevention measure in North America, the organization shifted its mission to "creating a society inclusive of people with physical disabilities".[2]

More commonly, however, mission and strategy can become disconnected when organizations shift their core services in order to pursue available funding even though they are unrelated to the stated mission. Governments and foundations provide funding consistent with their own objectives and cash-strapped small nonprofits may find themselves applying for programs that only marginally fit with their mission. Nonprofit organizations thus need to protect and support their

---

[2] Online at: <http://www.marchofdimes.ca/EN/AboutUs/Documents/Annual%20Reports/0102_AR.pdf>.

mission through well-integrated strategies. Significant economic pressures that force organizations to move beyond their immediate mission and engage in social entrepreneurship may also influence missions.

Strategy is central to successful decision-making in the private sector. Michael Porter famously articulated business strategy and its principles many years ago in his book on competitive strategy. Porter recommended that firms make conscious decisions about how to position themselves in the market by selecting one of three competitive strategies: low-cost leadership, differentiation and focus (Porter (1980)). More recently, the development and execution of strategies have been conceptualized as "strategic management". Strategic management consists of two different components: strategic thinking and strategic planning. Mintzberg explains that strategic thinking involves synthesis — encouraging intuitive, innovative and creative thinking at all levels of the organization; strategic planning concerns analysis — establishing and formalizing systems and procedures (Mintzberg (1994a)). Tim O'Shannassy has proposed a model that shows the breakdown of strategic management into strategic thinking and strategic planning. He has also connected the two processes in a continuous feedback loop. The model has been reproduced in Figure 1.

Figure 1: Strategic Management Process

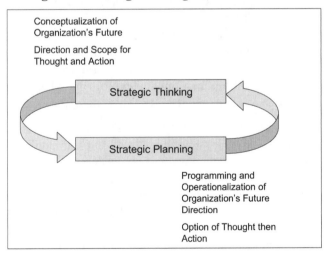

Source: Adapted from Tim O'Shannassy, "Modern Strategic Management: Balancing Strategic Thinking and Strategic Planning for Internal and External Stakeholders" *Singapore Management Review*, 25:1 (2003) 53-67 at 55.

Liedtka (1998) and Graetz (2002) have developed similar models. Liedtka (1998) has identified five major attributes of strategic thinking that should be of interest to nonprofit leaders. They are generic and can be equally applied in the private and nonprofit sector.

1. Strategic thinking is holistic in that it looks at all parts of the organization and their interrelationships.

2. Strategic thinking is characterized by strategic intent, which is the force that mobilizes leaders to think beyond the current capacity of the organization.

3. In addition to future oriented strategic intent, strategic thinkers make connections between the past, present and future.

4. Strategic thinking involves asking "what if" questions. Strategic thinkers develop hypotheses about different scenarios and are prepared to test them.

5. Strategic thinking requires leaders to be intelligently opportunistic. They will remain open to alternative strategies even after they have developed a strategic path for the organization (Liedtka (1998)).

To some extent, research on strategic thinking has been influenced by critiques leveled at constraints imposed by rigid strategic planning processes (*e.g.*, Mintzberg (1994b)). This is not surprising since, historically, strategic planning has its roots in the military and referred to the management of large-scale military operations. As a result, early efforts at strategic planning were characterized by a highly controlled process determined at the top of the organization. Formal documents would result from intensive analysis, and decisions on strategies and their associated projects would move down strict vertical hierarchical lines in the organization. Implementation of the plan was closely monitored through frequent and detailed reporting to the executive.

Strategic planning of this kind was adopted by business organizations in the early 1950s. It gained popularity until the mid-1970s, after which this form of it went into a steady decline. This decline was reversed in the 1990s when globalization and increased competition presented new challenges for business and the notion of strategic thinking began to replace the creation of formal long-term plan documents. This was also the period during which public sector organizations and nonprofit organizations started to plan "strategically". Now, because newer models of strategic planning include a certain amount of "visioning" as part of the planning process, nonprofit leaders are able to apply their strategic thinking to strategic planning. More and more nonprofit organizations formalize their vision in a strategic plan, which in turn provides the framework for initiatives and projects.

STRATEGIC PLANNING

One of the major challenges of strategic planning is how to prevent strategic plans from languishing on the shelf in well-designed binders that nobody ever looks at! Strategic planning demands executive involvement, employee commitment and, above all, should be relevant to the organization's day-to-day functioning. Nonprofit leaders also need to pay attention to the "political" dimension of strategic planning. The Board of Directors must be convinced, politicians' requirements must be met, stakeholders' sensitivities must be respected and employees must be persuaded to buy in to the process. The formal creation of a strategic plan is a technique, but the development of an effective strategic planning process is an art.

Most nonprofits in Canada, however, are small organizations, with the majority of them employing less than 10 people. As a result, they often lack the expertise in developing and implementing a strategic plan and so have to rely on outside expertise. In doing this, executive directors may ask advice from other nonprofits or may turn to consultants to help them with various components of strategic planning. Consultants may be hired as:

- Facilitators: to prepare for and manage strategic planning retreats or other key meetings;

- Researchers: to carry out time-consuming, highly specialized work such as environmental scans;

- Writers: to prepare successive drafts of the strategic plan; and

- Coaches/guides: to help participants become more effective in the strategic planning process by providing individual support.

Good consultants can be beneficial because they are able to dedicate their full attention to the planning process, something that is usually not possible for people within the organizations of all sizes. They can also provide an objective perspective on the process and mediate between people with divergent opinions. Management consultants are also well versed in techniques used to help groups make complex and difficult decisions. Of course, hiring outside consultants also means that the organization does not develop its own inhouse expertise, nor will there be a corporate memory of the process. CEOs will have to weigh this loss of knowledge against the advantages of bringing in someone with experience.

A visual representation of the strategic planning process appears as a linear journey through a process that is anything but linear. Strategic planning is circular, often circuitous, iterative and problematic. For the sake of expediency, the model is presented as if it were a straight line with step-by-step logic that proceeds systematically through the strategic planning process. Bryson (2004) has done seminal work in strategic planning for the nonprofit sector and much of the discussion that follows is based on his model. A modified version of the model is shown in Figure 2.

Figure 2: Strategic Planning Process

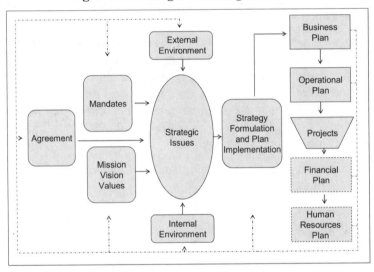

Source: Adapted from J.M. Bryson, *Strategic Planning for Public and Nonprofit Organizations: A Guide to Strengthening and Sustaining Organizational Achievement*, 3d ed. (San Francisco: Jossey-Bass, 2004) at 33.

The model shows a number of discrete stages, starting with the agreement and ending with a series of projects that flow from the strategies and goals and, where appropriate, from strategic and operational plans. The first part of the framework is primarily concerned with information collection, strategic thinking about mission, vision, and values, and the creation of strategic issues. The second part is mainly concerned with giving form to the strategic issues, translating them into "doable" strategies in a strategic plan and implementing the plan through an appropriate set of projects or programs. Depending upon the nature of the plan there may be many projects or just a few. In this chapter, we will concentrate on a project that involves the redesign of the organization.

Get Agreement on the Strategic Planning Process

It is useful to start the planning process by formally agreeing to do so. Agreements are likely to have different forms and different names. They may be called charters, contracts, or planning documents. They may be very detailed or consist of a simple letter of intent, indicating that strategic planning will take place, what its objectives are and who will be involved. Not all agreements need be very specific. However, the greater the specificity, the more guidance it can provide for the process. A formal document of agreement provides legitimacy and authority for the planning effort, demonstrates that the CEO is committed to the process and will assist in getting buy-in from the employees.

Nonprofit leaders will need the dedicated support of a team to create the strategic plan, even if an outside adviser supports the organization. If possible, team members should be appointed at the agreement stage and should be held directly accountable to the CEO.

Confirm Mandate and Conduct Stakeholder Analysis

The first step in the actual planning process itself should consist of those involved formally confirming the organization's mandate (even though the executive may be crystal clear about it). The mandate states what the organization is, what the limits are within which it is legally allowed to function and what it is required to do. In addition to its formal mandate, nonprofit leaders need to consider the organization's informal mandate. Informal mandates relate to the — often unspoken — expectations that stakeholders have, including internal stakeholders.

Stakeholders are "any person, group, or organization that can place a claim on an organization's (or other entity's) attention, resources, or output or that is affected by that output" (Bryson (2004, at 35)). Internal stakeholders, *e.g.*, the Board of Directors and the staff and volunteers working in the organization, have their own ideas about the informal mandate of the organization. Their views may be more restricted than the official mandate or they may believe that the organization's tasks go beyond that mandate and are looking to broaden the agency's range of activities. Outside stakeholders too, may expect an organization to take on responsibilities that, strictly speaking, do not fall within its mandate. An internal and external stakeholder analysis will assist nonprofit leaders in assessing their mandate as perceived by the stakeholders.

A stakeholder analysis should identify each stakeholder, describe the relationship between the stakeholder and the organization (and, if applicable, the relationship between the stakeholders and other stakeholders), and group stakeholders in accordance with their relative importance to the organization. In addition, it is important to describe, as precisely as possible, the expectations that the stakeholders have of the organization. Internal stakeholders may have very different expectations than external stakeholders. It is advisable to create a simple diagram that shows the relative importance of the stakeholders. The diagram could show for example, that funders and clients (members, service recipients and the community) are key stakeholders by showing them in large boxes and in close proximity to the organization.

Stakeholders are of great importance to an organization because it is they who must be satisfied if the organization is to continue a successful existence. Attention to stakeholders has been common in the private sector but has received greater attention in the nonprofit sector only in the past decade. For example, Fletcher *et al.* (2003) reported on the results of an empirical investigation of the stakeholders of the Australian Red Cross Blood Service. Using a methodology of value contribution they were able to aggregate a large number of stakeholders' priorities with respect to the agency. This allowed the agency to reconsider its mandate, mission and vision.

Review Mission, Vision and Values

Mission

Once the organization has established (or redefined) its mandate and has carried out a stakeholder analysis, it is ready to review its mission. Of course, most nonprofits already have a mission before they undertake a strategic planning exercise. However, leaders need to review the existing mission to ensure that it still meets both the organization's mandate and stakeholders' expectations. Compare for example the mission statement published on the Internet by Volunteer Calgary in its 2006-2008 Strategic Plan with that in the 2010-2012 Strategic Plan.

2006 Mission Statement

Engaging more people, more effectively to volunteer in the community.

2010 Mission Statement

Leading, promoting, connecting and strengthening volunteerism

Volunteer Calgary indicates that the mission statement was changed to capture "the four pillars of activity by which volunteer centres across Canada organize their activity". The effect of the mission restatement is a clarification of what is meant by "engaging" but it no longer reflects the organization's desire to do so "more effectively".

Consider also the different mission statements published on the Internet by the Victoria Cool Aid Society. This organization provides services in housing, shelters, health and dental care, and various services for people with mental illness. Its 2000-2001 strategic plan stated its mission as:

> The Victoria Cool Aid Society responds with care to the life needs of children, youth, men and women in adverse situations. By creating and supporting a range of effective immediate to long-term services, we build hope, lives and community.[3]

But note the different mission statement in the 2004-2005 plan:

> We work to eliminate homelessness by working in partnership with others to develop community based solutions. We are committed to working in a nonjudgmental way with people who are marginalized, homeless and hard to house. We advocate for and provide emergency shelter, supportive housing and integrated healthcare service to marginalized adults in the Victoria area.[4]

Clearly, the Victoria Cool Aid Society has shifted its services to adults but the mission statement also reflects a shift in emphasis from "services" to "housing", and its tone seems more practical and less idealistic.

Vision

Recently, the author of this chapter reviewed about 50 strategic plans of nonprofit organizations and was surprised to find that about 15 per cent of them did not include a vision statement. It is hard to imagine a strategic planning exercise without having a vision for the organization in place. An organization's vision is the beacon directing and guiding the nonprofit organization towards its desired future. The development of a vision for the organization comes closest to the realm of "strategic thinking" discussed earlier. Executive directors must be able to provide a description of what a successful organization should look like once it has reached its full potential. The vision statement should "emphasize purposes, behaviour, performance criteria, and decision

---

[3]   Online at: <http://coolaid.org/wp-content/uploads/2013/09/2000_2001_CoolaidAnnualReport.pdf>.
[4]   Online at: <http://coolaid.org/wp-content/uploads/2013/09/2004-05AnnualReport.pdf>.

rules that service the public, rather than the organization, and create public value" (Bryson (2004, at 226)). This conception of success should be widely shared within the organization to mobilize in employees a sense of commitment to the organization's goals. It should also be shared with the stakeholders to ensure a thorough understanding of the organization's objectives by interested outsiders.

Values

Explicit statements of values and principles often accompany mission and vision statements. Values are those conditions that the Board of Directors considers desirable for the organization to meet in executing its mandate. For example, a social service agency might hold as a value "unconditional respect for all our clients" or "transparency in all our operations". Values can be stated as principles that become the rules or standards that guide employee behaviour. The value of "respect" in a social agency, for instance, might dictate a number of principles which will lead staff to refrain from such actions as asking personal questions unless absolutely necessary for the provision of service. "Respect" in a half-way house could translate into a principle of zero tolerance for drugs. An organization's mission and vision should be strongly supported by values and principles that are more than just lofty statements. Nonprofit leaders should make an effort to create meaningful values and principles that are directly relevant to the mission and vision to guide the organization.

External and Internal Environmental Analysis

External Scan

The next step in the planning process is to carry out an analysis of the internal and external environments (referred to as an environmental scan). Environmental analyses can be quite extensive and many small organizations that attempt strategic planning prefer to engage a consultant for this work. Outside assistance might also be helpful when the organization attempts an environmental scan the first time. Ongoing and routine scanning can then be taken over by employees.

Conceptually, the environmental scan is broken down into three phases: scanning for emerging issues, monitoring priority issues, and forecasting trends. *Scanning for emerging issues* consists of picking up (sometimes quite weak) signals of the first expression of new ideas or pressures. An example in the nonprofit sector would be an increased emphasis by funders on accountability requirements for community service agencies. Such requirements may lead to demands for such things as quality assurance through accreditation. Ideas around accountability might have been "out there" for quite a while before they became articulated as new requirements for measuring and reporting on inputs, outputs, and outcomes. The idea of scanning the external environment is to identify such issues early enough to determine whether a future strategic response may be needed.

Monitoring occurs after scanning activities have identified emerging issues. It involves keeping track of them and clarifying them in sufficient detail to actually formulate a strategic response.

Forecasting trends is based on scanning and monitoring but goes beyond the capacity of scanning and monitoring by projecting different scenarios into the future.

In addition to these three phases of environmental analysis, it is also important for nonprofit leaders to assess the complexity of the environment and the risks it poses to the organization. The larger the scope of its programs, the greater is likely to be the complexity of its environment. For example, a national program operates in a more complex environment than a local or regional program. Likewise, the more heterogeneous the programs, the greater the complexity of the environment within which the programs operate. Finally, the greater the rate of change in the environment, the greater the risks it creates for the organization. Historically, many in the nonprofit sector enjoyed relative environmental stability and consequently operated in a low-risk environment for a long time. However, the late 20th century heralded a period of accelerating change that has made the environment in the future much more uncertain.

Internal Scan

While the external environment is extremely important, CEOs and other nonprofit leaders should not ignore the organization's internal environment. An internal scan involves the assessment of the organization's people and financial resources. Leaders should determine its current information technology, the competencies that staff possess and the prevailing culture. An assessment should also be made of the current overall strategy and, in the case of large organizations, their departmental and unit strategies. Finally, an internal scan includes examining current performance using existing indicators, history, or specially prepared reports such as a balanced scorecard. Small, voluntary organizations or large nonprofits that rely to some degree on volunteer labour should also complete an assessment of volunteers.

Strength, Weaknesses, Opportunities and Threats (SWOT)

The result of external and internal information gathering is a SWOT analysis. A SWOT analysis might best be presented in a table. A possible SWOT table for an agency promoting literacy in a medium-sized city is presented in Table 1.

Table 1: Partial SWOT Analysis

External		Internal	
Opportunities	**Threats**	**Strengths**	**Weaknesses**
Seen as a municipal resource	New or increased competition by other providers of literacy services	Central geographic location in populated area	Lack of space for volunteers and information collections
Good Internet connections – access, connectivity	Internet connections – access, connectivity	Well-connected with other agencies	High staff turnover
Culturally diverse population	Culturally diverse population	Expertise in locating resources	No fundraising strategy

From this example it can be seen that opportunities may be a threat but that threats may also be opportunities. A culturally diverse population is an opportunity because it creates a rich environment in which clients learn about each other's culture. At the same time, a culturally diverse population may be a threat because the methods that the organization uses may not be universal enough to support multiple cultures. Clients may experience loneliness and even alienation if they cannot relate to the mode of operation the agency employs.

A potential problem with SWOT analysis is that tables, such as in Table 1, may be very large and contain a great many boxes. Priorities are not always obvious and sometimes CEOs and their strategic management team feel overloaded with information and unable to make the best use of the analysis. The key is to remember that whether something is an opportunity or a threat is directly related to the organization's strengths and weaknesses. For example, good Internet connections are only an opportunity if the organization has computer-literate staff or volunteers. Otherwise, it will likely be a threat.

DEFINITION OF STRATEGIC ISSUES

We have now come to the central point in the strategic planning process: determining the organization's strategic issues. As Figure 2 above, indicates, all foregoing activities are completed in the service of this important step. Strategic issues are key questions facing the organization that most fundamentally affect its policies, programs and services. Figure 3 provides a schematic overview of strategic issues and their relationship to strategic planning.

Figure 3: Strategic Issues

Factors Influencing Strategic Issues	Characteristics of Strategic Issues	Responding to Strategic Issues
Organization's vision and mission and values determine the essence of the organization.	Developments that affect the core (essence) of the organization	Organization develops options to address strategic issues.
Organization's mandate sets upper and lower limits of its existence.	Need to be addressed soon. Must be described in: − a single paragraph − as a question − that leaves solution open	If there is more than one issue the organization develops a prioritized list to address the issues.
Environmental external and internal scan provides insight into external threats and internal weaknesses.	Assumes that the organization has the capacity to respond to the issue.	If no satisfactory solution can be found the organization may adjust its mission to minimize the effect.

Let us consider a well-known volunteer problem in the Canadian nonprofit sector. As a strategic issue it can be framed as follows: "How do we to ensure continued participation by volunteers in the sector?" This strategic issue is the result of a number of factors that an environmental scan would readily reveal. For example:

- Volunteers are moving from long-term volunteering with a single organization to short-term commitments to several organizations. More and more volunteers will commit for a specific, limited period of time but may or may not do so repeatedly.

- The volunteer pool has become increasingly diverse. New Canadians may not be familiar with the concept of volunteerism, leading to a reduction of total number of volunteers.

- Increased sophistication and education levels of volunteers have resulted in individuals seeking more meaningful, challenging and interesting volunteer opportunities. Nonprofits may not be aware of this shift or do not have exciting jobs to offer.

- The majority of volunteers today are working people and likely to come from families where both parents are employed. As a result there is an increasing interest in opportunities that can include or involve the entire family.

- With the advent of personal computers and the Internet come opportunities to change the way volunteering is managed and the programs being offered. The use of technology can impact volunteer job design and activity through home-based involvement (sometimes known as "virtual volunteering") (Renz (2005)).

The continuing reduction in volunteer hours since 1997 and the fact that volunteer labour is equivalent to about one million jobs in the nonprofit sector makes this a strategic issue for the sector as a whole. It is also a strategic issue for the leadership of individual nonprofit organizations because they have an opportunity to do something about it by responding creatively to the issue. The degree to which volunteers are a strategic issue for any one nonprofit organization however, will depend on more than the external environmental scan. Nonprofit leaders need to take into account the organization's internal strengths and weaknesses with respect to volunteers, the role envisioned for volunteers in the mission and vision statement and the relationship between volunteers and major stakeholders.

The identification and definition of strategic issues should be firmly connected to the vision statement. A collective picture of the future in which the organization has successfully met its mission will provide a clear point of reference for framing strategic issues. Within this context leaders have to ask a number of questions. Not surprisingly, the first one is: "What is the issue?" For example, if the organization does not use volunteers or anticipate using them in the future (*i.e.*, volunteers are not part of the vision of success), changes in the volunteer population will be of no consequence. Strategic issues should be framed as questions the organization can do something about. If the answer to the strategic issue is beyond its control, it does not qualify as a strategic issue.

The next question asks what factors (mandates, stakeholders and environmental forces) make this a strategic issue. Sometimes, but not always, it is useful to ask the additional question: "What happens when the strategic issue is *not* addressed?" The answer to this question would be most helpful if there are numerous strategic issues and the CEO and the strategic management team have to rank them in order of importance or urgency or both.

An alternative method to approaching strategic issues is called "scenario building" or "scenario planning". Scenario building is a technique that allows leaders to imagine and build on different possible futures (Schwartz (1991); Bradfield *et al.* (2005)). It introduces a new step between the environmental scan and the final identification of strategic issues. One of the three components of environmental scanning is the forecasting of trends. Forecasting is based on informed guesses and implied probabilities of events occurring. Scenario planning makes these probabilities explicit by imagining and articulating mutually exclusive, relevant futures. Figure 4 shows an example of possible scenarios for the non-profit sector based on recent trends.

Figure 4: Strategic Issues

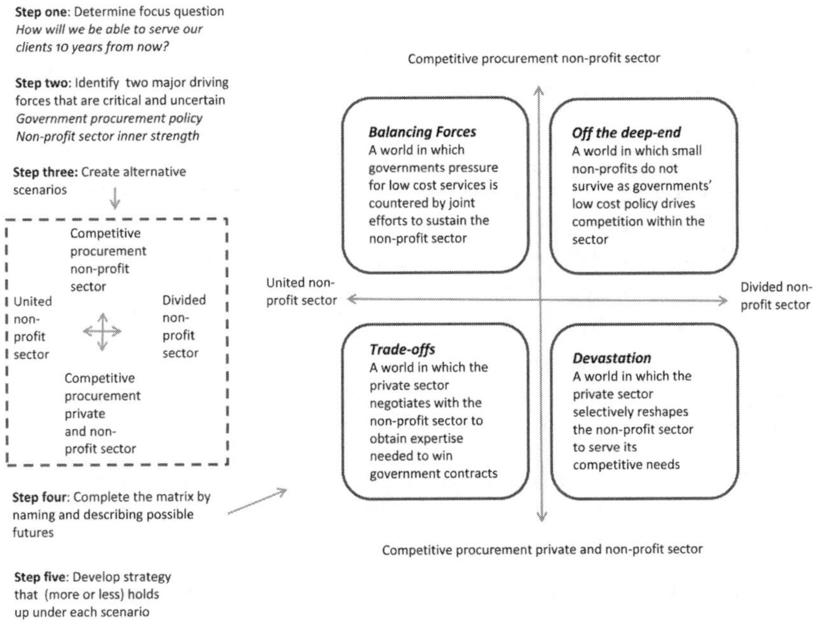
Step one: Determine focus question
How will we be able to serve our clients 10 years from now?
Step two: Identify two major driving forces that are critical and uncertain
Government procurement policy
Non-profit sector inner strength
Step three: Create alternative scenarios
Competitive procurement non-profit sector
United non-profit sector
Divided non-profit sector
Competitive procurement private and non-profit sector
Step four: Complete the matrix by naming and describing possible futures
Step five: Develop strategy that (more or less) holds up under each scenario
Competitive procurement non-profit sector
Balancing Forces
A world in which governments pressure for low cost services is countered by joint efforts to sustain the non-profit sector
Off the deep-end
A world in which small non-profits do not survive as governments' low cost policy drives competition within the sector
United non-profit sector
Divided non-profit sector
Trade-offs
A world in which the private sector negotiates with the non-profit sector to obtain expertise needed to win government contracts
Devastation
A world in which the private sector selectively reshapes the non-profit sector to serve its competitive needs
Competitive procurement private and non-profit sector

From the Figure we note that scenario planning involves a number of steps that start with an initial strategic question. For example, an agency providing shelter to homeless adults may wonder about its current strategy of relying on government grants and contracts to fulfill its mandate. The question might be whether this strategy should be replaced with a more market-based strategy that sees the organization securing mortgage financing to build revenue-generating apartment buildings. The revenue would be used to finance the shelters. In order to flesh out the scenario, next steps would involve the identification of trends in the housing market, the rate of increase in the homeless population and current government funding strategies. This information would be available from the environmental scan. Then, different scenarios could be developed on the basis of possible trends being realized. For example, real estate prices may increase, decrease, or stay the same. The effect on the alternative financing strategy will vary with each scenario. Other driving forces expected to be related to each of these price variations will be added to the scenarios until the scenarios are complete. Finally, each of the scenarios will form a specific strategic issue for the organization. Scenario planning techniques answer "what if" questions and enhance the nonprofit leaders' ability to add strategic thinking to the strategic planning process. In times of large economic fluctuations scenario planning could be pursued in more detail to identify strategic issues that are relatively robust, *i.e.*, they take more than one possible scenario into account.

STRATEGY FORMULATION AND PLAN IMPLEMENTATION

Once the strategic issues have been identified, the next step in the strategic planning process is to design a strategic plan to address these issues. The strategic plan is a blueprint for realizing the organization's vision. It formulates the specific goals and objectives to be achieved. The Canadian Mental Health Association of Ontario (CMHAO), for example, has identified that it will "promote mental health in collaboration with others" as one of its strategic directions in its 2010-2013 strategic plan. Within this area, the organization has identified four major strategies as follows:

1. We will advance implementation of public policies that increase access to resources that can promote health in individuals recovering from mental illness.

2. We will propose strategies that increase social inclusion.

3. We will develop and participate in opportunities to promote mental health in settings that can make a difference.

4.   We will support and be a resource for whole-of-government and inter-sectoral approaches to build healthy communities in Ontario. (Canadian Mental Health Association, 2010).

These strategies were to be implemented over the next three years, which brings us to the topic of implementation. Plan implementation is qualitatively different from the process of arriving at the strategic plan and its rate of success tends to be rather low (Mintzberg (1994b)). Implementation is an entirely new undertaking. It is the point where planning ends and reality starts. Implementation is also the most vulnerable stage since much of the excitement that went into putting the plan together and coming up with creative ideas and strategies to deal with the organization's future diminishes as the planning phase draws to a close.

Implementation requires nonprofit leaders to provide new energy and possibly new players who can invigorate the process of realizing the strategic plan. In addition, the skills associated with plan implementation are quite different from those needed for planning. Good implementers are people who take a highly structured approach to their work and pay sufficient attention to detail without losing sight of the larger picture. Their talents will include the management of sometimes very large teams from different parts of the organization who may have their own objectives for the plan's implementation. Most small nonprofits do not have employees with the requisite range of skills but, on the other hand, their involvement with complex organizational issues will be less demanding. Successfully implementing strategic plans also demands solid budgeting, scheduling, monitoring and evaluation skills. In short, nonprofit leaders who take strategic planning to the implementation stage must possess competencies that have a broad range as well as significant depth.

Implementation is also the point of transition between strategic planning, business plans, operational plans and project management, as shown in Figure 2, above. Most organizations use their strategic plan as a blueprint for their business plan with the only difference being the level of detail, especially if the strategic plan covers a relatively short period of time, *e.g.*, three years. Operational plans may contain more detail than business plans but are most often a representation of the business plan (or strategic plan) for one fiscal or calendar year. In some cases non-profits develop a strategic plan in sufficient detail to skip the business and operational plans and move directly to projects. A project, whether resulting directly from a strategic planning process or flowing from a business or operational plan, is defined as "a unique complex of activities aimed at achieving a jointly predetermined, unique result that must be realized with limited means" (Kor & Wijnen (2000, at 17)).

Regardless of how the projects were arrived at project management should also trigger a feedback process (shown as a dotted line in Figure 2) to ensure experiences during the implementation phase are evaluated and interpreted into possible implications for the strategic planning process. Feedback loops encourage ongoing learning and reflection on the plan and the planning process that will be useful for future strategic plans.

The literature on strategic plan implementation and project management contains many articles about the failure to implement plans successfully. Indeed, according to Raps (2004) only 10 per cent to 30 per cent of all implementation efforts succeed (at 49). Nonprofit leaders need to be particularly vigilant during the project management phase or all the efforts to create an exciting strategic plan will have been in vain.

PROJECT MANAGEMENT

There are two types of projects: those that flow from a strategic planning effort and those that are undertaken independently. In the private sector, emergent projects may come in the form of, say, large engineering assignments such as building a tunnel under the English Channel or dealing with the implications of a natural disaster. In the public sector, projects may emerge from government decisions in response to crises such as the 2003 SARS outbreak in Canada, or in response to otherwise unanticipated circumstances. In the nonprofit sector, projects may be the result of changes in governments' fiscal, economic, or social policies. In British Columbia, for example, the provincial government made several attempts to consolidate nonprofit organizations involved with delivering family services — a large project. Other changes in the funding environment may result in different networks having to be established. New accountability regimes may require the capturing of additional electronic information from more sources. Technological change may also drive projects as computer systems may no longer be supported by vendors and may need to be replaced. Clearly, nonprofit leaders are often faced with projects other than those following from the strategic plan and one of the ongoing challenges is to sustain the focus on strategic projects rather than constantly "putting out fires". It seems appropriate therefore to briefly review the main components of project management (Kor & Wijnen (2000)) and to provide a brief overview in Figure 5:

Figure 5: Project Management Overview

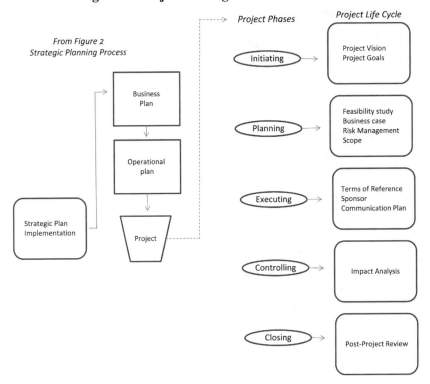

Project Life Cycle

A project life cycle is the sequence of stages that a project might progress through, from the time that it emerges from a strategic plan to the point that its objectives have been accomplished.

Feasibility Study. A feasibility study is an early, high-level assessment of whether it would be practicable and worthwhile to pursue an opportunity or a solution to a problem and, if so, how. It should identify and evaluate optional solutions, their justification and viability, and how one might implement each. The study needs to provide sufficient information to justify any recommendations on whether and how to proceed. Feasibility studies would normally precede a business case. When there are limited resources, feasibility studies will assist in selecting from among competing strategies.

Business Case. The business case is the documented justification for setting up a project, defining the benefits being sought, the likely investment, the constraints, and the timescales, all of which go to answer the question: "Why should we do this project?"

Risk Management. A project risk is a possible future event or situation that, if it happens, will affect the ability of a project to arrive at its intended outcome. Procedures should be put in place to identify those factors that might throw the project off-course, and result in measures to deal with them.

Scope. This is the definition of what the project needs to deliver (in terms of specific outputs) to identified stakeholders for a pre-defined purpose within a pre-defined period. It is often helpful to explicitly state in advance what is in and out of scope so that expectations about deliverables remain within the parameters of the project.

Terms of Reference. Written terms of reference are used to indicate the parameters of a particular project. They are important for defining the expectations of those working within the project and for accountability purposes.

Sponsor. In the project environment, a sponsor describes a senior individual in the organization, normally a person who will see his or her part of the organization benefit from the project's outputs. Usually the CEO is the ultimate authority on a project but this may be delegated depending on its scope and importance.

Communication Plan. A communication plan is that part of the project plan designed to ensure that internal and external stakeholders know what is going on, when and why, and enabling feedback from them. Large, lengthy and complicated projects are particularly in need of a communications plan since much of a project's success depends on the level of satisfaction of many stakeholders, not just the sponsor.

Impact Analysis. An impact analysis is conducted to understand the effect of requested changes to the project. It is used to forecast the possible effects of any proposed or imposed changes and the justification, schedule, budget, risks and issues. This will allow the board of directors the opportunity to consider the full implications before committing to a course of action.

Post-project Review. A post-project review is an appraisal to determine whether the expected benefits, as documented in the business case (or any other authorized documents showing expected results) have been achieved. The business case should also have identified how the benefits should eventually be measured, so this is a vital input to any review process.

There are quite a few similarities between the strategic planning process and project management. All projects can be broken down into five distinct phases:

1. Initiating — the development of a vision for a project and the establishment of overall project goals.

2. Planning — definition of financial and human resources, development of a schedule, and specification of detailed project objectives.

3. Executing — management and co-ordination of the project team and the resources allocated to the project as agreed to in the terms of reference or project charter.

4. Controlling — monitoring the project for deviations from the plan and taking remedial action as and when required.

5. Closing — bringing formal closure to the project through completion of all deliverables, disbanding of the team, and the production of final reports.

In the nonprofit sector strategies and projects are for the most part formulated within the current structure of the organization. Organization structures constrain the type of strategies that the CEO may wish to pursue, *i.e.*, those strategies that flow logically from the strategies issues. It may therefore be desirable to redesign the organization to achieve those ends. The next section of this chapter examines elements of organizational form and organizational design.

ORGANIZATIONAL FORM

This volume is dedicated to nonprofit organizations in Canada and to the nonprofit *form*[5] of organization, *i.e.*, governance by a voluntary board of directors, use of volunteers, and benefits that accrue to either the membership or the community. However, this is not the only form traditionally "pure" nonprofit organizations can take. Reductions in funding, increasing social and economic pressures, greater competition within the nonprofit sector, and the encroachment of the private sector have pushed some into the realm of "social entrepreneurship", which may generate other forms of organizations:

---

[5] Organizational form refers to the legal status of the organization; it is different from organizational design, which denotes the configuration of structures and processes. Organizational design is discussed in the next section.

Table 2: Examples of Organizational Forms

Pure Nonprofit (may or may not be a Registered Charity)	Social Entrepreneurship (charges for direct or indirect services)	Hybrid Form	Community Interest Company
Uses funds to provide services or goods to the community	Provide expert services to other non-profits Organize conferences and training programs Sell donated goods Provide client labour services to organizations	Holding company of a revenue generating business Participant in joint ventures	A for-profit organization that dedicates its profits to provide goods or services to the community

Social entrepreneurship occurs when nonprofit organizations establish or enter into profit-making ventures to finance their nonprofit operations. Nonprofits may use their expertise to sell their services to other nonprofit organizations. For example, an organization that manages a large number of properties may use its expertise to assist other nonprofit organizations with property financing and management. Others may have special expertise in communications that they offer in the community on a fee-for-service basis. The benefits appear to be mutual; the service-providing organization gains even greater expertise and the service-receiving organization does not have to develop its own expertise and obtains services at relatively low prices.

Nonprofits may offer services by employing their clients and selling their labour, *e.g.*, mental health clients. Clients may provide landscaping services, manufacture products for sale, or cater events. Provider clients gain because they get work experience and increase their ability to function independently, and receiving organizations benefit because they obtain services at a reduced cost. Other entrepreneurial activities may include organizing events such as conferences, workshops and training programs.

What these activities have in common is that they are intended to create revenue in the form of profit for the nonprofit organization. In order for such activities to be successful, the social entrepreneur has to build capacity, *i.e.*, acquire employees with business skills that are not necessarily aligned with the organization's mission and vision.

Social entrepreneurship may also lead to nonprofit organizations entering into subcontracts to provide programmatic expertise with private sector firms that have won government contracts through privatization. They may enter into partnerships with the for-profit sector through the creation of new (for-profit) companies. Some cases may even convert to for-profit status in order to carry out their mission.

As a result of these kinds of social entrepreneurial activities, nonprofit organizations may adopt non-traditional organizational hybrid forms. Holding companies and joint ventures are new forms that allow the nonprofit organization to generate additional funding while at the same time remaining true to its mission. An example of a holding company would be a university operating a real estate company or a hospital owning parking lots. A hospital could also restructure by "creating a nonprofit parent, a nonprofit hospital subsidiary, and for-profit ambulatory surgery centers and diagnostic laboratories" (Tuckman (1998, at 188)). In other words, joint ventures may be created between nonprofit organizations for the purpose of making a profit but the organizations would remain structured as nonprofits.

In 2012, the Nova Scotia government passed the *Community Interest Companies Act*,[6] introducing a new form of organization. The Act permits businesses formed under the *Companies Act* to be designated as community interest companies. This form, which has been in place in the United Kingdom since 2005, makes it easier for organizations to create businesses dedicated to the public good. A similar change is anticipated in British Columbia.

The strategic vision and key strategic issues in a strategic plan may contemplate a deviation from the traditional nonprofit form through entering into social entrepreneurial initiatives. In this case, leaders should be prepared to operate in a paradoxical environment. Staff and volunteers will have to be trained to become more business-focused in one area while upholding the organization's mission, values, and principles at the same time. This is particularly important in small organizations where the skills of organizational members are usually related only to the organization's service objectives.

ORGANIZATIONAL DESIGN

Organizational design refers to the grouping of organizational functions within an organization. An organization's basic design is the

---

[6] S.N.S. 2012, c. 38 [not yet proclaimed in force].

backbone of its structure, which comprises "the various processes technologies, systems, and coordination and control mechanisms necessary to allow individuals to perform tasks in an integrated manner" (Shoichet (1998, at 77)).

One of the most common designs is the functional grouping. "Functional grouping places employees together who perform similar function or work processes or who bring similar knowledge and skills to bear" (Daft (2004, at 97)). Thus some nonprofits may be designed around the primary functions served by the organization. They may have a nursing department staffed by nurses and nurse assistants and a social work department that houses probation officers, counsellors and child protection workers.

More often, however, nonprofits are organized by programs. A social service agency for example, may be organized around a shelter program, an addiction program, a half-way house and an employment program. Each program is headed by a program manager who has employees reporting to him or her. Programs may be in the same building or may be physically separate and located in special centres to be closer to the clientele. Program managers usually have their own budget, goals and objectives for the program. In small organizations functions and programs may be organized around individuals. For example, one nurse may be employed who, by definition, fulfills the nursing function. But she or he may also be responsible for a program that includes home visits, addiction counselling and a small recreation unit.

Regardless of whether a nonprofit is organized by program or function, if it is large enough, it usually has separate (functional) departments responsible for finance, information systems, human resources and public relations. Again, in small organizations these functions may be bundled and carried out by one or two people. These departments or individuals perform what are known as "staff" functions, i.e., they provide services to other parts of the organization. Programs and functions directly concerned with meeting organizational objectives are called "line" functions. Line functions are carried out by employees who directly serve the purpose of the organization and staff functions are carried out by employees who support line managers in doing their job.

Nonprofit leaders may have to deal with conflicts between line and staff functions when, for example, the financial manager attempts to influence the way a particular program is delivered because he or she feels that money can be saved by serving clients differently.

Disputes may also arise when the person responsible for human resources puts severe restrictions on a line manager in terms of attracting staff or when the systems analyst puts the efficiency of the system before the ease of managing the system by field staff.

Tensions may occur as a result of confusion about the authority and responsibility of staff and line positions or may be the result of poor organizational design. For example, groupings of staff functions and line programs may be overlapping, reporting relationships may be unclear or bottlenecks may exist that prevent efficient decision-making. Organizational design may either facilitate or obstruct efficient and effective operations. However, there is no perfect design that will work for all organizations, nor will an organization's design guarantee successful outcomes. Of course, size may limit the flexibility of the organization in assigning individuals to either a staff role or a line role. The important point for CEOs is to ensure that a clear distinction is made between the line and staff responsibilities and authority.

MECHANISTIC AND ORGANIC DESIGN

The very existence of organizations depends on the nature of their environment. In the private sector this environment is primarily framed by technological advances and competition. Political, legal and regulatory regimes have traditionally been the environmental forces that most strongly influence the existence of nonprofit organizations. However, over the past 20 years competition from other nonprofits, economic and social conditions, and technological developments are having an increasing effect.

In 1961, Burns and Stalker observed that for-profit organizations tended towards either mechanistic or organic structures as a function of the relative stability of their environment. In stable environments with high levels of certainty, structures tended to be *mechanistic*. Mechanistic structures exercised strict hierarchical control, *i.e.*, were highly centralized. Employees' tasks were strictly circumscribed and employees had little or no flexibility or discretion in carrying out their work. In unstable, uncertain environments however, organizations tended to be more flexible and their structure became more *organic*. In organic structures authority is decentralized, communication happens across the organization rather than from the top down and employees have more discretion in decision-making and work more in interdependent teams. The characteristics of mechanistic and organic structures are compared in Table 3 below.

Table 3: Mechanistic versus Organic Structures

Mechanistic	Organic
Tasks are broken down into specialized, separate parts.	Employees contribute to the common tasks of the organization.
Tasks are rigidly defined.	Tasks are adjusted and redefined through employee teamwork.
There is a strict hierarchy of authority and control, and there are many rules (high formalization).	There is less hierarchy of authority and control, and there are few rules (low formalization).
Knowledge and control of tasks are centralized at the top of the organization.	Knowledge and control of tasks are located anywhere in the organization.
Communication is vertical.	Communication is horizontal.

Source: Adapted from Gerald Zaltman, Robert Duncan & Johnny Holbek, *Innovations and Organizations* (New York: Wiley, 1973) at 131.

It would probably be fair to say that today most Canadian nonprofit organizations exist within a dynamic and changing environment where nothing much is certain and the future is anything but predictable. In addition, many nonprofits are greatly affected by public policy and must deal with highly charged and politicized environments. Given these conditions, it is suggested that the characteristics of organically structured organizations would appeal to the leaders of such organizations. It is also the case that smaller nonprofits would be more conducive to organic designs simply because they lack the resources to build extensive specialized staffs and hierarchies. Conversely, executives who run their organizations based on more traditional mechanistic principles may discover that they need to rethink the organization's structure to bring it in line with the prevailing forces in the environment. Again, there is no perfect structure but organizations that fail to align themselves with the demands of their environment will be less successful than those that do.

VERTICAL AND HORIZONTAL STRUCTURES

Vertical Structures

An organization's design can be further analyzed (and managed) by looking at its vertical and horizontal structures. The vertical structure comprises two major (control) mechanisms: hierarchy and formalization.

The horizontal structure includes two central (co-ordination) devices: information systems and cross-functional teams and task forces. Figure 6 shows an example of a vertically structured organization

Figure 6: Vertical Organization Structure

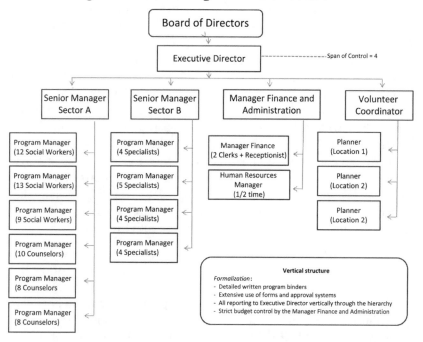

Hierarchy

The chain of command emanates from the top (CEO or Executive Director), and flows down through the management layers to the front-line workers who provide services to the clients, community, or members. This chain of command is expressed in organization charts (sometimes called organigrams), showing the employee names and titles in boxes connected by lines to other boxes below them. The lines indicate the reporting relationship within the organization's hierarchy. The Board of Directors is usually shown on the organization chart but the Board is (or should be) concerned with governance, not opera-tions.[7] The organization chart illustrates who is "in charge". Directions flow from the top of the organization, and problems and queries are

---

[7]   This separation of governance and operations may be difficult to achieve in very small operations where board members tend to do volunteer work. See Chapter 3.

referred to upwards for resolution. Therefore the lines of authority also reflect the organization's communication channels.

The number of employees who report to a particular position constitute that position's *span of control*. The span of control at the top is usually narrow, *e.g.*, in midsize organizations three or four senior managers may report to the Executive Director. At the lower end of the organization the span of control tends to be wide. Each senior manager may be responsible for five to seven different programs or functions and program managers may have a dozen or more professionals reporting to them. This is also the reason why organization charts typically take the form of a pyramid. The number of direct reports may vary from organization to organization depending on the complexity of the work being done. Organizations that have an overall narrow span of control (few people reporting to individual managers) have a *tall* hierarchy. The greater the number of layers between the CEO and the lowest employee in the hierarchy, the taller the organization. Organizations that have an overall wide span of control (many employees reporting to individual managers) have a *flat* hierarchy. Many small nonprofits are very flat, in that most employees report directly to the executive director.

One of the ways in which medium and large nonprofit organizations can become more efficient is through increasing spans of control, thereby reducing the number of managers in the organization. This "flattening" may reduce costs since fewer people have to be employed to do the same amount of work, but may negatively impact effectiveness since managers will have less time to deal with problems that need resolution and may generally feel overworked and under-compensated.

It is possible to find different organizations with the same hierarchy and span of control but with different loci of authority. Organizations in which the top executive makes most of the decisions without involving staff have highly centralized authority; they are *centralized*. In organizations where employees at the lower levels are permitted (and sometimes actively encouraged) to make the day-to-day decisions, authority is *decentralized*. The ability and willingness of the CEO to delegate authority to lower levels in the organization is mainly dependent on the real or perceived competency of employees, the personality of the CEO and the programs delivered by the organization. The degree to which authority is centralized is an indicator of organizational control.

Not all nonprofit organizations are structured in a pyramidal fashion. Some nonprofit leaders strongly believe in non-hierarchical structures. Such organizations are set up and managed in accordance with broad democratic principles, decisions tend to be made collectively and active participation by all staff is encouraged. In terms of organizational structure such organizations are very flat and decentralized. In small organizations operating on these principles everyone reports to the Executive Director. Medium and larger organizations may appoint team leaders rather than managers and staff may rotate in and out of these positions.

Formalization

The number of rules, regulations and operational procedures in place in an organization represents how formalized its structure is. One of the most commonly used sets of formal procedures is the departmental or program budget. A well-structured budget will allow employees to carry out their responsibilities within clear parameters. Other examples of formalization are detailed job descriptions, protocols for the treatments of clients, health and safety regulations, disciplinary procedures, and many more.

Nonprofit organizations that employ large numbers of professionals, such as museums and research organizations, usually have a low degree of formalization. This is based on the premise that professionals are assumed to have been trained before they joined the organization and so do not require a high level of control. They are believed capable of setting their own goals and objectives within the parameters set out in the organization's vision and mission statement. On the other hand, very large nonprofits with many programs staffed by a wide range of occupational groups would likely need a high degree of formalization to co-ordinate them and to ensure a standard level of performance in all parts of the organization.

Formalization may also be directly related to the type of nonprofit organization. A study by Hillel Schmid (2002), for example, showed that residential boarding schools for troubled children were characterized by a moderate to high degree of formalization, which "substantiates the argument that boarding schools are committed to formal patterns that dictate the life of the professional staff and children" (at 388). On the other hand, home care service organizations tended to have low levels of formalization combined with strong centralized management control. Schmid concluded that the high degree of control "is appropriate for the type and level of staff in home care organizations, which rely almost exclusively on an unskilled, non-nursing, female labor force" (at 389). In other words, plans, rules and procedures provide less control than direct oversight by those in authority.

Leaders of nonprofit organizations must match the amount and type of control needed in the organization with the capacity of its employees and the nature of the organization's programs.

Horizontal Structure

The horizontal structure of an organization refers to the formal linkages *across* the vertical hierarchy. They are the means used by leaders to co-ordinate work and overcome gaps and barriers that arise from the hierarchy and the division of labour by organizational functions or programs. For example, the exhibit unit, the outreach department, and the marketing department in a cultural organization may all serve the same objectives, but unless they co-ordinate their work and communicate their ideas to each other, objectives may not be achieved. Cross-functional teams and task forces are the major tools used in the private sector and can be used to advance the objectives and strategic issues of nonprofits. Figure 7 provides an example of a horizontal structure.

Figure 7: Horizontal Organization Structure

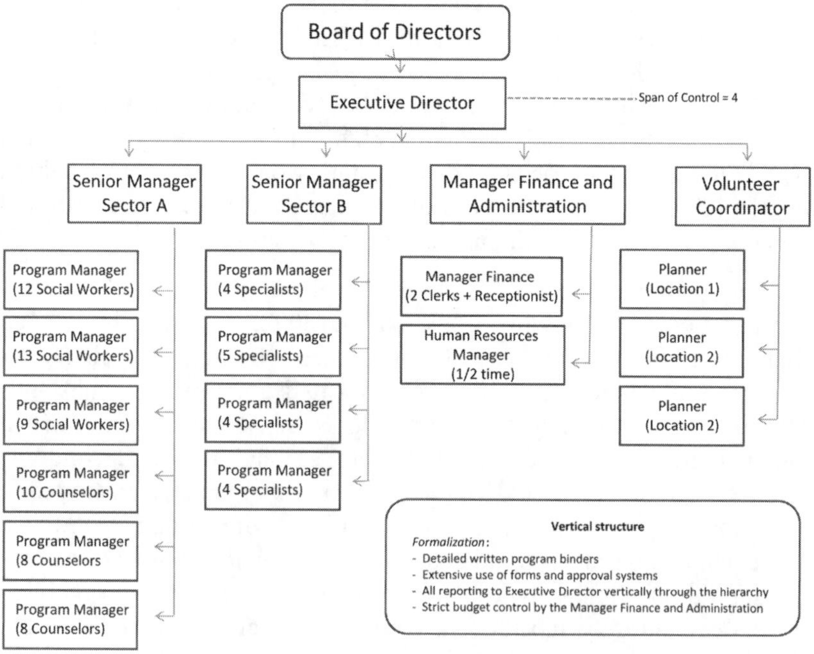

Information Systems

It is probably fair to say that today electronic information systems permeate all aspects of Canadians' personal and professional lives. In organizations, information systems have taken on different meanings over time. Today, information systems typically refer to computerized data processing for programmatic, financial, or other purposes. Computerized information systems play a central role in an organization's structure and operations, not just to collect, store and retrieve information but also to provide linkages across departments and programs. In addition to serving vertical communication, tools such as electronic mail create the opportunity for employees (and volunteers) at all levels of the organization to communicate with each other. Electronic message boards allow employees to stay in touch on emerging issues. Employees are also able to create communities of practice using Web-based technology in order to share information about problems they face in their professional area. Organizations can also use personnel databases (subject to confidentiality provisions) to bring people together with common backgrounds and interests.

Program databases can provide information on clients (again subject to confidentiality provisions) to be used by managers who are responsible for different programs but who service the same group of clients. In this way managers can stay in touch to ensure integrated services are provided to clients even though clients make use of different programs. Information systems can also be used as a central coordinating mechanism to link activities within the organization's strategic plan, thereby ensuring appropriate and timely input and the dissemination on the progress of the strategic plan and its related activities. For more on the use of information technology in nonprofit management, see Chapter 12.

Task Forces and Cross-functional Teams

Task forces or work teams fall under the general rubric of "committees". They are created for a specified time and are usually charged with the responsibility for completing a large project or dealing with an important problem that affects the organization across functional and program units. For example, a library can put a task force together to deal with a recurring problem of theft and vandalism. Task force members may be drawn from librarians, support staff, volunteers and technical staff. The task force may be led by one of the representatives or by a member of the executive and would be required to present options to management to reduce theft while maintaining an open and welcoming atmosphere in the library.

The creation of a task force to address a particular problem acknowledges that solutions should be created though different parts of the organization working together. In the case of strategic planning, the task force would be the employee team supporting the CEO in putting the strategic plan together.

Cross-functional teams can be seen as permanent task forces. Again, they are similar to committees. They are highly task-directed and consist of members from different programs and will sometimes include line and staff representatives. Cross-functional teams may be charged with the responsibility for projects that require strong co-ordination over a long period of time. In the case of a three-year strategic plan they would be responsible for the implementation and maintenance of the plan during the three years. Or, they may be responsible for the co-ordination of client services across different programs. Another example would be creating a cross-functional team to attract and manage volunteers and review volunteer policies to ensure the volunteer population continues to serve the mission of the organization. Cross-functional teams do not take the place of the CEO; rather they support the organization by providing a bridge between organizational components at the employee and managerial level.

CONCLUSION

Strategy and structure are closely related concepts. Strategic planning gives form and content to the strategic vision of nonprofit leaders. A well-constructed and carefully implemented strategic plan will enable the achievement of the organization's future vision of success. However, in order to successfully achieve strategic objectives the nonprofit organization needs a structure that is aligned with the strategy. If strategic goals cannot be achieved with the current structure, then structural redesign is called for. The description of the different features of organizational structure presented in this chapter is intended to assist nonprofit leaders in redesigning structures to meet the goals of the organization.

REFERENCES

R. Bradfield *et al.*, "The Origins and Evolution of Scenario Techniques in Long Range Business Planning" (2005) 37:8 Futures 795-812.

J.M. Bryson, *Strategic Planning for Public and Nonprofit Organizations: A Guide to Strengthening and Sustaining Organizational Achievement*, 3d ed. (San Francisco: Jossey-Bass, 2004).

T. Burns & G.M. Stalker (1961), *The Management of Innovation* (London: Tavistock Publications, 1961).

Canadian Mental Health Association, Ontario (2010), *Strategic Plan 2010-2013*, online at: <http://ontario.cmha.ca/files/2012/08/cmha_ontario_strategic_plan_2010-2013_summary.pdf > at 4.

R.L. Daft, *Organization Theory and Design*, 8th ed. (Mason, OH: Thomson/South-Western, 2004).

A. Fletcher *et al.*, "Mapping Stakeholder Perceptions for a Third Sector Organization" (2003) 4:4 Journal of Intellectual Capital 505-527.

F. Graetz, "Strategic Thinking Versus Strategic Planning: Towards Understanding the Complementarities" (2002) 40:5 Management Decision 456-462.

R. Kor & G. Wijnen, *50 Checklists for Project and Programme Managers* (Brookfield, VT: Gower, 2000).

J. Liedtka, "Linking Strategic Thinking with Strategic Planning" (1998) 26:4 Strategy and Leadership 30-35.

H. Mintzberg, "The Fall and Rise of Strategic Planning" (1994) 72:1 Harvard Business Review 107-114.

H. Mintzberg, *The Rise and Fall of Strategic Planning: Reconceiving Roles for Planning, Plans, Planners* (Toronto: Maxwell Macmillan, 1994).

T. O'Shannassy, "Modern Strategic Management: Balancing Strategic Thinking and Strategic Planning for Internal and External Stakeholders" (2003) 25:1 Singapore Management Review 53-67.

M.E. Porter, *Competitive Strategy: Techniques for Analyzing Industries and Competitors* (New York: Free Press, 1980).

V.K. Rangan, "Lofty Missions, Down-to-Earth Plans" (2004) 82:3 Harvard Business Review 112-119.

A. Raps, "Implementing Strategy" (2004) 85:12 Strategic Finance 49-53.

H. Renz, "The Changing Nature of Volunteerism in the 21st Century" (2005) [unpublished].

H. Schmid, "Relationships Between Organizational Properties and Organizational Effectiveness in Three Types of Nonprofit Human Service Organizations" (2002) 31:3 Public Personnel Management 377-395.

P. Schwartz, *The Art of the Long View: Planning for the Future in an Uncertain World* (New York: Doubleday/Currency, 1991).

R. Shoichet, "An Organization Design Model for Nonprofits" (1998) 9:1 Nonprofit Management and Leadership 71-88.

H.P. Tuckman, "Competition, Commercialization, and the Evolution of Nonprofit Organizational Structures" (1998) 17:2 Journal of Policy Analysis and Management 175-194.

G. Zaltman, R. Duncan & J. Holbek, *Innovations and Organizations* (New York: Wiley, 1973).

Chapter 9

PREPARING FOR IMPACT: THE EVOLUTION OF EVALUATION IN CANADA'S NONPROFIT SECTOR

Susan D. Phillips*
Carleton University

INTRODUCTION

"Impact" seems to be everywhere in the nonprofit sector. The Government of Canada, following the lead of the United Kingdom, has announced it will implement "social impact bonds" which tie funding to performance (Globe & Mail (2013)). Many United Ways and private foundations are transforming themselves into "impact funders", interested in making systemic change by addressing root causes of social issues, making grants more strategically to organizations that can deliver results on this change agenda, and assessing performance in producing results (Fulton *et al.* (2010)). International networks and a cottage industry have grown up around the measurement of "social return on investment" (SROI) — an outcome-based offshoot of cost-benefit analysis and social accounting — that seeks to help nonprofits "understand and quantify the social, environmental and economic value they are creating" (Nef (n.d.)). The online sector watchdog, Charity Navigator, now rates charities on the plausibility and evidence backing their theory of change, on publication of evaluation reports and whether they explain what they have changed as a consequence of evaluation findings (Charity Navigator (2012)). Its

* This chapter draws on earlier versions for this volume which were co-authored with Tatyana Teplova. The contributions of Dr. Teplova (currently with the OECD in Paris) remain central to the chapter and are gratefully recognized.

online cousin, GuideStar, recently added a feature of an "impact" tab on its Website that enables crowdsourcing, supposedly by experts, of assessments of a charity's strengths and performance. Although neither Charity Navigator nor GuideStar rate Canadian charities, this type of regulation-by-transparency is indicative of the wave of interest in measuring and reporting on performance.

This focus on performance evaluation is by no means new for the charitable and nonprofit sector. Indeed, 15 years ago the sector's own blue ribbon panel on accountability (Broadbent Panel 1999) noted the challenges of outcome measurement, which were hotly debated in consultations across the country. However, the pressures for performance assessment have arguably multiplied since that time as governments, a variety of funders and third parties begin to demand more sophisticated measurement and accountability through various means. Much of this is accountability in a narrow sense, primarily accountability as control (see, Aucoin and Heintzman (2000); Aucoin and Jarvis (2005); Perrin (2002)). However, as nonprofits seek to make more effective use of scarce resources and demonstrate their value to stakeholders and the public in a competitive environment, they need to make more effective use of performance measurement as a means of learning and as a basis for self-improvement.

This chapter takes a critical look at performance assessment as a strategic management tool and explores some of the key challenges involved. It focuses specifically on evaluating programs and the organization as a whole, rather than on the details of broader accountability and regulatory regimes — *e.g.*, rules governing registration of charities, political activities, and funding — that are discussed in Chapters 5 and 6 of this volume.

The main challenges of performance assessment as accountability for learning do not lie in finding the "right" measurement tools or management techniques. There are a plethora of methods available and, indeed, the branding and selling of an array of new techniques to voluntary organizations has built a substantial evaluation consulting industry. So, the point is not to extoll the virtues of SROI or the balanced scorecard over any of the other helpful and not-so-helpful techniques that are available and marketed to voluntary organizations these days. In an important sense, measurement is the easy part of evaluation. The harder part lies in addressing the meta-questions, such as when and why to evaluate what, in dealing with the political implications of evaluation, making effective use of evaluation results, and building the capacity to become a self-improving, learning organization. These meta-issues are the focus of this chapter.

The chapter begins with defining some of the key terms used in this field because language is often confused, and confusing, especially for the manager of a voluntary organization who simply wants to figure out how to do things better. It then provide a brief overview of the current state of performance assessment in the nonprofit sector, drawing on both Canadian and international research. The focus then turns to the meta-questions and challenges involved in using evaluation as a management tool with an eye to providing some practical guidance to those working in this sector. Performance assessment is not without its darker side, however, and the conclusion gives a glimpse of some of these shadows. It also offers some suggestions for ways of enhancing evaluation and accountability as a process of learning rather than as control.

IDENTIFYING THE TERRAIN

The assessment of performance is to some extent clouded by language, which itself has been subject to changing interests and fashions. Table 1 explains the primary terms in this field, beginning with the narrower concept of *audit*, which is focused on determining compliance, to *performance management*, which has been introduced to emphasize the strategic use of performance systems for ongoing improvement and facilitating change.

Table 1: Scales of Assessment

Term	Definition	Purpose
Audit	An independent assurance activity to determine compliance with and effectiveness of an organization's risk management systems) (Quesnel (2006)).	Verify compliance with rules and procedures.
Monitoring	A continuing, routine function that provides managers and stakeholders with early and ongoing indicators about progress (UNDP 2002).	Obtain feedback on whether implementation is going according to plan, and identify gaps and obstacles to make mid-course adjustments in a timely manner.

Evaluation	Evidence-based periodic assessment that is as systematic, impartial, and credible as possible, aimed at determining the relevance, impact, cost effectiveness, efficiency, and sustainability of the project or program and which attempts to identify best alternatives so as to inform an organization's strategic decision-making (see UNEG (2005)).	Determine if the organization is: 1) doing the right things; 2) doing it right; and 3) can find better ways of doing it (Quesnel (2006)).
Performance Assessment	More encompassing than evaluation, designating an ongoing, routinized process rather than an episodic snapshot. It often includes monitoring, benchmarking, and the use of indicators in addition to policy and program evaluation, and emphasizes the measurement of results rather than activities.	Potentially applicable to all aspects of an organization, including assessment of the organization as a whole, performance assessment systems are "designed and implemented with the intention of providing regular and continuing information for program and organizational purposes" (McDavid and Hawthorn (2006, at 9–6)).
Performance Management	Encompass broad issues of institutional design, co-ordination, and organizational culture that enable assessment to be not only a driver of change, but a common language for achieving collective goals (Kettl (2005)).	The focus shifts upward to the broader process of strategic planning and building the organizational systems for ongoing improvement. Encompasses performance assessment and evaluation (Davies (1999); Broadbent Panel (1999); English and Lindquist (1998)).

In the late 1990s, the language of program evaluation began to be displaced by the concept of *performance assessment* to signify a more encompassing set of processes, including monitoring and benchmarking in addition to evaluation, and to recognize that the subject might be the organization as a whole, rather than a program or project. Evaluation and performance assessment are obviously interdependent as evaluation is a mechanism for developing appropriate measures and indicators for ongoing monitoring and performance assessment, and ongoing assessment often generates data that can be used in evaluation (European Commission (1997); Davies (1999)). At the broadest level, the language of *performance management* has been introduced to expand the discussion beyond methodologies to wider processes of strategic planning and building the organizational systems for ongoing improvement (Davies (1999, at 151); English and Lindquist (1998)). The challenge in making evaluation a foundation for performance management, and thus for ongoing learning and self-improvement, is to use it as a strategic management tool.

In the Canadian context, "evaluation" retains a strong claim as a general concept for the assessment of projects, programs, policies and organizations because it is widely used by the Government of Canada and as a professional designation by the Canadian Evaluation Society. This chapter focuses primarily on evaluation and on how to embed evaluation in organizational governance and management systems more effectively.

A second aspect in need of clarification is the components and potential focus of evaluation, as set out in Table 2. As discussed later, there are heightened expectations for outcome and impact measurement, but the actual evaluations often assess only outputs.

Table 2: Basic Concepts Defined

Concept	Definition
Inputs	resources invested (*e.g.*, dollars, staff time, equipment)
Outputs	direct products or services generated from the inputs and activities (*e.g.*, "units of service" such as number of meals served, training sessions completed)

Concept	Definition
Outcomes	changes that result from the program outputs, usually in the shorter term (*e.g.*, increased awareness, improved skills)
Impacts	longer term changes that result (*e.g.*, change of state in a target population)

A TIDE OF RISING EXPECTATIONS: EVALUATION PRACTICES IN THE NONPROFIT SECTOR

The pressures for accountability and evaluation have grown significantly in recent years. These pressures for more *and* better evaluation are driven both internally, by boards, staff and volunteers concerned about making effective use of scarce resources, and externally, mainly by a variety of funders and by the need to demonstrate value in a crowded public space. Although most nonprofits conduct evaluations of their own volition and as part of their routine operations, rather than because they are required to do so by funders, it is important to consider the external drivers, particularly changes in the accountability requirements of the federal government, as the actions of governments have been shown to be an important factor in shaping the behavior of nonprofits (Carman (2009, at 386). In this section, we take a brief look at the current environment and state of practice for performance assessment in Canada's voluntary sector.

A Changing Environment

The introduction of New Public Management (NPM) with its emphasis on consumers, privatization, contracting out, and market-based policy instruments, created an "explosion" (Power (1994); Phillips and Smith (2012)) in auditing in Canada as elsewhere. Across large parts of government at all levels, the role of managers shifted from supervising and delivering programs directly to managing contracts for services provided by third parties — both voluntary organizations and private-sector firms. Assurances of quality in the expanded contracting culture created under NPM were provided by extended reporting requirements and by increased demands for evaluation of programs and projects. Performance assessment was by no means a new thing for NPM. Indeed, waves of budgeting and public sector reform over several decades had advocated different systems for assessing and managing performance, creating a virtual alphabet soup of techniques. What changed was the controlling role of government as a funder and contractor of services over the evaluation activities of a wide range of third parties.

With concomitant funding cuts and the increased demand for services that occurred in the late 1980s and early 1990s, voluntary organizations needed to make tough decisions among programs, sometimes rationalizing or even closing programs (Toronto Agency Survey (2004)). Evaluation took on new importance in this context, although the extent to which it was actually used for decision-making varied enormously.

The focus of what to evaluate also changed over the course of the 1990s with the rise of outcome or results-based measurement. Whereas evaluation had tended to focus on activities and *outputs* (what was produced), the new demands were for evidence of *outcomes* (what actual changes were realized in the lives of users and beneficiaries). Although the interest in outcome measurement emanated in part from the field of evaluation itself and flowed through internationally connected networks, such as the United Way movement,[1] the real pressures set in when provincial and federal governments began to adopt results-based management.

In March 2000, the federal government adopted a comprehensive management framework known as *Results for Canadians* that committed departments to be more results-oriented and was dedicated to responsible spending. As indicated in this Treasury Board document, the new management framework meant that "public service managers are expected to define strategic outcomes, continually focus attention on results achievement, measure performance regularly and objectively, learn from this information and adjust to improve efficiency and effectiveness".[2] Several provinces, notably Alberta, were already ahead of the federal curve. By the mid-1990s, they had already begun to incorporate business planning and performance measurement into their budget planning processes and develop "results-based cultures".[3]

---

[1] Several large American funders, notably the United Way of America and the Kellogg Foundation, produced handbooks for evaluation that circulated and were used quite widely in Canada. In particular, see Hatry *et al.* (1996) and Carman & Fredericks (2010) on the influence of the United Way in the United States.

[2] From the Treasury Board of Canada Secretariat "Guide for the Development of Results-based Management and Accountability Frameworks", online: <http://www.tbs-sct.gc.ca/cee/tools-outils/rmaf-cgrr/guide01-eng.asp>.

[3] Alberta was the leader in developing a government-wide performance measurement system in the early 1990s. For example, its 1995 report, *Measuring Up*, reported on 22 core government performance measures. See, Ogata *et al.* (1998).

At all levels, then, the policy environment became enamoured with a results focus and with the production of standardized population-level performance indicators. The fact that relatively few of the indicators produced by governments were actually outcome measures was irrelevant: the policy and political environment — and the expectations created for the voluntary sector — had shifted considerably.

Leaders in Canada's voluntary sector were cognizant of the potential impact of the growing concern with accountability. In addition to pressures for greater performance measurement, there was an active campaign in the early 1990s by a federal Liberal backbench MP to severely tighten the regulatory regime. The vicarious effects of several major scandals among nonprofits south of the border illustrated both the importance and the fragility of public trust. In 1997, the Voluntary Sector Roundtable, an unincorporated group of national associations and networks that broadly represented all parts of the sector and that had formed to provide policy leadership, commissioned a panel of six (volunteer) experts to review and make recommendations on issues of accountability. The Panel on Accountability and Governance in the Voluntary Sector (PAGVS), chaired by Hon. Ed Broadbent, was charged with reviewing, consulting, and making recommendations on how the sector could improve its own practices.

The Panel took a very broad perspective on accountability, considering both internal and external accountabilities and giving significant attention to the sector's relationship with government, particularly the federal government, which holds the main responsibility for the regulation of charities. Its 1999 report paved the way for the creation of the Voluntary Sector Initiative (VSI), a collaborative process established by the Government of Canada in 2000 to encourage a better relationship and enhance capacity in the sector. However, the key concerns voiced in the Panel's national consultations with voluntary organizations related not to the relationship with government, but to evaluation.[4] Of all the briefs submitted and the discussions held, the Panel probably heard more about outcome measurement and how voluntary organizations feared being carried away by a tidal wave of unrealistic expectations about evaluation than any other topic.

The report of the PAGVS recognized that results-based performance assessment was here to stay, at least for the foreseeable

---

[4]   Personal observation. I was Research Director for the Panel and attended many of the consultations held across the country.

future, and it encouraged voluntary organizations to begin to develop their own sets of appropriate indicators before less appropriate ones were imposed on them. The Panel also noted, however, that better performance measurement had to be a joint effort with funders, with a strong supporting role played by intermediary organizations (the federations, umbrellas and research organizations that serve the sector). In this regard, it called upon funders to use more multi-year funding, cover the costs of evaluation and consider more core funding, which helps build the capacity for performance assessment, and, perhaps most importantly, to begin a sustained dialogue with voluntary organizations related to evaluation.

Serious follow-through on sector-wide or collaborative actions related to performance measurement was derailed by two things, one more positive than the other. When the VSI was established in 2000, sector leaders became consumed with that process, leaving little time for other issues. The VSI facilitated some excellent research on the voluntary sector, developed an *Accord* (2001) with the Government of Canada, which was soon defunct, and made modest steps in regulatory reform. It did not, and was not explicitly mandated to, advance the state of accountability and evaluation. But neither did it hurt.

A second development — the establishment of a very stringent, control-based accountability regime focused on financial reporting on federal funding that came as a response to a scandal over grants and contributions at the largest federal department in 2000 — was a major setback to performance assessment as learning (Good (2004)). Financial reporting became *the* consuming focus of accountability while little was done to encourage better evaluation of programs and their impacts (Phillips and Levasseur (2004)). The *Federal Accountability Act* in 2006,[5] itself a response to the sponsorship scandal involving inappropriate contracting (with the private sector) imposed further controls on recipients of government funding and contracts, strengthened auditing practices within departments, and required that grant and contribution programs be evaluated every five years. The "web of rules" had become broader and denser.

The recognition within the federal government of the stultifying effect of these rules and their associated reporting burden on both voluntary organizations and government departments led to the creation of an independent Blue Ribbon Panel in June 2006. Its mandate was to make the delivery of grant and contribution programs

---

[5]   S.C. 2006, c. 9.

more efficient while ensuring greater accountability (Blue Ribbon Panel (2006, at iv)). Panel members reported being quite shocked at the negative impact of "the excessive and apparently redundant reporting required at every step of the grant and contribution process — duplicative audits, repeated performance reports, the obligation to collect data for apparently obscure reasons or to measure results even where these do not seem measurable" (Blue Ribbon Panel (2006 at 31)). The Panel concluded quite emphatically that "the present culture of over-control does nothing to strengthen accountability" (Blue Ribbon Panel (2006 at 44)). The Panel's recommendations, released in early 2007, stressed the importance of establishing genuine risk management processes in which administrative regimes are flexible and tailored to the degree of risk involved. They included the need to review the federal transfer policy and the rules on grants and contributions and suggested that multi-year funding for recipients should be explored. In terms of evaluation, the Panel recommended that the five-year reviews of the relevance and effectiveness of grant and contribution programs, as proposed in the *Federal Accountability Act,* be implemented. Evaluations needed to be more focused on larger program areas instead of the relatively *pro forma*, program-specific evaluations that had been mandatory, and data collection and reporting requirements needed to be reasonable and demonstrably relevant to meaningful program evaluation.

In response to the report, the Government of Canada developed a new policy on transfer payments, and designated vanguard departments were to implement changes to the way each designs, manages, and accounts for its grant and contribution programs, but follow through quietly faded away. A new federal Evaluation Policy was announced by the Treasury Board in April 2009, with full implementation in 2013. This policy aims to give the evaluation function more neutrality and independence and places greater responsibility on deputy heads for providing leadership for evaluation in their departments. It requires robust evaluation of all ongoing programs of grants and contributions every five years, based on a rolling five-year evaluation plan and supported by ongoing performance measurement for all initiatives. It also aims to enhance the competencies of evaluators and set more consistent standards for evaluation.

At the same time, an important change was under way within the evaluation community that would further enhance its professionalization. The Canadian Evaluation Society (CES) was the first in the world to move toward introducing a professional designation for evaluators that would define a credential and associated set of competencies expected of a credentialed evaluator. The benefit for voluntary organizations is that some of the guesswork involved in hiring an evaluator should be reduced, as there should be greater consistency in competencies across the profession.

The more recent pressures for evaluation come in part from governments' interest in social financing, which links funding to performance and the ability to attract additional investors, and from foundation and corporate funders who seek "impact" or are pursuing impact investing strategies. At a global scale, impact investing — investments made in nonprofits, companies and funds that are intended to produce "measurable social and environmental impact alongside a financial return"[6] — was projected to grow from an industry of USD $8 billion in 2012 to USD $9 billion in just one year (J.P. Morgan (2013 at 3)). In 2012, Canada largest bank announced a $10 million capital fund, the RBC Impact Fund, to support projects by organizations and entrepreneurs "tackling social and environmental challenges".[7] The significance of social finance for evaluation is that it relies on metrics, increasing the demand for the reporting of results in quantitative terms.

The United Way in many Canadian cities now sees itself as being "in the community impact business," focusing on addressing causes of social problems and "working to effect long-term changes that can be sustained over time".[8] In addition, many community and private foundations have situated themselves as "impact funders", some more rhetorically than in practice, but the implication is a new approach to grant-making that they will make fewer, larger grants over long periods, but determining which charities to fund in the first place, or continue supporting, will depend to a much great extent on demonstrated results — on performance assessments that go beyond number of people served to measuring changes in their lives. Although foundations account for a relatively small proportion of overall funding for the Canadian charitable sector, and Canadian foundations are just beginning to enter the impact space, for many charities, the funder-fundee relationship is likely to change quite significantly in coming years (see Greenwald (2009); Hedley, Lumley and Pavey (2011); Mayhew (2012)).

---

[6]   GIIN, <http://www.thegiin.org/cgi-bin/iowa/home/index.html>.

[7]   RBC, <http://www.rbc.com/newsroom/2012/0124-social-finance.html>.

[8]   For example, United Way of Winnipeg, <http://unitedwaywinnipeg.ca/impact/>.

The State of the Art: Evaluation Practices of the Nonprofit Sector

What effects have all these changes had on the voluntary sector? How is evaluation currently practiced? First, it is apparent from the surveys in Canada and internationally, that evaluation is being conducted widely in this sector. There is no sector-wide consistency, but considerable variation in approaches to evaluation. A national survey of almost 2,000 Canadian charities and nonprofits and over 300 funders conducted in 2003 by the Voluntary Sector Evaluation Research Project (VSERP) (M.H. Hall *et al.* (2003)) found that 73 per cent indicated that they do evaluation routinely, using a wide range of formal and informal approaches.[9] Smaller organizations, as noted in a 2012 U.S. survey (Innovation Network (2012 at 2)), are less likely to evaluate their work than larger ones: 78 per cent of small organizations (with budgets under $500,000) reported evaluating their work compared to 90 per cent of large organizations (budgets over $5 million). Even in large organizations, however, the status of performance assessment is often quite weak, (see the 2008 U.K. study by Ellis and Gregory (2008); also Arvidson (2009)).

While capacity — time, staff and financial resources, and expertise — is a factor in a commitment to evaluation, the more significant predictor is governance, specifically, leadership by the board. For instance, in a survey followed by intensive interviews, Carman (2010) identified three clusters of U.S. nonprofits: those that embraced and made extensive use of evaluation; those that associated it with compliance with funder requirements; and those that had significant challenges with evaluation which was largely associated with limited capacity. The distinguishing features of the first group were that: evaluation was linked with strategic planning and broader management systems; boards required regular reporting on performance; and data were collected on an ongoing basis. Similarly, MacIndoe and Barman (2012 at 732) found that while funders and other external stakeholders may lead to the adoption of a budget line for outcome measurement, nonprofits only substantively implement such measurement when internal stakeholders, particularly managers, perceive it to be important. In examining whether nonprofits actually use evaluation for strategic decision-making, LeRoux and Wright

---

[9]   VSERP operated from 2000 to 2006 as a Social Sciences and Humanities Research Council (SSHRC) funded partnership of national and community organizations, led by Carleton University and the Canadian Centre for Philanthropy (which later became Imagine Canada).

(2010) come to the same conclusion: an effective board and a more highly educated executive director are essential.

Four important findings emerged from the Canadian survey, which are reinforced by the international literature. First, there is confusion over terminology, particularly over the concept of "outcomes" and "impacts". It was surprising that three-quarters of the voluntary organizations surveyed indicated that they collect information on outcomes and that this was relatively easy to do so, as well as fairly easy to analyze and interpret such information. This is wildly out of step with the literature, which indicates the complexity of identifying the right outcomes and in collecting data on such indicators in a timely manner. What became evident in follow-up interviews is that the concept of "outcomes" has become enormously elastic and thus imprecise. In effect, "outcome measurement" had essentially come to be equated with any kind of performance assessment. Thus, while nonprofits may be claiming to collect outcome and impact data, they may well actually mean outputs (for similar results see Arvidson (2009); Ogain *et al.* (2012).

Second, expectations and pressures on the part of funders for evaluation have increased in recent years, in terms of both the amount and the type of information expected. Almost half of the organizations surveyed said that funder expectations had risen over the previous three years. Almost as many (44 per cent) indicated that funders are requiring more information than they had three years previously and 49 per cent said they are requiring information about outcomes or impacts. And, funders agreed; they too said they are expecting more by way of evaluation. As part of their funding packages, almost half of funders indicated that they require evaluations and 40 reported that they "encourage" but do not require evaluations. Although government funders reported greater increases in expectations than foundations, particularly in financial reporting and program evaluation, requirements for assessment have risen across the board. These were felt somewhat more acutely by larger voluntary organizations, probably because they have multiple funders so are facing not only more but potentially competing demands.

Figure 1: Increasing Funder Evaluation Expectations Over the Past Three Years

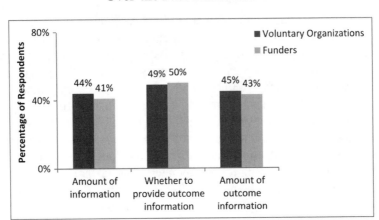

Third, the extent to which boards of directors play an active leadership role in Canadian nonprofits varies considerably but is not overwhelmingly impressive: in 20 per cent of organizations surveyed the board had no involvement at all, while for 35 per cent, the board had both requested and reviewed the evaluation information and in 33 per cent the board at least reviewed the results of evaluations.

Figure 2: Board Involvement in Evaluation

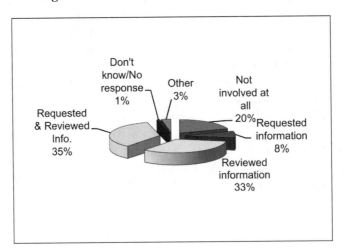

The final concern, which goes to the credibility of evaluation, is the extent to which it is used in decision-making, either by nonprofits or their funders. In general, voluntary organizations were satisfied with the quality and accuracy of the evaluations they had produced and about three-quarters indicated they have made effective use of the results. If the board at least reviewed the evaluation information, the likelihood that it was used very effectively increased significantly (M.H. Hall *et al.* (2003, at 26)). The use made of evaluation was mainly to improve programs and services (68 per cent) and for purposes of strategic planning (55 per cent). Although used to report to funders, the tendency was that evaluation results were not widely shared with others (only 15 per cent indicated they effectively shared such information).

Interestingly, funders felt they were less effective at using the evaluation information submitted to them than they could be (less than half said they made either effective or very effective use of such information). They said that this depended in part on the quality of information they received, and over one-third felt that the information was often not what they had asked for. Their limited use of evaluation information also reflects a lack of internal capacity, both a lack of time and resources, with more than one-quarter of funders citing capacity issues for such review.

Even if they used the information effectively, funders did not seem to be communicating very well how they use such information. Almost 20 per cent of voluntary organizations believed that funders used their evaluation reports for "administrative purposes" only — that is, to close the file. There was also a considerable discrepancy over perceptions of the extent to which evaluation was used by funders to help improve the performance of the organizations they fund. While 60 per cent of funders said they used evaluation information in this manner, only 20 per cent of voluntary organizations perceived this to be the case. The sense of evaluation as a paper exercise by a fairly large segment of voluntary organizations surveyed, combined with a reported fear that evaluations with unfavourable results would lead to a loss of funding, points to serious underlying challenges that are more political than technical in nature.

Figure 3: How Effectively Each Thinks Evaluation is

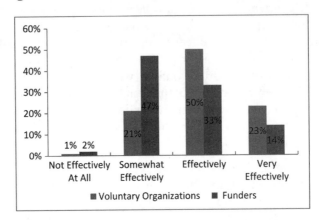

Both funders and voluntary organizations agreed on the main challenges of performance assessment — overwhelmingly, a lack of internal capacity and money. Although funder demands for evaluation have risen, there was no corresponding increase in resources to support such evaluation. The perceived ways in which evaluation could be improved relate to filling these gaps in capacity through more financial resources, access to better technology, and better staff training.

We can conclude that the state of the art in evaluation is a mixed record for the voluntary sector, with increasing demands for more sophisticated measurement and its strategic use in decision-making. How does an organization move from doing occasional evaluations of programs or other activities to being capable of ongoing performance assessment and management and of learning from this process for self-improvement? The first step is becoming competent and confident in doing evaluations of a variety of activities, from assessing programs to the organization overall. This involves knowing when and how to evaluate what — the "meta-questions". The second step is to build assessment into governance processes and the management systems of an organization, and develop the capacity as the organization (and ultimately as a sector) to do this. The rest of this chapter examines, in a practical way, the key issues involved first in evaluation and then in the institutionalization of performance management.

EVALUATION ISSUES: THE META-QUESTIONS

Evaluation design depends on what decisions need to be made with regard to the program, what information is needed to make these decisions and what kinds of resources are available to managers. Thus the key consideration in effective evaluation is aligning measurement with mission (Ebrahim and Rangan (2010)). This necessitates addressing:

- *Evaluation purpose and audience*: Why is the evaluation being done and what should be decided as a result? Who will be the main users of the evaluation results, *e.g.*, clients, funders, board, management, staff?

- *Program readiness*: Is the program ready to be evaluated?

- *Focus of evaluation*: What should be the focus of evaluation, *e.g.*, is it process or outcomes? What kind of information is needed to answer the evaluation questions (information on how the program was delivered or the effect of the program on clients and community at large)?

- *Choice of evaluator*: Who will conduct evaluation: external or internal evaluators? Who else needs to be involved?

- *Data collection methods and sources of information*: How can the requisite data be collected, *e.g.*, surveys, interviews, focus groups, *etc.*? What are the possible sources of information, *e.g.*, employees, users, existing program documentation?

Why: Evaluation Purpose and Audience

The first evaluation question that needs to be asked is *why* evaluation is being undertaken. Understanding the purpose of evaluation will help determine what should be evaluated, using what methodology, who should be engaged and when the best time is to evaluate. Typically evaluations are undertaken to serve one or more of three general purposes, as shown in Table 3.

Table 3: Purposes of Evaluation

Type	Purpose of Evaluation	Primary Driver/Audience
Accountability	Demonstrate the results of programs and account for the use of resources	External, particularly funders
Program planning or improvement	Identify strengths and weaknesses of a program or process, as well as appropriate changes to make (*e.g.*, redefine eligibility criteria,	Internal first, external second

Type	Purpose of Evaluation	Primary Driver/Audience
	add new categories of staff, improve guidelines, *etc.*)	
Knowledge generation or enlightenment	Create a new understanding about what works and what does not, understand the nature of specific social interventions and generate new knowledge (Patton (1997)).	Internal and external

Evaluation for accountability purposes is often externally driven and frequently referred to as *summative* evaluation. Summative evaluations are done at the end of a program or project and are designed for decision-making purposes about whether to continue or end a program, extend it to other sites, or cut it back (Perrin (2002)). The limitations and pitfalls of evaluation done for accountability purposes can be significant. If an evaluation is conducted strictly to demonstrate accountability for the use of money to external funders and fails to address "how" and "why" information, it probably cannot provide the information needed to assist with decisions about future directions (Perrin (2002)). Furthermore, evaluations that are done strictly for accountability purposes may result in the diversion of resources from program improvement to report writing and compliance auditing. It may compel program managers to focus more on the justification of programs as opposed to what can be improved in the future. Finally, it may lead to distortion of program activities in its attempt to reduce them to a small number of quantitative indicators when the reality may have been much messier than this.

Evaluation for program improvement is often referred to as *formative* evaluation. This type of evaluation is consistent with a focus on learning. Formative evaluations are designed to assist in the early stages those who are developing programs and can be used as management tools for identifying what works and what does not, and how things can be improved. As the national VSERP survey (M.H. Hall *et al.* (2003)) indicates, the majority of voluntary organizations in Canada utilize some form of formative evaluation, even if very informal, for management and planning purposes.

Audiences for evaluation findings range from funders, policymakers and the general public to program clients, association members, program staff and boards of directors. Accordingly, expectations for the evaluation vary with a stakeholder's position. For instance, funders tend to ask for information that helps them make decisions about their support of a program (*e.g.*, to continue or cut), while program managers require information to help them run the program. These distinctions matter as they affect the overall evaluation design and methodology as well as the eventual use of the evaluation results.

When: Program Readiness

The "when to evaluate" question can be systematically thought about through a procedure called *evaluability assessment*. Initially developed by Wholey (1979), evaluability assessment seeks to determine in a systematic way whether or not programs are ready for evaluation. Wholey (1979) recommended evaluability assessment as an initial step to evaluating programs in order to increase the likelihood that evaluations will provide timely, relevant, and responsive findings for decision-makers:

> The products of evaluability assessment are: (1) a set of agreed-on program objectives, side effects, and performance indicators on which the program can realistically be held accountable; and (2) a set of evaluation/management options which represent ways in which management can change program activities, objectives, or uses of information in ways likely to improve program performance.

(Trevisan and Huang (2003)).

Readiness for evaluation is assessed against three main criteria: (a) does the program operate as intended? (b) is it relatively stable? and (c) does it seem to be achieving positive outcomes? (Weiss (1998, at 74)). Assessing a program against these criteria requires clarifying the goals, boundaries and theory of the program; interviewing stakeholders and identifying their needs, concerns and differences in perceptions; determining the plausibility of a program model (how it is believed to work); and making specific recommendations with regard to evaluability of the program (Smith (1989); Trevisan and Huang (2003); Thurston and Potvin (2003)). The evaluator clarifies the series of assumptions that link program activities with program goals and examines the logical plausibility of the linkages. The main caution in this process is against oversimplification of program reality or using depictions of program theory as all-encompassing illustrations of the program. It needs to be kept in mind that programs can often be recursive rather than linear and represent a complex set of outcomes, both intended and unintended.

Evaluability assessment can be time-consuming and expensive for various reasons. It may be difficult to get commitments from key stakeholders. Program documentation may be unorganized. The process may require building a team that includes stakeholder groups and program implementers. The proper use of evaluability assessment, however, may increase the probability that actual evaluations will be timely, relevant and responsive (Trevisan and Huang (2003); Leviton *et al.* (2010)).

What: Focus of Evaluation

On a fairly regular basis, voluntary organizations evaluate most aspects of their operations, including organizational performance, programs and services, fundraising activities, the experiences of their volunteers, the performance of their boards of directors, and their products (M.H. Hall *et al.* (2003)). Although the literature has been dominated by a focus on *program* evaluation, it is not particularly useful to carve up evaluation approaches according to which activity is being evaluated. A more helpful distinction is to think of evaluation by contexts, processes and outcomes or impacts.

Table 4: Focus of Evaluation

Focus	Characteristics /Issues	Purpose
Context Evaluation	• conducted prior to the beginning of a program. • may also have to be undertaken in later phases as a project or program matures, when contextual information is required to modify plans and explain deviations from planned process and outcomes. • focuses on the characteristics of communities, stakeholders and broad social, economic, and environmental factors.	• plan relevant and effective interventions and increases the likelihood that they will be supported by community leaders and other organizations (Kellogg Foundation (1998)).

Focus	Characteristics /Issues	Purpose
	• aims to assess the needs, assets, and resources of a target community and identify its political environment and human services context.	
Process Evaluation	• while a program is still being implemented to enhance its likelihood of success by providing indications of what is happening and why (may be part of a formative evaluation). • may also be a part of the summative evaluation. • focus on *how* the program actually works to shed light on why certain results or outcomes are or are not achieved. It is distinguished from formative evaluation by its focus (an analysis of how things work) rather than its timing. • how things are actually working is seldom documented and perceptions of participants may differ considerably (Funnell (2000); Brinkerhoff (2002)).	• identify and maximize strengths of the process and minimize barriers to implementing activities; • determine the nature of interactions between staff and clients or users; • measure the performance, perceptions, and satisfaction of staff and volunteers, and the adequacy of organizational control and delivery systems; • monitor users' and other stakeholders' experiences with the project, and their satisfaction with and utilization of project services; and

Focus	Characteristics /Issues	Purpose
		• assess whether available resources can sustain project activities (Kellogg Foundation (1998, at 25)).
Outcome/Impact Evaluation	• assesses the short/medium term (outcomes) and long-term (impacts) on the conditions, lives or behaviour • may focus on: individuals/users; program and system-level; or community level outcomes (Kellogg Foundation (1998)).	• understand what difference the program made over the longer. • answer questions about what works, for whom, and in what circumstances.

The Limits of Outcome Measurement

The recent interest in measuring outcomes and impacts is that such assessments enable a voluntary organization to demonstrate its value, not just its good intentions or amount of activity, and they provide guidance as to where to direct resources with the greatest effect. There is often an implicit, sometimes quite explicit, assumption that outcome measurement is the "gold standard" — what every organization should strive for. The challenges associated with outcome measurement are significant, however, and it is not always feasible, appropriate, or needed. As Ebrahim and Rangan (2010 at 29) argue in their caution that the desirability of outcome measurement is contingent upon the environment in which a nonprofit operates, "measuring impacts makes sense under a severely limited set of circumstances — when an organization operates at an ecosystem level, and yet can exercise sufficient control over results to attribute impacts to its work."

One of the key issues is revealing the link between cause (activities) and effects (OECD (2004)). The complex, multi-layered nature of programs and the dynamic character of relationships among people, systems, and communities often make it very difficult to ascertain the exact cause of an outcome (Brinkerhoff (2002); Leeuw and Vaessen (2009)). Attribution requires a detailed analysis of cause-and-effect relationships, and even after such analysis, attribution may be problematic. Outcome measures also encounter the problems of timing. Particularly in preventative programs, the actual outcomes may take years to be realized, long after the evaluation period has ended. Also, good outcome measures may be expensive and time-consuming to collect and analyze, and lack of skills can be a significant limitation (Harlock (2013)). As well, due to the complex nature of community change, programs often produce *unintended* outcomes that may take extensive research at multiple levels to identify let alone measure (Kellogg Foundation (1998)).

Finally, an exclusive focus on outcomes may lead to overlooking equally important aspects of evaluation, such as understanding how and why the program works or does not work, and what factors and circumstances shape the program (see Brinkerhoff (2002, at 216); Arvidson (2009)). Indeed, outcomes may fail to provide information on how to improve service delivery and enhance efficiency, especially when results are disappointing. As Perrin (1998, at 374) notes:

> A program may fail to meet its performance targets because the program theory is wrong, in which case it should be replaced with something else. But it also may fail to do so for a variety of other reasons such as: inappropriate targets or measures which are not identifying other possible program outcomes; faulty management or implementation, under (or over) funding, unique circumstances (e.g. an employment training program during a recession or when the only employer in a single-industry town closes); the right program in the wrong situation (e.g. effective for some, but not all, of the types of clients it has been serving), measurement of outcomes attempted too soon or at the wrong time, faulty statistics, and so on.

Outcome measurement has become fashionable, even faddish in evaluation in recent years, and is increasingly required by funders and espoused by governments as a means of accountability and managing public expectations. A challenge for voluntary organization is to avoid the bandwagon effect. In many cases, outcome measurement may simply be overkill. It may in fact not answer the desired questions or all, or do so at such expense that it is not the best investment of resources. If the question is to understand whether volunteers are satisfied and doing a good job, for example, one does not need to know how volunteering has changed their lives. In many cases, a good process evaluation or assessment of outputs may be fully adequate, indeed more appropriate, and the time and money saved better directed toward program improvement. When outcome evaluation *is* warranted, voluntary organizations are generally well advised to have some control or input into the nature of these measures, rather than having them imposed by third parties.

Logic Models as a Means of Linking Contexts, Processes and Outcomes

Logic models are perhaps the most feared or at least seemingly mysterious part of evaluation for many voluntary organizations. If one thinks of logic models as simply theories — or hypotheses or hunches — about change, they are not nearly so abstruse.

A logic model is a means of connecting context, process, and outcomes, and attributing cause and effect. It is important, as Mayne (2003) notes, "not to definitively prove that the program has made a difference but to build over time a convincing case of plausible association between the results observed and the activities and outputs of the program, as more and more evidence is gathered".

Figure 4: Elements of A Logic Model

A logic model ties together:

- *Context*. The relevant physical, social, economic, cultural, or political circumstances in which a program or other activity is set.

- *Inputs*. The resources (*e.g.*, human, financial) that are required to implement the program.

- *Activities*. The processes, tools, events, technology and actions that are an intentional part of the program implementation.

- *Outputs*. The immediate products or consequences of program activities (such as number of workshops offered, personnel trained, *etc.*).

- *Outcomes*. The actual changes that are realized when the outputs are used. Outcomes may unfold over time and are thus differentiated on several time scales from *initial* (outcomes that can be directly attributed to the program activities) to *intermediate* (changes in behaviour once the immediate outcomes have been achieved) to *final outcomes or impacts* (longer term and organizational or system level change as an overall result of the program).[10]

An effective logic model is developed early, and continuously refined and changed throughout the program assessment process in order to reflect the changing nature of the environment and knowledge about what works and what does not (Kellogg Foundation (1998); see McDavid and Hawthorn (2006)).[11] Logic models, which have become virtually ubiquitous in evaluation, have attracted both staunch defenders and critics. The critics argue that the logic of logic models often supplants reality and that we need to keep in mind that they are in fact *models*, that is representations of reality, not reality itself. The risk lies in being lulled into a false confidence that in simply depicting the model, the job is done. Thus evaluators often do not put its logic to the test by critically examining whether it is meaningful, plausible, doable and testable. In addition, by presenting programs as a coherent sequence from objectives to outcomes, logic models imply linearity whereas the reality may be much more complex, dynamic and circular.

While supporters acknowledge many of its limitations, they argue that, as a heuristic for sorting out causes and effects, logic models are about the best that evaluation has to offer. The challenge comes in how the tool is used, not with the tool itself.

Who: Choice of Evaluator and Participant Involvement

Insiders or Outsiders?

Are evaluations better conducted by internal or external evaluators? Many evaluators would argue that it is not true evaluation unless it is independent; for others, the answer to this question largely depends on the purpose of evaluation, as well as available resources. If the primary aim of the assessment is to maximize learning and use of evaluation results in order to improve programs or operations, it may be preferable to have the assessment done internally. In this case, performance assessment may be integrated into the program cycle in

---

[10] OECD, 2004; Treasury Board of Canada Secretariat (TBS), "Results-Based Management Lexicon" online at: <http://www.tbs-sct.gc.ca/ rma/lex-lex_e.asp>.

[11] Building a logic model and identifying causal relationships may reduce but not eliminate problems associated with attributing outcomes to specific causes. Other techniques to assess program contribution to the results include using multiple lines of evidence, exploring and discussing plausible alternative explanations, and gathering additional relevant evidence (Mayne (1999)). On theories of change, see also Kubisch *et al.* (1998).

order to give feedback on actions taken. The trade-off is impartiality: can those responsible for the program dispassionately and effectively evaluate it?

Both approaches offer a number of advantages and disadvantages and the choice needs to balance the purpose of evaluation with other considerations (see Table 5). Traditionally, evaluations are done by external experts in order to ensure the objectivity, impartiality and credibility of the findings. However, the ongoing *monitoring* function is necessarily an inhouse function, and internal evaluations are also being used more widely. Internal evaluators, in most cases, have better "insider" knowledge of how the program works and can help increase the likelihood of utilization of evaluation results. External evaluations may or may not be more costly, but do require internal personnel to manage consultants. Combining both internal and external assessment is another option that might allow voluntary organizations to obtain an external quality check "without losing the benefit of the internal evaluator's firsthand knowledge of the project" (OECD (2004, at 18)).

Table 5: Advantages and Disadvantages of Internal and External Assessment

	Internal Assessment	External Assessment
Advantages	• Maximizes learning; benefits stay in the organization • Findings can be put to use immediately • Can be adjusted according to new needs and new findings • Increases organizational skills and capacities	• Impartiality • External consultants have assessment competence; can buy rather than grow such skills • May increase perceived legitimacy of results • Usually faster • Can be subject to competitive bidding (may be less costly) • Brings new perspectives
Disadvantages	• Lack of impartiality • Can obscure negative findings • Skills may be limited	• Can be expensive • Difficult to change the process • Less ownership by stakeholders • Gap with decision-makers;

	Internal Assessment	External Assessment
	• Takes staff time • Necessitates ongoing commitment	harder to use results

Source: Kim Forss, "Evaluation framework for information, consultation and participation in policy-making". A study commissioned by the OECD (January 2003).

Participatory Evaluation

The decision as to who should be involved does not stop with determining the evaluator. In order to maximize the usefulness of evaluation, program stakeholders need to buy into the evaluation process and its results, requiring the collaboration of stakeholders in evaluation design, identification of indicators, data collection and interpretation, and use of results. In addition, such participation is a means to empowering the stakeholders (Fetterman and Wandersman (2007)).

Stakeholder involvement in evaluation may prove to be a challenging task, however. First, such engagement increases the number of people involved in discussions and meetings, which potentially complicates evaluation activities, increases timelines and reduces work quality. Second, key participants such as senior officials, managers and staff members must reach a certain level of agreement about program and evaluation goals and ways to achieve them, while often having diverse needs with regard to the evaluation (Fine *et al.* (2000); Wholey (1979); DeLancer Julnes (2001)). For instance, managers and staff members are inclined to focus on inputs and outputs over which they have more control; decision-makers at the policy level tend to focus on inputs and outcomes; and advocates for particular interests tend to focus on intended and unintended outcomes (Wholey (1979); DeLancer Julnes (2001, at 404)). Third, collaboration also requires new roles for evaluators, such as an ability to work with diverse stakeholders, educate them about measurement, and facilitate their participation and input. Finally, stakeholder involvement blurs the line between professional evaluators and users with the risk of losing the objectivity that traditionally detaches evaluators from the environments they assess (Annie E. Casey Foundation (1997); Forss *et al.* (2006)).

Despite the difficulty of getting various stakeholders to agree on performance measures, it can prove to be highly beneficial to the process of performance management. For example, participatory assessment can enable evaluators to ask the right questions in the first place. Participation may raise stakeholders' expectations that the research results will be noticed, considered, valued and acted on (Annie E. Casey Foundation (1997)). It may "result in positive staff development, a feeling of empowerment, and a sense of competence in evaluation issues and procedures" (Lafleur (1995, at 53)) and improve evaluation validity and credibility (Thayer, Fine, Cousins and Whitmore (1998)). Finally, it also increases interaction and communication between funders and voluntary organizations that can lead to improved dialogue around the needs and complexities of performance assessment.

How: Data Collection Methods and Sources of Information

Once one gets to the *how* question, many of the tough issues have already been addressed. That said, decisions about which methods to use and their design probably consume more time than any other aspect of evaluation. There are a variety of evaluation methods available to voluntary organizations, ranging from informal staff and volunteer meetings to more formal methods such as focus groups, surveys, interviews and experimental design. The guiding determinant in the selection of measurement tools is to obtain the most valuable and credible information in the most appropriate and realistic manner.

Other factors that influence the choice of data collection methods, besides the intended use of the evaluation findings and nature of users, include:

- accuracy, credibility and sufficiency of data;

- political sensitivity of collecting data;

- complexity of collecting, interpreting and analyzing data; and

- costs of collecting data (*e.g.*, money, timeframe, *etc.*).[12]

Most organizations use more than one evaluation method. For example, the VSERP study (M.H. Hall *et al.* (2003)) revealed that the vast majority of survey respondents (84 per cent) reported that they used informal methods (such as staff and volunteer meetings) as well as more formal methods. This reflects the fact that different techniques

---

[12] See OECD, 2004; McNamara (1998b).

are better suited to different research questions and capabilities. Thus measurement generally should be approached from a variety of perspectives and we can expect to capture the full story by using a toolbox of methods and approaches, as appropriate to what we want to know and how much time and resources we have to find out. As Murray (2003) argues (see also Bamburger, Rugh and Mabry (2006)), the choice of how formal and elaborate a method to use should be made on the basis of how much time, money and skill an organization has, but more importantly on how much it needs large amounts of high quality, detailed information for making internal policy decisions or influencing important external stakeholders. Table 6 provides an overview of the major methods used for collecting data during evaluations.

Table 6: A Sample of Data Collection Methods

Method	Overall Purpose	Advantages	Challenges
Questionnaires, surveys, checklists	Get a slice of information from many people in a non-threatening way	• Can get data from many people, representative of a population • Can be completed anonymously • Relatively inexpensive to administer • Easy to compare and analyze	• Might not get careful feedback • Low response rates • Wording can bias participant's responses • May need sampling expert • Doesn't get full story, gets a thin slice of information
Interviews	Fully understand interviewees' impressions or experiences, or learn more about their answers to questionnaires	• Get rich range and depth of information • Develops relationship with participants • Can be flexible, more	• Can take considerable time • Can be hard to analyze and compare • Can be costly • Interviewer can bias

Method	Overall Purpose	Advantages	Challenges
		opportunity to follow up questions not anticipated	participant's responses
Documentation review	Understand how program was designed and officially operates without interrupting the program; preliminary step for other measurement	• Get comprehensive and historical information • Doesn't interrupt program or participant's routine in program • Information already exists • Few biases about information	• Information may be incomplete; gives "official" story • Not flexible means to get data; restricted to what already exists
Observation	Understand first hand how a program actually operates, particularly about processes	• View operations of a program as they are actually occurring • Can adapt to events as they occur	• Can be difficult to interpret observed behaviours without interviews • Can influence behaviours of program participants • Can be expensive and time-consuming
Focus groups	Explore a topic in depth through group discussion, e.g., about reactions to an experience or suggestion, understanding common	• Quickly get common impressions • Can be efficient way to get considerable range and depth of information in short time • Can convey key	• Can be hard to analyze responses; challenge of moving between group and individual level analyses • Need good facilitator for

Method	Overall Purpose	Advantages	Challenges
	complaints, *etc.*	information about programs	safety and closure • Difficult to schedule six to eight people together
Case studies	Understand or depict in detail participant's experiences in a program, and conduct comprehensive examination through cross comparison of cases	• Fully depicts participant's experience in program input, process, and results • Powerful means to portray program to outsiders	• Usually quite time-consuming to collect, organize, and describe • Represents depth of information, rather than breadth • May be highly selective, not representative

Source: McNamara (1998c).

Data collection is as much about process as expertise. Often programs require measurement across multiple systems and at multiple levels, over long periods of time, and of outcomes that are hard to capture (Annie E. Casey Foundation (1997)). In order to meet these challenges, evaluators need to refine and adapt their tools and methods for measuring program process and success. In addition, the involvement of stakeholders in the choice and design of instruments both helps in identifying the right questions and indicators and in building confidence and credibility that meaningful information has been collected, and thus is more likely to be used (Annie E. Casey Foundation (1997)).

USING EVALUATION FOR ORGANIZATIONAL LEARNING

The difference between an organization that can do good evaluation when needed and one that actually uses evaluation as a means of learning and self-improvement hinges on making effective use of the results of evaluation, dealing with the political dimensions, and developing the capacity for performance assessment.

Using Evaluation Results

Evaluation information can be a powerful tool for a variety of stakeholders, including program managers, funders and clients/users. The information can be used to improve program effectiveness and service delivery, increase awareness of the organization and facilitate information sharing, inform strategic planning and guide fundraising, as well as to report to funders. For their part, funders can ensure that they are funding effective programs, help funded organizations improve their programs through identifying best practices and facilitate their own strategic planning (Carman (2009); Thomson (2010)). The question of how the evaluation information will be used is best considered at the very beginning of a project, not only at the end, as is often the case. Planning *different* ways of using evaluation findings helps ensure evaluation is conducted and the results reported in a way that actually meets people's needs. By involving various stakeholders from the beginning, their commitment and ability to use the results is considerably enhanced (Fine and Thayer (2000)).

Several strategies can help promote the effective use of the evaluation data:

- *Ensuring high quality of evaluation information.* Evaluation information should be adequate and legitimate, and meet stakeholder needs and expectations. For example, the VSERP study suggests that a little over one-third of funders agreed (32 per cent) or strongly agreed (4 per cent) that the information they receive is often not what they had asked for. The low quality of information may be due to "voluntary organizations' confusion about outcome evaluation and to their lack of clarity about funder expectations" (M.H. Hall *et al.* (2003, at 26)).

- *Presenting evaluation results as a systematic, cumulative study of links between activities and outcomes.* This may help demonstrate credibility of findings and provide information on both process and program effectiveness.

- *Keeping specific audiences in mind in reporting evaluation results.* Data should be presented in a way accessible and useful for the people who are going to use it. Data presentation may range from simple fact sheets to lengthy and complex research papers; it could involve limited circulation to key decision-makers to widespread communication on the Web and through other technology to strategic face-to-face briefings with local decision-makers and news media.

- *Building stakeholder capacity to interpret, disseminate and maximize information.* There is a need to build capacity of stakeholders to use evaluation information, which may entail several strategies. For example, data can be used to develop action plans to address some of the issues revealed in the evaluation with input from stakeholders. Community members can be engaged in continuous program planning and management. Once community members start to use data, they begin to see more types of information that would be useful and more ways they can use the data to make their own decisions (Annie E. Casey Foundation (1997)).

- *Using strategies that anticipate and reduce opposition.* In the case of sensitive or controversial findings, holding meetings with interested stakeholders and keeping the focus on issues rather than on people and personalities may help find ways for the negative findings to inspire improvements.

- *Ensuring that data are used fairly.* Information sometimes can be used for harmful purposes, and it is the role of evaluators to protect the information so it cannot be misused. For example, when evaluation information is of a sensitive or controversial nature, one strategy would be to release it to all stakeholders simultaneously explaining what it means and what it can and cannot affirm (Annie E. Casey Foundation (1997)).

The Political Dimensions of Performance Assessment

Finding the appropriate evaluation techniques and measures can certainly be demanding and complex in their own right. It would be a mistake, however, to see the main challenges of evaluation to be only or even primarily technical in nature. Evaluation is not an objective, value-free process, but one that is inherently political. It often necessitates serious debates and conflicts over values and strategies. "Why are we doing this?" How would we define success?" "So what?" These are political rather than technical questions that run through performance assessment from its inception to the use of results for program or organizational change.

The political dimensions of evaluation may be manifest in several ways, some quite overt and others almost inadvertent. The most obvious ones range from the mere fact that evaluations involve *people* (*e.g.*, decision-makers, funders, consultants, program staff) with specific and different values, perceptions, and interests who may interpret assessment measurement in different ways. Cutt and Murray (2000) suggest that the phenomenon of *subjective interpretation of reality* arises when evaluation data have to be interpreted, and again when decisions need to be made. "When it comes to analyzing almost any aspect of human behaviour, there are too many variables and there is too little control over those variables to permit solid conclusions about causal connections" (Cutt and Murray (2000, at 40)). In addition, there may be many different, perhaps competing theories of change and beliefs about what works or does not work. Yet, decisions need to be made and the results of performance measurement figure in such decisions. Thus boards and staff, particularly if they have been close to a program or project and are committed to it, may tend to revert to pre-existing attitudes about what they "know" works.

Sometimes the politics are more conscious and intentional. Murray (2003) suggests that political behaviour may arise at each stage of the evaluation process, particularly when evaluators, evaluatees, and other interested parties disagree on various aspects of evaluation. For example, during the design and implementation stage, the stakeholders may have quite different perceptions of the real purpose of evaluation — whether to identify strengths and weaknesses for better decision-making (the official reason) or to identify aspects to cut (the feared reason).

Particularly when funders are driving evaluation or in performance contracting (when payment is provided only after the achievement of some pre-specified outcomes), there may be a more structural dimension to politics. This is the reluctance to present "bad" results, or the *Look-Good-Avoid-Blame* factor, as Cutt and Murray (2000, at 39-40) call it. If an evaluation reveals problems or if the results are not as expected, a natural concern is that funding may be terminated. So, the temptation is to make the results look as good as possible or explain failures as being beyond the organization's control. This politicization of evaluation is likely to occur when the environment has little tolerance for failure, as is the case in many governments today. Not only is innovation likely to be stifled in the first place, because innovative programs are by definition riskier, but it becomes more difficult to learn from innovation when it does occur because successes and failures are not reported openly and fully. There has been a growing interest in recent years in mandatory "failure reports", thus legitimizing the need to report on what did not work and recognizing that innovation necessarily involves some failures (Bansal (2012)).

A different kind of political problem arises internally, particularly in small, collegial organizations. Boards are often reluctant to push for evaluation as it might be seen as portending a lack of confidence in staff and the executive director in particular, whom they often know well, consider a friend, or have a great deal of deference toward. As a result, suggests Murray (2003), boards often fail badly in their governance roles related to performance assessment and in their fiduciary duties to hold management accountable.

Although politics in evaluation is inevitable, the solution is not to abandon evaluation. Rather, knowing that political dimensions exist is a precondition for usable evaluations (Guba and Lincoln (1989)). Murray (2003) suggests that there are three routes for dealing with political behaviour. The first is to build trust among the interested parties. In most cases, trust is built over time. If a prior relationship does not exist, there is a need for an open and participatory approach to evaluation in order to minimize the likelihood of political games. Such participation may be a process of co-operation, but it may also be one of negotiation. Indeed, Guba and Lincoln (1989) maintain that in evaluation all parties should negotiate their rights. This implies that the role of the evaluator is to solicit the co-operation of each party in return for a particular *quid pro quo*. Such negotiation gives the evaluator insight into the "obstacles and opportunities that impinge upon the evaluative effort, and the limitations and possibilities for putting the results to work — only with sensitivity to the politics of evaluation research — can the evaluator be as creative and strategically useful" (Weiss (1998, at 94)).

A second means is to pay more attention to articulating a clear logic model, that is, a theory about change, and ensure that it is agreed to by most stakeholders. A third path is better training for boards of directors so that they can minimize the political games, but also fulfill their responsibilities. This does not mean reverting to a strong accountability by control role, but encouraging them to develop appropriate assessment systems or mechanisms and establishing clear expectations regarding their interest and role in assessment.

These factors, even though falling short of completely eliminating the political nature of evaluation, may help create a non-threatening, trusting environment in which to more fully realize the benefits of a good evaluation.

Building the Capacity for Evaluation

The biggest barrier to effective evaluation in Canada is not political but a lack of capacity (M.H. Hall *et al.* (2003, at 32)). Capacity issues include financial constraints, lack of skills and knowledge in conducting evaluations, and inadequate staff and time (see Carman and Fredericks (2010); Innovation Network (2012)). The magnitude and frequency with which capacity was mentioned as a problem in the VSERP survey points to an acute need to enhance the infrastructure of voluntary organizations to conduct evaluation. Capacity for evaluation can be built through training, knowledge and information sharing, financial support, and closer collaboration and advice from funders.

Besides building the organizational capacity to undertake evaluation, it is important to build the capacity to involve stakeholders, including program staff, community organizations, clients and funders, in evaluation. Inculcating a leadership role into the governance of a voluntary organization, through the way in which the board understands its role in performance assessment, is critical. Creating greater capacity extends beyond individual organizations, however, to fostering greater collective and shared capacity at the community level and across the voluntary sector as a whole.

CONCLUSION

In an environment that expects to see results and in which accountability has become a major concern, the pressures for evaluation and reporting on all aspects of a nonprofit's operations have grown dramatically in recent years. In large part, this pressure is generated by external forces, but it is also being driven internally as boards and staff seek creative ways of demonstrating their value and of making strategic choices among competing claims on time and resources. Not only the pressures but the resources for evaluation have increased in recent years. A plethora of Websites provides advice on evaluation methods and a substantial consulting industry has developed around performance assessment. The main issues of evaluation are not so much technical in nature as they are the meta questions involving trade-offs of what an organization needs to know and how much time and resources it has to dedicate to finding out.

While there are clear benefits to evaluation, there is also a darker side. The transaction costs mean that the resources spent on measurement are probably diverted from service and other activities, which may not necessarily bring a long-term reward in performance improvement. As we saw from the VSERP national survey, funders are increasingly expecting evaluation to be conducted, but without providing financial support to cover the costs of it. Depending on how results are used, the possibility of goal displacement has been well documented. If funding is tied to positive results, as in performance contracts, and if indicators become the objectives, there may be a tendency to cherry-pick the easiest people to serve or stick to the tried and true, rather than innovating or adapting.

A key challenge for the voluntary sector is to bring evaluation closer to governance so that boards of directors are more actively involved in making policy decisions about performance management. A related challenge is to build greater capacity for evaluation, both at the organizational and the sectoral level. This involves a greater role for intermediary organizations in providing expertise, information sharing, and convening various interested parties. It also entails greater dialogue among funders *and* between funders and the organizations they fund in order to establish shared expectations, greater consistency in evaluation requirements and common terminology.

The most ominous prospect is that the current political environment is so focused on performance assessment and accountability as control and is so risk averse that it crowds out the potential for evaluation as learning. There is little room to have something go wrong or not according to plan, particularly when dealing with government funders, and thus there is limited scope for innovation, adaptation to changing conditions, or learning.

The emerging challenge is to start to connect the dots of evaluation — to encourage nonprofits to be collaborative in assessing collective or cumulative impacts on big, systemic, wicked issues (Kania and Kramer (2011); Hanleybrown, Kania and Kramer (2013); New Philanthropic Capital (2013)). If nonprofits were feeling pressures of performance to date, combing impact with collaboration on issues of systemic proportions will take evaluation to a new plane.

REFERENCES

Annie E. Casey Foundation (1997), *Evaluating Comprehensive Community Change. Research and Evaluation Conference*, online at: <http://www.aecf.org/upload/PublicationFiles/community%20change.pdf>.

M. Arvidson, *Impact and Evaluation in the UK Third Sector: Reviewing Literature and Exploring Ideas*, Third Sector Research Centre Working Paper (27 December 2009).

P. Aucoin & M. Jarvis (2005), *Modernizing Government Accountability: A Framework for Reform*, online at: Canada School of Public Service <http://publications.gc.ca/collections/collection_2008/csps-efpc/SC103-15-2005E.pdf>.

P. Aucoin & R. Heintzman, "The Dialectics of Accountability for Performance in Public Management Reform" (2000) 66:1 International Review of Administrative Sciences 45-56.

M. Bamberger, J. Rugh & L. Mabry, *Real World Evaluation: Working under Budget, Time, Data and Political Constraints* (Thousand Oaks, CA: Sage Publications, 2012).

S. Bansal, "The Power of Failure" *New York Times* (28 November 2012), online at: <http://opinionator.blogs.nytimes.com/2012/11/28/the-power-of-failure-2/?_r=0>.

Blue Ribbon Panel, *From Red Tape to Clear Results: The Report of the Blue Ribbon Panel on Grants and Contribution Programs* (Ottawa: Treasury Board Secretariat, 2006).

J. Brinkerhoff, "Assessing and Improving Partnership Relationships and Outcomes: A Proposed Framework" (2002) 25:3 Evaluation and Program Planning 215-231.

J.G. Carman, "Nonprofits, Funders, and Evaluation: Accountability in Action" (2009) 39:4 The American Review of Public Administration 374-390.

J.G. Carman & K.A Fredericks, "Evaluation Capacity and Nonprofit Organizations: Is the Glass Half-Empty or Half-Full?" (2010) 31:1 American Journal of Evaluation 84-104.

Charity Navigator (2012), *CN 3.0 Concept Note: The Evaluation of Reporting Results*, online at: <http://www.charitynavigator.org/__asset__/_articles_/2012/CN3_Concept_Note_FINAL%2012-15-2012.pdf>.

City of Toronto, *Cracks in the Foundation: Community Agency Survey 2003* (Toronto: City of Toronto Community and Neighbourhood Services, 2004).

J. Cutt & V. Murray (2000), *Accountability and Effectiveness Evaluation in Nonprofit Organizations* (London: Routledge, 2000).

I.C. Davies, "Evaluation and Performance Management in Government" (1999) 5:2 Evaluation 150-159.

P. DeLancer Julnes, "Does Participation Increase Perceptions of Usefulness? An Evaluation of a Participatory Approach to the Development of Performance Measures" (2001) 24:4 Public Performance & Management Review 403-418.

A. Ebrahim & V.K. Rangan (2010), "The Limits of Nonprofit Impact: A Contingency Framework for Measuring Social Performance" Working Paper 10-099, Harvard Business School.

J. Ellis & T. Gregory, *Accountability and Learning: Developing Monitoring and Evaluation in the Third Sector* (London: Charities Evaluation Services, 2009).

J. English & E. Lindquist (1998), "Performance Management: Linking Results to Public Debate", *IPAC New Directions – Number 2*.

European Commission, *Evaluating EU Expenditure Programmes: A Guide to Ex Post and Intermediate Evaluation* (Luxembourg: European Commission, 1997).

D. Fetterman & A. Wandersman, "Empowerment Evaluation: Yesterday, Today and Tomorrow" (2007) 28:2 American Journal of Evaluation 179-198.

A.H. Fine & C.E. Thayer, "Evaluation and Outcome Measurement in the Non-profit Sector: Stakeholder Participation" (2000) 24:1 Evaluation and Program Planning 103-108.

A.H. Fine, C.E. Thayer & A.T. Coghlan, "Program Evaluation Practice in the Nonprofit Sector" (2000) 10:3 Nonprofit Management and Leadership 331-339.

K. Forss *et al.*, "Chasing a ghost? An essay on participatory evaluation and capacity development" (2006) 12:1 Evaluation 128-144.

K. Fulton, G. Kasper & B. Kibbe, *What's Next for Philanthropy? Acting Bigger, Adapting Better in a Networked World* (New York: Monitor Institute, 2010).

P. Frumkin, *On Being Nonprofit* (Cambridge, MA: Harvard University Press, 2002).

S.C. Funnell, "Developing and using a program theory matrix for program evaluation and performance monitoring" (2000) 87 New Directions for Evaluation 91-101.

"Ottawa Throws its Weight behind Social Investing" *The Globe and Mail* (6 May 2013), online at: <http://www.theglobeandmail.com/news/politics/ottawa-throws-its-weight-behind-social-investing/article11743660/>.

D.A. Good, *The Politics of Public Management* (Toronto: IPAC, 2003).

H.P. Greenwald, "Increasing Evaluation Impact: A Survey of US Philanthropic Foundations" (The Center on Philanthropy and Public Policy, University of Southern California, Paper 32 (2009)).

E.G. Guba & Y.S. Lincoln, *Fourth Generation Evaluation* (London: Sage Publications, 1989).

M.H. Hall *et al.*, *Assessing Performance: Evaluation Practices & Perspectives in Canada's Voluntary Sector* (Toronto; Ottawa: Canadian Centre for Philanthropy and Centre for Voluntary Sector Research and Development, 2003).

F. Hanleybrown, J. Kania & M. Kramer, "Channeling Change: Making Collective Impact Work" (2012) Stanford Social Innovation Review, online at: <http://www.ssireview.org/blog/entry/channeling_change_making_collective_impact_work>.

J. Harlock, *Impact Measurement Practice in the UK Third Sector: A Review of Emerging Evidence*, Third Sector Research Centre (Working Paper 106, Third Sector Research Centre, University of Birmingham, July 2013).

H. Hatry *et al.*, *Measuring Program Outcomes: A Practical Approach* (Alexandria, VA: United Way of America, 1996).

S. Hedley, T. Lumley & H. Pavey, *Helping Grantees Focus on Impact* (London: New Philanthropy Capital, 2011).

Innovation Network Inc., *State of Evaluation 2012* (New York: Innovation Network, 2012).

J.P. Morgan, Per*spectives on Progress: The Impact Investor Survey* (New York: J.P. Morgan and the Global Impact Investing Network, 2013), online at: <http://www.thegiin.org/cgi-bin/iowa/download?row=489&field=gated_download_1>.

J. Kania & M. Kramer, "Collective Impact" (2011) 9:1 Stanford Social Innovation Review, online at: <http://www.ssireview.org/articles/entry/collective_impact>.

D.F. Kettl, *The Next Government of the United States: Challenges for Performance in the 21st Century* (Washington, DC: IBM Center for the Business of Government, 2005).

A.C. Kubisch, K. Fulbright-Anderson & J.P. Connell, "Evaluating Community Initiatives: A Progress Report" in K. Fulbright-Anderson, A.C. Kubisch & J.P. Connell, eds., *New Approaches to Evaluating Community Initiatives, Vol. 2: Theory, Measurement, and Analysis* (Washington, DC: The Aspen Institute, 1998), online at: <http://www.aspeninstitute.org/Programt3.asp?bid=1264>.

C. Lafleur, "A Participatory Approach to District-level Program Evaluation: The Dynamics of Internal Evaluation" in J.B. Cousins & L.M. Earl, eds., *Participatory Evaluation in Education: Studies in Evaluation Use and Organizational Learning* (London: Falmer, 1995) at 33-54.

F. Leeuw & J. Vaessen, *Impact evaluations and development: NONIE guidance on impact evaluation* (Washington, DC: NONIE, 2009).

K. LeRoux & N.S. Wright, "Does Performance Measurement Improve Strategic Decision Making? Findings From a National Survey of Nonprofit Social Service Agencies" (2010) 39:4 Nonprofit and Voluntary Sector Quarterly 571-587.

L.C. Leviton *et al.*, "Evaluability Assessment to Improve Public Health Policies, Programs, and Practices" (2010) 31 Annual Review of Public Health 213-233.

H. MacIndoe & E. Barman (2012), "How Organizational Stakeholders Shape Performance Measurement in Nonprofits: Exploring a Multidimensional Measure" (2012) 42:4 Nonprofit and Voluntary Sector Quarterly 716-738.

F. Mayhew "Aligning for Impact: The Influence of the Funder–Fundee Relationship on Evaluation Utilization" (2012) 23:2 Nonprofit Management and Leadership 193-217.

J. Mayne "Addressing Attribution Through Contribution Analysis: Using Performance Measures Sensibly" (Office of the Auditor General of Canada, June 1999), online at: <http://www.oag-bvg.gc.ca/internet/docs/99dp1_e.pdf>.

J. Mayne "Reporting on Outcomes: Setting Performance Expectations and Telling Performance Stories" (Office of the Auditor General of Canada, April 2003), online at: <http://oag-bvg.gc.ca/internet/docs/200305dp1_e.pdf>.

J.C. McDavid & L. Hawthorn, *Program Evaluation and Performance Measurement: An Introduction to Practice* (Thousand Oaks, CA: Sage Publications, 2006).

C. McNamara, "Where Program Evaluation is Helpful" in *Basic Guide to Program Evaluation* (1998), online at: <http://managementhelp.org/evaluation/program-evaluation-guide.htm>.

C. McNamara, "Selecting Which Methods to Use" in *Basic Guide to Program Evaluation* (1998), online at: <http://managementhelp.org/evaluation/program-evaluation-guide.htm>.

C. McNamara, "Overview of Methods to Collect Information" in *Basic Guide to Program Evaluation* (1998), online at: <http://managementhelp.org/evaluation/program-evaluation-guide.htm>.

V. Murray, "Evaluation Games: The Political Dimension in Evaluation and Accountability Relationships", online at: <http://www.academia.edu/3613949/Evaluation_Games>.

New Economics Foundation (Nef) "Proving and Improving", online at: <http://www.proveandimprove.org/tools/sroi.php>.

New Philanthropic Capital, *Blueprint for Shared Measurement: Developing, Designing and Implementing Shared Approaches to Impact Measurement* (London: NPC, 2013).

OECD, *Measures for Promoting Integrity and Preventing Corruption: How to Assess?* Report prepared for the 30th Session of the Public Governance Committee (Paris: OECD, October 13, 2004).

K. Ogata & R. Goodkey, *Redefining Government Performance* (Cambridge paper presented July 16, 1998). Online at: <http://www.finance.gov.ab.ca/publications/measuring/cambridge_paper.html>.

E.N. Ogain, T. Lumley & D. Pritchard, *Making an Impact* (London: New Philanthropic Capital (NPC), 2012).

Panel on Accountability and Governance for the Voluntary Sector (PAGVS), *Building on Strength: Improving Governance and Accountability in Canada's Voluntary Sector* (Ottawa: PAGVS, 1999).

M.Q. Patton, *Utilization-focused Evaluation: the New Century Text*, 3d ed. (Thousand Oaks, CA: Sage Publications, 1997).

B. Perrin, "Effective Use and Misuse of Performance Measurement" (1998) 19:3 American Journal of Evaluation 367-379.

B. Perrin, "Towards a New View of Accountability" (Paper presented to the European Evaluation Society annual conference, Seville, Spain (October 2002), as part of a symposium on *Promoting Organizational Learning via Evaluation: The New Accountability?*).

S.D. Phillips, "SUFA and Citizen Engagement: Fake or Genuine Masterpiece?" in S. Fortin, A. Nöel & F. St-Hilaire, eds., *Forging the Canadian Social Union: SUFA and Beyond* (Montreal: Institute for Research on Public Policy, 2003) 93-124.

S.D. Phillips & K. Levasseur, "The Snakes and Ladders of Accountability: Contradictions between Contracting and Collaboration for Canada's Voluntary Sector" (2004) 47:4 Canadian Public Administration 451-474.

S.D. Phillips & S.R. Smith, *Governance and Regulation in the Third Sector: International Perspectives* (London: Routledge, 2011).

M. Power, *The Audit Explosion* (London: Demos, 1994).

J.S. Quesnel, Presentation to the United Nations Evaluation Group (2006), online at: <http://cfapp1-docs-public.undp.org/eo/evaldocs1/uneg_2006/eo_doc_483020410.ppt#1>.

D. Saint-Martin, *Coordinating Interdependence: Governance and Social Policy Redesign in Britain, the European Union and Canada* (Ottawa: Canadian Policy Research Networks, 2004).

M.F. Smith, *Evaluability Assessment: A Practical Approach* (Boston: Kluwer Academic, 1989).

Social Development Canada, *The Voluntary Sector Initiative Process Evaluation, Final Evaluation Report* (2004), online at: <http://www.vsi-isbc.org/eng/relationship/pdf/process_evaluation.pdf>.

M. Taylor, "Between Public and Private: Accountability in Voluntary Organisations" (1996) 24:1 Policy and Politics 57-72.

C.E. Thayer *et al.*, "Framing Participatory Evaluation" (1998) 80 New Directions for Evaluation 5-23.

D.E. Thomson, "Exploring the Role of Funders' Performance Reporting Mandates in Nonprofit Performance Measurement" (1989) 39:4 Nonprofit and Voluntary Sector Quarterly 611-629.

W.E. Thurston & L. Potvin, "Evaluability Assessment: A Tool for Incorporating Evaluation in Social Change Programmes" (2003) 9:4 Evaluation 453-469.

M.S. Trevisan & Yi Min Huang, "Evaluability Assessment: a Primer" (2003) 8:20 Practical Assessment, Research & Evaluation, online at: <http://PAREonline.net/getvn.asp?v=8&n=20>.

United Nations Evaluation Group (UNEG), *Norms for Evaluation in the UN System* (New York: United Nations, 2005).

Voluntary Sector Initiative (*Accord*), *An Accord Between the Government of Canada and the Voluntary Sector* (Ottawa: Voluntary Sector Task Force, Privy Council Office, 2001).

Voluntary Sector Initiative (*Code on Funding*), *A Code of Good Practice on Funding* (Canada: Joint Accord Table, 2002).

Voluntary Sector Initiative (*Code on Policy*), *A Code of Good Practice on Policy Dialogue* (Canada: Joint Accord Table, 2002).

W.K. Kellogg Foundation, *Evaluation Handbook: Philosophy and Expectations* (1998), online at: <http://cyc.brandeis.edu/pdfs/reports/EvaluationHandbook.pdf>.

C.H. Weiss, *Evaluation: Methods for Studying Programs and Policies*, 2d ed. (Upper Saddle River, NJ: Prentice Hall, 1998).

J.S. Wholey, *Evaluation: Promise and Performance* (Washington, DC: The Urban Institute, 1979).

Chapter 10

FINANCIAL MANAGEMENT IN NONPROFIT ORGANIZATIONS

Carolyn Bodnar-Evans
Canadian Partnership Against Cancer

INTRODUCTION

Financial management in nonprofit organizations has become increasingly important and complex. There are numerous challenges in managing both revenues and expenditures due to changes nonprofits face in their external environment. For example, competition for funds and, in some areas, competition with for-profit organizations is creating pressure to paint a favourable financial picture. Donors and the public increasingly equate financial efficiency (or the percentage of expenses spent on programs and services) with organizational effectiveness. Scandals in both the nonprofit and for-profit worlds have created a demand for increased scrutiny and accountability.[1] Finally, information about nonprofits is more accessible to the public; for example, more people are accessing the annual information returns for registered charities that are readily available on Canada Revenue Agency's Website.[2]

This chapter will look at the basic elements of sound financial management. It will answer such questions as: what is financial management, who is responsible for it, and how can it help organizations achieve their

---

[1] In The Muttart Foundation's report, *Talking about Charities 2008*, available online at: <http://www.muttart.org/surveys>, nearly all those surveyed agreed that charities should be more transparent as to how donations are spent and almost half of those surveyed do research prior to donating, which includes reviewing financial statements.

[2] <http://www.cra-arc.gc.ca>.

missions in our increasingly accountable environment as well as help them to better respond to the challenges in their communities.

Financial management focuses on generating financial information that can be used to improve decision-making oriented towards achieving the goals of an organization as well as maintaining a healthy financial situation. It encompasses the broad areas of:

1.   Managerial accounting, which relates to the generation of any financial information that managers find useful for the internal management of the organization. It incorporates activities such as developing and implementing budgets and forecasts as well as various analytic techniques to support management decision-making.

2.   Financial accounting, which is concerned with providing retrospective financial information to those both internal and external to an organization. It produces regular reports from the accounting system regarding the financial status of the organization at any point in time.

3.   Finance, which focuses on sources, *e.g.*, donations, grants and uses, *e.g.*, program expenditures, purchase of a building, of an organization's financial resources such as cash and investments.

One study has argued that the future economic success of a nonprofit will depend not only on the quality of its social and economic activities but also its ability to improve its internal accounting decisions and communicate results from its financial reporting systems to its stakeholder community (see Keating & Frumkin (2003)). Inherent in this is the notion that financial management is not an end in itself but rather a tool in the overall pursuit of the mission, albeit an increasingly essential and powerful one. Financial management provides an understanding of the current financial status of an organization — how well it is doing financially and what it can or cannot afford to do. Suffice it to say, without adequate financial resources an organization cannot achieve its mission. Financial management is also concerned with effectiveness (whether an organization is accomplishing its mission), and efficiency (whether an organization uses the minimum resources required to accomplish its mission).

RESPONSIBILITY FOR FINANCIAL MANAGEMENT

Ultimately, the board of directors is responsible for the prudent management of a nonprofit's funds and assets. It cannot delegate this responsibility to employees or financial consultants but it can rely on the advice and assistance of such people. While day-to-day financial management duties are usually undertaken by staff, the board remains responsible and must maintain proper supervision and control of the work of the employees (see Ministry of the Attorney General (2004a)). The board's work in this area may be led by a finance committee, headed up by a treasurer. Depending upon the needs of the organization, the board may also create a separate audit committee. The responsibilities of these committees are discussed in more detail later in this chapter.

Except in all-volunteer organizations, the board usually delegates the responsibility for carrying out many of the financial management duties to the Executive Director (ED) or Chief Executive Officer (CEO), who in turn may delegate further to other professional staff. Often there is a bookkeeper, accountant, or finance manager who undertakes many of these duties, such as the preparation of the financial information needed for board and management decision-making, progress-tracking, and reporting to the organization's stake-holders. However, it is not the role of accounting or financial managers to decide what an organization should do based on the information they provide. Financial information is but one input to the decision-making process.

In small nonprofit organizations without access to professional accounting staff, the board of directors usually must retain the responsibilities more commonly played by staff in larger organizations. To assist them it is worth focusing effort on attracting a treasurer to keep the financial records of the organization or perhaps to oversee a part-time bookkeeper. More detail regarding roles and responsibilities for financial management is contained in each of the three main sections of this chapter, and further information on the responsibility for financial management may be found in the Muttart Foundation's publication *Financial Responsibilities of Not-for-Profit Boards: A Self-Guided Workbook* referenced at the end of the chapter.

HOW THIS CHAPTER IS ORGANIZED

The first section, "Budgeting — The Financial Component of the Planning Process", discusses the budgeting process, including pitfalls to avoid, types of budgets, who should be involved and steps in the process. The second section, "Internal Control", discusses the scope and importance of an internal control system, provides examples of controls, and describes the role of finance and audit committees. To illustrate its importance it also presents a case study concerning the discovery of fraud. The third and final section, "Financial Reporting", touches on basic financial statement concepts and those unique to nonprofit organizations, the roles of those responsible for it, and some key reporting issues in the sector today.

BUDGETING — THE FINANCIAL COMPONENT OF THE PLANNING PROCESS

Budgeting is an important step in the overall planning process. It follows from an organization's strategy for accomplishing its mission and a plan setting out its non-financial and financial objectives. The budget is a specific and detailed plan for the fiscal year that defines the resources needed to accomplish its goals and objectives, where the resources will come from, and how they will be used.

At its simplest, the budget is a plan expressed in monetary terms but, much more than this, it is a useful management tool to motivate, monitor and measure financial performance, and to assist in managing operations, revenues and costs. Budgets can also act as an accountability tool for the organization's stakeholders, board of directors and managers.

However, used unwisely, a budget also has the ability to unnecessarily limit an organization. For example, budgets should not act as a constraint on what the organization can and cannot do, or prevent it from doing the right things. No budget is perfect as none of us can predict the future with any certainty. For this reason many accountants view budgets as being out of date soon after they are assembled and therefore urge that they be treated as guidelines rather than rigid rules. To get the most from the budgeting process, it is important to know what the ideal process should be and how to avoid some of the pitfalls that can arise in it. There are four elements to the ideal process, shown in Table 1, below:

Table 1: Elements of a Successful Budgeting Process

Element	Description
Involve all staff levels	Should involve the CEO and senior executives, as well as program managers & other staff.
Focused connection to the organization's strategy	Should be reflective of how funds will be expended to reach the strategy's goals.
High degree of engagement	Should include mechanisms to promote staff engagement.
Flexibility	Should recognize that changes to the budget are inevitable.

First, appropriate *involvement of staff* is important. If senior management, starting with the ED or CEO, and senior financial manager (henceforth to be referred to as the CFO or chief financial officer) are not sufficiently engaged in the process then budgets may get short shrift from front-line managers and others involved in the process. The tone is set at the top. However, budgeting is not the sole domain of the CFO and therefore should not be viewed as simply an exercise in adjusting expense numbers to equal revenue numbers. Virtually all managers should become involved in creating and using budgets. If staff feel personally vested in how well the organization does, the chances of a good outcome are substantially improved. Finance staff should therefore be focused on providing information that will support program managers to set financial targets that will assist in meeting those outcomes.

Second, budgeting requires a significant amount of *time and energy*. It can typically take one to three months in small organizations and four to six months in a larger organization. Some have estimated that 20 to 30 per cent of the time of senior managers can be taken up by budgeting; therefore in order to be worthwhile, budgets have to be intimately connected to the plan and goals of the organization. Too often budgeting becomes an exercise in number crunching, separated from the planning process. A budget should reflect the way the organization's strategy will be implemented in terms of how funds will be spent to reach desired goals.

To prevent a budget from becoming too inwardly focused on negotiated targets, sufficient attention should be given to the client or donor served by the organization. It may also help for a budget not to focus just on inputs such as staff time or needed supplies, but to link the budgetary resources to the outputs and outcomes generated by such inputs (these are discussed in more detail in Chapter 9).

Third, the process of developing the budget should be *engaging*, especially for line managers such as program and department heads. These managers are often reluctant to get sufficiently involved in the budgeting process, seeing it as a low-value activity compared to their primary mission-related responsibilities. Yet their participation in devising, reviewing and analyzing the budget ensures the creation of something that is of value to them and the other users of the budget. Connecting the budget to the strategic priorities of the organization will help line managers see how the budget better serves the mission of the organization.

One way to involve managers in the budgeting process is by adopting a bottom-up approach, which starts by having managers provide specific targets or outputs that their programs or departments can accomplish in line with the organization's strategic plan. They then prepare the corresponding budget allocation request required to meet these targets. This kind of approach can also be combined with a partial top-down approach whereby the CEO provides the overall budget number that each program or department must work within and based on this, the line managers then prepare targets and their detailed budget information. Aside from the process itself, managers may feel more engaged if they are evaluated in terms of their contribution towards budget objectives, again connected with the mission.

Finally, the budget process should be *flexible*. It should contain appropriate procedures for approving changes when required so that it enables rather than disables the organization's ability to adapt to changing conditions. Too often budgets are treated as rigid rules with many organizations being unwilling to change their budgets within the fiscal year in spite of changing conditions. Fear of being punished for missing budget targets can lower service quality and inhibit needed innovation. It may also reinforce a dependency culture that encourages people to meet the target rather than exceed the target so improvements are only incremental. Another typical budget behaviour associated with inflexibility is the "use it or lose it" or protectionist mindset, which occurs when managers are penalized for not using their total budget allocation by having their next year's budget reduced. Managers with this mindset are therefore motivated to expend their total budget despite sometimes not really needing the funds. This kind of behaviour not only creates waste and inefficiency but also results in missed opportunities to reallocate resources to take advantage of circumstances that unexpectedly arise to further the mission.

Trying to accurately predict what will happen in 12 months and budgeting accordingly is an exercise in futility. Thus it is important that the budget process strikes the right balance between flexibility and control. This can be done by ensuring that everyone understands what the purpose of the budget is and what the process is for creating and changing it.

In some cases the board may decide to be more "hands on" and thus exercise more control and less flexibility when an organization's financial situation is more precarious. In other circumstances, where the financial situation is good and management has a solid track record, the board may agree that more flexibility is required such that the CEO can operate within the total budget and only when there are changes to the overall bottom line surplus or deficit, would board approval be needed.[3] The CEO may apply a similar principle to managers with budget responsibility. Some organizations have adopted a rolling budget process such that the approved budget is reviewed regularly and revised budget goals are agreed upon during the year within parameters set by the board.

So how does an organization get the most from its budgeting process? First it is important to more fully appreciate what a budget can do, then to understand the different types of budgets, and finally to be clear about the role of the people involved and the process itself.

Characteristics of a Well-prepared Budget

A well-prepared budget allows an organization to adjust plans, activities and spending as needed; spend money cost-effectively; reach specific goals it has set; receive clean audits; and avoid incurring questioned or disallowed costs or cost overruns that it may have to pay for from other funds. It also lets everyone in the organization know the goals to be achieved, the work to be done to reach the goals, the resources (people and things) available, the timetable for getting

---

[3]   The various options for a board's involvement in budgeting are further explained later in this chapter. Also refer to Chapter 3 on the role of the board.

specific work done, and the individuals responsible and accountable for doing it.

More specifically a well-prepared budget:

- provides the financial and operational guidance needed to implement policies and directives established by the board of directors;

- allows management to measure and guide immediate and long-term financial health and operational effectiveness;

- guides the acquisition and use of resources;

- anticipates operational expenses and identifies income to pay for such expenses;

- is a tool for controlling spending and avoiding unplanned deficits;

- helps to integrate administrative staff, with program activities;

- allows monitoring of actual income and expenses against those that were budgeted so management can assess the overall financial situation and alter plans as needed; and

- serves as one of the bases for performance reviews and in some cases, compensation.

Types of Budgets

While budgets are most commonly thought of in terms of an operating budget which shows revenues and expenses, there are two other types of budgets which are related and should be prepared as part of the overall budgeting process. These are:

1. The capital budget — a plan for the acquisition of capital assets such as buildings, equipment and vehicles that provide benefits for more than one year.

2. The cash budget — a plan for expected cash receipts and expenses that alerts management to those times when there will be excess cash to invest or a shortage of cash to make up.

Capital Budget

This budget shows what capital assets are required for an organization to operate and the effects of these acquisitions on the operating budget. Because the capital budget often details large costs for major pieces of equipment and buildings, it is important that it discuss the implications of these expenses for current and future operating costs and for the organization's cash flow. Depending on the results of this analysis, it may be necessary to make special arrangements to finance these acquisitions.

One of the most significant effects it has on the operating budget is through the inclusion of amortization or depreciation expenses. For example, while the full cost of a van or the major improvement of a building will be accounted for in the capital budget, only a one-year portion of the cost will be included as an expense in the operating budget for each year that the van or the major building improvement is expected to provide useful service to an organization's mission. This one-year portion is called amortization expense and it recognizes that the addition of a capital asset has a future benefit to the organization and therefore it is not reasonable to charge the full cost of the asset's purchase as an expense in the year purchased.

The capital budget of some organizations also identifies purchases of specific items for the coming year, while other organizations may approve an overall dollar value for capital spending and then evaluate and approve individual items for acquisition throughout the year as the need for those items arises. The capital budgeting process may require a thorough review of the proposed purchase and a search for alternative options. This usually involves a detailed financial analysis of the impact of the purchase on the organization's mission and financial situation over the purchase's lifetime.

Decisions regarding the purchase of an expensive piece of equipment used in a program and whether it should be purchased outright, leased, or shared with another organization require this kind of analysis. As a practical matter, limits are set such that only items over a certain dollar limit would be capitalized and amortized. A cut-off of $500 or $1,000 is a reasonable level for many nonprofits. Those purchases falling below the cut-off would be accounted for as an expense that is deducted from revenues in the statement of revenues and expenditures at the time of purchase.

Cash Budget

Regardless of whether a cash budget is required by the board, it is a good idea to prepare one to reveal times when there may be a shortage of cash to pay regular operating costs such as salaries and rent. This allows specific financing arrangements to be made well ahead of any potential cash shortages or, alternatively, management can try to speed up the timing of cash receipts and slow down disbursements so no shortage occurs. If a shortage necessitates borrowing from the organization's banker, sufficient lead-time will be required to make these arrangements and for the board to provide formal approval if this is required by the organization's by-laws. On the flip side, the cash budget will also identify those times when excess cash may be on hand and available for investment. The cash budget takes the information in both the operating and capital budgets and translates revenues and expenditures, as well as capital asset acquisitions and disposals, into cash flow showing when cash outflows will exceed cash inflows and vice versa.[4]

Operating Budget

The operating budget is based on a set of detailed assumptions about what the organization wishes to accomplish in the next fiscal year modified by an analysis of likely external influences on the organization's income and expenses, such as the state of the economy, inflation, employment market and interest rates. It should be based on the "accrual" method of accounting, which means that the revenues and expenses arising from providing the services of the organization are both recorded in the same fiscal year even though the cash associated with these revenues and expenses may be received or paid in a different fiscal year. The accrual method must be used in order to conform to generally accepted accounting principles.

An organization should be attentive to budgeting either a surplus or deficit. While some stakeholders may frown on the prospect of a surplus, the organization may be planning a new program in the following year and require additional resources from the current year to accomplish this. It may also be acceptable for organizations with accumulated surpluses from prior years to incur a deficit in order to apply those accumulated resources for special needs such as expanding a program.

The preparation of operating budgets is often an iterative process of top-down and bottom-up budgeting so in many cases it does not matter whether organizations budget for revenues or expenses first

---

[4] For more information regarding cash budgets and cash flow management refer to the reference at the end of this chapter — Dropkin & Hayden , *The Cash Flow Management Book for Nonprofits: A Step-by-Step Guide for Managers, Consultants, and Boards* (2001).

since revisions are likely to be needed to arrive at an acceptable final product. Operating budgets may be prepared for a fiscal period on many bases — monthly, quarterly, or even annually (although if prepared annually the value of the budget as a management tool will be limited). The time period applied will be determined by the particular needs of the organization.

Board and Staff Roles and Responsibilities in Budgeting

The roles played by board and staff will vary depending on a nonprofit's size, organizational structure and revenue structure. However, whatever the division of responsibility, it is important to follow a specified process that is tailored to the organization. Ideally, budgeting policies and procedures should be understood by all those involved. Also, as previously noted, budgets are best developed collaboratively using the skills and knowledge of those at a number of levels in the organization.

Board of Directors

Ultimately the board is legally responsible for ensuring that budgets meet applicable laws and regulations, are fiscally sound, and will further the organization's mission. The Canada Revenue Agency establishes and monitors many of the financial regulations that nonprofits must comply with such as the remittance of various withholding taxes and other amounts from employees as well as requirements for annual filings. As an example, charities must file a T3010 form annually and comply with the disbursement quota,[5] and advocacy expenditure maximum. More information regarding these regulations and filing requirements can be found on Canada Revenue Agency's Website.

As noted earlier, some boards restrict their role in budgeting to that of reviewing and approving, while others participate in budget preparation from the beginning. The extent of the board's role will depend on many factors. If management's financial expertise is limited

---

[5]   A detailed description of the disbursement quota is beyond the scope of this text but in general a charity meets the quota when it expends on charitable activities at least the sum of 3.5 per cent of all assets not currently used in charitable programs or administration if these assets exceed $100,000. This is to stop charities from accumulating funds without a stated purpose.

(or there are no paid staff) or the organization finds itself in a financial crisis, then a board could decide to take on roles that might normally be considered those of management. In either case there is usually value in creating a finance or budget committee with the specific responsibility for reviewing budgets before subjecting them to a formal review by the full board.

One of the key responsibilities of all boards is to establish general budget policies. Such policies would, for example, state that budgets must be balanced (and note any exceptions to this rule) and specify the use or development of reserve funds. The board should also set the framework for budgeting by making general policy decisions about new programs, capital projects, major fundraising efforts, salary increases, and changes to the overall staff complement.

Following the approval of the budget, the board should receive regular updates on its implementation from the ED or CEO and, where appropriate, approve any significant changes to the budget that become necessary during the year.

CEO (or ED)

The CEO's role is to facilitate and oversee the preparation and approval of the budget as well as its implementation once approved. This includes:

- arranging and staffing early strategic planning sessions with the board;

- preparing options and recommendations to guide budget development;

- ensuring the budget is accurate and adheres to board policies and that the budgeting schedule is met;

- reviewing draft budgets and making resource allocation decisions; and

- presenting the recommended budget to the board, explaining its provisions and possible consequences, and answering the board's questions.

Upon approval it is the responsibility of the CEO to work with the CFO or senior finance manager and others to implement the budget. This includes clearly communicating the approved budget to the management and front-line staff so they understand it and the part they play. Monitoring includes reviewing financial reports that compare actual with budgeted results so that variances can be determined and corrective action taken as appropriate. It is very important that the CEO communicate financial results and any corrective action he or she has taken to the board. Depending upon the situation, the CEO may seek the board's input and/or approval for needed fiscal or program changes.

CFO or Senior Financial Manager

The CFO plays a major and sustained role, often having day-to-day responsibility for co-ordinating budget development, implementation and monitoring. This would include:

- creating the budget development calendar and ensuring deadlines are met;

- communicating budgeting policies and procedures to managers and line staff;

- establishing the format for budget drafts;

- developing revenue and expense forecasts based on reviews of economic and competitive trends when applicable;

- collaborating in setting expense and revenue targets in line with strategic plan and programs;

- evaluating draft budgets from program or unit managers for accuracy, reasonableness, applicable guidelines and anticipated resources;

- discussing draft budgets with the CEO and other managers as needed;

- writing up recommendations for reducing, increasing, or reallocating requested resources;

- preparing the budget document once the CEO's budget decisions are made and possibly helping to present it to the board; and

- once approved, overseeing its implementation and monitoring, which includes preparing and analyzing budgeted versus actual income and expense reports, and overseeing any corrective actions needed.

In organizations that do not have a dedicated financial person, this role may be fulfilled by a combination of people such as the CEO, part-time bookkeeper, office or business manager, treasurer, or other qualified program staff.

Program, Unit, Activity or Department Managers

Usually it is program managers (including those involved in fundraising and administrative functions) who are best equipped to provide information on current program needs, revenues, costs and the effects of reducing or expanding individual programs. Thus their involvement is essential to developing budgets that accurately reflect reality. Ideally they are responsible for developing draft budgets for their areas, consulting with other staff to evaluate revenue potential, current or new programs, operating costs, and staff and equipment needs. They should meet with the CFO or CEO to review draft budgets, explore options for change and, once the budget is approved, inform staff about program and operational requirements for meeting the budget. They must also be held accountable for the allocated resources by regularly reviewing financial reports prepared by the CFO and developing corrective action plans when problems arise.

Others

Depending on the nature of the organization, others may be involved in the budgeting process such as clerical staff, selected clients or volunteers, and consultants or other outside specialists. The role of these others is usually to provide information or advice but, in any case, should be clear to all those involved in the process.

Steps in the Budget Preparation Process

Although the budget preparation process can generally be described as bottom-up and iterative, this is not the only approach. The steps that follow are general and, while typical in a traditional budgeting process, can be altered. There are also other methods of budget preparation and these are summarized at the end of this section. Employing these other methods would require changes to the process as described in this section.

A set of assumptions and guidelines is prepared that create the context within which managers will develop detailed budgets for their areas. The CEO, working with the CFO, will generally provide policies, goals and performance expectations stemming from the policies and strategy established by the board.

In many cases there is a requirement that budgets be prepared using a predetermined format to make it easier to aggregate them across the organization. It is also desirable to require that the budget be accompanied by a proposed work plan that can be evaluated along with the budget request. The plan should clearly link the work to be carried out the next year and how it will contribute to meeting the organization's strategic outcomes.

Sometimes those preparing budgets are told to focus only on the operating fund without including any restricted funds but, in order to make decisions regarding the best allocation of all the resources available to the organization, budgets should be prepared taking into consideration all the funds or resources of the organization.

The assumptions and guidelines that are provided at the beginning of the budget preparation process should reflect the organization's strategic plan and take into consideration its projected revenue and expenses for the coming year. For example, the organization could be having a bad year and need to make up for an unplanned deficit with a surplus the following year. Assumptions and guidelines may also include specific program objectives and priorities, reserve fund targets or limits, policies governing the creation of new programs or positions, and projections of personnel costs. An organization could also have a guideline requiring those doing the preparation to provide measures of what will be accomplished with the money they receive — indicators such as the number of counselling sessions to be conducted, the hours of service to be delivered or the participants to be served that link the budget outputs and outcomes to be achieved.

Sometimes organizations have budget formats that distinguish between those for internal reports (to staff, volunteers and the board) and those for external reports to stakeholders. For example, in the year-end audited financial statements to stakeholders, some administration expenses may be allocated to the cost of programs or fundraising, while, for the internal budget, administration may be categorized separately to facilitate its management by the person(s) responsible. In this case, the board may want to see both versions of the budget, the internally used version that may be more helpful to the board's oversight role and the externally used version so that it is aware of how the organization's stakeholders will view the financials. In addition, depending upon the funding structure, certain funders may require budget information in their own format to consider when making their decisions on funding.

The co-existence of budgets in different formats can get very confusing for managers and the board as well as adding to administrative complexity and cost. However, while settling on one format may seem ideal, if it does not provide value to the organization it could be worth producing more than one. If this is the case then, at minimum, the translation between internally and externally oriented budgets should be as simple as possible.

Budget Review and Adoption

Once the budgets for the responsibility areas are complete, they are aggregated. It is very common that the total of all spending requests exceeds projected revenues. Thus begins a process of negotiation to eliminate any inefficiency in the budget and then to find more revenue or reduce expenses. Choices must be made to focus on the highest priorities of the organization in order to minimize the impact on accomplishing the organization's goals and objectives. Through this negotiation process managers should be given the opportunity to provide a rationale for why their budget requests fit with the priorities and should not be among the first things cut. It may also be necessary to rethink certain aspects of the strategic plan because of information that comes to light during the budgeting process.

In the budget review process it is important that a good understanding of "hard and soft revenues and expenses" be developed so that there is some sense as to the degree of flexibility and risk inherent in the budget. "Hard" revenues are those that have a relatively high degree of certainty such as membership or tuition fees or fundraising revenue from a long-standing donor base. Hard expenses include salary and benefit expenses of permanent staff in core programs and rent payments. "Soft" revenues may include variable donation revenue from general sources, a challenge target or bequests. Soft expenses are those that, if the organization had to make mid-year budget cuts, could be reduced, eliminated, or deferred until the next year, without severe consequences, such as temporary staff and non-essential program expenses. Ideally an organization would not plan to make long-term commitments with soft revenue.

Budget Implementation

An effective budget presentation in written form communicates to managers the amount that can be spent and what it can be spent on. It assists the board in keeping management accountable. Managers will need additional detail that breaks down the budget at the account level. As we will see, an effective system of internal control can help an organization achieve its plan, as can effective financial reporting.

Evaluation

A comparison of variances from budgeted to actual results should be done on a periodic basis, typically monthly or quarterly, so that problems can be identified and corrected midstream. Things do not always go as planned and it is important to understand why and whether it is simply something that should be recognized and corrected, or something that is beyond the control of the organization.

Other Budget-setting Methods

There are other methods for the setting of budgets, and while a detailed discussion of these is beyond the scope of this book, they are briefly described below. As noted earlier, employing any one of these techniques would require changes to the process described earlier.

Zero-based Budgeting

This budget-setting method asks the question: "If we were not doing this program or activity today, would we start it?" The focus is on a thorough re-evaluation of every facet of an organization's operation to determine whether it should be continued; thus it assumes that the organization is starting from zero. Employing this type of budget-setting method is very time-consuming, requires reliable and detailed cost information about the organization's activities, and can be very threatening to managers and staff involved in the process. While the approach has its merits, unless an organization has the resources to do it right, its application is most appropriate during periods of financial crisis when it is important to reduce costs with the least damage to vital services. In this situation the zero-sum method forces careful consideration of what is "vital" and what is not.

Rolling Budgets

This is a relatively new approach to budgeting being employed by some business organizations looking for improvements to the traditional budgeting process. Rather than creating an annual budget that remains static for the year, a budget is prepared and reviewed regularly (*e.g.*, monthly or quarterly) and updated. Unlike the periodic reviews in the traditional process, which may yield occasional changes here and there, in this case the entire budget is systematically recalculated at each review period. In some circumstances the rolling budget is prepared for an 18-month period rather than a 12-month period so that the budget always provides a view into the next fiscal year. While it may provide better information since the budget for the current and future periods are regularly reviewed, it is more time-consuming. It also requires constant and effective communication to ensure that the goals, which are updated as needed, are clear. It would be worth investigating for those nonprofit organizations existing in very dynamic environments in which costs and revenue can vacillate extensively over short periods of time.

Activity-based Budgets

The focus here is on developing budgets for clusters of activities such as a particular program or a specific fundraising campaign, rather than the traditional method of line item costs. This approach allows the organization to know how much it is spending on what, thus informing resource allocation decisions differently than a traditional budget process. It forces managers to consider what resources are actually needed for programs and functions since it is based on the activities carried out by the organization. The process would start out with a determination of how many clients are to be served by a given program and proceed to a detailed analysis of the total cost, *i.e.*, *all* the direct and indirect expenses required to provide this level of service. For example, the complete cost of an activity includes the associated overhead costs such as a proportion of the rent, or a CEO's salary that is devoted to supporting the program. Thus, key decisions regarding cost allocations as well as reliable and detailed accounting information are critical. The chief benefit of this approach to budgeting is that it allows the organization to do a more thorough comparison of costs and benefits for its various programs and functions. This kind of information is also very valuable when it comes to making applications for grants. It also helps in negotiating contracts with governments or other funders who want only to fund direct costs but are unwilling to consider indirect costs necessary to support programs. The difficulty with this budgeting method is that there are no universally agreed-upon standards for calculating these indirect costs and deciding on the proportions that can be allocated to given programs.

INTERNAL CONTROL

Internal control used to be considered the sole domain of an organization's auditor or accountant. But this is no longer true and a much broader definition of internal control has emerged in the last decade. The following definition of "internal control" was developed by the U.S.-based Committee of Sponsoring Organizations (COSO)[6] in its publication *Internal Control — Integrated Framework*:

> Internal control is developed to allow an organization to achieve plans, protect resources, motivate employees, evaluate performance, alert management to variations from the plan, and take corrective action. It can be defined as a process, effected by an organization's board of directors, management and other personnel, designed to provide reasonable assurance regarding the achievement of objectives in three categories:
>
> 1. Effectiveness (moves the organization towards its goals or objectives) and efficiency of operations (accomplishes its goals at the lowest possible cost).
> 2. Reliability of financial reporting.
> 3. Compliance with applicable laws and regulations.[7]

The COSO Framework consists of five components that form an integrated system that can react to changing conditions. The internal control system is intertwined with the organization's operating activities and is most effective when controls are built into the infrastructure of the organization.

---

[6] The Committee of Sponsoring Organizations (COSO) Framework. COSO consists of the American Institute of Certified Public Accountants, the Institute of Management Accountants, the Institute of Internal Auditors, Financial Executives International, and the American Accounting Association.

[7] The Committee of Sponsoring Organizations of the Treadway Commission, *Internal Control — Integrated Framework* (Durham NC: American Institute of Certified Public Accountants, 2013) at 3.

1. *Control environment.* Sometimes referred to as the "tone at the top" of the organization, this refers to statements about the integrity, ethical values, and competence of the organization's people, including management's philosophy and operating style (*e.g.*, the way it assigns authority and responsibility); and the attention and direction provided by the board of directors. It is the foundation for all other components of internal control.

2. *Risk assessment.* The identification and analysis of risks, both inside and outside the organization that threaten the ability of the organization to achieve its objectives. This assessment forms the basis for developing a plan for minimizing the most serious of the risks identified.

3. *Control activities.* Policies and procedures that help ensure that management directives are carried out. Control activities occur throughout the organization at all levels in all functions. These include policies on what needs approval, verification or reconciliation of balance sheet and income statement accounts, and what reviews should be made of operating performance, security of assets, and segregation of duties.

4. *Information and communication.* Information systems within the organization are key to an effective system of internal control. Internal information, as well as information about external events, activities, and conditions must be communicated in useful ways to enable management to make informed decisions. It is also vital for meeting the accountability requirements of external stakeholders. For example, the control system surrounding the activity of putting on a fundraising event would consist of the budget for the event, the planned amount to be raised, the record of the expenses incurred in putting it on and the record of ticket sales. These sources of information would likely be recorded in various places but are of little value unless they are brought together and communicated to the responsible mangers in a clear and useful fashion. Only in this way can the information help them monitor how successful the event was compared to the planned outcome and decide whether it should be dropped or changed in the future.

5. *Monitoring activities.* The internal control system (all of the above four components) must be regularly monitored and evaluated by management and the board of directors to ensure that it is working as planned. The failure to carry out and act on this kind of evaluation of control systems is in large part responsible for

many of the scandals that have plagued both the business and nonprofit world from time to time in recent years.

Elements of an Internal Control System

Specific examples of the elements of an internal control system are discussed below. It should be recognized that this list is far from exhaustive and is only provided to give a sense of the breadth of controls that may be considered.

A clear audit trail. It should be possible to trace any transaction in the accounting system back to its source, *e.g.*, if an expense is significantly more than budget, one should be able to look at a detailed listing of expenses from the accounting system to see how much was spent on what. The audit trail should be documented and, in order to be effective as a control, it should be regularly used to identify and examine discrepancies or unusual spending patterns.

Reliable personnel. The organization must have a group of employees that are capable, trustworthy and appropriately supervised.

Segregation of duties. This is one of the most common elements albeit difficult to accomplish in small organizations. The person who approves the bills should not be the same person that writes the cheques (this could be the board member who is Treasurer in smaller organizations). The benefit of segregation is that one person may catch a problem missed by another; however it cannot help in the instance where there is collusion among several persons and therefore it goes back to the element of having reliable people in place.

Proper authorization. All spending must be supported by proper authorization. Authorization limits should be established so operations are not bogged down. Established authorization practices should extend to contracts that commit an organization's resources.

Proper procedures. To reduce errors, internal control systems rely heavily on standard operating procedures in the form of policy and procedure manuals. To be effective, both the procedures and manuals should be kept current and staff should be made fully aware of them.

Physical safeguards. Cash should be kept in the bank. Deposits should be made regularly, daily if possible. Blank cheques should be locked up when not in use. Computer backups should be kept in a separate location. Inventory should be locked up with appropriate access controls.

Other elements of internal control systems may be suggested by the organization's auditors or found in resources such as the workbook published by The Muttart Foundation, *Board Development: Financial Responsibilities of Not-for-Profit Boards*, which includes a section called "Making Sure the Accounts are in Order", of particular relevance to smaller organizations. Larger organizations may find the American Institute of Certified Public Accountant's *Audit Committee Toolkit for Nonprofit Organizations* a useful resource.

What an Internal Control System Cannot Do

The design of an internal control system is a function of the resources available, implying that its cost must be at least equal to the benefits derived from it. Because of this, even the best internal control system can only provide *reasonable* assurance to management and the board about the organization's progress, or lack of progress in achieving its mission. Breakdowns in the internal control system can occur due to a simple error as well as faulty judgments that could be made at any level of the organization. There is also a possibility that internal controls will be circumvented by collusion or management override. Breaches of the internal control system that lead to fraud are discussed later on in this chapter.

Responsibility for Internal Control Systems

Everyone in the organization has a role to play in the organization's internal control system.

Board of Directors. The primary role of the board is one of oversight of the internal control system. This is best carried out by its *Audit Committee*. For specific examples on what a board can do to fulfill its role, see the section called "*Audit Committee*" further on in this chapter.

CEO. The CEO has the ultimate responsibility for the internal control system. The CEO sets the "tone at the top" thus affecting the integrity, ethics and other factors that create the positive control environment needed for the internal control system to thrive. However, much of the day-to-day operation of the system would normally be delegated to other senior managers in the organization if they are available.

CFO or Senior Financial Manager (if available). The chief responsibility of this person is to provide critical technical leadership in the development, implementation and maintenance of the internal control system since much of the internal control structure flows through the accounting and finance area of the organization.

All other personnel. All other staff should understand why control systems are necessary, how they work, and their responsibility for supporting the system through their own actions.

The Role of Board Committees

Finance Committee

The board of a nonprofit organization often has a finance committee that can provide support to both the volunteer treasurer and staff. In smaller organizations unable to afford professional finance staff, this committee can play an important part in the internal control system. These responsibilities may include monitoring performance against budget, providing advice on investment policies, making investment decisions on behalf of the organization, and reviewing or deciding insurance coverage plans, unusual fundraising matters, or expense reimbursements.

For the past decade, the spotlight has been on standards of governance relating to the oversight of financial transactions and auditing procedures because of a number of very public corporate accounting scandals. Certain legislated measures have been taken in both Canada[8] and the United States to rebuild public trust in the for-profit sector, one of which is improved standards for audit committees. While nonprofits are not directly affected by these, some have suggested that it may be worthwhile for them to examine their practices as a precaution. Certainly if an organization subjects itself to an annual audit, best practice dictates that the board create an audit committee. The existence of an audit committee may also provide greater assurance to an organization's stakeholders of the integrity of its financial statements and the internal processes that guide the expenditure of funds on the mission. In lieu of having a separate audit committee, the finance

---

[8]   In Canada these measures have been taken by the Ontario Securities Commission; the Canadian Securities Administrators — a group that works to better harmonize securities regulation across Canada; and the Canadian Public Accountability Board — a group that helps ensure public confidence in the integrity of the financial reporting of public companies.

committee may be constituted twice a year or on an as-needed basis as an audit committee. In any case, it's a good idea that both management and the Board of Directors discuss how the organization can withstand increased public scrutiny. To help guide this discussion the Canadian Institute of Chartered Accountants has created a publication "Increasing Public Scrutiny of Not-for-Profit Organizations — Questions for Directors to Ask".[9]

Audit Committee

In general an audit committee has two main responsibilities: first, to assist the board of directors in assuring itself that appropriate accounting policies and internal controls are established and followed, and that financial statements and reports are issued on time and in accordance with regulatory obligations; and second, to encourage and facilitate communication among the board, management and external auditors.

The audit committee should meet at least twice a year, before and after the audit, and then on an as-needed basis to fulfill its responsibilities. The basic functions of an audit committee are as follows:

1. *Audit planning and preparation.* The committee should plan with the auditors the scope of the upcoming audit, including areas of identified risk or potential error. It should also ensure that appropriate assistance is provided by the staff, review control weaknesses, and determine whether all practical steps have been taken to overcome them, and approve the auditor's engagement letter, including fees and expenses.

2. *Oversight of information and control systems.* This includes assessing control system changes during the year, the condition of records, the adequacy of resources committed to accounting and control, and responding to any unanticipated financial risks that occur during the year.

3. *Review of annual financial statements.* This includes assessing accounting policies (particularly those applicable to the nonprofit sector) and reviewing the methods used to account for unusual or significant transactions such as when pledges of funds may be

---

[9]   R. Devitt, "Increasing Public Scrutiny of Not-for-Profit Organizations — Questions for Directors to Ask", online: <http://www.cica.ca/focus-on-practice-areas/governance-strategy-and-risk/not-for-profit-director-series/director-alerts/item38362.pdf>.

accounted for as receivables, or how to handle a large grant made by a foundation to an affiliated organization.

4. *Review of audit results.* This includes looking over the auditor's proposed report and commenting on the appropriateness of accounting policies such as when to account for pledges or bequests as revenue. It also reviews management's behaviour during the audit looking for significant adjustments, misstatements or irregularities, attempts to restrict the scope of the auditor's examination and evidence of illegal acts or fraud.

5. *Appointment of auditors.* Enquire as to the experience, capabilities, objectivity, and independence of individuals being proposed to conduct the audit, then recommend to the board the auditors to be appointed for the following year.[10]

Other functions may include: reviewing compliance with funders' regulations; ensuring that the required documentation has been sent to Canada Revenue Agency (CRA) and other regulators to maintain the organization's nonprofit and/or charitable status; reviewing the organization's fundraising methods for their propriety and adherence to ethical codes and CRA guidelines regarding fundraising, which also list activities that are prohibited. Sometimes the audit committee is the best one to review human resources policies with a special emphasis on assessing the extent to which they reduce the risks of lawsuits for harassment, wrongful dismissal, or poorly written employment contracts.

In general, therefore, it has more and more become the case that the audit committee becomes the body that focuses on risk management for the board, since, even though risk management is a central challenge for both boards and CEOs, this committee, in many areas, is in the best position to assess the risks faced by the organization.

Membership in this committee should consist of three or more directors who are independent (who have no financial, family, or other personal ties to management) and financially literate. This means having the ability to read and understand the organization's financial statements and understand the audit process, and being willing and able to ask searching questions about the matters before them. If possible, one member should be a financial expert (*e.g.*, employed in

---

[10] For further information refer to: Deloitte LLP, *The Effective Not-for-Profit Board. A value-driving force* (Montreal, QC: Deloitte LLP, 2013). Online at: <http://www.deloitte.com/assets/Dcom-Canada/Local%20Assets/Documents/Public%20Sector/ca_en_gov_Effective-NPO-Board_061113.pdf>.

finance or accounting or possessing a professional certification in accounting).

Of course it is understood that it is sometimes difficult for the boards of small, grassroots organizations to find someone with this kind of financial expertise, in which case, what can they do? Difficult though it may be, the board members themselves must do their best to understand their financial role by consulting various information sources available such as this book and The Muttart Foundation's publication on financial responsibilities of boards cited earlier in the chapter. It might also be possible to enlist someone in the community who might not be willing to join the board but might provide some volunteer consulting on financial matters. Local branches of professional accounting associations and organizations like local Volunteer Centres and service clubs or business associations might be helpful in identifying these kinds of volunteer resources. The "Accountants on Board: A guide to becoming a director of a not-for-profit organization" publication by the Canadian Institute of Chartered Accountants is also helpful.[11]

What to Expect from an External Audit

The role of an audit by external professionals is to obtain reasonable (not absolute) assurance that management's financial statements fairly present the financial position of the organization in accordance with generally accepted accounting principles (GAAP), which include Accounting Standards for Not-for-Profit Organizations. GAAP is explained later in this chapter. It is important to note that it is not always possible for an auditor to verify the completeness of all of an organization's cash receipts due to their nature. For example, if a door-to-door campaign is conducted and cash is collected, there are no tests that an auditor can do to ensure that all the cash collected in the campaign was actually deposited into the organization's bank account.

An alternative to an audit is a "review engagement", the product of which is a statement that nothing has come to the attention of the public accountants performing the review that would cause them to believe that the financial statements are not in accordance with GAAP. It is primarily done using procedures that are less intensive than those used in an audit, and based on information supplied by the organization. Because

---

[11] Available online at: <http://www.cica.ca/publications/list-of-publications/manual/item61633.pdf>.

of this, review engagements cost less than audits but they are mostly reserved for specific purposes such as complying with regulations attached to government funding contracts or foundation grants.

In general, it is not recommended that a review be used as a replacement for an annual audit. How a nonprofit is initially registered as a legal entity and the terms of its Letters Patent will determine whether an annual audit is required. It is also possible that certain funders may require an audit as a condition of receiving their funds.

Fraud

Fraud does not occur simply because of a poor internal control system, but ineffective controls can certainly make it easier for it to happen. One theory (which is captured by the acronym "GONE") is that the probability of fraud increases when there is a combination of Greed, Opportunity (presented by poor internal controls), Need (fuelled, for example, by a gambling problem or excessive debts), and Expectation (the perception that one will not be caught).

Fraud can have a significant impact on an organization's continued viability not only due to monetary losses but also due to the reduction in public support that generally results from publicized allegations of impropriety. Although there is no research to determine whether the incidence of fraud is higher or lower in nonprofits than for-profit enterprises, several factors make nonprofits especially vulnerable to fraud: an atmosphere of trust within the organization in which it is considered unnecessary to check on matters related to finance; the existence of donations which, because they do not involve an exchange for goods or services, cannot always be tracked; reliance on sometimes inexperienced volunteers to perform important tasks related to finance; unpaid boards of directors with little or no financial expertise; and lack of income to hire staff with appropriate experience and skills in the financial area.

It is important to understand that it is not the job of an external auditor to detect mismanagement or fraud. Rather, the board of directors is ultimately responsible and the audit or finance committee is key in fulfilling this responsibility.

Several steps can be taken to help reduce the occurrence of fraud.

1. Ensure that the organization has implemented an effective ethics and compliance program such as a signed code of ethics or code of conduct at the time of employment.

2. Ensure that the audit committee and management are creating internal controls that address the appropriate risk areas and are functioning as designed.

3. Maintain oversight of significant funding arrangements.

4. Make a member of the audit or finance committee one of the signatories on all large cheque payments.

5. Ensure that there is continuous and open communication between management and the auditor such that all financial and internal control systems issues are addressed on a timely basis.

6. Maintain an open door policy towards fraud such that employees feel free to report suspected fraud to upper-level management or the board of directors. A formal "whistle-blower" policy may also be developed.

7. Develop a clear understanding of what is in each revenue and expense account, then compare actual to budgeted expenses and, when there are differences, insist on plausible explanations and further investigation of things not satisfactorily explained.

8. Train and develop board members in their duties as financial overseers of the organization.

What Happens When Fraud Is Discovered?

It is not often that organizations want to disclose a case of fraudulent action, but much can be learned from an article that appeared in *The Nonprofit Quarterly* (see Erickson (2005)). By fluke it was discovered that the trusted bookkeeper of a mid-sized nonprofit organization had embezzled a significant sum of money over the three years she was employed. The strategy adopted by the board was to:

*   Immediately institute internal controls to minimize the chance of embezzlement ever happening again.

*   Contract with an accounting firm to conduct an audit.

*   Assemble a team of volunteers to review and reconcile all bank statements during the period of the embezzlement.

*   Implement a complete recovery plan to help the organization to operate while dealing with the realities of the embezzlement, including seeking restitution through the bonding insurance policy, launching a civil suit against the embezzler, negotiating with the bank, and developing a communications plan.

In this particular case the fraud occurred because of pressure to reduce administrative costs, insufficient independent verification of the general ledger and financial statements, and the use of a "review engagement" by an accounting firm instead of a full audit, to save money.

The organization learned several lessons from its unfortunate experience:

- When a crisis like this happens, tell the truth to your members.

- Be sure that independent bank reconciliations and other random verifications of invoices and receipts are done on a monthly basis.

- Conduct yearly audits.

- Reinforce to board members their fiduciary and legal responsibilities.

- Make sure your financial and administrative employees share the values of the organization.

- Be sure to train management staff as well as volunteer treasurers in financial procedures.

- Good administrative and financial controls are expensive but worth it.

- Maintaining good relationships among the board, management, members, funders and donors is critical in building and funding an organization, especially in times of crisis.

FINANCIAL REPORTING

The financial reporting process may be thought of as the concluding phase of the cycle that begins with planning then moves to implementing and controlling. Reporting helps managers, the board and outsiders understand the current financial status of the organization. Managers want to know if they are on track and if the organization has sufficient financial resources to be viable. Donors want to know whether donated resources are put to good use. Creditors want to know whether the organization is a good credit risk. Foundations and corporations require support for funding requests. The Canada Revenue Agency wants to know that sufficient expenditures are being made on charitable programs and that the organization has not expended more than 10 per cent of its income on advocacy activities.

Many different reports may be created to satisfy the needs of these stakeholders for financial information. This section deals mostly with general purpose financial statements that are reported to the board, membership, donors, funders, government and the public. Quite often a nonprofit organization does not have the resources to produce several different reports on a regular basis, and therefore the general purpose financial statements produced either monthly or quarterly normally must meet several needs. Ideally they should be adapted for the required level of detail; managers need more detail than the board of directors who, in turn need more information than the general public. Of course the accounting system should be able to produce supplementary information whenever needed for managers and directors alike.

Board members should expect that the information they require will be presented in an understandable way. Financial reports can make a board's financial responsibilities more difficult to carry out if they are in different formats, do not contain sufficient detail or contain too much detail. It is inadequate, for example, for a report to contain a statement of operations only, without the balance sheet and other corresponding statements.

Generally Accepted Accounting Principles

It is advisable that all financial reports be prepared using generally accepted accounting principles or GAAP so that they are readily understandable by their users and somewhat comparable from organization to organization. It is important to understand that GAAP is not a set of prescriptive rules. GAAP does not specify how a particular expense must be accounted for or how expenses have to be shown within the financial statements. GAAP encompasses broad principles with some specific rules and procedures that are spelled out in the *Canadian Institute of Chartered Accountant's (CICA) Handbook*.

Effective January 1, 2012 new standards were issued for not-for-profits. Government not-for-profits are now required to use public sector accounting standards as the basis of reporting. All others, *i.e.*, non-government not-for-profits, are considered private sector not-for-profit organizations and have a choice of applying Accounting Standards for Not-for-Profit Organizations (ASNPO) or International Financial Reporting Standards (IFRS). IFRS is the globally accepted reporting standard for for-profit organizations. As IFRS does not address unique aspects of not-for-profits, the majority of non-government not-for-profit organizations have chosen to use ASNPO. Thus the remainder of the section will focus on ASNPO.

The new standard, ASNPO, is not significantly different from the old one. Accounting policy choices are still possible under ASNPO and these, like before, can impact the financial position of an organization. For example, as we will see later, the choice an organization makes to account for contributions (donations, grants *etc.*) using the restricted fund method or the deferral method of accounting will impact its bottom line. This is because there is a timing difference related to when contributions are recorded in the statement of operations as revenue. Choices must also be made in selecting accounting procedures, which affect the degree to which the financial statements are accurate. For example, accurately calculating the cost of printed documents made with a printer shared among multiple functions or programs would necessitate procedures to keep track of the number of print copies made for each function or program. However, this may not be worth the time staff must take to do it and some staff may fail to record all the print copies they make. Thus it may be determined that the cost of printing will be established with an approximation based on something like the relative proportion of staff in each function or program. The end result may be that the cost of each function or program is not totally accurate but is deemed to be good enough so as not to represent a significant financial misstatement in the overall cost of programs. Organizations that choose to allocate costs from one function to another such as in the case above, printing costs from general support costs to other functions or programs, must adhere to disclosure guidelines issued by the CICA, which are briefly mentioned later on in this section.

Another element of choice in deciding how to present an organization's financial statements is the grouping of accounts. Certain financial information must be disclosed in a certain fashion but in general an organization has a significant amount of latitude, particularly in the disclosure of revenue and expense items. (See the discussion of financial statements below.)

These choices should be guided by what is most useful in making decisions as well as what the organization believes users would find most useful for their purposes. For example, an organization which places a high value on accountability may decide that the users of its financial statement should have more information than less and therefore choose to disclose expenses of various programs and services separately rather than lumping them into one expense line called "programs and services". This same organization's donors may want to know what the organization spends to fundraise, in which case it may choose to report these costs on a functional basis rather than a line-by-line basis (such as the costs of all printing, telephone and advertising expenses).

Financial Statements

Financial statements for a nonprofit organization normally include a set of four different types of statements.

Statement of Financial Position or Balance Sheet

This statement is a snapshot of the organization at a particular point in time, which could be either today or tomorrow, the end of the month, or the last day of the fiscal year. It helps in assessing whether an organization has the financial resources to continue. It has three components representing the basic accounting equation (thus the term balance sheet):

$$\text{Assets} = \text{Liabilities} + \text{Equity (or Net Assets)}$$

Assets are what the organization owns or what is owed to them. They are a result of past transactions or events and therefore represent the collective history of the organization from its beginning to the date of the balance sheet report. Common examples of assets are cash, investments, accounts receivable, prepaid amounts, and capital assets such as computer equipment, furniture and buildings.

Liabilities are what the organization owes to someone else. Common examples of liabilities are accounts payable, payroll payable, loans payable, and deferred grant revenue (advanced to the organization before a project's completion).

Equity (more commonly referred to as net assets or fund balances) is what is left over from the assets once all the liabilities have been paid. The net asset section shows unrestricted net assets as well as those whose use is restricted to a particular purpose, such as a scholarship fund, particular program, or endowment.

Statement of Operations

Also known as the Statement of Revenues and Expenditures or Income Statement, this statement shows what the organization received as revenue (income) and what was spent (expenditures) over a particular period of time. It shows the cost of operating the organization and whether the organization raised sufficient funds to pay for its expenses, and acts as a bridge between the balance sheets at two different points in time. Common examples of revenue include contributions, fee-for-service revenue, and investment income. Common examples of expenses include salaries, rent, insurance and printing. The difference between what was received as revenue and what was spent as expenses is either a surplus (more revenue than expenses) or a deficit (more expenses than revenue).

The only disclosure requirement for revenue is that contributions should be disclosed by major source. There are no disclosure requirements for expenditures, but typically an organization will report expenditures by function, for example, the costs for research, education, fundraising, or various programs. It may also choose to report by object or type of expense, for example, salaries, rent and utilities. Reporting by object is more common in organizations operating one or a few programs. Reporting by function, while requiring more judgment especially where costs are shared among several functions, may be more useful to financial statement users who want to know how much an organization spends in such areas as fundraising or costs of administration.

Nonprofit organizations that classify their expenses by function must adhere to disclosure principles regarding allocated expenses. If fundraising and general support expenses are allocated to functions other than fundraising or general support, the policy for and nature of these expenses as well as the basis on which the allocations have been made must be explained. Also, the amounts allocated from each of these functions and the amounts and functions to which they have been allocated must be disclosed. General support expenses are considered to be those that are administrative in nature such as general management, board of directors' meeting costs, finance and payroll administration, and human resources. They are either considered a function in their own right or are allocated to the relevant functions that they support. These guidelines will assist users of financial information to better compare costs among organizations and to see if an organization allocated fundraising or other costs to programs or other functions, and the extent of the dollars allocated.

Statement of Changes in Net Assets or Fund Balances

This statement is sometimes combined with the statement of revenues and expenses, and provides details regarding the changes between the opening and closing fund balances, including any transfers of resources between funds. Since they do not result in changes in the organization's overall economic resources, transfers between funds should not be recognized as revenues or expenses. In general, this statement will reveal the extent to which an organization's operations have added to or depleted its net assets. As a specific example, it will also reveal the result of board decisions regarding fund transfers; for example, it could show funds from the operating fund being "put aside" for a specific purpose in an internally restricted fund.

Statement of Cash Flows

The statement of cash flows, also known as the statement of changes in financial position, is a record of all funds coming into the organization and all funds flowing out of the organization during a particular period of time. Financial information is presented on a "cash" basis versus that of the statement of operations, which is presented on an "accrual" basis. This statement shows the organization's ability to raise cash from various sources such as from grants or donations or the sale of assets or investments, and how cash is used to support programs and services.

Unique Aspects of Nonprofit Accounting and Financial Reporting

The unique aspects of accounting and financial reporting for nonprofit organizations centre upon accounting for revenues from contributions; capital assets and collections held; and income from controlled and related entities (such as foundations set up solely to benefit the organization).

Contributions

One of the key aspects of nonprofit accounting is that contributors to nonprofit organizations, be they governments, individuals, corporations, or other nonprofits, can impose restrictions on how the resources they contribute can be used. This influences the bases of many nonprofit accounting and reporting practices. It is absolutely critical for organizations to honour these restrictions and distinguish them in their financial statements so that readers understand what resources an organization has to spend at its discretion and what resources are designated for specific purposes. This is the genesis of fund accounting.

Restrictions on contributions can only be imposed by a contributor from outside the organization. A restriction may be implicit in the fundraising appeal by the organization or contributors may have imposed restrictions of their own making. For example, if the organization raised funds that it said would be used for a specific purpose such as health research, these funds would then have an implied restriction.

(It should be noted that a board of directors may impose internal restrictions on contributions but these are generally referred to as appropriations and are treated differently from externally restricted contributions.)

Fund accounting is the breaking up of an organization's financial statements on the basis of the purposes of various funds. Funds are usually based on the requirements of the financial statement users. For example, separate funds could be established for general operations, research, capital assets and endowments. Elements of a fund can include assets, liabilities, net assets, revenues and expenses.

A key decision for any nonprofit is determining its accounting policy for contribution revenue. This policy not only determines the format of the financial statements but it also determines the bottom line, *i.e.*, it is possible that the number representing revenues less expenses (the annual surplus or deficit) will be different depending upon the policy selected. Two methods are permitted — the deferral method and the restricted fund method.

The two methods treat unrestricted contributions in the same manner in that they should be accounted for as revenue in the year received. The difference between them stems from the treatment of income from restricted funds and endowments. Under the deferral method, restricted contributions that cannot be expended in the year in which they are received (because of the nature of the restriction) must be deferred and accounted for as revenue in the year in which the related expenses are incurred. The balance of deferred contributions represents the accumulation of restricted resources subject to restrictions that have yet to be complied with.

Contributions to an endowment are accounted for as direct increases in net assets, *i.e.*, not revenue since these contributions are considered to be permanent and thus will never be available to meet expenses associated with the organization's service delivery activities (though of course the income from endowment funds would be available for this purpose depending how the donor of the endowment specifies its use).

Under the restricted fund method, contributions are accounted for as revenue in the year received regardless of whether the related expenses were incurred. The balance of the restricted funds represents the accumulation of resources subject to restrictions that have yet to be complied with. Endowment contributions, however, are accounted for as direct increases in net assets of that fund in the year received, *i.e.*, not as revenue, since contributions to endowments are seen as permanent. In cases where a restricted contribution is received but there is no corresponding restricted fund, these contributions should be accounted for in the general fund using the deferral method.

The differences in the methods can be illustrated as follows:

Operating Statement	Deferral Method	Restricted Fund Method
Unrestricted Contributions	$30,000	$30,000
Endowment Contributions	$0	$20,000
Restricted Contributions	$0	$10,000
Total Revenues	**$30,000**	**$60,000**
Expenses	$25,000	$25,000
Revenues less expenses	**$5,000**	**$35,000**
Balance Sheet		
Assets	**$35,000**	**$35,000**
Liabilities (deferred contributions)	**$10,000**	**$0**
Unrestricted Fund	$5,000	$5,000
Restricted Fund	$0	$10,000
Endowment Fund	$20,000	$20,000
Total Net Assets	**$25,000**	**$35,000**
Total Liabilities & Net Assets	**$35,000**	**$35,000**

The decision of which method to choose is entirely organization-dependent and there are pros and cons for both. An organization with limited accounting resources might find the restricted fund method easier since it does not entail keeping track of deferred contributions. On the other hand, some may consider financial statements prepared using the deferral method easier to understand since there is only one column of numbers for each fiscal year, and the revenue number is more representative of what was available to be spent in that year.

Another unique aspect of nonprofit accounting occurs when an organization receives a contribution of materials and/or services. Currently, a choice exists as to whether or not these will be accounted for but, if they are, a fair value must be estimated using market or appraisal values and the goods or services must be used in the normal course of the organization's operations. Except in the case of donations of capital assets, accounting for donated materials and services does not affect an organization's bottom line since their value counted as both a contribution and an expense. For example, a donation of legal fees might be accounted for as a corporate donation and correspondingly as an administrative expense. Some volunteer staffed organizations find it too cumbersome to track this information reliably. Others with a tracking system use the value of donation receipts to record a contribution as revenue and corresponding expense. However, the Canada Revenue Agency does not allow receipts to be issued for services and thus any tracking system must be for internal or public relations purposes only. For example, the value of volunteer services is normally not calculated due to the difficulty in determining what it should be. Nevertheless, some organizations like to make this estimation for certain special reports in which they seek to impress external stakeholders with the value of volunteer contributions. For more on how to calculate the approximate value of volunteer work, see Quarter, Mook & Richmond (2003).

Often organizations are conservative when it comes to accounting for contributions and in many instances account for them only on a cash basis, *i.e.*, when a cheque or cash is received. However, it *is* possible to recognize pledges as contribution revenue, *i.e.*, on an accrual basis if: (1) the amount to be received can be reasonably estimated; and (2) the ultimate collection is reasonably assured. Bequest revenue most often cannot meet these two criteria since wills must be probated and can be subject to legal challenges.

Financial Statement Analysis

As previously noted, the readers of a nonprofit's financial statements are a diverse group, but all are interested in understanding the general financial health of the organization. The following elements of financial statement analysis are generally considered useful for both external stakeholders and the organization's board members and CEO. Although the elements discussed here are generic to most nonprofits, several other types of analysis are possible that are unique only to certain subsectors such as the performing arts, health, or membership associations.

Comparative Financial Statements

Significant understandings can come from comparing two years or more of financial information with one another, on both the balance sheet and statement of operations. While general purpose financial statements generally only have the preceding year's information as a comparison, the interim financial statements circulated to management and the board should at least compare actual year-to-date results with the current budget as well as the actual for the previous year (covering the same time period). The board should expect reasonable explanations of any significant differences.

The Bottom Line

Interpreting the bottom line (annual surplus or deficit) from operations is tricky in a nonprofit. Nonprofits are not supposed to earn profits by their very nature so incurring more than an inconsequential surplus is generally frowned upon by contributors who want their contributions used, not sitting in a bank. On the other hand, deficits are also generally frowned upon as a sign of poor financial management. So what is the right bottom line? The answer is that it depends on the organization's situation, and financial statements do not usually provide the kind of information needed to properly assess this. There are valid reasons why an organization may be accumulating annual surpluses, for example, to establish a permanent financial reserve to assist with cash flow during the year or to "save up" for a major capital expenditure in the future. It may also be the case that a substantial unexpected unrestricted contribution was received during the year that could not be prudently expended in the same year. And, as we saw earlier in this chapter, the choice of accounting policies will also affect the bottom line.

Expense or Cost Ratios

These days more focus is being placed on administration and fundraising costs by donors and funders. It is suggested by some that donors ask several questions before giving (see Ministry of the Attorney General (2004b)). Two such questions are: "How much of my donation goes directly to helping others?" and "How much goes for administration and fundraising costs?" There are several ways to calculate this though no universal agreement exists as to which is the best one. The following are four examples:

Ratio of Program Expenses to Total Expenses. Dividing the program expenses by total expenses results in a percentage that indicates how much of every dollar spent is spent on programs. If an organization has more than one program area, these obviously need to be accumulated for purposes of this calculation.

Ratio of Administration Expenses to Total Expenses. Dividing the total administrative expenses by total expenses results in a percentage that indicates how much of every dollar spent by an organization is spent on administrative activities.

Ratio of Fundraising Expenses to Total Expenses. Dividing fundraising expenses by total expenses results in a percentage that indicates how much of every dollar spent is spent to raise money.

Ratio of Contribution Revenues to Fundraising Expenses. Dividing the total fundraising expenses by the total of all contributions or donated revenue indicates how much it costs to raise a dollar. This same formula can be applied to each type of fundraising revenue. For example, knowing special event revenue and expenses you can calculate how much it costs to raise a dollar using special events.

A word of caution — while these cost ratios may be important to know, they each have their limitations and shortcomings. First, there are many factors that influence these ratios that do not necessarily reflect the organization's efficiency in using its resources, for example: its size, its age, or the degree of involvement of volunteers in its operation. For instance, a relatively new organization trying to get established may have higher fundraising and administration costs than a more established one due to the degree of investment required to set up its programs and establish its base of donors.

Second, financial measurement is imprecise. There are no standards for what constitutes a program versus an administration versus a fundraising cost. The categorization of these costs is particularly troublesome in the case where some costs are shared. For example, how should the cost of rent incurred to operate the programs and house the administrative and fundraising functions be accounted for? Should this cost be allocated among these functions? If so, how? By determining the relative square footage occupied by these functions? By the relative number of staff assigned to these functions? What if some of the staff work in several functions? How should their costs be allocated?[12] While the CICA guidelines on allocated expenses will make it easier to compare amongst organizations, organizations will continue to apply a variety of allocation methodologies making accurate apples to apples comparisons virtually impossible.

Third, these measures may act as indicators of efficiency but this is not the same as effectiveness. An organization may have comparatively high costs of administration and higher-than-average fundraising expenses but be much more effective than others in actually achieving the results it was created to achieve.

Finally there is the question of how efficient is efficient? As we saw in the fraudulent action case cited in the "Internal Control" section, administration costs were in a sense too efficient in that they were too low, which led to poor control systems and thus made it easy for embezzlement to occur. The same might be said of fundraising costs. Allocating too few resources to fundraising may be detrimental to an organization in the long term.

How is all this attention on cost ratios affecting nonprofits? A study done by Peter Frumkin and Mark T. Kim at the Hauser Centre for Nonprofit Organizations at The Kennedy School of Government suggests that, while donors seem to be more interested in ratios, so far this bottom line management approach does not appear to be helping nonprofits attract more contributions (see Frumkin & Kim (2001)). The nature of the organization's mission and the personal commitment that donors have to it still matter more. However, some have challenged this notion arguing that cost ratios do affect how some donors assess their contributions to nonprofits.

In conclusion, while these ratios and other financial measures provide useful tools for examining a nonprofit's operations, it is important to understand their weaknesses and use them only in combination with other non-financial measures that address an organization's effectiveness in achieving its mission, and general information about the organization's plans for the future.

---

[12] A recent U.S. study revealed that tracking personnel time was a low priority for most organizations due to the low perceived benefit of the practice. When done at all, most of the organizations surveyed had one or two staff members make a judgment once a year about how everyone spent their time. The study questioned the value of these inaccurate cost ratios.

REFERENCES

Canadian Institute of Chartered Accountants, *Guide to Accounting Standards for Not-for-Profit Organizations in Canada* (Toronto: Canadian Institute of Chartered Accountants, 2012). Online at: <http://www.cica.ca/focus-on-practice-areas/small-and-medium-practices-(smp)/implementing-the-accounting-standards/item69429.pdf>.

Deloitte LLP, *The Effective Not-for-Profit Board. A value-driving force* (Montreal, QC: Deloitte LLP, 2013). Online at: <http://www.deloitte. com/assets/Dcom-Canada/Local%20Assets/Documents/Public%20Sector/ca_en_gov_Effective-NPO-Board_061113.pdf>.

T. Erickson, "How We Survived an Embezzlement" (2005) 12:2 The Nonprofit Quarterly, online at: <http://www.nonprofitquarterly.org/management/682-how-we-survived-an-embezzlement.html>.

P. Frumkin & M.T. Kim, "Strategic Positioning and the Financing of Nonprofit Organizations" (2001) 61:3 Public Administration Review 266-275.

K. Keating & P. Frumkin, "Reengineering Nonprofit Financial Accountability: Toward a More Reliable Foundation for Regulation" (2003) 63:1 Public Administration Review 3-15.

Ministry of the Attorney General, "Duties, Responsibilities and Powers of Directors and Trustees of Charities, Charities Bulletin #3", Information from the Public Guardian and Trustee's Charitable Property Program (Toronto, ON: Government of Ontario, 2004). Online at: <http://www.attorneygeneral.jus.gov.on.ca/english/family/pgt/charbullet/bullet3.asp>.

Ministry of the Attorney General, *Charitable Donations – Get the Facts Before You Give* (Toronto, ON: Government of Ontario, 2004). Online at: <http://www.attorneygeneral.jus.gov.on.ca/english/family/pgt/charitabledonations.pdf>.

J. Quarter, L. Mook & B.J. Richmond, *What Counts: Social Accounting for NonProfits and Cooperatives* (Toronto: Prentice Hall, 2003).

The Committee of Sponsoring Organizations of the Treadway Commission, *Internal Control — Integrated Framework* (Durham NC: American Institute of Certified Public Accountants, 2013).

FURTHER RESOURCES

This chapter has served as an introduction to the budgeting, controlling and reporting aspects of financial management. Additional resources are available for those who wish to pursue more in-depth studies. Among those the interested reader might consult are the following:

American Institute of Certified Public Accountants, *The AICPA Audit Committee Toolkit: Not-for-Profit Organizations*, 2d ed. (New York: AICPA, 2010).

R.N. Anthony & D.W. Young, *Management Control in Nonprofit Organizations*, 7th ed. (Boston: McGraw-Hill/Irwin, 2003).

D.H. Cornacchia, "Accountants on Board: A guide to becoming a director of a not-for-profit organization" (Canadian Institute of Chartered Accountants). Online at: <http://www.cica.ca/publications/list-of-publications/manual/item61633.pdf>.

B. Deazeley & R. Devitt, "Increasing Public Scrutiny of Not-for-Profit Organizations" (2010) 15 Director Journal 24-26.

M. Dropkin & A. Hayden, *The Cash Flow Management Book for Nonprofits: A Step-by-Step Guide for Managers, Consultants, and Boards* (San Francisco, CA: Jossey-Bass, 2001).

M. Dropkin, J. Halpin & B. LaTouche, *The Budget Building Book for Nonprofits: A Step-by-Step Guide for Managers and Boards* (San Francisco, CA: Jossey-Bass, 2007).

S.A. Finkler, *Financial Management for Public, Health, and Not-for-Profit Organizations*, 4th ed. (Upper Saddle River, NJ: Pearson Education Inc., 2013).

Imagine Canada, *Charity Tax Tools* (2013). Online at: <http://charitytax.imaginecanada.ca/>.

Muttart Foundation, *Financial Responsibilities of Not-for-Profit Boards: A Self-Guided Workbook* (Edmonton, AB: The Muttart Foundation, 2008). Online at: <http://www.muttart.org/sites/default/ files/downloads/publications/financial_responsibilities.pdf>.

S. Persaud & A. Mason, "Finance and Audit Committees Can Play a Key Role Both in Detecting Fraud and in Preventing It" *Canadian Fundraiser* (October 2000).

W. Ruppel, *Not-for-Profit Accounting Made Easy* (New York: John Wiley & Sons, 2003).

The Canadian Institute of Chartered Accountants, *CICA Handbook* (Toronto: CICA, 2013).

The Canadian Institute of Chartered Accountants (2013), *The Not-for-Profit (NPO) Director Series* (2013). Online at: <http://www.cica.ca/focus-on-practice-areas/governance-strategy-and-risk/not-for-profit-director-series/index.aspx>.

Voluntary Sector Initiative, *Resources for Accountability and Financial Management in the Voluntary Sector*, A Project of the Capacity Joint Table funded by the Government of Canada (2003). Online at: <http://www.vsi-isbc.org/eng/funding/financial_guide/resources_english.pdf>.

Chapter 11

MANAGING THE HUMAN DIMENSION IN NONPROFIT ORGANIZATIONS: PAID STAFF AND VOLUNTEERS

Agnes Meinhard
Ryerson University

INTRODUCTION

An organization is a complex social system comprising various groups of individuals working together towards a common purpose. A fundamental challenge for management is to co-ordinate the actions of these individuals in order to ensure the achievement of the organization's goals. At a minimum, this requires knowledge of the organization's technologies and specific task requisites in order to match the people best suited for the jobs. At a higher level, this entails understanding the diversity of individuals in the organization with respect to their personalities, cultural backgrounds, values, attitudes, emotions, abilities, motivations and ambitions; and being able to leverage this knowledge to ensure the smooth functioning of the organization. Whether or not an organization has a formal Human Resource (HR) department or manager, a foundation of good human resource practices is essential to the long-term success of an organization.

Although there is a common basis for good human resource practices that pertains to all organizations, nonprofit organizations differ with respect to several characteristics: governance structure, incentive structure and reliance on volunteers. These unique features warrant special consideration. Therefore, this chapter focuses on both identifying the basic concepts and discussing the unique aspects of managing the human dimension in nonprofit organizations. The chapter begins with a snapshot of volunteer and paid participation in the nonprofit sector in Canada. This is followed by a discussion of key concepts related to managing people in organizations, and the particular challenges faced by nonprofit organizations. Since volunteers are an integral part of most nonprofit organizations, the chapter's third section focuses on the special case of recruiting and managing volunteers. The chapter ends with some concluding observations on how nonprofit organizations can apply the insights raised in the chapter to benefit their operations, even in low-budget conditions.

LABOUR AND VOLUNTEER PARTICIPATION IN THE NONPROFIT SECTOR

The importance of the nonprofit and charitable sector in providing social, cultural and recreational benefits to Canadians has long been valued, however the size of its contribution to Canada's economy and job market is only now being recognized. Sixty-nine thousand out of approximately 160,000 nonprofit organizations employ 1.2 million Canadians, which comprises 7.2 per cent of workforce (HR Council for the Voluntary and Nonprofit Sector (2008a)). Mostly on the strength of the wages, salaries and supplementary income paid out by nonprofit organizations, the sector accounts for 6.8 per cent of the nation's GDP. This compares favourably to the contributions to GDP by the agriculture (1.5 per cent), mining, oil and gas (4.0 per cent), retail (5.0 per cent) or food and accommodation (2.3 per cent) sectors. Even without considering the contribution of hospitals and post-secondary institutions, which are the major employers of the nonprofit sector, the rest of the nonprofit sector still accounts for 3.9 per cent of the GDP (Statistics Canada (2004, Figure 2, at 6)).

Almost three-quarters of the jobs in the sector are concentrated in the largest 2 per cent of organizations; half of them are to be found in hospitals and universities (NSNVO, 2005). The majority of nonprofit organizations (63 per cent) are small and operate with an annual budget of less than $100,000. Only 30 per cent of these small organizations have paid staff and they generally number fewer than two full-time employees. Almost three quarters of the employees in the nonprofit sector are women, compared with less than half in the for-profit sector (HR Council (2008b)). The majority of managers in the sector are women as well, ranging from 50 per cent in hospitals and universities to 66 per cent in other nonprofits. This compares favourably with the for-profit sector, where only 36 per cent of managers are women (McMullen & Schellenberg (2002, at 40)). According to a recent survey of 2,043 employees of nonprofit organizations, members of Canada's ethnic and racial minorities are under-represented in the nonprofit workforce. Only 11 per cent self-identified as being members of minority racial/ethnic groups (HR Council (2008b)).

Most nonprofit organizations (54 per cent) rely exclusively on volunteers to carry out their missions (NSNVO (2005)). Twelve and a half million Canadians volunteer in nonprofit organizations (Imagine Canada 2009) but because many volunteer at several organizations, "nonprofit and voluntary organizations report a combined volunteer complement of over 19 million" (NSNVO (2005, at 32)). This translates into 2.1 billion hours of volunteer labour representing about 7.5 full-time jobs per voluntary organization for a total of 1.2 million full time jobs.

Figure 1: by the Numbers

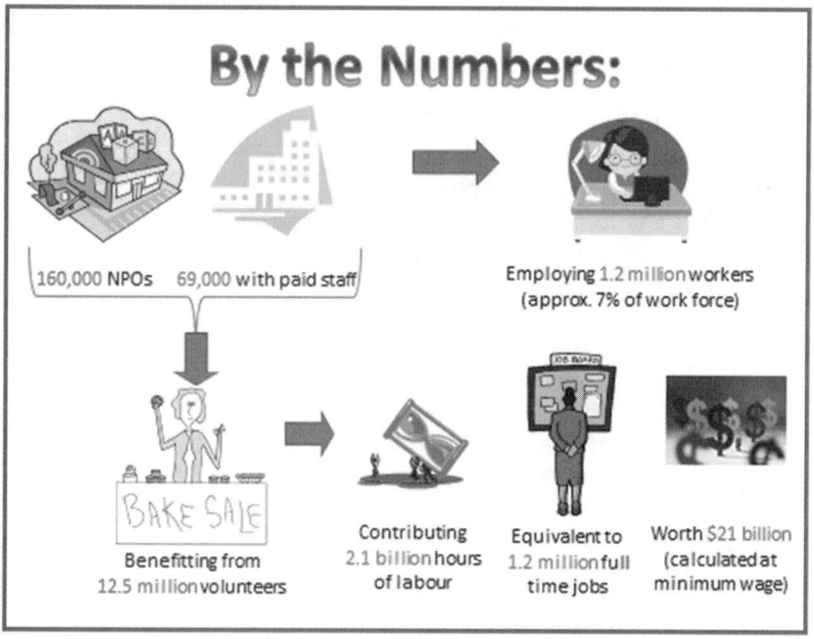

By the Numbers:

160,000 NPOs 69,000 with paid staff

Employing 1.2 million workers (approx. 7% of work force)

BAKE SALE

Benefitting from 12.5 million volunteers

Contributing 2.1 billion hours of labour

Equivalent to 1.2 million full time jobs

Worth $21 billion (calculated at minimum wage)

HUMAN RESOURCE MANAGEMENT IN CANADIAN NONPROFIT ORGANIZATIONS

In the broadest sense of the term, human resource management (HRM) refers to all management and leadership practices involving the co-ordination of paid and/or unpaid members of a social, political, cultural or economic enterprise, to work towards achieving organizational goals. In the narrowest sense of the term, it refers to a specialized field of organizational management dealing with the administrative functions associated with staffing an organization: hiring, training, compensation and firing. However, even in its narrowest sense it is far more complex, involving the creation of an organizational infrastructure that enables employees and volunteers to accomplish their tasks and reach their goals. This entails clearly defining the jobs, resources and skills needed to fulfill the organization's mission, ensuring a safe and positive work environment where people are treated fairly, providing mechanisms for managing conflict, maintaining open lines of communication, giving timely feedback and rewarding good work. It also involves finding people with the appropriate knowledge and abilities to accomplish required tasks, helping them navigate organizational change through training and development, and engaging in strategic human resource planning.

Figure 2: Basic Human Resource Functions

> Ensuring the organization has the right number of people with the necessary competencies to meet its goals.
> This is achieved through:
> - job analyses;
> - recruitment strategies;
> - selection protocols;
> - hiring procedures;
> - compensation packages and benefits,
> - orientation and training;
> - professional development;
> - performance evaluation;
> - disciplinary protocols;
> - termination procedures; and
> - ensuring a safe and welcoming workplace through:
>   - conflict management policies,
>   - health and safety protocols,
>   - discrimination and harassment policies, and
>   - mediating solutions to problems in the workplace.

The vast majority of nonprofit organizations do not have specialized HR units, nor even designated HR officers. It is not surprising then, that human resource management was earmarked by the Voluntary Sector Initiative (VSI) as an area that needs to be developed. With VSI funding, a thorough and informative Website was created providing detailed descriptions of the various HR functions. The site, called *Human Resources in the Voluntary Sector*, also has explicit "how to" instructions for organizations that are interested in developing and/or improving HR practices.[1]

A Brief Review of Basic Human Resource Functions

Human resource management has evolved from a "welfare officer's" position in the mid-19th century, created to help management comply with newly-passed workers' rights legislation, to a senior management position involving long term strategic planning (Torrington & Hall (1987)). Until the early third of the 20th century, despite being paid agents of the factory owners, welfare officers saw their role as representing the interests of the workers by advocating for ever more enlightened management practices. However, as unionization became more prevalent, the HR officer assumed the role of representing management in contract negotiations, and progressively became a more integrated player in the management team and in strategic planning (Torrington & Hall (1987)). Today, the basic human resource functions incorporate both the worker's welfare aspects and the strategic planning aspects.

In the Canadian nonprofit sector, human resource management tends to be focused more on workers' welfare issues than on strategic managerial practices (Haiven (1998)). Indeed, research indicates that in Canada, human resource management practices are not aligned with organizational strategy (Akingbola (2005)), rather, they appear to concentrate on mediating solutions to problems in the workplace and ensuring that workers' needs are met (Haiven (1998)).

Ultimately the main purpose of human resources management is to ensure that the organization has the right number of people with the necessary competencies to meet its goals and fulfill its mission. (Competencies can be defined as the abilities, individual values, personality traits and other personal characteristics that lead to superior

---

[1]   See online: <http://www.hrvs-rhsbc.ca/>.

performance in an organization.) In order to do this, an organization not only has to find the right people to help achieve its goals, but also to provide working conditions which will protect it from disruptive turnover rates. This spans a vast array of formalized HR functions: job analyses; recruitment strategies; selection protocols; hiring procedures; compensation packages including medical and dental benefits and vacation time; orientation and training; professional development; performance evaluation; disciplinary protocols; and termination procedures. HR management also involves ensuring a safe and welcoming workplace by having policies in place (*e.g.*, conflict management, health and safety, discrimination and harassment) that protect the employees' physical, intellectual and emotional wellbeing and provide them with help and resources when needed. The organization benefits when all of these functions are carried out well: a competent and satisfied workforce (paid and volunteer) increases the likelihood that the organization will be effective and efficient in carrying out its goals (Macaleer & Jones (2003)).

Each of the functions listed above involves specialized knowledge that is often not resident, nor indeed always necessary, in small nonprofit organizations (Meinhard, Sakinofsky & Matthews (2009). It is critically important for the leader of a nonprofit organization to recognize the salient role good HR management plays in determining the success of an organization. Today, information and support is increasingly accessible over the Internet, through seminars and continuing education courses geared to nonprofit organizations, and through a consortium-like sharing of outsourced HR services among several organizations. Unfortunately, many leaders are unaware of these resources (Meinhard *et al.* (2009)).

The Benefits of Human Resource Planning

Nonprofit organizations in Canada, as elsewhere, are working in an environment characterized by continuous change, uncertain and scarce financial resources, and increasing demands for services as the government continues to withdraw from directly providing a social safety net. In order to survive and fulfill their missions in such an environment, nonprofits cannot afford to waste any of their resources, especially human resources. They therefore have to anticipate organizational needs, avoiding both shortages and surpluses of human resources. They can control labour costs by determining the optimal complement of volunteers and staff. By planning ahead, they can co-ordinate recruitment campaigns to achieve cost efficiencies when hiring new workers or bringing in new volunteers. Well-developed HR planning helps to improve performance, increase productivity and reduce employee and volunteer dissatisfaction and turnover (Macaleer & Jones (2003)).

On the other hand, inadequate human resource planning can be both financially and organizationally costly. Without proper planning, organizations may be unable to fill their specific human resource needs, thus weakening their performance capabilities. For example, unfilled positions can be costly both from a productivity perspective — work not done, and from a human perspective — needed services are not provided. In such cases, additional stress is placed on remaining staff as they work extra hours to compensate for vacant positions. In large organizations, poor planning and/or lack of communication between departments about their anticipated needs can result in one department laying off individuals while another department in the same organization is acquiring individuals with the same or similar competencies. The impact on morale is immeasurable, but its disruptive effect on the social fabric of the organization is palpable. Given the benefits of forecasting human resources needs, and the potential costs to the organization of inadequate planning, it would seem negligent not to engage in strategic human resource management. Yet, for a variety reasons, most nonprofit organizations do not plan ahead.

Human resource planning involves three main activities: forecasting human resource needs, analyzing the availability of human resources both within the organization and in the general society, and balancing supply and demand.

- Forecasting an organization's current and future human resource needs involves determining: what activities are needed to carry out the organization's goals (job analysis); what competencies are required for accomplishing the activities (skills analysis); and what financial resources are necessary to support these activities.

- Analyzing the supply of human resources both within the organization and in the external environment involves monitoring changes in positions and skills and determining: whether current staff and volunteers have the skills necessary to forward the organization's goals (skills inventory); whether training can prepare current staff for the new organizational needs; or whether even with training and upgrading, new staff/volunteers will be required.

- Balancing supply and demand involves adjusting the organization's workforce in response to its needs. If the demand for staff and volunteers exceeds the internal supply, or the internal candidates are unsuitable, the organization must determine the markets from which best potential candidates may be attracted and set in motion the recruitment and section process. If the supply of potential staff and volunteers exceeds the demand for human resources rebalancing is necessary and may be achieved through any combination of the following: re-assigning employees and volunteers; reducing surplus through attrition; encouraging early retirement or buying out; job sharing, work sharing; reducing working week; temporarily laying people off; and terminating certain jobs.

With HR planning systems in place an organization can move quickly to effectively balance the human resource needs of the organization. (For more detail, see "Human Resources Management in a Dynamic Environment" and "Strategic Human Resources Management and Planning" in Joan E. Pynes, ed., *Human Resources Management for Public and Nonprofit Organizations* (San Francisco, CA: Jossey-Bass, 1997), at 5-16 and 17-28.)

Human Resource Management as Practised in Canadian Nonprofit Organizations

As already stated, few Canadian nonprofit organizations have formal HR departments or specially designated HR managers. However, despite the lack of formal HRM mechanisms, for the most part, nonprofit employers furnish their workers with good working conditions and opportunities for full participation. As a series of reports published by the Canadian Policy Research Network (CPRN) on nonprofit employers indicates, the smaller and less hierarchical workplaces in the nonprofit sector are more likely to create an atmosphere of mutual trust and respect through shared responsibility and decision-making practices. They are also more likely to provide personal and family support systems (McMullen & Brisbois (2003)), as well as offer their employees training opportunities, most of which occur outside the organization (McMullen & Schellenberg (2003, Table 11, at 28)). These positive working conditions are important because nonprofit organizations are often at a disadvantage in terms of their ability to offer salaries that are competitive with the for-profit and public sectors. In fact, employee satisfaction in the nonprofit sector is similar to that in the for-profit sector, despite significant wage differentials (McMullen & Schellenberg (2003)).

Figure 3: Challenges of HR management in nonprofit organization

> 1. A dearth of relevant guidelines for managing human resources;
> 2. A lack of HR management training;
> 3. Insufficient financial resources;
> 4. Employment uncertainty under project funding; and
> 5. Tension between volunteers and paid staff.

The Challenge of Human Resource Management for Nonprofit Organizations

Nonprofit managers face several challenges in creating an infrastructure that provides optimal conditions for maximizing their human resource potential: (1) a dearth of relevant guidelines for managing human resources; (2) a lack of HR management training; (3) insufficient financial resources; (4) employment uncertainty under project funding; and (5) tension between volunteers and paid staff.

Dearth of Relevant Guidelines

There are few, if any, guidelines written specifically for nonprofit organizations. This is not surprising as more than half of all nonprofit organizations rely exclusively on volunteer labour. Only 20 per cent of nonprofit organizations have more than four paid employees (NSNVO (2005)). Textbooks on human resource management and practices focus on the corporate sector. This does not reflect the reality of the smaller nonprofits with limited funds and very few employees. Nevertheless, HR management is relevant to all organizations.

Lack of HR Management Training

In all but large nonprofit organizations HR functions are left to the executive director, who is rarely trained in HR management (Brudney (1999)), and/or a committee of the organization's Board of Directors. In either case, the day-to-day HR issues that arise are the concern of the executive director. Lacking HR training, many of the necessary mechanisms for such matters as recruitment and selection, harassment control and conflict management are not in place, sometimes leading to strained relations in the workplace. Most executive directors (EDs), trying to guide their organizations through changing conditions and dealing with higher priority problems, are understandably loath to add the tasks of HR management to their already heavy loads (Meinhard *et al.*, (2009)).

Insufficient Financial Resources

Most nonprofit organizations operate with very tight budgets, influencing not only the size of their employee component, but also their incentive structures. Salaries in the nonprofit sector are generally lower than in the for-profit sector. With the exception of hospitals and universities, managers in the nonprofit sector earn approximately 18 per cent less than those in the for-profit sector and professionals earn 14 per cent less, despite the fact that 28 per cent of nonprofit employees have university degrees as opposed to 15 per cent in the for-profit sector. Wages are equivalent at the clerical level (McMullen & Schellenberg (2003)). While for-profit organizations can offer their employees monetary incentives, in nonprofit organizations, there is little room for significant financial incentives; nonprofits therefore rely on the goodwill and dedication of their paid workers. As one employee stated: "I was hired to work half-time, but there is no way the work can get done on a half-time position, so I basically volunteer the rest of the hours I need to complete the work" (Meinhard *et al.* (2004)). In nonprofit organizations, preventing employee burnout is more of a problem than motivating them.

Employment Uncertainty under Project Funding

By and large, governments are increasingly funding individual projects rather than providing stable, long-term operational grants (Pal (1997)). Because nonprofit organizations are so heavily reliant on government funding, the uncertainty inherent in these new funding practices makes it more difficult for them to plan their human resource needs, and attract skilled people (Akingbola (2005)). This is as true for the larger organizations with a formal HR department as it is for the small organizations. In the smaller organizations, the situation is exacerbated as the juggling of hiring and firing decisions is placed on the shoulders of an already over-extended executive director. In a climate of increasing accountability concerns, governments and other funders are demanding more frequent and more detailed reports. This is also placing a strain on nonprofit organizations, as employee time spent on preparing reports is at the expense of time spent on mission activities. This leads to frustration, dissatisfaction and a drop in productivity.

Tension between Volunteers and Paid Staff

Tensions between volunteers and paid staff can occur at two levels. First, there may be tension among employees and volunteers at the front lines where paid employees and volunteers are often doing similar work. This will be discussed in more detail later in the chapter. A second source of tension and conflict lies in the governance structure of nonprofit organizations, which is characterized by a shared, but legally unequal, leadership between the chairperson of the volunteer board and the paid professional executive director. As O'Connell (1985, at 52) points out, "The greatest source of friction and breakdown in voluntary organizations of all types, sizes, ages and relative degrees of sophistication and excellence relates to misunderstandings and differing perceptions between the voluntary board president and staff directors." This creates role ambiguity and role conflict. Role ambiguity occurs when boundaries between board and staff are blurred and people are uncertain about their job duties, performance expectations, level of authority and other job conditions. Often volunteer board members misinterpret their responsibilities and try to micromanage the organization's paid employees. In small nonprofit organizations the tasks of governance, management and operations are undifferentiated as everyone chips in to fulfill the organization's mission and goals. As an organization grows and recruits professional staff, management is delegated to the executive director. However, often board members continue to "work in the trenches". This mixing of roles can often lead to conflict. On the other hand, lack of involvement in the organization by board members may cause paid employees to feel directionless.

Many of these challenges are being addressed. The dearth of human resource guidelines specifically tailored for the nonprofit sector is being rectified through easily accessible HR information repositories such as the HRSV. In addition, during the past decade several Canadian universities and colleges have begun to offer programs in nonprofit management studies to address the lack of management skills among leaders in the nonprofit sector. With respect to insufficient financial resources and reliance on government funding, recent statistics and surveys indicate that nonprofit organizations are increasingly seeking partnerships with corporations (Meinhard & Foster (2003)) and diversifying resources in order to decrease their dependence on government (Foster & Meinhard (2005)). The most recently available statistics indicate that between 1996 and 2003, the corporate sector's share of support for the voluntary sector has increased from 1 per cent to 3 per cent of the total nonprofit revenue. The nonprofit sector's earned income, from dues, sales, rentals and other commercial activities now accounts for 35 per cent of the proportion of income to the sector, up from 30 per cent, while the government's share is down to 49 per cent from 56 per cent (Standing Committee on Finance (1996); NSNVO (2005)). This trend in revenue diversification has implications for greater independence for at least some nonprofits and their ability to plan for their human resource needs. Finally, as suggested in the following section, there are ways to mitigate the tensions created by the leadership duality that is characteristic of nonprofit organizations.

The Role of the Board in Human Resource Management

Canadian law stipulates that nonprofit boards are fully responsible for the affairs of the organization and the conduct of all its members. They have ultimate jurisdiction over staff. Normally the board delegates this responsibility to a chief executive officer if there is one; however, if the organization is too small to have a staff, the board can fulfill the HR functions itself usually through an HR committee with, if possible, an HR expert to sit on it.

In any case, well-functioning nonprofit boards set the tone for their entire organization. First, they must ensure that the organization is in compliance with the various provincial and federal laws governing employment relationships such as employment standards, collective agreements and labour standards, occupational health and safety, pension benefits, pay equity, employment equity and human rights. Second, the board is responsible for ensuring that the quality of work life for those in the organization is high. This means fair compensation and benefits, good working hours, and policies that ensure equitable treatment of staff and volunteers. These are the cornerstones of a good workplace. Furthermore, the board should ensure that the organization has in place systems that lead to performance evaluation of staff and volunteers and enable them to receive feedback about organizational effectiveness and staff morale. It is also the board's job to ensure that the organization's work values and ethics are conveyed to all their members, both paid staff and volunteers. This is critical in the case of organizations that serve vulnerable clients such as people with disabilities, at-risk children and youth, and abused women and children, to name but a few.

Much of the role ambiguity found in nonprofit organizations stems from the lack of clearly defined role descriptions for members of the board and staff. When the roles of board members and staff are clearly delineated, and feedback mechanisms are in place, there is less room for role ambiguity. And when the relationship between the board and the executive director is more realistically defined as a partnership, rather than a hierarchy of power, role conflict may be averted. A partnership model of governance recognizes that EDs are the *de facto* leaders, given that they have information and expertise about how their organizations operate on a day-to-day basis. The organization is more central in their lives than it is in the lives of the board members they serve, many of whom hold other jobs and may not have been members for a long time (Herman & Heimovics (1991)). Therefore, realistically, it is EDs who assure that the governance function is properly organized and maintained (Herman & Heimovics (1991); Drucker (1990)). Executive directors are expected not to usurp the board's role, but to work with it, not only on decision-making and policy formulation, but also in providing criteria for the evaluation of programs and individual performance. The challenge is to find the middle ground between a rubber-stamp board that abdicates its responsibilities to the ED, and an overbearing, micro-managing board that creates tension among the staff. Regular board development sessions, and board orientation programs for new board members can go a long way to enhance board and staff members' understanding of their roles in the organization. (See Chapter 3 for more on boards.)

THE SPECIAL CASE OF VOLUNTEERS

As the statistics at the beginning of this chapter indicate, volunteers are the backbone of the nonprofit sector. No estimates of their financial worth can truly gauge the value of their contribution to Canadian society. They invigorate our communities, preserve our parks and waterways, champion our arts and cultural institutions and support recreational facilities and amateur sports. They also help immigrants settle in their new communities and enrich the lives of our less fortunate citizens, thus strengthening Canada's social capital.

The noun "volunteer" is commonly understood to refer to someone who engages in an activity of his or her own free will for the benefit of others, without receiving monetary remuneration. There is some controversy in the literature with respect to the parameters of the term (Wilson (2000)), as the word is often used in ways that extend beyond this basic meaning. A prime example of this would be high school students who "volunteer" in order to fulfill curriculum requirements, or experts who "volunteer" their time to give free advice but accept symbolic monetary honoraria. Cnaan and associates (1996) identified four dimensions that underlie the concept of volunteering: (a) free choice (is there any coercion?); (b) remuneration (is any reward of monetary value received in exchange for an activity?); (c) context (does the activity take place in a formal or informal setting?); and (d) beneficiaries (who benefits from the activity?).

In this chapter, the term "volunteer" is used in a broad sense to include all those who freely engage in an activity within a nonprofit organizational context to benefit others in some way, without receiving monetary compensation. Volunteers serve their chosen organizations in many ways: providing direct service to clients, helping with administrative activities, contributing expertise, and serving as a director on an organization's board.

Formal volunteering most likely originated in religious institutions. It was an active expression of the religious obligation of performing charitable deeds — a cornerstone of all religions (de Schweinitz (1943)). As institutions run by religious orders were set up to help care for the physical needs of the sick, the orphaned and the handicapped, lay people began to contribute time as well as alms to the poor (de Schweinitz (1943); Feingold (1987); Martin (1985)). Because of the nature of the work, most of these early volunteers were women. Voluntary association was one of the few socially sanctioned extra-domestic activities available to women. Thus, for many, volunteerism played a liberating role in their lives, giving them their only experience in the public realm (McCarthy (1990)). Eventually, women began forming their own associations and by the mid-1800s, they were administering organizations in the fields of philanthropy, arts and sciences, and social reform (Kaminer (1984)), that were both efficient and effective in carrying out their missions (Scott (1990)). These organizations laid the foundations of the modern voluntary sector (Lewis (1994); Odendahl (1994)) and strongly influenced the creation of the social welfare state (O'Neill (1994)). By the beginning of the twentieth century, helping the poor and the handicapped became more secularized and professionalized as social workers and other professionally trained workers gradually replaced volunteers. Congregational voluntary action declined as the state formed a partnership with nonprofit organizations to provide essential social and cultural services (Cnaan et al. (1993)). With generous funding, some nonprofit organizations were able to hire professionals; in these organizations, volunteers became adjuncts. However, the bulk of organizations now, as then, still rely on volunteers.

Figure 4: Reasons for volunteering

1. Helping others
2. Fulfilling religious or social obligation
3. Identification with a "good cause"
4. Instrumental benefit: Acquiring skills, experience, social recognition
5. Affective benefit: New friendships and social network

Indeed, 12 million Canadians (45 per cent of people 15 years and older) volunteer two billion hours of their time in nonprofit organizations. This averages to 168 hours per volunteer, but these hours are not distributed equally among the volunteers. One-quarter of volunteers contribute more than three-quarters of volunteer hours. This means that voluntary organizations in Canada rely on 11 per cent of the population to do the bulk of volunteering.

Despite these encouraging numbers, many organizations claim they are facing "a crisis in volunteering". In fact, almost three quarters of all volunteers are engaged by only 6 per cent of nonprofit organizations (NSNVO (2005)). The earliest signs of this crisis coincided with the entry of women into the workforce in large numbers in the late 1970s and 1980s. At that time, both the number of women volunteers, and total volunteer hours, dropped substantially (Kaminer (1984); Masi (1981)). And although the number of volunteers has increased significantly since the 1980s, its growth has not been commensurate with the demand (Beerli, Diaz & Martin (2004)). Fears of a deepening crisis are mitigated in part by hopeful projections that the downward trend in volunteering will be reversed when the baby boomers start retiring *en masse* (Independent Sector (2003)). This hope may be based on a common misconception that there are legions of retirees volunteering. In truth, in 2000 the 65+ cohort accounts for the lowest volunteering rate: 18 per cent compared to 30 per cent among the 35-44 and 45-55 age cohorts. However, their low participation rate is tempered by the fact that they contribute the largest amount of time, averaging more than 269 hours per year (M.H. Hall *et al.* (2001)). According to the 1980 and 1987 statistics (Duchesne (1989)), this same cohort volunteered in greater numbers when they were younger, so their volunteering rates have decreased as they aged. It is therefore not a foregone conclusion that baby boomers will volunteer in greater numbers when they retire, than current retirees. As a matter of fact, baby boomers are not volunteering at the rates at which current retirees volunteered when they were younger. Ambitious campaigns are being planned in the United States to attract this cohort (Mareck (2004)).

Who Volunteers and Why?

Two questions have long intrigued researchers: who volunteers, and why do they volunteer? There is a broad consensus in research findings from many countries that the most important predictors of adult volunteering are related to three factors: whether their parents volunteered, whether they volunteered as children or young adults, and whether they are affiliated with a religious institution (Reed & Selbee (1999); Hodgkinson & Weitzman (1997)). Additionally, being a woman, having a university education and holding a job also increase the likelihood of volunteering. Age plays a role as well: adults between the ages of 35 and 44 make up the highest proportion of volunteers.[2] This may partly be a reflection of their participation in child-related activities in sports, education, music and arts.

So, why do people volunteer? There are many theories that attempt to answer this question. (For a thorough review of theories, see Wilson (2000)). An idea central to volunteering is altruism — giving without expectation of reward and indeed "helping others" is the most frequently cited reason given for voluntary affiliation (Duchesne (1989); Carter (1975); Beerli (2004)). This notwithstanding, more probing investigations suggest that altruism is only a minor motivator (Smith (1982); Gluck (1975); Clary et al. (1996)). Social catharsis (Langton (1982)), such as fulfilling a religious or social obligation, and collective identification with a "good cause" (Kramer (1981); Duchesne (1989)) are other reasons for volunteering. Some researchers suggest that volunteering, like other human behaviour, is best explained as the pursuit of personal benefits and rewards. These may be either instrumental, such as acquiring skills and job experience, building one's resume or gaining social recognition (Olson (1965); Clark & Wilson (1961); Flynn & Webb (1975); Masi (1981); Taylor (1989)); or affective, such as gaining new friendships and establishing social networks (Knoke (1986); Flynn & Webb (1975); Gluck (1975); Beerli (2004)).

---

[2]   Calculated from aggregated statistics from 1980, 1987, 1997 and 2000.

No doubt, all of these incentives play a role in determining volunteering behaviour, but at certain times, different factors will predominate. For example, when embarking on a new career, volunteer-volunteering may help round out resumes or provide skills needed to gain a competitive edge in the job market. Volunteering also opens possibilities for new friendships after moving to a new city or neighbourhood. Parents volunteer to organize or help in their children's recreational and educational groups. Often people join groups when invited to by a friend. Finally, there are times, such as in disaster situations, when people are moved by altruism and join in an effort to help irrespective of personal benefit.

The latest theories and research have identified two separate clusters of reasons for volunteering. The first may be labelled as "traditional" and involves collectivist values, with a focus on institutional loyalty and the collective common good. This is closely related to affective incentives. The second may be labelled "modern" and is characterized by individualistic values expressed in self-organized and/or program-based volunteering, with a focus on instrumental incentives and personal gains (Hustinx & Lammertyn (2003)).

Figure 5: Traditional and Modern Volunteer Clusters

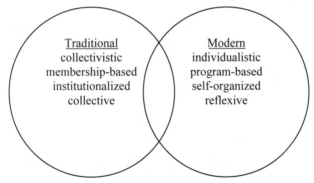

These clusters are not mutually exclusive, and an individual may hold both traditional and modern values, but research indicates that younger volunteers fall more clearly into the "modern" cluster. There has been a shift from group/community induced volunteering, characteristic of older volunteers, to more individual self-serving volunteering defining the younger generation. Whereas in the past, people volunteered because they were, or aspired to be, members of a group that served a cause that they believed in (for example, being a life member of Rotary Club or the National Council of Women), today's young volunteers seek to benefit both the organization and themselves. They fulfill that purpose by working on a specific project without a long-term commitment to the group. Or alternatively, because they tend to mistrust institutions, they may self-organize for a specific project and then disband. Whether this is a distinguishing characteristic of the current cohort of young volunteers that will define them even as they age, or whether this is a phenomenon related to life cycles, is yet to be seen.

Attracting Volunteers

Attracting volunteers has been a major challenge for the nonprofit sector. Volunteer recruitment manuals and Internet Websites abound with common sense advice aimed at appealing to both the affective and the instrumental needs of potential volunteers. For example, they urge recruiters to be personable, friendly and enthusiastic (Schindler-Rainman & Lippitt (1977); Routh (1972)), while suggesting that organizations set up peer programs and encourage members to bring along their friends (The Economist (2005)). On the instrumental side, these manuals recommend that organizations create interesting programs (Jackson (2005)), define tasks and jobs carefully, and offer training opportunities (Jackson (2005)). Finally they advise organizations to know their target population (Beerli, Diaz & Martin (2004)), advertise (Izon (2005)), and market themselves much like they would a product (Beerli *et al.* (2004)). This last strategy is now a recurring theme in the literature; there are even journals dedicated to the subject of the marketing for nonprofit organizations.[3]

Essentially, there are two different ways in which nonprofit organizations appeal to prospective volunteers. One is through focusing on membership orientation, where the emphasis is on satisfying the affective needs of the volunteer (*i.e.*, needs that relate to emotions and feelings); the other is through a task/program orientation, where the focus is on instrumental gains — for example, the practical benefits of volunteering for making contacts or learning skills (Meijs & Hoogstad (2001)).

---

[3]   For example, International Journal of Nonprofit and Voluntary Sector Marketing, Journal of Nonprofit & Public Sector Marketing.

Membership Orientation

In organizations characterized by membership orientation, the primary focus is on the needs and goals of the members. Initially this is what defines the organization's mission. New members join because they either identify with the organization's mission or have an affinity with the other members. Loyalty is cultivated through informal socialization rather than formal training. Membership organizations seek equilibrium between individual and organizational goals by emphasizing the pleasure of social activity while doing good. There is a progression of involvement from passive membership to active volunteering. Over time, membership in the organization becomes a part of the individual's identity. Service clubs (*e.g.*, Kiwanis, Rotary, Lions) and churches are examples of membership-oriented organizations (Meijs & Hoogstad (2001)).

Task/program Orientation

In these organizations the focus is on tasks and programs. Volunteers are sought, not to become members of the organization, but to complete specific tasks. Emphasis is on training to provide the volunteer with new skill sets. Task accomplishment takes priority over social activities. In the absence of demands for organizational loyalty, organizations find it easier to attract people to do specific, but time-limited jobs. The task/program management orientation seeks equilibrium between individual and organizational goals by encouraging individual gain, with an emphasis on training, work experience and merit reward, all for a good cause. Volunteers tend not to identify with the organization as much. Examples of these kinds of organizations would be food banks, hospitals or social service agencies (Meijs & Hoogstad (2001)).

Recruitment strategies for organizations with a membership orientation target people who share the organization's values, and emphasize the social and friendship benefits the organization can offer. Organizations with a program orientation are more likely to seek individuals with skills needed by their organization. They offer instrumental incentives such as learning new skills and the opportunity to enhance personal benefits (Meijs & Hoogstad (2001)).

In the past it was generally believed that "the cause" was the main source of attracting volunteers, and that those who identified with it would join the organization, form friendships, become loyal members and do whatever task was necessary to help the organization achieve its mission. The emphasis was on the shared effort towards furthering the mission. Indeed, this was a strategy that seemed to work quite well until recently. Most organizations are still geared to that kind of recruitment despite the fact that research shows a growing trend toward episodic volunteering for instrumental gains.

New Trends

As funding for social and cultural services continues to decrease (Hall & Banting (2000)), provincial and federal governments have encouraged increased volunteerism by supporting initiatives such as the 1998 Ontario Voluntary Forum and the 2001 International Year of the Volunteer. In some sectors however, there is strong opposition to any suggestions of replacing professional services with volunteer labour. High volunteer turnover rates, high costs of training, threat of job losses for paid employees, and the risks involved in replacing university-trained professionals by volunteers, are all potent arguments that have been put forward against the replacement of paid staff by volunteers (e.g., Lefebvre (1996)). And, in fact, there is little evidence that any large-scale replacement of paid staff has taken place (NSNVO (2004)).

Nevertheless, given severe funding cuts, organizations may benefit from a larger and better-educated pool of volunteers. Indeed, in a recent study of the value added contribution of hospital volunteers, Handy and Srinivasan (2004) calculated that for every dollar spent on the volunteer program, the hospital derived an average of $6.84 in value. Volunteers provided invaluable non-medical support to patients while freeing professionals to spend more time on medical care. Several new volunteer initiatives are occurring in Canada. The largest and most ambitious of these are government-mandated programs in the secondary schools of several provinces. Other initiatives include employee volunteer programs sponsored by corporations, and social-entrepreneurial ventures aimed at enticing young people to volunteer.

Education

Although during the past decade the voluntary sector has become more visible thanks to increased media attention, greater research interest and the establishment of various graduate and undergraduate nonprofit management programs, many members of the general public are still not aware of the size and importance of the voluntary sector. Education is essential not only to increase awareness of the critical role of the voluntary sector for societal well-being, but also to help develop an ethos of giving and participating (Salamon & Anheier (1996)). This has traditionally been a role played by religious institutions, however in an increasingly secularized society it is unrealistic to rely solely on religious institutions to encourage community involvement and social action (Cnaan *et al.* (1993); Wuthnow (1991)). Evidence from school-based "service learning" programs in the United States indicates that schools can play a significant role in encouraging civic responsibility. The concept of service learning dates back to the turn of the last century when John Dewey wrote about the "importance of social and not just intellectual development; and the value of actions directed towards the welfare of others" (Kraft (1996, at 133)). "Service learning" links community service directly to the school curriculum. It has enjoyed renewed interest in the latter decades of the twentieth century as a potential brake to the worrisome decline in civic participation (Barber (1992); Bellah *et al.* (1985); Putnam (2000)).

In many Canadian provinces, community service programs have long existed as part of co-op placements, extracurricular activities, and specific courses. Nonetheless, Ontario and British Columbia are the only provinces with mandated community service requirements for high school graduation. Technically, high school students who volunteer in nonprofit organizations in order to fulfill credit require-ments would not fall into the category of volunteer as defined above. However, a recent study of the Ontario program indicates that many of the students were already volunteers before the program, and many actually continued freely volunteering more than their required hours (Meinhard *et al.* (2006)).

These relatively new programs highlight government interest in playing a more active role in socializing youth to the importance of community involvement and charitable giving. For example, the stated intention of the service component in Ontario is to "encourage students to develop awareness and understanding of civic responsibility and of the role they can play in supporting and strengthening their communities" (Ontario Ministry of Education (1999, at 9)). In fact, a lack of aware-ness — "not knowing" where to volunteer — is the most common reason given by young people for not volunteering (M.H. Hall *et al.* (2001)). This barrier has been effectively eliminated by the new program, as schools and parents help students organize their volunteer-ing activities to fulfill their requirements.

Although the long-term success of this program is not yet known, other studies show that the greatest benefits occur when community service is linked to a structured school activity, and when placements are arranged in active partnership with nonprofit agencies. (Meinhard & Foster (1999); Foster & Meinhard (2000); Raskoff & Sundeen (1998)). Simply requiring 40 hours of service over four years of high school in the absence of a structured program is not likely to achieve the intended long-term results of increased civic-mindedness and community participation.

Employer-supported Volunteering

While the government has been cutting funding to the nonprofit sector, the corporate sector has increased its involvement. The most recently available statistics indicate that the corporate sector has more than doubled its support of the voluntary sector from $1.2 billion in 1996 (Standing Committee on Finance (1996)) to $2.8 billion in 2003 (Statistics Canada (2003, at 23)). This relatively newfound sense of corporate social responsibility is, in part, in response to shareholder concerns for community involvement and social responsibility (Austen (2000); Schmid & Meinhard (2000)), and in part a result of an increased realization of the marketing potential of such involvement (Berger *et al.* (2005a)). To this end, organizations try to offer support in different, and at times innovative, ways, both through direct giving and by facilitating employee volunteer programs. These volunteer programs include: volunteer recognition events, making donations to the volunteers' charities in recognition of their work, sponsoring events that employees organize, providing time off, arranging flexible scheduling, and "lending" employees to nonprofit organizations for periods of time.

One of Canada's major banks has just launched an innovative paid leave of absence program where employees can request a secondment to a nonprofit organization for a period of from three to 12 months. The bank will not only pay the employees' salaries and guarantee equivalent movement in the ranks when they return, it will also give a $5,000 grant to the nonprofit organization to cover space and equipment costs. Other programs capitalize on the widespread use of the Internet by providing a service to match volunteers from the corporation with nonprofit boards in need of their skills.

Employer-supported volunteering is a three-way partnership that benefits all involved as summarized in Table 1.

Table 1: Mutual Benefits from Employer-supported Volunteering

Nonprofits gain from:	Businesses	New partnerships and sponsorships, support and better understanding
	Employees	A supply of volunteers with needed skills, exposure to their cause
Businesses gain from:	Nonprofits	Improved image, which leads to increased sales and greater customer loyalty
	Employees	More loyal workforce, better morale and pride in organization
Employees gain from:	Nonprofits	New skills, sense of giving back, social network
	Business	Recognition, support for community work, time off to volunteer

Entrepreneurial Initiatives

There are many individual efforts by young people to get their peers involved in volunteering and community activity. One example is the creation of the Framework Foundation, conceived and executed by a young man who was worried about the lack of community participation among his peers. He engaged several of his friends and with them organized a unique art auction to attract 22- to 35-year-olds to volunteer. Called a *Timeraiser*, people pledge volunteering hours, instead of bidding money, to purchase paintings by young Canadian artists. The art is purchased by Framework Foundation with money raised through corporate sponsorships and fundraising. Everyone gains, the artists get important exposure and sell their paintings, the corporate donors and partners get exposure and recognition, voluntary agencies get skilled and educated volunteers, and volunteers not only get to purchase art but also contribute to their community and learn about its needs. In the words of the Framework Foundation:

> The Framework Foundation empowers Canadians between the ages of 22 and 35 to "get in the picture" and help build stronger communities through volunteer involvement. Our Framework Foundation "picture" celebrates the

power of collective dedication, recognizing its importance in addressing community needs.[4]

The first *Timeraiser* was launched in 2004 in Toronto and was a great success with almost 10,000 hours of volunteering completed at over 40 agencies. Volunteers and agencies track their hours by a computerized tracking system that was specially devised for this project. In 2006 *Timeraisers* are planned for other Canadian cities.

Volunteer Diversity

As noted above, volunteer participation rates in Canada are decreasing just as voluntary organizations are becoming more reliant on volunteers. In order to expand the pool of volunteers and supporters, leaders of nonprofit organizations are increasingly recognizing the need to engage Canada's growing ethnic communities. Currently, the participation rate among Canada's newer ethnic communities is lower than that of older, more established communities. The challenge for nonprofit organizations is to find a way to reach out to these groups. This means recognizing that volunteering is a function of many interrelated factors: prevailing cultural norms and values, available opportunities, individual and societal barriers, and past experience, all of which influence personal attitudes. These factors may differ among the various ethnic communities. Thus, for example, in a culture where volunteering has a connotation of "forced labour" as in Communist China, where individuals were forced to "volunteer" to engage in an activity deemed necessary by the authorities, volunteering outside the home or family may have little appeal.

When members of various ethnic groups were asked why they do not volunteer, the two main reasons given were lack of time and not being asked (M.H. Hall *et al.*, 2001). Lack of time, although not unique to newer Canadians, is all the more pertinent to immigrants who are struggling to make ends meet. "Not being asked" may be an indication of subtle social barriers that may exist in the recruitment of volunteers. Thus, while members of some social groups may be actively courted by voluntary organizations, thereby increasing their knowledge of where and how to volunteer, members of other groups may receive no attention or may be approached in culturally inappropriate ways, thereby impeding intentions to volunteer. Recruiters must

---

[4]   <http://www.frameworkfoundation.ca/about/index.php>.

recognize these subtle barriers and mitigate them by learning more about the myriad ethnic communities in Canada today.

Diversity is also an issue when it comes to the composition of nonprofit boards. Although there is no definitive Canadian count, American studies estimate the extent of minority representation on boards to be between 12 per cent to 16 per cent (Constance-Huggins & Bangs (2003)). This trend continues, despite clauses in the by-laws of many nonprofit organizations calling for a board composition representative of the community's population. In Canada, ethnic diversity in the nonprofit sector is reflected by the diversity of ethno-cultural organizations across the sector rather than diversity within individual organizations, which means that the problem here is probably as great as in the United States.

Volunteering in nonprofit organizations can play a bridging role in helping new Canadians integrate into society. Thus, a concerted effort by voluntary organizations to attract new immigrants serves not only the organization but also society as a whole, not to mention the newcomer (Onyx & Maclean (1996)). However, new immigrants are more likely to volunteer and join organizations within their ethnic community. This may provide them with important bonding experiences, especially in a new and strange country, but it can also delay their integration into Canadian society (Berger et al. (2005b)). Low volunteering rates among certain ethnic minorities continue even into the second generation, indicating that cultural and normative influences, as well as discriminatory barriers, have deep roots in a country that encourages the celebration of multiculturalism (Berger et al. (2005b)).

It is perhaps in the area of gender diversity that the voluntary sector has made the greatest strides. Although women were always active in voluntary organizations, access to leadership was denied them. In their frustration, they founded and led their own organizations. Today, many nonprofit organizations, including large national ones, have women at their helm. For example, data from a large Canadian study (Meinhard & Foster (2003)) involving more than 300 organizations that were not specifically serving women or advocating their causes, indicate that 53 per cent of them were led by women in either paid or unpaid positions. This figure dropped to 48 per cent when considering only those organizations with revenues exceeding one million dollars. On the other hand, women's representation on boards of directors is considerably lower, averaging around 36 per cent in American studies (Mayorova (1995)) and 43 per cent in the Canadian one, including the large organizations (Meinhard & Foster (2003)). However, compared to the corporate sector, these figures are encouraging.

The concept of diversity on boards is not limited to gender and ethno-racial background. Diversity in terms of age, education, economic status and type of work will give boards access to a variety of different perspectives that will help them function better in Canada's diverse environment. Achieving diversity is not an easy task and can only be accomplished if the board deliberately sets policy to attract people of various backgrounds.

Managing Volunteers

The ultimate challenge in employee management is how to improve worker productivity. Organizational behaviour literature identifies two separate but related avenues for achieving high performance from workers. One is devising an appropriate and fair incentive structure. This must be coupled with creating a favourable workplace climate and attractive job design. These two pillars of management are pertinent for volunteers as well, but the emphasis and balance between them is different.

Incentive Structure

Organizational management practices are predicated on the principle of exchanging rewards for services rendered to the organization in pursuit of its goals. The rewards are primarily monetary in nature, although they may also include promotion through the ranks and non-tangible reinforcements such as recognition and praise. In addition, there may be intrinsic rewards associated with an activity, such as feeling good about an outcome or enjoying the activity itself. Various theories of motivation describe the relationship of human performance to the satisfaction of basic needs and the achievement of desired rewards (Hertzberg *et al.* (1959)). These theories posit that as basic needs for food and security are fulfilled through the performance of certain activities, humans strive to satisfy more complex ones such as needs for affiliation, esteem, achievement power and self-actualization (Alderfer (1972); Maslow (1943); McClelland (1961)). Whether or not they continue to pursue certain activities depends on the value of the extrinsic and/or intrinsic rewards associated with the activity (Lawler (1973)). In a paid workplace, mundane, uninteresting work may be well tolerated in exchange for sufficient monetary compensation, which acts as an incentive to perform the task. However, even in the workplace, increasing monetary rewards has diminishing returns after a certain level of reward satisfaction has been reached (McShane (2004)). Therefore, in order to improve performance it is often the case that the answer lies in improving the structure and characteristics of the job and/or the workplace.

Workplace Climate and Job Design

Often called simply job design, this refers to a combination of factors that together affect the performance of an individual. The key components are: clarity of the task (*i.e.*, what exactly needs to be done); level and variety of skills needed (*i.e.*, mundane and boring versus challenging and varied work); perceived significance of the work (*i.e.*, the importance to key stakeholders); level of autonomy (*i.e.*, is the job highly standardized or does one have discretion to make decisions?); identification with the completed task (*i.e.*, participation in the entire process versus performing a specific part exclusively); and finally, level and quality of feedback (Hackman & Oldham (1980)). In theory, the better the job design, and the more socially fulfilling the workplace, the more satisfied the worker will be, which in turn increases motivation and ultimately leads to better performance.

In the case of volunteers, monetary reward is not a motivator, nor is the activity undertaken by the volunteer to satisfy basic existence needs. Therefore, the challenge for management is to find the right combination of incentives and job characteristics that will induce the volunteer to stay interested in helping the organization. In terms of incentives, both the academic and practitioner literature has identified the following "best practices":

- Understand the volunteers' needs and match them with the appropriate job (Wilson & Pimm (1996)).

- Emphasize and communicate the social meaningfulness of the activity (Onyx & Maclean (1996)).

- Link the activity to generalizable skills (Janey *et al.* (1991)).

- Value their time, give them feedback, publicly and privately recognize their contributions, and reimburse their expenses (Brudney (1999)).

Furthermore, job and workplace characteristics take on added importance in managing volunteers. Although there are many non-monetary incentives related to volunteering, such as those discussed above, they may not be enough to mitigate the deleterious effects of poor workplace/job characteristics. The academic and practitioner literature identifies the following work and job factors as important and beneficial for a volunteer program:

- Provide a budget for a dedicated volunteer manager (Brudney (1999)).

- Train paid staff members in how to work with volunteers (Brudney (1999)).

- Train volunteers to lead other volunteers (Brudney (1999)).

- Clearly communicate roles and define jobs (Ross (1992)).

- Provide orientation and job training (Wilson & Pimm (1996)).

- Ensure work variety and delegate responsibility (Netting *et al.* (2005); Wilson & Pimm (1996)).

- Create a positive ambiance in the workplace (Puffer & Meindl (1995)).

Effective volunteer management is highly correlated with a volunteer's commitment to continue volunteering with the organization (Farmer & Fedor (1999)). On the organizational side, time devoted to managing volunteers is strongly related to organizational benefits accruing from the use of volunteers (Brudney (1999)). This notwithstanding, evidence from a study of 1,800 nonprofit organizations suggests that 80 per cent of organizations using volunteers lack the capacity to manage them effectively (GUI Program News (2005)). Budgetary constraint is the foremost reason put forward as preventing organizations from instituting structured volunteer programs with trained managers whose primary focus is the volunteer contingent (Hager & Brudney (2004)).

Besides the size of the budget, there are three other determinants of whether or not an organization adopts formal volunteer management practices: task variety, size of volunteer contingent and type of organization. The greater the variety of tasks performed by volunteers and the greater the number of volunteers, the more likely that the organization will adopt formal volunteer management practices. Additionally, the type of organization will also be a determinant; for example, health and human service organizations were found to be more likely to adopt a formally structured volunteer program than educational and arts institutions (Brudney & Nezhina (2005)).

Challenges for managing volunteers differ depending on whether the organization's activities are performed for the most part by volunteers, or whether they are carried out by paid employees, with some additional help from volunteers (Adams & Shepherd (1996)). In the former, it is usually volunteer leaders who organize other volunteers. The foremost problems incurred in these situations are related to lack of leadership training in managing others and lack of job descriptions and role clarity (Adams & Shepherd (1996)).

In organizations where volunteers and paid staff members work together, the success of the volunteer program depends on the relationship between volunteers and paid staff (Adams & Shepherd (1996); Colomy *et al.* (1987); Mausner (1988)). Tension between the two tends to be higher in organizations without trained volunteer managers, where volunteers are often supervised by staff managers who, on average, devote less than one-third of their time to volunteer co-ordination (Brudney (1999), and who are often unfamiliar with the characteristics of volunteers (Wilson (1981)). Wilson and Pimm (1996) identify three main areas of misunderstanding. The first relates to mutual misperceptions. Employees often fear that they may be replaced by volunteers and resent the favoured treatment that they believe is afforded to volunteers. On the other hand, volunteers often feel exploited, believing they are given the least important, least interesting jobs and experience higher role uncertainty (Farmer & Fedor (1999)). The second involves managerial discomfort as supervisors recognize the limits of their authority with respect to volunteers. This leads to attitudes among staff that "volunteers are a nuisance, work has to be found to occupy them and then resources diverted to supervise them" (Wilson & Pimm (1996, at 27)). The third misunderstanding stems from a clash of values with respect to paid and volunteer labour, the latter generally considered of higher moral value.

Each of these areas of misunderstanding can be overcome with good volunteer management practices that involve open communications clearly identifying the roles of volunteers and staff members as mutually supportive (Adams & Shepherd (1996)), building a relationship of trust between supervisors and their volunteers (Farmer & Fedor (1999)), and reiterating the importance of both volunteers and employees in furthering the mission of their organizations.

BOARD, STAFF AND VOLUNTEERS WORKING TOGETHER FOR ORGANIZATIONAL SUCCESS

In many nonprofit organizations, the sandwiching of paid professional staff between a voluntary board of directors and volunteer workers presents a situation prone to role ambiguity and role conflict. On the one hand there may be tensions between staff and board members over the direction of the organization in light of an imbalance between knowledge and information on the part of the part-time board volunteers and the full-time paid organizational leadership. Conflict may also occur over issues of supervision, as boards may be prone to micro-managing their staff. On the other hand, tensions may arise between paid employees and volunteer workers over misperceptions about their respective roles and miscommunication in the work they do together. Solutions are not simple, but problems can be minimized and their impact mitigated through the application of sound human resource practices. Interestingly, with the exception of a few articles, most treatises on how to best recruit and manage volunteers do not mention the importance of having basic human resource management structures in place.

Basic Human Resource Functions

"Board, staff and volunteers working together for organizational success" is not a just cliché when an organization has guidelines to address human resource challenges and opportunities. Using Wilson's & Pimm's (1996) framework, the seven basic HR functions will be reviewed and their applicability to all levels of the organization — board, staff and volunteers — will be demonstrated.

Recruitment

Finding the right people for the right job is basic to all organizations, however in nonprofit organizations finding a fit with the organization, its cause and its people often has more weight than job skills. Recruitment entails preparation and planning in terms of predicting organizational needs, identifying target markets, clearly defining the purpose and content of the job or jobs, devising a profile of the ideal person, marketing the organization through informative advertisements that appeal both to the instrumental benefits of participating and to the affective benefits of belonging to the organization, and finding the right channels through which to communicate. Even in membership organizations, where recruitment for a specific job will target the organization's own membership, such planning and segmentation of potential recruits is recommended (Wilson & Pimm (1996)). A common problem in nonprofit organizations is that without an HR structure, response to applications is slow and people go elsewhere. Proper recruitment helps to forestall later problems associated with lack of fit. These principles apply not only to the recruitment of volunteer workers, but also to board volunteers and staff members.

Selection

Although the nonprofit literature is replete with recruitment suggestions, selection processes are barely mentioned. Yet this is a key element of HRM, as not all potential recruits are suited for the job. In the for-profit world there are many tools for selection, depending on the job. In nonprofit organizations the most viable tool is the structured job interview. The interview should not only be a means for the interviewer to gauge the suitability of the prospective volunteer or employee, it should also include an opportunity for the organization to clearly define the parameters (task, skills needed, time required, flexibility, *etc.*) of the activities the volunteer will be engaged in. This will give potential recruits a chance to (re)consider their application if the parameters do not fit with their needs and abilities. It also gives both parties the opportunity to explore shared values. The selection process should be completed for board members as well as staff and volunteers. As with recruitment, proper selection processes mitigate the chance of a poor fit. This is important because frequent turnover is disruptive, but also can lead to disaffection among the existing employees and volunteers.

Orientation

Once the selection process is complete, the most important, and often most neglected part of the HRM process, especially where there is no one designated to oversee these functions, is orientation (Wilson & Pimm (1996)). Formal orientation serves many purposes, but basically it is a process of organizational socialization (McShane (2004)), in which new members learn about the organization, its values, and how things are done. They meet key people and see how their activities fit in with the rest of the organization. During the orientation, new members should be informed about the organization's policies with respect to their rights and obligations, and be informed about the organization's liability insurance. Most importantly, a formal orientation is an opportunity to revisit the job description, and to clearly understand the reporting relationships and performance expectations. Without a formal orientation, the learning process is extended and it takes longer for the new member to play an active and beneficial role in the organization. Formal orientation can also be an opportunity for self-selection, without incurring large costs to either the leaving member or the organization. Orientation of new board members is a crucial board activity as well, as so many people who join nonprofit boards have little experience and knowledge of boards in general, and certainly not of the specific board.

Supervision

This not only involves providing direction and oversight for the work to be done, it also includes training in both technical skills pertaining to the job and leadership skills for filling leadership positions and supervising volunteers in the future. In the absence of direct control mechanisms through managerial authority, supervision of volunteers requires more negotiation and persuasion than direction. Thus, training supervisory staff is important. They need to learn that volunteers have different needs and values associated with their voluntary work, and that therefore, they have to be approached in different ways. In addition, they need to respect constraints facing volunteers, and not overburden them during busy times. On the other hand, in times of low activity, they must keep their volunteers involved in the affairs of the organization, to prevent them from leaving. Training staff members in how to supervise and work with volunteers paves the way for smoother staff-volunteer relations. Boards should be training their members as well, outlining the limits of their authority vis-à-vis staff.

Performance Appraisals

This is perhaps the most neglected HR function in nonprofit organizations. There is often a reluctance to give negative feedback to a volunteer in fear of losing their support. But poor performance has ripple effects that can lead to covert and even overt conflict, a lowering of work norms among other volunteers and staff, and a decrease in morale. Formal performance evaluations for the purposes of wage or career advancement should be instituted for every staff member. However, formal appraisals may be counter-productive with respect to volunteers (Wilson & Pimm (1996)). In their case, it may be more beneficial to provide feedback through informal chats. Asking them how things are going, whether they are happy in their work and how the organization is treating them, can lead to openings where the supervisor can suggest how things can be improved and express their concerns without discrediting volunteers' work. Supervisors need training in this as well.

Performance evaluation of the ED by the board of directors is another oft-neglected task. Here the opposite is true. The board should engage in regularly scheduled formal evaluations. For more on this see Chapter 3.

Termination

Informing an organizational member that his or her services are no longer needed is always a difficult task, except when circumstances involve illegal or immoral activities. It is even more difficult with respect to volunteers. Paid supervisors may find the task less daunting, but voluntary staff members or board members find it almost impossible as there may be social and personal repercussions. However, keeping a poorly functioning volunteer is detrimental to the organization. It takes skill to terminate a voluntary relationship in a way that will hurt neither the volunteer nor the organization. These skills have to be learned and practised. Fortunately it is more often the case that volunteers initiate the termination. An exit interview to determine the reasons for withdrawal is an important tool to improving recruitment and selection practices.

CONCLUSION

Knowledge and application of basic human resource practices is beneficial to nonprofit organizations not only with respect to paid staff members, but also with respect to volunteers and volunteer board members. That these practices are not widespread, especially in smaller, volunteer-driven organizations, is often a function of budgetary constraints. However, there is a distinct lack of awareness on the part of many voluntary organizations of the importance and benefits of exercising human resource practices. There is sometimes a mistaken belief that the attraction of a voluntary organization is its informality and lack of professionalism, and that adding formal HR practices may detract from the organization's appeal. It is not essential for a small organization to have a paid, trained person designated for HR issues. However, since the board has ultimate legal responsibility for what happens in the organization, it is in its interests to pay more attention to HR issues. Therefore, as part of their resource planning, they should consider sending their volunteer leaders or staff supervisors to attend seminars and workshops that teach basic HR practices. Sometimes simply by raising awareness of HR issues, relations among board, volunteers and paid staff can be improved for future organizational success.

This chapter has highlighted some of the basic issues around managing human resources in voluntary and nonprofit organizations. The overarching goal of HRM is to bring together the various groups of players in ways that enhance an organization's capacity to pursue its mission efficiently and effectively. Although many of the practices are similar to those in the private sector, the dimensions of the challenge are magnified because of the dual nature of nonprofit governance, the budgetary constraints so many of them face, the reliance on voluntary commitment to carry out goals, and the relatively undeveloped state of human resource practices in nonprofit organizations.

REFERENCES

C.H. Adams & G.J. Shepherd, "Managing Volunteer Performance: Face Support and Situational Features as Predictors of Volunteers' Evaluations of Regulative Messages" (1996) 9:4 Management Communication Quarterly 363-389.

O. Akingbola, *Strategy, Human Resource Management and Government Funding in Nonprofit Organizations* (Doctoral Dissertation, University of Toronto, 2005 (unpublished)).

C.P. Alderfer, *Existence, Relatedness and Growth* (New York: The Free Press, 1972).

J.E. Austin, "Strategic Collaboration Between Nonprofits and Businesses" (2000) 29:1 Nonprofit and Voluntary Sector Quarterly 69-97.

B. Barber, *An Aristocracy of Everyone* (New York: Ballantine, 1992).

M. Beer *et al.*, *Managing Human Assets* (New York: Free Press, 1984).

A. Beerli, G. Diaz & J.D. Martin, "The Behavioral Consequences of Self-Congruency in Volunteers" (2004) 9:1 International Journal of Nonprofit and Voluntary Sector Marketing 28-48.

R. Bellah *et al.*, *Habits of the Heart* (Berkeley: University of California Press, 1985).

I.E. Berger *et al.*, *Ethnicity, Voluntary Behaviour and Social Integration* (Proceedings of the Annual Conference of the Administrative Sciences Association of Canada, Toronto, ON).

I.E. Berger, P.H. Cunningham & M.E. Drumwright, "Social Alliances: Company/Nonprofit Collaboration" (2005) 47:1 California Management Review 58-90.

J.L. Brudney, "The Effective Use of Volunteers: Best Practices for the Public Sector" (1999) 62:4 Law and Contemporary Problems 219-255.

J.L. Brudney & T.G. Nezhina, "What is Old is New Again: Achieving Effectiveness with Volunteer Programs in Kazakhstan" (2005) 16:3 Voluntas 293-308.

N. Carter, *Trends in Voluntary Support for Non-Governmental Social Service Agencies* (Ottawa: Canadian Council on Social Development, 1975).

P.B. Clark & J.Q. Wilson, "Incentive Systems: A Theory of Organizations" (1961) 6:2 Administrative Sciences Quarterly 129-166.

E.G. Clary, M. Snyder & A.A. Stukas, "Volunteers' Motivations: Findings from a National Survey" (1996) 25:4 Nonprofit and Voluntary Sector Quarterly 485-505.

R. Cnaan, A. Kasternakis & R.J. Wineburg, "Religious People, Religious Congregations, and Volunteerism in Human Services: Is There a Link?" (1993) 22:1 Nonprofit and Voluntary Sector Quarterly 33-51.

R. Cnaan, F. Handy & M. Wadsworth, "Defining Who is a Volunteer: Conceptual and Empirical Considerations" (1996) 25:3 Nonprofit and Voluntary Sector Quarterly 364-383.

P. Colomy, H. Chen & G.L. Andrews, "Situational Facilities and Volunteer Work" (1987) 6:2 Journal of Volunteer Administration 20-25.

M. Constance-Huggins & R.L. Bangs, *Diversity Within and Among Nonprofit Boards in Allegheny County* (Pittsburgh: University Center for Social and Urban Research, University of Pittsburgh, 2003).

K. de Schweinitz, *England's Road to Social Security* (New York: Barnes, 1943).

E. Dreesen, *What Do We Know About the Voluntary Sector? An Overview.* Statistics Canada, Cat. No. 75F0048MIE-No. 06. Online at: <http://www.statcan.ca/english/research/75F0048MIE/75F0048 MIE2002006.pdf>.

P.F. Drucker, "Lessons for Successful Nonprofit Governance" (1990) 1:1 Nonprofit Management and Leadership 7-14.

D. Duchesne, *Giving Freely: Volunteers in Canada.* Statistics Canada, Labour Analytic Report, Cat. No.: 71-535 No. 4 (Ottawa: Minister of Supply and Services, 1989).

Economist, The, "Britain: Volunteering – Subsidising Virtue" *The Economist* 374:8417 (12 March 2005) 57.

S.M. Farmer & D.B. Fedor, "Volunteer Participation and Withdrawal" (1999) 9:4 Nonprofit Management and Leadership 349-368.

M. Feingold, "Philanthropy, Pomp and Patronage: Historical Reflections upon the Endowment of Culture" *Daedalus* 116:1 (1987) 155-178.

J.P. Flynn & G.E. Webb, "Women's Incentives for Community Participation in Policy Issues" (1975) 4:3-4 Journal of Voluntary Action Research 137-145.

M.K. Foster & A.G. Meinhard, "Diversifying Revenue Sources in Canada: Are Women's Voluntary Organizations Different?" (2005) 16:1 Nonprofit Management & Leadership .

M.K. Foster & A.G. Meinhard, *Structuring Student Volunteering Programs to the Benefit of Students and the Community* (Presented at the Fourth International Conference of the International Society for Third Sector Research, Dublin, Ireland) (2000).

M.K. Foster & A.G. Meinhard, *Toward Transforming Social Service Organizations in Ontario* (Presented at the Babson Conference on Entrepreneurship, Seattle, WA) (1996).

R. Gluck, "An Exchange Theory of Incentives of Urban Political Party Organization" (1975) 4:1-2 Journal of Voluntary Action Research 104-115.

GUI Program News (April 1, 2005). "New Fundraiser Volunteer Module Eases Management Tasks", 16(4) *GUI Program News.*

J.R. Hackman & G.R. Oldham, *Work Redesign* (Reading, MA: Addison-Wesley, 1980).

M. Hager & J.L. Brudney, *Volunteer Management Practices and Retention of Volunteers* (Washington, DC: The Urban Institute, 2004).

J. Haiven, *The Right People for the Job: The Not-For-Profit Sector and its Human Element* (Presented at the Association for Research on Nonprofit Organizations and Voluntary Action Conference, Seattle, Washington) (1998).

M.H. Hall & K.G. Banting, "The Nonprofit Sector in Canada: An Introduction" in K.G. Banting, ed., *The Nonprofit Sector in Canada: Roles and Relationships* (Montreal and Kingston: School of Policy Studies, Queen's University, 2000).

M.H. Hall, L. McKeown & K. Roberts, *Caring Canadians, Involved Canadians: Highlights from the 2000 National Survey of Giving, Volunteering and Participating.* Catalogue No. 71-542-XIE (Ottawa: Statistics Canada, 2001). Online at: <http://sectorsource.ca/ resource/file/caring-canadians-involved-canadians-highlights-2000-national-survey-giving>.

M.H. Hall *et al.*, *Caring Canadians, Involved Canadians: Highlights from the 2004 CSGVP* (Ottawa: Ministry of Industry, 2006).

F. Handy & N. Srinivasan, Valuing Volunteers: An Economic Evaluation of the Net Benefits of Hospital Volunteers" (2004) 33:1 Nonprofit and Voluntary Sector Quarterly 28-54.

R.D. Herman & D.R. Heimovics, *Executive Leadership in Non-Profit Organizations* (Oxford: Jossey-Bass Publishers, 1991).

F. Hertzberg, B. Mausner & B.B. Snyderman, *The Motivation to Work* (New York: Wiley, 1959).

V.A. Hodgkinson & M.S. Weitzman, *Volunteering and Giving Among American Teenagers 14 to 17 Years of Age: 1996 edition* (Washington, DC: Independent Sector, 1997).

Human Resources Council for the Voluntary/Non-profit Sector (2008), *Toward a Labour Force Strategy for Canada's Voluntary and Non-profit Sector, Report #1.* Online at: <http://hrcouncil.ca/about/HRC_ Labour_Force_Study_R1.pdf.pdf>.

Human Resources Council for the Voluntary/Non-profit Sector (2008), *Toward a Labour Force Strategy for Canada's Voluntary and Non-profit Sector, Report #2.* Online at: <http://hrcouncil.ca/about/ documents/ LFS_ R2_web_001.pdf>.

Human Resources Council for the Voluntary/Non-profit Sector (2005), *The Canadian Centre for Philanthropy and the Canadian Policy Research Networks*. Online at: <http://www.hrvs-rhsbc.ca/hr_ overview/pg001_e.cfm>.

L. Hustinx & Frans Lammertyn, "Collective and Reflexive Styles of Volunteering: A Sociological Modernization Perspective", (2003) 14:2 Voluntas 168-187.

Independent Sector, Press Release, "Independent Sector Report Illustrates Philanthropic Potential of the American Baby Boom Generation" (4 November 2003), online at: <http://www.independentsector.org/media/ experiencePR.html>.

L. Izon, "Volunteer Vacations Target the Tsunami Zone" *The Globe & Mail* (15 January 2005) T2.

J. Jackson, "Volunteers: Not Free Labour" (2005) 115:4 Municipal World 39-40.

J.P. Janey, J.E. Tuckwiller & L.E. Lonnquist, "Skill Transferal Benefits from Volunteer Experiences" (1991) 20:1 Nonprofit and Voluntary Sector Quarterly 71-79.

W. Kaminer, *Women Volunteering* (Garden City, NY: Anchor Press, 1984).

D. Knoke, "Associations and Interest Groups" (1986) 12 Annual Review of Sociology 1-20.

R. Kraft, "Service Learning: An Introduction to Its Theory, Practice and Effects" (1996) 28:2 Education and Urban Society 131-159.

R. Kramer, *Voluntary Agencies in the Welfare State* (Berkeley: University of California Press, 1981).

S. Langton, "The New Voluntarism" in J.D. Harman, ed., *Volunteerism in the Eighties: Fundamental Issues in Voluntary Action* (Washington, DC: University Press of America, 1982) 3-22.

E.E. Lawler, *Motivation in Work Organizations* (Monterey, CA: Brooks/Cole, 1973).

B. Lefebvre. From Minutes of the Standing Committee on General Government (Timmins, ON: Government of Ontario, June 16, 1996).

J. Lewis, "Gender, the Family and Women's Agency in the Building of the 'Welfare States': The British Case" (1994) 19:1 Social History 37-55.

B. Macaleer & S. Jones, "Does HR Planning Improve Business Performance?" (2003) 45:1 Industrial Management 14-21.

A.C. Marek, "Volunteer" *U.S. News & World Report* 137:23 (2004) 84.

S. Martin, *An Essential Grace: Funding Canada's Health Care, Education, Welfare, Religion and Culture* (Toronto: McClelland and Stewart, 1985).

D.A. Masi, *Organizing for Women: Issues, Strategies, and Services* (Lexington, MA: Lexington Books, 1981).

A. Maslow, "A Theory of Human Motivation" (1943) 50:4 Psychological Review 370-396.

C. Mausner, "The Underlying Dynamics of Staff Volunteer Relationships" (1988) 5:3 The Journal of Volunteer Administration 5-9.

E. Mayo, *The Social Problems of an Industrial Civilization* (Boston: Harvard University, 1945).

O.V. Mayorova, *Corporate and Nonprofit Boards: Have Women Gained Power?* (MA Thesis submitted to the Graduate School of the University of Louisville (1995)).

K.D. McCarthy, ed., *Lady Bountiful Revisited: Women, Philanthropy, and Power* (New Brunswick, NJ: Rutgers University Press, 1990).

D. McClelland, *The Achieving Society* (New York: Van Nostrand, 1961).

K. McMullen & R. Brisbois, *Coping With Change: Human Resource Management in Canada's Non-Profit Sector*, CPRN Research Series on Human Resources in the Non-profit Sector, No. 4 (Ottawa: Canadian Policy Research Networks, 2003).

K. McMullen & G. Schellenberg, *Job Quality in the Non-Profit Sector*, CPRN Research Series on Human Resources in the Non-profit Sector, No. 2. Ottawa: Canadian Policy Research Networks, 2003).

K. McMullen & G. Schellenberg, *Mapping the Non-Profit Sector*. CPRN Research Series on Human Resources in the Non-profit Sector, No. 1 (Ottawa: Canadian Policy Research Networks, 2002).

S.L. McShane, *Canadian Organizational Behaviour*, 5th ed. (Toronto: McGraw-Hill Ryerson, 2004).

L. Meijs & E. Hoogstad, "New Ways of Managing Volunteers: Combining Membership Management and Programme Management" (2001) 3:3 Voluntary Action 41-61.

A.G. Meinhard, I. Sakinofsky & G. Matthews, *Human Resource Management in Small Nonprofit Organizations*. Centre for Voluntary Sector Studies, Working Paper Series (2009). Online at: <http://www.ryerson.ca/cvss/working_papers>.

A.G. Meinhard & M.K. Foster, "Differences in the Responses of Women's Voluntary Organizations to Shifts in Canadian Public Policy" (2003) 32:3 Nonprofit and Voluntary Sector Quarterly 366-396.

A.G. Meinhard & M.K. Foster, *The Impact of Community Service Programs on Students in Toronto's Secondary Schools* (Presented at the annual conference of the Association for Research on Nonprofit Organizations and Voluntary Action, Washington, DC (1999)).

A.G. Meinhard & M.K. Foster, *Women's Voluntary Organizations and the Restructuring of Canada's Voluntary Sector: A Theoretical Perspective* (Proceedings of the Annual Conference of the Administrative Sciences Association of Canada, St. John's, NL (1997).

A.G. Meinhard, M.K. Foster & I. Berger, *The Process of Institutional Isomorphism in Ontario's Voluntary Sector* (Presented at the annual conference of the Administrative Sciences Association of Canada, Quebec City, Quebec (2004)).

A.G. Meinhard, M.K. Foster & P. Wright, "Rethinking School-Based Community Service: The Importance of a Structured Program" (2006) 20:1 The Philanthropist 5-22.

F.E. Netting *et al.*, "Mixing and Phasing of Roles Among Volunteers, Staff, and Participants in Faith-Based Programs" (2005) 34:2 Nonprofit and Voluntary Sector Quarterly 179-205.

NSNVO (2005), *Cornerstones of community: Highlights of the National Survey of Nonprofit and Voluntary Organizations*, Catalogue No. 61-533-XIE (Ottawa: Statistics Canada, Minister of Industry, 2005). Online at: <http://sectorsource.ca/sites/default/files/nsnvo_report_english.pdf >.

B. O'Connell, *The Board Member's Book: Making a Difference in Voluntary Organizations* (New York: Foundation Center, 1985).

T. Odendahl, "Women's Power, Nonprofits and the Future" in T. Odendahl & M. O'Neill, eds., *Women and Power in the Nonprofit Sector* (San Francisco, CA: Jossey-Bass, 1994) 183-222.

M. Olson, *The Logic of Collective Action: Public Goods and the Theory of Groups* (Cambridge, MA: Harvard University Press, 1965).

M. O'Neill, "The Paradox of Women and Power in the Nonprofit Sector" in T. Odendahl & M. O'Neill, eds., *Women and Power in the Nonprofit Sector* (San Francisco, CA: Jossey-Bass, 1994) 1-16.

Ontario Ministry of Education, *Ontario Secondary Schools, Grades 9 to 12: Program and Diploma Requirements* (Toronto: Queen's Printer, 1999). Online at: <http://www.edu.gov.on.ca/eng/document/ curricul/ secondary/oss/oss.pdf>.

J. Onyx & M. Maclean, "Careers in the Third Sector" (1996) 6:4 Nonprofit Management and Leadership 331-345.

L.A. Pal, "Civic Re-alignment: NGOs and the Contemporary Welfare State" in R.B. Blake, P.E. Bryden, & J.F. Strain, eds., *The Welfare State in Canada: Past, Present and Future* (Concord, ON: Irwin Publishing, 1997) 88-104.

S. Puffer & J. Meindl, "Volunteers from Corporations: Work Cultures Reflect Values Similar to the Voluntary Organizations" (1995) 5:4 Nonprofit Management and Leadership 359-376.

R.D. Putnam, *Bowling Alone: The Collapse and Revival of American Community* (Toronto: Simon & Schuster, 2000).

S. Raskoff & R. Sundeen, "Youth socialization and civic participation: The role of secondary schools in promoting community service in southern California" (1998) 27:1 Nonprofit and Voluntary Sector Quarterly 66-87.

P. Reed & K. Selbee, *Distinguishing Characteristics of Active Volunteers in Canada: Nonprofit Sector Knowledge Base Project* (Ottawa: Statistics Canada, 1999).

D. Ross, "Managing Volunteers: When the Carrot is not a Paycheque" *CMA Magazine* 66:9 (1992) 30.

T. Routh, *The Volunteer and Community Agencies* (Springfield, IL: Thomas Books, 1972).

L.M. Salamon & H.K. Anheier, *The Emerging Nonprofit Sector: An Overview* (Manchester: Manchester University Press, 1996).

E. Schindler-Rainman & R. Lippitt, *The Volunteer Community: Creative Use of Human Resources*, 2d ed. (La Jolla, CA: University Associates, 1977).

H. Schmid & A.G. Meinhard, *A Comparative Analysis of Emerging Partnerships Between Corporations and Nonprofit Social Service*

Organizations in Canada and Israel (Presented at the annual conference of the Association for Research on Nonprofit Organizations and Voluntary Action, New Orleans, LA (2000)).

A.F. Scott, "Women's Voluntary Associations: From Charity to Reform" in K. McCarthy, ed., *Lady Bountiful Revisited: Women, Philanthropy, and Power* (New Brunswick, NJ: Rutgers University Press, 1990) 35-54.

D.H. Smith, "Altruism, Volunteers, and Volunteerism" in J.D. Harman, ed., *Volunteerism in the Eighties: Fundamental Issues in Voluntary Action* (Washington DC: University Press of America, 1982) 23-44.

Standing Committee on Finance, *The 1997 Budget and Beyond: Finish the Job.* Fifth Report of the Standing Committee on Finance, December 1996. Online at: <http://www.parl.gc.ca/Content/HOC/Archives/Committee/352/fine/reports/05_1996-12/fine-05-cov-e.html>.

Statistics Canada, *Business Dynamics in Canada, 2001*, Catalogue No. 61-534-XIE (Ottawa: Minister of Industry, 2005).

Statistics Canada, *Satellite Account of Nonprofit Institutions and Volunteering*, Catalogue No. 13-015-XIE (Ottawa: Minister of Industry, 2004). Online at: <http://www.statcan.ca/english/freepub/13-015-XIE/13-015-XIE2004000.pdf>.

F.W. Taylor, *The Principles of Scientific Management* (New York: Harper Brothers, 1911).

H.L. Taylor, "Volunteer Work Develops Many Skills: Keys to Effective Management" (1989) 14:2 Canadian Manager 27.

D. Torrington & L. Hall, *Personnel Management: A new Approach* (London: Prentice-Hall, 1987).

J. Wilson, "Volunteering" (2000) 26 Annual Review of Sociology 215-240.

M. Wilson, "Reversing the Resistance of Staff to Volunteers" Voluntary Action Leadership (1981 Spring) 21-24.

A. Wilson & G. Pimm, "The Tyranny of the Volunteer: The Care and Feeding of Voluntary Workforces" (1996) 34:4 Management Decision 24-39.

R. Wuthnow, *Acts of Compassion: Caring for Others and Helping Ourselves* (Princeton, NJ: Princeton University Press, 1991).

Chapter 12

OPTIMIZING THE POTENTIAL OF INFORMATION AND COMMUNICATIONS TECHNOLOGY IN NONPROFIT ORGANIZATIONS

Yvonne Harrison
University at Albany, SUNY

INTRODUCTION

In his book, *Making Nonprofits Work*, new governance scholar Paul Light (2000) concludes that nonprofit work is more difficult now than ever before. He points to "funders, be they governments, charitable foundations, or individual givers ... [being] so insistent about economy and results" and "clients, be they communities or individuals . . . [being] more demanding about efficiency and responsiveness" (p. v). With the global economic recession, nonprofit organizations throughout the world have had to respond more rapidly to changing conditions in the economic, social, technological, and political environments in which they operate. These pressures have renewed emphasis on the need to be more responsive to stakeholder needs and to be more efficient, effective and accountable. One of the major tools with the potential for providing help in doing this is information and communications technology (ICT).

Generally, the normative literature on ICT use in nonprofit and voluntary sector work is enthusiastic and supportive. Numerous studies point to the benefits of ICT use on a number of levels, including increases in organizational efficiency and effectiveness and enhanced relationships with constituents (*e.g.*, Blau (2001); Burt & Taylor (2000; 2003); Mele (2008); Saxton & Game (2001); Te'eni & Young (2003)). In the United Kingdom, Burt & Taylor (2000) report that the benefits "extend beyond conventional enhancements of administration and operational efficiency and effectiveness ...'. Embedded within electronic networks is the potential to reshape organizations internally, reconfigure relationships across networks of organizations, and redefine relationships with individual citizens" (at 131). In spite of this enthusiasm, however, the extent to which ICT tools have actually helped nonprofits meet their missions is a question that remains unanswered (Saidel & Cour (2003)).

A review of the literature on ICT adoption suggests that Canada is a world leader in the adoption of the Internet (OECD (2012)) and, more particularly, in its adoption by the voluntary sector (Parmegiani & Sachdeva (2000)). Nevertheless, there is mounting evidence that not all nonprofits are making full use of these resources, nor are they benefiting from them to the same degree (*e.g.*, Blau (2002); A. Hall (2001); Ipsos Reid (2001); Kirschenbaum & Kunamneni (2001); Ludgate & Surman (2004); Nonprofits' Policy and Technology Project (1998); Murray & Harrison (2004); Harrison & Murray (2007); Pitkin & Manzo (2002); and Ticher, Maison & Jones (2002)). Of course this problem is not confined to the non-profit and voluntary sector. It has been a concern to all those who study the "new economy" for some time (*e.g.*, Cooper (2004); McLoughlin & Harris (1997); OECD (2004); Te'eni & Young (2003); and Zuboff (1988)).

Te'eni & Young (2003) describe how the new economy[1] challenges and changes the role of nonprofits by "making disclosed information more readily available and also raising the expectations of consumers ..." (at 403). They caution that those who do not adopt the technology that lies behind this new economy will suffer serious consequences including a loss of "relative advantages ... compared to business and government, in providing services ..." (at 397). Failure to make use of ICT effectively also results in a waste of the money and time invested (Quinn (2005); Van Grembergen (2000)).

While ICT can act as a "double-edged sword" depending on how well it is used, the question nonprofits must be concerned with in the

---

[1]   Te'eni & Young (2003) define the new economy as the "general trend toward global organizations and marketplaces, a move from mainly tangible to combinations of tangible and intangible goods, and a leap into an intensely interlinked network of goods and agents"(at 397).

new economy is not "should we or shouldn't we adopt ICT?" but rather, *why* should we adopt it and how do we get the most out of what it has to offer?" Typical is this comment from Charity Channel's Stephen Nill (2005) in his review of Hart, Greenfield & Johnston's (2005) book, *Nonprofit Internet Strategies*:

> The simple truth is that the use of technology is one of the more challenging aspects facing those who manage nonprofit organizations. First, it is complicated ... Second, it is hard to have a clear idea of how to think about technology in the unique context of running a nonprofit organization. Third, it is hard to determine the best way to implement technological solutions when there are so many being thrown at us. Lastly, how can we be sure we're following best practices?[2]

This chapter draws from the growing literature on ICT adoption and use in the nonprofit and voluntary sector. It will address four questions non-profit and voluntary organizations face with regard to new ICT tools:

1. What is information and communications technology (ICT)?

2. What are the common types of ICT applications and how do we get the most out of them?

3. What factors influence the adoption and use of ICT?

4. How should we approach the management of ICT change?

WHAT IS INFORMATION AND COMMUNICATIONS TECHNOLOGY (ICT)?

While there is no generally accepted definition of ICT, one way to understand it is to look at the makeup of the ICT sector, delineated by the Organisation for Economic Cooperation and Development (OECD) (2008) as "the production of goods and services ... to fulfill or enable the function of information processing and communication by electronic means, including transmission and display" (at 34). Table 1 below illustrates the goods and services produced by the ICT sector in OECD categories.

---

[2]   See online at: <http://www.in.gov/arts/2447.htm>.

Table 1: ICT Sector as Defined by the OECD (2008)

ICT Sector	ICT
ICT Goods:	• Telecommunications equipment • Computer and related equipment • Network infrastructure, *e.g.*, wired, wireless, broadband cable and modems • Electronics components • Audio and video equipment • Other related goods (at 344)
ICT Services:	• Internet and Web services • Data hosting and software services • Other ICT services, *e.g.*, consulting, database, membership or subscriptions (at 343)

On a personal or business computing level, ICT includes the following components:

- Hardware (*e.g.*, laptop, desktop or handheld personal computer, mobile phone, audio and digital recorder, hard storage devices);

- Operating system software (*e.g.*, the operating systems like Windows, Mac OS, GNU/Linux);

- Software applications (off-the-shelf computer-based programs and Web-based software that is accessed from remote servers over the Internet, including free "open source",[3] software); and

- Network infrastructure, wired or wireless, such as the Internet or an Intranet that makes information sharing between computers and mobile devices possible.

While ICT can be separated into specific goods and services, when connected or combined in a network (*e.g.*, computer, software, and the Internet), they form what is known in the literature as an information system (IS) (Clarke (2001)).

The OECD (2000) reports that ICT is an example of a new general-purpose technology that has had pervasive effects on practically all sectors of the economy. Furthermore, a larger proportion of investment is now spent on ICT than all other general-purpose

---

[3]   For information on "open source" see online at: <http://directory.fsf.org/>.

technologies making the case for the emergence of a new economy. Lim (2001) refers to it as a "phenomenon ... where the main goods and energy of a social economy is converted to information through the revolution of high data communication technology and utilizing information produced by gathering, processing and distributing data within the vast fields of the society (National Computerization Agency [NCA], 1997)" (at 144 as cited in Lim, 2001).

With advancements in the World Wide Web (WWW), organizations are making more use of ICT. With the introduction of Web-based communications technology, new ICT applications have emerged that have redefined the nature of business and organization. The purpose of these tools is to transform work in order to increase organizational efficiency and effectiveness while decreasing overall costs (Cooper, (2004)). Arnant (2002) has pointed out that this "'redefining' process can be applied to just about any area of a business or organization: sales and marketing, accounting and finance, training and education, customer service, manufacturing or new business development" (at 7). For nonprofit and voluntary organizations, the process includes these and other organizational functions (*e.g.*, volunteerism, advocacy, fundraising, donor and stakeholder relations, and community development, *etc.*) (see Cravens & Jackson (2012), Clerkin & Gronbjerg (2007); Brainard & Brinkeroff (2004); Harrison & Murray (2007); McNutt (2007); Mele (2008); Nunn (2007); Saxton & Wang (2013); Saxton & Guo (2013); and Saidel & Cour (2003)).

No longer considered tools to conduct the work of organizations, the WWW has evolved to the level of social interaction. This is sometimes called "Web 2". Alexander (2006) defines "Web 2" as a set of ICT tools that are "profoundly social, as listservs, Usenet groups, discussion software, groupware, and Web-based communities have linked people around the world" (at 33). Facebook, Twitter, YouTube and Flikr are examples of Web 2.0 technologies designed to share news, events, videos and photos with others who are part of the same network.

These new tools represent a fundamental shift in the nature of information sharing on the WWW. In 2005, when the first edition of this book was written, the WWW was primarily used to *push* information to Web-users. In 2009 when the book was updated, the WWW was used to "pull" information from Web-users (*e.g.*, posting information on a blog, a status update on Facebook, content added to a Wiki). In 2005, most information on the WWW was organized in a directory specified and controlled by the Web owner. In 2009, Web-users used Web 2.0 tools to create content on the WWW as well as manage and organize it in ways that further developed and made sense of it. In economic terms, Tapscott & Williams (2008) suggest the changes in the WWW empowered users to "become their own supplier — in effect to become an economy unto themselves" (at 46). Though Alexander suggests that the content users contribute through Web 2.0 tools have been around for decades, the way these tools aggregate content is new (*e.g.*, from the contributions of many Web-users). Tapscott and Williams (2008) refer to Web 2.0 as a tool for "collective intelligence", while others suggest it is the ideal forum for collaboration. Whatever the term applied, Web 2.0 has evolved the WWW from a *closed* space where information-sharing was under the control of Web-owners to an *open* space where Web-users play a key role in sharing, organizing, and creating the information that is available on the WWW (O'Reilly (2009); Alexander (2006)).

The OECD (2012) predicts "a large expansion" of networks connecting "anywhere from ten to a hundred devices per family and thousands or potentially millions of devices per company" (at 7). As "economies and societies become increasingly intermeshed with devices that continuously communicate with each other and provide information to users", the Web has evolved further (OECD, 2012, at 7). A central feature of the "third wave" of the WWW is data processing "across multiple devices and networks" to inform people about their surroundings but also to provide information about people to third parties" (at 7). While the benefit to users is "personalized" content, the emergence of Web 3 tools raises privacy concerns and questions about data ownership and access (OECD, 2012) (See Table 2 below for differences between Web 1.0, 2.0 and 3.0 tools).

Table 2: Comparison of Web 1, 2 and 3

Web 1 "Closed System"	Web 2 "Open System"	Web 3 "Networks"
Owner Control	User Control	Technology Control
Content Pushed (*e.g.*, Website)	Content Pulled (*e.g.*, Blogs)	Content Shared (e.g., Databases)
Content Managed (Content Management Tools)	Content Created (Content Development Tools)	Content Generated (Web Applications)
Content Organized/Presented (Data Directories)	Content Developed/Streamed (Data Tagging)	Content Personalized (Data Mining)

A review of the literature suggests non-profit and voluntary organizations have significant advantages over other actors (*e.g.*, government and business) in the network economy. Kingsley (2007) suggests the non-profit sector is ideally suited to take on a leadership role in the new network economy because the sector is more "reflexive" and responsive, as well as "dynamic and eclectic in its relationships due to the very nature of the diverse actors ... that constitute its parts" (at 20). Te'eni and Young (2003) suggest non-profits have an information advantage over government because they are closest to citizens.

By way of example, many grassroots organizations that interact with citizens occupy virtual spaces (Kingsley, 2007). Melucci suggests a "planetary action system" of non-profit organizations has emerged where individual "stars" are being drawn into constellations, in which Keane (2003) suggests is "the first genuinely bottom-up transnational order, a global civil society in which millions of people come to realize, in effect, that they are incarnations of World Wide Webs of interdependence, whose complexity is riddled with opportunity as well as danger" (as cited by Kingsley, 2007, at 21).

In their 2008 book, *Wikinomics*, Tapscott & Williams suggest that the WWW is only now beginning to fulfill its "great promise of an Alexandrian library of all past and present information and a platform for collaboration to unite communities of all stripes in any conceivable art of creative enterprise" (at 37). With the collective generation of the Internet now upon us, nonprofit and voluntary organizations should be rethinking their institutional arrangements in order to "combine the advantages of small scale with the economies of scale provided by 'clusters' and networks" (Antonelli, Geuna & Steinmueller (2000, at 90)). In this new collective context, "innovation is fed by the interaction among a variety of learning players within multidisciplinary technological networks" (Antonelli *et al.*, at 90). It is this combination that "has emerged as the dominant mode of organization and the production of new knowledge" in the new economy (Antonelli *et al.*, at 90). At the same time, Rainee and Wellman remind us of two paradoxes in the networked economy:

- The tools "that connect people will also threaten to overload them with extra work" (l. 386).

- The tools that liberate people will require a greater investment of time and effort as the networks they belong to will "no longer take care of them" (l. 386).

According to sociologist Manuel Castells (1999), another challenge for human society is adaptability in an era of rapid technological change.

Simply put, technology can adapt to change in ways humans cannot. Additionally, the capability of technology to "link up everything that is valuable according to dominant values and interests, while disconnecting everything that is not valuable or becomes devalued … this simultaneous capacity to include and exclude people … leads to social underdevelopment, precisely at the threshold of the potentially most promising era of human fulfillment" (p. 2).

WHAT ARE THE COMMON TYPES OF ICT APPLICATIONS AND HOW DO YOU GET THE MOST OUT OF THEM?

There are two main types of ICT applications — those that primarily impact the way we interact with *people* and those that primarily make *organizations* perform more efficiently and effectively.

People

There are a number of ICT applications on the market designed for the purpose of engaging and managing people. Email, text and instant messaging are examples of *direct applications* that have transformed the way people share information and interact. *Indirect applications*, on the other hand, facilitate information sharing between people by way of a third party. For example, information is shared with a large number of people through an ICT service provider such as Website owner, Web forum, Web blog, Social Network (*e.g.*, Twitter), or Real Simple Service (RSS) feed (*i.e.*, digital audio feed that can be downloaded from the Internet and played on a personal digital audio device like an iPod). In some cases, ICT applications enhance traditional forms of engagement (*e.g.*, chat or meeting). In others, they extend or involve new forms of engagement (*e.g.*, podcasting, crowdsourcing and micro-volunteering).

Direct Applications

Communication

Defined by some as "a method of composing, sending, storing and receiving messages over electronic communication systems" (*i.e.*, through a computer, email software application, and Internet network), email brings people who are physically or geographically separated, together (Wikipedia, (2005)). In 2013, The Radicati Group estimated the number of email accounts worldwide at 3.9 billion with 4.9 billion expected by 2019. Email use, on the other hand, is at 100 billion messages per day (sent and received) with an expected annual growth of 7 per cent to 132 billion by 2017. Consumer email use on the other hand, is expected to decline by 3 to 4 per cent annually as text, instant messaging and communications through social media applications increase.[4]

In Canada, email is generally widely adopted in organizations. According to a 2007 Statistics Canada survey, 100 per cent of public sector organizations used email, with 81 per cent of the private sector using it. Within the private sector, arts and recreation sectors used it the most (86 per cent) followed by health and social service agencies (79 per cent).[5] A 2012 Statistics Canada survey of Digital Technology and Internet Use by Canadian private enterprises provides evidence of a shift in communications technology adoption with large enterprises (100 or more full-time equivalent (FTE)) significantly more likely to adopt Customer Relationship Management (CRM) (41 per cent) and Enterprise Resource Planning (ERP) (35 per cent) software than small-to medium-sized enterprises (less than 100 FTE) (12 per cent CRM and 5 per cent ERP).[6]

While CRM, ERT, and social networking applications "might displace email", Delany (2011) suggests email "is still by far the most widely used supporter-contact tool".[7] In his 2003 book, *The Basics of Nonprofit Email*, leading nonprofit ICT consultant Michael Gilbert questions whether email is having as positive an impact on nonprofits as it could. Though he and Forum One's Managing Director, Andrew Cohen refer to email as the "killer application" of the Internet, Gilbert is quick to point out that nonprofits "have only scratched the surface" of email use and usefulness; that a number of factors continue to stand in the way of increased email effectiveness.[8] He suggests that nonprofits should use email to build relationships, share (*e.g.*, electronic newsletters) and collect information (*e.g.*, electronic questionnaires), connect with prospective and traditional donors, and promote the sale of goods and services ("e-commerce"). However, he cautions against being "disingenuous" (*e.g.*, sending out "email blasts".[9]

---

[4]   See <http://www.radicati.com/wp/wp-content/uploads/2013/04/Email-Statistics-Report-2013-2017-Executive-Summary.pdf>.

[5]   See online: <http://www40.statcan.gc.ca/l01/cst01/econ146a-eng.htm>.

[6]   See online at: <http://www.statcan.gc.ca/daily-quotidien/130612/dq130612a-eng.htm>. For more information on use of CRM in nonprofit and voluntary organizations see <http://www.techsoup.org/support/articles-and-how-tos/few-good-crm-tools>.

[7]   See online at: <http://www.epolitics.com/2006/07/03/online-advocacy-tools-email-lists/>.

[8]   See online at: <http://forumone.com/blogs/post/12-big-trends-nonprofit-technology-2012>.

[9]   See online at: <http://news.gilbert.org/EmailBlastSyndrome>.

With one report showing nonprofit email response rates on the decline,[10] Gilbert's (2003) advice to nonprofits wanting to increase effectiveness through email communication may be more important than ever. The following key words provide a framework for Gilbert's best practice email advice to nonprofits:

Humanize

Communicate in the online world the same way you would in the offline world. Gilbert argues for a "human" response to email communications. He cites Locke, Levine, Searls & Weinberger (2001) who emphasize "genuineness in communication between people" even when some of those communications take place in the online world (at 34). Gilbert describes how communications in the online world can be thought of "as the very lifeblood of an organization … an invitation to deeper engagement" (at 34).

Relationship

Use email to build relationships first, content second. Gilbert describes an overabundance of "issue heads" in nonprofit and voluntary organizations. He defines an "issue head" as someone "deeply engaged with the subject matter of his or her work" (at 37). He claims that being "issue" oriented "can lead nonprofits to have a deeper relationship with the content that they send to their supporters, rather than with the supporters themselves" (at 37). He argues that the direction of email communications should flow from relationship to content, not the other way around. At the same time, Delany (2008) cautions that email communication must contain "content [that] is going to be worth the effort" for the receiver to respond (at 6). Delany suggests email messages should contain links that allow subscribers to unsubscribe as well as mail forward (within networks) and advocacy functions (*e.g.*, to write to elected officials about causes).[11]

Responsible

Take responsibility for email by safeguarding your contacts and accessing new ones responsibly. Gilbert cautions against purchasing email lists as they "create the slippery slope toward becoming a

---

[10] See <http://e-benchmarksstudy.com/> for a copy of the 2013 eNonprofit Benchmarks Study by M-R Strategic Services and NTEN.

[11] See online at: <http://www.epolitics.com/onlinepolitics101.pdf>.

spammer" (at 33). To establish new email relationships, Gilbert suggests asking stakeholders to introduce you to their contacts. New relationships are more likely to develop if an existing relationship is in place. If an email list is purchased, Delany (2008) advises that it contain the names of "opt-ins" or the people who agreed to be on the list (at 17).

Trusting

Manage email relationships in a way that builds trust. Gilbert suggests giving stakeholders control over how they wish to be involved. According to Friedman, Kahn & Howe (2000), giving stakeholders control over how they wish to be involved in the online environment helps to build trusting relationships by "easing cooperation among people and fostering reciprocal care-taking" (at 34). Another way to build trust electronically is to let stakeholders know that your organization has adopted a code of ethics for online conduct. There are several useful codes of conduct available to assist nonprofits in this regard. One code that relates to email comes from TRUSTe, a nonprofit email accrediting organization that offers a privacy seal based on an assessment of an organization's email practices.

Collect

Never pass up an opportunity to collect an email address. Gilbert describes access to email addresses as the "most important level of engagement" (at 32). He suggests nonprofit Websites be set up so as to collect email addresses on each Web page. As well, nonprofits should ensure that in every form of communication, the opportunity to collect email addresses is presented.[12]

Respond

Treat email as you would the telephone. In the private sector, many managers believe that not answering a telephone call from a customer translates into loss of the customer. Not answering email is similar. Gilbert suggests, "people expect email to be returned on much the same schedule as they expect phone messages to be returned, but many organizations fail to meet that expectation" (at 34). In the context of online recruitment of volunteers, Harrison & Murray (2007) report that nonprofit managers who fail to use ICT in volunteerism effectively will

---

[12] For information on the use of email marketing see online at: <http://www.epolitics.com/2006/07/03/online-advocacy-tools-email-lists/>.

not only lose contact with the prospective volunteer but may suffer the negative consequence of having the prospective volunteer say negative things about their volunteer experience.

Apart from email usage patterns, nonprofits also need to address the security and privacy aspects of their email communications. For a summary of the CAN-SPAM Act[13] and practical information on avoiding spam in nonprofit email see the "CAN-SPAM Compliance Checklist" published by Return Path.[14]

Messaging

Defined by some as "the act of instantly communicating between two or more people over a network" by way of a computer or a mobile phone, Instant and Text Messaging (I/TM) is different from email in that it can put users in "real-time" person-to-person communication with one another.[15] One application of I/TM is in the area of volunteer management as a way of contacting volunteers, or putting them in touch with one another, especially at certain times, such as while a special event or campaign is under way or in times of disaster. Former United Nations Volunteers co-ordinator Jayne Cravens has stated she prefers IM to email because it is much easier "to build a relationship with a volunteer and get much more of an idea of his or her personality via IM than email".

Another application of it is in the area of building support for a campaign. A notable example comes from the 2008 and 2012 U.S. presidential campaigns where candidate Barack Obama used it as "part of a mobile marketing strategy" to develop relationships with prospective volunteers, inform and collect donations from them, as well as mobilize them and their friends. Referred to in the literature as "micro-volunteering", mobile messaging helped him form real-time relationships as well as build a database of supporters. Specific details of the Obama strategy included options for prospective volunteers to join the campaign (*e.g.*, to subscribe or unsubscribe), options for them to help grow the campaign (*e.g.*, have the volunteer "tell a friend") as well as to get involved in the campaign (*e.g.*, by sending volunteers to an interface where they could engage in specific activities associated with it). Embedded in every message was the capability to collect

---

[13] *Controlling the Assault of Non-solicited Pornography and Marketing*, 15 U.S.C., c. 103.

[14] Online at: <http://www.returnpath.com/wp-content/uploads/resource/can-spam-compliance-checklist/Return-Path-CAN-SPAM-Reference-9_12.pdf>.

[15] See online at: <http://en.wikipedia.org/wiki/Instant_messaging>.

information (*e.g.*, phone numbers, email addresses, and zip codes).[16] With global access to mobile phones on the rise, I/TM is fast becoming the "killer app" for International Development. The United Nations Development Programme (UNDP) estimates that over three-quarters of the global population (5.4 out of 7 billion people) have access to a mobile phone with 80 to 90 per cent of those in the poorest regions having at least some access. The UNDP elaborates on the benefits of mobile strategies,

> ... mobile technologies offer portable, real-time communication and information access for people who previously had little to no access to affordable communication channels. Mobiles have relatively low physical infrastructure requirements and can reach remote areas in a more cost-effective fashion than other ICTs such as the Internet or fixed phone lines. In some places, mobile devices are simply the only option available. And mobile phones require only basic literacy, making the barriers to entry much lower than with other modern ICTs.[17]

While there are a growing number of uses for I/TM as described above, Richards (2001) cautions against using it for file sharing because of copyright violation. He recommends that managers become aware of the legal implications of file sharing and adopt ethical file-sharing practices to ensure compliance with copyright law (Richards (2001)). The author of *Instant Messaging Rules*, Nancy Flynn (2004) goes one step further in suggesting organizations consider the security (use of multiple and unsecure systems) and privacy risks (records of IM) associated with it. In addition, there are other risks associated with computer identity theft, viruses, worms, and other malicious software, and SPIM, a form of SPAM for IM that may contain pornographic information.

Collaborating

Most Web-conferencing software applications, which can be downloaded and accessed over the Internet for a fee or within an existing application, provide virtual facilities that a traditional onsite meeting would provide (*e.g.*, meeting room, white board, file-sharing, IM, email discussion, *etc.*). When combined with a free Internet Voice Over IP telephone service such as Skype,[18] these applications can provide nonprofit and voluntary organizations with a low-cost collaborating and meeting device.

---

[16] See online at: <http://e-strategyblog.com/2008/08/texting-the-vp-barack-obamas-mobile-marketing-effort/>.

[17] See online: <http://issuu.com/undp/docs/mobile_technologies_and_empowerment_en> 8.

[18] See <http://www.skype.com>.

Web-conferencing decreases the cost of travel and increases the connectivity of the organization internally and externally. The effectiveness of Web-conferencing depends on a number of factors, including the technological speed at which meeting participants can connect their computers to the conference. Some Web-conferencing applications allow the moderating organization to set the connection speed, which is important in ensuring participants experience the same audio and video quality. This is especially important when working with organizations in rural areas or internationally in places with limited access to the Internet (*e.g.*, dial-up connection only; limited bandwidth because Internet traffic prevents high quality connection).

While there are technological considerations in planning Web conferences and meetings, special attention should be paid to leadership in the planning and facilitation of online meetings. This means, those who chair online meetings should be considered by others to have the organization, communication (written and oral), and facilitation skills to move the virtual group toward shared goals, values, and meeting norms. In addition, Web-conference software vendor, Elluminate, recommends chairs demonstrate the following "habits of highly effective moderators":

1. Knowledgeable and enthusiastic about the benefits of the technology and use of it;

2. Schedule time for participants to log on early to the meeting to become familiar with the technology;

3. Coordinate IT support with participants prior to the meeting to troubleshoot potential technological problems (site or application specific);

4. Instruct participants on use of online features and encourage their use during the meeting;

5. Obtain feedback from participants on the effectiveness of the technology at the end of the meeting;

6. Recognize and summarize contributions to the meeting, including use of technology; and

7. Provide a recording of the meeting and documents produced from it.[19]

---

[19] See online at: <http://www.elluminate.com/downloads/whitepapers/Top-Ten-Habits-of-Highly-Effective-Elluminate-Moderators.pdf>.

In summary, while direct ICT applications like email, I/TM, and collaborating tools like Web conferencing provide nonprofits with the means to hold meetings, communicate and share work, the trend is toward "unifying communications" (UC) strategy, a "buzzword" Elliot Harmon says is used to describe the integration and alignment of ICT tools with business strategy. He suggests the size of the organization and scope of the work involved should be considered before adopting a UC approach.[20]

Communities of Practice

An online community of practice (COP) is a "designed community that uses network technology" (Johnson, 2001, at 45). A key feature of the kind of COP advocated by Johnson is that learning and development of new knowledge emerge from them. Johnson identifies three features that distinguish online from traditionally organized communities of practice:

1. There is no hierarchy. They include within them different levels of expertise that are simultaneously present in the community of practice.

2. There is fluidity of movement within the community "that symbolizes the progression from being a novice to an expert".

3. The communication that occurs within them is "completely authentic" (at 45).

An example of an online COP is The Global Solidarity Network Study e.Broad Program (GSNSEB),[21] a participatory learning community that connects students and faculty in some higher education institutions in the United States to Catholic Relief Services (CRS) policy experts and staff working on the front lines of social injustice (*e.g.*, human migration, food security, disaster relief, peace and conflict) in developing countries. This online COP provides members (faculty, students, NGO staff) with a collaborative space to access information, discuss critical social justice issues, and interact with CRS policy experts and staff around the world. An evaluation of this COP by Harrison *et al.* showed that while it increased student knowledge and understanding of the diversity of perspectives of the issues discussed and generated feelings of compassion and advocacy

---

[20] See online at: <http://www.techsoup.org/support/articles-and-how-tos/unified-communications-options-for-nonprofits>.

[21] See <http://university.crs.org/gsn/>.

for those affected by them, not all users (institutions, faculty and students) were keen to join and engage in the participatory learning community. Clearly communicating the purpose for engagement and having a well-designed structure to engage online as well as addressing fundamental barriers to engagement (*e.g.*, lack of time) were some of the recommendations made to increase the effectiveness of this COP (see Harrison *et al.* (2010) for more information).

While the GSNSEB is an example of a network of formal institutions organizing to deliver an online global social justice educational program, Brainard & Brinkerhoff (2004) describe two informal cases of cyber grassroots organizations (CGOs) that used the Internet to create community. In the CGOs they studied, they found that while CGOs "performed the same set of functions" and facilitated "highly personal communication" as grassroots organizations in the physical world, they were completely different in that they "included little or no face-to-face interaction" (at 50). They predict that as globalization and technology advances so too will our understandings of community. Specifically, it will "blur the demarcations between communities and categories thereby facilitating a CGO's ability to provide multiple benefits simultaneously to members and non-members alike" (at 50). It is this aspect of community that they link to the development of social capital as the online community interacts (bonds) and engages (bridges) in shared goals. They say the challenge for CGOs in developing social capital will increase with formalization (at 48). In these cases, they suggest the community "operate on the basis of norms rather than formal rules, and these norms continue to be developed by members through debating and enacting them" (at 48).

Knowledge Management

In the "knowledge economy", a number of applications exist to inform and educate managers about nonprofits and voluntary sector work. Among them is the library of Imagine Canada. This site will direct the reader to nonprofit and voluntary sector research and best practice reports.[22]

Outside of access to expert information and advice, online training programs have emerged in Canada to provide practical advice to nonprofit leaders in a number of areas. One example is Imagine Canada's, *Strengthening Organizations: Webinar Series for Nonprofits*

---

[22] <http://sectorsource.ca/>.

and Charities. This series offers online courses for a fee to help nonprofits meet Imagine Canada standards in nonprofit governance, finance and fundraising and human resources management. Users typically register and participate online by purchasing a "seat" in the online training application.[23]

For working professionals looking for a formal academic credential, two new nonprofit graduate degree programs have emerged in Canada that blend online and face-to-face onsite residency programs. In western Canada, University of Victoria offers the Master of Arts in Community Development (MACD) to "help communities address the challenges of a rapidly changing world".[24]

In eastern Canada, working professionals now have access to Carlton University's, Master of Philanthropy and Nonprofit Leadership (MPNL), a six credit, 11 course graduate degree program with a mission to "create innovators and leaders for those who work in or interact with nonprofit and voluntary organizations.[25]

With the emergence of *Massive Online Open Courses* (MOOCs), some U.S. institutions of higher education are partnering with third party technology providers (*e.g.*, for profit Coursera, Udacity; nonprofit EdX) to offer academic courses online to their students and the public for free. While the business model specifying how revenue will be earned from free courses is still being worked out, MOOCs have the potential to bridge the divide between those who can afford higher education and those who cannot. In theory, although making courses available to those for whom education can truly make a difference makes sense, concerns have been raised about the quality of MOOCs, particularly the low level of discourse and student push back over course costs (*e.g.*, purchasing course materials and time to do course work). Some have also questioned the utility of MOOCs when the completion rate is so low (Kolowich, 2013, at A6). One response to addressing these concerns has been to step up the quality of online instruction and the amount of end-user technology support. As Steven Kolowich (2013) recently reported in the *Chronicle of Higher Education*, this strategy will increase academic quality and decrease the cost of MOOCs and online learning platforms as competition within the technology education marketplace increases.

---

[23] See online: <http://www.imaginecanada.ca/> for more information.

[24] See online: <http://ring.uvic.ca/10jul/macd.html>; <http://www.uvic.ca/hsd/publicadmin/programs/graduate/maInCommunityDevelopment/>.

[25] See online: <http://www6.carleton.ca/mpnl/>.

One MOOC that may be of considerable interest to members of the nonprofit and voluntary sector is the Metaliteracy MOOC offered by the University at Albany, SUNY and Empire State College. Through the Metaliteracy MOOC, undergraduate and graduate students in these New York institutions and members of the public will explore and engage in "emerging technologies ... to effectively participate in social media and online learning communities".[26]

With respect to the effectiveness of online learning, Dziuban, Moskal & Dziuban (2000) claim that these programs have created a new context for learning. Within this context, end user and content deliverer roles have shifted. For users, the role is that of responsible "life-long learners" who are in charge of what they learn and how they interact with the new media. For the content deliverer, the role is of "facilitator of incremental and interactive cyber pedagogy" (at 174). While the learning context has changed, they present research that shows most learners prefer a "mixed" learning environment that combines online and traditional pedagogy often referred to as hybrid or blending learning (see Dziuban, Hartman & Moskal (2004)).

These authors suggest that blended learning may be a first step for most organizations contemplating online learning models. They found the most successful blended learning models were those that ...

1. Shifted learning from lecture to interactive instruction;

2. Increased student-instructor interaction; and

3. Increased summative and formative assessment.

In addition, they claim success was maximized when there was "high quality faculty development, course development assistance, learner support, and ongoing formative and summative assessment" (at 3).

Fundraising

Of all the nonprofit ICT applications on the market, online giving or e-philanthropy appear to have generated the most interest and success. While no estimates are available for Canada, Network for Good, a nonprofit organization with the mission to increase online fundraising capacity that acquired ePhilanthropy in 2008, reports that private giving reached over five billion dollars worldwide with online giving representing approximately half of this amount (USD $2.62 billion).

---

[26] For more information on Metaliteracy and the MOOC see online at: <http://metaliteracy.cdlprojects.com/what.htm>.

The size of online giving is related to "significant increases in online giving for both small and large organizations and the unprecedented use of the Internet for tsunami and hurricane relief efforts ...".[27] Shaver (2006) offers the following statistics as a way of predicting the acceptance of online giving in Canadian nonprofits:

> The estimated 45 per cent of donations to Hurricane Katrina made online was higher than the 22 per cent for the tsunami, which in turn was higher than the percentage for any previous disaster — including 9/11. Nonprofits are taking note, and fewer will be on the digital sidelines in 2006.[28]

A report by the Chronicle of Philanthropy showed the amount of money raised online through global relief efforts for the Haitian earthquake in 2010 exceeded 9/11 and the tsunami disasters but was close to the amount raised for Hurricane Katrina (USD $520 million versus USD $568 million). While the amount was similar, a major difference between the Haitian and Hurricane relief efforts was the use of smart phones and social media applications to collect donations. Referred to in the normative literature as micro-volunteering, the use of smart phone technology to support causes is on the rise. In the Haitian earthquake social media was used to *collect* donations *and* to provide a *forum* for donors to communicate donation preferences.[29]

In 2009, firstgiving.com, a private online fundraising organization reported collecting USD $94,748,794 for 24,781 nonprofits listed on Guidestar, a public charity that keeps a database of records (*e.g.*, tax and charitable giving information) on U.S. nonprofits. U.S. President Obama used ICT to fundraise with some estimating that donations reached half a billion dollars in the two years of his presidential campaign.[30]

While most nonprofit Websites have a link to online giving, Grobman (2001) cautions that nonprofits consider the following factors[31] prior to adopting an online giving/fundraising strategy:

1. *Legal.* New Antiterrorism legislation adopted in Canada after the September 11, 2001 attacks on the United States includes

---

[27] Accessed online from: <http://www.imakenews.com/ephilanthropy/e_article000413576.cfm?x=b5wpwKf, b3D0cyPh,w>.

[28] See online at: <http://www.supportingadvancement.com/vendors/canadian_fundraiser/articles/online_fundraising.htm>.

[29] See <http://philanthropy.com/article/Social-Media-Aid-Efforts-to/63566/>.

[30] For "Online Fundraising Tips" and best practices, click on the following link: <http://www.fundraising123.org/fundraising>.

[31] Grobman's considerations are expanded to reflect the Canadian nonprofit context.

money-laundering legislation. The federal government of Canada has set up a Financial Action Task Force (FATF) to sort through the policy implications of the legislation. According to its Website: "the FATF is an intergovernmental body whose purpose is the development and promotion of national and international policies to combat money laundering and terrorist financing".[32] As part of their "due diligence", nonprofits will need to review and consider the implications of this legislation before hiring fundraising professionals and engaging in e-commerce activities.

2. *Ethical*. Nonprofits should also be aware of the threat that online fundraising may be used fraudulently. It is up to nonprofit managers and boards of directors to protect individual donors. One way to ensure authenticity is to adopt Imagine Canada's Ethical Fundraising and Financial Accountability Code.[33] The Salvation Army, for example, has adopted this code, which lays out SA's fundraising "obligations" for individual donors.[34]

3. *Tax*. As of 2005, the Canada Revenue Agency (CRA) requires that registered charities include the CRA's Website on all charitable donation receipts. The CRA also requires that all online receipts be delivered in an unalterable format (*e.g.*, PDF document).

4. *Service Provider*. Nonprofits must consider the costs associated with collecting donations online. Many e-commerce providers are private technology companies that take a percentage of the donation to make a profit (*e.g.*, to facilitate the transaction between the donor and the bank). The banks also take a percentage of the transaction to cover profit and processing costs. It is important to know that while e-commerce is a standard and "seamless" practice, it involves a host of costs and business relationships.

5. *Marketing*. Once the e-commerce service is operational, nonprofits must be sure to market it vigorously. Promoting online sites through direct email marketing (*e.g.*, by using a third party provider in Constant Contact) is important as is ensuring Website

---

[32] See online: <http://www.fatf-gafi.org/media/fatf/documents/reports/Corruption%20Reference%20Guide%20and%20Information%20Note%202012.pdf>.

[33] See online: <http://www.imaginecanada.ca/ethicalcode>.

[34] See online: <http://www.salvationarmy.ca/fundraisingethics>.

search engines are updated with the appropriate key words or "meta tags".[35]

For tips on selecting an online fundraising database see online: <http://www.idealware.org/articles/ten_common_mistakes_in_selecting_donor_databases.php>; for an online giving software report see online: <http://www.idealware.org/donations/idealware_online_donations.pdf>.

Indirect ICT Applications

Blogging

WordPress, Tumblr, Blogging, Twitter are all examples of free blogging or micro-blogging applications. Smith, Kearns, & Fine (2005) has defined this relatively recent phenomenon as "web-based applications used to post journal-like commentaries" (at 36) hence the name "blogs" stands for "Web logs". "Bloggers" are individuals who informally publish their opinions in the online environment using text, images, media objects and data. While no numbers are available for Canada, Sifry estimated in 2005 there were 22 to 26 million U.S. blogs with 184 million worldwide.[36] According to Wortham (2013), the free micro-blogging company, "Twitter has more than 200 million monthly active users [while] Facebook has more than a billion".

Rudolf (2005) describes two types of blogs: "aggregation" and "open-ended". Aggregation blogs are issue-specific whereas open-ended blogs place no restriction on blogger content. Open-ended blogs allow for free access (*i.e.*, any blogger can participate) while issue-specific blogs may place restrictions on participation (*e.g.*, must be a registered or approved blogger to join). Nonprofits can make use of blogs to become informed about issues or to engage the involvement of those concerned about their issues. On another level, blogs are an important tool for nonprofits to engage constituents, especially donors and volunteers, who want to stay engaged or have little time to attend nonprofit events.

According to Rohit Bhargava, author of the marketing book, *Personality Not Included*, event blogging is a great way to drive traffic to Websites especially when they are costly (*e.g.*, a nonprofit conference or fundraiser). He says the key to creating quality blog

---

[35] See Network for Good's non-profit marketing checklist online: <http://www.fundraising123. org/article/laying-good-foundation-short-term-priorities-nonprofits#.UijIEO1uHzI>.

[36] Accessed online: <http://technorati.com/blogging/state-of-the-blogosphere>.

content from an event is to consider the content against the framework of the following questions:

- Does the content have a purpose? He suggests that the blogger think about the purpose of the blog for those that they will connect with (through the blog) to ensure that they find meaning in it.

- Is the content accurate and timely? For example, does the content reflect what is going on at the event and when? Is it designed for the intended audience? He suggests that Twitter is an effective tool for "sending out information on the best sound bites of an event ... with tags for content using the keywords used by people at the event".

- Is the content the right amount? Bhargava suggests that bloggers consider the length of their content. Recall that bloggers are in a relationship with Web-users so they should strive to produce content as short conversations rather than "manifestos". For example, with Twitter shorter is "Tweeter" when it comes to length.

- Does the content provide a perspective? While the blogger represents the information, the tools should be used to share their own perspective on the event/topic they are covering as well as the perspectives of others.

- Does the blog summarize the content? (*e.g.*, all of the tweets posted during the event). This is an important step in reviewing and synthesizing the content in a way that recaps the event and extends it by raising new questions or insights about an issue coming out of an event.[37]

For a listing of open-source blogging applications see online: <http://directory.fsf.org/search/fsd-search.py?q=blogging>. For tools to edit and organize blogs see online: <http://www.hongkiat.com/blog/blogging-application-tools/>.

Podcasting

"Podcasting's essence is about creating content (audio and video) for an audience that wants to listen or watch when they want, where they want, and how they want."[38] Really Simple Syndication (RSS) and XML (Extensible Markup Language) provide the tools to create audio and video content that can be accessed over the Internet from

---

[37] See online: <http://rohitbhargava.typepad.com/weblog/2009/05/how-to-live-blog-or-twitter-an-event-effectively.html> for the full blog.

[38] Accessed online from: <http://en.wikipedia.org/wiki/ Podcasting>.

podcaster Websites. Not confined to audio and video, PodZinger has created a tool to transform audio into digital text. The tools are so freely available that many nonprofit organizations have become "podcasters", creating their own podcasts and making them accessible (*e.g.*, on their Websites or in the iTunes store) for download.

While podcasts can be downloaded and played on a computer, a mobile phone or personal audio device (*e.g.*, mp3 player), it is the iPod that is responsible for the podcasting phenomenon (*e.g.*, in 2005 the New Oxford Dictionary declared "podcast" word of the year) (Pew Internet, 2006). While no data exists on the use of podcasts by nonprofits, the rate of adoption of RSS feeds is staggering. Hart, Pierson & Hull (2005) cite statistics that showed over 1,700 RSS feeds were available for podcasting within the six months of being made available.[39] In 2009, PodcastAlley — a private online podcast directory, claims to have 62,000 podcasts — a remarkable number given that it reported only 1,000 in 2004.[40] In 2013, Pew's Research Center for Excellence in Journalism published a report that showed the number of podcasts, which increased significantly between 2009 and 2011 (from 65,000 to over 90,000 podcasts), has stabilized at 91, 765 with no significant growth since 2011.[41]

With regard to use of podcasts, Madden of the Pew Internet Project reported in 2006 that 12 per cent of the Internet users they surveyed[42] had downloaded a podcast with only 1 per cent (n=28) downloading them frequently. In 2008 adoption had increased to 19 per cent and 3 per cent respectively.[43] While still low in adoption and use, podcasting is a potentially useful tool for nonprofits for a number of reasons:

1. It reduces the amount of work by providing a means of translating audio into digital feeds that can be stored and shared electronically over a large network (*e.g.*, externally in the iTunes store, or internally with staff, the board, stakeholders).

2. It provides busy managers with an opportunity to listen to information that they have little time to read (*e.g.*, listen to minutes of board meetings in the car radio by way of a personal audio device and an FM transmitter).

---

[39] Accessed online: <http://www.burningdoor.com/feedburner/archives/001029.html>.

[40] See online: <http://www.podcastalley.com>.

[41] See online: <http://stateofthemedia.org/2013/audio-digital-drives-listener-experience/12-number-of-podcasts-stood-at-virtual-standstill-in-2012/>.

[42] Twelve per cent represents 338 of the 2,822 Internet users surveyed.

[43] Accessed online: <http:///www.pewinternet.org/files/old-media//Files/Reports/2008/PIP_Podcast_2008_Memo.pdf.pdf>.

3.   It can increase knowledge and transparency (*e.g.*, creating podcasts on specific topics and posting them on the organization's Website).

4.   They can help market and grow the brand of the nonprofit and provide another forum for communication.

For information on podcasting and downloading audio and video podcasts see online: <http://en.wikipedia.org/wiki/Uses_of_podcasting>; and <http://www.wikihow.com/Use-Podcasting>.

Social Networking

With the evolution of the WWW and Web 2 tools (*e.g.*, Facebook, MySpace, Twitter and a host of other social media applications, *etc.*), Websites have provided a platform for organizations and forum for people to share information and communicate (*e.g.*, opinions, photos, music, *etc.*) within a social network (Karlin (2007)). Notley (2008) defines a social network as an "internet-based environment that requires membership for participation whereby membership facilitates a relationship through which resources (both material and immaterial) can be mobilized" (at 20-21). Boyd & Ellison (2007, at 211) define it further as a type of ICT application that allow individuals to:

1.   Construct a public or semi-public profile within a bounded system;

2.   Articulate a list of other users with whom they share a connection; and

3.   View and traverse their list of connections and those made by others within the system.[44]

With regard to adoption of social networking applications in Canada, the following statistics are noteworthy:

•   Half of Canadians over the age of 55 have established a social network profile compared to 86 per cent of 18- to 24-year-olds (Dewing, 2013).

•   Canadian men use the Internet more at home whereas women are more likely to use social media as part of their daily routines. Also, 92 per cent of Canadian women have a Facebook profile compared to 75 per cent of men (Dewing, 2013).

With respect to the adoption of social media and networking applications by nonprofits, Hart & Greenwell (2009) report that

---

[44]   See online: <http://jcmc.indiana.edu/vol13/issue1/boyd.ellison.html>.

235,000 nonprofit organizations were members of Facebook: "More than 25 million active users of Facebook's 200 million worldwide members have signed on as supporters of at least one [nonprofit] cause, making it the third most popular of the more than 52,000 applications on the site" (at 1).

An April 2009 Nonprofit Technology Network (NTEN), Common Knowledge, and ThePort survey of nonprofits about their use of social networks defined social networks into two types:

1. Commercial Social Networks — a social network owned and operated by a private corporation from its Website (*e.g.*, Facebook, Twitter, MySpace).

2. House Social Networks — a social network owned and operated by a nonprofit organization from its own website.

They asked nonprofits (n=980) about their use of social networking applications and Websites, including the purpose, amount of time allocated to managing them, the number of members, how much revenue they generated for the organization, as well as characteristics of responding organizations. They report the following usage statistics:

- 74.1 per cent of respondents reported establishing a presence on Facebook, a popular commercial social network. Ninety four per cent of nonprofits used Twitter.

- One-third of the nonprofits they studied had developed "their own house social networks from a variety of social network software vendors" (at 2).

- The average size of nonprofit house social networks (10,000) was twice as large as commercial social networks (5,391).

- Nonprofits allocated little staffing (<.25 FTE) and no financial resources to 40 per cent of them. Of those that allocated resources only 8 per cent allocated more than USD $10,000.

- Social networks were not revenue generators with only 40 per cent raising funds and less than one-third of that amount raising more than $500 (annual) (*e.g.*, when used as fundraising or advertising tools). Eighty-eight had raised more than $10,000 and only one of the 235,000 nonprofit Facebook members had raised more than $100,000. This finding is in keeping with Hart & Greenwell (2009) who found few nonprofits had fundraised successfully through them.

Beth Kanter (2014), lead author of the 2012 book *Measuring the Net-worked Nonprofit*, claims it is the heavy user of social media that is the most likely to donate to a cause after learning about it through social media. Not only is the heavy user more likely to donate to the cause, they are also more likely to use their social network to tell others about it. These donors are also more likely to be new voluntarism suggesting a market to be tapped. Kanter supports these assertions with empirical data drawn from a large-scale quantitative study she and Vancouver-based market research firm, Vision Critical conducted that examined the relationship between donor social media use and donations in Canada and the United States (see <http://www.slideshare.net/visioncritical/smdata> for a summary of the study and results).

The findings above support the assertion of Murray and Harrison (2002a), Harrison, Murray, and MacGreogor (2004), Harrison (2005), and Veenhof *et al.* (2008) made about Internet users in Canada, that is, those who spend time online tend to be "civically and socially engaged using the Internet to find out about opportunities and make contact with others" about them (p. 4).

Social networks are potentially very useful for nonprofits for a number of reasons, but primarily for the reason Boyd & Ellison (2007, at 211) describe,

> What is unique about them is not that they allow individuals to meet strangers, but rather that they enable users to articulate and make visible their social networks. This can result in connections between individuals that would not otherwise be made.

These tools have the potential to grow constituent databases, help to establish a brand, communicate with stakeholders about important events, and mobilize them as volunteers, as well as to solicit money from them for causes they believe in. Convio (2010, at 7) summed up the "Key Benefits of Social Media for Nonprofits" as follows:

1.   Learn what your supporters are saying and sharing about your organization.

2.   Drive traffic to your various web properties — website, blog, Facebook, *etc.*

3.   Improve results on search engine result pages with keyword rich content.

4.   Drive visitors to online donation pages.

5.   Enable supporters to distribute messages about your organization through their social web presence.

6. Empower your most passionate and influential supporters to promote your organization.

7. Enable grassroots movements in real-time and rapidly respond to unforeseen events.

8. Humanize your organization by not limiting communications to traditional methods or messages.

9. Acquire new contacts and build your email housefile.

10. Increase trust and loyalty from your supporters by allowing them to share their voice through feedback forums.

While social networks have numerous benefits for non-profit organizations, they also expose them to risks. Short (2008) notes that most organizations have limited knowledge about who enters their networks exposing them to malicious attacks from hackers who may engage in personal attacks or impersonation. For this reason, organizations must manage social networks as diligently as traditional networks.

For more information on social networking in nonprofit organizations, see Kanter & Fine's (2010) book, *Networked Nonprofit: Connecting with Social Media to Drive* Change (San Francisco, CA: Jossey-Bass, 2010).

Websites

The evolution of the Internet and its billions of Websites has become more and more diverse and sophisticated in recent years. This makes the value of Websites for performing and managing many aspects of nonprofit and voluntary sector work more important than ever.

Cukier & Middleton (2003) report that nonprofits in Canada use Websites to share information, fundraise, conduct advocacy, provide member support, develop community, and recruit volunteers. However, 80 per cent of these sites are used for "information provision and organizational promotion" only (at 109). Harrison, Murray & MacGregor (2004) assessed how NPOs in Canada were making use of Websites specifically for the purpose of managing their volunteer program according to the following four levels of "e-connectivity":

•   Level 1: Websites used for "hosting information" about the volunteer program.

•   Level 2: Websites used for hosting information as well as interactive features such as online volunteer applications, listservs, or online survey capabilities.

- Level 3: Level 2 features as well as the capability of accessing databases remotely by those within the organization.

- Level 4: Level 3 features as well as accessing databases by those external to the organization.

While overall access to Websites in the volunteer programs they surveyed (total n=494) was high (90 per cent in a national e-enabled sample (n=365); 78 per cent in a regional traditional sample (n=129)), the overall level of e-connectivity was low at 1.5. This finding indicates that most volunteer programs were making use of their Websites solely to host information about their volunteer programs, building in some interactivity. Fewer were using their sites to interact with their members and volunteers (level 2, interactivity, was 20 per cent) and a very small percentage use them to share information vertically (within) and horizontally across organizations.

Kang & Norton (2004) who reviewed how large U.S. nonprofit organization were making use of their Websites (n=100) found the majority were using them to push information to the public. Over 80 per cent of the Websites reviewed posted information about the organization (*e.g.*, logo, mission, vision, policy statements, strategic goals, how to donate money, *etc.*). Less than 10 per cent "included interactive functions such as discussion forums, chat rooms, online polls and surveys". Even fewer "provided statements inviting visitors to return (only 2 per cent) and encouraged visitors to bookmark their site (1 per cent) (at 281). This review, like others, suggests nonprofits are not making the most out of their Websites.

In 2011, Lee and Bhattacherjee examined nonprofit and voluntary sector organization adoption and use of the Web. Table 3 below shows the types of problems and goals nonprofits were using Websites to resolve/realize:

Table 3: Nonprofit Website Use

Problems	Goals
Reduced government funding	Generate Revenue
Decreased civic participation	Recruit Volunteers
Corruption and Fraud	Increase Accountability
Increased demand for programs and services	New programs and services delivery models

While one could argue there has never been a better time for nonprofit and voluntary organizations to adopt the Web, Lee and Bhattacherie (2011) suggest that many will NOT resolve their problems and achieve their goals because of "a lack of organizational and technological capacity" (at 103). Particularly at risk, they say, is the small- to medium-sized rural nonprofit. To be more effective users of the Web, Lee and Bhattacherie suggest nonprofit leaders assess ICT effectiveness within the following framework of governance and management questions:

- Governance Questions

  - Do leaders understand the value of the Web as a means of achieving strategic goals?

  - Has the organization clearly articulated a Web strategy?

  - Is the Web strategy aligned with the organization's strategic plan?

- Management Questions

  - Does the organization have the capacity (knowledge, skills, attitudes of its people) to implement the Web strategy/plan?

  - Does it have the technological infrastructure to support it?

  - Given the current capacity/infrastructure, should the Web strategies/goals be adjusted?

The key to getting the most value out of an organizational Website is to think of it as a means to an end in terms of meeting performance goals and objectives. Once performance goals and objectives have been established and agreed upon, ICT strategies should be identified to achieve them. With respect to what kinds of strategies should be incorporated into Websites, nonprofits should consider Web 1 (push), 2 (pull) and 3 (network) strategies and applications to increase their connectivity to people and organizations. In addition, nonprofits should pay attention to the *design* of their Website, the speed at which it loads, its scalability (how easily it can grow with increased traffic), and its capability for facilitating nonprofit work and governance functions.

Whereas in Web 1 having a recognizable domain *name* was important, in Web 2.0, the name is less important because finding a domain name on the WWW is much easier with the evolution of search engine optimization tools. As we enter the era of Web 3.0, Schultz & Fristedt (2005) suggest that nonprofits monitor the popularity of their Websites and determine whether they are "optimized — that is easily found among the multitude of other sites a seeker may happen upon" (at 8). Nonprofits can check on the optimization level of their Websites through a process Schultz and Fristedt refer to as "search engine optimization (SEO)". This process provides the nonprofit with information about the likelihood that their Website will be found if actively searched.[45]

Virtual Volunteering

As described above, ICT can be a useful means to facilitate different activities associated with the volunteering process. Whereas in traditional volunteering, each step of the process is carried out through face-to-face interaction with those in the voluntary organization, now the individual volunteer can use ICT to search for volunteer opportunities, select an organization to volunteer for, and perform specific forms of work at a physical distance from the organization. For the manager of volunteer resources, the process is similar. The virtual volunteer manager may use ICT to perform any or all necessary functions at a physical distance from the volunteer, from identifying the need for volunteers and the nature of the work required to searching for and locating a potential pool of volunteers (recruitment), making selections, putting them to work, and overseeing their performance. The hope is that the use of ICT will increase volunteering by providing volunteer program managers with new tools to reach and recruit more volunteers from traditional sources and from new sources such as the ICT community, youth, those who are housebound or those who face time and travel restrictions.

The extent to which ICT is used to find and perform volunteer work at a physical distance is very low in Canada as it is in the U.S. (Brudney (1999); Murray & Harrison (2002b)). Murray & Harrison report that while "pure" virtual volunteering is rare, the majority of volunteers use a combination of online and on site work. In a study conducted prior to the 2010 national survey of volunteering in Canada, Vezina and Crompton (2012) reported similar findings with volunteers using ICT more often to perform volunteer work (25 per cent in 2010 up from 20 per cent in 2004) than to search for it (14 per cent up from 8 per cent in 2004). (See <http://www.statcan.gc.ca/pub/11-008-x/2012001/article/11638-eng. htm#n2>). The same holds true for managers of volunteer programs in

---

[45]   To check Website optimization levels see online: <http://www.linkpopularitycheck.com/>.

that they use ICT to recruit volunteers to do work on site (see Murray & Harrison 2002a; Harrison, Murray, an& MacGregor, 2004).

When ICT is used to perform volunteer work, the typical tasks are those that involve the use of ICT such as:

- Desktop publishing;

- Research (*e.g.*, literature reviews);

- Writing, editing and translating documents;

- Creating and editing pictures, videos and podcasts;

- Website development and maintenance;

- Advocacy;

- Fundraising; and

- Marketing.

In addition to these tasks, it has been shown that virtual volunteers can also perform direct service delivery work such as counselling, tutoring, and mentoring (Cravens (2000); Cravens & Ellis (2013); Mele (2008); Pena-Lopez (2007)). This suggests that, in addition to those tasks that require ICT use, it is possible to re-engineer volunteer work to include tasks that have typically been thought of as requiring face-to-face interaction. This will require that managers identify volunteer needs, time commitment (*e.g.*, is it long-term, short-term, or a one-time task also referred to in the literature as micro-volunteering) and position requirements first, ensure the technological infrastructure is in place to meet them, then actively recruit virtual volunteers with the capability and manage them as they would any other volunteer — albeit through technological means (*i.e.*, use ICT to communicate about a position or schedule, gather information, provide support, track and monitor work, and provide recognition).

In 2012 Jayne Cravens and Rob Jackson surveyed managers of volunteer resources throughout the world to learn about the types of software applications they were using in their work. As you can see from Table 4 below, a combination of spreadsheet and volunteer management specific software applications were used. Similar to the findings of Murray and Harrison (2002a), Cravens and Jackson found that adoption of volunteer management software varied by size of the volunteer program with larger sized programs demonstrating the most need (*e.g.*, Cravens and Jackson found programs with 100 volunteers or more versus 75 or more in the Canadian volunteer programs Murray and Harrison assessed). They also found most applications were being used to track volunteers rather than to schedule them. Over half of the applications reported could be accessed over the Internet ("the cloud") with some allowing volunteers to enter their own data. When choosing volunteer management software applications, Cravens and Jackson recommend that each agency consider the functions and features of each volunteer management software application relative to volunteer and program needs as "different people like different features; a software loved by one organization may be loathed by another" (at 4).

Table 4: Applications Used to Manage Volunteers

Application Type	Adoption by Manager (n=240)
Spreadsheets (*e.g.*, Microsoft Excel, Open Office, Google Docs *etc.*)	21%
Volgistics	19%
Volunteer Impact/Volunteer Squared	15%
Volunteer	7%
Raisers Edge	6%
Samaritan	6%
Microsoft Access	5%
V-Base	4%

With respect to demographics, adopters of online recruitment sites in Canada are more likely than volunteers who find work in traditional ways to be younger, newer to volunteering, female, educated, and motivated to volunteer in order to learn new skills or find paid employment (Murray & Harrison (2002b, 2005)).

Though virtual volunteers can be found in existing volunteer programs, the best source of them is online. Murray & Harrison (2002b) found that users of online recruitment systems were significantly more likely than traditional volunteers to have virtual volunteer experience. The key to "landing" a virtual volunteer is to use ICT to contact them. About half of the prospective volunteers that had been in email contact with a volunteer agency about a volunteer position were recruited.[46]

Recent books on this topic include Adams & Smith (2008), Kollock & Smith (1999), Rheingold (2000), and Song (2009). There is also a dissertation (see Harrison, 2005), book chapters (see Harrison & Murray, 2005; 2007), journal articles (see Harrison & Murray, 2004; Pena-Lopez, 2007); research reports (see Harrison & Murray, 2002a; 2002b; Harrison, Murray, & MacGregor, 2004); and practical guidelines on how to develop and manage this type of volunteering (see Ellis & Cravens, 2000; 2012).

Crowdsourcing

As connectivity increases, organizations are turning to the Internet and Web applications to search through "crowds" of people for donations (Kanter, 2014) and volunteers to perform nonprofit work. Saxton *et al.* (2013, at 29) elaborate further on the nature of the crowdsourcing phenomenon:

> Although online community users play the role of producers, innovators, and problems solvers, they are, unlike in traditional organizations, not *employees* of crowdsourcing networks. They are only temporarily connected to the organization for a specific task or project. Therefore, the management focus in crowdsourcing is not on the enhancement of potential workers' skill or on employee retention. Rather, its management strategy is to uncover and leverage the skills and knowledge of potential workers, and for drawing more intelligent, diverse, and capable people into the crowdsourcing platform.

The concept of crowdsourcing is not unlike pure virtual volunteering, where ICT tools are used to search for a position/find volunteers and perform volunteer work virtually at a distance from the organization. The kinds of "outsourced" tasks crowds take on include fundraising, Website and software development (*e.g.*, open-source), marketing (*e.g.*, creating a logo or brand), and problem solving. Table 5 below shows just a few of the many applications individuals and organizations are using to meets needs for volunteering and perform a range of organizational functions in "the crowd".

---

[46] For more information on how to build and manage a virtual volunteer program see online: <http://www.serviceleader.org>.

Table 5: Types of Crowdsourcing ICT Applications

Application	URL	Use
Crowdrise	http://www.crowdrise.com/	Fundraising
Kickstarter	http://www.kickstarter.com/	Fundraising
IndieGoGo	http://www.indiegogo.com/	Fundraising
OpenIDEO	http://www.openideo.com/	Problem-Solving
Sparked	http://hello.sparked.com/	Volunteering
Ushahidi	http://www.ushahidi.com/	Software Development

For more information about the "crowd" and the phenomenon of "sharing" in the collaborative economy, see the following Vision Critical (March 2014) report: <http://www.slideshare.net/jeremiah_owyang/sharingnewbuying>.

Performance Management and Measurement

Performance management is an aspect of nonprofit reform that places emphasis on accountability and value for money (Light (2000); Cutt & Murray (2000)). Light notes that the call for greater accountability and levels of performance comes from a number of sources, including current reforms in the government and business sectors, government legislation, and funders and clients wanting to determine the appropriateness and responsiveness of services. ICT provides nonprofits with new means to manage and measure performance, including "the number of clients served, client demographics, satisfaction of clients, and initial and immediate outcomes" (Collins (2003, at 3)). While manual methods can be used to collect and keep track of information, Collins states that the use of ICT allows nonprofits to "streamline" what is often perceived as a difficult and time-consuming process. He provides four reasons why performance management ICT applications should be adopted by nonprofit organizations:

1. Digital information can be indexed, sorted, and cross-tabulated in more complex ways than are feasible in a manual system.

2. Computerized systems can store far more data much faster and, given an appropriate back-up system, more securely.

3. Computerized systems can standardize data collection, much like using forms does, but also offers opportunities to integrate data

systems from other areas in the agency, such as billing to create an enterprise-wide database that reduces redundant work efforts.

4. ICT applications have been developed for the collection and analysis of quantitative and qualitative or "soft" data (*e.g.*, Collins describes that qualitative data can be collected systematically as a result of data "coding", while analysis can produce outcomes by way of "results mapping"; SPSS Text Analysis is an example of this type of application).

While Collins (2003) recommends that nonprofits adopt these applications, he also suggests that they do not adopt them blindly. He advocates due diligence in determining the suitability of performance measurement ICT applications by:

(a) Reviewing the capability of existing ICT applications;

(b) Reviewing other ICT applications in relation to existing applications;

(c) Involving staff and stakeholders in the purchase and/or design, training, and evaluation of new ICT applications, and the development of performance measures. For example, in the area of board performance measurement and management, boardcheckup.com (<http://www.boardcheckup.com>) provides boards of directors of non-profit and voluntary organizations throughout the world with a free board performance assessment tool to measure and manage board performance. This tool, which is a University at Albany, SUNY sponsored research project designed to assess the issues that challenge boards and the impacts of board performance, requires no technical expertise in performance assessment. The only requirement is that the board identify a coordinator who has access to the Internet and is confident in use of basic Web applications (*e.g.*, Internet and email) (Harrison & Murray, 2013). Other Web-based service technologies like SurveyMonkey and Zoomerang provide nonprofits with sophisticated tools to design, collect, store and analyze hard and soft survey data in one application. While these tools are convenient and cost-effective, their use by nonprofits does not guarantee success (*i.e.*, respondents will want to respond to them, that they will provide answers to important questions). To increase effectiveness of these tools, nonprofits need a basic knowledge of survey research.

While all too often the responsibility for ICT rests in the hands of technical experts (*e.g.*, developers and vendors), Collins claims, "careful planning, implementation flexibility, and a clear strategy will guide the process towards creating maximum value" (at 7). In considering the management of ICT success, Van Grembergen (2000) suggests that user organizations ask governance types of ICT questions:

1.   How does management get ICT to return value to the organization?

2.   How does top management make sure the resources invested do not result in failed projects?

3.   How does top management control and evaluate ICT use within and beyond the organization?

One way to ensure that the use of ICT applications adds business value to the nonprofit organization is to adopt an IT performance management framework. A good example is the IT balanced scorecard (IT BSC) (Van Grembergen, 2000). Van Grembergen (2000) derived the IT BSC from Kaplan & Norton's (1992) balanced scorecard approach (BSC), a framework to organize and monitor an organization's performance in relation to its strategic plan. The IT BSC includes a variety of performance measures at different levels of analysis, including the level of the user, operations, business contribution, and future orientation. The critical feature of the IT BSC framework is the linkage between performance objectives and benchmarks within ICT scorecards (*e.g.*, development and strategic) and the organization's balanced scorecard.

WHAT FACTORS INFLUENCE THE ADOPTION AND USE OF ICT APPLICATIONS?

One recent approach to understanding adoption and use of ICT can be found in the research of Harrison and Murray (see Murray & Harrison (2002a); Harrison, Murray & MacGregor (2004); Harrison & Murray (2007)). This work found that barriers to adoption and use of ICT exist along several dimensions. For example, in volunteer management, Harrison (2005) found evidence of barriers at the level of the *individual* (*e.g.*, ICT experience and literacy), the *organization* (*e.g.*, size of budget, job stress), the *social group* (*e.g.*, ICT training and involvement in decisions to use new applications), and the *technical systems* (*e.g.*, access and ease of use of ICT) levels. Moreover, different barriers influence access and use of different types of ICTs resulting in different patterns of ICT effectiveness suggesting it is not a singular but rather, a multidimensional construct. This work also found that levels of adoption and effective use of ICT applications varied according by ICT application type. This is consistent with the innovation diffusion literature, which contends that the factors associated with the adoption of innovations change over time as they become more accepted and used (Rogers (2003); van Dijk & Hacker (2003)). It is also consistent with the information system success literature, which supports the notion that different usage contexts and ICT tools will have different measures of effectiveness (Seddon, Staples, Patnayakuni & Bowtell (1999)).

By way of example, Nah & Saxton (2013) examined the question of what factors drive the adoption and use of social networking applications like Facebook and Twitter in large nonprofit organizations. Table 6 below shows the factors they found were predictors of adoption and use of these social media tools.

Table 6: Predictors of Adoption and Use of Social Media

Level of Analysis/ Variables	Facebook Presence	Twitter Presence	Frequency of Facebook Updates	Twitter Updates	Social Media Utilizations
Strategy					
Fee for Service	X	X	X	X	
Lobbying Expenditures	X				
Capacity					
Website Reach	X	X	X	X	
Governance					
Membership	X				

Level of Analysis/ Variables	Facebook Presence	Twitter Presence	Frequency of Facebook Updates	Twitter Updates	Social Media Utilizations
Board Size		X			
Efficiency	X		X	X	X
External Pressures Donor Dependence	X	X	X		X

Their research findings suggest adoption and use of social media by large nonprofit organizations is related to need (*i.e.*, to accomplish a strategy, to increase efficiency, and to respond to external pressures) and capacity to use ICT (*e.g.*, Website reach).

HOW SHOULD THE MANAGEMENT OF ICT CHANGE BE APPROACHED BY NONPROFITS?

While advances in the WWW and ICT applications have provided nonprofits with improved tools for conducting their work, developing new knowledge, and engaging stakeholders both internally and externally within networks, the research shows not all nonprofit and voluntary organizations will adopt and make the most effective use of them. To become effective users of ICT requires nonprofit and voluntary organizations manage ICT applications and technological change. Several practical suggestions come to mind to assist in this regard:

1. Attention should be given to the governance of ICT. At the policy level, this means developing and aligning ICT tools with strategy. Consider appointing an ICT leader at all levels of the organization (*e.g.*, board director with responsibility for ICT; and executive manager responsible for ICT (Lim (2001); and user groups) to

integrate ICT with the work, strategy, and mission of the organization (see: Van Grembergen (2000) for linking ICT to the organization's balanced score card). In addition, establish policy surrounding development and ownership of ICT (*e.g.*, intellectual property specifying ownership in employment and volunteer contracts) and guidelines for appropriate and inappropriate use of ICT in the organization (*e.g.*, business and personal distinctions). Consider a policy on information sharing, with a special section for working with vulnerable populations (*e.g.*, youth, prison, elderly, disabled clients) if applicable.

2. ICT Involvement strategies should target individuals who are not predisposed to wanting to adopt new ICT applications in their work. Among managers, this group would include those who have been in the job for more than five years and/or who lack experience using ICT applications in the usage context. The critical success factor is that users gain experience with ICT both formally — in such activities as the design, training and evaluation stages of new ICT applications — and informally with other users in the organization. Making experienced users into "champions" of ICT change within the organization will increase trust in ICT tools as well as feelings of capability among those that lack experience. Each of these efforts will help create positive attitudes toward ICT change within the organization.

3. The need for ICT change should be communicated and introduced in manageable pieces so that it does not seem overwhelming. Another purpose of managing change in this way is to build opportunities for learning, with one successful change setting the stage for another as managers and users gain experience with ICT.

4. The role of the ICT support or technical assistant specialist should be redefined to "facilitator of change" rather than lone problem-solver who hands out solutions for others' difficulties. By playing this new role, the ICT specialist becomes an advisor/coach, thus encouraging users to develop their own ICT capabilities and confidence.

5. Special attention should be paid to making sure that ICT applications are relevant, easy to learn, user friendly, and rewarding, so users perceive them as adding positive value to nonprofit and voluntary sector work.

6. The ICT budget should contain sufficient resources to cover the hard and soft costs of ICT goods and services as well as strategic planning and proper training and management processes. NPower, a nonprofit technology assistance provider, recommends a one-third ICT equipment; two-thirds training and support budget allocation.

7. It is always necessary to monitor, measure, and communicate progress. An IT BSC is a useful framework in this regard.

Failure to manage ICT change in the ways suggested might result in a digitally deficient organization — one that lacks the capacity to meet the demands of operating in the new economy.

CONCLUSION

Increasing the capacity of nonprofit and voluntary sector organizations to meet the demands of the new network economy requires that they understand ICT, the range of tools available, and the factors that challenge their adoption. To be effective users of ICT, it is important that nonprofit leaders recognize that there is no "one size fits all" application or strategy for ICT change and that there will be competing interests and needs surrounding the adoption and use of ICT applications. Managing ICT is thus as much about managing technological and organizational change as it is about knowing every ICT application that exists on the market. While managing technological and organizational change may seem daunting, the research suggests that it is worth undertaking because of the many benefits that well-planned and implemented ICT strategies can provide organizations in need of resources, clients in need of more efficient and responsive services, regulators in need of accountability, stakeholders in need of involvement, and citizens seeking to satisfy their needs for civic engagement.

REFERENCES

T.L. Adams & S.A. Smith, *Electronic Tribes: The Virtual Worlds of Geeks, Gamers, Shamans, and Scammers* (Austin, TX: University of Texas Press, 2008).

B. Alexander, "Web 2.0: A New Wave of Innovation for Teaching and Learning" *EDUCAUSEreview* (March/April 2006) 33-44. Online at: <https://net.educause.edu/ir/library/pdf/ERM0621.pdf>.

C. Antonelli, A. Geuna & W.E. Steinmueller, "Information and Communication Technologies and the Production, Distribution and Use of Knowledge" (2000) 20:1/2 International Journal of Technology 72-94.

G. Arnant, "At the dawn of the e-evolution" *Globe and Mail Report on Business* (21 November 2002) 6-11.

A. Blau, "More than Bit Players: How Information Technology Will Change the Ways Nonprofits and Foundations Work and Thrive in the Information Age" (New York: Surdna Foundation, 2001). Online at: <http://www.surdna.org>.

D.M. Boyd & N.B. Ellison, "Social Network Sites: Definition, History, and Scholarship" (2008) 13:1 Journal of Computer-Mediated Communication 210-230.

L.A. Brainard & J.M. Brinkeroff, "Lost in Cyberspace: Shedding Light on the Dark Matter of Grassroots Organizations" (2004) 33:3 Nonprofit and Voluntary Sector Quarterly 32S-53S.

K.L. Brock, "Antagonists and Allies: Voluntary Organizations, Business and the Policy Process" (Paper presented at the Institute of Public Administration of Canada Meetings, Halifax, 27 August 2002).

J. Brudney "Effective Use of Volunteers: Best Practices for the Public Sector" (1999) 62:4 Law and Contemporary Problems 219-255.

E. Burt & J.A. Taylor, "Information and Communication Technologies: Reshaping Voluntary Organizations" (2000) 11:2 Nonprofit Management and Leadership 131-143.

E. Burt & J.A. Taylor, "New Technologies, Embedded Values, and Strategic Change: Evidence from the U.K. Voluntary Sector" (2003) 32:1 Nonprofit and Voluntary Sector Quarterly 115-127.

A. Carvin, "Tim Berners Lee: Weaving a Semantic Web" (Newton, MA: EDC Center for Media & Community, 2005). Online at: <http://www.digitaldivide.net/articles/view.php?ArticleID=20>.

J. Casey, "Card-Based Purchasing and Effective Government" (1998) 1:4 The Business of Government 7.

S. Clarke, *Information Systems Strategic Management* (London: Routledge, 2001).

R.M. Clerkin & K.A. Gronbjerg, "Infrastructure and Activities: Relating IT to the Work of Nonprofits Organizations" in M. Cortès & K.M. Rafter, eds., *Nonprofits & Technology: Emerging Research for Usable Knowledge* (Chicago: Lyceum, 2007) 3-20.

M. Collins, "Wanted: Information Technology Solutions for Problems of Measuring Outcomes" (2003) [unpublished].

D.R. Compeau, C.A. Higgins & S. Huff, "Social Cognitive Theory and Individual Reactions to Computing Technology: A Longitudinal Study" (1999) 23:2 MIS Quarterly 145-158.

D.R. Compeau & C.A. Higgins, "Computer Self-Efficacy: Development of a Measure and Initial Test" (1995) 19:2 MIS Quarterly 189-211.

comScore, "The Next Big Things: Mobile Internet & Applications – Gaining Momentum" (2009) (PowerPoint Slide Presentation, online at: <http://www.comscore.com>.

Convio, *Going Social, Tapping into Social Media for Nonprofit Success* (Guidebook) (2010) 1-37. Online at: <http://www.councilofnonprofits. org/files/Convio_Social-Media-Guide.pdf>.

J.C. Cooper, "The Price of Efficiency" *Business Week* (22 March 2004) 38-46.

J. Cooper & K.D. Weaver, *Gender and Computers: Understanding the Digital Divide* (Manwah, NJ: Lawrence Erlbaum Associates, 2003).

J. Cravens, "Virtual Volunteering: Online Volunteers Providing Assistance to Human Services" (2000) 17:2/3 Journal of Computers in Human Services 119-136.

J. Cravens & S. Ellis, *The Last Virtual Volunteering Guidebook* (Philadelphia: Energize Inc., 2013).

J. Cravens & R. Jackson, "Survey of Software Tools to Manage and Track Volunteer Information" (2012) [unpublished]. Online at: <http://www.coyotecommunications.com/tech/volmanagesoftware.pdf>.

W. Cukier & C. Middleton, "Evaluating the Web Presence of Voluntary Sector Organizations: An Assessment of Canadian Web Sites" (2003) 1:3 IT & Society 102-130.

J. Cutt & V. Murray, *Accountability and Effectiveness Evaluations in Nonprofit Organizations* (London: Routledge, 2000).

R. De' & B. Mathew, "Issues in the Management of Web Technologies: A Conceptual Framework" (1999) 19:6 International Journal of Information Management 427-447.

M. Dewing, "Social Media: Who Uses Them?" Publication 2010-05-E (Ottawa: Library of Parliament, 2013).

C. Dziuban, P. Moskal & E. Dziuban, "Reactive Behavior Patterns Go Online" (2000) 17:3 Journal of Staff, Program, & Organizational Development 171-182.

R.E. Ferndig & K.D. Trammell, "Content Delivery in the 'Blogosphere'" (2004) 3:7 T.H.E. Journal 12-20.

N. Flynn, *Instant Messaging Rules: A Business Guide to Managing Policies, Security, and Legal Issues for Safe IM Communication* (New York: American Management Association, 2004).

J. Fountain, *Building the Virtual State: Information Technology and Institutional Change* (Washington, DC: Brookings Institution Press, 2001).

B. Friedman, P.H. Kahn & D.C. Howe, "Trust Online" (2000) 43:12 Communications of the ACM 34-40.

M. Gilbert, *The Basics of Nonprofit Email* (Seattle: Gilbert Center, 2003).

P. Glen, "Five Clues that your Project is Headed for Trouble" Computer Management World, online at: <http://www.computerworld.com/s/article/337716/Five_Clues_a_Project_Is_Headed_for_Trouble>.

P. Goodyear, "eLearning, Knowledge Work and Working Knowledge" Lancaster University, CSALT Documents: Center for Studies in Advanced Learning Technology, accessed online at: <http://domino.lancs.ac.uk/edres/csaltdocs.nsf>.

Government of Canada, Parliament, House of Commons, Speech from the Throne (Adrienne Clarkson), Debates and Proceedings (Hansard). 37th Parliament, 1st Session, October 12, 1999 (Ottawa: Public Works and Government Services, 1999). Accessed online at: <http://www.pco-bcp.gc.ca/default.asp?Language=E&Page=InformationResources&sub=sftddt&doc=sftddt1999_e.htm>.

G. Grobman, *The Nonprofit Organization's Guide to E-commerce* (Harrisburg, PA: White Hat Communications, 2001).

A. Hall, *E-enabling the Voluntary and Community Sectors: Final Report*. Glasgow: U.K. Government Online, Office of the E-envoy. Accessed online at: <http://www.e-envoy.gov.uk/reports-e-enabling-top/$file/index.htm>.

K. Hampton & B. Wellman, "Neighboring in Netville: How the Internet Supports Community and Social Capital in a Wired Suburb" (2003) 2:4 City and Community 277-311.

Y.D. Harrison, "Motivated to Adopt: Understanding the Digital Effectiveness Divide (DED) in Volunteerism" (The University of Victoria, Doctoral Dissertation, 2005), online at: <http://dspace. library.uvic.ca:8080/bitstream/handle/1828/757/harrison_2005.pdf?seq uence=1>.

Y.D. Harrison *et al.*, "Globalization of Social Justice Education: The Case of the Global Solidarity Network Study e-Broad Program" (2010) 13:3 Internet and Higher Education 115-126.

Y.D. Harrison, V. Murray & J. MacGregor, *The Impact of ICT on the Management of Canadian Volunteer Programs, Information and Communications Technology: Beyond Anecdotes* (Toronto: Canadian Centre for Philanthropy, 2004).

Y.D. Harrison & V. Murray, "Bridging the Effectiveness Divide in ICT Use: The Case of Volunteer Recruitment in Canada" in M. Cortès & K.M. Rafter, eds., *Nonprofits & Technology: Emerging Research for Usable Knowledge* (Chicago: Lyceum, 2007) 68-84.

K. Hart & M. Greenwell , "'Causes' Social Networking May Be All Talk, No Cash for Nonprofits Seeking Funds" *The Washington Post* (22 April 2009).

P.E. Hart, K. Pierson & J.J. Hull, "Refocusing Multimedia Research on Short Clips" (2005) 12:3 IEEE Multimedia 8-13.

Industry Canada (2002), *VolNet Final Report* (Ottawa: Government of Canada, 2002).

Interview of Julianna Cafik Principal, Stonebridge Solutions (January 10, 2006).

Ipsos Reid, *Volunteer Opportunities Exchange (VOE): Summary of Findings* (Ottawa: Ipsos Reid, 2001).

C. Johnson, "A Survey of Current Research on Online Communities of Practice" (2001) 4:1 Internet and Higher Education 45-60.

S. Kang & H.E. Norton, "Nonprofit Organizations' Use of the World Wide Web: Are they Sufficiently Fulfilling Organizational Goals?" (2004) 30:3 Public Relations Review 279-284.

B. Kanter, "What Social Media Analytics and Data Can't Tell You" (March 2014). Online at: Beth's blog <http://www.bethkanter.org/sxsw-analytics/>.

R.S. Kaplan, "Strategic Performance Measurement and Management in Nonprofit Organizations" (2001) 11:3 Nonprofit Management & Leadership 353-370.

R.S. Kaplan & D.P. Norton, "The Balanced Scorecard – Measures that Drive Performance" (1992) 70:1 Harvard Business Review 71-79.

S. Karlin, "Examining How Youth Interact Online" Education Digest 73 (December 2007) 7-9.

C. Kimble, F. Li & A. Barlow, "Effective Virtual Teams Through Communities of Practice" Research Paper No. 2000/9, (2000) Management Science 1-15.

D. Kingsley, "Technologies of Civil Society – Communication, Participation, Mobilization" (2007) 20:1 Innovation 19-34.

J. Kirschenbaum & R. Kunamneni, Bridging the Organizational Divide: Toward a Comprehensive Approach to the Digital Divide (Oakland, CA: Policy Link, 2001).

P. Kollock & M. Smith, eds., Communities in Cyberspace (New York: Routledge, 1999).

S. Kolowich, "The MOOC 'Disruption' Proves Less Than Revolutionary After All" The Chronicle of Higher Education (16 August 2013) A6.

J. Langford & Y. Harrison, "Partnering to Produce Electronic Government" (2000) 44:4 Canadian Public Administration 393-416.

J. Langford & K. Seaborne, "To Click or Not to Click: E-learning for the Public Sector" (2003) 46:1 Canadian Public Administration 50-75.

R.L. Lee & A. Bhattacherjee, "A Theoretical Framework for Strategic Use of the Web Among Nonprofit Organizations" (Proceedings of Southern Association for Information Systems Conference, Atlanta, Georgia, March 25-26, 2011, at 103-108).

P.C. Light, Making Nonprofits Work. A Report on the Tides of Nonprofit Management Reform (Washington, DC: The Brookings Institution, 2000).

S.K. Lim, "A Framework to Evaluate the Informatization Level" Chapter IX in W. Van Grembergen, ed., Information Technology Evaluation Methods and Management (Hershey, PA: Idea Group Publishing, 2001) 144-152.

C. Locke et al., The Cluetrain Manifesto (New York: Perseus Publishing, 2001).

C. Ludgate & M. Surman, *Beyond the Box*: *Thinking Strategically about Technology Grantmaking in Canada's Voluntary Sector* (Ottawa: Government of Canada through the Voluntary Sector Initiative, 2004).

M. Madden, "Pew Internet Project Podcast Downloading", online at: <http://www.pewinternet.org/files/old-media//Files/Reports/2008/PIP_Podcast_2008_Memo.pdf.pdf>.

D. McDonald, *Web Services Technologies Report*. For the JISC Technology Watch Service, online at: <http://www.jisc.ac.uk/uploaded_documents/tsw_03-04.pdf>.

I. McLoughlin & M. Harris, *Innovation, Organizational Change and Technology* (London: International Thomson Business Press, 1997).

J. McNutt, "Adoption of New-Wave Electronic Advocacy Techniques by Nonprofit Child Advocacy Organizations" in M. Cortès & K.M. Rafter, eds., *Nonprofits & Technology: Emerging Research for Usable Knowledge* (Chicago: Lyceum, 2007) 33-48.

V. Mele, "Streamlining Volunteer Management Through Information and Communications Technologies" in M. Liao-Troth, ed., *Challenges in Volunteer Management* (Charlotte, NC: Information Age Publishing, 2008) at 69-90.

C.A. Meyer, "The Political Economy of NGOs and Information Sharing" (1997) 25:7 World Development 1127-1140.

J. Murray, *The Connector*. Online at: <http://firstsearch.oclc.org.ezproxy.library.uvic.ca/WebZ/FSPage?pagetype=return_frameset:sessionid=sp02sw11-34270-e8hq42ws-29z6z5:entitypagenum=29:0:entityframedurl=http%3A%2F%2Fgateway.uvic.ca:entityframedtitle=:linktype=librarylink:entityframedtimeout=15:entityopenTitle=:entityopenAuthor=:entityopenNumber=:>.

V. Murray & Y.D. Harrison, "The Impact of Information and Communications Technology (ICT) on Volunteer Management" (Toronto: Canadian Centre for Philanthropy, 2002(a)).

V. Murray & Y.D. Harrison, "Virtual Volunteering: Current Status and Future Prospects" (Toronto: Canadian Centre for Philanthropy, 2002(b)).

V. Murray & Y.D. Harrison, "Virtual Volunteering, Current Status and Future Prospects", Chapter 5 in J. Brudney, ed., *Emerging Areas of Volunteering* (Indiana: Association for Research in Nonprofit Organizations and Voluntary Action (ARNOVA), 2005).

S. Nah & G.D. Saxton "Modeling the Adoption and Use of Social Media by Nonprofit Organizations" (2013) 15:2 *New Media & Society* 294-313.

S.C. Nill, Book Review of *Nonprofit Internet Strategies: Best Practices for Marketing, Communications, and Fundraising Success* by T. Hart, J.M. Greenfield & M. Johnston, eds. (New Jersey: John Wiley & Sons, 2005). Online at: <http://charitychannel.com>.

Nonprofits Policy and Technology Project, *Speaking up in the Internet Age: Use and Value of Constituent E-mail and Congressional Web Sites* (Washington DC: OMB Watch, 1998).

T.M. Notley, "Online Network Use in Schools: Social and Educational Opportunities" (2008) 27:3 Youth Studies Australia 20-29.

NTEN, Common Knowledge & ThePort, "Nonprofit Social Network Survey Report" (2009), accessed online at: <http://www.nonprofitsocialnetworksurvey.com>.

T. O'Reilly, "What is Web 2.0: Design Patterns and Business Models for the Next Generation of Software" (20 March 2009) online at: <http://www.oreilly.com/web2/archive/what-is-web-20.html>.

Organisation for Economic Co-operation and Development, "Use of information and communications technologies at work" DSTI/ICCP/IE ((1997)8/FINAL) (Paris: OECD, 1997).

Organisation for Economic Co-operation and Development, "Science, Technology and Innovation in the New Economy" (Policy brief) (Paris: OECD, September 2000).

Organisation for Economic Co-operation and Development, *OECD Information Technology Outlook* (Report) (2004), online at: <http://www.oecd.org/sti/ieconomy/37620123.pdf>.

Organisation for Economic Co-operation and Development, *OECD Information Technology Outlook* (Report) (2008), available online: <http://www.oecd-ilibrary.org/content/book/it_outlook-2008-en>.

Organisation for Economic Co-Operation and Development, OECD Internet Economy Outlook 2012 (Highlights), online at: <http://www.oecd.org/sti/ieconomy/internet-economy-outlook-2012-highlights.pdf>.

J. Paylor, "Micro-Volunteering, Doing Some Good through Smartphones?" (Institute for Volunteering Research, 2012), online at: <http://www.ivr.org.uk/images/stories/Micro-volunteering_bulletin_final_version_June.pdf>.

M. Parmegiani & T. Sachdeva, *Information and Public Policy Concerning Voluntary Sector Use of Information Technologies, the Internet and the World Wide Web: An International Report* (Toronto: Canadian Centre for Philanthropy, 2000).

Pew Internet, "Podcast Downloading" (2006), online at: <http://pewinternet.org/2006/11/22/podcast-downloading/>.

S. Phillips, *Renewing Governance: Voluntary Sector Network Support Program (VolNet): Citizen Engagement Through Information and Communication Technology* (Ottawa: Industry Canada, 2000). Accessed online at: <http://www.volnet.org/english/Sue_Phillips_report:_Renewing_Governance.html>.

J.C. Pierce & N.P. Lovrich, "Internet Technology Transfer and Social Capital, Aggregate and Individual Relationships in American Cities" (2003) 1:1 Comparative Technology Transfer and Society 49-71.

B. Pitkin & P. Manzo, *The IT Revolution and Nonprofit Organizations in Los Angeles* (Los Angeles: Center for Nonprofit Management in partnership with the School of Social Policy and Research, UCLA Advanced Policy Institute, 2002).

Princeton Survey Research Associates, *Wired, Willing and Ready: Nonprofit Human Service Organizations' Adoption of Information Technology* (Princeton, NJ: Independent Sector and Cisco Systems, 2001).

L.S. Quinn, "*Software Costs and Usage: Findings of a Nonprofit Sector Survey*" Idealware (2005), online at: <http://www.idealware.org/sites/idealware.org/files/documents/IW_software_survey_report.pdf>.

Radicati Group Inc., "A Quantitative Summary of All Key Market Segments" Covered by The Radicati Group Inc. Releases Q1 2008 Market Numbers (April 7, 2008), online at: <http://www.radicati.com/wp/wp-content/uploads/2008/08/q1-2008_pr.pdf>.

Radicati Group Inc., "Email Statistics Report, 2013-2017" (2013), online at: <http://www.radicati.com/wp/wp-content/uploads/2013/04/Email-Statistics-Report-2013-2017-Executive-Summary.pdf>.

L. Rainee & B. Wellman, *Networked: The New Social Operating System* (Cambridge: The MIT Press, 2012).

M. Remenyi, T. White & M. Sherwood-Smith, "Language and a Post-modern Management Approach to Information Systems" (1999) 19:1 International Journal of Information Management 17-32.

H. Rheingold, *The Virtual Community*, rev. ed. (Cambridge, MA: MIT Press, 2000).

H. Richards, Jr., "Is the Whole Greater than the Sum of Its Parts? The Applicability of the Fair Use Doctrine to the New Breed of Instant Messaging Software" (2001) 8:2 The Richmond Journal of Law and Technology 15, online at: <http://www.law.richmond.edu/jolt/v8i2/article3.html>.

B. Rocheleau, "The Political Dimensions of Information Systems in Public Administration" in D.G. Garson, ed., *Information Technology and Computer Applications in Public Administration* (Hershey, PA: Idea Group Publishing, 1999) 23-40.

E.M. Rogers, *Diffusion of Innovations*, 5th ed. (New York: Free Press, 2003).

W. Rudolph, "Engaging Citizens in On-Line Politics: Technology Tools in On-Line Community" (Paper presented to the ARNOVA conference, Washington, DC, 19 November 2005).

J.R. Saidel & S. Cour "Information Technology and the Voluntary Sector Workplace" (2003) 32:1 Nonprofit and Voluntary Sector Quarterly 5-24.

G.D. Saxton & C. Guo, "Conceptualizing Web-based Stakeholder Communication: The Organizational Website as a Stakeholder Relations Tool" Communication & Science Journal (18 December 2012) (forthcoming).

G.D. Saxton & L. Wang, The Social Network Effect: The Determinants of Giving Through Social Media, (2013) Nonprofit and Voluntary Sector Quarterly, DOI: 10.1177/0899764013485159.

G.D. Saxton, O. Onook & R. Kishore, "Rules of Crowdsourcing: Models, Issues and Systems of Control" (2013) 30:1 Information Systems Management 2-20.

J. Saxton & S. Game, *Virtual Promise: Are Charities Making the Most of the Internet Revolution?* (London: Third Sector, 2001). Accessed online at: <http://www.virtualpromise.net/vp_docs/Complete.pdf>.

J. Schneider, "Small, Minority-Based Nonprofits in the Information Age" (2003) 13:4 NonProfit Management and Leadership 383-399.

J. Schultz & J. Fristedt, "Calling All Search Engines" *Association Management, Supplement* (June 2005) 8-13.

P.B. Seddon *et al.*, "Dimensions of Information Systems Success" (1999) 2:3 Communications of the AIS 165-176.

L. Segil, *FastAlliances: Power your e-business* (New York: Wiley & Sons, 2001).

Z.S. Shah, "What's a Blog, and Why Should Nonprofits Care?" *Nonprofit Quarterly* 10 (Winter 2003) 1-5.

N. Shaver, "Online Fundraising" (2006). Online at: <http://www. supportingadvancement.com/vendors/canadian_fundraisers/articles/online _fundraising.htm>.

D.V. Shaw, N. Kwak & R.L. Holbert, "'Connecting' and 'Disconnecting' with Civic Life: Patterns of Internet Use and the Production of Social Capital" (2001) 18:2 Political Communication 141-162.

J. Short, "Risks in a Web 2.0 World" (2008) 55:10 Risk Management 28-31.

D.L. Sifry, "The State of the Blogosphere" (Powerpoint presentation, October 2005) (Technorati, Inc.).

J. Smith, M. Kearns & A. Fine, *Power to the Edges: Trends and Opportunities in Online Civic Engagement*, e-Volve Foundation (2005). Online at: <http://www.justvote.org/press/Pushing_Power_to_ the_Edges.pdf>.

F.W. Song, *Virtual Communities: Bowling Alone, Online Together* (New York: Peter Lang Publishing, 2009).

Statistics Canada, "Digital Technology and Internet Use" (2012), online at: <http://www.statcan.gc.ca/daily-quotidien/130612/dq130612a-eng.htm>.

D. Tapscott & A.D. Williams, *Wikinomics* (London: Atlantic Books, 2008).

D. Te'eni & D.R. Young, "The Changing Role of Nonprofits in the Network Economy" (2003) 32:3 Nonprofit and Voluntary Sector Quarterly 397-414.

P. Ticher, A. Maison & M. Jones, *Leading the Way to ... ICT Success* (London: The Baring Foundation, 2002).

TimeBank.org, "About Giving Time: Virtual Volunteering" (12 January 2005), online at: <http://www.timebank.org.uk/aboutgiving/virtual.htm>.

R. Tyler, "Online Volunteering" Digital Journal (15 November 2002), accessed online at: <http://www.digitaljournal.com>.

UN Volunteers, "Online Volunteering: What Is It?" (2005), online at: <http://www.unvolunteers.org/volunteers/options/online/whatisov.htm>.

J. Van Dijk & K. Hacker, "The Digital Divide as a Complex and Dynamic Phenomenon" (2003) 19:4 The Information Society 315-326.

W. Van Grembergen, "The Balanced Scorecard and IT Governance" (2000) 2 Information Systems Control Journal 40-43. Online at: <http://www.isaca.org/Certification/CGEIT-Certified-in-the-Governance-of-Enterprise-IT/Prepare-for-the-Exam/Study-Materials/Documents/The-Balanced-Scorecard-and-IT-Governance.pdf>.

B. Veenhof *et al.*, "How Canadian's Use of the Internet Affects Social Life and Civic Participation" (2008), online at: <http://unpan1.un.org/intradoc/groups/public/documents/un-dpadm/unpan038448.pdf>.

M. Vezina & S. Crompton, "Volunteering in Canada" (2012), accessed online at: <http://www.statcan.gc.ca/pub/11-008-x/2012001/article/11638-eng.pdf>.

VisionCritical, "Sharing is the New Buying: How to Win in the New Collaborative Economy" (14 March 2014), report online at: <http://www.slideshare.net/jeremiah_owyang/sharingnewbuying/>.

Y. Vogiazou, *Wireless Presence and Instant Messaging* (United Kingdom: Knowledge Media Institute, Open University, 2002). Online at: <http://www.jisc.ac.uk/uploaded_documents/tsw_02-07.pdf>.

Volunteers on line, "Making it Work for Volunteers" (2001), accessed online at: <http://www.volunteersonline.ca/news/environmentalscan.htm>.

M.A. Warren & L.F. Weschler, "Electronic Governance on the Internet" in D.G. Garson, ed., *Information Technology and Computer Applications in Public Administration: Issues and Trends* (Hershey, PA: Idea Group Publishing, 1999) 118-136.

Webroot (2008), "State of Internet Security: Protecting Business Email", online at: <http://www.idc-online.com/technical_references/pdfs/information_technology/Email%20Security.pdf>.

B. Wellman *et al.*, "Does the Internet Increase, Decrease or Supplement Social Capital?" (2001) 45:3 American Behavioural Scientist 436-455.

Wikipedia: <http://en.wikipedia.org/wiki>.

J. Wortham, "Twitter vs. Facebook: A Tale of Two Sites" (2013), accessed from the *New York Times* online at: <http://bits.blogs.nytimes.com/2013/09/13/twitter-vs-facebook-a-tale-of-two-sites/>.

S. Zuboff, *In the Age of the Smart Machine: The Future of Work and Power* (New York: Basic Books, 1988).

Chapter 13

SOCIAL ACCOUNTING[1]

Laurie Mook
Arizona State University

INTRODUCTION

When nonprofit organizations prepare conventional accounting statements, they use formats developed for profit-oriented businesses. Yet, as we know, the primary mission of a nonprofit organization is social, and as such their accounting statements miss a critical feature — that their social impact is a vital part of their performance story. In addition, nonprofit organizations rely in varying degrees on volunteers and members, yet the value of this unpaid service is normally excluded from accounting statements.

Indeed, conventional accounting reflects primarily the needs of owners and managers of profit-oriented businesses (Hines, 1988; Morgan, 1988; Tinker, 1985). However, there is nothing inherent in accounting that limits it to this set of interests. Social accounting has attempted to reorient accounting to a broader set of social variables and social interests.

Experimentation with different social accounting statements emerged in the 1970s as public demand for information related to the social impacts of expenditures grew (Dilley & Weygandt (1973)). At that time, predictions were made that social audits would be required for businesses within the next ten years (Linowes (1972)). These were pioneering attempts, but all focused on the business sector (see Abt and Associates (1974); Belkaoui (1984); Estes (1976); Flamholtz (1985); Linowes (1972); Seidler (1973)). Although these attempts did

---

[1] This chapter draws heavily on Chapter 9 of J. Quarter, L. Mook & A. Armstrong, *Understanding the Social Economy: A Canadian Perspective* (Toronto: University of Toronto Press, 2009).

not take hold in the accounting world, they have inspired the re-emergence of social accounting in the 21st century, including models that apply to social economy organizations such as nonprofits, co-operatives and social enterprises (Mook, Quarter & Richmond (2007)).

There are varying definitions of social accounting. All share the common feature of expanding the range of criteria that are taken into consideration when measuring performance and looking at the organization in relation to its surrounding environment, both social and natural. Additionally, they stress that the audience for social accounting is broader and may differ from that of other forms of accounting. We define social accounting as "a systematic analysis of the effects of an organization on its communities of interest or stakeholders, with stakeholder input as part of the data that are analyzed for the accounting statement" (Mook *et al.* (2007, at 2)). Mook *et al.* (2007) also argue that accounting is a driver of behaviour, and that social accounting can be used as a driver of social change.

Inherent in the social accounting approach is a stakeholder perspective in both looking at how stakeholders contribute to the organization and how they are impacted by it. Freeman (1984, at 46) presents the most widely used definition of a stakeholder: "any group or individual who can affect or is affected by the achievement of the organization's objectives." This definition casts a wide net and is refined by Clarkson (1995), who subdivides stakeholders into primary and secondary. In his words, "A primary stakeholder group is one without whose continuing participation the corporation cannot survive as a going concern" (1995, at 106). He identifies primary stakeholders as: employees, customers, suppliers, investors, and governments and communities that supply laws, regulations, infrastructure and markets.

Clarkson's list is directed to profit-oriented businesses, but it can be adapted for nonprofit organizations. For example, volunteers and members play an important role. We also include the community and the natural environment to signify their importance both to the organization and to a social accounting framework. That said, accounting, and particularly social accounting, has an obligation to go beyond mirroring the power dynamics of an organization, internally and externally. The accounting analysis should present the organization within its broadest context and examine its impact on a variety of stakeholders, including those with the least power.

In this chapter, we will look at how social accounting can be used to better tell the performance story of nonprofit organizations. We will consider the role of accounting in accountability and control and also in driving behaviours that move us towards the economic, social, and environmental sustainability of the organization and of society. Three models of social accounting are reviewed, and the challenges and opportunities of this type of accounting are discussed.

FROM CONVENTIONAL ACCOUNTING TO SOCIAL ACCOUNTING

The prevailing definitions of conventional accounting present it as identifying, gathering, measuring, summarizing and analysing financial data in order to support economic decision-making (American Accounting Association (1990; 1992)). Overall, accounting education treats the discipline as a neutral, technical, and value-free activity, and presents accounting decisions in businesses as being made to achieve the goal of maximizing shareholder wealth (Ferguson, Collison, Power & Stevenson (2005; 2006); Hopwood (1990); Lewis, Humphrey & Owen (1992)). This traditional approach to accounting is reflected in teaching and professional development, which tends to focus on technique acquisition (Gray, Bebbington & McPhail (1994); Roslender & Dillard (2003)).

Sustained criticisms to conventional accounting emerged in the 1960s and 1970s and gave birth to a second approach known as critical accounting. Scholars of critical accounting began to systematically question the assumptions underlying conventional accounting, arguing that accounting practices are neither objective, neutral, nor value-free, and that they create, sustain, and change social reality (Cooper & Neu (2001); Craig & Amernic (2004); Gray (2002); Hines (1988); Hopper, Storey & Willmott (1987); Llewellyn (1994); Lodh & Gaffikin (1997); Mathews (1997); Morgan (1988); Tinker (1985)). For instance, critical accountants argue that, by the very act of counting certain things and excluding others, accounting shapes a particular interpretation of social reality. This interpretation, which corresponds to particular assumptions about how society functions and should function, has in turn implications for decision-making and policy (Hines (1988); Tinker Merino & Neimark (1982)).

Critical accounting also urges us to reflect on the conditions and consequences of accounting, and to consider accounting within a broad, societal context (Lodh & Gaffikin (1997); Roslender & Dillard (2003)). Critical accounting asserts that organizations have an impact on a wide group of stakeholders and that accountability to these groups is a desirable democratic mechanism (Gray, Dey, Owen, Evans & Zadek (1997)).

Critical accounting seeks not only to understand the world but also to change it, a fundamental difference from traditional accounting. In theory, critical accounting aims to "engender progressive change within the conceptual, institutional, practical, and political territories of accounting" through all evaluative forms of social praxis (Tinker, (2005 at 100)). Yet, this goal is hypothetical more than real, as most often, critical accounting theorists develop critiques without suggesting alternative models to address issues of economic, social and ecological justice in everyday life (Cooper, 2000; Cooper & Hopper (2006); Dey (2000; (2002); Gray (1998)). This emphasis on theoretical critique does not detract from the merits of critical accounting. In fact, its contributions have raised important insights to understanding accounting frameworks and practices from a critical perspective. However, for the most part, this approach does not provide accountants with working strategies and tools that challenge traditional accounting practices. This is precisely the intent of social accounting.

Social accounting is a broad term that includes a variety of alternative accounting models, including expanded value added accounting, environmental accounting and sustainability accounting. It shares most of the critiques raised by critical accounting, but at the same time provides a working framework that considers a broader range of factors and actors in the accounting process. This broadening is of particular importance to nonprofit organizations because the statements used in traditional accounting, as noted previously, were developed for profit-oriented businesses and then applied to other organizations. Therefore, by creating alternative accounting frameworks, social accounting addresses an important need.

Accountants thus have the option of continuing with the current accounting systems that sustain the status quo, or creating more democratic, transparent, and participatory accounting practices in the context of a broader strategy for social change. The assumption underlying the approach presented in this chapter is that accounting can be an agent of social change, and, moreover, this point is of partic-ular importance to accounting practices for nonprofit organizations, which as noted, are set up for different purposes than profit-oriented businesses. Before we look at some of the innovations in social accounting, we look at the concept of accountability and discuss how it applies to nonprofit organizations.

NONPROFIT ORGANIZATIONS AND ACCOUNTABILITY

It is important to note that accountability in nonprofit organizations differs from that in the private and public sectors. In the for-profit sector, organizations are ultimately accountable to one stakeholder, the shareholder or owner, whose primary concern is return on investment, and the competitive marketplace provides a mechanism for accountability (Herzlinger (1996)). In the public sector, governments are held to account to voters by mechanisms such as political constituencies, public mandates, oversight agencies, media scrutiny, and checks and balances (Kearns (1994)).

For nonprofit organizations, there are multiple accountabilities involving numerous actors, mechanisms, and standards of performance (Ebrahim (2003)). Generally, for nonprofit organizations, there are four important issues to address in terms of accountability: effectiveness (achieving mission), efficiency (getting the most out of resources), risk (minimizing), and corruption (guarding against individuals benefiting excessively) (Herzlinger (1996)).

Approaches to accountability can be either reactive or proactive. Reactive responses often occur as a result of internal crises, damage control, shifting societal values and expectations, or obligations such as with grants and contracts. These obligations are typical for public sector nonprofit organizations, community economic development organizations, and others relying on external funds (Abraham (2006)). For example, outside stakeholders such as funders establish rules to monitor organizations and ensure they are in compliance with those rules (Ebrahim (2003)). Each funder may have its own rules and reporting requirements. Accounting is thus used as a way of tracking and monitoring how the organization spends the funds that have been entrusted to it. Proactive accountability is driven by the desire to influence and shape the environment in which the organization operates. In some cases, it is done to define and shape standards that eventually may become mandated.

Accountability mechanisms can also be functional or strategic. Most common accountability mechanisms are functional, such as accounting for fund expenditures or to seek out cost efficiencies. Most often, these mechanisms are designed to support and facilitate organizational objectives, and take a short-term perspective on impacts. Strategic mechanisms, by comparison, are more visionary and require a broader approach. This may involve umbrella organizations in national-level policy debates to support or facilitate the pursuit of sector objectives or the development of long-term approaches to sustainability (Ebrahim (2003); Gray (2000); Mook & Sumner (2010)).

Social accounting can be connected to both accountability and control. Social accounting designed to support and facilitate organizational objectives includes: assessing risk, managing stakeholders, image management, public relations, seeking out efficiencies and maintaining legitimacy. Social accounting designed to support and facilitate the pursuit of societal objectives would include stakeholder rights to information, transparency, openness, and describing the social and environmental costs of economic success (Gray (2000)). Several models of social accounting are presented next.

SOCIAL ACCOUNTING IN PRACTICE

Social accounting often requires that we place a monetary value on items that are not financial. In order to do so, we need to establish proxies for this value. We cover this topic next and then look at three models of social accounting used by nonprofits.

Determining a Market Value for Outputs

Determining the market value for the outputs of a for-profit firm is relatively straightforward — it is simply the amount of revenues received through sales, or in other words, the amount people have paid for those goods or services in the market. However, for some nonprofit organizations revenues are seen as inputs[2] and the term "outputs" is generally used to mean the direct products of its activities, for example, such services as mentorship and counselling for clients or running a soup kitchen.

Determining the market value for the outputs of a nonprofit organization presents special challenges because some of its goods and services may not involve market transactions, and non-financial items such as contributions of volunteer labour are generally ignored. In order to assign a comparative market value (a reasonable rate if it were exchanged in the market) to the outputs of nonprofit organizations, the following procedure can be used (Richmond (1999)):

---

[2]   The characterization of revenues as inputs might not apply to all nonprofits, *e.g.*, those that earn their revenues from market transactions.

Look to the market to find a comparative market value for similar goods/services produced in the private sector (*e.g.*, for a nonprofit organization delivering employment training services, the cost of similar private sector training could be used).

If there are no equivalents in the private sector, compare with public sector goods (in the case of employment training, the cost of federal employment training programs could be used).

If that value is not available, compare with other nonprofit sector goods/services, using fees that they receive from government for providing the services. For example, a comparison could be made with fees paid by a government department to an employment-training agency to provide specialized training. In this case, the fees actually do go through the market. However, it has been argued that because the service is delivered by a nonprofit organization, which is subsidized by government and uses volunteers, the fees for the service are not an accurate reflection of their real cost in the market.

Another method is to assign the value according to the cost of the resources going into creating the goods and services plus the value of in-kind and volunteer contributions. This can also be thought of as the revenues that might be received in the market, less the allocation for profit.

Estes (1976) also proposed a number of techniques to assign a monetary value to outputs. His examples are largely in relation to profit-oriented businesses, but they are also relevant to nonprofit organizations:

Surrogate Valuation. "When a desired value cannot be directly determined, we may estimate instead the value of a surrogate — some item or phenomenon that is logically expected to involve approximately the same utility or sacrifice as the item in which we are interested" (Estes (1976 at 110)). He gives the example of estimating the value of building facilities loaned to civic groups and suggests as a surrogate the rent that would be paid for commercial facilities of a similar quality. Another example is establishing a surrogate value for the personal growth and development of volunteers from participating in a nonprofit organization. As a surrogate, we have used the cost of a community college course in personal development (Mook *et al.* (2007)).

Survey Techniques. This procedure involves asking participants what a service is worth to them. To assist in establishing an accurate estimate, Estes (1976) suggests using, as a prompt, a list of either prices or consumer items and asking the respondents to situate the service in relation to others on the list.

Restoration or Avoidance Cost. "Certain social costs may be valued by estimating the monetary outlay necessary to undo or prevent the damage" (Estes (1976 at 115)). Road salt corrodes automobiles, but frequent washings can prevent the damage, something that can be easily priced. Similarly, it is possible to estimate the cost of restoring environmentally damaged land to either industrial or residential use. In the event of a plant closure, many governments require a cleanup of the work site to residential standards, a liability that can be determined.

Determining a Market Value for Volunteer Contributions

In order to place a value on volunteer labour contributions, there are two general schools of thought. The first is based on what economists refer to as "opportunity costs" and the second is "replacement costs". The opportunity costs approach assumes that "the cost of volunteering is time that could have been spent in other ways, including earning money that could, after taxes, be spent on desired goods and services" (Brown (1999 at 10)). Because time might have been spent generating income, the opportunity cost is tied to the hourly compensation that volunteers normally receive from paid jobs that they hold. However, this procedure could be problematic from an organization perspective because the skills associated with a volunteer service may differ substantially from those for which a salary is being received (Brown (1999)). The hourly rate that Mark Zuckerberg receives from Facebook for his services would not be an appropriate standard if he were to spend a day volunteering at a local food bank. An opposite problem might arise if the food bank volunteer were unemployed and, therefore, without an hourly wage. It would be incorrect to suggest that the service is worth nothing. After considering the complexities of estimating opportunity costs, including the portion of a paid worker's hourly wage that goes to taxes, and after adjusting for any fringe benefits, Brown (1999 at 11) suggests that volunteer time "be valued at roughly one half to six sevenths of the average hourly wage". In her view, higher values should be applied when volunteers have increased responsibilities relative to their paid work and lower values should be applied in the opposite circumstance.

Variations of Brown's (1999) procedure to estimate opportunity costs of volunteers have been undertaken by Wolfe, Weisbrod & Bird (1993) and Handy & Srinivasan (2004). Wolfe *et al.* estimated the marginal opportunity costs by asking volunteers what they would have received if they had worked additional hours for pay. Volunteers not in the labour market (retired, students, unemployed) "were asked what they believed they could earn if they decided to seek paid employment" (1993 at 31). Handy & Srinivasan (2004) also asked volunteers to estimate how much their tasks were worth, thereby arriving at a lower figure than the marginal opportunity cost. These procedures vary, but they share the common feature of looking at the value of volunteering from the perspective of the volunteer and what an hour is worth to that person.

The second approach is called the replacement cost method. This method looks at volunteer value from the perspective of the organization. This procedure, which is favoured by the accounting profession in cases where estimation for volunteer value is permitted, assumes that volunteers could be replaced by wage earners as substitutes in terms of skills and productivity.

There are three approaches to estimating replacement costs: the generalist approach; the specialist approach; and the modified specialist approach (Mook & Quarter (2004)). The generalist approach makes the assumption that all volunteer tasks should be treated equally, and is the simplest of the three methods to apply. For example, the Independent Sector — an advocacy organization for nonprofits in the United States — utilizes the average hourly wage for non-agricultural workers published in the Economic Report of the President, plus 12 per cent for fringe benefits (Independent Sector (2013)). For Canada, Ross (1994) suggested a weighted average of hourly and salaried wages based on Statistics Canada data for employment earnings. He calculated both national and provincial averages.

The specialist approach, by comparison, targets the value of a volunteer's role to the market value of the exact task (Brudney (1990); Community Literacy of Ontario (1998); Gaskin (1999); Gaskin & Dobson (1997); Karn (1983)). For example, Community Literacy of Ontario uses an hourly rate for volunteer literacy workers based on a survey of the average annual salary of full-time support staff of 94 community organizations that supply training. Its strength is its precision — comparisons are made for each volunteer task and the market rate for paid work in that category is used. These rates can be found in labour market data generated by government agencies. The limitations are that organizations may not have access to the information needed to make such comparisons and may lack the personnel do the analysis.

The modified specialist approach targets the rate for a volunteer task to an organization as well as to the general skill level of the volunteer task. This approach is simpler than the specialist approach and, arguably, more practical. One method is to use the Statistics Canada wage rates based on the North American Industry Classification System (NAICS). This classification system (jointly developed by the statistics agencies of Canada, the United States and Mexico) classifies organizations (such as businesses, government institutions, unions, and charitable and nonprofit organizations) according to economic activity.

The NAICS classification combines all levels of tasks for a class such as sub-sector 624, social assistance. This sub-sector includes organizations engaged in a variety of services such as food and housing within the community and emergency and other forms of relief both to the individual and family. The NAICS classification combines all the tasks for a sub-sector and puts forward an average wage rate for all levels of occupation in that category, making its subsequent use straightforward. For volunteer activities requiring a high level of professional skills, the rate for salaried employees can be used. For those activities requiring basic skills, the rate for hourly employees can be used. For those activities using a mixture of skills, the two rates can be averaged.

In Practice: Canadian Crossroads International

Canadian Crossroads International (CCI) is an international nonprofit that recruits, trains and places volunteers from Canada and 12 partner countries in international development projects and internships in those countries, as well as in community development projects within Canada. Its mission is "to create a more equitable and sustainable world by engaging and strengthening individuals, organizations and communities through mutual learning, solidarity and collective action" (CCI (2013, at 22)). CCI is funded primarily through the Canadian International Development Agency (CIDA) and through fundraising.

Each year, CCI recruits, trains, and sends over 100 volunteers on international development projects and internships in partner countries and Canada. Participants are matched to a variety of community-based activities run by local non-governmental organizations working to eradicate poverty and advance women's rights. Pre-departure orientation, post-placement debriefing and re-entry training, fund-raising, civic engagement, and education on development issues are all integral components of a CCI placement or internship. Travel, accommodation, and related costs are paid by CCI. Volunteers also serve as trainers, on the board of directors, and on many different national, regional, local and country committees governing the various programs.

To place a value on volunteer contributions of hours for their accounting statement, Statistics Canada wage rates based on the North American Industry Classification System (NAICS) were used. The activities of the majority of the volunteers of CCI were classified under NAICS sub-sector 54, "professional, scientific and technical services". This category includes organizations engaged in activities in which knowledge and skills are the major input and in which much of the expertise requires a university or college education. Wages rates for both hourly paid employees and salaried employees are calculated by Statistics Canada.[3] For volunteer activities requiring a high level of professional skills, the rate for salaried employees was used. For those activities requiring basic skills, the rate for hourly employees was used. For the year ending March 31, 2013, the total value of volunteer contributions was calculated to be $2,342,718. Financial revenues for the same period were $3,927,594. Together, these amounted to $6,270,312, with volunteer contributions comprising over 37 per cent of the total resources (CCI (2013)).

Three Models of Social Accounting

Three models of social accounting are presented next to illustrate the range of social accounting approaches that have been implemented by nonprofit organizations: (1) the expanded value added statement (EVAS); (2) the Global Reporting Initiative (GRI); and (3) The Natural Step (TNS).

The first approach, the EVAS, integrates social, environmental and economic data. In other words, the economic, social and environmental dimensions are not supplemental to the financial accounts; rather, together they are integral. We use the term "integrated social accounting" to refer to this approach. The last two

---

[3]   For 2012, the wage rate for hourly paid employees in this category for Canada was $27.47. For salaried employees in this job category, the hourly equivalent was $35.54. Source: Statistics Canada Table 281-0030 and 281-0036.

approaches are generally found in what we call "supplemental social accounting" reports, which separate financial and sustainability reporting (New Economics Foundation (1998); Sillanpää (1998); Zadek (1998)).

Expanded Value Added Statement

The expanded value added statement (EVAS) is an integrated approach to social accounting, and focuses on economic, social, and environmental impacts, instead of just the "bottom line" of financial surpluses or deficits (Mook (2007)). For instance, an EVAS analysis of a housing co-operative was able to identify key aspects of the organization's functioning that were not apparent from traditional financial statements alone. These key aspects included the impact of unpaid labour (*i.e.*, volunteers), the role of the organization in providing employment, skills development, and personal growth for its members, and the contribution of the organization to society through service provision and tax payments (Richmond & Mook (2001)).

The expanded value added statement puts together information from audited financial statements along with monetized social and environmental data to calculate the value added it creates. Value added is a measure of wealth that an organization creates by adding value to raw materials, products and services through the use of labour and capital. In contrast to profit, which is the wealth created for only one group — owners or shareholders — value added represents the wealth created for a larger group of stakeholders including employees, society, government and the organization itself. Indeed, traditional accounting for socially minded organizations falls short in two important areas. First, traditional accounting is incomplete as it ignores a significant source of inputs, in particular, volunteer labour. Second, it is incomplete as it ignores a significant part of its outputs, particularly social and environmental outputs. Because of these two features, traditional accounting leaves much to be desired in helping socially minded organizations measure their performance according to their combined social and economic objectives.

The EVAS also emphasizes the collective effort needed for an organization to achieve its goals, viewing each primary stakeholder as important to its viability as a socially and economically responsible organization. For example, including volunteers and society as stakeholders presents an alternative perspective of an organization than focusing solely on its ability to spend its financial resources. By combining financial and social value added, the EVAS also emphasizes the interconnectedness and interdependence of the economy, community and environment (Mook, Quarter & Richmond (2007)).

In Practice: Putting Together an EVAS: PARO Centre for Women's Enterprise

In 2007, Carleton University researchers applied the expanded value added method to The PARO Centre for Women's Enterprise, a non-profit organization located in Thunder Bay, Ontario (Babcock (2007)). PARO was started in 1995 to serve communities across the northern Ontario region in order to "empower women within their communities, strengthen small business and promote community economic development (CED) through integrated and women-centred program delivery" (PARO (2008)). It provides training and business coaching, organizes networking events and peer lending circles, and operates a retail store with the goal of increasing the self-sufficiency and success of women, families, and communities in the North.

For the fiscal year analysed,[4] PARO received $440,019 in revenue, of which $439,493 was spent on programming and administration, and the remainder transferred to its surplus account for the following year. Of those expenses, $254,364 went to employee wages and benefits for 10.5 full-time equivalent paid employee positions. The remainder, $185,129, was spent on purchasing external goods and services.

Six social value added factors were quantified for PARO (for de-tailed calculations, see Babcock (2007)).

1. The skills development of the 18 volunteers, both board members and non-board members, was measured, and a cost of one course at the local community college ($275) was used as a proxy value. The total of this was calculated to be $4,950.

2. Artisan volunteers who sold their products at the PARO retail store did so at a lower commission rate, and the value of this was estimated to be $1,100.

3. Volunteer hours were determined for board members, non-board members and artisans. The nine-member board contributed 678 hours in the fiscal period analysed, while non-board members contributed an additional 661 hours. These hours were calculated

---

[4] Due to a change in fiscal year end, the period covered by this analysis is 11 months rather than the typical 12 months.

to have a replacement value of $12,120 and $10,905 respectively. Artisans working in the PARO retail outlet volunteered 1,386 hours, which was valued at $13,860. The total value of volunteer hours thus was $36,885.

4.   A value was also placed on the mentorship that the 150 loan circle members received, considered equivalent to a membership at the local Chamber of Commerce ($230). This amounted to $34,500.

5.   In additions, speakers at PARO conferences frequently waived their speaking fees, which would have been $20,000.

6.   The executive director of PARO frequently provided unpaid consultations and support to other organizations in the CED sector, to the amount of $35,200 for the fiscal period, based on a total of 880 hours multiplied by $40 per hour.

In total, the social factors that were quantified amounted to $132,635. This is the amount that will be shown in the "Social" column in the EVAS presented in Table 1, below.

Table 1: Expanded Value Added Statement (Partial) for PARO for the Period Ended March 31, 2006[5]

		Financial	Social	Combined
Outputs		$447,019	$132,635	$579,654
Purchases of external goods and services		$192,655		$192,655
Value added created		$254,364	$132,635	$386,999
Stakeholders				
Employees	Wages and benefits	$254,364		$254,364
Volunteers	Skills development (1)		$4,950	$4,950
Artisan member volunteers	Lower commissions (2)		$1,100	$1,100

---

[5]   As PARO was in the process of changing its year-end, this statement covers an 11-month period, from 30 April 2005 to 31 March 2006.

		Financial	Social	Combined
Program participants	Volunteer contributions (3)		$36,885	$36,885
	Mentorship (4)		$34,500	$34,500
	Donated speaker time (5)		$20,000	$20,000
CED sector	Consultations (6)		$35,200	$35,200
Value added distributed		$254,364	$132,635	$386,999

The expanded value added statement consists of two sections: value added created and value added distributed. The first section estimates the value added created by the organization and the second shows the distribution of the value added to the key stakeholders associated with the organization. For the analysis of the value added that is created by the organization, the table is divided into three columns: (1) financial, using information from audited financial statements; (2) social and environmental contributions for which a market-comparison monetary value is estimated; and (3) combined (the addition of the first two columns).

The second part of the statement shows how the value added that was created is distributed to different stakeholders. For instance, employees received payments for wages and benefits in the amount of $254,364; volunteers received skills development valued at $4,950; artisan member volunteers also benefited by having to pay a lower commission for the sale of their wares ($1,100); program participants received benefits from volunteer contributions, mentorship, and donated speaker time ($91,385); the community economic development sector benefited by consultations given by the executive director of PARO valued at $35,200. In total, the amount of value added distributed is equal to the amount of value added created.

In contrast, PARO's Statement of Revenues and Expenditures shows that it spent slightly less than it received, resulting in a surplus of $1,486 (see Table 2, below). This is important because it indicates that the organization is living within its means. However, this statement does not fully show the contribution that PARO is making to the surrounding community. The EVAS, by contrast, indicates that for every dollar spent on external goods and services, PARO generated expanded value added of $2.01, which is 52 per cent higher than had we used financial information only.

Table 2: Statement of Revenues and Expenditures for PARO for the Period Ended March 31 2006[6]

Revenues	
Government grants	$365,711
Sales of goods and services	$74,915
Donations	$7,203
Other	$676
Total	$448,505
Expenditures	
Advertising and promotion	$9,423
Travel and vehicle	$11,471
Interest and bank charges	$1,253
Office supplies and expenses	$22,171
Occupancy costs	$42,507
Professional and consulting fees	$5,907
Education and training	$21,312
Wages and benefits	$254,364
Other	$78,611
Total	$447,019
Surplus	$1,486

---

[6] Source: 2006 T3010 online at: http://www.cra-arc.gc.ca>. As PARO was in the process of changing its year-end, this statement covers an 11-month period, from 30 April 2005 to 31 March 2006.

Discussion

Social goods and services, ones that are not given a monetary value, are often a large part of the operations of a nonprofit organization. Without taking these goods and services into account, there is neither a clear picture of a nonprofit's performance nor the contributions made by its volunteers. The expanded value added statement is a methodology to broaden the accounting for nonprofits to include social indicators. The EVAS tells a different story than the financial statements alone — and to a different audience. The EVAS helps various stakeholders, particularly volunteers, to see what value they have added to an organization and what value they have received.

The strengths of the EVAS lies in its ability to take a broader look at the organization and the role of volunteers within it and to put this in a larger social-economic perspective. The challenges faced by the EVAS are shared by other forms of alternative accounting and economics — quantifying and placing a value on goods and services that are seen as "free". The EVAS model attempts to integrate financial information for which there are strict methods of accounting, with non-financial or social information — and to develop a methodology that supports this.

The limitations of the EVAS are those that affect the nonprofit sector as a whole: there are few resources to track free goods and services. The EVAS method attempts to place a reasonable market value on items and activities that do not pass through the market. Much more research and application will be required to refine this process. However, as the report of PARO shows, the EVAS currently captures and displays information that other forms of accounting or evaluation do not. This information can be used by the organization and its stakeholders to better understand the role and value of volunteers. Indeed, since the report was generated, the executive director of PARO has been able to demonstrate to funders and other CED organizations that PARO generates a large contribution of social value added for every dollar it receives from grants and other sources. By comparison, traditional accounting statements undertaken with nonprofits like PARO portray them as the users of grants and other forms of funding, and show how they use the funds (expenditure categories) without portraying the value (both social and financial) that they add. This is a fundamental difference, as it strikes at the essence of nonprofit organizations — their social mission.

The EVAS is unique because it is a form of integrated social accounting. Other forms of social accounting are also important, but as noted, are supplemental to the financial statements. Although providing useful information, supplemental social accounting reports often receive secondary status (Coupland (2006)). It is also difficult with supplemental reports to judge the relative materiality of social and environmental actions with respect to financial performance. As a result, social and environmental reports published by an increasing number of corporations (especially for-profit) are frequently dismissed as "greenwashing" or "specious gloss" (Laufer (2003); Owen & Swift (2001at 5)). We look at two forms of supplemental social accounting next.

Global Reporting Initiative

The second social accounting approach, the Global Reporting Initiative, or GRI, is used by organizations in the for-profit, public, and social economy sectors. The GRI does not challenge conventional accounting formats, but provides a framework to communicate economic, social, and environmental performance in order to measure, disclose, and discharge accountability (GRI (2006, at 40)):

> Sustainability reporting is the practice of measuring, disclosing, and being accountable for organizational performance while working towards the goal of sustainable development. A sustainability report provides a balanced and reasonable representation of the sustainability performance of the reporting organization, including both positive and negative contributions.

Stichting Global Reporting Initiative[7] is the nonprofit organization that coordinates the networks that come together to develop the Global Reporting Initiative framework. It is headquartered in the Netherlands, and its mission is "to make sustainability report standard practice by providing guidance and support to organizations" (GRI (2012, at 2)). The organization was started in 1997 as a partnership between the Coalition for Environmentally Responsible Economies (CERES) in Boston and the United Nations Environment Program (UNEP). It published its first guidelines in 2000. Today, using a global, multi-stakeholder consensus-seeking approach, the guidelines are now in their fourth version (G4), and numerous sector supplements have been developed to provide specialized guidance, including for nonprofit organizations (GRI (2013)). More than 1,000 organizations (private, public, and nonprofit) have self-declared their

---

[7] Stichting is the Dutch word for "foundation".

use of the GRI guidelines in their sustainability reports. Many others use the guidelines on a more informal basis.

The GRI framework also provides important guidance on the materiality aspect of social and environmental reporting, as discussed below. Its ultimate goal is to develop globally accepted sustainability reporting principles (GRI (2013a)).

Materiality

Accounting bodies have issued statements on materiality as they relate to the financial accounts. The Canadian Institute of Chartered Accountants refers to materiality in section 1000.17 of its Handbook (CICA (2003)): accountants are to use professional judgment in deciding if an item of information or its aggregate that is omitted or misstated would influence or change a decision.

The International Accounting Standards Board (IASB (2006 at 15-16)) also defines materiality:

> Omissions or misstatements of items are material if they could, individually or collectively, influence the economic decisions of users taken on the basis of the financial statements. Materiality depends on the size and nature of the omission or misstatement judged in the surrounding circumstances. The size or nature of the item, or a combination of both, could be the determining factor.

Materiality is also an important concept in sustainability reporting, but it is concerned with a wider range of impacts and stakeholders. When determining materiality for a sustainability report, external and internal factors taken into account include (GRI (2013b at 12)):

External Factors

- Main sustainability interests/topics and indicators raised by stake-holders.

- Main topics and future challenges for the sector reported by peers and competitors.

- Relevant laws, regulations, international agreements, or voluntary agreements with strategic significance to the organization and its stakeholders.

- Reasonably estimable sustainability impacts, risks, or opportunities (*e.g.*, global warming, HIV-AIDS, poverty) identified through sound investigation by people with recognized expertise, or by expert bodies with recognized credentials in the field.

Internal Factors

- Key organizational values, policies, strategies, operational management systems, goals, and targets.

- The interests/expectations of stakeholders specifically invested in the success of the organization (*e.g.*, employees, shareholders, and suppliers).

- Significant risks to the organization.

- Critical factors for enabling organizational success.

- The core competencies of the organization and the manner in which they can or could contribute to sustainable development.

These are important guidelines that, if followed, help organizations avoid producing reports that are just simply public relations exercises, or "greenwashing".

Indicator Protocols

The Global Reporting Initiative provides protocols for indicators in three categories: economic, environmental and social. The category Social is further broken down into the sub-categories of labour practices and decent work, human rights, society, and product responsibility. Each of the categories and sub-categories is further broken down into aspects, which currently number 58. In addition to reporting on the indicators, organizations also provide disclosures in a number of other areas. These include strategy and analysis, organizational profile, identified material aspects and boundaries, stakeholder engagement, report profile, governance, ethics and integrity (GRI (2013a)).

In Practice: Société de développement Angus (SDA)

The Société de développement Angus (SDA) is a non-profit development corporation located in Montreal with a mission to create local jobs and encourage sustainable development. Founded in 1995, SDA operates according to the values of sustainable development principles, social economy development, and transparency. To monitor and report on its performance, it commissions a third party to report on its economic, social and environmental impacts using the Global Reporting Initiative guidelines.

SDA completed its first GRI sustainability report in 2010, covering the years 2008 to 2010, and its second in 2012, covering the years 2010 to 2012. The GRI sets out 79 different indicators and SDA has responded to all of them. As a result, their report is an "A" level report. The report details SDA's economic, environmental and social performance over a two-year period. At the end of the report, all of the GRI indicators are listed, and the page number in the report where the indicator was reported on is indicated. The reports are also checked by GRI to confirm that they are complete before the organization can attach the *"A" GRI Report, GRI Checked* logo.

Part of the GRI process is the inclusion of stakeholder input. Stakeholders are those who influence the work of the organization, or are influenced by the work of the organization. In this regard, three key stakeholder groups were identified for SDA: its employees, its tenants, and the community of Rosemont where the organization is located. These stakeholders were interviewed as to their perception of the organization's impact, as well as asked about their expectations for future performance. Surveys are also used to gather material. For instance, tenants are surveyed every two years as to their satisfaction with items such as communications, reduction of greenhouse gases, and business relationships. Employees are also surveyed as to their satisfaction with the quality of their work life (SDA (2012)).

The following are examples of some of the items that SDA reported on in its 2010-2012 sustainability report following the GRI guidelines (SDA (2012)). The notation that follows each item in brackets is the GRI indicator code.

In additional to showing a traditional Statement of Activities, or income statement, the organization reports on the wealth (or "value added") that was distributed to employees, providers of capital (creditors), local government (through taxes), and retained by the organization (Figure 1) (EC1: Direct economic value generated and distributed, including revenues, operating costs, employee compensation, donations and other community investments, retained earnings, and payments to capital providers and government).

For its environment performance, SDA has concentrated on waste management, energy use and commuting of employees. It has a policy to use goods made from recycled materials and notes that by

2012 it had almost eliminated all non-renewable materials in its management activities (EN2: Percentage of materials used that are recycled input materials). Over 95 per cent of waste from its management activities, such as paper, plastic, and computer components, was recycled or recovered (EN27: Percentage of products and their packaging materials that are reclaimed by category).

In terms of energy use, SDA reports on its use of natural gas for heating (EN3: Direct energy consumption), and its electricity use (EN4: Indirect energy consumption). It also monitors automobile use by its employees and has indicated that this is a priority item for them (EN29: Significant environmental impacts of transporting members of the workforce). As a result, it is developing programs to encourage the use of alternative transportation rather than driving alone to work.

Figure 1: Breakdown Of The Distribution Of The Wealth Created By SDA For The Year June 1, 2011 To May 31, 2012

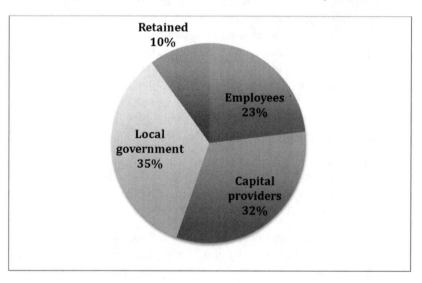

A notable achievement for SDA is in local employment. In 2012, over 40 per cent of SDA's employees lived less than five kilometres from their workplace. This has both a positive environmental and social impact. SDA also supports several work reintegration programs: one for young people lacking education, and one for people with mental health issues. Its housekeeping company provides employment to people with disabilities.

SDA notes that 18 per cent of its purchases are made from tenant organizations within its buildings, and 70 per cent from suppliers in the Montreal area. The remainder of purchases are for items that are hard to find in the local area (EC6: Policy, practices and proportion of spending on locally based suppliers).

SDA provides detailed information on employment and wages, including an analysis by gender and age for management, middle management and administrative levels (LA2: Total number and rate of employee turnover by age group, gender and region; LA14: Ratio of basic salary of men to women by employee category). The lowest salary it pays is more than twice the minimum required (EC5: Range of ratios of standard entry level wage compared to local minimum wage).

The Natural Step Framework

The third approach to social accounting illustrated in this chapter is the Natural Step Framework, developed in Sweden in 1989 by Dr. Karl-Henrik Robèrt, a medical doctor and cancer scientist. Robèrt worked with over 50 Swedish scientists to develop a consensus document that set out a framework for organizations to follow to institute policies and procedures that would move them towards becoming more sustainable. The document describes how the biosphere functions, how society influences and is a part of natural systems, how societies are threatening these systems, and what opportunities exist to reverse unsustainable behaviours. Four conditions were identified that must be satisfied in order to move towards sustainability (Broman, Holmberg & Robèrt (2000)):

To become a sustainable society we must:

1. Eliminate our contribution to the progressive buildup of substances extracted from the Earth's crust (for example, heavy metals and fossil fuels).

2. Eliminate our contribution to the progressive buildup of chemicals and compounds produced by society (for example, dioxins, PCBs and DDT).

3. Eliminate our contribution to the progressive physical degradation and destruction of nature and natural processes (for example, over harvesting forests and paving over critical wildlife habitat).

4.   Eliminate our contribution to conditions that undermine people's capacity to meet their basic human needs (for example, unsafe working conditions and not enough pay to live on).[8]

In order to develop a strategic approach for sustainable development, a process called "backcasting" is used. A future is envisioned where the organization is complying with system conditions, and then you work backwards. Once organizations understand the framework and their role in it, they undertake a baseline assessment, noting where they are contravening the principles of sustainability and designing a program for change that will take them from where they are today to their future vision (Broman *et al.* (2000)). These baseline measurements and future measurements are reported in a sustainability report.

This is the process followed by the Co-operators and hundreds of other organizations and municipalities including IKEA, the town of Canmore, Alberta, the National Film Board, the resort municipality of Whistler in British Columbia, Santropol Roulant in Montreal, the David Suzuki Foundation, the Co-operative Housing Federation of Canada, and the government of Canada.

In Practice: The Natural Step Canada

The Natural Step Canada is a national nonprofit organization founded and incorporated in 1996. It provides sustainability training for businesses and community groups, as well as community-wide and regional capacity building and engagement programs. It is one of over 10 international offices of The Natural Step founded by Karl-Henrik Robèrt. In 2008, it had a staff of 12, and financial expenditures of $1,330,255. In addition, it received donations of volunteer time (The Natural Step Canada (2008)).

Following the same framework it uses to train others organizations, The Natural Step Canada set strategic goals in order to become a sustainable nonprofit (TNS (2008)). These goals are:

1.   Our operations are energy efficient and rely on 100% renewable energy;

2.   We use resource efficient transportation;

3.   We produce zero waste;

---

[8]   See online at: <http://www.naturalstep.ca/four-system-conditions>.

4. Every purchasing decision we make has a positive sustainability impact;

5. We create conditions that empower our employees and contractors to meet their needs;

6. We contribute to a vibrant local community.[9]

Taking It Further: Connecting the GRI to The Natural Step Framework

One of the main criticisms of sustainability reports is they have nothing to do with sustainability (Gray (2000)). As part of their Master's program in Strategic Leadership towards Sustainability at the Blekinge Institute of Technology in Karlskrona, Sweden, Ronan Chester and Jennifer Woofter took up this challenge and evaluated the 2002 Global Reporting Initiative Sustainability Reporting Guidelines against The Natural Step principles of sustainability. By doing this, they created indicators based on science that would report the organization's contribution to unsustainability. Examples of these indicators, which they call GRI+, included the following principles (Chester & Woofter (2005, at 27-28)):

Principle one

Report on how your organization contributes to systematically increasing concentrations of substances extracted from the lithosphere:

(1) mining of metals or minerals; (2) extraction of petroleum-based materials; (3) reliance on metals, minerals, or petroleum-based materials in manufacturing, logistics, *etc.*; and (4) life cycle analysis of relevant metal/mineral/petroleum products.

Principle two

Report on how your organization contributes to systematically increasing concentrations of substances produced by society: (1) carbon dioxide, (2) nitrous oxides, (3) chlorofluourocarbons (CFCs), and (4) any other persistent unnatural compounds.

---

[9] TNS (2008 at 19).

Principle three

Report on how your organization contributes to systematically increasing degradation by physical means: (1) strip mining; (2) timber harvesting; (3) land use changes; and (4) biodiversity.

Principle four

Report on how your organization contributes to conditions that systematically undermine people's capacity to meet their needs: (1) child labour; (2) women's rights; (3) human rights, and (4) fair wage.

CONCLUSION

As can be seen, social accounting can include a broad range of activities from formats such as the expanded value added statement and the Global Reporting Initiative, to The Natural Step. Although these approaches differ, they share the common goal of broadening the framework of traditional accounting and attempting to understand the impact that an organization has on the communities to which it relates and the physical environment. Decisions to follow one or more of these approaches are made based on the values of the organization and its leadership, and also on the cost and benefits of doing so. In some cases, leadership may not be aware of social accounting, but once they are, take steps to implement it. Smaller organizations may not have the resources to follow fully some of these approaches, but there may be aspects that can be incorporated into their operations and strategic thinking.

Social accounting, therefore, is useful for nonprofit organizations as they are created to fulfill a social mission. Ignoring their social impact, as traditional accounting does, misses an essential feature of their performance story. In an age when so many demands are being made of nonprofit organizations, having tools that assess their accountability and their social impact is *sine qua non* for survival.

REFERENCES

A. Abraham, "Financial management in the nonprofit sector: A mission-based approach to ratio analysis in membership organizations" (2006) 9:2 Journal of American Academy of Business 212-217.

Abt and Associates Inc., "The Abt model" in D. Blake, W. Frederick & M. Meyers, eds., *Evaluating the Impact of Corporate Programs* (New York: Praeger, 1974) 149-157.

American Accounting Association (AAA) (1990), "Objectives of Education for Accountants". online at: <http://aaahq.org/AECC/ PositionsandIssues/pos1.htm>.

American Accounting Association (AAA), "Position Statement No. Two: The First Course in Accounting" (1992), online at: <http://aaahq.org/ AECC/PositionsandIssues/pos2.htm>.

K. Babcock, PARO Centre for Women's Enterprise: Measuring Social Impact (2007), online at: <http://www.ccednet-rcdec.ca/files/ccednet/ PWP-11.pdf>.

A. Belkaoui, *Socio-economic Accounting* (Westport, CT: Quorum Books, 1984).

G. Broman, J. Holmberg & K.-H. Robèrt, "Simplicity Without Reduction: Thinking Upstream Towards the Sustainable Society" (2000) 30:3 Interfaces: International Journal of the Institute for Operations Research and the Management Sciences. Online at: <http://www.naturalstep.org/ en/system/files/3a-Simplicityreduction.pdf>.

E. Brown, "Assessing the value of volunteer activity" (1999) 28:1 Nonprofit and Voluntary Sector Quarterly 3-17.

J. Brudney, *Fostering Volunteer Programs in the Public Sector* (San Francisco, CA: Jossey-Bass, 1990).

Canadian Crossroads International (CCI), *Annual Report, 2012-2013.* Online at: <http://www.cintl.org/document.doc?id=907>.

Canadian Institute of Chartered Accountants (CICA), *CICA Handbook* (Toronto: Author, 2003).

R.J. Chester & J.K. Woofter, *Non-financial Disclosure and Strategic Planning: Sustainability Reporting for Good Corporate Governance* (Master's thesis, Blekinge Institute of Technology, Sweden, 2005) [unpublished].

M. Clarkson, "A stakeholder framework for analyzing and evaluating corporate social performance" (1995) 20:1 Academy of Management Review 92-117.

Community Literacy of Ontario, *The Economic Value of Volunteers in Community Literacy Agencies in Ontario* (Barrie, ON: Community Literacy of Ontario, 1998).

D.J. Cooper & T. Hopper, "Critical Theorizing in Strategic Management Accounting Research" (Paper presented at the Eighth Interdisciplinary Perspectives on Accounting Conference, Cardiff Business School, Cardiff University, 10-12 July 2006).

D.J. Cooper & D. Neu, "Critical accounting interventions" (2001) 12:6 Critical Perspectives on Accounting 735-762.

G. Cooper, *Online Assistance for Problem Gamblers* (Doctoral dissertation, University of Toronto (2000)) [unpublished].

C. Coupland, "Corporate social and environmental responsibility in web-based reports: Currency in the banking sector?" (2006) 17:7 Critical Perspectives on Accounting 865-881.

R. Craig & J. Amernic, "The deployment of accounting-related rhetoric in the prelude to a privatization" (2004) 17:1 Accounting, Auditing and Accountability Journal 41-58.

C.R. Dey, "Bookkeeping and ethnography at Traidcraft plc: A review of an experiment in social accounting" (2000) 20:1 Social and Environmental Accounting Journal 16-18.

C.R. Dey, "Methodological issues: The use of ethnography as an active research methodology" (2002) 15:1 Accounting, Auditing and Accountability Journal 106-121.

S.C. Dilley & J.J. Weygandt, "Measuring social responsibility: An empirical test. (1973) 136:3 Journal of Accountancy 62-70.

A. Ebrahim, "Accountability in practice: Mechanisms for NGOs" (2003) 31:5 World Development 813-829.

R. Estes, *Corporate Social Accounting* (New York: Wiley, 1976).

J. Ferguson *et al.*, "What are recommended textbooks teaching students about corporate stakeholders?" (2005) 38:1 British Accounting Review 23-46.

J. Ferguson *et al.*, "Accounting textbooks: Exploring the production of a cultural and political artefact" (2006) 15:3 Accounting Education 243-260.

E. Flamholtz, *Human Resource Accounting*, 2d ed. (San Francisco, CA: Jossey-Bass, 1985).

R.E. Freeman, *Strategic Management: A Stakeholder Approach* (Boston: Pitman, 1984).

K. Gaskin, "Valuing volunteers in Europe: A comparative study of the Voluntary Investment and Value Audit (VIVA)" (1999) 2:1 Voluntary Action: The Journal of Active Volunteering Research 35-48.

K. Gaskin & B. Dobson, "The economic equation of volunteering" (2007), online at: <http://www.jrf.org.uk/knowledge/findings/socialpolicy/SP110.asp>.

Global Reporting Initiative (GRI), G4 Sustainability Reporting Guidelines: Reporting Principles and Standard Disclosures (2013a). Online at: <https://www.globalreporting.org/resourcelibrary/GRIG4-Part1-Reporting-Principles-and-Standard-Disclosures.pdf>.

Global Reporting Initiative (GRI), G4 Sustainability Reporting Guidelines: Implementation Manual (2013b). Online at: <https://www.globalreporting.org/resourcelibrary/GRIG4-Part2-Implementation-Manual.pdf>.

Global Reporting Initiative, *Sustainability Reporting Guidelines* (2006). Online at: <https://www.globalreporting.org/resourcelibrary/G3-Guidelines-Incl-Technical-Protocol.pdf>.

Global Reporting Initiative, *Annual Report 2011/12* (2012). Online at: <https://www.globalreporting.org/resourcelibrary/GRI-Annual-Report-2011-2012.pdf>.

Global Reporting Initiative, "What is GRI?" (2013). Online at: <https://www.globalreporting.org/information/about-gri/what-is-GRI/Pages/default.aspx>.

R. Gray, "Imagination, a bowl of petunias and social accounting" (1998) 9:2 Critical Perspectives on Accounting 205-216.

R. Gray, "Current developments and trends in social and environmental auditing, reporting and attestation: A review and comment" (2000) 4:3 International Journal of Auditing 247-268.

R. Gray, "The social accounting project and *Accounting, Organizations and Society:* Privileging engagement, imaginings, new accountings and pragmatism over critique?" (2002) 27:7 Accounting, Organizations and Society 687-708.

R. Gray *et al.*, "Struggling with the praxis of social accounting: Stakeholders, accountability, audits and procedures" (1997) 10:3 Accounting, Auditing and Accountability Journal 325-364.

R.H. Gray, J. Bebbington & K. McPhail, "Teaching ethics and the ethics of teaching: Educating for immorality and a possible case for social and environmental accounting" (1994) 3:1 Accounting Education 51-75.

F. Handy & N. Srinivasan, "Improving quality while reducing costs? An economic evaluation of the net benefits of hospital volunteers" (2004) 33:1 Nonprofit and Voluntary Sector Quarterly 28-54.

R.E. Herzlinger, "Can public trust in non-profits and government be restored?" (1996) 74:2 Harvard Business Review 97-107.

R.D. Hines, "Financial accounting: In communicating reality, we construct reality" (1988) 13:3 Accounting, Organizations and Society 251-261.

T. Hopper, J. Storey & H. Willmott, "Accounting for accounting: Towards the development of a dialectical view" (1987) 12:5 Accounting, Organizations and Society 437-456.

A.G. Hopwood, "Ambiguity, knowledge and territorial claims: Some observations on the doctrine of substance over form–a review essay" (1990) 22:1 British Accounting Review 79-88.

IASB, *Exposure Draft of Proposed Amendments to IAS 1: Presentation of Financial Statements* (London: IASB, 2006). Online at: <http://www.ifrs.org/Current-Projects/IASB-Projects/Financial-Statement-Presentation/ED2006/Documents/EDAmdmtstoIAS1.pdf>.

Independent Sector, (2013) Volunteer Time. Online at: <http://www.independentsector.org/volunteer_time>.

G.N. Karn, "Money talks: A guide to establishing the true dollar value of volunteer time, Part 1" (1983) 1:2 Journal of Volunteer Administration 1-19.

K.P. Kearns, "The strategic management of accountability in nonprofit organizations: An analytical framework" (1994) 54:2 Administration Review 185-192.

W.S. Laufer, "Social accountability and corporate greenwashing" (2003) 43:3 Journal of Business Ethics 253-261.

L. Lewis, C. Humphrey & D. Owen, "Accounting and the social: A pedagogic perspective" (1992) 24:3 British Accounting Review 219-233.

D. Linowes, "An approach to socio-economic accounting" (1972) 9:11 Conference Board Record 58-61.

S. Llewellyn, "Managing the boundary: How accounting is implicated in maintaining the organization" (1994) 7:4 Accounting, Auditing and Accountability 4-23.

S.C. Lodh & M.J.R. Gaffikin, "Critical studies in accounting research, rationality and Habermas: A methodological reflection" (1997) 8:5 Critical Perspectives on Accounting 433-474.

M.R. Mathews, "Twenty-five years of social and environmental accounting research: Is there a silver jubilee to celebrate?" (1997) 10:4 Accounting, Auditing and Accountability Journal 481-531.

L. Mook & J. Quarter, *How to Assign a Monetary Value to Volunteer Contributions* (Toronto: CCP, 2004).

L. Mook & J. Sumner, "Social accounting for sustainability in the social economy" in J.J. McMurtry, ed., *Living Economics: Perspectives on Canada's Social Economy* (Toronto: Emond Montgomery, 2010) 157-178.

L. Mook, J. Quarter & B.J. Richmond, *What Counts: Social Accounting for Non-profits and Cooperatives*, 2d ed. (London: Sigel Press, 2007).

G. Morgan, "Accounting as reality construction: Towards a new epistemology for accounting practice" (1988) 13:5 Accounting, Organizations and Society 477-485.

New Economics Foundation, *Briefing Paper on Social Auditing* (London: Author, 1998).

D. Owen & T. Swift, "Introduction: Social accounting, reporting and auditing: Beyond the rhetoric?" (2001) 10:1 Business Ethics: A European Review 4-8.

PARO Centre for Women's Enterprise. (2008). "About Us", online at: <http://www.paro.ca/index.php?pid=8>.

B.J. Richmond & L. Mook, *Social Audit for WCRI* (Toronto: Author, 2001).

B.J. Richmond, *Counting on Each Other: A Social Audit Model to Assess the Impact of Nonprofit Organizations* (Ph.D. dissertation, University of Toronto) [unpublished].

R. Roslender & J.F. Dillard, "Reflections on the interdisciplinary perspectives on accounting project" (2003) 14:3 Critical Perspectives on Accounting 325-351.

D. Ross, *How to Estimate the Economic Contribution of Volunteer Work* (Ottawa: Department of Canadian Heritage, 1994).

L. Seidler, "Dollar values in the social income statement" in A. Belkaoui, ed., *Socio-economic accounting* (Westport, CT: Quorum Books, 1973) 167.

M. Sillanpää, "The Body Shop values report: Towards integrated stakeholder auditing" (1998) 17:13 Journal of Business Ethics 1443-1456.

Société de développement Angus (SDA), *Rapport de développement durable 2010-2012* (2012). Online at: <http://sda-angus.com/medias/download?f=/datas/5148d7257a84c/7985-sda-rapport-gri-4-lr.pdf>.

Statistics Canada. Table 281-0030 – Average hourly earnings for employees paid by the hour (SEPH), for selected industries classified using the North American Industry Classification System (NAICS), annual (current dollars), CANSIM (database), online at: <http://www5.statcan.gc.ca/cansim/home-accueil?lang=eng>.

Statistics Canada. Table 281-0036 – Average hourly earnings for salaried employees (paid a fixed salary) (SEPH), including overtime, for selected industries classified using the North American Industry Classification System (NAICS), annual (current dollars), CANSIM (database), online at: <http://www5.statcan.gc.ca/cansim/home-accueil?lang=eng>.

The Natural Step Canada (TSN), *Annual Report, 2008*. Online at: <http://www.naturalstep.ca/sites/default/files/annual_report_2008.pdf>.

A.M. Tinker, B.D. Merino & M.D. Neimark, "The normative origins of positive theories: Ideology and accounting thought" (1982) 7:2 Accounting, Organizations and Society 167-200.

T. Tinker, *Paper Prophets: A Social Critique of Accounting* (New York: Praeger, 1985).

T. Tinker, "The withering of criticism: A review of professional, Foucauldian, ethnographic, and epistemic studies in accounting" (2005) 18:1 Accounting, Auditing and Accountability Journal 100-135.

N. Wolfe, B. Weisbrod & E. Bird, "The supply of volunteer labor: The case of hospitals" (1993) 4:1 Nonprofit Management and Leadership 23-45.

S. Zadek, "Balancing performance, ethics, and accountability" (1998) 17:13 Journal of Business Ethics 1421-1441.

INDEX

H

O